Mastering Generative AI Systems Engineering

Design, Train, and Deploy Powerful Generative Models Across Vision, Language, and Multimodal AI Workflows

Praveen Kumar

www.orangeava.com

First Published: February 2026

Published By: Orange Education Pvt Ltd, AVA®

Address: 9, Daryaganj, Delhi, 110002, India

275 New North Road Islington Suite 1314 London,
N1 7AA, United Kingdom

ISBN (PBK): 978-93-49887-94-7
ISBN (E-BOOK): 978-93-49887-67-1

Scan the QR code to explore our entire catalogue

www.orangeava.com

Get a Free eBook

We hope you're enjoying your recent book purchase! Your feedback is incredibly valuable to us and helps other readers discover books that truly make a difference.

If you found this book useful or enjoyable, we'd greatly appreciate it if you could leave a short review with a 5-star rating on Amazon. Your review supports our work and allows us to reach more learners worldwide.

As a thank-you, we're happy to offer you a **free digital copy of this book** plus a **30% discount code** for your next purchase on our official websites:

www.orangeava.com

www.orangeava.in (For the Indian Subcontinent).

☑ How it works:

Leave your review on Amazon, take a screenshot of the confirmation or use the following link to submit the claim and email it to **info@orangeava.com.** Once received the required detail, we will send your rewards within 24 hours, **along with one month free subcription to the book on AVA SkillShelf!**

Claim Form

https://rebrand.ly/4d2477

Thank you for your support—it truly means a lot to us.

Enjoy 1 Month of Free Access to AVA SkillShelf!

The future belongs to lifelong learners. With AVA SkillShelf, you go beyond reading books and start building real, job-ready skills curated by industry experts.

Your membership unlocks **200+ learning products** covering AI, Cloud, Python, Cybersecurity, Data Science, DevOps, and more—all in one platform. Our bestselling technical books are transformed into structured courses designed for practical, real-world application.

Learn directly from experienced professionals and published authors, with no filler—just actionable insights. Earn **verified digital certifications** to strengthen your CV, LinkedIn profile, and professional credibility.

Learn anytime, anywhere, on any device, at your own pace. Ideal for students, professionals, career switchers, and tech leaders.

For full access to all current and future courses, choose our **Annual Membership**. Simply scan the QR to get started!

For 1 month Free access, simply refer to the steps on the previous page titled: Get a Free ebook!

https://www.avaskillshelf.com/

Downloading the code bundles and colored images

Please follow the links or scan the QR codes to download the ***Code Bundles and Images*** of the book:

https://github.com/ava-orange-education/Mastering-Generative-AI-Systems-Engineering

The code bundles and images of the book are also hosted on ***https://rebrand.ly/1b5eea***

In case there's an update to the code, it will be updated on the existing GitHub repository.

Errata

We take immense pride in our work at **Orange Education Pvt Ltd,** and follow best practices to ensure the accuracy of our content to provide an indulging reading experience to our subscribers. Our readers are our mirrors, and we use their inputs to reflect and improve upon human errors, if any, that may have occurred during the publishing processes involved. To let us maintain the quality and help us reach out to any readers who might be having difficulties due to any unforeseen errors, please write to us at :

errata@orangeava.com

Your support, suggestions, and feedback are highly appreciated.

Dedicated To

My Beloved Parents,

Smt. Keerthi Kulkarni and
Shri Krishnarao Kulkarni

And

Naveen, Shilpa and Mahi.

About the Author

Praveen Kumar is a seasoned global technology leader with over 27 years of experience in the IT industry. He has held senior leadership roles, including CTO, Vice President, and Enterprise Architect across multiple countries, including the USA, Canada, China, and Europe. He has also led cross-cultural teams in Serbia, Brazil, Mexico, Nigeria, Germany, the Netherlands, and Singapore. This international exposure has given him a unique perspective on global technology landscapes, enterprise challenges, and the nuances of leading diverse teams.

Praveen is a hands-on technologist with expertise spanning AI, ML, Generative AI, Big Data, cloud technologies, Python, Microsoft .NET, AWS, Java, and modern JavaScript frameworks. He has successfully led the design, development, and deployment of large-scale AI and software solutions across industries, mentoring teams, while fostering innovation. He has collaborated with major clients such as Verizon, Toronto Stock Exchange, Intelsat, RBC, RelayHealth, Wells Fargo, TravelClick, Quantumzyme and more, spanning sectors such as healthcare, finance, biotechnology, hospitality, and travel. He has demonstrated strong entrepreneurial acumen by co-founding several startups, combining business vision with technological expertise.

Originally from Bengaluru, Praveen earned a degree from the prestigious BMS College of Engineering. He has also been recognized with national and state awards for his outstanding contributions to software development, highlighting his ability to translate technical mastery into impactful outcomes.

Praveen has delivered numerous technology talks, workshops, and training sessions, mentoring hundreds of developers in Generative AI, Agentic AI, RPA, and cloud computing. He emphasizes practical learning with hands-on implementation, helping others convert theoretical concepts into real-world solutions.

This book, ***Mastering Generative AI Systems Engineering***, reflects Praveen's passion for AI, practical learning, and mentorship. By combining foundational concepts, mathematical principles, and hands-on projects, he provides readers with a comprehensive understanding of Generative AI models and their applications. His goal is to equip both aspiring and experienced developers with the skills, confidence, and practical expertise needed to navigate the rapidly evolving AI landscape, build innovative solutions, and make meaningful contributions in their professional careers.

About the Technical Reviewer

Rahul Vats is a distinguished Data and AI engineering leader with over 15 years of experience in architecting and delivering innovative, AI-driven solutions for Fortune 500 clients. He specializes in Generative AI, Microsoft Copilot development, Retrieval-Augmented Generation (RAG) architecture, and Agentic AI systems, enabling enterprises to implement scalable, intelligent, and cost-efficient solutions.

Currently serving as a Senior Lead (Manager) at Capital One, Rahul provides technical leadership in establishing robust guardrails and standards to remediate and control non-compliance across diverse cloud environments, including AWS, Azure, and GCP.

Throughout his career, his technical and strategic initiatives have driven impactful advancements in Microsoft Copilot integrations, significantly enhancing productivity through intuitive, AI-driven experiences. Rahul's expertise in RAG architecture has been pivotal in building scalable knowledge retrieval pipelines that empower enterprise search, customer support automation, and decision-support systems. By implementing modular and adaptive frameworks, he has enhanced system scalability, improved contextual relevance, and streamlined information retrieval for enterprise users.

Rahul's deep technical proficiency, coupled with his leadership in AI engineering, has established him as a trusted partner in driving innovation, empowering teams, and delivering impactful business outcomes.

Acknowledgments

I express my heartfelt gratitude to all those who supported me throughout the writing of this book. First and foremost, I thank my family – my mom, who has been the foundation of everything I am; my dad, from whom I inherit patience; my dear brother, Naveen, who gives me great confidence; Shilpa Ramdurg, whose support and positivity have been invaluable; and Mahi Kulkarni, who has always been a source of joy and motivation. Their constant support and encouragement actually made this book possible!

I am deeply grateful to several individuals and teams who contributed to the successful completion of this book. First and foremost, I would like to acknowledge Varun Walvekar, Srinidhi MR, and Vivek Joseph for their intellectual discussions, debates, and perspectives through the rights and wrongs of Generative AI concepts. I also sincerely thank Nikhil Karnam, Sagar Gopinath, Sanjay, Sandeep, Pratham Joshi, Sadananda, and others for their invaluable support with editing, rework, image processing, formatting, and much more. Finally, I am highly grateful to the talented individuals at Zummit Infolabs and Digital Nexus AI for technical discussions, war room sessions, and continued support throughout this journey. I offer my heartfelt gratitude to Mr. Rahul Vats for his review and validation as his expertise and perspective reinforced my confidence that the book was on the right track.

I am extremely thankful to Satish Kulkarni and his family, the Terwad family, Mr. Ramesh and his family, the Alwandikar family, and the Joshi family for graciously providing a peaceful and welcoming environment during moments, when I needed solitude to collect my thoughts and reflect, which proved invaluable in developing ideas for the book.

My heartfelt gratitude also goes to the editorial team at Orange Education Pvt. Ltd. for their unwavering support, patience, and flexibility throughout the completion of this book. I greatly appreciate their meticulous attention to detail in proofreading, corrections, and guidance. Working with this prestigious Publishing House has been a rewarding experience indeed!

Preface

Generative Artificial Intelligence (AI) has grown from a focused research area into one of the most powerful and exciting fields in technology today. This book, ***Mastering Generative AI Systems Engineering***, is written to give readers both the basic understanding and the practical experience needed to learn and apply generative models effectively.

The book begins with the key ideas and mathematical concepts that form the base of generative modeling, and then moves through important architectures such as Variational Autoencoders (VAEs) and Generative Adversarial Networks (GANs). It later covers advanced versions such as DCGANs, Conditional GANs, CycleGANs, StyleGANs, and Diffusion Models – each explained with hands-on examples in TensorFlow and PyTorch. The following sections go beyond image generation to show real-world uses in Natural Language Processing (NLP), data augmentation, and model deployment. The final part connects these models to today's Generative AI systems and Large Language Models (LLMs), including GPT, LangChain, RAG, and Agentic AI tools – helping readers understand how modern AI applications are designed and improved.

Throughout the book, the focus remains on clear explanations, practical coding, and responsible use of AI. Each chapter is meant to build your technical skills, and help you develop a deeper appreciation for creativity and ethics in AI.

Chapter 1 will introduce you to the world of generative models, and explain why they play such an important role in modern artificial intelligence. You will learn what generative models are, how they work, and how they differ from traditional machine learning approaches. The chapter will explain the evolution of generative modeling–from early statistical techniques to advanced deep learning architectures such as VAEs, GANs, and Diffusion Models. You will also understand where these models are applied in real-world AI systems, including image generation, data synthesis, and text creation. The chapter will further introduce the main tools used throughout this book, such as Python, TensorFlow, PyTorch, NumPy, and Matplotlib, and explain how they help in implementing and visualizing generative models.

Chapter 2 will cover the key mathematical concepts that form the base of generative modeling. You will learn the fundamentals of probability theory, statistics, and information theory that help understand how generative models learn patterns, and create new data. The chapter will also explain important optimization techniques used for training neural networks, such as gradient descent and backpropagation, in a simple and intuitive way. You will explore how mathematical concepts such as entropy, KL divergence, and likelihood estimation play an essential role in VAEs and GANs. This chapter will introduce the basic structure of neural networks which act as the foundation for deep generative architectures. Using libraries such as NumPy and SciPy, you will gain hands-on experience applying these mathematical principles.

Chapter 3 will introduce Variational Autoencoders (VAEs), one of the most important types of generative models. You will learn how VAEs combine deep learning with probability to generate new data similar to what they were trained on. The chapter will explain the core architecture of VAEs, including the encoder, decoder, and latent space, along with the mathematical concepts of loss functions and KL divergence. You will implement a simple VAE using TensorFlow and PyTorch, and visualize how it learns to represent data in a lower-dimensional space.

Chapter 4 will introduce Generative Adversarial Networks (GANs), one of the most influential generative architectures. You will learn how GANs use two competing networks–the generator and the discriminator–to create realistic data. The chapter explains their mathematical foundation, loss functions, and training process, followed by a hands-on implementation in TensorFlow and PyTorch.

Chapter 5 will build upon the basic GANs by introducing Deep Convolutional GANs (DCGANs). You will learn how convolutional layers improve image quality and model stability. The chapter will guide you in creating a DCGAN using TensorFlow or PyTorch, explaining how feature maps and up-sampling work together to generate realistic images. You will also visualize the training progress and generated outputs.

Chapter 6 will focus on Conditional GANs, which allow controlled data generation based on specific inputs or labels. You will learn how conditioning helps the model generate images or text that match a given class or description. This chapter includes hands-on implementation and examples such as generating digits or objects conditioned on class labels.

Chapter 7 will cover CycleGANs, which enable unpaired image-to-image translation without needing matching datasets. You will also learn how two generators and discriminators work in a cycle-consistent manner to convert images from one domain to another. Practical examples such as photo enhancement and style transfer will help solidify the concept.

Chapter 8 will introduce StyleGANs, known for generating high-quality, photorealistic images. You will explore how StyleGAN separates different levels of detail, and controls style features during generation. The chapter will include practical experiments using pre-trained models to generate human faces and other realistic images.

Chapter 9 will revisit VAEs, and introduce advanced versions like β-VAE and Conditional VAE (CVAE). You will learn how these variations help in achieving better control and disentanglement of features in generated data. The chapter will also guide you through implementing these models and visualizing their latent representations.

Chapter 10 explains Diffusion Models, a recent breakthrough in generative AI. You will understand how these models iteratively refine noise to create clear, realistic images. The chapter will cover the training process, noise scheduling, and sampling techniques, along with simple implementations and visual examples.

Chapter 11 will show how generative models like GANs and VAEs can enhance datasets through synthetic data generation. You will learn techniques to improve model robustness, and handle data imbalance using data augmentation. The chapter includes practical examples such as generating additional training images for classification tasks.

Chapter 12 will explore the use of generative models in NLP. You will learn how VAEs and GANs can be applied for text generation, dialogue systems, and creative writing. The chapter introduces NLP tools such as NLTK, spaCy, and Hugging Face Transformers for preprocessing and model development.

Chapter 13 will focus on evaluating and improving generative models. You will learn qualitative and quantitative evaluation methods such as Inception Score and FID. The chapter will also explain optimization techniques and model comparison strategies to enhance performance and output quality.

Chapter 14 will teach how to deploy generative models for real-world use. You will explore tools such as TensorFlow Serving, PyTorch Serve, and Docker for deploying models efficiently. The chapter also introduces cloud deployment options using AWS and Google Cloud for scalability and production readiness.

Chapter 15 will discuss the ethical challenges and responsibilities of using generative models. You will learn about fairness, bias, and the misuse of AI-generated content. The chapter will also provide insights into the future of generative AI and emerging research directions.

Chapter 16 will introduce Large Language Models (LLMs), and explain how they process and generate natural language. You will learn the principles of tokenization, attention, and transformer-based architectures. This chapter sets the foundation for understanding advanced models like GPT and their role in modern AI systems.

Chapter 17 will explore GPT models in detail, explaining how they are trained and fine-tuned for various applications. You will learn how GPT architectures work, how pre-training and transfer learning function, and how to use them for text generation, summarization, and reasoning tasks.

Chapter 18 will show how to integrate LLMs into applications using the LangChain framework. You will learn to build conversational AI systems, automate workflows, and connect multiple tools through LangChain. Hands-on examples will demonstrate how to design and deploy functional AI-powered apps.

Chapter 19 will teach prompt engineering techniques and Retrieval-Augmented Generation (RAG) methods for improving LLM responses. You will also learn fine-tuning strategies to adapt pre-trained models for specific use cases such as chatbots and enterprise AI assistants.

Chapter 20 will explore emerging ideas in AI such as Multi-Context Prompting (MCP), agentic AI systems, and AI tool integrations. You will understand how autonomous AI agents interact with tools and environments to perform complex tasks with minimal supervision.

Chapter 21 will summarize the key lessons from the book, and share practical tips for working with generative models. You will learn how to troubleshoot training issues, optimize performance, and maintain ethical standards, while developing real-world AI applications.

DID YOU KNOW

Did you know that Orange Education Pvt Ltd offers eBook versions of every book published, with PDF and ePub files available? You can upgrade to the eBook version at **www.orangeava.com** and as a print book customer, you are entitled to a discount on the eBook copy. Get in touch with us at: **info@orangeava.com** for more details.

At **www.orangeava.com**, you can also read a collection of free technical articles, sign up for a range of free newsletters, and receive exclusive discounts and offers on Print Books and eBooks.

PIRACY

If you come across any illegal copies of our works in any form on the internet, we would be grateful if you would provide us with the location address or website name. Please contact us at **info@orangeava.com** with a link to the material.

ARE YOU INTERESTED IN AUTHORING WITH US?

If there is a topic that you have expertise in, and you are interested in either writing or contributing to a book, please write to us at **business@orangeava.com**. We are on a journey to help developers and tech professionals to gain insights on the present technological advancements and innovations happening across the globe and build a community that believes Knowledge is best acquired by sharing and learning with others. Please reach out to us to learn what our audience demands and how you can be part of this educational reform. We also welcome ideas from tech experts and help them build learning and development content for their domains.

REVIEWS

Please leave a review. Once you have read and used this book, why not leave a review on the site that you purchased it from? Potential readers can then see and use your unbiased opinion to make purchase decisions. We at Orange Education would love to know what you think about our products, and our authors can learn from your feedback. Thank you!

For more information about Orange Education, please visit **www.orangeava.com**.

Table of Contents

CHAPTER 1
Introduction to Generative Models

Introduction

The purpose of this chapter is to take the reader through an introduction to the basic concepts that underlie generative models, thereby setting solid grounds for the advanced topics covered in subsequent chapters. We will start with the explanation of what generative models are, some essential properties thereof, and why generative models are important in modern AI. After that, we will take a brief look at the historical evolution of these models, from early approaches into cutting-edge techniques. Finally, we will look at some of the most impactful real-world applications of generative models, which will set the stage for the practical, hands-on projects in later chapters.

Structure

In this chapter, we will discuss the following topics:

- **The Future of Creation – Generative Models in Action**
- **What are Generative Models?**
  - Definition and Core Concepts
  - Understanding Latent Space Using an Analogy: The Recipe Book
  - How Generative Models Differ from Other AI Models
  - Practical Applications of Generative Models
  - Key Challenges in Generative Modeling
- **Historical Overview and Evolution**
  - Early Generative Models (RBMs, Autoencoders)
  - Breakthrough with GANs and VAEs
  - Modern Advancements in Generative AI
- **Applications and Impact of Generative Models**
  - Image Synthesis and Style Transfer
  - Text Generation and Natural Language Processing (NLP)
  - 3D Design and Printing (Architecture, Medical)
  - Music Generation and Media
  - Healthcare – Drug Discovery and Medical Imaging
  - Gaming – Procedural Content Generation
  - Finance – Synthetic Data Generation
  - Impact of Generative Models

- **Key Tools and Technologies**
  - Python: The Primary Programming Language
  - TensorFlow and PyTorch for Model Implementation
  - Essential Libraries: NumPy, Matplotlib, and so on

The Future of Creation – Generative Models in Action

What if you could teach a machine to create? From generating realistic images to writing coherent text, generative models are revolutionizing industries far beyond the research lab. Imagine designing a 3D model of a house in minutes, just as well as a certified architect.

Figure 1.1: *Turning Data into Creativity!*

How about crafting music that sounds like a Green Day's song, or generating new anime characters with expressive emotions? Take a look at the creation of a plaster or cast that fits the patient perfectly through 3D printing. These are not only future possibilities; they happen right now, thanks to the power of generative models.

Generative models are reshaping fields such as architecture, entertainment, healthcare, and art. Thus, by the end of this book, you will not only understand how these technologies work but also how to apply them in your own projects. You will be able to harness the same techniques driving these innovations, and leverage them to solve creative and technical problems. So, welcome to a world where machines create alongside us.

Understanding Generative Models

Generative models belong to a class of machine learning models that produce new data samples based on the learned patterns. They are a step beyond AI techniques, where most of them are limited to classification or prediction based on previously known data. Generative models can actually create new, unseen examples, and this makes them particularly powerful in creativity, simulation, and data augmentation tasks.

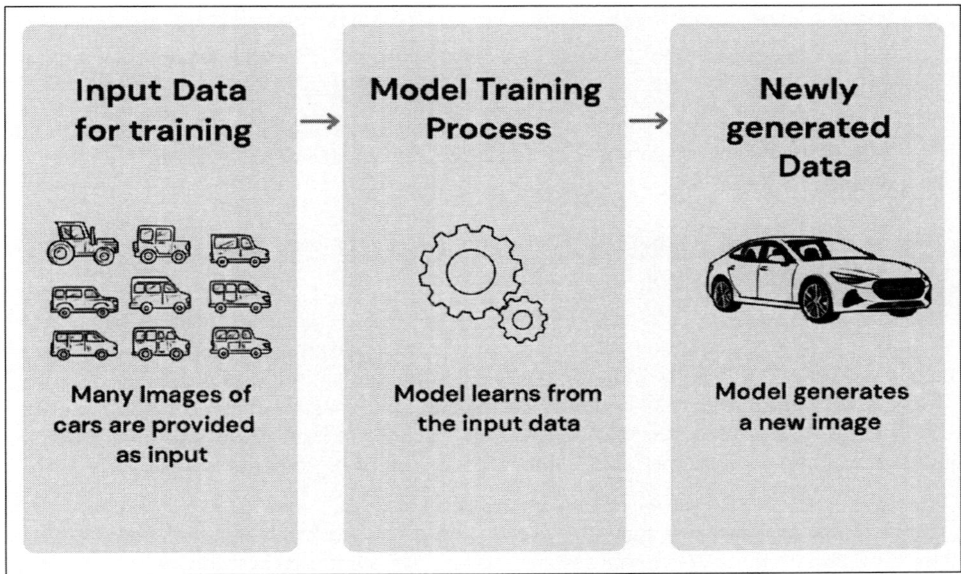

Figure 1.2: *Generative Models at Work*

Core Concepts of Generative Models

In fact, generative models can generate novel, unseen examples, and that is what makes them particularly strong in creativity, simulation, and data augmentation tasks.

At their heart, generative models learn a data distribution, and then draw samples from that distribution in order to generate new data points. For example, instead of just identifying the picture of an image as "*cat*" or "*dog*," a generative model could make altogether new images of cats or dogs by learning and reproducing the patterns underlying the features of these objects.

How Do Generative Models Work Internally?

To understand the inner workings of generative models, it is important to explore their training process, the concept of latent space representation, and the sampling mechanism that enables them to create new data. Here is a detailed breakdown:

- **Training Process:**
  - Similar to teaching an artist to paint based on a humongous collection of images, text, or sounds, training a generative model represents a process of study from the given dataset, learning patterns, structures, and relationships within the given data. This continues until it fine-tunes its understanding to generate outputs that are relatively close to the real thing.
  - For example, consider a model trained on thousands of human faces. It does not memorize them like a photo album—it learns common shapes, textures, and features that define a face. Then, when asked to create a new face, it blends what it has learned to produce something entirely unique—realistic, yet never before seen.
- **Latent Space Representation:**
  - The latent space is the compressed, lower-dimensional representation of the input that defines the key concepts in generative models. The model will learn to map its input data into this low-dimensional latent space, where different regions correspond to different types of generated outputs.

    - For instance, in an image-generating model, parts of the latent space may perhaps correspond to variations in lighting, pose, or facial expressions.
- **Sampling:**
    - At the end, the model samples from the latent space, and generates new data. This new data is then decoded to get back the original inputs as data, say images or text, into the output.

Understanding Latent Space Using an Analogy: The Recipe Book

Suppose, you have a huge cookbook with hundreds of recipes around the world-ranging from Italian pasta dishes to French pastries to Indian curries. Each recipe is unique to a specific dish, but many recipes have common ingredients like flour, salt, butter, and spices. Now, rather than viewing each recipe in its entirety, a tendency would be to distill that information down into only the essence of ingredients describing each recipe. This reduced collection of ingredients is analogous to the latent space.

- **Ingredients as Features:** Just like every recipe can be broken down into a collection of ingredients (flour, butter, tomatoes, and so on), data can be broken down into features. With images, for instance, these features might include colors, shapes, and textures.
- **The Recipe's Essence:** In essence, the latent space is some hidden "*recipe essence*" such that each dish is expressed in terms of basic features combined in some unique way. Pizza could be translated in the latent space as being represented by ingredients like dough, cheese, and sauce. A picture of a cat might represent ears, texture, and fur on the shape, and eyes of a cat.
- **Navigating the Latent Space: Create Your Own Dish:** Suppose, you can mix and match these ingredients like rice, cheese and sauce without following any specific formula or recipe. In the latent space, you can generate completely new dishes that no one has seen before by adjusting the proportions of different ingredients. If you mix dough, cheese, and spices, you might get something like pizza or breadsticks. Similarly, in generative models, by adjusting these values in the latent space, you can create totally new and unique images that resemble originals, however, they are completely new.
- **Finding Similar Dishes:** Food items and dishes that are similar to each other or belong to the same category such as a margherita pizza and a pepperoni pizza, would be placed close together in the latent space, just like similar images (for example, two pictures of cats) are grouped together. Dishes that are totally different, such as a fried rice and a chocolate cake, would be far apart, like how an image of a cat and a dog are apart in the latent space.

In machine learning, when we reduce the full recipe of a dish into core ingredients, it can be compared to the concept of dimensionality reduction. In latent space, we compress complex data into a smaller set of representations (very similar to reducing a recipe into a list of ingredients). This compressed representation will still capture the essence of the data, and allow it to be manipulated more easily.

How Generative Models Differ from Other AI Models

Predictive models try to predict the outcome or classify data based on the training that it undergoes, but generative models focus on generating new data from patterns that it learns while going through the training. A predictive model will be able to tell if an image is a cat or dog, but a generative model will create a totally new, unique image of a cat or a dog from scratch. This distinction makes generative models incredibly powerful for creative and innovative tasks, and this is the reason why it has become so popular even among people who are not tech-savvy.

In the following comparison table, you can see the key differences between traditional machine learning models and generative models. Traditional models focus mostly on predictive tasks, like classification and regression, using labeled data to learn decision boundaries or patterns. Generative models are specifically designed to create new, unseen data samples by learning the underlying distribution of the input data, and generally working in unsupervised or semi-supervised settings. While traditional models excel in use cases like medical diagnosis or stock prediction, generative models are more appropriate for creative applications like image synthesis, text generation, and music composition. Both approaches have different challenges, and demand different tools and evaluation metrics.

Aspect	**Traditional ML Models**	**Generative Models**
Primary Function	Classify, predict, or estimate based on existing data	Create new data samples that resemble training data
Output Type	Predicts labels or categories, outputs numerical values	Generates new, unseen examples (e.g., images, text)
Examples	Decision Trees, SVM, Linear Regression, KNN	GANs, VAEs, Autoencoders
Learning Objective	Learn decision boundaries or patterns for prediction	Learn the underlying data distribution to generate new samples
Common Applications	Classification, regression, clustering, recommendation	Image synthesis, text generation, 3D design, music composition
Core Components	Input features, output labels, and cost functions	Generator, Discriminator (GANs), Encoder, Decoder (VAEs)
Data Requirement	Can work with smaller datasets depending on the task	Requires large datasets to capture the full distribution

Table 1.1: *Comparison of Generative Models and Traditional ML Models*

Practical Applications of Generative Models

The models have shown much potential in multiple domains, thereby changing the ways we approach creativity, productivity, and innovation. Some of the key applications include:

Product Design: Generative models are applied in product design to speed up creativity and innovation. Designers can input parameters such as color schemes, shapes, and materials, and the model can come up with different variations of a product, which could be a car, chair, or clothes.

- **How it helps:** Designers can quickly prototype different styles and test new ideas by letting a generative model explore the vast design space. This helps companies innovate faster, and test concepts without manually creating hundreds of prototypes.

Deepfakes: One of the most well-known (and controversial) applications of generative models is in creating deepfakes. By using models like GANs, AI can generate highly realistic videos or images of people doing or saying things they never actually did. These deepfakes have raised significant concerns about digital media authenticity but also highlight the sheer power of generative models in creating photorealistic content.

- **How it works:** A generative model trained on hours of video footage of a person can learn their facial expressions, voice, and mannerisms. By feeding new inputs into the model (such as audio or a script), the model can generate realistic video footage of the person speaking or acting.

AI-Generated Art: Generative models are also making waves in the world of art. AI-generated art is being created through models like StyleGAN, which can blend artistic styles or generate entirely new images in the style of famous painters.

- **Example:** A generative model trained on Renaissance paintings can learn the specific textures, brushstrokes, and color palettes used in that era. Once trained, it can create a completely new painting that looks as though it was crafted by a Renaissance artist, yet it is a unique piece of art that never existed before.

Text-to-Image Generation: Generative models such as DALL·E can convert textual descriptions into images. This application is especially useful in areas like advertising, content creation, and entertainment, where designers and creators can generate visual content based on written input.

- **How it helps:** Text-to-image generation allows companies to create custom images or designs without needing a graphic designer. For example, a simple text input such as "a futuristic city skyline at sunset" could generate an AI-generated image based on that description, speeding up content production.

Content and Code Generation: Generative models are increasingly being used for automatic content and code generation. AI models like GPT (Generative Pre-trained Transformer) can generate articles, blogs, or technical documentation based on minimal input, while tools such as V0 Vercel, Claude AI, and GitHub Copilot assist developers by generating code snippets or even entire functions based on comments or code descriptions.

- **How it helps:** In content creation, AI models can generate written content, saving time for marketers, writers, and businesses that need bulk content. For code generation, developers can quickly prototype solutions, reduce errors, and increase productivity by using AI-assisted coding, making it easier to write boilerplate code or debug programs.

Key Challenges in Generative Modeling

While generative models hold immense potential, they also come with certain challenges such as:

- **Mode Collapse:** Where the model generates limited types of outputs, reducing its diversity. For instance, if the goal is to generate diverse images of cats, a GAN suffering from mode collapse might only generate images of a few cat variations, ignoring others. This lack of diversity can be problematic when the model is expected to generate a wide range of outputs.
- **Training Instability:** The training process of models such as GANs can be unstable due to the adversarial nature of two competing networks. Training instability in GANs is like a chess player and coach training together. If the coach is too strong, the constant defeats may demotivate the player, making it harder to improve. If the player is too strong, there is not much to learn from a coach, and they do not face any real challenge. The goal is to balance their skills so that each side learns and improves.
- **Quality of Generated Outputs:** Ensuring that the generated data is of high-quality and realistic remains a technical challenge. Making sure that the generated outputs are good quality is like making sure a chef can cook a great dish every time using the same recipe. It is not just about having the right ingredients and instructions (data), but also making sure that the model (the chef) can follow the process correctly, without making mistakes or skipping steps.

These challenges have been a focus of research and development in the field of AI, leading to many of the advancements that you will explore in this book.

Historical Overview and Evolution

Generative models have a fascinating history, beginning with early attempts to model data in an unsupervised way and evolving into today's sophisticated deep learning techniques. To truly appreciate the state-of-the-art, it is important to understand the key milestones that led us here.

Early Generative Models (RBMs, Autoencoders)

Before Generative Adversarial Networks (GANs) and Variational Autoencoders (VAEs) took center stage, early models such as Restricted Boltzmann Machines (RBMs) and Autoencoders laid the groundwork for generative AI.

- **Restricted Boltzmann Machines (RBMs):** One of the earliest breakthroughs in generative models came with the introduction of Restricted Boltzmann Machines (RBMs) by Geoffrey Hinton in the 1980s. Introduced as a way to model the complex data distributions, RBMs were among the first attempts to use unsupervised learning to generate data. However, their complexity and limited scalability made them less suitable for modern applications.
  - RBMs are shallow, two-layer networks that are trained to reconstruct the input data. They were a precursor to deep generative models, as they laid the foundation for unsupervised learning techniques that do not require labeled data.
  - A key development came in 2006 when Hinton and his collaborators introduced Deep Belief Networks (DBNs). DBNs stacked multiple layers of RBMs to create deep, hierarchical representations of data, enabling them to model more complex patterns (refer to *Hinton et al.*, 2006).
- **Autoencoders:** These represent a significant breakthrough in machine learning and generative models. Their core architecture consists of two primary components: an encoder, which compresses the input data into a low-dimensional latent space, and a decoder, which reconstructs the data back to its original form. This process allows the model to learn an efficient representation of the data, capturing its most essential features, while discarding unnecessary details. This ability to reduce data to a latent space, without losing critical information, paved the way for more advanced applications in generative modeling and beyond.
  - Initially developed as a method for dimensionality reduction and data reconstruction, autoencoders have found widespread use in various tasks, including anomaly detection, denoising, and feature extraction. Although autoencoders themselves are not fully generative in the sense that they do not inherently produce new data samples such as GANs (Generative Adversarial Networks), they introduced the idea of learning an efficient and compact representation of data, which is fundamental to generative modeling.
- **Variational Autoencoders:** A major advancement over traditional autoencoders came with the introduction of Variational Autoencoders (VAEs), which introduced a probabilistic approach to generating new data. VAEs encode data by incorporating probability distributions, and then decode these probabilistic representations into values, allowing the model to generate new outputs that were not part of the original input. Unlike standard autoencoders, VAEs introduce stochastic elements into the encoding process, ensuring that the latent space is continuous and allowing for smoother transitions between different data points. This structured latent space makes it easier to generate new data that closely resembles the original input, providing greater control over the generation process.
  - By adding this probabilistic twist, VAEs allow for more flexible and continuous data generation, making them highly effective for tasks such as image synthesis, where smooth and realistic transitions between different data samples are essential. VAEs have thus become a powerful tool in the generative model landscape, enabling applications ranging from medical imaging to creative tasks like generating art or music. Their combination of efficiency and flexibility has established autoencoders as a foundational building block for many modern generative models (see *Kingma & Welling*, 2013).

Generative Adversarial Networks (GANs): A Revolution in Image Synthesis

One of the most significant breakthroughs in generative models came in 2014, when Ian Goodfellow and his colleagues introduced Generative Adversarial Networks (GANs). GANs introduced a competitive two-network system—one generating content (the generator) and the other evaluating it (the discriminator)—leading to rapid advancements in image synthesis and data generation.

The original GAN model has since inspired many variations, including Deep Convolutional GANs (DCGANs), which improved the quality of generated images by leveraging convolutional layers. GANs have been applied to a wide range of tasks, including image synthesis, style transfer, and text-to-image generation.

StyleGAN: Generating Highly Detailed Images

In 2018, StyleGAN, developed by researchers at NVIDIA, took GANs to a new level by introducing a method that allows for more control over the generated image's style. StyleGAN's key innovation was the separation of content and style during generation, enabling users to control attributes such as lighting, facial features, and color. This model became famous for generating photorealistic human faces (*Karras et al.*, 2019).

At the same time, **Variational Autoencoders (VAEs)** brought a probabilistic approach to data generation, producing smoother and more realistic results compared to earlier models. VAEs allowed for a more structured representation of the latent space, which was a significant step forward in generative modeling (*Goodfellow et al.*, 2014).

Modern Advancements in Generative AI

Since the introduction of GANs and VAEs, generative AI has continued to evolve. Researchers have refined these models to improve stability, performance, and applicability to real-world tasks.

- **Deep Convolutional GANs (DCGANs):** By leveraging convolutional layers, DCGANs brought significant improvements to image generation, making it possible to generate high-resolution images.
- **Conditional GANs (CGANs):** CGANs are a variation of GANs where both the generator and discriminator are conditioned on additional information such as class labels or data attributes. This allows for more controlled data generation such as generating images of specific objects or applying styles based on user inputs. For instance, a CGAN trained on the MNIST dataset can generate images of a specific digit, like '3' or '7,' based on the label provided.
- **CycleGANs and StyleGANs:** These models take generative AI even further by allowing for style transfer between images (CycleGANs) or generating highly detailed and customizable images (StyleGANs). **StyleGANs** in particular have become famous for their ability to generate human faces that are nearly indistinguishable from real photographs.
- **BigGAN**: BigGAN introduced scalability to GAN models, enabling the generation of extremely high-resolution images with greater diversity. This advancement allowed researchers to produce large-scale, realistic images that were difficult to achieve with earlier GAN architectures.
- **Diffusion Models**: A more recent breakthrough, diffusion models approach data generation by progressively adding noise to the training data, and then learning to reverse the noise to generate realistic samples. These models have shown great promise in generating high-quality images, and are considered a strong alternative to GANs.

Applications and Impact of Generative Models

Generative models are transforming industries by enabling machines to create images, text, music, source code and even 3D designs. Their ability to generate content has opened up numerous possibilities for innovation. So, let us explore some key applications of these models:

Image Synthesis and Style Transfer

One of the most impressive capabilities of generative models is their ability to create hyper-realistic images or transfer the style of one image to another. This has applications in various industries:

- **Architecture:** Imagine generating realistic 3D designs of houses or even entire neighborhoods. Generative models allow architects to rapidly prototype different designs, visualize them in 3D, and tweak them as needed.
- **Art and Design:** Artists can use models like StyleGAN to generate new artworks by merging various styles or transforming existing works. Style transfer can take a famous painting's style and apply it to a modern photograph, blending the old with the new.
- **Fashion:** Generative models are being used to create unique clothing designs by combining different textures, colors, and styles. This allows fashion designers to experiment with countless iterations without manual labor.

Text Generation and Natural Language Processing (NLP)

Generative models have had a significant impact on **Natural Language Processing (NLP)**, allowing for the creation of text that reads as though a human wrote it. By learning from massive datasets, these models can generate articles, stories, poems, and even code. Some of the prominent applications include:

- **Automated Content Creation:** Companies use generative models to automatically generate product descriptions, social media posts, or even news articles. This reduces time and effort, while maintaining a human-like tone and structure.
- **Chatbots and Virtual Assistants:** NLP-powered generative models are used to create virtual assistants such as Google Assistant, Alexa, and Siri. These systems can understand and respond to natural language, making them more intuitive and user-friendly.
- **Generative Pre-trained Transformers (GPT)**: OpenAI's GPT series, including GPT-3, GPT-4, GPT-4o, and Omni can generate long-form text, images, video, presentations, have conversations, and even write codes. They are some of the most powerful language models, transforming how we interact with machines.

3D Design and Printing (Architecture, Medical)

Generative models have also found their way into 3D design and printing, making it easier to create highly customized objects, from prosthetic limbs to architectural models.

- **Architecture and Urban Design:** Generative models can produce detailed 3D models of buildings, furniture, and even urban landscapes. By learning from the existing designs, these models can propose new architectural solutions, enabling architects to visualize their ideas more efficiently.
- **Medical Applications:** Generative models are playing a critical role in designing patient-specific medical items such as casts, prosthetics, and implants. For example, a cast generated by a model can be 3D printed to perfectly fit a patient's unique anatomy, providing more

comfort and a faster healing process. These customized medical devices are more accurate, improving patient outcomes.

Music Generation and Media

Generative models are making waves in the music industry as well. AI systems can learn from the works of famous musicians, and create entirely new compositions that resemble a particular style, genre, or artist.

- **Music Composition:** Models like **MuseNet** by OpenAI can generate music across multiple genres, from classical to jazz. These systems understand musical patterns, styles, and rules, allowing them to compose original pieces. This opens up new possibilities for composers and artists looking for inspiration.
- **Soundtrack Generation:** Generative models are being used to create soundtracks for video games, films, and even advertisements. By providing input, such as mood or tempo, the model can generate music that fits the scene or product, speeding up the creative process.

Healthcare – Drug Discovery and Medical Imaging

Generative models are revolutionizing the healthcare industry, particularly in the areas of drug discovery and medical imaging. By generating potential molecular structures and synthetic medical images, these models are speeding up research and improving diagnostic accuracy.

- **Discovery:** Generative models are used to generate new molecular structures that can be tested for potential therapeutic effects. This accelerates the drug discovery process by narrowing down promising candidates for further research.
- **Medical Imaging:** In medical imaging, generative models create synthetic datasets that can be used to train AI models for tasks like detecting tumors in radiology scans. This improves the accuracy of AI diagnostics by providing more diverse training data.

Gaming – Procedural Content Generation

In the gaming industry, generative models are used for procedural content generation, which allows for the automatic creation of game levels, characters, and environments. This enhances player experiences by offering unique, customizable game content, without manual input.

- **Game Levels:** Generative models can create entire game levels or worlds dynamically, allowing for endless possibilities and challenges for players. Each playthrough can offer a new experience based on the model's content generation.
- **Character and Environment Creation:** These models can also generate diverse characters and environments, providing game developers with endless assets to build richer, more immersive worlds.

Finance – Synthetic Data Generation

Generative models are valuable in the finance industry for generating synthetic financial data. This is particularly useful for training AI models when real-world data is limited, sensitive, or unavailable.

- **Financial Data Generation:** Models can generate synthetic datasets that mimic real financial data, enabling companies to train models for stock price predictions, risk assessment, or portfolio simulation.
- **Risk Assessment and Fraud Detection:** Generative models help improve AI systems that

assess risks and detect fraudulent activities by creating more varied and diverse training data, reducing model bias.

Impact of Generative Models

Generative models are having a profound impact across various industries by driving innovation and efficiency. In creative fields such as art, design, and entertainment, these models are enabling artists and designers to push the boundaries of creativity. AI-generated videos, music, images, and software are transforming how content is produced, allowing for faster prototyping and the creation of unique, never-before-seen works. In architecture, for example, generative models are helping designers create more personalized and functional spaces, accelerating the design process while enabling creative exploration. Additionally, industries such as gaming and filmmaking are using generative models to produce realistic environments, characters, and even entire scenes with minimal manual intervention.

In sectors such as healthcare and manufacturing, the impact of generative models extends beyond creativity to improving efficiency and personalization. In medicine, AI-generated models are being used to create patient-specific prosthetics, implants, and treatment plans, enhancing both precision and patient outcomes. Manufacturing industries are leveraging generative models to optimize product designs and processes, resulting in cost reductions and increased efficiency. By reducing human effort and introducing more automated solutions, generative models are helping industries innovate faster, improve decision-making, and explore entirely new possibilities for solving complex challenges.

Key Tools and Technologies

To build and implement generative models, we need to be familiar with several key tools and technologies. In this book, we will rely heavily on **Python** as the primary programming language, along with libraries like **TensorFlow** and **PyTorch** for model development and training. Hence, let us briefly explore each of these tools.

Python: The Primary Programming Language

Python is one of the most widely used languages in the world of machine learning and AI, and for good reason. It offers simplicity, readability, and an extensive ecosystem of libraries and tools that make it ideal for implementing generative models.

- **Why Python?** Python's vast collection of libraries for data manipulation, visualization, and deep learning make it the language of choice for AI development. Libraries such as NumPy, Matplotlib, and TensorFlow/PyTorch provide everything we need to build, and visualize generative models.

TensorFlow and PyTorch for Model Implementation

Two of the most popular deep learning frameworks used for building generative models are TensorFlow and PyTorch. Both provide the flexibility to design, train, and deploy deep learning models with ease.

- **TensorFlow:** Developed by Google, TensorFlow is known for its robustness and scalability. It is widely used in research and industry for building production-ready models. TensorFlow provides tools such as **Keras**, which simplifies the model-building process, making it easier for beginners and experts alike to create powerful models.
- **PyTorch:** PyTorch, developed by Facebook's AI Research lab, is highly favored in academic

research due to its dynamic computation graph, which allows for more flexibility during experimentation. It is great for fast prototyping, and is also gaining traction in the industry.

The following is a comparison table of TensorFlow and PyTorch:

Aspect	TensorFlow	PyTorch
Developer	Google	Facebook (Meta)
Release Year	2015	2016
Primary Use	Production deployment and scalability	Research and rapid prototyping
Ease of Use	Improved with TensorFlow 2.x, but initially more complex	Known for ease of use and Pythonic design
Performance	High performance, widely used in large-scale deployments	Excellent performance, particularly for research and experimentation
Deployment	Strong support for production deployment	Less native deployment support
Community and Ecosystem	Large community, including TensorFlow Hub, Keras	Strong research community, Lightning & Hugging Face
Visualization Tools	TensorBoard for detailed visualizations and tracking	3rd-party tools like Visdom TensorBoard and Matplotlib
Backward Compatibility	TensorFlow 1.x and 2.x have some incompatibility issues	Backward compatibility is generally strong
Popularity	More popular for industry use and production deployments	More popular in academia and research
Mobile and Edge Support	Strong mobile support with TensorFlow Lite	Less robust mobile support, Torch Mobile or ONNX
Integration with Cloud Platforms	Excellent integration with Google, AWS, and Azure	Less tightly integrated compared to TensorFlow

Table 1.2: *Tensorflow and PyTorch Comparison*

Sample TensorFlow Code: Generating an Image of a Car Using BigGAN

The following code demonstrates how to use a pretrained model from TensorFlow Hub to generate realistic images of vehicles such as a sports car. By specifying a known class label corresponding to the object you want to generate (in this case, class 817 for "*sports car*"), the model can generate a brand-new image of the specified object. This highlights the power of generative models in creating high-quality visuals from pretrained networks with minimal code. You can also experiment with different class labels to generate images of other vehicles such as a bus (class 779) or a taxi (class 468).

```
# Import the necessary Libraries
import tensorflow as tf
import tensorflow_hub as hub
import numpy as np
import PIL.Image        #Python Imaging Library

# Load the pretrained BigGAN model (BigGAN-deep-256) from TensorFlow Hub
model = hub.load('https://tfhub.dev/deepmind/biggan-deep-256/1')

# Class label for 'car' (ImageNet class 817 corresponds to "sports car")
car_class = 817  # You can also try other vehicle classes from ImageNet
```

```
# Generate a random noise vector (z) and use the class vector for 'car'
z = tf.random.normal([1, 128])  # Latent space vector
y = tf.convert_to_tensor([[car_class]])  # Class vector for car

"""
Note: The latent space is a mathematical space that the model uses to create
new images.
By changing the values of this random vector, we can generate different
variations
of images within the same class (e.g., different cars).
"""

# Generate the image
output = model(z, y)
output_image = (output.numpy().squeeze() + 1.0) / 2.0  # Normalize to [0, 1]
range

# Convert to a PIL image and display
PIL.Image.fromarray((output_image * 255).astype(np.uint8)).show()
```

Essential Libraries – NumPy, Matplotlib, and More

In addition to TensorFlow and PyTorch, several other Python libraries play a pivotal role in building, training, and evaluating generative models. These libraries simplify everything from data manipulation to visualization, which are critical components in understanding model performance.

NumPy for Data Manipulation

Numpy is a powerful library that provides support for large, multi-dimensional arrays and matrices, along with a collection of mathematical functions to operate on these data structures. It is the foundation for much of Python's scientific computing and machine learning ecosystem, making it indispensable for working with data in generative models.

- **Why Use NumPy?** Whether you are processing images, text, or 3D models, NumPy helps you to efficiently manipulate data. Its performance and ease of use make it the go-to library for handling datasets in machine learning projects.

Matplotlib for Data Visualization

Visualizing data and model outputs is an integral part of working with generative models. Matplotlib is one of the most widely used libraries for creating static, animated, and interactive visualizations in Python. From plotting loss curves to visualizing the output of your models, Matplotlib helps you gain insights into model performance and areas for improvement.

- **Why Matplotlib?** Matplotlib is flexible, and easy to integrate with other libraries such as NumPy and Pandas, making it the default choice for generating visualizations in AI projects. You can use it to create charts, graphs, and plots to track training performance, and visualize generated outputs.

Other Key Libraries

Pandas, OpenCV, and Scikit-learn are essential libraries frequently used in generative modeling. They play crucial roles in data manipulation, image processing, and model evaluation, making them indispensable when working with generative model applications.

- **Pandas:** Often used for data manipulation, particularly with tabular data.

- **OpenCV:** Useful for computer vision tasks, such as image preprocessing or manipulation before feeding data into generative models.
- **Scikit-learn:** While primarily used for traditional machine learning algorithms, Scikit-learn offers many preprocessing tools and metrics that are necessary for evaluating models.

Case Study: Exploring AI-Driven Hairstyling with StyleGAN for a European Hair Stylist

In this case study. a European hair stylist explores how StyleGAN can power a real-time virtual hairstyling experience that lets customers see realistic hairstyles on themselves instantly. It highlights the journey from concept to deployment as AI transforms a traditional salon visit into an interactive digital experience.

Problem: Enhancing Customer Experience with Virtual Hairstyling

A popular hair stylist in Europe sought a team of AI experts to provide an innovative customer experience by allowing clients to preview various creative hairstyles in real-time. The idea was simple: when a customer sat in front of the webcam at a salon, they could see themselves on the screen with different hairstyles applied virtually to their face. This solution aimed to personalize the styling experience, allowing customers to experiment with unique hair designs and colors before making a decision.

The challenge was to develop a seamless, real-time experience where the hairstyles would adjust dynamically based on the customer's head position and facial expressions. Traditional photo manipulation techniques were too slow and inflexible, requiring stylists to upload photos and manually adjust hairstyles for each client. The company needed a more efficient, automated solution that would allow customers to interactively try out different hairstyles, as if they were looking into a mirror.

Figure 1.3: *Generative Models at Work*

Solution Approach: Feasibility of StyleGAN for Real-Time Hairstyle Generation

In response, the AI experts team conducted an in-depth analysis of different solutions, and finally the potential of using StyleGAN, a generative model renowned for producing high-quality images. The research focused on designing an architecture that would integrate StyleGAN with real-time video processing, allowing hairstyles to be applied dynamically as customers viewed themselves on screen.

The solution worked by capturing the live video feed of a person's face in front of the webcam. StyleGAN was trained on a vast dataset of hairstyle images, encompassing various haircuts, colors, and styles from around the world. This allowed the model to learn the intricate details of different hair textures, lengths, and shapes. Using this dataset, StyleGAN could then generate highly realistic hairstyles that matched the customer's facial features in real-time.

Users could browse through multiple hairstyle options using an interface, selecting different styles and colors with the click of a button. The system would instantly apply the new hairstyle to the live image, giving clients a preview of how the haircut would look from different angles as they moved their heads.

Challenges: Real-Time Processing and Personalization

The biggest challenge in implementing the solution was ensuring that the system could operate in real-time. Processing live video feeds, applying the generated hairstyles, and adjusting them dynamically based on customer movements required significant computational power. Moreover, the system had to be fast enough to avoid delays, which could negatively affect the customer experience.

Another challenge was ensuring that the generated hairstyles matched the customer's face shape, hairline, and proportions accurately. Hairstyles that looked artificial or poorly aligned with the customer's head would undermine the effectiveness of the solution.

Solution: Optimization and Fine-Tuning

To address the real-time processing issue, the development team recommended using high-performance GPUs and optimized the StyleGAN model to reduce latency. This included transfer learning techniques to fine-tune the model on specific facial characteristics and hairstyles commonly requested by customers. This would allow the system to generate high-quality hairstyles more efficiently, minimizing the lag between user input and visual output.

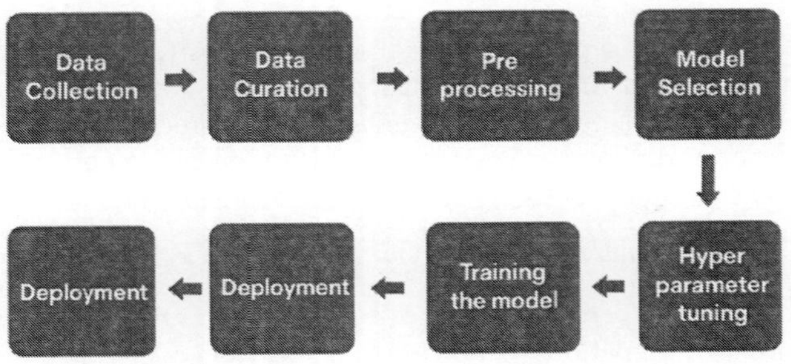

Figure 1.4: *Lifecycle of the Solution Steps*

As shown in the preceding figure, the overall solution involved data collection, data curation, preprocessing, and model selection (for example, CNN, DLib, and StyleGAN), hyper parameter tuning, training the model, testing the model, deployment and continuous training with human feedback. A quick explanation of each step is as follows:

- **Data Collection:** Gathering a large dataset of diverse hairstyle images, including different angles, lighting conditions, and hair types, to train the model.
- **Data Curation:** Cleaning and organizing the collected data, ensuring high-quality, labeled images, and removing irrelevant or low-quality data points.
- **Preprocessing:** Preparing the images for model training such as resizing, normalization, and augmenting the dataset to improve model robustness.
- **Model Selection:** Choosing appropriate models such as CNN for feature extraction, DLib for facial landmark detection, and StyleGAN for generating high-quality hairstyle images.
- **Hyperparameter Tuning:** Adjusting key model parameters (for example, learning rate, batch size, and so on) to optimize model performance, and ensure faster convergence during training.
- **Training the Model:** Feeding the preprocessed data into the selected models, and iterating through the training process to learn and generate new hairstyle images.
- **Testing the Model:** Evaluating the model's performance on a separate test dataset to ensure accuracy and consistency in generating realistic and aligned hairstyles.
- **Deployment:** Implementing the trained model into a real-world environment (such as a salon interface), where customers can view generated hairstyles in real-time based on their facial features.

Recommendations and Future Directions

Following the analysis, several recommendations were proposed to enhance the system's scalability, effectiveness, and personalization. It was suggested to further optimize StyleGAN by applying transfer learning techniques, fine-tuning the model to better recognize common facial features and hair types specific to the stylist chain's clientele. To ensure that the generated hairstyles were accurately aligned with the customer's face, facial landmark detection was recommended. This would allow the system to dynamically adjust the hairstyles based on different head angles and facial expressions, ensuring a natural and responsive experience as the customer moved or smiled.

To address the computational challenges, the research suggested using cloud-based GPU services to scale the solution, enabling real-time processing. The team recommended further testing and refinement through live customer interactions, which would help to ensure the system's responsiveness and accuracy.

Outcome and Future Potential

The solution and findings offered a promising vision for how AI-driven solutions could revolutionize the hairstyling industry. The use of AI-powered hairstyle previews not only help customers make more informed decisions but also attracts a broader audience interested in experimenting with creative styles. The recommendations outlined a clear path for further development, showing how technology like StyleGAN could create a highly engaging and personalized experience for clients.

Conclusion

We are now familiar with the foundational concepts of generative models, including how they function, their unique ability to create new data, and the practical applications that make them invaluable across industries. From deepfakes and AI-generated art to medical advancements and product design, generative models have already begun reshaping various sectors. We have also explored key technologies such as TensorFlow and PyTorch, which provide the necessary frameworks for building these models, along with libraries like NumPy and Matplotlib for data manipulation and visualization. With these tools and concepts in hand, you are well-prepared to embark on your journey into the world of generative AI.

In the next chapter, we will dive deeper into the mathematical foundations that underpin generative models. You will learn about probability distributions, latent variables, and optimization techniques, which are essential for understanding how these models generate data, and improve over time. These concepts will provide the technical foundation needed to build more advanced generative models, setting the stage for hands-on projects in the chapters to come. Thus, by mastering these fundamentals, you will be ready to tackle more complex and innovative applications of generative AI.

Points to Remember

- Generative models are designed to learn patterns from data, and generate new, unseen samples based on those learned patterns.
- The latent space is a key concept in generative models, representing data in a compressed form that the model uses to generate new outputs.
- GANs and VAEs are two of the most popular generative models, each with different approaches to generating new data.
- Tools such as TensorFlow and PyTorch are essential for building, training, and deploying generative models, while libraries like NumPy and Matplotlib support data manipulation and visualization.
- Generative models have a wide range of applications, from creating deepfakes and AI-generated art to synthesizing text and generating 3D models for product design.

Multiple Choice Questions

1. Which of the following is a key concept in generative models?
   a. Data Classification
   b. Feature Extraction
   c. Latent Space
   d. Overfitting
2. What is the primary function of the generator in a Generative Adversarial Network (GAN)?
   a. To generate new data samples
   b. To classify images
   c. To train on real data only
   d. To evaluate the generated data
3. Which of the following is an application of generative models?
   a. Sorting data
   b. Image synthesis
   c. Predicting stock prices
   d. Data compression

4. In the training of GANs, what does the discriminator do?
    a. It generates data samples.
    b. It evaluates whether the data is real or fake.
    c. It adjusts the latent space.
    d. It minimizes the loss function.
5. Which library is commonly used for manipulating multi-dimensional arrays in Python, particularly for generative modeling?
    a. PyTorch
    b. Matplotlib
    c. NumPy
    d. Scikit-learn
6. Which type of generative model uses a probabilistic approach to generate smoother outputs?
    a. GAN
    b. VAE
    c. CNN
    d. RNN

Answers

1. c
2. a
3. b
4. b
5. c
6. b

Questions

1. What is a generative model, and how does it differ from traditional machine learning models?
2. What are some practical applications of generative models in industries such as healthcare, art, and entertainment?
3. What is the purpose of the latent space in generative models?
4. How does the training process of a generative model work?
5. What is the role of sampling in generative models?
6. What are deepfakes, and how are they created using generative models?
7. How do Generative Adversarial Networks (GANs) and Variational Autoencoders (VAEs) differ in their approach to generating data?
8. How do TensorFlow and PyTorch support the implementation of generative models?

9. What is the significance of using libraries like NumPy and Matplotlib in the development and evaluation of generative models?
10. What are the key challenges in training generative models such as GANs?

Key Terms

- **Generative Model:** A type of machine learning model that learns from data and generates new, unseen samples that resemble the training data.
- **Latent Space:** A lower-dimensional representation of input data where the generative model maps features for efficient processing and data generation.
- **Training Process:** The phase where a generative model learns the underlying patterns in data by adjusting its parameters to minimize the difference between real and generated data.
- **Sampling:** The method by which a generative model selects points from the learned latent space to generate new data such as images or text.
- **Deepfake:** A synthetic media technique where generative models create realistic videos or images that can make people appear to do or say things they never did.
- **Autoencoder:** A neural network used for dimensionality reduction and reconstruction, often a precursor to more complex generative models.
- **Generative Adversarial Network (GAN):** A generative model that consists of two networks—a generator and a discriminator—competing against each other to create and evaluate the synthetic data.
- **Variational Autoencoder (VAE):** A type of autoencoder that uses a probabilistic approach to generate smoother, more structured outputs by learning the underlying data distribution.
- **Style Transfer:** A generative model technique used to apply the style of one image (for example, a painting) to another image, while maintaining the content of the second image.
- **Data Augmentation:** The process of artificially increasing the amount of data by generating new data points from the existing dataset using generative models.
- **TensorFlow:** A deep learning framework developed by Google used to build, train, and deploy machine learning models, including generative models.
- **PyTorch:** A flexible deep learning framework developed by Facebook, popular for its dynamic computation graph, and used widely in research and generative model development.
- **NumPy:** A library in Python for performing high-level mathematical functions and handling large, multi-dimensional arrays, often used in generative model workflows.
- **Matplotlib:** A Python library for creating visualizations such as plots, charts, and graphs, essential for tracking model performance, and visualizing generated outputs.

References

- Hinton, G. E., Osindero, S., and Teh, Y. W. (2006). A *fastlearning algorithm for deep belief nets*. Neural Computation, 18(7), 1527–1554.
- Kingma, D. P., & Welling, M. (2013). *Auto-encoding variational Bayes*. arXiv preprint arXiv:1312.6114.
- Karras, T., Laine, S., and Aila, T. (2019). A *style-based generator architecture for generative adversarial networks*. In Proceedings of the IEEE/CVF Conference on Computer Vision and Pattern Recognition, pp. 4401–4410.
- Goodfellow, I., Pouget-Abadie, J., Mirza, M., Xu, B., Warde-Farley, D., Ozair, S., ... and Bengio, Y. (2014). *Generative adversarial nets*. In Advances in neural information processing systems, pp. 2672–2680.

CHAPTER 2
Mathematical Foundations

Introduction

Generative models, like most advanced machine learning models, are built on a strong mathematical foundation. Hence, understanding key mathematical principles is crucial for developing, optimizing, and evaluating these models effectively. In this chapter, we explore the essential concepts of probability theory, information theory, and optimization techniques, all of which form the backbone of generative models such as GANs and VAEs. These models rely heavily on mathematical frameworks to understand data distributions, minimize errors, and improve performance during training. By mastering these foundational principles, you will be equipped to not only grasp how generative models function but also to apply these techniques to build your own models with greater accuracy and efficiency. This chapter will guide you through the core mathematical tools, from probability distributions to gradient descent, providing practical examples to reinforce your understanding.

Structure

In this chapter, we will discuss the following topics:

- **Overview of Mathematical Foundations in Generative Models**
- **Probability Theory and Statistics**
  - Definition and Core Concepts
  - Common Distributions in Generative Models
  - Types of Probabilities
  - Bayes' Theorem and Its Significance in Machine Learning (ML)
  - Sampling Techniques
- **Information Theory**
  - Definition of Entropy
  - Core Concepts
  - Practical Examples with Python
- **Optimization Techniques**
  - Introduction to Optimization in Machine Learning
  - Loss Functions
  - Gradient Descent
  - Stochastic Gradient Descent (SGD)
  - Backpropagation Overview
  - Implementing Gradient Descent Using NumPy

- **Introduction to Neural Networks**
  - Basic Neural Network Architecture
  - Forward and Backward Propagation
  - Common Activation Functions
  - A Simple Neural Network using NumPy
- **Case Study: Mathematical Foundations Applied to Generative Models**
  - Problem: Applying Mathematics to Solve Generative Modeling Challenges
  - Solution Approach: Probability, Information Theory for Model Performance
  - Challenges and Solutions

Overview of Mathematical Foundations in Generative Models

Generative models are a fascinating branch of Artificial Intelligence (AI), allowing machines to create new data that mirrors the distribution of real-world datasets. From generating images to synthesizing text and music, these models rely heavily on the underlying principles of mathematics. Understanding the mathematics behind generative models is key to unlocking their potential, and ensuring that they perform efficiently in real-world applications.

This chapter delves into the foundational mathematical concepts that underpin generative models. By the end of this chapter, you will understand how core areas such as probability theory, statistics, information theory, and optimization techniques provide the backbone for the design and functionality of generative AI.

Importance of Mathematical Principles in Generative Models

Mathematics is often the invisible force behind the amazing capabilities of generative models. Every generated image, every new piece of text, and every synthetic dataset that comes from a generative model relies on a deep mathematical structure. The key mathematical areas such as probability, statistics, and optimization techniques govern how these models learn patterns, adapt, and improve over time.

Figure 2.1: *Gen AI and Statistics!*

Here are some of the main reasons why understanding mathematical principles is crucial for working with generative models:

- **Learning from Data:** Generative models need to understand the underlying distribution of the training data to create new, plausible outputs. This requires a firm understanding of probability theory, as the model must capture patterns and nuances in the data distribution.
- **Handling Uncertainty:** In the real world, data is often incomplete or noisy. Statistics and information theory help generative models manage uncertainty, ensuring that even with imperfect data, the models can generate meaningful and realistic outputs.
- **Optimization**: Generative models are trained through iterative optimization processes, such as gradient descent. These optimization techniques minimize the difference between the generated output and the real data, improving the quality of the model over time.

How Mathematical Foundations Underpin Generative AI

Generative AI does not just "*happen*"; it is a structured process governed by precise mathematical rules. Thus, let us briefly introduce the key areas of mathematics that support generative AI:

- **Probability Theory:** At the heart of every generative model lies probability theory. Probability provides the foundation for how these models make predictions, generate new data, and manage uncertainty. In generative models, probability theory is used to model the distribution of data. This enables the model to generate outputs that closely resemble the training data, without producing the exact duplicates.

Key Concepts in Probability for Generative Models:

- **Random Variables:** A generative model treats the data as random variables drawn from a probability distribution. For example, a model that generates images treats each pixel as a random variable that can take on a certain value.
- **Probability Distributions:** Generative models work by learning the underlying distribution of the training data. The model's goal is to capture this distribution accurately enough so that it can generate new data points that are statistically similar to the original dataset.
- **Conditional Probability:** Many generative models such as Conditional GANs (CGANs), rely on conditional probability, where the model generates data based on certain conditions or inputs.

This simple code demonstrates how a generative model can sample from a distribution to generate data, a core function in probability-based models.

```
import numpy as np
from scipy.stats import norm  # normal random variable

# Example of probability distribution - sampling from a normal distribution
data = np.random.normal(0, 1, 1000)  # Generating 1000 samples from a normal
distribution (mean=0, std=1)

# Visualizing the probability distribution
import matplotlib.pyplot as plt
plt.hist(data, bins=30, density=True)
plt.title("Normal Distribution of Generated Data")
plt.show()
```

The outcome of this code will be a histogram showing the distribution of 1,000 samples that have been randomly generated from a normal distribution with a mean of 0 and a standard deviation of 1.

- **Statistics:** Statistics plays a critical role in understanding and modeling data for generative models. While probability theory focuses on predicting outcomes based on known distributions, statistics helps to make sense of the data, and identify patterns. For generative models, statistics answers key questions such as:

- What is the average pattern in the data?
- How much variability is there?
- How are different variables related to each other?

Statistical methods guide the model in learning the key features of the data, allowing the generative process to maintain the right balance between consistency and diversity. Concepts such as variance, correlation, and covariance are necessary tools in this process.

- **Variance:** Measures how much the data points in a dataset differ from the mean. Maintaining an appropriate level of variance is crucial for creating outputs that have both consistency and diversity.
- **Covariance and Correlation**: Covariance measures how two variables change together, while correlation normalizes this relationship to a range between -1 and 1. Thus, understanding correlations between features helps generative models produce more coherent outputs.

- **Information Theory:** Information theory provides a framework for measuring how much "*information*" is present in a dataset. It is a crucial concept for generative models because it helps manage uncertainty, and optimize the process of generating new data.

  Key concepts in information theory that are relevant to generative models include:

  - **Entropy:** A measure of uncertainty or randomness in a dataset. High entropy indicates more variability, while low entropy suggests that the data is more predictable.
  - **KL-Divergence:** A way to measure the difference between two probability distributions, typically used to compare the model's learned distribution with the actual data distribution.

  Information theory is particularly important in models like Variational Autoencoders (VAEs), which rely on minimizing the difference between learned and real data distributions.

- **Optimization Techniques:** Optimization is the engine that drives the learning process in generative models. The goal of optimization is to minimize the error between the model's generated outputs and the actual data. Techniques such as gradient descent help generative models gradually improve over time by adjusting the model parameters.
  - **Gradient Descent:** A popular optimization technique where the model's parameters are updated iteratively to minimize a cost function.
  - **Backpropagation:** Used in neural networks, backpropagation calculates the gradient of the loss function with respect to each weight by using the chain rule, essential for updating the model's parameters.

Probability Theory and Statistics

Understanding probability theory is crucial when building generative models, as it enables us to model uncertainty, make predictions, and estimate likelihoods in machine learning. Generative models rely heavily on probability theory and statistical measures to function effectively. These mathematical concepts allow models to generate new data by understanding and sampling from underlying data distributions. So, let us explore the key components that form the foundation of probability theory and statistics in the context of generative AI. This section covers the fundamental concepts of probability, essential distributions, sampling techniques, and how these concepts integrate into generative modeling.

Definition and Core Concepts

To build a strong foundation in generative models, it is necessary to understand the underlying mathematical principles, including random variables, probability distributions, and expected values. These core concepts enable generative models to represent, learn, and create data effectively.

Random Variables

A random variable is a variable whose possible values are determined by the outcomes of a random event or process. Its value is not fixed but varies based on the result of an underlying chance-based phenomenon. Random variables are used to represent elements of data, such as pixel values in an image or words in a sentence. In the context of generative models, random variables help represent uncertain quantities. They are categorized into:

- **Discrete random variables:** These take on distinct, countable values. For example, the outcome of rolling a die (1, 2, 3, ... 6) is a discrete random variable.
- **Continuous random variables:** These can take on any value within a given range. For instance, temperature readings over time or pixel intensity values in images are continuous random variables.
- **Example:** In an image generation model, each pixel can be considered a random variable that takes on a specific value from a distribution of possible pixel intensities.

Probability Distributions

A probability distribution explains how the possible values of a random variable are spread or distributed across different outcomes. It gives the likelihood of different outcomes. Generative models learn the probability distribution of the training data, and use this to generate new, realistic data points.

- **Expected Value:** The expected value of a random variable is the average value it would take on if the random experiment were repeated many times. It provides a central measure of the data. In generative models, the expected value helps the model understand the "*center*" of the data distribution, guiding the generation process toward more probable outputs.
  - **Key Formula:**

    Expected Value (for discrete variables):

    $$E[X] = \sum_{i=1}^{n} x_i P(x_i)$$

    Where x_i are possible values of the random variable, X and $P(x_i)$ is the probability of each outcome.

Common Distributions in Generative Models

Generative models use various probability distributions to represent data. So, let us explore some of the most common ones:

- **Normal Distribution (Gaussian Distribution)**: This is the most widely used distribution in generative models, especially when working with continuous data. It has a bell-shaped curve, with most data points clustered around the mean.

  $$f(x \mid \mu, \sigma) = \frac{1}{\sigma\sqrt{2\pi}} e^{-\frac{(x-\mu)^2}{2\sigma^2}}$$

  where μ is the mean and σ is the standard deviation.

- **Bernoulli Distribution**: This distribution is used when there are only two possible outcomes, such as success or failure, yes or no. It is commonly used in binary classification tasks.

$$P(X = 1) = p \text{ and } P(X = 0) = 1 - p$$

  where p is the probability of success.

- **Binomial Distribution**: The binomial distribution is an extension of the Bernoulli distribution to multiple trials. It represents the number of successes in a set number of independent and identical trials.

$$P(X = k) = (n, k)\, p^k (1 - p)^{n-k}$$

- **Multinomial Distribution**: This is a generalization of the binomial distribution where each trial can result in one of more than two outcomes. It is useful when generating categorical data.

$$P(X = (x_1, ..., x_k)) = \frac{n!}{x_1! \cdots x_k!} p_1^{x_1} \ldots p_k^{x_k}$$

- **Uniform Distribution:** The uniform distribution assigns equal probability to all outcomes within a given range. It is commonly used in generative models to initialize weights, sample noise vectors, or generate latent variables from a broad and unbiased range. This helps to ensure that the model explores the space without prior bias.

$$f(x) = \frac{1}{b-a} \text{ for } a \leq x \leq b$$

Types of Probabilities

Probabilities form the foundation of generative models, enabling them to represent and learn data distributions. Different types of probabilities play specific roles in these models, helping to manage complex relationships between variables, and handle uncertainty effectively. Here is an overview:

- **Joint Probability:** The probability of two or more events occurring together. For example, in generative models, we often model the joint probability of features and labels.
- **Conditional Probability:** The likelihood of an event happening, assuming that another event has already taken place. It is represented as P(A|B), and it is used in generative models to update beliefs based on the observed data.
- **Marginalization:** This refers to the process of summing or integrating over a variable to obtain the marginal probability of another variable. It is a fundamental technique in probabilistic models to handle the hidden or unobserved variables.

Bayes' Theorem and Its Significance in Machine Learning

Bayes' Theorem relates joint and conditional probabilities, providing a mechanism for updating probabilities based on new data. It is expressed as:

$$P(A \mid B) = \frac{P(B \mid A)\ P(A)}{P(B)}$$

Here is what each part represents:

- **P(A|B):** This is the posterior probability. It represents the probability of event A occurring given that event B has already happened. This is what we want to calculate or update—our belief about A after knowing B.
- **P(B|A):** This is the likelihood. It represents the probability of observing event B given that event A has occurred.
- **P(A):** This is the prior probability of A. It represents our initial belief about the probability of A happening before we have any information about B.
- **P(B):** This is the marginal probability of B, also known as the evidence. It is the overall probability of observing event B across all possible scenarios.

Example to understand Bayes' theorem: Is it a Cat or Dog in the Box?

Imagine we have a box, and we want to determine whether it contains a cat or a dog based on the sound we hear coming from the box. Let us say we hear a meow, and we want to figure out the probability that the animal inside the box is a cat given that we heard the meow. Bayes' Theorem allows us to revise or update our belief based on new information.

***Figure 2.2**: Is it a Cat or Dog in the Box?*

Let us make the following assumptions:

- A represents the statement, "*There might be a cat in the box.*"
- B represents the statement, "*We hear a meow.*"

We want to find:

- P(Cat|Meow), which is the probability that there is a cat in the box given that we heard a meow.

To use Bayes' Theorem, we need the following:

- **P(Meow|Cat)**: This is the likelihood, the probability of hearing a meow if there is a cat in the box. Let us say this is quite high, like 0.9 (since cats meow often).
- **P(Cat)**: This is the prior probability that the box contains a cat. Let us say that before we hear anything, we think the box is equally likely to have a cat or a dog, so P(Cat)=0.5.
- **P(Meow|Dog)**: We also need the probability of hearing a meow if there is a dog in the box (since dogs rarely meow, this will be very low). Let us assume it is 0.05.

- **P(Meow)**: This is the overall probability of hearing a meow. We can calculate this as the total probability of hearing a meow across both scenarios (cat or dog in the box): `P(Meow) = P(Meow|Cat) * P(Cat) + P(Meow|Dog) * P(Dog)`

Using the numbers we assumed earlier:

```
P(Meow) = (0.9 * 0.5) + (0.05 * 0.5) = 0.45 + 0.025 = 0.475
```

Now, using Bayes' Theorem, we can compute the posterior probability

$$P(Cat \mid Meow) = \frac{P(Meow \mid Cat) \,.\, P(Cat)}{P(Meow)}$$

Substituting the values:

So, the probability that the box contains a cat given that we heard a meow is 94.7%. Our initial belief (prior) was 50%, but after hearing the meow, we update our belief using Bayes' Theorem, making it much more likely that there is a cat in the box.

$$P(Cat \mid Meow) = \frac{0.9 \,.\, 0.5}{0.475} = \frac{0.45}{0.475} \simeq 0.947$$

Sampling Techniques

Sampling from probability distributions is crucial in generative models to create new data points or to approximate complex integrals that cannot be computed analytically.

- **Monte Carlo Sampling:** This is a technique used to approximate probability distributions through random sampling. It is particularly useful when dealing with high-dimensional spaces where direct computation is difficult to control. In generative models, Monte Carlo methods are often used to estimate expectations or optimize models such as GANs and VAEs.
- **Importance of Sampling:** This technique improves the efficiency of Monte Carlo sampling by drawing samples from a distribution that is easier to sample from, and then weighting them to reflect the desired distribution. This is particularly useful in variational inference and other probabilistic generative models where direct sampling may be difficult.

Expectation and Variance

- **Expectation:** The expectation (or expected value) of a random variable gives the long-term average outcome of that variable. In the context of generative models, the expectation helps in computing the average output of a model or the expected loss. Mathematically, the expectation of a random variable X is defined as:

$$E[X] = \sum_x P(x) \cdot x$$

- **Variance**: Variance measures the spread or dispersion of a random variable's possible outcomes. In generative models, variance is necessary for understanding uncertainty, and for tuning models. The variance of a random variable X is given by:

$$Var(X) = E[(X - E[X])^2]$$

In generative models, the concepts of expectation and variance are widely used in defining loss functions (for example, mean squared error) and in modeling uncertainty in the data. For example, in VAEs, minimizing the variance between the predicted and true data distribution is key to generating high-quality outputs.

Information Theory

Information theory is the mathematical study of data encoding, transmission, and storage. In the context of generative models, it helps quantify the amount of information a model holds and transmits during training and inference. The foundational concept of **entropy** is used to measure uncertainty, which plays a crucial role in understanding how well a generative model can predict or generate data.

Information theory is widely used in generative models like VAEs, where we aim to minimize the difference between the learned distribution and the true data distribution, a task directly linked to minimizing the amount of "*surprise*" or uncertainty (high entropy) in the system.

Definition of Entropy

The core idea in information theory, entropy, is a measure of unpredictability or uncertainty. In the context of a generative model, entropy helps us understand how much uncertainty is in the output. High entropy means the model is highly uncertain about the prediction or generation, while low entropy implies more certainty.

- **Mathematical Formula:**

  $$H(X) = -\sum_{i=1}^{n} p(x_i) \log p(x_i)$$

  where $p(x_i)$ is the probability of an event x_i

  In generative models, entropy helps in quantifying the uncertainty in the data and the latent variables. Lower entropy implies that the model has learned to generate more predictable and realistic data.

- **Entropy as a Measure of Uncertainty:** In machine learning, entropy is used to assess the degree of uncertainty in the predictions made by a model. If the entropy is high, it indicates that the model is uncertain about the outcome. Entropy is widely used in decision trees, where it helps in determining which feature to split on, as well as in probabilistic generative models such as VAEs, where it quantifies the uncertainty in the latent space.

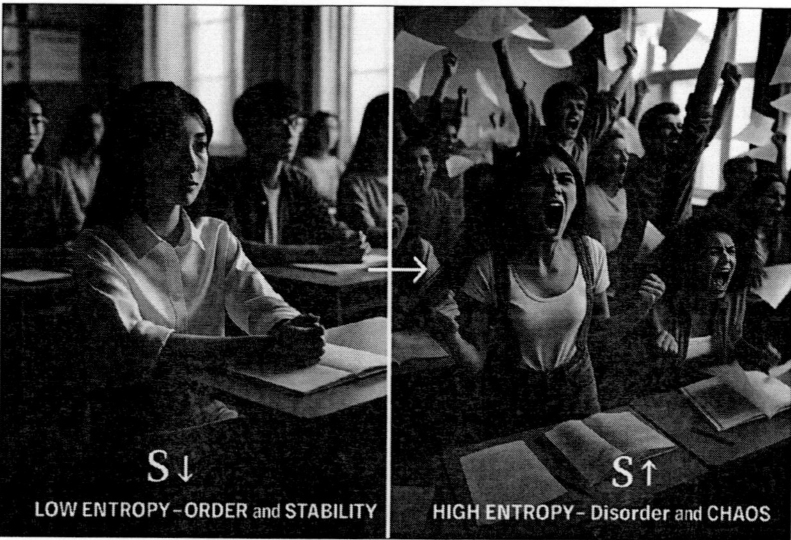

Figure 2.3: *Quiet Classroom (Low Entropy) and Noisy Classroom (High Entropy)*

Imagine a classroom where students either remain quiet or become noisy, depending on whether the teacher is present or not.

- **Quiet Classroom (Teacher is Present):** When the teacher is in the classroom, the students are generally quiet. The behavior of the class is very predictable – almost everyone stays quiet. There is very little uncertainty because we know what will happen (students will remain quiet). In this case, the entropy (a measure of uncertainty or unpredictability) is low because the situation is very ordered, and the outcome is predictable.
- **Noisy Classroom (Teacher is Absent):** When the teacher leaves the classroom, the students' behavior becomes less predictable. Some students might start talking, others might yell, and a few might still remain quiet. There is a lot more uncertainty about what the students will do. In this case, the classroom's behavior is less predictable and more random, so the entropy is high because there is more disorder and unpredictability.

In summary, entropy is a measure of unpredictability. A quiet classroom with the teacher present has low entropy because it is predictable and ordered. A noisy classroom with the teacher absent has high entropy because it is chaotic and uncertain.

Kullback-Leibler (KL) Divergence: A metric that indicates how much one probability distribution differs from another, is expected probability distribution. In generative models such as VAEs, minimizing the KL Divergence between the learned distribution and the true data distribution helps make the model's output more realistic.

Mathematical Formula:

$$DKL\,(P\,||\,Q) = \sum_i P(xi)\,log\,\frac{P(x_i)}{Q(x_i)}$$

where $P(x_i)$ and $Q(x_i)$ are the probability distributions.

How It is Used in Generative Models (for example, in VAEs)

In Variational Autoencoders (VAEs), KL divergence plays a critical role. VAEs aim to approximate a complex, intractable (difficult to control) distribution by using a simpler distribution (for example, Gaussian). The goal is to minimize the KL divergence between the approximate posterior and the true prior distribution. By doing so, VAEs ensure that the generated data remains close to the original data distribution, while also learning meaningful representations of the latent space.

Core Concepts

In this section, we lay the groundwork for understanding the mathematical ideas that power modern generative models. These concepts act like the quiet machinery behind the scenes, shaping how models learn patterns, preserve information, and produce realistic outputs. They give us a clearer view of why generative systems behave the way they do and how to guide them toward better performance.

Mutual Information

Mutual information measures the amount of information obtained about one random variable by observing another. It measures how much uncertainty about one variable is reduced when information about the other variable is known. In generative models, this concept helps ensure that generated data retains certain key attributes from the input data, for example image features in an image-to-image translation task. If you know that the weather (Y) is sunny, then you gain some information on the clothes (Y) a person might wear, like a t-shirt and not a jacket.

Mathematical Formula:

```
I(X; Y) = H(X) - H(X | Y)
```

where H(X) is the entropy of X and H(X|Y) is the conditional entropy of X given Y.

In model learning, maximizing mutual information can help improve the quality of the generated data by ensuring that the latent representations capture useful, interpretable features of the input data.

Cross-Entropy Loss

Explanation and Connection to Generative Models (for example, in GANs)

Cross-entropy is a widely used loss function in machine learning, particularly in classification tasks. It measures the difference between two probability distributions: the true distribution (ground truth) and the predicted distribution (model output). In generative models, cross-entropy is used to optimize how well the model generates the realistic data.

In Generative Adversarial Networks (GANs), cross-entropy loss is used in both the generator and discriminator. The discriminator is trained to minimize the cross-entropy between real and fake data, while the generator is trained to fool the discriminator into predicting that generated data is real. The competition between these two networks is optimized using cross-entropy, driving the generator to produce more realistic outputs.

Practical Examples with Python

We can demonstrate the core concepts of information theory using Python. Here is a simple example to calculate entropy for a given distribution using the scipy library:

```
import numpy as np
from scipy.stats import entropy

# Define a simple probability distribution
probability_distribution = [0.2, 0.5, 0.3]

# Calculate entropy
entropy_value = entropy(probability_distribution, base=2)
print(f"Entropy: {entropy_value}")
```

Similarly, we can calculate KL Divergence between two distributions:

```
import numpy as np
from scipy.special import rel_entr # relative entropy

# Define two probability distributions
P = [0.4, 0.6]
Q = [0.5, 0.5]

# Calculate KL Divergence = Sum of element wise relative entropy
kl_divergence = np.sum(rel_entr(P, Q))
print(f"KL Divergence: {kl_divergence}")
```

Outcome of the Program

The first part of the code calculates the entropy of the probability distribution [0.2, 0.5, 0.3] using base 2. The calculated entropy will be printed to the console as something like:

```
Entropy: 1.4854752972273344 (High Entropy)
```

The second part of the code calculates the KL divergence between two probability distributions, P = [0.4, 0.6] and Q = [0.5, 0.5]. The calculated KL divergence will be printed to the console, and the output will be something like:

```
KL Divergence: 0.020410407324513063 (Low divergence)
```

Optimization Techniques

Optimization is a critical aspect of training machine learning models, particularly generative models such as GANs and VAEs. In generative models, optimization helps to minimize the difference between the model's predictions, and the true data distribution, ensuring that the model generates realistic outputs. This section covers essential optimization techniques and their application in machine learning.

Introduction to Optimization in Machine Learning

Optimization refers to the process of adjusting the model's parameters to minimize a loss function, which measures the difference between the predicted and actual data. For generative models, this can be thought of as guiding the model to generate data that is as close as possible to real-world examples.

In generative modeling, optimization techniques such as Gradient Descent and its variants are used to update the model's parameters iteratively until the model produces high-quality output.

Loss Functions

Loss functions are used to measure the discrepancy between the model's predictions and the actual data distribution, which helps the optimization process. Choosing the right loss function depends on the architecture and objective, especially in Generative models–for instance, GANs use something called as adversarial losses to distinguish the real from the generated data, while VAEs rely on a concept called as reconstruction loss combined with a KL divergence term to regularize the latent space. Loss functions ensure that the model learns meaningful patterns, and generates high-quality samples.

Gradient Descent

Gradient Descent is the backbone of most of the optimization techniques in machine learning. It iteratively updates the model's parameters to minimize the loss function by calculating the gradient (derivative) of the loss function with respect to the model's parameters. The gradient indicates the direction of the steepest ascent, and taking steps in the opposite direction minimizes the loss.

- **Mathematical Formula:**

  $$\theta = \theta - \alpha \cdot \nabla_{\theta} J(\theta)$$

  where:

  a. Theta θ represents the model parameters.

  b. Alpha α is the learning rate (step size).

  c. $\nabla_{\theta} J(\theta)$ is the gradient of the loss function $J(\theta)$.

- **Key Parameters:**
  - **Learning Rate:** Determines the step size during each iteration. A smaller learning rate ensures stable convergence but may take longer, while a large learning rate could overshoot the optimal solution.

  - **Convergence:** Gradient Descent converges when the gradient becomes very small, indicating that the model has reached a point where further updates have little effect.

Stochastic Gradient Descent (SGD)

Stochastic Gradient Descent is a variant of Gradient Descent that updates the model's parameters for each data point, rather than using the entire dataset. This makes it more efficient, and allows for faster iterations, particularly when dealing with large datasets common in generative modeling.

- **Key Difference:** In standard gradient descent, we calculate the gradient for the whole dataset. In SGD, the gradient is calculated for one random sample at a time, speeding up the training process, but introducing more noise.
- **Mathematical Formula**:

$$\theta = \theta - \alpha \cdot \nabla_{\theta} J\ (\theta;\ x^{(i)},\ y^{(i)})$$

  where $x^{(i)}$, $y^{(i)}$ are a single data point and label.

Backpropagation Overview

Backpropagation is the algorithm used in combination with Gradient Descent to optimize neural networks. It involves calculating the gradient of the loss function with respect to each weight in the network, and updating the weights accordingly. This is like fixing errors after seeing an outcome.

- **Steps of Backpropagation:**
  a. **Forward Pass:** Compute the output of the neural network by passing the input data through each layer.
  b. **Compute Loss:** Calculate the error by comparing the predicted output to the true label.
  c. **Backward Pass:** Calculate the gradients of the loss function with respect to the weights by propagating the error backward through the network.
  d. **Update Weights:** Use Gradient Descent or SGD to update the model's weights, and reduce the error.

Backpropagation allows neural networks to learn complex representations by iteratively adjusting weights to minimize the errors.

Implementing Gradient Descent Using NumPy

Here is a simple implementation of gradient descent in python using NumPy:

```
import numpy as np

# Define a simple linear model: y = mx + c
def model(x, m, c):
    return m * x + c

# Define the loss function: Mean Squared Error (MSE)
def loss_function(y_true, y_pred):
    return np.mean((y_true - y_pred) ** 2)

# Gradient Descent Algorithm
def gradient_descent(x, y, learning_rate, epochs):
    m, c = 0, 0  # Initial parameters
    n = len(x)   # Number of data points
```

```
    for _ in range(epochs):
        y_pred = model(x, m, c)
        dm = -(2/n) * np.sum(x * (y - y_pred))  # Gradient for m
        dc = -(2/n) * np.sum(y - y_pred)        # Gradient for c

        m = m - learning_rate * dm  # Update m
        c = c - learning_rate * dc  # Update c

    return m, c

# Sample data
x = np.array([1, 2, 3, 4, 5])
y = np.array([5, 7, 9, 11, 13])

# Perform gradient descent
m, c = gradient_descent(x, y, learning_rate=0.01, epochs=1000)
print(f"Optimized Parameters: m = {m}, c = {c}")
```

This example demonstrates a basic application of gradient descent to a simple linear model, optimizing the slope, m and intercept, c.

Introduction to Neural Networks

Neural networks are the fundamental building blocks of many generative models, especially GANs and VAEs. Understanding how they function will provide the necessary background to comprehend how generative models learn to represent and generate data.

Basic Neural Network Architecture

A neural network consists of multiple layers of interconnected nodes, or neurons. Each neuron in a layer receives inputs, applies an activation function to process them, and forwards the output to the subsequent layer. The architecture typically consists of:

- **Input Layer:** The first layer that receives the input data.
- **Hidden Layers:** Intermediate layers where the data is transformed using weights and biases. In generative models, these hidden layers are key in learning the complex patterns in data.
- **Output Layer:** The final layer that produces the output, such as a generated image or a predicted class.

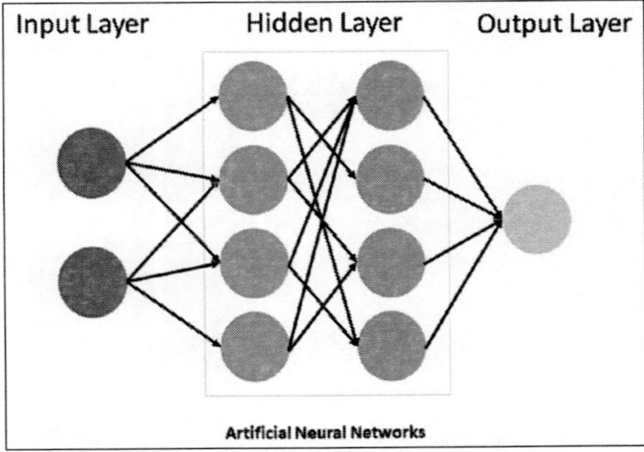

Figure 2.4: *Artificial Neural Networks with Different Layers*

Each connection between neurons is associated with a weight, which the network learns during training. The neural network's objective is to find the optimal set of weights that minimize the loss function.

Forward and Backward Propagation

Forward and backward propagation are fundamental processes in training neural networks. They work together to enable the model to learn from data by minimizing errors, and updating weights effectively.

- **Forward Propagation:** This is the process where the input data is passed through the network, layer by layer, until the output is generated. During forward propagation, each layer transforms the input using weights, biases, and activation functions.
- **Backward Propagation:** After calculating the output, and comparing it to the true label (using a loss function), backpropagation calculates the gradient of the loss function with respect to each weight. These gradients are used to update the weights, reducing the errors, and improving the model's performance in future iterations.

Backpropagation ensures that each weight in the network is updated to reduce the overall error.

Common Activation Functions

Activation functions introduce non-linearity into the network, allowing it to model complex patterns. Here are some common activation functions:

- **Sigmoid:**

$$f(x) = \frac{1}{1 + e^{-x}}$$

  - Output is between 0 and 1.
  - Sigmoid is commonly used in binary classification tasks but may suffer from a problem called vanishing gradients.
- **ReLU (Rectified Linear Unit):**

$$f(x) = max(0, x)$$

  - Most widely used activation function.
  - Allows the network to converge faster by only passing positive values.
- **Tanh:**

$$f(x) = \frac{(e^{x} - e^{-x})}{(e^{x} + e^{-x})}$$

  - Output is between -1 and 1.
  - Like Sigmoid, but scales values more effectively.
- **Softmax:**

$$f(x_i) = \frac{e^{x_i}}{\Sigma_{j=1}^{n} e^{x_j}}$$

  - It takes a list of any numbers (for example: [3, 1, -2]) and converts them into a list of probabilities (like [0.84, 0.11, 0.05]).

- This is essential for multi-class classification, where the highest input number will become the highest probability, and all probabilities adding up to 1.

A Simple Neural Network Using NumPy

Here is an example of implementing a basic neural network using NumPy to predict a binary output.

```
import numpy as np

# Sigmoid activation function
def sigmoid(x):
    return 1 / (1 + np.exp(-x))

# Derivative of the sigmoid function
def sigmoid_derivative(x):
    return x * (1 - x)

# Training data: inputs and corresponding outputs
inputs = np.array([[0, 0], [0, 1], [1, 0], [1, 1]])
outputs = np.array([[0], [1], [1], [0]])

# Initialize weights randomly with mean 0
np.random.seed(1)
weights = 2 * np.random.random((2, 1)) - 1
bias = np.random.random(1)

# Learning rate and number of epochs
learning_rate = 0.1
epochs = 10000

# Training loop
for epoch in range(epochs):
    # Forward propagation
    input_layer = inputs
    output_layer = sigmoid(np.dot(input_layer, weights) + bias)

    # Calculate error
    error = outputs - output_layer

    # Backpropagation
    adjustments = error * sigmoid_derivative(output_layer)
    weights += np.dot(input_layer.T, adjustments) * learning_rate
    bias += np.sum(adjustments) * learning_rate

# Final output after training
print(f"Trained Output: \n{output_layer}")
```

This code implements a single-layer neural network (also known as a perceptron) with sigmoid activation and backpropagation for training. The model predicts the XOR function based on the inputs.

Case Study: Mathematical Foundations Applied to Generative Models

Objective: To apply the key mathematical principles–probability theory, information theory, and optimization techniques–in the development of a FashionGAN model that generates new custom-designed t-shirts. The aim was to produce high-quality, unique designs, while ensuring the model could be trained efficiently, and handle common challenges.

Problem: Using Math to Solve Fashion GAN

The project involved building a GAN based solution that could generate custom t-shirt designs based on a user's preferences such as colors, patterns, and styles. Before development, several mathematical challenges needed to be addressed:

1. **Learning Complex Design Patterns:** The model needed to capture and generate intricate patterns, textures, and features common in fashion design.
2. **Ensuring Design Diversity:** The GAN had to avoid generating similar designs repeatedly (mode collapse), ensuring a wide variety of unique t-shirt designs.
3. **Balancing Efficiency and Quality:** Training the model required computational efficiency, without compromising the quality of the generated outputs, which could result in blurry or unrealistic designs.

Solution Approach: Key Concepts behind Generative Models

Generative models such as GANs and VAEs rely heavily on mathematical principles to generate new data that closely resembles real-world data. A solid understanding of the underlying mathematics, such as probability theory, optimization techniques, and information theory, would help achieve these goals.

In this case study, we will explore how these mathematical concepts are applied to real-world generative models, addressing common challenges that arise during training and model evaluation.

Probability Theory: Understanding and Generating Fashion Data

In generative models, probability theory helps in defining and understanding data distribution. For instance, VAEs learn to approximate the underlying probability distribution of the data using variational inference. This involves calculating the likelihood of generating specific data points based on latent variables.

- **GAN's Adversarial Process:** The generator in FashionGAN was trained to produce new t-shirt designs from a latent space, while the discriminator was tasked with distinguishing real designs from the generated ones. Probability theory played a key role in modeling the distribution of real-world fashion designs.

  Outcome: By optimizing the GAN to approximate the probability distribution of real t-shirt designs, the model successfully generated realistic outputs that closely resembled designs from our training dataset, which included thousands of images of custom t-shirts.

- **Latent Space Representation:** Probability theory was used to understand the latent space, where random noise was mapped to different fashion design features such as sleeve length, collar type, and color combinations.

  Outcome: The model learned to map these random variables to meaningful, diverse t-shirt designs, generating a variety of styles without repetition.

  Additionally, GANs use probability in the adversarial process between the generator and discriminator. The generator tries to produce samples from a distribution similar to the real data, while the discriminator estimates the probability that a given sample is real or fake.

Information Theory: Ensuring Diversity and Realism in Fashion Designs

Information theory plays a key role in ensuring that generative models are efficient in their task of data generation. In VAEs, minimizing KL Divergence ensures that the learned distribution (the model's output) is as close as possible to the actual data distribution. This helps the model generate realistic data, while maintaining diversity.

- **Minimizing KL Divergence:** In early tests with the FashionGAN, we explored VAEs alongside GANs to maintain diversity in the generated designs. Minimizing KL Divergence ensured that the distribution of generated t-shirts was diverse and did not collapse into a narrow set of similar designs.

  Outcome: By minimizing the KL Divergence between the learned distribution and the true distribution of fashion designs, the model was able to generate unique t-shirt designs that captured various fashion trends, from minimalist patterns to complex prints.

- **Entropy Control:** Controlling entropy was crucial for maintaining the balance between predictable (standard) designs and more experimental, creative outputs.

  Outcome: Managing the entropy helped the model create a blend of conventional designs and innovative ones, allowing the application to offer both classic and trendy t-shirts that users could customize.

  Additionally, the concept of entropy is used to quantify the uncertainty in the model's predictions. In some cases, controlling the entropy can lead to more stable models that generate higher-quality samples.

Optimization Techniques: Improving Efficiency and Quality in Design Generation

Training generative models requires efficient optimization methods to minimize the error between the generated data and the actual data. In GANs, the optimization process is adversarial: the generator and discriminator are optimized simultaneously in a min-max game. The generator is optimized to minimize the error of the discriminator, while the discriminator is optimized to detect whether the generated data is real or fake.

- **Gradient Descent in FashionGAN:** The optimization process involved tuning the generator and discriminator simultaneously. We used the Adam optimizer to ensure smooth and efficient updates to the model's parameters. This reduced the risk of the GAN becoming unstable, where the discriminator could overpower the generator.

  Outcome: Efficient optimization resulted in quicker convergence, allowing the model to generate high-quality designs within a reasonable training time. Designs became more accurate in capturing details such as fabric texture, pattern alignment, and symmetry.

- **Backpropagation and Regularization:** We utilized backpropagation to ensure that the model could calculate and update gradients efficiently during training. Batch normalization helped stabilize training, especially when generating complex designs such as abstract patterns.

  Outcome: The use of these techniques helped avoid overfitting and vanishing gradients, leading to more consistent quality in the generated designs.

VAEs, on the other hand, use Stochastic Gradient Descent (SGD) to minimize a combined loss function that includes both the reconstruction loss and KL divergence. Optimization techniques like gradient descent ensure that the model's parameters are updated in a way that reduces the error with every iteration.

Challenges and Solutions

Common Difficulties in Training Models and How Optimization helps Training generative models is filled with challenges, especially when it comes to balancing performance, stability, and accuracy. The following are some common difficulties encountered in practice, along with the solutions provided by optimization techniques:

- **Mode Collapse in FashionGAN**: One of the most notorious issues in GANs is mode collapse, where the generator produces limited variations of the same data. This happens because the generator finds a way to fool the discriminator with a specific set of outputs, rather than learning the full data distribution.
    - **Challenge:** In the early stages, the generator produced a limited variety of t-shirt designs, repeating the same patterns and color schemes.
    - **Solution:** Various techniques such as mini-batch discrimination, label smoothing, and unrolled GANs have been proposed to address mode collapse by encouraging the generator to explore a wider range of data distributions.
    - **Concrete Outcome:** After applying this solution, the model started generating diverse designs, including a range of styles such as crew-neck, V-neck, and various sleeve lengths.
- **Vanishing Gradients:** In deep networks, vanishing gradients can hinder the training process, especially during backpropagation. When gradients become very small, they no longer provide the necessary information to update the model's parameters.
    - **Challenge:** During the training of FashionGAN, we faced the vanishing gradients problem, where gradients became too small during backpropagation, preventing effective updates to the model's parameters. This caused the generator to struggle in learning, resulting in slow progress and low-quality t-shirt designs.
    - **Solution:** We addressed the vanishing gradients problem by using the ReLU (Rectified Linear Unit) activation function in both the generator and discriminator, allowing gradients to flow freely without being squashed. We also applied Batch Normalization to stabilize and normalize gradients, ensuring they remained effective as they propagated through the network.
    - **Concrete Outcome**: The model achieved smoother gradient flow and faster convergence. It began generating sharper, more detailed t-shirt designs, with distinct fabric textures and logos. The training process became more efficient, reducing the time required for high-quality results.
- **Instability in GAN Training:** GANs are notoriously difficult to train due to the adversarial nature of their optimization. If the discriminator becomes too strong, the generator may fail to learn, leading to unstable training dynamics.
    - **Challenge:** Training the GAN was unstable at times, with the discriminator becoming too effective, leading to the generator's failure to learn.
    - **Solution:** We applied a solution called Wasserstein GAN with gradient penalty (WGAN-GP) to stabilize the training process by enforcing smooth updates to the generator and discriminator, reducing instability in the adversarial process.
    - **Concrete Outcome:** The training stabilized, and the generator improved its ability to create high-quality, varied t-shirt designs that mimicked real-world fashion collections.

- **Balancing Reconstruction and Divergence in VAEs:** VAEs must strike a balance between reconstructing the data accurately and maintaining diversity in the latent space. This can be difficult, as too much focus on reconstruction can lead to overfitting, while too much focus on latent space regularization can lead to blurry outputs.
    - **Challenge:** The generated t-shirt designs either lacked detail or became too repetitive. It was difficult to strike a balance between the model accurately capturing intricate design details and maintaining variety.
    - **Solution:** By tuning the loss function and adjusting the trade-off between the adversarial loss (for realism) and a regularization term (to ensure variety), we were able to improve both the quality and diversity of the designs.
    - **Concrete Outcome:** The final FashionGAN model was able to generate a mix of detailed designs that included fine details such as embroidery or logo placement while still maintaining a diverse output set.

Key Takeaways from Mathematical Foundations in Practical Generative Model Training

Understanding the mathematical foundations of generative models is crucial for both designing and optimizing these models. Key takeaways from this case study include:

- **Probability theory:** This enabled the model to map random variables to diverse t-shirt design features, ensuring variety in the outputs.
- **Information theory:** This played a key role in minimizing divergence and maximizing diversity in the generated designs, producing t-shirts that spanned a range of fashion styles.
- **Optimization techniques**: This helped stabilize and improve the quality of the generated outputs through techniques such as gradient descent and backpropagation.

Thus, by mastering these mathematical concepts, machine learning engineers can overcome the common challenges in generative model training, and unlock the full potential of models like GANs and VAEs.

Conclusion

In this chapter, we delved into the core mathematical foundations that underpin generative models such as GANs and VAEs. A strong grasp of these mathematical principles allows machine learning engineers to not only understand how generative models work but also improve their performance through proper application of techniques like probability theory, optimization, and information theory.

In the next chapter, we will dive into the core principles and mechanics behind Variational Autoencoders (VAEs), one of the most important types of generative models. VAEs extend traditional autoencoders by introducing a probabilistic approach to the latent space, enabling them to generate new data that closely resembles the input data. We will explore the architecture of VAEs, including the roles of the encoder, decoder, and latent variables, while also discussing the mathematical foundations such as KL divergence and the reparameterization trick. Additionally, we will walk through practical implementations of VAEs using TensorFlow and PyTorch, highlighting their applications in areas such as image generation, anomaly detection, and data augmentation. Therefore, by the end of this chapter, you will have a solid understanding of how VAEs work, and how they can be used to build powerful generative models.

Points to Remember

- Probability theory is crucial for understanding how generative models handle data distributions, especially in models like VAEs that learn to generate new data points by approximating real-world distributions.
- Bayesian probability plays an important role in incorporating prior knowledge into generative models, helping to improve predictions based on previously observed data.
- KL Divergence is commonly used in VAEs to measure how much the learned distribution diverges from the true data distribution, guiding the model toward generating more accurate data.
- Information theory concepts such as entropy and mutual information help in understanding how much uncertainty exists in predictions, and improving the quality of the generated data.
- Optimization techniques such as gradient descent and stochastic gradient descent are fundamental in training generative models efficiently by minimizing the loss function, and ensuring that the model parameters converge to optimal values.
- Neural networks provide the structural foundation for generative models like GANs and VAEs, using layers of interconnected neurons to learn complex patterns in data through forward and backward propagation.

Multiple Choice Questions

1. What does gradient descent aim to achieve during the training of generative models?
    a. Maximize the output of the model
    b. Minimize the loss function
    c. Increase the variance of the data
    d. Introduce randomness into the model
2. In which context is KL Divergence used in generative models?
    a. To measure the output accuracy of GANs
    b. To compute the difference between two probability distributions
    c. To increase the entropy of the data
    d. To optimize the learning rate in backpropagation
3. Which of the following is a key advantage of using Stochastic Gradient Descent (SGD)?
    a. It speeds up training by updating model parameters after every data point.
    b. It computes gradients for the entire dataset at once.
    c. It reduces the noise in the data.
    d. It is only applicable for small datasets.
4. What role does entropy play in information theory for generative models?
    a. It measures the amount of uncertainty or randomness in a data distribution.
    b. It increases the accuracy of backpropagation.

   c. It defines the speed of gradient descent.

   d. It helps in computing activation functions.

5. Which activation function is most commonly used to prevent the vanishing gradient problem in deep neural networks?

   a. Sigmoid

   b. Tanh

   c. ReLU

   d. Softmax

6. What is the purpose of backpropagation in neural networks?

   a. To compute the loss during the forward pass

   b. To apply information theory concepts in the model

   c. To increase the learning rate

   d. To adjust weights by calculating the gradient of the loss function with respect to the weights

Answers

1. b
2. b
3. a
4. a
5. c
6. d

Questions

1. What role does probability theory play in generative models, and how does it help in modeling data distributions?
2. How is KL Divergence used in generative models like VAEs, and why is it important for aligning the learned distribution with the real data distribution?
3. What is the significance of information theory in generative models, and how does the concept of entropy impact model performance?
4. Explain how gradient descent works as an optimization technique in training generative models. Why is it necessary to minimize the loss function?
5. How does Stochastic Gradient Descent (SGD) differ from traditional gradient descent, and when would you use SGD in training generative models?
6. What is the purpose of backpropagation in neural networks, and how does it contribute to the optimization of generative models like GANs and VAEs?
7. How do activation functions such as ReLU and Sigmoid impact the performance of neural networks in generative models? Why is ReLU often preferred?

8. What challenges arise from mode collapse in GANs, and what optimization techniques can be used to mitigate this issue?
9. In what ways does Bayesian probability enhance the generative modeling process, particularly when prior knowledge is available?
10. How does the concept of mutual information ensure that key attributes of input data are retained during the generation process in generative models?

Key Terms

- **Entropy:** A measure of uncertainty or unpredictability in a system. In the context of generative models, it quantifies how much information is in a data distribution.
- **KL Divergence:** A measure of how one probability distribution diverges from a second, expected probability distribution. It is frequently used in VAEs to guide the model in learning the correct data distribution.
- **Gradient Descent:** An optimization algorithm used to minimize the loss function by iteratively adjusting the model parameters.
- **Stochastic Gradient Descent (SGD):** A variant of gradient descent where the model's parameters are updated for each data point, enabling faster and more efficient training.
- **Backpropagation:** A key algorithm for training neural networks that calculates the gradient of the loss function with respect to each weight by propagating the error backward through the network.
- **Mutual Information:** In information theory, it measures the amount of information obtained about one random variable by observing another. In generative models, it helps preserve the key attributes during data generation.
- **Activation Function:** A function used in neural networks to introduce non-linearity into the model. Common examples include Sigmoid, Tanh, ReLU, and Softmax.
- **Bayesian Probability:** A method in probability theory that updates the probability of a hypothesis as more evidence or information becomes available.
- **ReLU (Rectified Linear Unit):** A popular activation function that allows for faster convergence in neural networks by only passing positive values, and zeroing out negatives.
- **Loss Function:** A function that measures the difference between the predicted and actual output. Generative models aim to minimize this function to improve the accuracy of the generated data.

CHAPTER 3
Introduction to Variational Autoencoders

Introduction

In this chapter, we will dive into the core principles and mechanics behind Variational Autoencoders (VAEs), one of the most important types of generative models. VAEs differ from normal autoencoders by introducing a probabilistic approach to the latent space, enabling them to generate new data that closely resembles the input data. We will explore the architecture of VAEs, including the roles of the encoder, decoder, and latent variables, while also discussing the mathematical foundations such as KL divergence and a concept called reparameterization trick. We will also learn the practical implementations of VAEs using TensorFlow and PyTorch, highlighting their applications in areas such as image generation, anomaly detection, and data augmentation. By the end of this chapter, you will have a solid understanding of how VAEs work, and how they can be used to build powerful generative models.

Structure

In this chapter, we will discuss the following topics:

- **Variational Autoencoders (VAEs)**
  - Core Concepts of VAEs
  - The Concept of Latent Space
  - KL Divergence and Variational Inference
  - The Reparameterization Trick
- **Mathematical Foundations of VAEs**
  - Latent Space Representation and Distributions
  - VAE Loss Function
  - Optimization of the VAE
- **Architecture of VAEs**
  - Encoder and Decoder Architecture
  - Latent Variables and Their Role
  - Comparison with Traditional Autoencoders
- **Implementation of a Basic VAE**
  - Building a VAE in TensorFlow
  - Building a VAE in PyTorch
  - Differences from TensorFlow Implementation
  - Visualizing Results with Matplotlib

- **Challenges and Common Pitfalls**
  - Training Instabilities
  - Balancing Reconstruction and KL Loss
  - Latent Space Overlap and Overfitting
- **Practical Applications of VAEs**
  - Image Generation
  - Anomaly Detection
  - Data Augmentation
- **Case Study: Using VAEs for Anomaly Detection in Manufacturing**

Variational Autoencoders (VAEs)

Variational Autoencoders (VAEs) are a powerful class of generative models designed to learn a latent space from a given dataset. Think of VAEs as an extension of traditional autoencoders, but instead of mapping the input to a single set of numbers (latent code), VAEs map it to a probability distribution. This allows for more flexibility and generative capabilities, as the decoder can sample from the latent space to produce new data points that closely resemble the original dataset.

The key difference between a VAE and a traditional autoencoder lies in this probabilistic mapping. A traditional autoencoder learns a direct transformation from input (x) to a compressed representation (z) in the first step. This is followed by reconstructing (x) again from the compressed representation (z) in the second step. In contrast, a VAE learns to map (x) to a distribution over possible latent variables (z), and the decoder samples from this distribution to reconstruct (x).

By training a VAE on a dataset, such as images, the model cannot only compress and reconstruct the data but also generate entirely new images by sampling from the learned latent space.

Core Concepts of VAEs

VAEs aim to achieve a balance between two competing objectives:

Reconstruction: The decoder must be able to reconstruct the input data as accurately as possible from the latent representation, ensuring that the important features of the input are preserved.

Regularization: The latent space must be regularized to follow a predefined distribution, typically a multivariate Gaussian distribution. This ensures that the learned representations in the latent space are smooth, and can be easily sampled from, even for inputs that the model has not seen during training. VAEs introduced a regularization term (KL divergence) into the loss function, which ensures that the latent space follows a continuous, smooth distribution.

This regularization is crucial because it allows the model to interpolate between different points in the latent space, and generate new, realistic data samples.

Encoders and Decoders: A traditional autoencoder consists of two main components: An encoder and a decoder as seen in the following *Figure 3.1*. The encoder takes the input data (X) and compresses it into a fixed latent representation (Z), which is often a lower-dimensional vector.

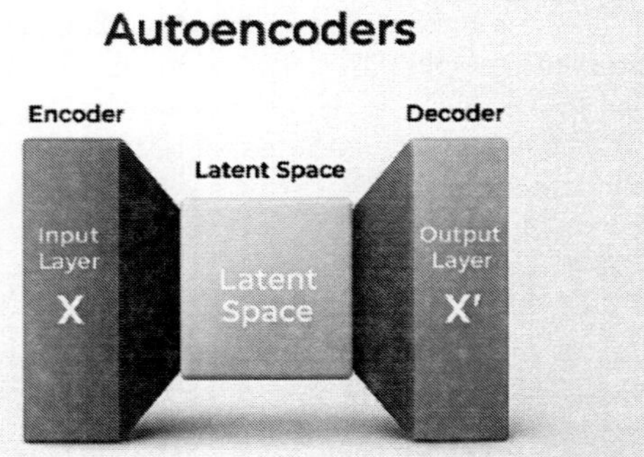

***Figure* 3.1:** *Traditional Autoencoder*

This latent space represents the "*essence*" or compressed form of the input data, which can be as simple as a reduced set of features or key patterns within the data. The decoder then takes this compressed latent code, and reconstructs the original input (X') from it. This compression-reconstruction cycle makes autoencoders useful for tasks such as data compression, noise reduction, and dimensionality reduction.

However, one of the limitations of traditional autoencoders is that the latent space they learn is deterministic. This means that each input data point is mapped to a single, fixed point in the latent space, and this mapping does not necessarily have a meaningful structure. For example, two input data points that are semantically similar (for example, two different images of the same object) may be mapped to very distant points in the latent space, and points that are close to each other in latent space do not always correspond to small variations in the output. This lack of structure in the latent space makes traditional autoencoders unsuitable for tasks that require the generation of new data, as they are only trained to reconstruct the existing data.

Probabilistic Approach: Variational Autoencoders (VAEs) address the limitations of traditional autoencoders by introducing a probabilistic approach to the latent space. Instead of compressing the input data into a fixed point in the latent space, the encoder outputs a distribution–specifically, a mean and variance for each dimension of the latent space. These values define a Gaussian distribution for each latent variable. The decoder then samples from this distribution to generate the output. This approach allows the VAE to generate new data points by sampling from the latent space, rather than just reconstructing the existing data points.

The key advantage of the VAE's latent space is that it is continuous and structured. The regularization imposed by the Kullback-Leibler (KL) divergence term in the VAE's loss function ensures that the latent space follows a standard normal distribution. As a result, nearby points in the latent space correspond to small variations in the output, making the latent space smooth and interpretable.

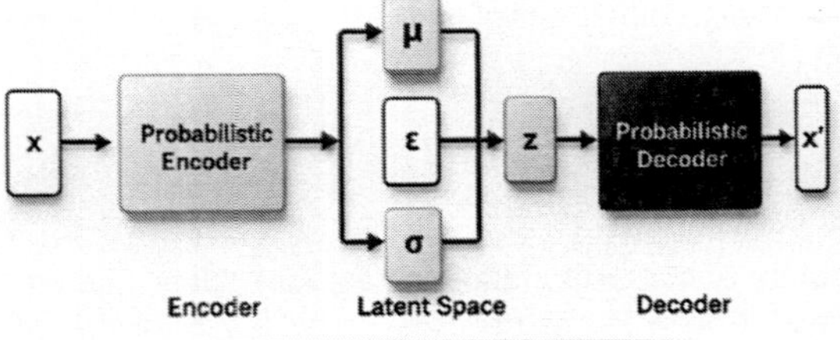

***Figure* 3.2**: *Variational Autoencoder*

Another advantage of the VAE is its ability to generate entirely new data points by sampling from the latent space. Since the latent space follows a continuous and structured distribution, the model can sample points from this space, even those not seen during training, and generate new, plausible outputs. This generative capability makes VAEs suitable for tasks such as image generation, data augmentation, and anomaly detection.

The Concept of Latent Space in VAEs

Latent simply means *hidden* or *underlying*. In machine learning, the concept of latent space refers to the compressed representation of data in a lower-dimensional space. In traditional Autoencoders, latent space is deterministic, which means there is no randomness or uncertainty. A specific input is mapped to a single point in the latent space. However, in a VAE, the encoder learns to map the input data to a distribution over the latent space. This distribution is often Gaussian, with each input data point being represented by a mean vector μ, and a variance vector σ^2.

***Figure 3.3**: Humor - VAEs and Latent Space*

The goal of the VAE is to learn a latent space that captures the important features of the input data in a smooth and continuous manner. This means that points that are close together in the latent space should correspond to similar inputs in the original data space. For example, in the case of a VAE trained on images of handwritten digits, points in the latent space that are close together might correspond to different variations of the same digit (for example, different styles of the number "3"). One of the key advantages of VAEs is that by regularizing the latent space to follow a continuous distribution (such as a Gaussian), it becomes possible to generate entirely new data points by sampling from this space. This makes VAEs highly effective for tasks such as image generation, where the goal is to produce new images that are similar to those in the training set but not identical.

Sampling from Latent Space

In a traditional autoencoder, the encoder compresses the input into a fixed point in the latent space, making it difficult to generate new data from the latent space. In contrast, VAEs treat the latent representation as a probability distribution, allowing for sampling. The encoder outputs the mean μ and variance σ^2 of this distribution, and the decoder samples latent variables z from the distribution $z \sim N(\mu, \sigma^2)$.

By sampling from this latent space, the VAE can generate new data points that are similar to the original data but are not identical. This ability to generate new data from the latent space is one of the key advantages of VAEs over traditional autoencoders.

The following diagram illustrates how the latent space is structured in a VAE. Points that are close together in the latent space correspond to similar data points in the original input space. By sampling from different regions of the latent space, we can generate new data that exhibits different characteristics.

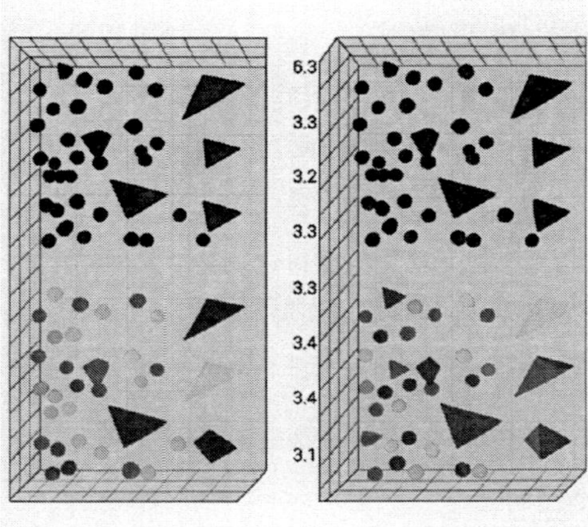

Figure 3.4: *VAEs Need Latent Space*

- **Latent Space (Left Side):** The left part of the image represents a grid of points within the latent space. Each point in this space corresponds to a potential representation of data, with the closeness of points indicating similar characteristics. The points are scattered across the grid, showing that the latent space is continuous and structured, allowing for smooth transitions between different regions.
- **Generated Data (Right Side):** The right part of the image shows abstract shapes or objects that represent the data generated from the corresponding points in the latent space. Each shape varies in form, size, and color, demonstrating how different areas of the latent space correspond to distinct characteristics in the generated data. Points that are close together in the latent space generate similar-looking shapes, illustrating the idea that similar latent variables produce similar data points.

Together, these two parts highlight the relationship between the latent space and the generated output in a VAE. Sampling from different regions of the latent space allows the VAE to generate new and varied data with controlled characteristics.

KL Divergence in VAEs

Kullback-Leibler (KL) Divergence is a measure of how one probability distribution diverges from another, and it plays a crucial role in the training of VAEs. In the context of VAEs, KL divergence is used to regularize the latent space by ensuring that the learned distribution q(z|x) is as close as possible to a standard normal distribution p(z).

Mathematically, KL divergence is given by:

$$D_{KL}(q(z|x) \; || \; p(z)) = \int q(z|x) \; \log\left(\frac{q(z|x)}{p(z)}\right) \, dz$$

This term is added to the VAE's loss function to encourage the encoder to produce latent variables that follow a standard Gaussian distribution. Without this regularization, the latent space could become too sparse or too clustered, making it difficult to sample new, meaningful data points.

Variational Inference

The posterior distribution p(z|x) represents the probability distribution of the latent variable *z* given an observed variable x. In Bayesian terms, the posterior distribution provides updated beliefs about the latent variable *z* after observing the data x.

In traditional inference, we would calculate the posterior distribution p(z|x) directly, but this is often not feasible due to the complexity of the model. Instead, VAEs use variational inference, which approximates p(z|x) with a simpler distribution q(z|x). The goal is to minimize the difference between the true posterior and the approximate posterior, and this is where the KL divergence term comes in.

The Reparameterization Trick

One of the challenges in training VAEs is that the encoder produces a distribution over the latent variables, rather than a fixed point. Sampling from this distribution introduces stochasticity, which makes backpropagation difficult. To overcome this, VAEs use a technique known as the reparameterization trick.

The reparameterization trick allows us to rewrite the sampling process in a way that is differentiable, enabling the use of gradient-based optimization methods like backpropagation. Instead of sampling directly from the learned distribution $z \sim N(\mu, \sigma^2)$ where z follows a normal distribution with mean μ and variance σ^2, we reparameterize the sampling as $z = \mu + \sigma \cdot \epsilon$ where $\epsilon \sim N(0,$ is a random sample from a standard normal distribution.)

This technique separates the random sampling process from the fixed, predictable parts of the model. By doing this, it lets the model's internal calculations update smoothly and effectively during training. In simpler terms, it allows the learning signals (gradients) to pass through the model, without being blocked by randomness, so that the model can learn better from each training step.

Mathematical Foundations of VAEs

Variational Autoencoders (VAEs) represent a powerful generative framework that marries probabilistic inference with deep learning. Unlike traditional autoencoders that compress data to a fixed, deterministic latent space, VAEs model the latent space probabilistically, allowing for more flexible data generation and interpolation. Understanding the mathematical principles underlying VAEs such as latent space representation, loss functions, and optimization is essential for effectively building and training these models.

Latent Space Representation and Distribution

As mentioned earlier, the latent space is not a fixed vector of values as in traditional autoencoders but rather a probabilistic representation of the input data. The encoder network in a VAE maps each input data point to a distribution over the latent space, which allows the model to capture uncertainty and variability in the data. This flexibility is crucial for generating new data points that are similar but not identical to the training data.

Multivariate Gaussian Distribution

The most common distribution used to model the latent space in VAEs is the multivariate Gaussian distribution. For each input data point, the encoder network outputs two vectors:

- A **mean vector** μ
- A **variance vector** σ^2

These two vectors define the parameters of the Gaussian distribution in the latent space. Instead of mapping an input to a single point, the VAE samples from this Gaussian distribution to obtain a latent variable z, which is then fed into the decoder network to reconstruct the input data. The sampling process introduces randomness, allowing for diverse data generation.

The distribution for each input x is represented as:

$$q(z|x) = \mathcal{N}(\mu(x), \sigma^2(x))$$

where $\mu(x)$ and $\sigma^2(x)$ are the outputs of the encoder for a given input x.

Regularization with Prior Distribution

To ensure that the learned latent space is continuous and structured, VAEs introduce a prior distribution over the latent variables. Typically, this prior distribution is a standard Gaussian distribution $p(z) = N(0, I)$. Here 'I' represents the identity matrix.

This prior ensures that the learned latent variables are centered around 0, and follow a smooth distribution, enabling meaningful interpolation between different data points in the latent space. During training, the KL divergence term ensures that the distribution $q(z|x)$ (learned by the encoder) is as close as possible to the prior $p(z)$. This regularization prevents the latent space from becoming too fragmented or sparse.

VAE Loss Function

The loss function of a VAE is crucial to ensuring both good data reconstruction and a well-structured latent space. It consists of two main components: Reconstruction loss and KL divergence loss.

Reconstruction Loss

The reconstruction loss measures how well the decoder is able to reconstruct the input data x from the latent variables z. It is similar to the loss function used in traditional autoencoders. The goal is to minimize the difference between the original input data and the data reconstructed by the decoder.

For continuous data, the reconstruction loss is typically the Mean Squared Error (MSE):

$$L_{recon} = \text{MSE}(x, \hat{x}) = \frac{1}{n} \sum_{i=1}^{n} (x_i - \hat{x}_i)^2$$

where x is the original input, and is the reconstructed output.

For binary data (for example, pixel values in black-and-white images), the reconstruction loss is often the Binary Cross-Entropy (BCE):

$$L_{recon} = -\sum_i [x_i \, log\,(\hat{x}_i) + (1 - x_i)\, log\,(1 - \hat{x}_i)]$$

The reconstruction loss ensures that the model is capable of reproducing the input data as closely as possible from the compressed latent representation.

KL Divergence Loss

The KL divergence loss measures the distance between the learned latent distribution q(z|x) and the prior distribution p(z), which is usually a standard Gaussian distribution N(0, 1). The KL divergence is a regularization term which ensures that the learned latent space follows the prior distribution, preventing overfitting and ensuring a smooth latent space for sampling.

The KL divergence for a Gaussian distribution can be computed as:

$$L_{KL} = D_{KL}(q(z|x) \,||\, p(z)) = \frac{1}{2}\sum_{i=1}^{d}(1 + \log(\sigma_i^2) - \mu_i^2 - \sigma_i^2)$$

where μ_i and σ_i^2 are the mean and variance for each dimension of the latent space.

The KL divergence ensures that the latent variables are distributed according to the standard Gaussian, enabling the model to generate new data by sampling from this space. It also prevents overfitting by regularizing the latent space, and ensuring that the model does not memorize the input data.

Total VAE Loss

The total loss for the VAE is the sum of the reconstruction loss, and the KL divergence loss is calculated as $L_{VAE} = L_{recon} + L_{KL.}$

The reconstruction loss ensures that the VAE accurately reconstructs the input, while the KL divergence loss ensures that the latent space is well-structured and regularized.

Optimization of the VAE

Training a VAE involves minimizing the total loss function (reconstruction loss + KL divergence) with respect to the parameters of the encoder and decoder networks. This is typically done using gradient-based optimization methods such as stochastic gradient descent (SGD) or the Adam optimizer-a variant of SGD that includes momentum and adaptive learning rates.

Challenges in Balancing Loss Terms

One of the key challenges in training VAEs is finding the right balance between the reconstruction loss and the KL divergence loss. If the reconstruction loss dominates, the model may focus too much on reconstructing the input data, and fail to learn a meaningful latent space, leading to overfitting. On the other hand, if the KL divergence loss dominates, the latent space may become too regularized, resulting in poor reconstruction and blurry outputs.

To achieve the right balance, practitioners often use techniques such as:

- **KL Annealing**: This involves gradually increasing the weight of the KL divergence term during training. Initially, the model focuses more on minimizing the reconstruction loss, and as training progresses, the KL divergence term is given more weight to regularize the latent space.
- **β-VAE**: In a β-VAE, the KL divergence term is multiplied by a hyperparameter β, which controls the strength of the regularization. A larger β increases the influence of the KL divergence, encouraging more separated and independent features in the latent space.

Choosing the Right Loss Function

The choice of the reconstruction loss function depends on the type of data being used. For continuous data, such as images or sound waves, the Mean Squared Error is commonly used. This loss measures the average squared difference between the original and reconstructed data, making it suitable for the real-valued data. However, for binary data or categorical data (for example, black-and-white images or discrete labels), the Binary Cross-Entropy (BCE) or categorical cross-entropy is more appropriate.

The KL divergence loss is more standardized, as it is primarily used to enforce a Gaussian prior on the latent space. The combination of these two losses is what gives the VAE its generative power, allowing it to both reconstruct the existing data, and generate entirely new data samples from the latent space.

Common Pitfalls and Solutions in Training VAEs

- **Blurry Reconstructions:** One common problem with VAEs is that they can sometimes produce blurry reconstructions. This is often a result of the KL divergence dominating the loss function, causing the latent space to be overly regularized. In such cases, the model sacrifices reconstruction accuracy for latent space smoothness. One solution to this problem is to decrease the weight of the KL divergence term, or to use KL annealing to slowly introduce the KL divergence term during training.
- **Overfitting:** Like other neural networks, VAEs are prone to overfitting, especially when trained on small datasets. Overfitting occurs when the model memorizes the training data instead of learning general patterns. Techniques such as dropout, early stopping, and data augmentation can help mitigate overfitting. Additionally, the KL divergence term itself acts as a form of regularization, preventing the model from overfitting to the latent space.
- **Training Instabilities:** Training VAEs can be unstable, particularly when using large networks or complex datasets. The stochastic nature of the reparameterization trick can introduce noise, leading to unstable gradient updates. Techniques such as gradient clipping, batch normalization, and learning rate scheduling can help stabilize training.

Architecture of VAEs

Variational Autoencoders (VAEs) are built on the foundational principles of autoencoders but extend their capabilities by introducing probabilistic modeling into the latent space. The architecture of a VAE consists of two primary components: The encoder and the decoder, which work together to transform data into a probabilistic latent space, and then reconstruct data points by sampling from that space. This process allows the VAE to capture meaningful features from the input data, generate diverse outputs, and create new data points by leveraging the variability encoded in the latent distribution.

Encoder and Decoder Architecture

The architecture of VAEs is centered around the ability to encode data into a latent representation, and then decode it back into the original or a similar form. Understanding the roles of the encoder and decoder in this architecture is key to grasping how VAEs learn, reconstruct, and generate new data.

Encoder Architecture

The encoder is responsible for transforming the input data into a distribution in the latent space, rather than a fixed point, which is common in traditional autoencoders. The encoder takes an input data point x, and maps it to a latent variable representation z by outputting two vectors:

- **Mean Vector** μ

- **Variance Vector σ^2**

These vectors represent the parameters of a Gaussian distribution from which the latent variable z will be sampled. The key role of the encoder is not only to compress the input into a lower-dimensional space (like in a traditional autoencoder) but also to ensure that this space is continuous and smooth, allowing for interpolation and sampling.

Most VAEs use neural networks as the encoder. This network consists of several hidden layers, typically with nonlinear activation functions like ReLU, to capture complex features of the input data. The final layer outputs the mean and variance, which define the distribution over the latent space. These values are then used to sample from the latent space, adding an element of randomness to the encoding process. The following is the mathematical representation of the Encoder:

$$q(z|x) = \mathcal{N}(\mu(x), \sigma^2(x))$$

The encoder approximates the posterior distribution $q(z|x)$, where:

The outputs-mean $\mu(x)$ and variance $\sigma^2(x)$ are learned from the data through backpropagation, and are used to sample a latent variable z.

Decoder Architecture

The decoder takes a sample z from the latent space, and maps it back to the original data space, generating a new data point that closely resembles the original input. The decoder can be thought of as the generative part of the VAE, responsible for reconstructing the input from the latent variables, and producing new, similar data points by sampling from the learned latent distribution.

The decoder is also typically a neural network, mirroring the structure of the encoder but working in the opposite direction. It starts with the latent variable z, and applies several layers of transformations (usually dense or convolutional layers) to generate the reconstructed output $x^\wedge$.

The goal of the decoder is to generate data that closely matches the original input. However, because the latent space is probabilistic, the decoder can generate slightly different outputs each time it samples from the latent space. This introduces variability in the generated data, and allows the VAE to produce diverse outputs, even from the same latent space representation.

The decoder approximates the likelihood $p(x \mid z)$, where: $p(x \mid z) = \text{Decoder}(z)$

The output is a probability distribution over the possible reconstructed values of x, which the decoder learns to generate from samples z.

Latent Variables and Their Role

The latent variables z in a VAE represent the compressed, underlying structure of the input data. These variables are not directly observed but are inferred by the encoder. They play a crucial role in the VAE's ability to generate new data points, as the decoder relies on samples from the latent space to produce new outputs.

Latent Space Structure

The latent space in a VAE is continuous and multidimensional. This means that each latent variable z is represented as a point in this space, and small changes in the latent variables result in small changes in the generated data. This structure allows for smooth interpolation between different points in the latent space, enabling the generation of new data that resembles the input data but contains variations.

For example, if the VAE is trained on a dataset of faces, small changes in the latent variables could result in the generation of new faces with slightly different features, such as hair color, facial expression, or lighting. This capability to generate diverse data points from a continuous latent space is one of the defining features of VAEs.

Generative Capability

The generative capability of a VAE comes from its ability to sample from the latent space, and decode the sampled values into new data points. By varying the values of the latent variables, the decoder can generate different versions of the input data or even entirely new data points. This generative power is particularly useful for tasks such as:

- **Image generation**: Generating new images that resemble those in the training dataset.
- **Data augmentation**: Creating new training data to improve the performance of machine learning models.
- **Anomaly detection**: Detecting outliers by comparing the reconstructed data with the original input.

As the latent space is structured probabilistically, the VAE can generate new data points by sampling from this space in a meaningful way, enabling the creation of realistic and diverse outputs.

Comparison with Traditional Autoencoders

While VAEs and traditional autoencoders share some similarities in their architecture, there are several key differences that set them apart. These differences primarily lie in how the latent space is structured (refer *Figure* 3.2) and the generative capabilities of each model.

Deterministic vs. Probabilistic Encoding

In traditional autoencoders, the encoder maps the input data to a fixed point in the latent space. This deterministic encoding means that each input corresponds to a single, specific point in the latent space, and the decoder uses this point to reconstruct the input. While this is useful for tasks such as data compression, it limits the model's ability to generate new data.

In contrast, VAEs use a probabilistic encoding. Instead of mapping the input to a single point, the encoder maps the input to a distribution in the latent space. The decoder samples from this distribution to generate the output, allowing for variability in the reconstructed data. This probabilistic encoding is what enables VAEs to generate new data points by sampling from the latent space, which is not possible with traditional autoencoders.

Latent Space Structure

The latent space in traditional autoencoders is deterministic and unstructured. This means that there is no meaningful relationship between points in the latent space. For example, two similar input data points may be mapped to distant points in the latent space, making it difficult to interpolate between them.

In contrast, the latent space in VAEs is structured and regularized. The KL divergence term in the VAE's loss function ensures that the learned latent distribution follows a standard Gaussian distribution, which allows for smooth interpolation between points in the latent space. This structure makes it possible to generate meaningful data points by sampling from the latent space, something that traditional autoencoders are not designed to do.

Generative Power

Traditional autoencoders are primarily used for tasks such as data compression and reconstruction, where the goal is to reproduce the input data as accurately as possible. However, they lack the ability to generate new data points. VAEs, on the other hand, are designed for generative tasks. By sampling from the learned latent space, VAEs can generate new data points that are similar to the input data but contain variations. This generative power makes VAEs more versatile than traditional autoencoders, as they can be used for tasks such as image generation, data augmentation, and unsupervised learning.

Implementation of a Basic VAE

In this section, we will walk through the implementation of a basic VAE using two popular deep learning frameworks: **TensorFlow** and **PyTorch**. We'll cover the architectural components of VAEs (encoder, latent space, and decoder) and how to build and train these models. Additionally, we will discuss how the VAE loss function is constructed to balance reconstruction accuracy and latent space regularization. Finally, we will visualize the results of the VAE using the Matplotlib library.

Building a VAE in TensorFlow

Variational Autoencoders (VAEs) are a class of generative models that leverage probabilistic latent spaces to generate data resembling the input dataset. This guide walks through building a VAE in TensorFlow step by step.

Step 1. Model Design Overview

The VAE consists of three core components:

- **Encoder**: Compresses the input data to a latent space represented by a mean vector μ and a variance vector σ^2.
- **Latent Space**: The latent variables are sampled using the reparameterization trick, which ensures that gradients can flow through the sampling process during training.
- **Decoder**: The decoder maps the latent variables back to the data space, generating reconstructed data points.

Each component is built as a neural network using Keras layers in TensorFlow. Below is the step-by-step process.

Step 2. Encoder Architecture in TensorFlow

The encoder is responsible for mapping the input data x to a distribution in the latent space. This distribution is defined by the mean μ and variance σ^2 of the latent variables. The following code demonstrates how to build an encoder using fully connected layers:

```
import tensorflow as tf

def build_encoder(input_shape, latent_dim):
    # Define the input layer
    inputs = tf.keras.layers.Input(shape=input_shape)

    # Flatten the input data (especially useful for images)
    x = tf.keras.layers.Flatten()(inputs)

    # Fully connected hidden layer with ReLU activation
    x = tf.keras.layers.Dense(128, activation='relu')(x)

    # The mean of the latent distribution
    z_mean = tf.keras.layers.Dense(latent_dim)(x)
```

```
    # The log variance of the latent distribution
    z_log_var = tf.keras.layers.Dense(latent_dim)(x)

    # Return the encoder model
    return tf.keras.Model(inputs, [z_mean, z_log_var])
```

Explanation:

a. The **Input layer** takes in data of the shape **input_shape**. For example, in image data, this shape could be (28, 28, 1) for grayscale images like MNIST.

b. The input is **flattened** into a single vector (for image data, this turns the 2D image into a 1D vector).

c. The next step involves a fully connected **Dense layer** with 128 units and the **ReLU activation function**. This layer helps extract features from the input data.

d. The final layer outputs the **mean** and **log variance** for the latent space. These two parameters define the Gaussian distribution from which we will sample latent variables.

Step 3. Latent Space with Reparameterization Trick

In VAEs, latent variables are sampled using a technique called the reparameterization trick. This trick allows gradients to propagate through the sampling process, enabling backpropagation to optimize the entire VAE. The following code defines the sampling process:

```
def sampling(z_mean, z_log_var):
    # Random normal distribution with the shape of the mean vector
    epsilon = tf.keras.backend.random_normal(shape=tf.shape(z_mean))

    # Reparameterization trick: z = mean + std * epsilon
    return z_mean + tf.exp(0.5 * z_log_var) * epsilon
```

Explanation:

a. **Epsilon** is sampled from a standard normal distribution, which is then scaled by the standard deviation of the latent variable.

b. The mean μ and standard deviation σ are used to compute the latent variable z, where: $z = \mu + \sigma \cdot \epsilon$

c. This ensures that the stochastic sampling process can be differentiated, enabling the VAE to be trained with gradient-based methods.

Step 4. Decoder Architecture in TensorFlow

The decoder takes a sample from the latent space and maps it back to the original data space, generating new or reconstructed data. Here is how the decoder is implemented:

```
def build_decoder(latent_dim, output_shape):
    # Define the input for the latent variable z
    latent_inputs = tf.keras.layers.Input(shape=(latent_dim,))

    # Fully connected hidden layer with ReLU activation
    x = tf.keras.layers.Dense(128, activation='relu')(latent_inputs)

    # Output layer to generate final data point, reshaped back to the original
shape
    outputs = tf.keras.layers.Dense(np.prod(output_shape), activation='
sigmoid')(x)
```

```
    outputs = tf.keras.layers.Reshape(output_shape)(outputs)

    # Return the decoder model
    return tf.keras.Model(latent_inputs, outputs)
```

Explanation:

a. The **latent inputs** are passed into a fully connected layer with 128 units and **ReLU activation**.

b. The output of the decoder is reshaped back into the original input shape (for example, image dimensions). This is done by using the **Dense layer** with the sigmoid activation, which is ideal for generating values between 0 and 1 (useful for normalized data like images).

c. The final layer reshapes the output to the original input dimensions using Reshape.

Loss Function in TensorFlow

The VAE's loss function is composed of two key components:

1. **Reconstruction Loss**: Measures how well the decoder can reconstruct the original input from the latent variables.

2. **KL Divergence**: Encourages the learned latent distribution to be close to a standard normal distribution.

```
def vae_loss(x, x_decoded, z_mean, z_log_var):
    # Compute the reconstruction loss (MSE)
    reconstruction_loss = tf.keras.losses.mean_squared_error(x, x_decoded)
    reconstruction_loss *= input_shape[0] * input_shape[1]  # Scale by image
dimensions

    # Compute the KL divergence loss
    kl_loss = 1 + z_log_var - tf.square(z_mean) - tf.exp(z_log_var)
    kl_loss = tf.reduce_mean(kl_loss) * -0.5

    # Return the total VAE loss
    return reconstruction_loss + kl_loss
```

- **Reconstruction Loss:** For continuous data, **mean squared error (MSE)** is commonly used. It calculates the squared differences between the original data and the reconstructed output.
- **KL Divergence:** This term regularizes the latent space, ensuring that the learned distribution is close to a standard normal distribution.

Training the Model

Once the encoder, decoder, and loss function are defined, we can compile and train the VAE using the **Adam optimizer**:

```
vae = tf.keras.Model(inputs, outputs)
vae.compile(optimizer='adam', loss=vae_loss)

# Train the VAE model on the dataset
vae.fit(x_train, x_train, epochs=50, batch_size=128)
```

Explanation:

a. The **`vae.compile`** method configures the VAE model for training. The optimizer chosen here is **Adam**, which is commonly used for its adaptive learning rate, and the ability to handle sparse gradients.

b. The model is trained for 50 epochs on the training dataset, with a batch size of 128.

c. In Variational Autoencoders (VAEs), the model learns to reconstruct the input data. So, in this case, both the input and the target output are the same data, **`x_train`**. This setup is typical for autoencoders because the goal is to have the model recreate the original input data after passing it through the encoder and decoder.

Building a VAE in PyTorch

The structure of a VAE in PyTorch follows the same fundamental architecture as other implementations, but leverages PyTorch's distinctive syntax and framework conventions. Like the TensorFlow approach, PyTorch implementations construct Variational Autoencoders (VAEs) as generative models that utilize probabilistic latent spaces to produce new data samples resembling the original dataset.

Differences from TensorFlow Implementation

In PyTorch, the encoder is built using torch.nn layers, which form the neural network for mapping the input data to the latent space.

Encoder in PyTorch

```
class Encoder(nn.Module):
    def __init__(self, input_dim, latent_dim):
        super(Encoder, self).__init__()
        self.fc1 = nn.Linear(input_dim, 128)
        self.fc_mean = nn.Linear(128, latent_dim)
        self.fc_logvar = nn.Linear(128, latent_dim)

    def forward(self, x):
        h = F.relu(self.fc1(x))
        z_mean = self.fc_mean(h)
        z_logvar = self.fc_logvar(h)
        return z_mean, z_logvar
```

Explanation:

a. The **`Encoder`** class inherits from nn.Module, which is the base class for all neural network modules in PyTorch.

b. Similar to the TensorFlow version, it includes a fully connected layer followed by outputs for the mean and variance of the latent distribution.

Decoder in PyTorch

The PyTorch decoder differs from TensorFlow primarily in its explicit, imperative style–activation functions are applied manually in the forward pass, rather than being embedded in layer definitions, and the entire model structure is defined through Python code with explicit class inheritance from nn.Module. Unlike TensorFlow's declarative approach where activations are often specified as layer parameters, PyTorch requires explicit function calls for each transformation, giving more granular control but requiring more verbose code. Additionally, PyTorch uses torch namespace functions like **`torch.sigmoid()`** instead of TensorFlow's tf.keras.activations.

```
# Decoder
class Decoder(nn.Module):
    def __init__(self, latent_dim, output_dim):
        super(Decoder, self).__init__()
```

```
        self.fc1 = nn.Linear(latent_dim, 128)  # No activation parameter
        self.fc2 = nn.Linear(128, output_dim)  # No activation parameter

    def forward(self, z):
        h = F.relu(self.fc1(z))  # Manual activation application
        x_reconstructed = torch.sigmoid(self.fc2(h))  # Explicit function call
        return x_reconstructed
```

Training Process in PyTorch

In PyTorch, the training loop is explicit, and requires manual loss computation and backpropagation for each batch of data.

```
optimizer = torch.optim.Adam(vae.parameters(), lr=1e-3)
for epoch in range(epochs):
    for batch in data_loader:
        # Forward pass, compute loss, and backpropagate
        loss = compute_loss(vae, batch)
        optimizer.zero_grad()
        loss.backward()
        optimizer.step()
```

Explanation:

a. The optimizer (**`torch.optim.Adam`**) updates the parameters by minimizing the loss.

b. The loop iterates over each epoch and batch of data, manually computing the loss, and performing backpropagation with **`loss.backward()`**.

Visualizing Results with Matplotlib

Once the VAE has been trained, the results can be visualized using **Matplotlib**. Here is how to visualize the original, reconstructed, and generated images:

```
plt.figure(figsize=(10, 5))

# Plot the original image
plt.subplot(1, 3, 1)
plt.imshow(original_image)
plt.title('Original')

# Plot the reconstructed image
plt.subplot(1, 3, 2)
plt.imshow(reconstructed_image)
plt.title('Reconstructed')

# Plot the generated image from the latent space
plt.subplot(1, 3, 3)
plt.imshow(generated_image)
plt.title('Generated')
plt.show()
```

Explanation:

a. This code creates a figure with three subplots: one for the original image, one for the reconstructed image, and one for the generated image.

b. The images are displayed using plt.imshow(), with titles indicating the type of image (original, reconstructed, or generated).

c. The original image is the actual input data from the dataset (for example, an MNIST digit) that the VAE is trained to encode, and then recreate.

d. The reconstructed image is the VAE's final output, generated by decoding the latent representation. Its similarity to the original image indicates how well the model has learned to compress and recreate data.

e. A generated image is created by sampling random points from the latent space, and decoding them. This tests the VAE's ability to produce new, realistic images from its learned data distribution.

Challenges and Common Pitfalls

In this section, we take a look at some of the common challenges that we encounter when working with VAEs. These difficulties primarily stem from modeling the latent space as a probability distribution, rather than using fixed points, and from the delicate balance, the model must learn between two competing objectives.

Training Instabilities

A key challenge is training instability during optimization. VAEs must balance two competing goals: minimizing reconstruction loss, while regularizing the latent space via KL divergence. Poor management of this balance causes unstable training and suboptimal results.

Some of the key reasons for training instability in VAEs include:

- **Vanishing gradients:** This can happen if the KL divergence term dominates, causing the gradients from the reconstruction loss to vanish.
- **Mode collapse:** If the latent space becomes too regularized, the VAE might generate only a limited variety of outputs, leading to mode collapse where the model generates similar samples regardless of the input.

To mitigate these issues, techniques such as gradually annealing the KL divergence term during training, or using better weight initializations can help stabilize training.

Balancing Reconstruction and KL Loss

The total VAE loss is a combination of the reconstruction loss (measuring how well the model can recreate the input) and the KL divergence loss (measuring how well the latent distribution matches the prior). If the balance between these two losses is not correctly tuned, the model may either fail to generate meaningful data (if the KL loss dominates) or overfit to the training data (if the reconstruction loss dominates).

To strike the right balance, researchers often experiment with different weightings for the two loss components. A common approach as discussed earlier, is to introduce a hyperparameter β that scales the KL divergence term, known as the β-VAE approach: $L_{VAE} = L_{recon} + \beta_{LKL}$

Setting $\beta < 1$ can reduce the influence of the KL loss during early training, allowing the model to focus on reconstruction. Once the model is able to reconstruct the data well, β can be gradually increased to emphasize regularization.

Latent Space Overlap and Overfitting

In an ideal VAE, the latent space is regularized such that points sampled from different regions of the space correspond to different, but plausible, variations of the data. However, if the latent space is not properly regularized, there can be too much overlap between regions of the latent space, causing the model to generate confusing or blurry outputs.

To address this, VAEs use the KL divergence to encourage the latent space to follow a continuous, smooth distribution. This ensures that nearby points in the latent space correspond to similar data points, reducing overlap, and improving the quality of generated samples.

Like many machine learning models, VAEs are prone to overfitting, particularly when trained on small datasets. Overfitting occurs when the model learns to reconstruct the training data perfectly but fails to generalize to new, unseen data. This is especially problematic in generative models, as the goal is to generate new data, rather than merely reconstruct existing data. Regularization techniques, such as early stopping, dropout, and the use of the KL divergence term, can help mitigate overfitting in VAEs. Additionally, data augmentation techniques can help increase the diversity of the training data, reducing the likelihood of overfitting.

Practical Applications of VAEs

Variational Autoencoders (VAEs) have emerged as a highly versatile tool across several fields, offering both generative and analytical capabilities. From generating new images to detecting anomalies and augmenting datasets, VAEs provide a robust approach to solving real-world problems in machine learning and artificial intelligence. In this section, we shall explore some of the key practical applications of VAEs, such as image generation, anomaly detection, and data augmentation, and how their unique architecture makes them suitable for these tasks.

Image Generation

One of the most prominent applications of VAEs is in the field of image generation. The probabilistic nature of VAEs, coupled with their ability to learn meaningful latent space representations, makes them an excellent tool for creating new, diverse images. VAEs are commonly trained on large image datasets, such as those containing faces, handwritten digits, or objects, and can generate entirely new images by sampling from the latent space.

How Image Generation Works in VAEs

When a VAE is trained on a dataset of images, such as the MNIST dataset of handwritten digits, it learns to encode each image into a latent representation. The encoder compresses the high-dimensional input data into a lower-dimensional latent space, capturing essential features such as digit shapes or orientations. The decoder then learns to reconstruct the images from this latent space. Once trained, the VAE can generate new images by sampling from the latent space, and decoding the samples into meaningful images.

- **Example: Handwritten Digits (MNIST Dataset):** A VAE trained on MNIST can generate novel handwritten digits by sampling points in the latent space. Each sample corresponds to a potential digit that shares characteristics with the digits in the training set but is not an exact copy of any digit seen during training.

Latent Space Interpolation and Creativity

One of the most powerful features of VAEs is their ability to interpolate between different data points in the latent space. Interpolation refers to generating intermediate data points by navigating between two known points in the latent space. For image data, this results in smooth transitions between two images, with each intermediate step representing a new image that gradually changes from one to the other.

- **Latent Space Interpolation Example**: Consider two images of handwritten digits, one of a “3” and the other of an "8." By sampling points in the latent space between the two corresponding latent variables, the VAE can generate a series of images that smoothly transition from the digit "3" to the digit "8." Each interpolated image represents a blend of the two digits, showing how the latent space captures both the structure and variability of the data.

This interpolation capability extends beyond digits, and applies to more complex tasks, such as Art and Synthetic Data Generation. When trained on face datasets, a VAE can generate faces with various features, such as changes in hair color, facial expressions, or lighting conditions, simply by moving through the latent space.

Anomaly Detection

Another significant application of VAEs is in anomaly detection, where the model is trained to recognize and reconstruct normal patterns in the data. By learning a probabilistic model of the normal data distribution, VAEs can detect anomalies by identifying instances where the reconstruction error is high, indicating that the input data deviates significantly from the normal patterns, the VAE has learned.

How VAEs Detect Anomalies

When a VAE is trained on a dataset consisting of normal data, it learns to reconstruct the data with high accuracy. The reconstruction loss, which measures how well the VAE can recreate the input data from the latent space, is low for normal data points. However, when the model encounters anomalous data or the data that is significantly different from the training data–the reconstruction error is higher. This is because the VAE has not learned how to represent the anomalous data in the latent space, leading to poor reconstructions.

- **Reconstruction Error as an Anomaly Signal**: The VAE's reconstruction error can be used as a signal to detect anomalies. If the error is above a certain threshold, the data point can be flagged as anomalous. This technique is useful in a wide range of industries where identifying rare, unexpected events is critical.

Applications of VAEs in Anomaly Detection

VAEs are applied in various fields for detecting anomalies, particularly in areas where abnormal behavior is rare but critical to detect. Some examples include:

- **Manufacturing:** VAEs can be trained on sensor data or images of normal, defect-free products. When a defective product is presented to the model, it will exhibit a high reconstruction error, indicating an anomaly. This approach is valuable in automated quality control, where VAEs can help detect faulty products before they reach consumers.
- **Healthcare:** In medical imaging, VAEs are used to detect anomalies that may signify the presence of rare diseases or conditions. For example, VAEs trained on normal MRI scans can detect abnormalities in brain scans, assisting in early diagnosis of conditions such as tumors or lesions. The ability to detect subtle deviations from normal patterns makes VAEs useful in a range of medical applications.
- **Cybersecurity:** In cybersecurity, VAEs are employed to detect unusual network activity, which may indicate a security breach or cyber-attack. By training on normal network traffic, the VAE can identify anomalous behavior, such as unauthorized access or unusual data transfers, by flagging instances with high reconstruction error.

Data Augmentation

Data augmentation is the process of increasing the size and diversity of a training dataset by generating additional data points. VAEs excel at this task due to their generative capabilities. By sampling from the learned latent space, VAEs can generate new data points that are similar to the original training data but introduce subtle variations. This augmentation process is particularly valuable in machine learning tasks where large, diverse datasets are essential for model training.

Generating Additional Training Data

In many machine learning applications, especially image classification, the size of the dataset plays a critical role in the model's performance. However, collecting and labeling large datasets is often expensive and time-consuming. VAEs provide a solution by generating additional training samples that are representative of the underlying data distribution. These new samples can be used to improve the model's ability to generalize to new, unseen data.

- **Image Classification Example:** Suppose a VAE is trained on a dataset of images for an object recognition task. By sampling from the latent space, the VAE can generate new images of the object with slight variations, such as changes in color, lighting, or orientation. These new images augment the training dataset, providing the model with more diverse examples, and improving its performance.
- **Handling Imbalanced Datasets:** Data augmentation using VAEs can also address the issue of imbalanced datasets, where certain classes are underrepresented. For example, if a dataset contains significantly fewer images of a particular category, a VAE can be used to generate additional images for that category, balancing the dataset and reducing the bias in the model's predictions.

VAEs for Time Series Data Augmentation

VAEs are not limited to image data; they are also effective at augmenting other types of data, such as time series data. Time series data, common in fields like finance, healthcare, and sensor data analysis, often suffers from limited availability of diverse training examples. VAEs trained on time series data can generate new sequences that mimic the temporal patterns in the original dataset, helping improve model robustness and performance in predictive tasks.

Case Study: Using VAEs for Anomaly Detection in Manufacturing

In this case study, we will explore how generative models such as β-VAE and CVAE can be used to generate images with specific, controllable attributes, such as modifying facial features in human images. We will delve into the design and training of a β-VAE to achieve disentangled representations, and leverage CVAE for attribute-specific control. Additionally, we will address challenges like balancing β and reconstruction loss in β-VAE, and preventing overfitting with limited labeled data in CVAE. By the end, we will showcase visual examples demonstrating the controlled generation of images, and discuss the practical implications of these techniques.

Problem

In manufacturing, the timely detection of faulty products is critical to ensuring product quality, and minimizing waste. Traditional methods of anomaly detection, such as manual inspection or rule-based systems, can be inefficient, costly, and prone to human error. These approaches often fail to scale with increased production volumes, and the complexity of modern manufacturing processes makes it difficult for rule-based systems to detect all possible defects.

Figure 3.5: *Surface Defect Detection Using VAEs*

The manual inspection of products, particularly in industries that deal with thousands or millions of units, is not only labor-intensive but also unreliable, as human inspectors can miss subtle defects or experience fatigue over time.

Moreover, certain defects in products may not be immediately visible to the human eye. For example, internal defects in materials, slight variations in sensor readings, or early signs of wear in mechanical components may go undetected by traditional methods. As a result, faulty products may slip through the cracks, leading to customer dissatisfaction, product recalls, and increased costs for the manufacturer.

In this context, there is a growing need for automated, scalable, and reliable anomaly detection systems that can operate in real-time, identifying defects as soon as they occur. A system that can learn normal product behavior, and automatically flag deviations would allow manufacturers to take corrective action before faulty products reach the market, reducing waste, and improving the overall efficiency.

Solution Approach

Variational Autoencoders (VAEs) offer a promising solution for anomaly detection in manufacturing by leveraging their ability to learn the distribution of normal data, and detect deviations from it. The key insight behind using VAEs for this task is that they can be trained to model the behavior of non-faulty (normal) products. When presented with normal data, the VAE reconstructs the input data with a low error, indicating that the product is behaving as expected. However, when the VAE is presented with faulty or anomalous products, the reconstruction error increases, signaling that the product deviates from the normal distribution learned by the VAE.

The VAE learns a compressed representation (latent space) of the normal data, and its decoder reconstructs the input from this representation. When faulty data is inputted into the model, it fails to generate an accurate reconstruction because the faulty product does not follow the same distribution as the normal data. As a result, the reconstruction error (the difference between the original and the reconstructed data) increases, which can be used to flag the product as defective.

Thus, the VAE is particularly well-suited for this task because it handles the inherent variability in normal product behavior. By modeling normal variations, such as small changes in size, shape, or sensor readings, the VAE avoids over-flagging minor deviations that are not actual defects. Additionally, the VAE's ability to generate smooth latent space representations allows it to generalize well to unseen, non-faulty products.

The process of applying a VAE to manufacturing anomaly detection can be summarized as follows:

1. **Data Collection:** Collect data from sensors, cameras, or other monitoring systems that capture the characteristics of normal products during production.
2. **Training the VAE:** Train the VAE on the collected normal product data, allowing the model to learn the underlying distribution of non-faulty products.
3. **Reconstruction and Anomaly Detection:** During production, the input data from new products into the trained VAE. If the reconstruction error exceeds a certain threshold, the product is flagged as faulty.
4. **Real-Time Monitoring:** Integrate the VAE into the production line for real-time monitoring and anomaly detection.

Challenges

While VAEs are highly effective in detecting anomalies, their application in real-world manufacturing environments presents several challenges. One of the most significant challenges is the balance between the reconstruction loss and the KL divergence during training. The reconstruction loss ensures that the VAE can accurately reconstruct the normal data, while the KL divergence term regularizes the latent space to follow a standard Gaussian distribution. Striking the right balance between these two objectives is critical for the VAE to generalize well to the unseen data, and avoid overfitting to the training set.

- **Overfitting:** If the reconstruction loss is focused more in the training process, the VAE may overfit to the normal data, learning to reconstruct the specific characteristics of the training set, rather than capturing the general distribution of normal products. In this case, the VAE may fail to generalize to new products or minor variations in normal product behavior, leading to an increase in false positives (flagging normal products as faulty).
- **Noisy Data:** Another challenge is the presence of noise in the data. Manufacturing environments often involve noisy sensor readings or image data due to variations in lighting, temperature, or sensor sensitivity. This noise can make it difficult for the VAE to distinguish between normal variations and actual defects. If the model is not robust to noise, it may incorrectly flag products with slight variations as faulty, leading to an increase in false positives.
- **Fault Variety:** In some manufacturing settings, defects can vary significantly in nature, from minor cosmetic flaws to major structural defects. Training a VAE to detect all types of defects can be challenging, especially when the number of faulty products in the training set is limited.

Solution

To address these challenges, several strategies can be implemented:

1. **Fine-Tuning the KL Divergence Term:** The balance between reconstruction loss and KL divergence can be adjusted by introducing a hyperparameter β which controls the weight of the KL divergence term in the loss function (as in β-VAE). By fine-tuning this parameter, manufacturers can ensure that the VAE captures the general distribution of normal products, without overfitting to specific characteristics of the training data.

2. **Noise Robustness Techniques:** To improve the model's ability to handle noisy data, noise robustness techniques can be introduced during training. One approach is to augment the training data with noise, allowing the VAE to learn to distinguish between normal variations and true defects. Additionally, techniques such as dropout or batch normalization can help regularize the model, and improve its robustness to noise.
3. **Data Augmentation:** Given the variability in product defects, increasing the diversity of the training set through data augmentation can help the VAE generalize better to unseen defects. By generating additional training data that includes various types of normal product behavior, manufacturers can reduce the likelihood of false positives, and improve the model's ability to detect true anomalies.
4. **Threshold Tuning:** In the anomaly detection phase, manufacturers can fine-tune the threshold for reconstruction errors to determine whether a product is flagged as faulty. By adjusting this threshold based on production requirements–for example, setting a higher threshold for critical components and a lower threshold for cosmetic defects–manufacturers can adopt a more customized and adaptable approach to quality control.

Conclusion

This chapter has provided a comprehensive introduction to Variational Autoencoders (VAEs), covering their foundational concepts, architecture, and practical implementation. By exploring the mathematical underpinnings and the structure of VAEs, we have seen how they differ from traditional autoencoders, and enable powerful generative capabilities. Through step-by-step implementations in TensorFlow and PyTorch, this chapter has offered hands-on insights into building and training VAEs, addressing common challenges and pitfalls in the process. With a solid understanding of VAEs, you are now prepared to apply them to real-world tasks, such as image generation and anomaly detection, using a structured and probabilistic approach to data representation.

In the next chapter, we delve into Generative Adversarial Networks (GANs), a revolutionary approach to machine learning that has transformed the field of generative modeling. You will explore the adversarial dynamic between the generator and discriminator, understanding how their interplay drives the creation of highly realistic data. The chapter includes hands-on exercises to build and train a GAN using TensorFlow and PyTorch, leveraging Keras for streamlined model design and Matplotlib for visualizing results. Thus, by the end of the chapter, you will have the skills to design, train, and fine-tune GANs, mastering their unique loss functions, and applying them to cutting-edge generative tasks.

Points to Remember

- VAEs encode input data into a continuous, probabilistic latent space, allowing for smooth sampling and interpolation between points, unlike traditional autoencoders with a fixed latent representation.
- The KL divergence term is crucial for regularizing the latent space, ensuring that the learned distribution is close to a standard Gaussian, which helps in smooth and interpretable data generation.
- Reparameterization trick allows for differentiable sampling from the latent space by separating the randomness from the learned parameters, enabling backpropagation through the stochastic process and allowing the model to be optimized using gradient-based methods.
- The total VAE loss function combines the reconstruction loss, which measures how well the decoder can recreate the input data, and the KL divergence, which regularizes the latent space.

- Unlike traditional autoencoders, VAEs can generate entirely new data points by sampling from the learned latent space, making them useful for generative tasks like image synthesis and text generation.
- The latent space of a VAE is continuous and structured, meaning nearby points correspond to similar data points, which allows for effective interpolation and smooth transitions between generated outputs.
- VAEs introduce variability in the data generation process, allowing for the generation of diverse outputs by sampling different points in the latent space, rather than reconstructing exact input data.
- VAEs are widely used in real-world applications such as image generation, anomaly detection in manufacturing and healthcare, data augmentation for machine learning models, and unsupervised learning for tasks like clustering.

Multiple Choice Questions

1. What is the main difference between traditional autoencoders and VAEs?
   a. VAEs use a probabilistic latent space.
   b. VAEs use a deterministic latent space.
   c. VAEs cannot generate new data.
   d. VAEs do not regularize the latent space.
2. What is the purpose of the KL divergence term in VAEs?
   a. To minimize the reconstruction loss
   b. To ensure that the latent space follows a continuous distribution
   c. To improve backpropagation
   d. To reduce overfitting
3. Which of the following is a common application of VAEs?
   a. Data compression
   b. Reinforcement learning
   c. Time series prediction
   d. Anomaly detection
4. What is the function of the reparameterization trick in VAEs?
   a. To reduce the complexity of the model
   b. To allow backpropagation through the sampling process
   c. To enforce regularization of the latent space
   d. To directly optimize the KL divergence term
5. Which component is responsible for generating new data from the latent space?
   a. The encoder.
   b. The reparameterization trick.

   c. The decoder.

   d. The KL divergence term.

6. What happens if the KL divergence term in a VAE is too large during training?

   a. The model overfits to the training data.

   b. The model generates poor reconstructions.

   c. The latent space becomes too sparse.

   d. The reparameterization trick becomes unstable.

Answers

1. a
2. b
3. d
4. b
5. c
6. b

Key Terms

- **Latent Space:** A lower-dimensional space where the VAE encodes the key features of the input, allowing for meaningful interpolation and generation of new data points.
- **KL Divergence:** A regularization term in the VAE's loss function that measures how closely the learned latent distribution approximates a standard Gaussian distribution.
- **Reconstruction Loss:** The part of the VAE's loss function that measures how accurately the decoder can reconstruct the original input from the latent variables, commonly using Mean Squared Error (MSE) or Binary Cross-Entropy (BCE).
- **Encoder:** The neural network in a VAE responsible for compressing the input into a probabilistic latent space, outputting the mean and variance vectors for each point.
- **Decoder:** The neural network in a VAE that takes samples from the latent space, and generates new data points based on the latent variables.
- **Anomaly Detection:** A practical application of VAEs where the model identifies unusual or out-of-distribution data points by measuring reconstruction error, which is higher for the anomalous data compared to the normal data.
- **Data Augmentation:** The process of generating new training data points using VAEs by sampling from the latent space, helping to increase the size and diversity of datasets for machine learning tasks.

CHAPTER 4
Introduction to Generative Adversarial Networks

Introduction

Generative Adversarial Networks (GANs) represent a groundbreaking approach to machine learning, enabling machines to create data that closely mirrors reality. In this chapter, we dive into the fascinating world of GANs, uncovering the powerful synergy between the generator, which crafts new data, and the discriminator, which critiques it. Together, they form an adversarial duo, driving each other toward producing highly realistic outputs. Through hands-on exercises, you will construct and train a GAN from the ground up using TensorFlow and PyTorch, harnessing Keras for simplified model building and Matplotlib for visual insights. By the chapter's end, you will gain the foundational skills to design and fine-tune a GAN, mastering the generator-discriminator interplay, and the intricacies of GAN-specific loss functions to build compelling applications.

Structure

In this chapter, we will discuss the following topics:

- **The Concept of GAN: Redefining Creativity**
  - The Dual Network Structure of GAN
- **Importance of GAN**
  - Core Concepts around GAN
  - Generator vs Discriminator: An Analogy
  - How GANs Differ from Other AI Models
- **Mathematical Foundations of GANs**
  - Probabilistic Foundations
  - Optimization
- **Architecture of GANs**
  - Overview of GAN Architecture
  - Building Blocks of GANs
- **Implementing a Basic GAN: Step-by-Step**
  - Building Your First GAN Model
  - Training the GAN

The Concept of GAN: Redefining Creativity

Generative Adversarial Networks (GANs) have become a transformative force in Artificial Intelligence (AI), particularly in fields where creativity and data generation are essential. GANs were first introduced by **Ian Goodfellow** and his team in 2014. The key innovation lies in the ability of GANs to generate new data that looks indistinguishable from the real data, such as photorealistic images, synthetic music, or even human speech. This capability opens up a wealth of possibilities in fields like art, entertainment, and data augmentation.

Unlike traditional machine learning models that typically perform tasks such as classification or prediction, GANs push the boundaries of what AI can achieve by creating entirely new content. This makes them a critical tool for applications that require high-quality, realistic outputs. Hence, whether you want to generate artwork that resembles the style of famous painters, create deepfake videos, or synthesize voices that sound human, GANs provide the framework for such innovations.

The Dual Network Structure of GAN

At the heart of GANs is the interplay between two neural networks: the **generator** and the **discriminator**. The generator's task is to create data that closely mimics the real data, such as images, videos, or text. It starts with random noise from a latent space—essentially a lower-dimensional vector space filled with random values—and transforms this noise into meaningful data. The discriminator, on the other hand, is tasked with identifying whether the data it receives is real (from the training dataset) or fake (generated by the generator). The two networks engage in a game where the generator tries to fool the discriminator, and the discriminator tries to catch the fake data.

The adversarial nature of this process is key to the success of GANs. In the beginning, the generator's outputs are random, and easily detected by the discriminator. However, over time, the generator improves as it learns from the feedback provided by the discriminator. The discriminator also becomes more skilled at identifying the fake data. This **minimax game** continues until the generator produces data that the discriminator can no longer easily distinguish from the real data.

Importance of GAN

GANs have found applications across a wide range of fields. In the creative arts, for instance, GANs are used to generate artwork that closely mimics famous artists, creating paintings or styles that would have otherwise been impossible without human intervention. In the film industry, GANs are used to create lifelike digital characters, and in music, they help compose songs in the style of well-known composers.

Figure 4.1: *These People Do not Exist. Generated Fake Images Using GAN*

Another key application is in the field of data augmentation. GANs are used to create synthetic data for training ML models, especially when the real data is scarce. For example, GANs can generate additional medical images for healthcare applications, allowing models to improve accuracy by training on a larger dataset. Similarly, GANs are used in self-driving car development to generate varied driving scenarios that the car's AI must learn to handle.

Core Concepts around GAN

In this section, we take a closer look at the core ideas that drive the generator–discriminator duel. These concepts explain how creation and evaluation work together as one learning system, shaping the unique behavior of GANs. By keeping the discussion rooted in the basics, we see more clearly why GANs differ from other generative models and how their adversarial design pushes them toward highly realistic outputs.

The Generator: Creating Synthetic Data

The generator is the creative force behind a GAN. It starts with a random noise vector sampled from a latent space—a space in which each point represents a potential pattern that can be transformed into the real data. The generator learns to map these noise vectors into meaningful data points, such as an image, video, or sound clip.

For example, in the case of image generation, the generator might take a random noise vector, and use a series of transformations to turn this noise into a 28x28 pixel image that looks like a handwritten digit. Initially, the generated images will be far from realistic, often resembling random noise. However, as the generator receives feedback from the discriminator, it learns to make subtle adjustments to improve the realism of the generated data. Over time, the generator becomes skilled at producing images that mimic the actual training data (for example, the MNIST dataset for handwritten digits).

Each step of the generator involves **convolutional layers** (in the case of images) or fully connected layers (for other types of data) that gradually refine the random input into a coherent output. The success of the generator is measured by how well it can produce data that fools the discriminator.

The Discriminator: Evaluating Real vs. Fake Data

The discriminator is the evaluator in the GAN framework. Its job is to classify data as either real (that is, from the training set) or fake (that is, generated by the generator). Initially, this task is straightforward because the generator's outputs are random and unconvincing. However, as the generator improves, the discriminator must also evolve to keep up with the increasingly realistic fake data.

The discriminator typically uses a binary classification framework, where it outputs a probability between 0 and 1, indicating how likely it believes the input data is real. If the input data is from the real dataset, the probability should be close to 1; if the data is from the generator, the probability should be close to 0.

The discriminator's role is critical in providing feedback to the generator. Every time the discriminator successfully identifies fake data, it sends a signal to the generator, indicating where the fake data fell short. This adversarial relationship between the two networks creates a feedback loop that drives the learning process.

Understanding Adversarial Networks

In an adversarial network, two models play opposing roles, much like the relationship between Batman and Joker. Imagine Batman as the *discriminator*, constantly scrutinizing everything around him, aiming to differentiate between real and falsehoods in Gotham City. Joker, on the other hand, plays the role of the *generator*, relentlessly trying to deceive Batman by creating clever illusions that resemble reality.

The generator and discriminator are locked in an intense, ongoing battle, each improving their skills through this competition. This adversarial relationship fuels the training process in GANs, as the generator becomes better at creating realistic outputs, while the discriminator sharpens its ability to distinguish between the real and generated data.

Figure 4.2: *A Battle of Wits Like Batman vs. Joker, GANs Pit Creation against Critique*

Generator versus Discriminator - An Analogy

One of the easiest ways to conceptualize the dynamic between the generator and the discriminator is by imagining Batman and Joker locked in a continuous duel of deception and detection.

- **The Joker (Generator):** In this scenario, the generator can be seen as Joker, always scheming to create convincing illusions that could pass as reality. He starts with crude tricks, easily spotted by Batman. But with every encounter, Joker learns more about what it takes to fool his adversary, refining his illusions to make them more believable. Over time, Joker's schemes become so intricate that even Batman finds it challenging to see through them.
- **Batman (Discriminator):** Batman, representing the discriminator, is the watchful detective whose task is to distinguish reality from Joker's tricks. In the beginning, Joker's illusions are simple, and Batman can easily detect them. However, as Joker becomes more skilled, Batman is forced to hone his own abilities, refining his detection skills to keep up. The better Batman becomes at spotting Joker's deceptions, the more cunning Joker has to be to succeed.
- **The Adversarial Process:** This continuous struggle between the Batman and Joker captures the essence of GANs' adversarial training. Joker, as the generator, constantly seeks to deceive, while Batman, as the discriminator, strives to see through the deception. With each iteration, Joker learns to create more realistic illusions, and Batman becomes more adept at detection. Eventually, Joker's illusions become so lifelike that even Batman struggles to tell the real from the fake–indicating the GAN has achieved its goal of generating highly realistic data.

Distinguishing Features of GANs Compared to Other AI Models

GANs are part of a broader family of generative models, but they are unique in several key ways when compared to models like Autoencoders (AEs) and Variational Autoencoders (VAEs).

- **Autoencoders (AEs):** Autoencoders are designed to compress the data into a lower-dimensional latent space (encoding), and then reconstruct the original data (decoding). While autoencoders are good at creating compressed representations, they are not designed to generate new, novel data from scratch. Their goal is to recreate the input data as accurately as possible, rather than producing something entirely new.
- **Variational Autoencoders (VAEs):** VAEs build on autoencoders by introducing probabilistic reasoning into the latent space. Instead of mapping data to a single point in the latent space, VAEs map data to a probability distribution, allowing for more varied data generation. However, even VAEs struggle to generate the high-quality, photorealistic data that GANs are known for, primarily because VAEs are trained to minimize reconstruction loss, not to fool a discriminator.

Key Differences between GANs and Other Models:

Generative Adversarial Networks (GANs) stand out from other generative models such as Autoencoders (AEs) and Variational Autoencoders (VAEs) due to their unique training dynamics, and the quality of their outputs. Unlike AEs and VAEs, which focus on reconstruction and probabilistic modeling, GANs leverage an adversarial framework where two networks compete to achieve optimal results. This section highlights the distinct characteristics of GANs, comparing their training process, output realism, and practical use cases to those of other models.

1. **Training Process:** The adversarial training process sets GANs apart. In GANs, the generator and discriminator are constantly learning from each other's mistakes. This game-like setup drives both networks to improve, resulting in highly realistic data. In contrast, AEs and VAEs focus on minimizing the reconstruction errors, which tend to produce smoother but less realistic outputs.
2. **Realism of Generated Data:** GANs excel at generating data that is nearly indistinguishable from the real-world data. The discriminator's role ensures that the generator continually improves

until the generated data can pass as real. AEs and VAEs, on the other hand, focus more on creating smooth transitions between data points, which often results in less photorealism.

3. **Use Cases**: GANs are particularly suited for tasks that require the generation of high-quality images, videos, and audio. They have been used in deepfake creation, generating realistic avatars, and even synthesizing voices for digital assistants. VAEs, while still useful, are better suited for applications where diversity in the generated data is more important than realism, such as in data augmentation or style variation tasks.

Mathematical Foundations of GANs

To fully understand and leverage Generative Adversarial Networks (GANs), it is necessary to grasp the mathematical principles that form their backbone. GANs are built on concepts from probability theory and optimization, which enable the generator and discriminator to work together in an adversarial setup. This section delves into the probabilistic foundations and optimization techniques that underpin GANs, providing a deeper understanding of how these models learn to generate the realistic data.

Probabilistic Foundations

Generative Adversarial Networks (GANs) operate on probabilistic principles, where the goal is to generate new data that closely resembles the real data by learning an underlying data distribution. The generator tries to approximate the true data distribution by transforming random noise sampled from a latent space into data that mirrors the training data. This idea of probabilistic modeling is central to how GANs function.

Latent Space and Noise Sampling

In a typical GAN setup, the generator starts with a latent space, which is a lower-dimensional space populated with random noise vectors. These noise vectors are drawn from a probability distribution, often Gaussian or uniform, and each point in this latent space corresponds to a potential output generated by the model. The task of the generator is to map these random noise points into realistic data points.

For example, in the case of image generation, each noise vector in the latent space could represent features of an image such as texture, color, and shape. Over time, the generator learns to associate these noise vectors with patterns that represent actual images, gradually producing outputs that resemble real images.

Joint Probability Distribution

In GANs, the training process revolves around two key distributions:

1. **Real Data Distribution** $p_{data}(x)$: This is the probability distribution from which the real data is sampled. Each data point x is a real example from the training dataset, such as a photograph of a face, a handwritten digit, or any other type of data.

2. **Generated Data Distribution** $p_g(x)$: This is the distribution of data produced by the generator. The generator receives random noise z from a prior distribution p(z), and maps it to a data point $x=G(z)$. The goal of GAN training is for the generator to adjust its parameters so that $p_g(x)$ becomes indistinguishable from $p_{data}(x)$.

Learning the Mapping

The generator learns a mapping G(z) that transforms the noise into data. During training, the generator is refined through the feedback provided by the discriminator which evaluates how close the generated data G(z) is to the real data. By optimizing this mapping, the generator attempts to generate data that matches the statistical properties of the real data distribution.

Game Theory Concepts and the Minimax Game

GANs are structured as a **two-player game** between the generator and the discriminator, inspired by the **game theory**. Each player (the generator and the discriminator) has opposing objectives. The generator's goal is to generate realistic data that fools the discriminator, while the discriminator aims to correctly classify whether the data is real or generated.

The Minimax Game

The adversarial process can be understood as a **minimax game**, where the generator and discriminator are both optimizing opposing objectives. The generator tries to minimize the discriminator's ability to distinguish between real and fake data, while the discriminator tries to maximize its accuracy in distinguishing the real from the generated data.

The minimax objective can be written as:

$$\min_G \max_D V(D, G) = E_{x \sim p_{data}(x)}[\log D(x)] + E_{z \sim p_{z(z)}}[\log(1 - D(G(z)))]$$

In this setup:

- D(x) is the discriminator's estimate of the probability that data x is real.
- G(z) is the generated data produced by the generator using random noise z.

  Discriminator Objective: The discriminator aims to maximize the likelihood of correctly classifying real data x as real, and generated data G(z) as fake. This is done by maximizing log D(x) for real data and minimizing log(1–D(G(z))) for fake data.

  Generator Objective: The generator, on the other hand, seeks to minimize log(1–D(G(z))). In simple terms, the generator wants to produce data G(z) that maximizes D(G(z)), that is, data that the discriminator believes is real.

This adversarial process between the generator and the discriminator forms the core of GAN training. The two networks constantly improve by playing this minimax game, with the generator getting better at creating realistic data, and the discriminator becoming more adept at distinguishing the real from the fake.

Nash Equilibrium in GANs

From a game theory perspective, GANs converge when they reach a **Nash equilibrium**, where neither the generator nor the discriminator can improve their strategy, given the strategy of the other. At this point, the generator produces data that is indistinguishable from the real data, and the discriminator is unable to make a better classification than random guessing (that is, assigning a probability of 0.5 for both real and fake data).

Objective Function and Loss Functions

Binary Cross-Entropy Loss in GANs: GANs are traditionally trained using **binary cross-entropy loss** for both the generator and the discriminator. The objective is for the discriminator to correctly classify the real data as real and the fake data as fake. For the generator, the objective is to generate the data that the discriminator incorrectly classifies as real.

The discriminator's loss function can be expressed as:

$$L_D = -(\mathbb{E}_{x\sim p_{data(x)}}[\log D(x)] + \mathbb{E}_{z\sim p_{z(z)}}[\log(1 - D(G(z)))])$$

This function encourages the discriminator to:

1. Maximize the likelihood of correctly identifying the real data by increasing D(x).
2. Minimize the likelihood of incorrectly classifying the generated data by decreasing D(G(z)).

   The generator's loss function is given by:

   $$L_G = -\mathbb{E}_{z\sim p_{z(z)}}[\log(D(G(z)))]$$

3. The generator aims to maximize D(G(z)), or in other words, it tries to generate data which increases the probability that the discriminator classifies it as real.

Alternative Loss Functions: While binary cross-entropy is the most commonly used loss function for GANs, but it is not without its challenges, particularly in terms of gradient flow and stability during training. Several alternative loss functions have been introduced to address these issues:

- **Wasserstein Loss**: The **Wasserstein GAN (WGAN)** uses a loss function based on the **Wasserstein distance**, which measures the distance between the real and the generated data distribution. This loss function mitigates the problem of vanishing gradients, and provides a smoother as well as more stable training process.
  - **Discriminator Loss:**

    $$L_D = \mathbb{E}_{x\sim p_{data(x)}}[D(x)] - \mathbb{E}_{z\sim p_{z(z)}}[D(G(z))]$$

  - **Generator Loss:**

    $$L_G = -\mathbb{E}_{z\sim p_{z(z)}}[D(G(z))]$$

  WGANs replace the binary cross-entropy loss with this Wasserstein distance-based loss, resulting in a more stable training process, and better gradient flow for the generator.

- **Least-Squares GAN Loss (LSGAN)**: The Least-Squares GAN (LSGAN) modifies the loss function to minimize the mean squared error between the discriminator's output, and the desired classification label. This smooths out the optimization process, and can lead to better visual quality in generated images.
  - **Discriminator Loss:**

    $$L_D = \frac{1}{2}\mathbb{E}_{x\sim p_{data(x)}}[(D(x) - 1)^2] + \frac{1}{2}\mathbb{E}_{z\sim p_{z(z)}}[(D(G(z)))^2]$$

  - **Generator Loss:**

    $$L_G = \frac{1}{2}\mathbb{E}_{z\sim p_{z(z)}}[(D(G(z)) - 1)^2]$$

  Thus, LSGANs result in more stable convergence, and can help generate more visually appealing outputs.

Optimization Challenges in GANs

Training GANs poses several significant optimization challenges, primarily due to the adversarial nature of the model. These challenges can make it difficult to stabilize GAN training, and achieve high-quality results:

- **Vanishing Gradients:** In the early stages of GAN training, the discriminator often becomes too strong, meaning that it easily identifies the fake data as fake. When the discriminator is too confident, the generator receives very little feedback, leading to vanishing gradients. As the gradients it receives during backpropagation are too small for meaningful updates.

Figure 4.3: *The Vanishing Gradient Problem*

  You can see a crude analogy of vanishing gradient problem in *Figure* 4.3, where people closer to the stage are getting more goodies, while people farther away get very little. In the vanishing gradient problem, the loss function's gradients diminish as they are backpropagated through the layers of a neural network. As a result, the weights of the layers closest to the output are updated effectively, while the layers farther from the output receive gradients that are too small, preventing proper weight updates and learning. This problem typically arises when the discriminator quickly learns to classify the real and the fake data, resulting in minimal error and, consequently, weak gradient signals for the generator.

- **Mode Collapse:** Another common challenge in GAN training is mode collapse, where the generator produces a limited variety of outputs, often repeating similar patterns or even identical images. For instance, in an image generation task, the generator might consistently produce a particular type of image (for example, cats of the same breed) that successfully fools the discriminator but fails to capture the full diversity (for example: cats of different breed) of the real data distribution.

  Mode collapse can significantly reduce the quality of the generated data, as the outputs lack variability and creativity. This issue occurs when the generator finds a shortcut that tricks the discriminator into believing it is generating diverse data, while in reality, it is only exploiting a small subset of patterns that consistently work.

***Figure 4.4**: Generated Images Have Better Variety with No Mode Collapse (left image)*

- **Instability in Training:** GANs are notoriously unstable during training due to the adversarial interaction between the generator and the discriminator. If one network (typically the discriminator) becomes too powerful, it dominates the training process, preventing the other network from learning effectively. This can result in oscillating loss values, where neither network converges, leading to poor quality generated data, or a failure of the GAN to train altogether.

Architecture of GANs

Generative Adversarial Networks (GANs) are composed of two key components–the generator and the discriminator–working together in an adversarial setup to create highly realistic data. Understanding the architecture of GANs involves breaking down their core building blocks, exploring how these components interact, and analyzing the iterative process that drives their training. This section provides a detailed overview of the GAN architecture and its fundamental building blocks, offering insights into their roles and significance in the generative process.

Overview of GAN Architecture

At its core, a GAN consists of two primary components: the **generator** and the **discriminator**. These components work in tandem, competing against each other in a zero-sum game, where the success of one network implies the failure of the other. The goal of this adversarial process is for the generator to produce realistic data that can fool the discriminator, while the discriminator continuously improves its ability to distinguish between the real and the fake data.

Generator

The generator is responsible for creating new data instances. It takes random noise as input, usually drawn from a prior distribution such as a uniform or Gaussian distribution, and transforms this noise into data that mimics the characteristics of the real dataset. The key function of the generator is to learn a mapping from the latent space (noise) to the data space (real data).

- **Key Role:** The generator's task is to create synthetic data that resembles the training data. It learns by receiving feedback from the discriminator on how realistic its outputs are.

- **Training Goal:** The generator is trained to minimize the ability of the discriminator to distinguish between the real and the generated data. In doing so, it continuously improves its outputs.

Discriminator

The discriminator acts as a binary classifier. It takes the input data, and outputs the probability that the input data is real (that is, from the dataset) or fake (that is, generated by the generator). The discriminator plays a crucial role in evaluating how well the generator performs and provides feedback that guides the training of the generator.

- **Key Role:** The discriminator's task is to maximize its accuracy in distinguishing the real data from the fake data.
- **Training Goal:** The discriminator is trained to maximize the likelihood of correctly identifying real versus generated data, making it progressively harder for the generator to fool it.

Interaction between Generator and Discriminator

The generator and discriminator are trained in an alternating fashion:

Step 1: The discriminator is trained on both real data and fake data generated by the generator. It updates its parameters to better classify the real versus the fake data.

Step 2: The generator is trained based on feedback from the discriminator. Its goal is to minimize the discriminator's ability to distinguish between the real and fake data.

This adversarial process continues until the generator becomes so proficient that the discriminator can no longer tell the difference between the real and the generated data.

Building Blocks of GANs

To understand how GANs function at a deeper level, we must look into the building blocks of each component. Both the generator and discriminator are neural networks composed of multiple layers that are fine-tuned to their respective tasks.

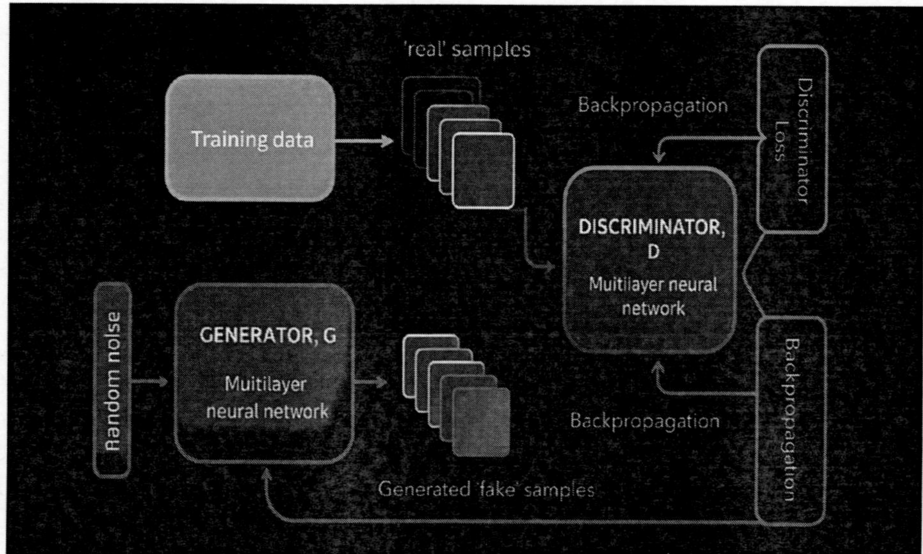

Figure 4.5: *Architecture of GAN*

Generator Layers

The generator typically uses a series of fully connected layers or convolutional layers to transform noise from the latent space into the realistic data. The key layers and techniques in the generator include:

- **Fully Connected Layers:** The initial transformation of noise often happens through fully connected layers that project the latent space vector into a higher-dimensional space.
- **Convolutional Layers:** In image-based GANs, convolutional layers are used to up sample the noise into an image. These layers increase the spatial resolution, and add complexity to the generated data.
- **Activation Functions:**
    - **LeakyReLU:** This activation function is commonly used in the generator's layers to introduce non-linearity. LeakyReLU is preferred over standard ReLU because it prevents the dying ReLU problem, where neurons can become inactive, and stop learning.
    - **Tanh:** The Tanh activation function is often applied at the output layer of the generator to map the generated data into the appropriate range (for example, pixel values between -1 and 1).

The following is a sample code that builds a typical generator component:

```
import tensorflow as tf

def build_generator(latent_dim):
    model = tf.keras.Sequential()
    model.add(tf.keras.layers.Dense(256, input_dim=latent_dim, activation='relu'))
    model.add(tf.keras.layers.BatchNormalization())
    model.add(tf.keras.layers.LeakyReLU(alpha=0.01))
    model.add(tf.keras.layers.Dense(512, activation='relu'))
    model.add(tf.keras.layers.BatchNormalization())
    model.add(tf.keras.layers.LeakyReLU(alpha=0.01))
    model.add(tf.keras.layers.Dense(1024, activation='relu'))
    model.add(tf.keras.layers.BatchNormalization())
    model.add(tf.keras.layers.LeakyReLU(alpha=0.01))
    # Output for MNIST images
    model.add(tf.keras.layers.Dense(28 * 28 * 1, activation='tanh'))
    return model
```

Discriminator Layers

The discriminator network is tasked with classifying the real and fake data, which makes its architecture fundamentally different from the generator. The key components of the discriminator include:

- **Convolutional Layers:** In image-based GANs, convolutional layers are used to downsample the input data, extracting the key features that allow the discriminator to differentiate the real data from the fake.
- **Fully Connected Layers:** After extracting the features through convolutional layers, fully connected layers process this information, and reduce it to a single probability value representing whether the data is real or fake.
- **Activation Functions:**
    - **Sigmoid:** The sigmoid activation function is typically used in the output layer of the discriminator, as it maps the output to a value between 0 and 1, representing the probability of the input being real.

- **LeakyReLU:** Similar to the generator, the discriminator uses LeakyReLU for intermediate layers to prevent the dying ReLU problem, and allow for better gradient flow.

The following is a sample code that builds a typical discriminator component:

```
def build_discriminator():
    model = tf.keras.Sequential()
    model.add(tf.keras.layers.Conv2D(64, kernel_size=3, strides=2,
input_shape=(28, 28, 1), padding="same"))
    model.add(tf.keras.layers.LeakyReLU(alpha=0.01))
    model.add(tf.keras.layers.Conv2D(128, kernel_size=3, strides=2,
padding="same"))
    model.add(tf.keras.layers.LeakyReLU(alpha=0.01))
    model.add(tf.keras.layers.Conv2D(256, kernel_size=3, strides=2,
padding="same"))
    model.add(tf.keras.layers.LeakyReLU(alpha=0.01))
    model.add(tf.keras.layers.Flatten())
    # Output real/fake probability
    model.add(tf.keras.layers.Dense(1, activation='sigmoid'))
    return model
```

Normalization Techniques

- **Batch Normalization:** To improve stability during training, GANs often use batch normalization in both the generator and discriminator. This technique normalizes the inputs to each layer, reducing the likelihood of vanishing/exploding gradients, and making the training process more stable.

Batch normalization ensures that the inputs to a given layer have a mean of 0, and a standard deviation of 1, which improves convergence rates, and helps prevent overfitting.

Latent Space Representation

The latent space in a GAN is the source of creativity. It is a lower-dimensional space from which the generator samples noise, which is then transformed into the realistic data. The latent space allows the generator to explore a variety of outputs by sampling different points in this space, each corresponding to a different potential output.

Mapping Random Noise to Meaningful Data: In the latent space, each vector represents a random point, and the generator learns to map this noise to the meaningful data. For example, in an image generation task, a point in the latent space might correspond to an image of a specific type of object (for example, a car, a face, and so on).

As training progresses, the generator becomes better at associating specific regions of the latent space with different features of the real data distribution. For instance, in a GAN trained on faces, moving in a particular direction in the latent space might correspond to changes in facial features, such as age or expression.

Dimensionality of the Latent Space: The dimensionality of the latent space is a hyperparameter that must be carefully chosen. A larger latent space allows for more complex and diverse data generation but can make training more difficult. A smaller latent space makes it easier to train but can limit the diversity of the generated data.

Implementing a Basic GAN: Step-by-Step

Building and training a Generative Adversarial Network (GAN) can seem complex, but breaking it down into manageable steps makes the process approachable. This section walks through the implementation of a basic GAN, starting with the construction of the generator and discriminator models. You will learn how to set up the adversarial training loop, adjust key hyperparameters, and monitor the progress of your GAN as it learns to generate the realistic data. Thus, by following this guide, you will gain hands-on experience in building your first GAN, and understand the mechanics of training these powerful models.

Building Your First GAN Model

Let us start by building the basic architecture of a GAN using TensorFlow and PyTorch. We will create two key components: the generator and the discriminator.

Generator Model

The generator is responsible for taking random noise from a latent space, and transforming it into synthetic data (such as images). In this example, we will use TensorFlow to build a generator that outputs 28x28 grayscale images, similar to the MNIST dataset.

TensorFlow Code:

```
import tensorflow as tf

def build_generator(latent_dim):
    model = tf.keras.Sequential()
    # Input layer - latent space
    model.add(tf.keras.layers.Dense(256, input_dim=latent_dim,
activation='relu'))
    # Adding BatchNormalization for stable training
    model.add(tf.keras.layers.BatchNormalization())
    model.add(tf.keras.layers.LeakyReLU(alpha=0.01))
    # Increase dimensionality for image data
    model.add(tf.keras.layers.Dense(512, activation='relu'))
    model.add(tf.keras.layers.BatchNormalization())
    model.add(tf.keras.layers.LeakyReLU(alpha=0.01))
    model.add(tf.keras.layers.Dense(1024, activation='relu'))
    model.add(tf.keras.layers.BatchNormalization())
    model.add(tf.keras.layers.LeakyReLU(alpha=0.01))
    # Output layer - reshape to 28x28 image
    model.add(tf.keras.layers.Dense(28 * 28 * 1, activation='tanh'))
    model.add(tf.keras.layers.Reshape((28, 28, 1)))
    return model
```

Explanation:

- The **latent_dim** represents the size of the noise vector that will be sampled from a prior distribution (usually Gaussian or uniform).
- **Dense layers** are used to project the latent vector into a higher-dimensional space.
- **LeakyReLU** is used to introduce non-linearity, which helps prevent issues like the dying ReLU problem.
- **BatchNormalization** stabilizes the training process by ensuring that the mean and variance of the inputs remain consistent.

PyTorch Code:

```
import torch
import torch.nn as nn

class Generator(nn.Module):
```

```
    def __init__(self, latent_dim):
        super(Generator, self).__init__()
        self.model = nn.Sequential(
            nn.Linear(latent_dim, 256),
            nn.ReLU(),
            nn.BatchNorm1d(256),
            nn.Linear(256, 512),
            nn.ReLU(),
            nn.BatchNorm1d(512),
            nn.Linear(512, 1024),
            nn.ReLU(),
            nn.BatchNorm1d(1024),
            nn.Linear(1024, 28 * 28),
            nn.Tanh()
        )

    def forward(self, z):
        img = self.model(z)
        img = img.view(img.size(0), 1, 28, 28)  # Reshape into image format
        return img
```

Discriminator Model

The discriminator's task is to classify images as real or fake. It takes an image (either from the dataset or generated by the generator) and outputs a probability indicating how likely it is that the image is real.

TensorFlow Code:

```
def build_discriminator():
    model = tf.keras.Sequential()
    # Input layer for 28x28 images
    model.add(tf.keras.layers.Flatten(input_shape=(28, 28, 1)))
    # Adding Dense layers for feature extraction
    model.add(tf.keras.layers.Dense(512, activation='relu'))
    model.add(tf.keras.layers.LeakyReLU(alpha=0.01))
    model.add(tf.keras.layers.Dense(256, activation='relu'))
    model.add(tf.keras.layers.LeakyReLU(alpha=0.01))
    # Output layer - binary classification (real/fake)
    model.add(tf.keras.layers.Dense(1, activation='sigmoid'))
    return model
```

Explanation:

a. **Flatten:** This layer flattens the 28x28 image into a 1D vector to be processed by the dense layers.

b. **Sigmoid activation:** The final output layer uses sigmoid activation to produce a probability value between 0 and 1.

PyTorch Code:

```
class Discriminator(nn.Module):
    def __init__(self):
        super(Discriminator, self).__init__()
        self.model = nn.Sequential(
            nn.Linear(28 * 28, 512),
            nn.LeakyReLU(0.2),
            nn.Linear(512, 256),
            nn.LeakyReLU(0.2),
```

```
                nn.Linear(256, 1),
                nn.Sigmoid()
            )

        def forward(self, img):
            img_flat = img.view(img.size(0), -1)  # Flatten the image
            validity = self.model(img_flat)
            return validity
```

Explanation:

a. The **LeakyReLU** activation with a small slope ensures better gradient flow.

b. The **Sigmoid** function outputs a binary classification probability indicating if the image is real or fake.

Training the GAN

Once the generator and discriminator are defined, the next step is to implement the training loop.

Define Loss Functions

Both the generator and the discriminator are trained using binary cross-entropy loss. The generator's objective is to minimize the discriminator's ability to detect fakes, while the discriminator tries to correctly classify the real and fake images.

```
# Binary cross-entropy loss function
loss_fn = tf.keras.losses.BinaryCrossentropy()
```

Optimizers

We use Stochastic Gradient Descent (SGD) or Adam optimizer for optimizing both networks. Adam is generally preferred for GANs because of its adaptability during training.

```
# Optimizers for generator and discriminator
gen_optimizer = tf.keras.optimizers.Adam(learning_rate=0.0002, beta_1=0.5)
disc_optimizer = tf.keras.optimizers.Adam(learning_rate=0.0002, beta_1=0.5)
```

Training Loop

The GAN training process involves alternating between training the discriminator and the generator. Here is the structure of the training loop:

Step 1: Train the Discriminator

a. Generate a batch of fake images using the generator.

b. Get a batch of real images from the dataset.

c. Calculate the discriminator loss using both real and fake images.

d. Update the discriminator's weights based on this loss.

Step 2: Train the Generator

a. Generate another batch of fake images.

b. Pass these images through the discriminator.

c. Calculate the generator loss based on how well it fooled the discriminator.

d. Update the generator's weights accordingly.

```
for epoch in range(epochs):
    # Step 1: Train Discriminator
    # Get real and fake images
    real_images = real_data_loader.next_batch(batch_size)
    noise = np.random.normal(0, 1, (batch_size, latent_dim))
    fake_images = generator.predict(noise)

    # Train on real and fake images
    d_loss_real = discriminator.train_on_batch(real_images,
np.ones((batch_size, 1)))
    d_loss_fake = discriminator.train_on_batch(fake_images,
np.zeros((batch_size, 1)))

    d_loss = 0.5 * np.add(d_loss_real, d_loss_fake)

    # Step 2: Train Generator
    noise = np.random.normal(0, 1, (batch_size, latent_dim))
    valid_y = np.ones((batch_size, 1))  # Generator wants to fool
discriminator

    g_loss = generator.train_on_batch(noise, valid_y)

    # Logging progress
    print(f"Epoch {epoch}: D loss: {d_loss}, G loss: {g_loss}")
```

Hyperparameters

- **Learning Rate:** Lower values (like 0.0002) are typically used for GANs to ensure stable convergence.
- **Batch Size:** Common values range from 32 to 128. Larger batch sizes provide more stable updates but require more computational power.

Explanation:

- **`d_loss`** measures how well the discriminator distinguishes the real from fake images.
- **`g_loss`** indicates how well the generator fools the discriminator.

Visualizing Generated Images with Matplotlib

Visualizing the generated images is crucial to track the progress of GAN training. Using Matplotlib, we can visualize how the images evolve over time.

```
import matplotlib.pyplot as plt

def visualize_images(epoch, generator, latent_dim):
    noise = np.random.normal(0, 1, (25, latent_dim))
    gen_images = generator.predict(noise)
    gen_images = 0.5 * gen_images + 0.5  # Rescale images 0-1

    plt.figure(figsize=(5, 5))
    for i in range(25):
        plt.subplot(5, 5, i + 1)
        plt.imshow(gen_images[i, :, :, 0], cmap='gray')
        plt.axis('off')
    plt.tight_layout()
    plt.savefig(f"generated_images_epoch_{epoch}.png")
    plt.show()
```

Explanation:

- We generate 25 images from random noise, and plot them using Matplotlib.
- This function should be called periodically (for example, every few epochs) to monitor the generator's progress.

Monitoring Training and Evaluation

1. Tracking Losses: Tracking the loss values for both the generator and discriminator is essential for diagnosing issues such as mode collapse or unstable training.

- **Discriminator Loss:** If the discriminator loss becomes too low, it indicates that the generator is failing to produce realistic images.
- **Generator Loss:** A high generator loss indicates that the discriminator is too strong, and the generator is not learning effectively.

```
plt.plot(d_loss_list, label='Discriminator Loss')
plt.plot(g_loss_list, label='Generator Loss')
plt.legend()
plt.show()
```

2. Evaluating GAN Performance: While losses provide some insight, evaluating the quality of generated images visually is often more effective. Save the generated images at intervals (for example, every 100 epochs) to compare how the quality improves.

3. Common Issues to Monitor:

- **Mode Collapse:** The generator produces a limited variety of images, often generating the same or similar images repeatedly. If this happens, consider using minibatch discrimination to encourage diversity in the generated samples.
- **Training Instability:** GANs are notoriously difficult to train. If the losses fluctuate wildly or do not converge, try adjusting the learning rate or using techniques like Wasserstein loss for more stable optimization.

Challenges and Pitfalls in Training GANs

Common Challenges: Mode Collapse, Vanishing Gradients, and Instability

Training GANs presents several unique challenges, making it notoriously difficult to achieve stable and efficient training. Let us recap some of the most common issues encountered when working with GANs:

Mode Collapse

Mode collapse occurs when the generator repeatedly produces a limited variety of outputs, failing to capture the full diversity of the real data.

Example: For example, if training a GAN to generate faces, a mode-collapsed generator might produce multiple faces with similar features, ignoring the diversity in the training data.

Why It Happens: The generator overfocuses on specific patterns that fools the discriminator, as the discriminator does not explicitly enforce diversity. Imbalances during training can further make this problem worse.

Impact: This problem leads to reduced variability in the generated samples, which is undesirable in most cases where diversity is essential.

Vanishing Gradients

Vanishing gradients occur when the discriminator becomes too effective early in training, causing the generator to receive minimal feedback during backpropagation, which hinders its learning.

Why It Happens: If the discriminator easily identifies fake data with high confidence, it sends weak feedback (low gradients) to the generator. This makes it difficult for the generator to make meaningful updates, slowing down the learning process.

Impact: Vanishing gradients can lead to the generator failing to improve or train effectively, resulting in poor-quality outputs.

Training Instability

GAN training is inherently unstable because of the adversarial nature of the two networks. Small imbalances in their performance can cause dramatic shifts in the learning dynamics.

Why It Happens: If the generator improves too quickly, the discriminator might not have enough time to learn effectively. Conversely, if the discriminator becomes too powerful, the generator struggles to learn and improve. These imbalances lead to oscillating loss values and unstable training trajectories.

Impact: Instability can manifest as large fluctuations in the loss curves of both the generator and the discriminator. This makes it difficult to track progress and achieve convergence.

Practical Solutions and Tips

There are several practical techniques that researchers and practitioners use to mitigate these common challenges and stabilize GAN training.

Label Smoothing

What It Does: Label smoothing is a technique where the labels for the real data are adjusted to values slightly less than 1 (for example, 0.9 instead of 1). This prevents the discriminator from becoming overly confident in distinguishing real data from fake data.

How It Helps: By smoothing the labels, the generator receives more useful gradients, helping to prevent vanishing gradients. It also makes the discriminator slightly less accurate, giving the generator more room to improve.

Code Example:

```
# Label smoothing example
real_labels = np.ones((batch_size, 1)) * 0.9  # Smoothing real labels to 0.9
fake_labels = np.zeros((batch_size, 1))       # Fake labels remain 0
```

Batch Normalization

What It Does: Batch normalization is applied to both the generator and the discriminator to stabilize the learning process. It normalizes the inputs to each layer, ensuring that the mean and variance remain consistent, which improves gradient flow and stabilizes training.

How It Helps: Normalizing the inputs prevents issues such as vanishing/exploding gradients, leading to smoother and more reliable learning. This technique is particularly useful in the generator, helping it produce more diverse outputs.

Code Example (in generator):

```
model.add(tf.keras.layers.BatchNormalization())
```

Code Example (in discriminator):

```
model.add(tf.keras.layers.BatchNormalization())
```

Gradient Penalty in WGAN-GP

What It Does: Introduces a gradient penalty term to the loss function, ensuring the discriminator's gradients maintain a controlled magnitude.

How It Helps: Enforces Lipschitz continuity, prevents the discriminator from overpowering the generator, and stabilizes training.

Code Example:

```
# Calculating the Discriminator Loss
L_D = D(real_data) - D(fake_data) + λ * (||gradients|| - 1)^2
```

The gradient penalty term $\lambda(||\nabla||-1)^2$ ensures that the discriminator's gradients remain close to 1, maintaining a balanced training process.

Note: *The term* ∇ *refers to the gradients of the discriminator with respect to the interpolated samples between real and fake data.*

Learning Rate Adjustments

What It Does: GANs are sensitive to learning rates, and using the same learning rate for both networks can lead to imbalances. A common solution is to use a lower learning rate for the discriminator compared to the generator.

How It Helps: Slowing down the learning rate for the discriminator prevents it from becoming too powerful early in the training process, allowing the generator to keep up.

Code Example:

```
# Different learning rates for generator and discriminator
gen_optimizer = tf.keras.optimizers.Adam(learning_rate=0.0001, beta_1=0.5)
disc_optimizer = tf.keras.optimizers.Adam(learning_rate=0.00005, beta_1=0.5)
```

Dropout and Regularization Techniques

What It Does: Regularization techniques such as Dropout can help prevent overfitting in the discriminator. Dropout randomly drops neurons during training, forcing the network to generalize better, rather than relying on memorizing specific features.

How It Helps: Dropout helps prevent the discriminator from becoming too strong, which would lead to vanishing gradients for the generator. It also reduces the risk of mode collapse by encouraging the generator to explore a wider range of outputs.

Code Example:

```
# Applying dropout in the discriminator (for eg: 40%)
model.add(tf.keras.layers.Dropout(0.4))
```

Minibatch Discrimination

What It Does: Introduces diversity in the generator's outputs by comparing generated samples within the same batch, and penalizing similarity.

How It Helps: Reduces the likelihood of mode collapse by encouraging the generator to produce a broader range of outputs.

Code Example:

```
# Psuedo code
For each sample in the batch:
    Compute similarity between the sample and all other samples in the batch
    Aggregate similarities into a diversity score
    Penalize the generator if the diversity score is too low
```

Case Study: Creating Synthetic Handwritten Digits with GANs

Problem: Generating Handwritten Digits Similar to MNIST

In this case study, we aim to generate synthetic handwritten digits using a GAN trained on the MNIST dataset. The MNIST dataset is a widely used benchmark in machine learning and computer vision, consisting of 60,000 training images and 10,000 test images of handwritten digits (0-9). Each image is 28×28 pixels in grayscale.

Why GANs? Traditional machine learning models focus on classification tasks, such as recognizing handwritten digits from the MNIST dataset. However, with GANs, the goal is to generate new, synthetic handwritten digits that resemble the real ones. This allows for:

- **Data augmentation:** GANs can create additional data for training models, improving performance in situations where the real data is limited.
- **Understanding latent representations:** GANs provide insight into the underlying structures of data by mapping random noise to coherent outputs.

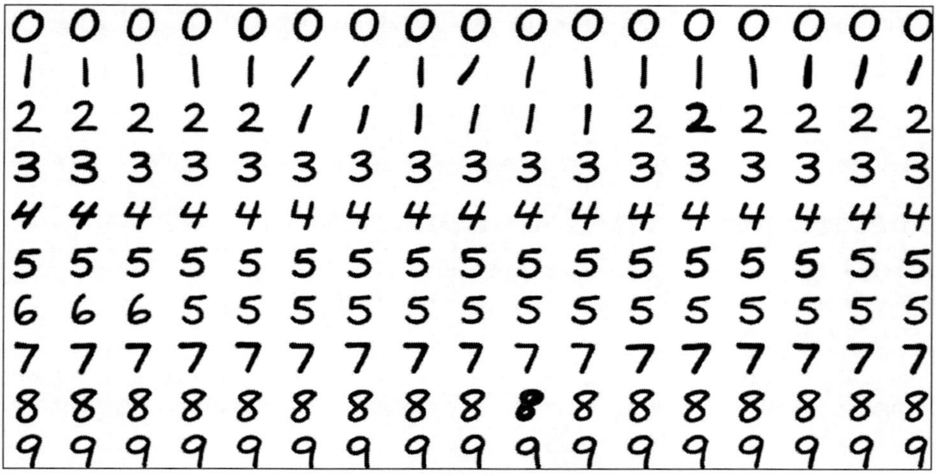

Figure 4.6: *Handwritten Digits Data (The MNIST Database)*

Solution Approach: Building a GAN

To solve this problem, we will build a basic GAN using TensorFlow. Our GAN consists of two components: the generator and the discriminator. The generator will learn to produce new digits, and the discriminator will learn to distinguish between the real and fake digits.

Step 1: Defining the Generator and Discriminator

Generator: The generator takes a vector of random noise, and transforms it into a 28×28 image. Here is the architecture:

```
import tensorflow as tf

def build_generator(latent_dim):
    model = tf.keras.Sequential()
    model.add(tf.keras.layers.Dense(256, input_dim=latent_dim, activation='relu'))
    model.add(tf.keras.layers.BatchNormalization())
    model.add(tf.keras.layers.LeakyReLU(alpha=0.01))
    model.add(tf.keras.layers.Dense(512, activation='relu'))
    model.add(tf.keras.layers.BatchNormalization())
    model.add(tf.keras.layers.LeakyReLU(alpha=0.01))
    model.add(tf.keras.layers.Dense(28 * 28 * 1, activation='tanh'))
    model.add(tf.keras.layers.Reshape((28, 28, 1)))
    return model
```

Discriminator: The discriminator takes an image (real or generated) and outputs a probability indicating whether the image is real or fake:

```
def build_discriminator():
    model = tf.keras.Sequential()
    model.add(tf.keras.layers.Flatten(input_shape=(28, 28, 1)))
    model.add(tf.keras.layers.Dense(512, activation='relu'))
    model.add(tf.keras.layers.LeakyReLU(alpha=0.01))
    model.add(tf.keras.layers.Dense(256, activation='relu'))
    model.add(tf.keras.layers.LeakyReLU(alpha=0.01))
    model.add(tf.keras.layers.Dense(1, activation='sigmoid'))  # Output real/fake
probability
    return model
```

Step 2: Training the GAN

The training process alternates between training the discriminator, and training the generator.

Training the Discriminator: The discriminator is trained to correctly classify real digits from the MNIST dataset as real, and the digits generated by the generator as fake. We use binary cross-entropy as the loss function.

```
# Binary cross-entropy loss function
loss_fn = tf.keras.losses.BinaryCrossentropy()

# Optimizers for generator and discriminator
gen_optimizer = tf.keras.optimizers.Adam(learning_rate=0.0002, beta_1=0.5)
disc_optimizer = tf.keras.optimizers.Adam(learning_rate=0.0002, beta_1=0.5)

# Training loop
for epoch in range(epochs):
    # Train discriminator
    real_images = real_data_loader.next_batch(batch_size)
    noise = np.random.normal(0, 1, (batch_size, latent_dim))
    fake_images = generator.predict(noise)

    # Real and fake labels
    real_labels = np.ones((batch_size, 1))
    fake_labels = np.zeros((batch_size, 1))
```

```
    # Train on real and fake images
    disc_loss_real = discriminator.train_on_batch(real_images, real_labels)
    disc_loss_fake = discriminator.train_on_batch(fake_images, fake_labels)
    disc_loss = 0.5 * np.add(disc_loss_real, disc_loss_fake)

    # Train generator
    noise = np.random.normal(0, 1, (batch_size, latent_dim))
    gen_loss = generator.train_on_batch(noise, real_labels)

    print(f'Epoch {epoch}, Disc Loss: {disc_loss}, Gen Loss: {gen_loss}')
```

Step 3: Visualizing Generated Digits

During training, it is important to visualize the generated digits to assess the progress of the generator. Here is how we use Matplotlib to visualize the generated digits.

```
import matplotlib.pyplot as plt

def visualize_images(epoch, generator, latent_dim):
    noise = np.random.normal(0, 1, (25, latent_dim))
    gen_images = generator.predict(noise)
    gen_images = 0.5 * gen_images + 0.5  # Rescale images to 0-1

    plt.figure(figsize=(5, 5))
    for i in range(25):
        plt.subplot(5, 5, i + 1)
        plt.imshow(gen_images[i, :, :, 0], cmap='gray')
        plt.axis('off')
    plt.tight_layout()
    plt.savefig(f'generated_images_epoch_{epoch}.png')
    plt.show()
```

Challenges Encountered:

- **Mode Collapse:** Initially, the generator struggled with mode collapse, where it produced a limited variety of digits (for example, consistently generating the digit "7"). This issue was addressed by adding batch normalization, and lowering the learning rate of the discriminator.
- **Convergence Issues:** We also encountered convergence problems where the generator's loss fluctuated heavily. We stabilized the training by adjusting the learning rate, and using label smoothing.

Results:

By the end of training, the generator successfully produced realistic handwritten digits. The diversity of the generated digits improved significantly after addressing mode collapse. The following figures show the progression of the generated digits:

- **Early Epochs:** Generated digits were blurry, and difficult to distinguish.
- **Mid Training:** Some digits became clearer, but there was still noticeable repetition of certain digits.
- **Late Epochs**: The generator produced a wide variety of digits that were highly realistic.

Conclusion

This chapter has established the foundational principles of Generative Adversarial Networks. We have explored their core architecture—the competing generator and discriminator networks—and the adversarial training process that enables data generation. You have also learned about the key challenges like training instability and mode collapse, which are critical in diagnosing and improving model performance. With a firm grasp of this dynamic framework, its common pitfalls, and its implementation in modern libraries, you now possess the essential knowledge to begin building and experimenting with these powerful models.

In the next chapter, we will advance from these core concepts to a practical, high-performing implementation: the Deep Convolutional GAN (DCGAN). You will learn how to integrate convolutional neural networks into the GAN framework to generate high-quality images. We will cover the specific architectural guidelines, stabilization techniques, and training tricks that make DCGAN a milestone in generative AI. This hands-on exploration will provide the crucial bridge from theory to a functional, impactful model.

Points to Remember

- A GAN consists of two neural networks, a Generator and a Discriminator, that are trained simultaneously in an adversarial game.
- The Generator's goal is to create realistic data from random noise, while the Discriminator's goal is to distinguish between the real data and the Generator's fake data.
- Training instability is a core challenge, often leading to issues like mode collapse, where the generator produces a limited variety of samples.
- The training process is a minimax game, where the generator tries to minimize the discriminator's ability to spot fakes, and the discriminator tries to maximize it.
- Unlike other models, GANs learn to generate data, without explicitly modeling the probability distribution of the training data (for example, they do not compute likelihoods).
- GANs have revolutionized image generation, enabling applications such as deep fake creation, photorealistic art, and data augmentation for other AI models.

Multiple Choice Questions

1. What is the primary role of the generator in a GAN?
   a. To classify input data and extract features
   b. To distinguish between real and augmented data
   c. To map random noise to realistic data samples
   d. To compress data into a lower-dimensional latent space
2. In a GAN, what is the primary objective of the discriminator?
   a. To create new, diverse data samples from noise
   b. To act as a critic, judging the authenticity of data as "*real*" or "*fake*"
   c. To minimize its own loss function by helping the generator
   d. To preprocess the training data for the generator
3. What is a common and significant challenge when training GANs?
   a. Underfitting and excessive regularization
   b. Rapid convergence leading to simple solutions
   c. Training instability and mode collapse
   d. Inability to handle large batch sizes

4. During the GAN training process, the generator and discriminator are in a state of:
    a. Collaborative fine-tuning
    b. Adversarial competition
    c. Sequential dependency
    d. Independent and parallel processing
5. Which of the following best describes "mode collapse" in a GAN?
    a. The discriminator becomes too accurate, and provides no useful gradient.
    b. The generator produces a wide variety of high-quality, novel outputs.
    c. The model's latent space becomes overly complex and disentangled.
    d. The generator fails to learn the entire data distribution, producing only a few types of samples.
6. What is the theoretical, and ideal outcome of the GAN minimax game?
    a. Nash equilibrium where the discriminator is guessing at random (50% confidence).
    b. The generator wins completely, fooling the discriminator on every sample.
    c. The discriminator wins completely, identifying fakes with 100% accuracy.
    d. Both networks converge to a joint, collaborative solution.

Answers

1. c
2. b
3. c
4. b
5. d
6. a

Questions

1. What is the core adversarial concept behind Generative Adversarial Networks (GANs), and how do the two networks compete?
2. What are the distinct roles and architectures of the generator and discriminator networks within a GAN?
3. How does the training process of a GAN differ from that of a traditional, single neural network?
4. What is "*mode collapse*," and why is it a particularly common and challenging problem in GAN training?
5. How can you diagnose training instability in a GAN by observing the generator and discriminator loss curves?
6. What is the significance of the discriminator's output in the GAN framework, and how is it used to train both networks?

7. Why is the choice of a random noise vector (the latent space) as input to the generator crucial for the diversity of its outputs?
8. What are some of the key architectural improvements (like those in DCGAN) that were introduced to stabilize GAN training, and improve output quality?
9. Beyond deepfakes and art, what are some practical, positive applications of GANs in fields like science and industry?
10. How does the concept of a "*Nash equilibrium*" relate to the theoretical goal of a perfectly trained GAN?

Key Terms

- **Generator:** The component of a GAN that creates new data samples. It takes a random noise vector from the latent space as input, and transforms it into a synthetic output, such as an image, with the goal of fooling the discriminator.
- **Discriminator:** The component of a GAN that acts as a critic. It takes a data sample (either real or generated) as input, and outputs a probability score estimating how likely it is that the sample came from the real training data, rather than the generator.
- **Adversarial Training:** The process of training a GAN where the generator and discriminator are pitted against each other in a competitive game, each improving in response to the other's progress.
- **Minimax Game:** The foundational theoretical framework for GANs, describing an optimization problem where the generator aims to minimize the discriminator's ability to correctly classify samples, while the discriminator aims to maximize it.
- **Mode Collapse:** A common and challenging failure mode in GAN training where the generator learns to produce only a very limited variety of outputs, or even a single type of output, failing to capture the full diversity of the training data.
- **Latent Space / Noise Vector (z):** A low-dimensional, compressed representation (often a random vector from a Gaussian distribution) that serves as the input to the generator. The model learns to map different points in this space to different features in the output data.
- **Vanishing Gradient:** A training problem that occurs when the discriminator becomes too successful, too quickly, providing gradients that are near zero, and thus offering the generator no meaningful signal to learn from.
- **Deep Convolutional GAN (DCGAN):** A landmark and highly influential GAN architecture that utilizes convolutional and transposed convolutional layers to stabilize training, and generate high-quality images.
- **Nash Equilibrium:** In the context of GANs, this is the theoretical ideal state where the generator produces perfect fakes, and the discriminator is forced to guess at random, resulting in a prediction of 50% for every sample.
- **Generator Loss:** The loss function for the generator, which is typically based on how successfully it fooled the discriminator (for example, the discriminator classifying its fakes as "*real*").
- **Discriminator Loss:** The loss function for the discriminator, which measures its ability to correctly distinguish between the real training data and the fake data produced by the generator.

Chapter 5
Deep Convolutional GANs

Introduction

Deep Convolutional Generative Adversarial Networks (DCGANs) mark a major advancement in the evolution of generative models, combining the foundational concepts of GANs with the power of Convolutional Neural Networks (CNNs). By leveraging the feature extraction capabilities of convolutions, DCGANs revolutionize the generation of high-quality, realistic images. In this chapter, we delve into the transformative world of DCGANs, exploring how their architectural innovations enhance the stability and scalability of GAN training. Through practical exercises, you will build and train a DCGAN step by step using TensorFlow and PyTorch. Thus, by the end of this chapter, you will not only master the core principles of DCGANs but also understand their unique strengths, enabling you to create sophisticated generative models capable of producing stunningly realistic images!

Structure

In this chapter, we will discuss the following topics:

- **Core Concepts of DCGANs: Redefining Generative Models with Deep Learning**
  - Definition and Evolution from Basic GANs
  - Why DCGANs Matter: Stability and Scalability
  - Key Differences between GANs and DCGANs
- **Background: Convolutional Neural Networks (CNNs)**
  - Convolutions Defined
  - Layers in CNNs
- **Architecture of DCGANs**
  - Components of DCGANs
  - Key Innovations in DCGANs
- **Working of DCGANs**
  - Data Flow through the Generator and Discriminator
  - Objective Functions Used in Training
- **Implementing a DCGAN: Step-by-Step**
  - Key Steps in Implementing a DCGAN
  - Example Code Snippet for Training a DCGAN
  - Visualizing Outputs
- **Challenges and Limitations**
- **Case Study: Creating High-Quality Synthetic Images with DCGANs**

Core Concepts of DCGANs

While GANs revolutionized synthetic data generation, they struggled with stability and output quality. DCGANs solved these challenges by integrating convolutional neural networks into the GAN framework. This breakthrough enabled stable training, higher-resolution outputs, and efficient feature learning - establishing DCGANs as the foundation for modern image generation. Hence, by combining GANs' adversarial training with CNNs' spatial processing, DCGANs created a robust framework powering everything from digital art to data augmentation.

Definition and Evolution from Basic GANs

Deep Convolutional Generative Adversarial Networks (DCGANs) are a specialized type of GANs that integrate Convolutional Neural Networks (CNNs) into the generator and discriminator, enabling more efficient and stable training. Introduced by Alec Radford, Luke Metz, and Soumith Chintala in 2015, DCGANs address some of the key limitations of traditional GANs, such as instability during training, and difficulty in generating high-quality images. By replacing fully connected layers with convolutional operations, DCGANs exploit spatial hierarchies in data, making them particularly effective for tasks like image synthesis, super-resolution, and style transfer.

The evolution of DCGANs marked a critical step in the development of generative models, bridging the gap between simple GAN architectures and more sophisticated approaches such as StyleGAN and BigGAN. The innovative use of convolutions allows DCGANs to generate realistic images with fine-grained details, while maintaining computational efficiency.

Why DCGANs Matter: Stability and Scalability

DCGANs have become a cornerstone of modern generative models due to their ability to overcome many of the challenges faced by traditional GANs. The stability of DCGANs arises from architectural innovations such as:

- **Convolutional Layers:** These layers capture spatial features effectively, enabling the generator to produce consistent outputs, and the discriminator to identify realistic patterns.
- **Batch Normalization:** This technique reduces the distribution of inputs to a layer during training, making it harder for the model to learn. By normalizing these inputs, the technique stabilizes training, ensuring that the model learns consistently, and it reaches optimal performance faster.
- **Leaky ReLU and Tanh Activation Functions**: These ensure smoother gradient flow, mitigating the vanishing gradient problem common in traditional GANs.

Figure 5.1: *DCGAN Uses Convolutional Networks to Generate Images*

Scalability is another key advantage of DCGANs. By utilizing convolutional operations, DCGANs can handle larger datasets, and generate higher-resolution images compared to the basic GANs. This scalability has made DCGANs the foundation for numerous advanced architectures and applications in fields such as computer vision, creative arts, and data augmentation.

Key Differences between GANs and DCGANs

Traditional GANs introduced great capabilities in generative modeling, but they often had trouble with training stability and low-resolution outputs. DCGANs come up as a refined architecture that addresses these limitations through important structural improvements. By incorporating convolutional neural networks and other key enhancements, DCGANs achieve more stable training, higher-quality outputs, and a varied number of real-world applications. The following are the key differences, and their impact on performance.

Structural Enhancements

Convolutional Layers vs. Fully Connected Layers:

- The basic GANs rely on fully connected layers, which lack the ability to leverage spatial hierarchies in data.
- DCGANs replace these with convolutional layers, enabling the model to learn spatial features, and produce more coherent images.

Transposed Convolution (Deconvolution):

- DCGANs use transposed convolutions in the generator for up-sampling, ensuring that outputs retain spatial consistency, and exhibit realistic textures.

Batch Normalization:

- Unlike basic GANs, DCGANs use batch normalization extensively in both the generator and discriminator. This helps in stabilizing training, and avoiding mode collapse.

Removal of Fully Connected Layers:

- DCGANs eliminate the fully connected layers in both the generator and discriminator, simplifying the architecture, and improving performance.

Impact on Performance and Applications

Improved Training Stability:

- DCGANs address the notorious training instability of GANs through architectural modifications, allowing for smoother and more reliable optimization.

Higher-Quality Outputs:

- By leveraging convolutional layers, DCGANs generate images with sharper edges, better textures, and enhanced overall quality compared to the basic GANs.

Broader Applicability:

- The scalability and stability of DCGANs have broadened their application scope to include tasks such as:
    - High-resolution image synthesis
    - Style transfer and artistic applications
    - Super-resolution for image enhancement
    - Semi-supervised learning to improve classification tasks

An Analogy to Understand DCGAN Better

Imagine you are in the world of fine arts. A **sculptor** (generator) is tasked with creating lifelike sculptures, but instead of using marble, they start with a random material to shape it based on their imagination. Their goal is to make them so realistic that they could belong in a museum.

On the other side, there is a **museum curator** (discriminator), whose job is to evaluate every sculpture, and decide whether it is museum-worthy. The curator has an eye for detail–with years studying real sculptures, from texture to proportions to intricate details.

Now, here's where the twist comes in: the sculptor is no ordinary artist–they have a toolbox of advanced carving tools (the convolutional layers). These tools allow the sculptor to capture tiny details such as the fine lines of a face or the delicate folds of fabric, that would not be possible with the basic tools.

Figure 5.2: *Analogy of a Sculptor and a Curator to Understand DCGANs*

The sculptor learns through the trial and error method:

1. They create a sculpture, and present it to the curator.
2. The curator critiques it, pointing out flaws like "*This does not look like a real nose!*" or "*The texture of this does not feel like marble.*"
3. The sculptor refines their technique based on the feedback, making the next sculpture even better.

Over time, the sculptor becomes incredibly skilled at using their tools, producing sculptures that fool even the most discerning curator. Eventually, the museum ends up filled with breathtaking works of art, indistinguishable from reality.

The Process Involved in DCGAN

The interplay between the generator and the discriminator in a DCGAN is compared to the evolving relationship between a sculptor and a curator as in the preceding analogy, locked in a continuous cycle of creation and critique.

The sculptor and curator engage in an iterative process of creation and critique:

- The generator starts with rough, basic samples, and refines them over time using advanced tools such as convolutional layers.
- The discriminator critiques each submission, driving the generator to improve the work.
- The generator refines its ability to create realistic images by learning from the feedback of the discriminator.
- The discriminator sharpens its ability to detect fakes, forcing the generator to improve with every iteration.
- Through this back-and-forth process, the generator learns to create samples that are so realistic that even the discriminator struggles to tell them apart from authentic pieces.
- Over time, this adversarial interplay leads to the creation of high-quality, lifelike outputs.

In the end, just as the sculptor strives to craft masterpieces that can fool even the most experienced curator, the generator in a DCGAN aims to produce images so convincing that the discriminator can no longer tell them apart from real-world samples. Thus, this balance of competition and improvement is the foundation of DCGANs' ability to generate realistic data.

Background of Convolutional Neural Networks

Convolutional Neural Networks (CNNs) have transformed the field of deep learning, particularly in applications involving visual data. By mimicking the way, the human brain processes visual information, CNNs excel at recognizing patterns, detecting features, and extracting meaningful information from images. Before diving into DCGANs, it is essential to understand the fundamentals of CNNs, as they form the backbone of DCGAN architectures.

Convolutions Defined

A convolution is a mathematical operation that combines two functions to produce a third function. In the context of image processing, it involves sliding a small matrix, called a filter or kernel, across an image to perform operations like edge detection, sharpening, or blurring as shown in *Figure* 5.3. The primary role of convolutions in CNNs is to detect features such as edges, textures and patterns within an image, enabling the network to understand its visual content.

Feature extraction is the cornerstone of CNNs. During a convolutional operation:

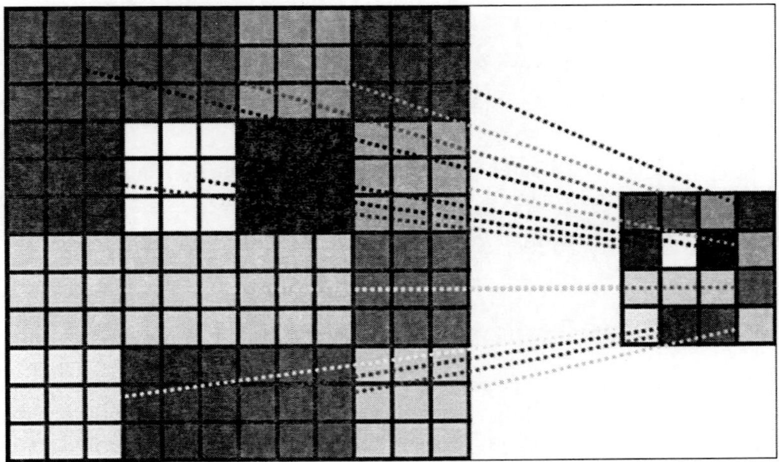

Figure 5.3: *Sliding a Small Matrix across an Input Image*

- A filter scans the input image pixel by pixel, computing the dot product between the filter values, and the corresponding pixel values in the image.
- The result is stored in an output matrix called the **feature map** or **activation map**, which highlights the presence of specific features.

For example, an edge-detection filter emphasizes the edges of objects within the image, while a texture-detection filter may highlight fine-grained patterns. By stacking multiple convolutional layers, CNNs can learn hierarchical features–starting from simple edges to complex shapes and patterns–necessary for tasks like object recognition.

Layers in CNNs

CNNs consist of several types of layers, each serving a unique purpose in the processing pipeline. These layers work together to transform the raw input data into a structured representation suitable for tasks like classification or detection.

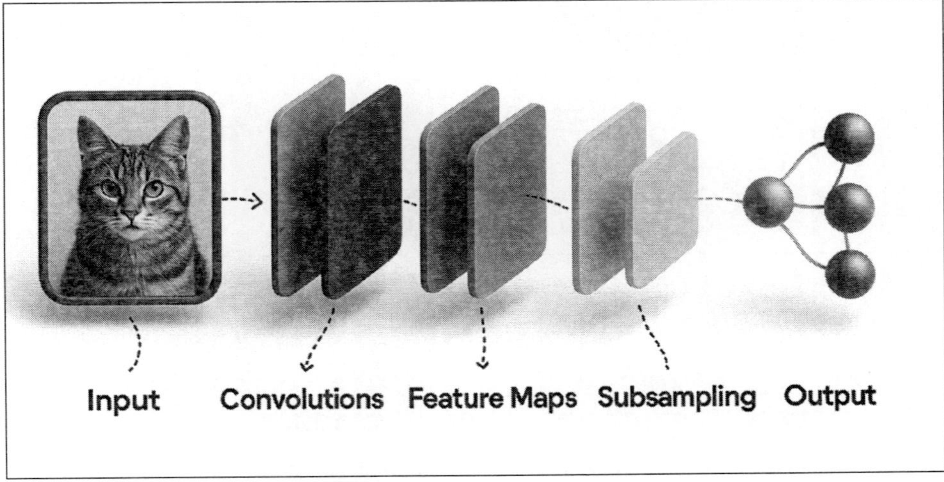

Figure 5.4: *Convolutional Neural Network Layers*

Convolutional Layers: Filters and Feature Maps

The convolutional layer is the foundational building block of CNNs. This layer applies a set of learnable filters to the input data, producing feature maps that emphasize different aspects of the image.

- **Convolutional Filters:** These are small matrices (for example, 3x3, 5x5) that slide over the input image to extract features such as edges or corners.
- **Feature Maps:** The output of applying a filter to the input image. Each feature map represents the activation of a specific feature in different regions of the image.

Multiple filters can be applied in a single convolutional layer, enabling the network to detect a wide variety of features.

Pooling Layers: MaxPooling and AveragePooling

Subsampling in CNNs, also known as down-sampling or pooling, is a technique used to reduce the spatial dimensions (height and width) of feature maps, while retaining important features. This not only decreases computational complexity but also makes the network more robust to variations like translations or distortions in the input image.

- **MaxPooling:** Retains the maximum value from a defined window (for example, 2×2) within the feature map. The following *Figure* 5.5 illustrates a 4x4 input feature map on the left. On the right, the 2×2 output feature map shows the result after max pooling. For the top-left 2×2 region [3, 7, 0, 2], the maximum value is **7**. For the top-right 2×2 region [7, 4, 2, 9], the maximum value is **9** and so on.
- **AveragePooling:** Instead of picking the maximum value, it computes the average value within a defined window, providing a smoother representation of the feature map.

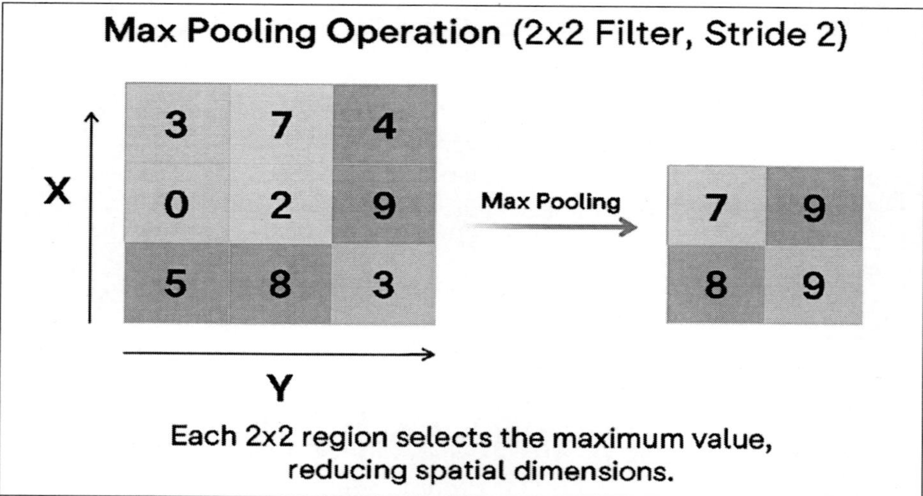

Figure 5.5: *Subsampling - Max Pooling Operation*

Pooling layers help the network focus on the most salient features of an image, discarding irrelevant details.

Fully Connected Layers and Their Purpose

Fully connected layers are used at the end of a CNN to combine the extracted features into a final decision. Unlike convolutional and pooling layers, which work spatially, fully connected layers treat the feature map as a flattened vector.

- Each neuron in a fully connected layer is connected to every neuron in the previous layer.
- These layers are responsible for learning the relationships between high-level features and the output labels, enabling tasks like classification or regression.

Applications of CNNs

CNNs have revolutionized a variety of fields by enabling machines to interpret the visual data with remarkable accuracy. The following are some of the key applications:

Image Classification CNNs are widely used for image classification tasks, where the goal is to assign a label to an input image. For example, a CNN can identify whether an image contains a cat, dog, or car by learning distinctive features for each category.

Object Detection: In object detection, CNNs not only classify objects within an image but also localize them by drawing boxes around the objects. Applications include autonomous vehicles (for example, detecting pedestrians) and security systems (for example, identifying unauthorized access).

Image Segmentation: Image segmentation involves partitioning an image into distinct regions or objects. CNN is widely used in medical imaging to identify tumors in MRI scans.

Super-Resolution and Image Enhancement: CNNs can improve the resolution and quality of images through super-resolution techniques. They reconstruct high-resolution images from low-resolution inputs, which is useful in fields like satellite imaging and forensics.

Style Transfer and Creative Applications: CNNs power artistic applications such as style transfer, where the style of one image (for example, Van Gogh's painting) is applied to another image.

Thus, by understanding the fundamentals of CNNs, we can appreciate their role in DCGANs. DCGANs use CNNs to generate high-quality, realistic images by leveraging the convolutional layer's ability to learn meaningful spatial features.

Architecture of DCGANs

DCGANs extend the traditional GAN framework by leveraging the power of CNNs in both the generator and discriminator. CNNs, known for their ability to extract meaningful features from visual data, form the backbone of DCGAN architectures. Thus, by integrating convolutional layers, they enable stable training while generating high-quality images. This section explores the key components, workflow, and concepts that make DCGANs innovative.

DCGAN Components and Workflow

As in any GAN, the DCGAN architecture also consists of two key components: the generator and the discriminator, which work in tandem through an adversarial process.

The Generator Architecture:

- Transforms random noise (latent vector) into realistic images.
- Uses *transpose convolutional layers* to up-sample the input, progressively increasing spatial resolution.
- Features such as *batch normalization* and *ReLU activations* ensure stable training, and prevent vanishing gradients.
- The final layer applies the *Tanh activation* function, with pixel values between –1 and 1.

Generator Pipeline:

- **Input:** Random noise vector sampled from a uniform or Gaussian distribution.
- Multiple transpose convolutional layers progressively up-sample the input.
- **Output**: A synthetic image matching the desired dimensions (for example, 64×64 RGB).

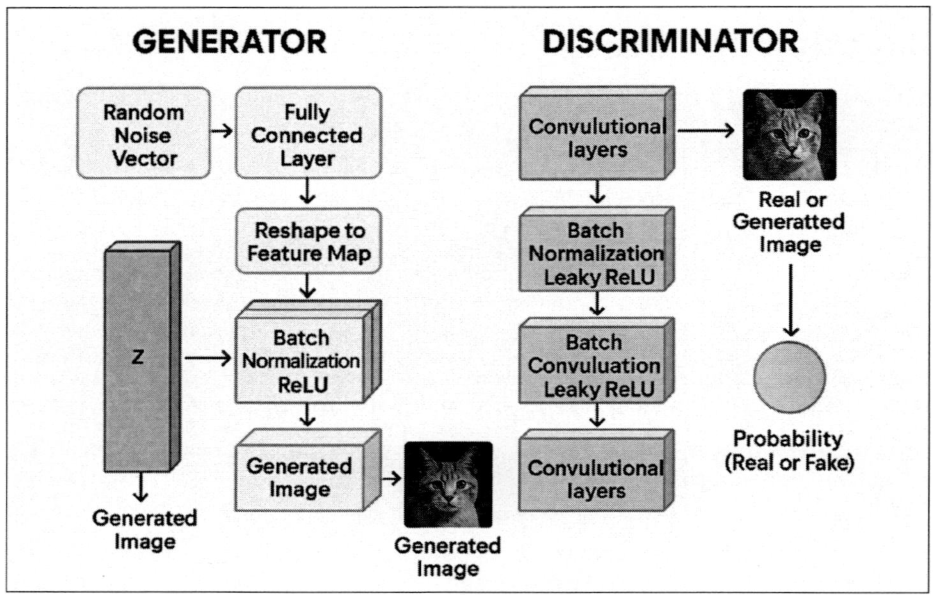

Figure 5.6: *DCGAN Architecture*

Key Features:

- **Transpose Convolutions (Deconvolutions):**
  - These layers expand the spatial dimensions of the input, allowing the generator to construct high-resolution images.
  - Each layer gradually turns abstract patterns into detailed parts of the image, keeping everything consistent and connected.
- **Batch Normalization:**
  - Used after every transpose convolution layer (except the output layer).
  - Stabilizes training and accelerates convergence by normalizing activations.
- **Activation Functions:**
  - **ReLU**: Used to introduce non-linearity and prevent vanishing gradients.
  - **Tanh**: Applied to the output layer to scale pixel values between −1 and 1.
- **The Discriminator Architecture:**
  - Acts as a binary classifier, distinguishing real images from generated ones.
  - Uses *convolutional layers* to down-sample images, while extracting hierarchical features.
  - Incorporates *batch normalization* to stabilize gradient flow and *Leaky ReLU* activations to prevent dead neurons.

Discriminator Pipeline:

- **Input**: An image (real or generated).

- Multiple convolutional layers reduce spatial dimensions, while learning the key features.
- **Output**: A scalar value indicating whether the input is real or fake.

Key Features:

- **Convolutional Layers:**
  - Extract hierarchical features such as edges, textures, and object shapes.
  - Down-sample the input image to learn spatial patterns.
- **Batch Normalization:**
  - Applied after each convolutional layer (except the input layer) to ensure stable gradient flow.
- **Leaky ReLU Activation:**
  - Introduces non-linearity, while allowing small gradients to pass through the negative values.
  - Prevents dead neurons, ensuring better feature learning.

Key Innovations in DCGANs

DCGANs introduced several architectural improvements that address the limitations of traditional GANs. These innovations are pivotal in enhancing training stability and output quality.

1. **Removal of Fully Connected Layers**
   - Traditional GANs rely on fully connected layers to map the latent vectors to image space. DCGANs eliminate these layers in both the generator and discriminator, simplifying the architecture, and improving spatial feature learning.
   - Instead, DCGANs use convolutional layers exclusively, ensuring that spatial hierarchies are preserved throughout the network.
2. **Use of Batch Normalization**
   - Batch normalization normalizes the activations in each layer, mitigating the risk of internal covariate shift.
   - It accelerates convergence and stabilizes training by ensuring consistent gradient flow.
   - Applied in both the generator and discriminator, batch normalization helps to maintain equilibrium in the adversarial training process.
3. **Transpose Convolutions for Up-sampling**
   - DCGANs replace simple up-sampling techniques with learnable transpose convolution layers in the generator.
   - These layers ensure that the up-sampling process keeps the spatial structure intact, producing high-quality, sharp images.
4. **All-Convolutional Architecture**
   - DCGANs adopt an all-convolutional design, eliminating the need for pooling layers. Instead, strided convolutions are used for down-sampling in the discriminator, and transpose convolutions for up-sampling in the generator.
   - This design choice prevents information loss associated with pooling layers, and enables the network to learn features more effectively.
5. **Activation Functions for Stability**
   - The generator uses ReLU activations in all layers except the output, where Tanh is applied.

- The discriminator employs Leaky ReLU activations, which allow small gradients for negative values, preventing dead neurons and improving training.

Thus, by integrating these architectural innovations, DCGANs achieve remarkable stability and scalability. They are capable of generating high-quality images across various domains, making them a foundational model for advanced generative architectures such as StyleGAN and BigGAN.

Working of DCGANs

Understanding how DCGANs work requires a clear grasp of the data flow between the generator and discriminator, as well as the objective functions that govern their training. So, let us explore these aspects in detail.

Data Flow through the Generator and Discriminator

Step 1: Input to the Generator

- The generator starts with a random noise vector sampled from a latent space (typically a Gaussian or uniform distribution). This serves as the seed for generating an image.
- Example: A 100-dimensional vector of random numbers.
- The generator uses transpose convolutional layers to gradually up-sample this noise into a structured image. Each layer refines the noise, introducing features and patterns that resemble the training data.

Step 2: Generator Output

- The generator produces a synthetic image that matches the dimensions of the real images in the dataset (for example, 64x64x3 for an RGB image).
- At this stage, the synthetic image might look incomplete or noisy, especially in the early training iterations.

Step 3: Input to the Discriminator

- The discriminator receives both real images from the training dataset and fake images generated by the generator.
- Each image passes through multiple convolutional layers in the discriminator, which extract hierarchical features like edges, textures, and shapes.

Step 4: Discriminator's Evaluation

- The discriminator outputs a probability score for each image, indicating whether it believes the image is real (close to 1) or fake (close to 0).
- This feedback is passed back to both the generator and discriminator to improve their performance.

Iterative Step:

- The generator aims to fool the discriminator by producing images that the discriminator classifies as real.
- The discriminator, in turn, strives to distinguish real images from fake ones. This adversarial process ensures that both networks improve over time.

The quality of generated images improves significantly as the generator learns to create features that mimic real data, and the discriminator becomes better at recognizing details.

Objective Functions Used in Training

The adversarial training of DCGANs is governed by carefully designed objective functions. These functions define the goals of the generator and discriminator, and ensure that they improve iteratively.

Standard GAN Objective Function

The original GAN objective function is formulated as a minimax game:

- The probability assigned by the discriminator to real images.
- The probability assigned by the discriminator to fake images generated by the generator.

This function represents a two-player game:

1. The discriminator maximizes its confidence in correctly classifying real images as real and fake images as fake.
2. The generator minimizes this objective, aiming to increase the discriminator's belief that fake images are real.

Generator's Objective

In practice, the generator's loss is often modified to improve gradient flow during training. Instead of minimizing, the generator maximizes. The loss function for the generator is given by:

$$L_G = -\mathbb{E}_{z \sim p_z(z)}[\log D(G(z))]$$

This formulation encourages the generator to produce images that maximize the discriminator's confidence in their realism.

Discriminator's Objective

The discriminator's goal is to maximize its ability to correctly classify real and fake images. Its loss function is given by:

$$L_D = -\mathbb{E}_{x \sim p_{data}(x)}[\log D(x)] - \mathbb{E}_{z \sim p_z(z)}[\log(1 - D(G(z)))]$$

This loss penalizes the discriminator for misclassifying real images as fake or fake images as real.

Training Process

1. **Update the Discriminator:** Train the discriminator to maximize its loss by correctly distinguishing the real images from the fake ones.
2. **Update the Generator:** Train the generator to minimize its loss by producing images that fool the discriminator.
3. **Alternate Updates:** The generator and the discriminator are updated alternately, ensuring balanced training.

Challenges in Objective Functions

Mode Collapse

- The generator may produce limited variations of images, leading to "*mode collapse*."

- This occurs when the generator exploits weaknesses in the discriminator, without truly learning the data distribution.

Training Instability

- GANs are prone to instability during training, as the generator and discriminator's objectives are inherently adversarial.
- Proper tuning of hyperparameters, such as learning rates and batch sizes, is crucial for stable training.

Solutions

1. **Batch Normalization**: Stabilizes gradient flow, ensuring smoother training.
2. **Modified Loss Functions**: Techniques like Wasserstein Loss mitigate instability by providing more informative gradients.

Implementing a DCGAN: Step-by-Step

Implementing a DCGAN involves constructing a generator and discriminator, training them in an adversarial framework, and visualizing the results to evaluate progress. This section will walk through the key steps, provide code snippets in TensorFlow and PyTorch, and demonstrate output visualization.

Key Steps in Implementing a DCGAN

1. **Prepare the Dataset:**
   - DCGANs are typically trained on image datasets. Datasets like CIFAR-10, MNIST, or CelebA are commonly used.
   - Normalize the pixel values to a range of [-1, 1] to match the output activation function (Tanh) used in the generator.
2. **Define the Generator:**
   - The generator transforms random noise (latent vector) into an image through transpose convolutional layers.
   - It progressively up-samples the latent vector to create realistic images.
3. **Define the Discriminator:**
   - The discriminator classifies images as real or fake using convolutional layers.
   - It down-samples the input and outputs a scalar probability value.
4. **Define the Loss Functions:**
   - Use binary cross-entropy loss for both the generator and discriminator.
   - The generator's loss encourages it to fool the discriminator, while the discriminator's loss ensures that it can distinguish the real from fake images.
5. **Set Up the Training Loop:**
   - Alternate between updating the discriminator and the generator.
   - Use an optimizer like Adam with appropriate learning rates for stable training.
6. **Visualize Generated Images:**
   - Periodically, save and visualize the generator's outputs to monitor progress.

Example Code Snippet for Training a DCGAN

TensorFlow Implementation

```
import tensorflow as tf
from tensorflow.keras import layers
import numpy as np
import matplotlib.pyplot as plt

# Generator Model
def build_generator():
    model = tf.keras.Sequential([
        layers.Dense(7 * 7 * 256, use_bias=False, input_shape=(100,)),
        layers.BatchNormalization(),
        layers.LeakyReLU(),

        layers.Reshape((7, 7, 256)),
        layers.Conv2DTranspose(128, (5, 5), strides=(1, 1), padding='same',
use_bias=False),
        layers.BatchNormalization(),
        layers.LeakyReLU(),

        layers.Conv2DTranspose(64, (5, 5), strides=(2, 2), padding='same',
use_bias=False),
        layers.BatchNormalization(),
        layers.LeakyReLU(),

        layers.Conv2DTranspose(1, (5, 5), strides=(2, 2), padding='same',
use_bias=False, activation='tanh')
    ])
    return model

# Discriminator Model
def build_discriminator():
    model = tf.keras.Sequential([
        layers.Conv2D(64, (5, 5), strides=(2, 2), padding='same', input_
shape=[28, 28, 1]),
        layers.LeakyReLU(),
        layers.Dropout(0.3),

        layers.Conv2D(128, (5, 5), strides=(2, 2), padding='same'),
        layers.LeakyReLU(),
        layers.Dropout(0.3),

        layers.Flatten(),
        layers.Dense(1, activation='sigmoid')
    ])
    return model

# Losses and Optimizers
generator = build_generator()
discriminator = build_discriminator()

cross_entropy = tf.keras.losses.BinaryCrossentropy()

def generator_loss(fake_output):
    return cross_entropy(tf.ones_like(fake_output), fake_output)
```

```
def discriminator_loss(real_output, fake_output):
    real_loss = cross_entropy(tf.ones_like(real_output), real_output)
    fake_loss = cross_entropy(tf.zeros_like(fake_output), fake_output)
    return real_loss + fake_loss

# Training Loop
def train(dataset, epochs):
    for epoch in range(epochs):
        for image_batch in dataset:
            noise = tf.random.normal([BATCH_SIZE, 100])
            generated_images = generator(noise, training=True)

            with tf.GradientTape() as disc_tape, tf.GradientTape() as gen_tape:
                real_output = discriminator(image_batch, training=True)
                fake_output = discriminator(generated_images, training=True)

                gen_loss = generator_loss(fake_output)
                disc_loss = discriminator_loss(real_output, fake_output)

            gradients_of_generator = gen_tape.gradient(gen_loss,
generator.trainable_variables)
            gradients_of_discriminator = disc_tape.gradient(disc_loss,
discriminator.trainable_variables)

            generator_optimizer.apply_gradients(zip(gradients_of_generator,
generator.trainable_variables))
            discriminator_optimizer.apply_gradients(zip(gradients_of_discrimina-
tor, discriminator.trainable_variables))

# Visualize Outputs
def generate_and_save_images(model, epoch, test_input):
    predictions = model(test_input, training=False)
    fig = plt.figure(figsize=(4, 4))
    for i in range(predictions.shape[0]):
        plt.subplot(4, 4, i + 1)
        plt.imshow(predictions[i, :, :, 0] * 127.5 + 127.5, cmap='gray')
        plt.axis('off')
    plt.savefig('image_at_epoch_{:04d}.png'.format(epoch))
    plt.show()
```

The preceding TensorFlow implementation code involves defining two primary models: the generator and the discriminator. The generator transforms a random noise vector (latent space) into a synthetic image through a series of transpose convolutional layers, with batch normalization and ReLU activations ensuring stable training and non-linear transformations. Its output layer uses a Tanh activation to generate pixel values in the range of [-1, 1]. The discriminator processes input images (real or fake) using convolutional layers, Leaky ReLU activations, and dropout for regularization, ultimately outputting a probability indicating whether the image is real or generated. The training loop alternates between updating the discriminator to accurately classify real and fake images, and training the generator to create images that fool the discriminator. The use of binary cross-entropy loss functions and the Adam optimizer with tuned learning rates ensures stable adversarial training, while generated outputs are periodically visualized to monitor progress.

PyTorch Implementation

```
import torch
import torch.nn as nn
import torch.optim as optim
```

```
from torchvision import datasets, transforms
import matplotlib.pyplot as plt

# Generator
class Generator(nn.Module):
    def __init__(self):
        super(Generator, self).__init__()
        self.model = nn.Sequential(
            nn.Linear(100, 256 * 7 * 7),
            nn.BatchNorm1d(256 * 7 * 7),
            nn.ReLU(inplace=True),
            nn.Unflatten(1, (256, 7, 7)),
            nn.ConvTranspose2d(256, 128, 4, stride=2, padding=1),
            nn.BatchNorm2d(128),
            nn.ReLU(inplace=True),
            nn.ConvTranspose2d(128, 64, 4, stride=2, padding=1),
            nn.BatchNorm2d(64),
            nn.ReLU(inplace=True),
            nn.ConvTranspose2d(64, 1, 4, stride=2, padding=1),
            nn.Tanh()
        )

    def forward(self, x):
        return self.model(x)

# Discriminator
class Discriminator(nn.Module):
    def __init__(self):
        super(Discriminator, self).__init__()
        self.model = nn.Sequential(
            nn.Conv2d(1, 64, 4, stride=2, padding=1),
            nn.LeakyReLU(0.2, inplace=True),
            nn.Conv2d(64, 128, 4, stride=2, padding=1),
            nn.BatchNorm2d(128),
            nn.LeakyReLU(0.2, inplace=True),
            nn.Flatten(),
            nn.Linear(128 * 7 * 7, 1),
            nn.Sigmoid()
        )

    def forward(self, x):
        return self.model(x)

# Initialize Models
generator = Generator()
discriminator = Discriminator()

# Loss and Optimizers
criterion = nn.BCELoss()
g_optimizer = optim.Adam(generator.parameters(), lr=0.0002)
d_optimizer = optim.Adam(discriminator.parameters(), lr=0.0002)

# Training Loop
def train_gan(generator, discriminator, data_loader, epochs):
    for epoch in range(epochs):
        for real_images, _ in data_loader:
            batch_size = real_images.size(0)
```

```
            real_labels = torch.ones(batch_size, 1)
            fake_labels = torch.zeros(batch_size, 1)

            # Train Discriminator
            d_optimizer.zero_grad()
            real_images = real_images.to(device)
            real_output = discriminator(real_images)
            real_loss = criterion(real_output, real_labels)

            noise = torch.randn(batch_size, 100).to(device)
            fake_images = generator(noise)
            fake_output = discriminator(fake_images.detach())
            fake_loss = criterion(fake_output, fake_labels)

            d_loss = real_loss + fake_loss
            d_loss.backward()
            d_optimizer.step()

            # Train Generator
            g_optimizer.zero_grad()
            fake_output = discriminator(fake_images)
            g_loss = criterion(fake_output, real_labels)
            g_loss.backward()
            g_optimizer.step()

# Visualizing Outputs
def visualize_output(generator, epoch, test_input):
    with torch.no_grad():
        fake_images = generator(test_input).cpu()
        fig, ax = plt.subplots(1, 10, figsize=(10, 1))
        for i in range(10):
            ax[i].imshow(fake_images[i].squeeze(), cmap='gray')
            ax[i].axis('off')
        plt.show()
```

The PyTorch implementation of a DCGAN follows a similar structure to the TensorFlow version but leverages PyTorch's dynamic computation graph and modular design. The generator uses linear layers to reshape the latent noise vector into a small spatial representation, which is progressively up-sampled using transpose convolutional layers, with BatchNorm and ReLU activations ensuring smooth training. The discriminator employs convolutional layers with Leaky ReLU activations to down-sample images and outputs a probability through a fully connected layer. A key difference in PyTorch is its flexibility in defining the training loop, where gradients are manually calculated using **`torch.autograd`**. Losses are computed using the Binary Cross-Entropy loss, and the Adam optimizer is applied with carefully tuned learning rates. Additionally, PyTorch allows explicit control over device placement (CPU/GPU), making it easier to monitor model performance and debug issues. This implementation is well-suited for researchers needing fine-grained control over the training process.

Visualizing Outputs

Visualizing the outputs generated by the DCGAN is crucial for monitoring the training process. By saving and inspecting the images created by the generator at different epochs, you can track how well the model is learning to replicate the patterns in the training data. It helps identify common issues such as mode collapse (where the generator produces limited variations) or overly noisy outputs. Visualization provides valuable insights into whether the model's training is progressing as expected or requires adjustments in the hyperparameters or architecture. Regularly evaluating these outputs ensures that the generator is moving closer to producing high-quality, realistic images.

Challenges and Limitations

DCGANs are a significant milestone in generative modeling, but like all machine learning frameworks, they come with their own set of challenges and limitations. Understanding these pitfalls is necessary for effectively training DCGANs and exploring methods to overcome these obstacles.

Mode Collapse

Mode collapse occurs when the generator produces a limited variety of outputs, often generating identical or highly similar images regardless of the input noise vector. This happens when the generator exploits weaknesses in the discriminator, creating outputs that consistently fool the discriminator but fail to represent the diversity of the data distribution.

Impact:

- The generator fails to learn the full data distribution.
- Generated images lack variety and fail to meet the goals of the training process.

Potential Solutions:

- **Noise Injection:** Introduce noise during training to encourage diversity in generated images.
- **Mini-Batch Discrimination:** Modify the discriminator to evaluate images in groups, making it harder for the generator to exploit specific weaknesses.
- **Improved Architectures:** Use variations like Wasserstein GANs (WGANs) or Progressive GANs to mitigate mode collapse.

Training Instability

DCGAN training involves a delicate balance between the generator and discriminator. Instability arises when one model outpaces the other, leading to either the discriminator dominating the training or the generator collapsing entirely.

Impact:

- Training becomes unpredictable and may fail to converge.
- Generated outputs oscillate between being realistic and nonsensical.

Potential Solutions:

- **Batch Normalization:** Normalize activations to stabilize gradient flow, and accelerate convergence.
- **Careful Hyperparameter Tuning:** Adjust learning rates, batch sizes, and optimizer settings for stable training.
- **Regularization Techniques:** Apply gradient penalty or weight clipping to avoid extreme parameter updates.

Sensitivity to Hyperparameters

The performance of DCGANs is highly sensitive to hyperparameter choices, including learning rates, batch sizes, and architecture configurations. Incorrect settings can lead to issues such as vanishing gradients, exploding gradients, or mode collapse.

Impact:

- Requires extensive experimentation to identify optimal settings.
- Increases computational cost and training time.

Potential Solutions:

- **Learning Rate Scheduling:** Use adaptive learning rate methods, such as learning rate decay or optimizers like Adam with adaptive momentum.
- **Grid Search or Bayesian Optimization:** Systematically search for the best hyperparameters.
- **Smaller Batch Sizes:** Smaller batches can lead to better generalization but may require longer training times.

Computational Complexity

DCGANs, especially when generating high-resolution images, demand significant computational resources. The generator and discriminator both require substantial memory and processing power, which can limit their scalability.

Impact:

- Prohibitive for researchers and developers with limited hardware resources.
- Increased training time, particularly for larger datasets.

Potential Solutions:

- **Model Compression:** Use techniques like pruning or quantization to reduce model size.
- **Distributed Training:** Leverage multi-GPU setups or cloud-based solutions to distribute the training workload.
- **Progressive Training:** Start with low-resolution images, and gradually increase resolution as the model learns.

Lack of Interpretability

GANs, including DCGANs, operate as black-box models. It is difficult to understand why a specific output is generated or why the training process behaves in a particular way.

Impact:

- Makes debugging and optimization challenging.
- Hinders the adoption of DCGANs in critical applications where explainability is essential.

Potential Solutions:

- **Visualization Tools:** Use techniques like t-SNE or feature map visualization to understand the learned representations.
- **Attention Mechanisms:** Incorporate attention layers to highlight which features influence the outputs.
- **Post-Hoc Analysis:** Use interpretability frameworks to analyze trained models.

Vulnerability to Overfitting

DCGANs can overfit small datasets, memorizing training samples rather than generalizing to new examples. This is particularly problematic when the training dataset lacks diversity.

Impact:

- The generator fails to create novel outputs.

- Discriminator performance degrades on unseen data.

Potential Solutions:

- **Data Augmentation:** Apply transformations like rotations, flips, or cropping to expand the training dataset.
- **Dropout:** Use dropout layers in the discriminator to prevent overfitting.
- **Regularization:** Apply L1 or L2 regularization to penalize overly complex models.

Ethical Concerns and Misuse

The high-quality images generated by DCGANs can be misused for unethical purposes, such as creating deepfakes or spreading misinformation.

Impact:

- Potential for harm in societal, political, and personal contexts.
- Raises concerns about the responsible use of generative AI technologies.

Potential Solutions:

- **Detection Algorithms:** Develop robust tools to identify synthetic media.
- **Policy and Regulation:** Implement guidelines for ethical use of generative models.
- **Transparency:** Encourage openness about the use of GAN-generated content.

While DCGANs are powerful tools for generative modeling, they are not without challenges. Mode collapse, training instability, and sensitivity to hyperparameters are common issues that require careful mitigation strategies. Computational complexity and lack of interpretability further complicate their usage. Addressing these challenges through innovative solutions and ethical considerations is key to unlocking the full potential of DCGANs in real-world applications.

Case Study: Creating High-Quality Synthetic Images with DCGANs

Generating realistic synthetic images has become a cornerstone of modern AI applications, from virtual assistants to personalized marketing. This case study explores how Deep Convolutional Generative Adversarial Networks (DCGANs) were leveraged to create culturally diverse, high-quality synthetic faces for an innovative Interview Bot system. Hence, by overcoming key challenges in diversity, realism, and stability, the project demonstrates how advanced generative modeling can deliver personalized experiences at scale, while maintaining ethical standards in synthetic media creation.

Problem: Generating Realistic Faces for Interviewers

The Interview Bot project aimed to enhance the candidate experience during virtual interviews by generating synthetic interviewer faces tailored to the candidate's locale and cultural background. This personalization was intended to make candidates feel more comfortable and engaged. Unlike generic avatars, these synthetic faces needed to capture diverse ethnic and cultural features while maintaining a high level of realism.

Key challenges in this problem included:

- Generating culturally appropriate and realistic faces for a wide range of locales.
- Ensuring diversity in features such as skin tone, hairstyles, and facial expressions.
- Avoiding artifacts or repetitive outputs that could diminish the interview experience.

Solution: Implementing a DCGAN for Image Synthesis

To address the problem, a DCGAN was developed and trained to generate high-quality synthetic faces suitable for the Interview Bot platform. The following steps outline the solution approach:

1. **Data Preparation**:
    a. **Dataset**: The CelebFaces Attributes Dataset (CelebA) was augmented with additional localized datasets to better represent diverse facial features across cultures.
    b. **Preprocessing**: Resize all images to 64×64 pixels to standardize input dimensions. Normalize pixel values to the range [-1, 1] to match the Tanh activation function used in the generator output. Categorize and label images based on locale for later conditioning.
2. **Model Architecture**:
    a. **Generator**:
        - **Input**: A 100-dimensional noise vector sampled from a Gaussian distribution.
        - Transpose convolutional layers progressively up-sample the noise to generate a 64x64 RGB image.
        - Batch normalization ensures stable training, while ReLU activations introduce non-linearity.
        - The final output layer uses a Tanh activation function.

    b. **Discriminator**:
        - **Input**: A 64×64 RGB image (real or generated).
        - Convolutional layers with strides down-sample the input while learning spatial features.
        - Leaky ReLU activations prevent dead neurons and improve gradient flow.
        - The output layer provides a scalar probability of whether the image is real or fake.
3. **Training Process**:
    a. **Adversarial Training Loop**:
        - Train the discriminator to correctly classify real and generated images.
        - Train the generator to produce images that fool the discriminator.

    b. **Loss Functions**: Binary cross-entropy loss for both generator and discriminator.
    c. **Adam optimizer**: A learning rate of 0.0002 and beta values of 0.5.
    d. Periodically save generated images for monitoring and evaluation.

Challenges: Fine-Tuning for Stability and Diversity

Implementing the DCGAN for Interview Bot required addressing the following challenges:

1. **Mode Collapse**: The generator occasionally produced faces with limited variations in features like skin tone or hairstyle.
    - **Solution**: Introduced mini-batch discrimination to encourage diversity. Augmented the dataset with culturally specific features to enhance variety.
2. **Training Instability**:
    - Loss values oscillated, leading to inconsistent quality in generated faces.

- **Solution**: Applied gradient penalty to stabilize training. Reduced learning rates dynamically during later epochs.

3. **Cultural Sensitivity**:
   - Generating culturally appropriate faces required careful representation of localized features.
   - **Solution**: Incorporated labeled subsets for conditional training to focus on specific locales. Ensured the generator learned balanced features across diverse ethnicities.

4. **High-Frequency Details**:
   - Fine details, such as hair texture and facial expressions, appeared noisy in early outputs.
   - **Solution**: Expanded the generator architecture to include skip connections for better feature retention. Trained the model for additional epochs with higher-resolution datasets.

Outcome: Generated Outputs and Improvements

After 100 epochs of training, the DCGAN produced synthetic interviewer faces that:

1. **Visual Quality**:
   - Early outputs were blurry and lacked coherence, but later epochs yielded sharp, detailed faces.
   - The final images displayed realistic skin tones, lighting, and expressions.

2. **Cultural Representation**:
   - The generator successfully produced faces reflecting diverse cultural and ethnic backgrounds.
   - Latent space interpolations showed smooth transitions between different locales, demonstrating robust learning.

3. **Challenges Addressed**:
   - Mode collapse was mitigated, and training stability improved significantly with architectural adjustments.

Future Directions: StyleGANs or Conditional DCGANs

While the DCGAN implementation met the requirements for the Interview Bot project, further advancements can enhance its capabilities:

1. **StyleGANs**:
   - StyleGANs provide greater control over image attributes, allowing users to customize interviewer features like age, gender, or attire.
   - Integrating StyleGANs could create more personalized interviewer profiles.

2. **Conditional GANs**:
   - Training with locale-specific labels could enable on-demand generation of culturally specific faces.
   - This approach would allow seamless adaptation to new regions or client requirements.

3. **High-Resolution Outputs**:
   - Scaling to higher resolutions (for example, 256×256) can improve the realism of generated faces, particularly for detailed applications.

   - Progressive growing techniques could help achieve this without introducing instability.
4. **Emotion and Expression Control**:
   - Extend the generator to allow customization of facial expressions, making the interview experience more engaging.

This case study demonstrates the potential of DCGANs in creating realistic and culturally tailored synthetic faces. By addressing challenges such as mode collapse and cultural sensitivity, the model achieved high-quality outputs that enhanced the candidate experience. Future work leveraging advanced GAN architectures like StyleGANs can further expand the capabilities of the Interview Bot, ensuring its adaptability and effectiveness in diverse applications.

Conclusion

In this chapter, we explored the architecture, working principles, and practical applications of DCGANs. DCGANs have emerged as a powerful generative model, leveraging convolutional layers to produce realistic images with remarkable detail and diversity. From generating synthetic face images to advancing applications in data augmentation and artistic synthesis, DCGANs demonstrate their versatility across industries. We also examined the challenges of training DCGANs, such as mode collapse and instability, and discussed strategies to overcome these issues using architectural innovations like batch normalization and Leaky ReLU activations.

With a solid understanding of DCGANs, including hands-on implementation in TensorFlow and PyTorch, you are well-equipped to apply these models to real-world problems. In the next chapter, we will delve into advanced generative models such as Conditional GANs, exploring how they build upon the foundations of GANs and DCGANs to achieve greater control and precision in generative tasks. Thus, by mastering these advanced techniques, you will unlock even more opportunities to innovate with generative AI.

Points to Remember

- DCGANs improve upon traditional GANs by incorporating convolutional layers, which excel at feature extraction and image generation.
- CNNs are widely used in Image classification, segmentation and many more real-world applications like face recognition and object detection.
- The generator uses transpose convolutional layers to up-sample noise into realistic images, while the discriminator evaluates their authenticity.
- Techniques such as batch normalization and Leaky ReLU activations stabilize training, and improve model performance.
- DCGANs have diverse applications, from synthetic image generation to data augmentation and artistic style transfer.

Multiple Choice Questions

1. What is the primary role of convolutional layers in DCGANs?
   a. Down-sample the latent space
   b. Extract features from data
   c. Up-sample noise into images
   d. Normalize data

2. Which activation function is commonly used in the output layer of a DCGAN generator?
   a. ReLU
   b. Sigmoid
   c. Tanh
   d. Leaky ReLU
3. Which optimization algorithm is frequently used in training DCGANs?
   a. Stochastic Gradient Descent (SGD)
   b. Adam Optimizer
   c. RMSprop
   d. Adagrad
4. What is mode collapse in the context of DCGANs?
   a. The generator produces limited variations of outputs.
   b. The discriminator overpowers the generator.
   c. The training process fails to converge.
   d. The generated images have high-frequency noise.
5. Which architectural feature helps DCGANs generate more realistic images compared to basic GANs??
   a. Use of fully connected layers
   b. Larger batch sizes
   c. Higher learning rates
   d. Transposed convolutions in the generator

Answers

1. b
2. c
3. b
4. a
5. d

Questions

1. What distinguishes DCGANs from traditional GANs, and how do convolutional layers contribute to their effectiveness?
2. How do transpose convolutional layers function in the generator architecture?
3. What challenges arise during the training of DCGANs, and what techniques can be used to address them?

4. Discuss the role of batch normalization and activation functions in stabilizing DCGAN training.
5. What are some practical applications of DCGANs in fields such as art, healthcare, and gaming?
6. How do the generator and discriminator interact in the adversarial training loop?
7. What strategies can be employed to mitigate mode collapse in DCGANs?
8. Why is the Adam optimizer commonly used in training DCGANs?
9. How can visualization of generated outputs help in monitoring the training progress of DCGANs?
10. What are the potential future advancements in DCGAN architectures?

Key Terms

- **Generator:** The component of a GAN that creates synthetic images from random noise.
- **Discriminator:** The component of a GAN that evaluates the authenticity of real and generated images.
- **Transpose Convolution:** A technique used in the generator to up-sample low-resolution inputs into higher-resolution outputs.
- **Batch Normalization:** A method to stabilize training by normalizing activations in the network.
- **Leaky ReLU:** An activation function that prevents dead neurons by allowing small gradients for negative values.
- **Mode Collapse:** A common issue in GAN training where the generator produces limited variations of outputs.
- **Adam Optimizer:** An optimization algorithm that combines the benefits of RMSprop and momentum for efficient training.
- **Data Augmentation:** The process of expanding a dataset by generating new samples using transformations or synthetic data.
- **Latent Space:** The compressed representation of input data from which new samples are generated.

Chapter 6
Conditional Generative Adversarial Networks

Introduction

Conditional Generative Adversarial Networks (cGANs) introduce a critical step forward in the growth of GANs by introducing assisted control within the generative process. While traditional GANs generate data in an unsupervised manner, cGANs enable the generation of data based on specific labels or features. This innovation allows users to manage the generative process, producing outputs tailored to desired categories or conditions, such as generating images of a particular object, class or style.

In this chapter, we shall explore the fascinating world of cGANs, diving into their architecture and the modifications that enable conditional generation. By combining input noise with additional information such as labels or class embeddings, cGANs unlock a wide range of applications in data synthesis, image-to-image translation, and more. Additionally, through hands-on exercises, you will learn to design, train, and evaluate a cGAN using TensorFlow and PyTorch, gaining practical experience in controlling this process. By the end of this chapter, you will not only understand the principles behind cGANs but also utilize the knowledge to create meaningful generative models tailored to your needs.

Structure

In this chapter, we will discuss the following topics:

- **Conditional GANs: Motivations and Applications**
  - Definition and Overview of Conditional GANs
  - The Benefits of Adding Conditions to GANs
- **Mathematical Foundations of Conditional GANs**
  - Objective Function of cGANs
  - Incorporating the Conditional Input
- **Architecture of Conditional GANs**
  - Overview of cGAN Architecture
  - Incorporating the Conditional Input
- **Implementing Conditional GANs**
  - Building a Conditional Generator
  - Building a Conditional Discriminator
  - Practical Implementation

- **Training Conditional GANs**
  - Training Process
  - Hyperparameters and Fine-Tuning
- **Applications of Conditional GANs**
  - Image-to-Image Translation
  - Text-to-Image Synthesis
  - Data Augmentation
  - Domain-Specific Applications
- **Challenges and Pitfalls in Conditional GANs**
  - Common Issues
  - Practical Solutions
- **Advanced Topics in Conditional GANs**
  - Extensions of cGANs
  - Combining cGANs with Other Models
  - State-of-the-Art cGAN Models
- **Case Study: Enhancing MRI Cancer Detection with Conditional GANs**

Conditional GANs: Motivations and Applications

GANs have revolutionized the field of generative modeling by enabling the creation of remarkably realistic data. However, while traditional GANs excel at generating diverse outputs from random noise, they lack the ability to control or direct the generative process toward specific outcomes. This limitation gave rise to Conditional GANs (cGANs), a powerful extension of GANs that allows for controlled data generation by conditioning the model on additional information.

Conditional GANs have brought unprecedented flexibility to generative modeling by enabling applications that demand precision and control. From generating images of specific objects to translating text descriptions into visuals, cGANs have opened new frontiers for creativity and functionality in AI-driven systems. This chapter delves into the world of Conditional GANs, starting with their foundational concepts, motivations for their development, and real-world applications.

Definition and Overview of Conditional GANs

Conditional GANs are an extension of traditional GANs, where the generation process is guided by additional input information referred to as the "*conditioning variable*." Unlike traditional GANs, which rely solely on random noise to produce outputs, cGANs incorporate auxiliary inputs—such as class labels, textual descriptions, or even other images—to generate data aligned with those conditions.

At their core, cGANs maintain the adversarial structure of GANs, consisting of two neural networks, the generator and the discriminator.

The conditioning mechanism adds an extra layer of control, enabling the model to produce outputs that correspond to specific attributes. For example, a cGAN conditioned on class labels can generate images of cats or dogs based on the input label.

Concept of Conditioning: Guiding Generation with Additional Inputs

Conditioning transforms GANs from an unsupervised model into a semi-supervised or supervised one. The generator's input is no longer just noise; it is a combination of noise and a conditioning vector. The discriminator is also conditioned, receiving both the real or fake data, and the associated conditioning vector.

Analogy of a Baker: The Cheesecake Connoisseur

Imagine you walk into a bakery which has two bakers. The first is a general baker (such as a standard GAN). They have a recipe book with a variety of cakes, and can make any cake from the menu. However, you are looking to order a special cheesecake, but he knows only one way of making a cheesecake.

Now, meet the second baker, who is a cheesecake connoisseur (such as a conditional GAN). This specialized baker has mastered the art of making cheesecakes. They do not just make random cheesecakes – they take your instructions, or conditions, and use them to craft the perfect dessert. You might ask for a cheesecake with fresh berries, a chocolate swirl cheesecake, or even a tropical cheesecake with mango and coconut. No matter the request, the base of the cake is always a cheesecake (the core condition), but the output is in alignment with your request and liking.

This process mirrors how cGANs work:

- The cheesecake base represents the conditioning variable (the essential feature that defines the structure of the output).
- The flavor, toppings, and presentation represent the added details specified by the conditioning vector, guiding the generator to create highly customized outputs.
- The customer's feedback is analogous to the discriminator's role, ensuring that the final product matches both the cheesecake base and the specific flavor requested.

Figure 6.1: *Bake a Cake, but the Condition is, it is Always a Cheesecake!*

In contrast to the general baker, who produces random cakes, the cheesecake connoisseur combines their expertise with your instructions to deliver exactly what you want. Similarly, Conditional GANs take in noise (creativity) and conditioning variables (instructions) to generate data with specific, targeted features.

The following are the two common techniques for incorporating conditioning information which include:

- **Concatenation:** Directly appending the conditioning vector to the input noise for the generator, or to the data for the discriminator.
- **Embedding:** Using embeddings to represent the conditioning variable, especially for categorical data, and combining these embeddings with other inputs.

This ability to condition outputs allows cGANs to produce data with targeted features, making them invaluable for applications where specificity and control are paramount.

The Benefits of Adding Conditions to GANs

The primary motivation for Conditional GANs is to address the inherent unpredictability of traditional GANs. While traditional GANs generate diverse outputs, they offer no control over the attributes or features of the generated data. By introducing conditioning variables, cGANs enable a precise control over the generative process, allowing the model to produce outputs aligned with user-defined criteria.

This level of control is particularly useful in scenarios where:

- **Specificity is Required:** Applications such as medical imaging or data augmentation demand the generation of data with precise characteristics.
- **Enhanced Realism is Needed:** Conditioning helps the model focus on relevant features, improving the quality and relevance of the generated data.
- **Targeted Creativity is Desired:** In fields such as art and design, cGANs allow creators to explore controlled variations of the content.

Real-World Examples: Targeted Data Synthesis and Enhanced Generation Control:

- **Image-to-Image Translation:** cGANs are used in tasks such as converting grayscale images to color, turning sketches into realistic images, or translating day-time images into night-time versions.
- **Text-to-Image Synthesis:** Models such as AttnGAN and DALL-E utilize cGANs to generate images based on textual descriptions, opening possibilities for creative tools and interactive systems. One of the best examples of text-to-image synthesis is the image of the Baker shown in *Figure* 6.1 that was generated by Dall-E.
- **Data Augmentation:** cGANs enhance datasets by generating labeled synthetic data, which is especially valuable in domains with limited real-world data, such as medical imaging or autonomous driving.

Mathematical Foundations of Conditional GANs

To fully understand cGANs, it is essential to delve into their mathematical underpinnings. At the heart of it is the incorporation of conditional information into the GAN framework, which modifies the loss functions and training dynamics to accommodate additional inputs. These foundations provide the basis for understanding that they achieve controlled generative outputs.

Objective Function of cGANs

The core idea of cGANs is to model the conditional distribution P(X|Y), where X represents the generated data (for example, an image) and Y is the conditional variable (for example, a label or class). Thus, by learning this conditional distribution, cGANs enable the generation of outputs tailored to specific conditions.

Mathematically, the objective function of a cGAN can be written as:

$$\min_G \max_D \mathbb{E}_{x,y\sim p_{data}(x,y)}[\log D(x, y)] + \mathbb{E}_{z\sim p_z(z),\ y\sim p_{data}(y)}[\log(1 - D(G(z, y), y))]$$

Here:

- $D(x, y)$: The discriminator's output, which predicts the probability that x is a real data sample conditioned on y.
- $G(z, y)$: The generator's output, which generates data x conditioned on y.
- $p_{data}(x, y)$: The joint distribution of real data and its associated conditions.
- $p_z(z)$: The distribution of noise input to the generator.
- $E_{x,y\sim pdata}(x,y)[\log D(x,y)]$: This term encourages the discriminator D to correctly classify real data x as real, given the condition y. E is the expectation operator.

This objective function modifies the traditional GAN formulation by incorporating y, the conditional input, into both the generator and the discriminator.

Explanation of Conditional Distributions P(X|Y)

In traditional GANs, the generator learns to model the marginal distribution P(X), which represents all possible data samples, without any conditions. In contrast, cGANs aim to model the conditional distribution P(X|Y). This additional constraint ensures that the generated data X is not only realistic but also aligns with the specific condition Y.

For example:

- In an image synthesis task, Y could be a label indicating the class of the image (for example, "*cat*" or "*dog*").
- The generator learns to produce an image of a cat or dog based on the label provided as Y, ensuring that the output matches the specified condition.

Mathematical Formulation of Generator and Discriminator Loss Functions

The generator and discriminator in cGANs have loss functions that incorporate the conditional variable Y. These loss functions are:

Generator Loss:

$$L_G = \mathbb{E}_{z\sim p_z(z),\ y\sim p_{data}(y)}[-\log D(G(z, y), y)]$$

- z: Random noise sampled from a prior distribution $pz(z)$, such as a uniform or Gaussian distribution.
- y: Conditioning variable (for example, labels) sampled from the data distribution $p_{data}(y)$.
- $G(z, y)$: The generator's output conditioned on y, aiming to create a data instance x that matches the real data distribution for that condition.

Here, the generator aims to minimize the discriminator's ability to distinguish between real and fake samples, while ensuring that the generated samples align with the condition y.

Discriminator Loss:

$$L_D = -E_{x,y\sim p_{data}(x,y)}[\log D(x, y)] - E_{z\sim p_z(z),\ y\sim p_{data}(y)}[\log(1 - D(G(z, y), y))]$$

- **`z`:** Random noise sampled from a prior distribution $p_z(z)$, such as a uniform or Gaussian distribution.
- **`y`:** Conditioning variable (for example, labels or attributes) sampled from the data distribution $p_{data}(y)$.
- **`D (x, y)`:** The generator's output when given a real sample `x` conditioned on `y`. This measures how well the discriminator can identify real samples as real.
- **`G (x, y)`:** The generator's output when given random noise `z` and the condition `y`. This generates fake samples conditioned on `y`.

The discriminator's objective is to minimize this loss function (L_D) to correctly classify real and fake samples. Simultaneously, the generator is trained to minimize its own loss, which typically depends on the logarithmic function. The discriminator maximizes its ability to correctly identify real samples `x`, while rejecting fake samples generated by `G`, all while considering the condition `y`.

Incorporating the Conditional Input

Conditioning in cGANs is achieved by incorporating the variable Y into both the generator and discriminator. This requires specific techniques to handle categorical, numerical, or continuous conditions effectively.

Embedding Categorical and Continuous Conditions

Categorical Conditions:

- For categorical variables (for example, class labels), a common approach is to use one-hot encoding or embedding layers to convert the labels into dense vectors.

Category	Apple	Banana	Cherry
Apple	1	0	0
Banana	0	1	0
Cherry	0	0	1

Figure 6.2: *Example of One Hot Encoding Categorical Variables*

- The resulting vectors are concatenated with the noise vector z (for the generator) or the input data x (for the discriminator).

Continuous Conditions:

- Continuous variables (for example, numerical attributes) can be normalized, and directly concatenated with z or x.
- Alternatively, embeddings can be learned for continuous variables to improve flexibility and representation.

Adapting Traditional GAN Loss Functions to Include Conditioning Variables

The inclusion of conditional inputs modifies the adversarial loss functions to ensure that both the generator and discriminator learn to incorporate the conditional variable Y.

- The generator loss penalizes outputs that do not align with Y, encouraging the model to produce conditionally accurate data.
- The discriminator evaluates the joint representation of the input data and the condition, distinguishing between real and fake pairs.

These adaptations ensure that cGANs can effectively learn the conditional distribution P(X|Y), resulting in controlled and precise generative outputs.

Architecture of Conditional GANs

The architecture of Conditional GANs (cGANs) builds upon the traditional GAN framework by integrating conditional inputs into both the generator and discriminator. This architectural innovation allows for controlled data generation by guiding the learning process with specific information, such as labels, attributes, or other features. Understanding the modifications introduced by cGANs is necessary for appreciating their versatility and applications.

Overview of cGAN Architecture

The cGAN architecture accommodates the conditional input (y) to the primary components:

- **Generator (G):**
  - The generator takes a noise vector z as input sampled from a latent distribution, and a conditional input y. It combines these inputs to generate data G(z, y) that aligns with the specified condition y.
  - Its goal is to produce realistic samples that the discriminator cannot distinguish from the real data, while ensuring that the generated samples adhere to the conditioning variable.
- **Discriminator (D):**
  - The discriminator evaluates whether an input sample is real or generated by the generator, while considering the associated conditional input y.
  - It takes both the data sample and the condition as input, ensuring that its evaluation is conditioned on the expected output.

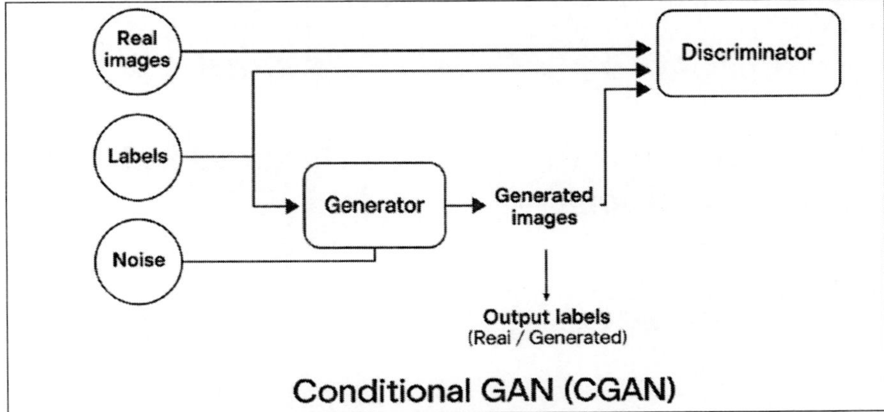

Figure 6.3: *Architecture of cGAN*

By incorporating y into both networks, cGANs introduce a dependency that enforces alignment between the generated data and the specified condition.

Roles of the Generator and Discriminator in cGANs

The roles of the generator and discriminator in cGANs are similar to those in traditional GANs, with the key difference being the integration of conditional information:

- **Generator**: Generates data samples conditioned on the input y. It aims to minimize the discriminator's ability to distinguish between real and fake data, while ensuring adherence to the condition.
- **Discriminator**: Evaluates the authenticity of input samples, while considering the condition y. It works as a classifier that predicts whether the input is real or generated, given the conditional input.

Key Differences from Traditional GANs:

- **Conditioning Mechanism**: Traditional GANs operate solely on random noise z, while cGANs combine z with conditional inputs y.
- **Modified Loss Functions**: The loss functions in cGANs incorporate the conditional inputs, influencing both the generator and the discriminator.
- **Training Dynamics**: cGANs require balanced handling of z and y, ensuring that the generated samples align with the conditioning variable.

Incorporating the Conditional Input

The inclusion of conditional inputs in cGANs necessitates specific techniques for integrating y into the generator and the discriminator:

Concatenation:

- The simplest and most common technique is to concatenate the conditional input y with the noise vector z (for the generator) or the data sample x (for the discriminator).
- For example, if y is a one-hot encoded label, it can be appended to z to form an extended input vector.

Embedding:

- Embedding layers can be used to map categorical or numerical conditions into dense vector representations. This approach is particularly useful for high-dimensional or complex conditions.
- For instance, class labels can be embedded into a continuous space, and then concatenated with z.

Input Representations for Categorical, Numerical, and Image-Based Conditions

Categorical Conditions:

- Represented as one-hot encodings or embeddings.
- **Example**: A label indicating a specific digit (for example, "3") in the MNIST dataset.

Numerical Conditions:

- Normalized values or embeddings of continuous variables.
- **Example**: Numerical attributes such as "*price*" or "*weight*".

Image-Based Conditions:

- Directly input as images or feature maps.
- **Example**: Using a sketch as a condition for generating a realistic image.

Implementing Conditional GANs

Implementing Conditional GANs (cGANs) involves designing both the generator and discriminator to incorporate conditional inputs effectively. This requires careful consideration of how labels or extra information are integrated into the architecture, and how these inputs influence the adversarial training process. In this section, we explore the design and practical implementation of cGANs, with explanations and code examples in TensorFlow and PyTorch.

Building a Conditional Generator

The generator in a cGAN is designed to produce data samples that align with the given conditional input. To achieve this, the labels or conditions must be embedded into the latent space, alongside the noise vector.

- **Input Configuration**: The generator takes two inputs: A random noise vector z and the conditional input y.
- **Embedding Conditional Inputs**: For categorical conditions, the labels are embedded into dense vectors. For continuous conditions, the values can be normalized, and directly concatenated with z.
- **Latent Space Fusion**: The unified input is passed through a series of layers (for example, fully connected, convolutional, or transposed convolutional) to generate the output data.

Strategies for Effective Conditioning:

- Use separate embedding layers for conditions to allow the network to learn meaningful representations of the labels.
- Regularize the embeddings to prevent overfitting on specific conditions.
- Experiment with different fusion methods, such as concatenation or element-wise multiplication, to determine the most effective approach for your dataset.

Building a Conditional Discriminator

The discriminator's role in a cGAN is to distinguish between real and generated data, while taking the conditional input into account. To achieve this, the discriminator incorporates the conditional input into its decision-making process.

- **Input Configuration**: The discriminator accepts two inputs: The data sample x (real or fake) and the conditional input y.
- **Label Conditioning Techniques**: The conditional input y is concatenated with the data sample x along the feature dimension. Alternatively, the conditional input is projected into the same space as x, and combined using element-wise multiplication.

Methods for Merging Labels with Real/Fake Data:

- **Concatenation-Based Merging**: Append the embedded labels to the data sample before feeding it into the network. For example, concatenate a one-hot encoded label with a flattened image vector.
- **Feature Map Fusion**: For image data, the conditional input can be replicated spatially, and

concatenated with the image's feature maps. For example, add a channel representing the condition to the input image.

Practical Implementation

In this section, we will explore how to build and train cGANs using both TensorFlow and PyTorch. Through practical code examples, we will walk through defining the generator and discriminator, conditioning the model on labels, and training the network step by step. Thus, whether you are working with image generation, style transfer, or text-to-image synthesis, this will provide a strong foundation for applying cGANs to real-world problems.

Code Example in TensorFlow

The following is a simplified implementation of a conditional Generator and Discriminator:

```
import tensorflow as tf
from tensorflow.keras import layers

# Conditional Generator
def build_generator(noise_dim, num_classes):
    noise = layers.Input(shape=(noise_dim,))
    label = layers.Input(shape=(num_classes,))

    # Combine noise and label
    combined_input = layers.Concatenate()([noise, label])
    x = layers.Dense(128, activation='relu')(combined_input)
    x = layers.Dense(256, activation='relu')(x)
    x = layers.Dense(784, activation='sigmoid')(x)

    return tf.keras.Model([noise, label], x)

# Conditional Discriminator
def build_discriminator(input_dim, num_classes):
    data = layers.Input(shape=(input_dim,))
    label = layers.Input(shape=(num_classes,))

    # Combine data and label
    combined_input = layers.Concatenate()([data, label])
    x = layers.Dense(256, activation='relu')(combined_input)
    x = layers.Dense(128, activation='relu')(x)
    x = layers.Dense(1, activation='sigmoid')(x)

    return tf.keras.Model([data, label], x)
```

Data Preprocessing for Conditional Inputs:

- **Preparing Labels:**
    - Encode categorical labels into one-hot vectors or use embedding layers for dimensionality reduction.
    - Normalize continuous labels to ensure that they fall within a comparable range.
- **Combining Data and Labels:**
    - Use the same preprocessing steps for real and generated data to maintain consistency.
    - Ensure that the conditional input is correctly paired with each data sample during training.

- **Batch Preparation:**
    - For each training step, create batches of real data, fake data, and their corresponding labels.
    - Ensure that the generator and discriminator receive their inputs in the correct format.

These design principles and implementation steps provide a robust foundation for building and training Conditional GANs, enabling controlled and targeted data generation across various applications.

Code Example in PyTorch

The following is a simplified implementation of a Conditional Generator and Discriminator:

```
import torch
import torch.nn as nn

# Conditional Generator
class Generator(nn.Module):
    def __init__(self, noise_dim, num_classes, output_dim):
        super(Generator, self).__init__()
        self.noise_dim = noise_dim
        self.num_classes = num_classes

        # Embedding layer for labels
        self.label_embedding = nn.Embedding(num_classes, num_classes)

        # Generator network
        self.model = nn.Sequential(
            nn.Linear(noise_dim + num_classes, 128),
            nn.ReLU(),
            nn.Linear(128, 256),
            nn.ReLU(),
            nn.Linear(256, output_dim),
            nn.Sigmoid()
        )

    def forward(self, noise, labels):
        label_embedding = self.label_embedding(labels)
        gen_input = torch.cat((noise, label_embedding), dim=1)
        return self.model(gen_input)

# Conditional Discriminator
class Discriminator(nn.Module):
    def __init__(self, input_dim, num_classes):
        super(Discriminator, self).__init__()
        self.num_classes = num_classes

        # Embedding layer for labels
        self.label_embedding = nn.Embedding(num_classes, num_classes)

        # Discriminator network
        self.model = nn.Sequential(
            nn.Linear(input_dim + num_classes, 256),
            nn.ReLU(),
            nn.Linear(256, 128),
            nn.ReLU(),
            nn.Linear(128, 1),
```

```
            nn.Sigmoid()
        )

    def forward(self, data, labels):
        label_embedding = self.label_embedding(labels)
        disc_input = torch.cat((data, label_embedding), dim=1)
        return self.model(disc_input)
```

Explanation of the Code:

- **Generator:**
  a. Takes a random noise vector (**`noise_dim`**) and a label (**`num_classes`**).
  b. The label is embedded into a dense representation.
  c. The noise and label embedding are concatenated and passed through fully connected layers.
  d. The output is a generated image (or any structured data).
- **Discriminator**:
  a. It takes an input sample (**`input_dim`**) and its label.
  b. The label is embedded and concatenated with the input data.
  c. The combined input is processed through fully connected layers.
  d. Outputs a probability (0-1) indicating whether the input is real or fake.

Training Conditional GANs

Training Conditional GANs (cGANs) requires an iterative process where the generator and discriminator are optimized alternately, ensuring that neither network becomes too dominant. Unlike traditional GANs, cGANs incorporate conditional inputs, meaning both the generator and discriminator must learn not only to generate the realistic data but also to align outputs with the specified conditions. Achieving this balance is crucial to prevent mode collapse, unstable gradients, or poor-quality generations.

To train a cGAN effectively, careful attention must be given to hyperparameter tuning, including learning rates, batch sizes, and loss function selection. Additionally, robust monitoring strategies—such as tracking losses, inspecting generated samples, and using evaluation metrics—are essential for ensuring convergence and high-quality outputs.

Training Process

The training of Conditional GANs (cGANs) follows an adversarial process where the generator and discriminator are updated alternately, ensuring that the generator learns to produce the realistic data that aligns with the specified conditions, while the discriminator improves its ability to distinguish between real and fake samples.

Discriminator Training

The discriminator D(x, y) is trained to correctly classify the real and generated (fake) data, conditioned on the input label y. It learns to maximize its ability to distinguish between the real and fake samples.

Steps in Discriminator Training:

1. The real data samples x are paired with their true labels y, and the discriminator is trained to classify them as real.
2. The generator produces fake data G(z, y) by taking random noise z and conditional input y. These fake samples are passed to the discriminator, along with the corresponding labels.
3. The discriminator is optimized to maximize the probability of correctly classifying real samples as real and fake samples as fake.
4. The discriminator's loss function is:

$$L_D = -E_{x,y \sim p_{data(x,y)}}[Log\ D(x, y)] - E_{z \sim p_{z(z)},\ y \sim p_{data(y)}}[Log(1 - D(G(z, y), y))]$$

   a. The first term represents how well the discriminator classifies the real data as real.
   b. The second term represents how well the discriminator classifies the generated (fake) data as fake.
   c. The discriminator aims to minimize this loss, improving its ability to distinguish between the real and fake samples.

Generator Training

The generator is trained to minimize the discriminator's ability to classify its outputs as fake, while ensuring that the outputs match the conditional input.

Steps in Generator Training:

1. The generator takes random noise z, and a condition y as input as well as produces a synthetic output G(z, y).
2. The generated output is passed to the discriminator, along with the condition y.
3. The generator is optimized to minimize the discriminator's ability to distinguish fake samples, encouraging it to assign a high probability to generated samples.
4. The generator's loss function is:

$$L_G = -E_{z \sim p_{z(z)},\ y \sim p_{data(y)}}\ [\log D(G(z, y), y)]$$

   - This loss encourages the generator to produce outputs that the discriminator misclassifies as real.
   - The generator aims to minimize this loss, improving its ability to generate realistic and correctly conditioned data.

The Role of Conditions in Training Stability

The inclusion of conditional inputs can significantly enhance training stability by providing additional context. Proper handling of these inputs ensures:

- **Guided Learning:** Conditions help the generator focus on relevant features, reducing ambiguity in the output space.
- **Improved Discrimination:** The discriminator evaluates samples with an added layer of complexity, enhancing its training dynamics.

Thus, to maintain stability, it is essential to:

- Use balanced datasets with well-represented conditional inputs.
- Regularize the conditional inputs to prevent overfitting or instability.

Hyperparameters and Fine-Tuning

Training a Conditional GAN (cGAN) effectively requires careful selection and tuning of hyperparameters. Since cGANs involve a delicate balance between the generator and the discriminator, improper tuning can lead to mode collapse, vanishing gradients, or training instability. The key hyperparameters and strategies for fine-tuning a cGAN model for optimal performance are as follows.

Learning Rates:

- The learning rate is crucial in balancing how fast each network (generator and discriminator) updates.
- A common approach is to use a slightly lower learning rate for the generator than the discriminator. This prevents the generator from making extreme updates before the discriminator has learned to distinguish real from fake samples.
- **Typical Choices:**
  - Discriminator learning rate: $\alpha_D = 4 \times 10^{-4}$
  - Generator learning rate: $\alpha_G = 2 \times 10^{-4}$

Optimizers such as Adam with betas = (0.5, 0.999) are commonly used to stabilize training.

Batch Sizes:

- Batch size affects the stability of gradient updates and training dynamics.
- Larger batch sizes (for example, 64, 128) help smooth gradients, and improve training stability, but they require more memory.
- Smaller batch sizes (for example, 16, 32) can introduce more noise but may lead to better generalization.
- **Common Choices:**
  - Small datasets: Batch size 32 (if computationally limited)
  - Medium to large datasets: Batch size 64–128 for smoother training

Conditional Regularization

Regularization techniques help prevent overfitting, and improve generalization, ensuring that both the generator and discriminator remain stable throughout training. There are multiple techniques to achieve this as follows.

Dropout Regularization

- **Purpose:** Reduces overfitting by randomly deactivating neurons during training, preventing reliance on specific patterns.
- **Implementation:**
  - Apply Dropout layers (0.3 - 0.5 probability) in both generator and discriminator networks.
  - Dropout is particularly useful in the discriminator to prevent it from memorizing real samples.

Label Smoothing

- **Purpose:** Prevents the discriminator from becoming too confident in its classifications, which stabilizes adversarial training.
- **Implementation:**
    - Replace hard labels (0 and 1) with smoothed labels:
        - **Real samples**: Use 0.9 instead of 1.0
        - **Fake samples**: Use 0.1 instead of 0.0
    - This encourages the discriminator to remain uncertain, allowing the generator a fair chance to improve.

Weight Initialization:

- Proper weight initialization ensures that both the generator and the discriminator start training on reasonable scales, without vanishing or exploding gradients.
- A common approach is **Xavier (Glorot) Initialization** or **He Initialization**, which is applied as:

```
def weights_init(m):
    if isinstance(m, nn.Linear) or isinstance(m, nn.Conv2d):
        nn.init.xavier_uniform_(m.weight)
```

Gradient Clipping:

- **Purpose:** Prevents gradients from growing too large, which can cause instability.
- **Implementation:** Apply gradient clipping to cap gradients at a maximum value (for example, 1.0).

  In PyTorch:

```
torch.nn.utils.clip_grad_norm_(generator.parameters(), max_norm=1.0)
```

Summary of Hyperparameter Guidelines:

Hyperparameter	Suggested Values / Techniques
Learning Rate (Discriminator)	4×10^{-4}
Learning Rate (Generator)	2×10^{-4}
Batch Size	32–128 (depending on dataset size)
Dropout Rate	0.3 – 0.5
Label Smoothing	0.9 for real, 0.1 for fake
Weight Initialization	Xavier or He Initialization
Gradient Clipping	Max norm = 1.0
Optimizer	Adam (betas = (0.5, 0.999))
Evaluation Metrics	Loss curves, FID, Inception Score

Figure 6.4: *Suggested Values of Hyperparameters for cGAN Training*

Monitoring Training

While training Conditional GANs (cGANs), it is essential to monitor both qualitative and quantitative aspects of the generated data. Thus, by employing visual inspection, quantitative metrics, and conditional accuracy evaluation, we can assess whether the model produces realistic and well-conditioned outputs.

Visual Inspection: The First Line of Evaluation

- Regularly generate samples for different conditions, and inspect their quality.
- Compare outputs with expected conditional labels to ensure proper alignment.
- Look for artifacts, distortions, or mode collapse where the generator produces repetitive or incorrect outputs.
- Save images at fixed intervals (for example, every few epochs) for side-by-side comparisons over time.

Best Practice: Maintain a progress log of generated samples to track improvements or regressions.

Quantitative Metrics: Measuring GAN Performance

To objectively assess performance, statistical measures help quantify realism and diversity:

- **Inception Score (IS):** The IS evaluates the diversity and realism of generated samples. A higher IS indicates that the generated images belong to distinct, recognizable classes, enhancing their credibility. However, a key limitation of IS is that it does not compare generated samples to real ones, making it less effective for assessing distribution alignment.
- **Fréchet Inception Distance (FID):** The FID measures how closely the distribution of generated samples align with the real data. Lower FID scores indicate better quality and realism. Unlike the Inception Score, FID directly compares the distribution of real and generated data, making it a more reliable metric for evaluating generative model performance.

Best Practice: Compute FID at different training checkpoints to detect quality drift.

Conditional Accuracy: Evaluating Class Consistency

Since cGANs generate samples based on conditional labels, an additional classifier can verify whether the generated images match the intended conditions.

- Train a pre-trained classifier (for example, ResNet, EfficientNet) on the original dataset.
- Pass generated images through the classifier, and compute classification accuracy.
- Higher accuracy indicates that the cGAN is correctly conditioning its outputs.

Best Practice: If accuracy is low, investigate whether conditional embeddings are being effectively utilized in the generator.

Thus, by carefully optimizing the training process, fine-tuning hyperparameters, and monitoring progress, you can harness the full potential of Conditional GANs, ensuring that the outputs are not only realistic but also aligned with their conditional inputs.

Applications of Conditional GANs

Conditional GANs (cGANs) have revolutionized the field of generative modeling by enabling the production of highly controlled and targeted outputs. Their ability to condition the generative process on auxiliary inputs has unlocked numerous applications. From creative tools to domain-specific innovations, cGANs have become an essential component of modern AI solutions.

Image-to-Image Translation

Image-to-image translation is one of the most prominent applications of cGANs, where the goal is to transform images from one domain to another, while preserving the key features.

***Figure* 6.5:** *Example of Image-to-image Translation Using cGAN*

Thus, by conditioning the output on specific attributes or domains, cGANs excel in tasks such as:

- **Sketch-to-Image Translation and Vice versa:** cGANs (for example, in Pix2Pix) transform simple hand-drawn sketches into detailed, realistic images, automating the addition of textures and colors. For example, a simple outline of a cat can be transformed into a photorealistic image of a cat with detailed textures and colors.
- **Artistic Style Transfer:** cGANs can apply the visual style of one image (for example, a Van Gogh painting) to another, enabling powerful photo and digital art filters for applying predefined or custom artistic styles.

Text-to-Image Synthesis

cGANs enable the generation of images based on textual descriptions, bridging the gap between language and visual content. This application is particularly useful for creating visual representations from abstract ideas or concepts.

- **Generating Images from Descriptions:**
    - By conditioning on text inputs, cGANs can generate images that align closely with the provided descriptions.
    - **Example:** A model conditioned on the text "*a red flower with yellow petals*" generates a corresponding image of the described flower.
- **Interactive Content Creation:**
    - **Text-to-image models powered by cGANs** are widely used in creative industries to generate custom visuals based on user-provided prompts.
    - **Use Case:** Applications such as AttnGAN and DALL-E utilize cGANs to create illustrations, advertisements, and other creative assets.

Data Augmentation

Data augmentation is another critical application of cGANs, especially in scenarios where labeled datasets are limited. By generating synthetic data that mimics real-world distribution, cGANs enhance the diversity and volume of training datasets.

- **Labeled Synthetic Data:**
    - **cGANs can generate realistic samples** for under-represented classes in datasets, improving model performance on imbalanced datasets.
    - **Example:** Generating synthetic images of rare diseases for medical datasets.
- **Improving Model Generalization:**
    - **Augmenting datasets with a variety of synthetic examples** reduces overfitting, and improves the generalization capabilities of machine learning models.
    - **Use Case:** In autonomous driving, cGANs generate variations of road scenes to train robust perception models.

Domain-Specific Applications

The versatility of Conditional GANs (cGANs) extends far beyond traditional generative tasks, finding applications in highly specialized fields that demand precise control over generated outputs. Conditional GANs allow for guided data generation based on specific input conditions, making them invaluable in domains where accuracy, customization, and controlled variability are critical. Whether enhancing medical imaging, advancing scientific research, or revolutionizing fashion and e-commerce, cGANs have proven to be a powerful tool for solving real-world challenges. The following are some key domains where cGANs are making a significant impact.

- **Medical Imaging:** cGANs are used to enhance and synthesize medical images, aiding in diagnosis and research. For example:
    - Generating MRI scans conditioned on specific anatomical features.
    - Enhancing low-resolution images for improved diagnostic accuracy.
- **Fashion and E-Commerce:** cGANs generate fashion designs based on textual descriptions, or adapt clothing designs to different styles and trends.
    - **Use Case:** Virtual try-on systems leverage cGANs to simulate how garments would look on different body types.
- **Scientific Research:** In fields like astronomy, cGANs generate simulations of cosmic phenomena conditioned on specific parameters, enabling researchers to study rare or theoretical events.
- **Gaming and Entertainment:** cGANs create game assets, such as characters or landscapes, based on design constraints or player input.
    - **Use Case:** Procedural content generation in video games to create unique and engaging environments.

Therefore, by enabling controlled and targeted data generation, cGANs have become an indispensable tool across a wide range of applications. Their ability to generate high-quality, conditionally accurate outputs continues to drive innovation in AI-powered solutions.

Challenges and Pitfalls in Conditional GANs

While Conditional GANs (cGANs) offer powerful capabilities for controlled data generation, they are not without their challenges. Training cGANs can be fraught with instability, mode collapse, and difficulty in learning complex conditions. Addressing these issues requires a combination of robust training practices, fine-tuning, and regularization techniques.

Common Issues

Training Instability:

- GANs, including cGANs, are notoriously difficult to train due to the adversarial setup between the generator and the discriminator.
- Instability arises when one network outpaces the other, leading to oscillations in loss values or failure to converge.
- Conditioning variables introduce additional complexity, as both networks must learn to process the conditions effectively.

Mode Collapse:

- Mode collapse occurs when the generator produces limited variations of outputs, failing to capture the full diversity of the target distribution.
- In cGANs, this can manifest as repetitive outputs that align with a subset of conditions, while ignoring others.

Difficulty in Learning Complex or Overlapping Conditions:

- cGANs struggle when conditions are highly complex or overlapping, as the generator may fail to produce distinct outputs for similar conditions.
- This issue is exacerbated in datasets with noisy or ambiguous labels, where the generator may confuse conditions or fail to generate coherent samples.

Practical Solutions

Label Smoothing:

- Label smoothing replaces binary labels (for example, 0 and 1) with slightly shifted values (for example, 0.1 and 0.9).
- Instead of training the discriminator to classify real samples as 1.0, it learns to classify them as 0.9, and instead of classifying fake samples as 0.0, it assigns them a label of 0.1. Notice the difference in the following equations before and after applying label smoothing.

$$L_D = -E_{x,y \sim p_{data(x,y)}} [\log D(x, y)] - E_{z \sim p_{z(z)},\, y \sim p_{data(y)}} [\log(1 - D(G(z, y), y))]$$

$$L_D = -E_{x,y \sim p_{data(x,y)}} [\log D(x, y) \cdot 0.9] - E_{z \sim p_{z(z)},\, y \sim p_{data(y)}} [\log(1 - D(G(z, y), y)) \cdot 0.1]$$

Feature Matching:

- This technique encourages the generator to match the statistics of intermediate features in the discriminator, rather than solely minimizing the adversarial loss.
- By aligning feature distributions, feature matching reduces instability, and improves the diversity of generated samples.

Regularization Techniques:

- **Dropout:** Applying dropout layers in the generator and discriminator prevents overfitting, and introduces variability in feature learning.

- **Gradient Penalty:** Adding a gradient penalty term to the discriminator loss stabilizes training by encouraging smooth gradients.

$$L_{D,GP} = L_D + \lambda\, E_{\hat{x}}\, [(\| \nabla_{\hat{x}} D(\hat{x}, y)\|_2 - 1)^2]$$

Thus, by incorporating dropout for regularization and gradient penalty for smooth optimization, this approach helps improve the training stability of cGANs, ensuring that both the generator and the discriminator learn effectively.

Balancing Diversity and Specificity in Conditional Outputs

To ensure diverse outputs that align with conditional inputs:

- Inject noise into the generator alongside the conditional inputs to promote variation.
- Introduce auxiliary objectives that encourage diversity, such as mutual information maximization between inputs and outputs.
- **Example:** `I(y; x) = H(y) - H(y | x)`

  `I(y;x)`: Mutual Information.

  `H(y)`: Entropy of y, which quantifies the total uncertainty in y.

  `H(y|x)`: Conditional entropy of y given x, which represents the remaining uncertainty in y after knowing x.

Maximize mutual information to strengthen the relationship between conditions, and the generated data.

Implementation Tips:

- Monitor loss values and sample outputs frequently to identify early signs of instability or mode collapse.
- Use adaptive learning rates or schedulers to balance the training pace of the generator and discriminator.
- Experiment with architectural modifications, such as spectral normalization or attention mechanisms, to enhance the networks' ability to handle complex conditions.

Thus, by addressing these challenges with targeted strategies, cGANs can achieve greater stability, diversity, and fidelity in their outputs. This paves the way for robust applications across domains that require precise and controlled generative capabilities.

Advanced Topics in Conditional GANs

Conditional GANs have been the foundation for significant advancements in controlled generative modeling. As the field progresses, researchers have developed various extensions and hybrid approaches to enhance the performance and versatility of cGANs. This section explores advanced topics, including extensions of cGANs, integration with other generative models, and state-of-the-art innovations.

Extensions of cGANs

Semi-Supervised cGANs extend the traditional framework by leveraging unlabeled data alongside the labeled data during training. This approach is particularly useful in scenarios where obtaining the labeled data is expensive or time-consuming.

- **Key Idea:** The discriminator is modified to function as both a classifier and a discriminator. It predicts the class labels for real samples, while distinguishing real samples from the generated ones.
- **Benefits:**
    - Improves the generalization of the generator.
    - Reduces the reliance on large labeled datasets.
- **Applications:** Image classification and generation in domains with sparsely labeled data, such as medical imaging or satellite imagery.

Multi-Modal cGANs aim to generate diverse outputs (text, image, video, and so on) for a given conditional input, addressing the limitations of producing only a single mode of data per condition.

- **Key Techniques:**
    - Introducing objectives that encourage diversity, such as maximizing mutual information between the latent variable and the output.
    - Adding additional latent variables to represent variations within a condition.
- **Example:** For instance, when conditioned on the text "*a futuristic city at night*," a multi-modal cGAN could generate a bustling neon-lit metropolis, a serene city with flying vehicles, or a rain-slicked cyberpunk alleyway, exploring multiple visual interpretations from a single prompt.

Combining cGANs with Other Models

Conditional GANs (cGANs) are powerful on their own, but their capabilities can be further enhanced when combined with other generative models. Thus, by integrating cGANs with architectures such as Variational Autoencoders (VAEs) and Diffusion Models, researchers have developed hybrid approaches that leverage the advantages of multiple techniques. These combinations enable more stable training, improved latent space representations, and higher-quality outputs. Let us now explore two notable hybrid models that incorporate cGANs for controlled and efficient data generation.

Variational Autoencoders (cVAE-GAN): cVAE-GANs combine the strengths of Variational Autoencoders (VAEs) and cGANs. The VAE captures the latent structure of the data, while the cGAN ensures high-quality outputs conditioned on specific attributes.

- **Architecture:** The encoder in the VAE maps the input data into a latent space conditioned on auxiliary information. The decoder (generator) reconstructs the data, while adhering to the conditions.
- **Applications:** Text-to-image synthesis where the latent space of the VAE captures textual semantics, and the cGAN refines the visual quality.

Diffusion Models with Conditions: Diffusion models are emerging as a robust alternative to GANs for high-quality image generation. Therefore, by incorporating conditions, these models enhance their applicability in controlled generation tasks.

- **Key Features:**
    - Gradual noise removal processes guided by the conditional input.
    - Superior training stability compared to GANs.
- **Applications:** High-resolution image synthesis, video generation, and artistic style applications.

State-of-the-Art cGAN Models

Conditional GANs have undergone rapid evolution, with breakthroughs in architecture, training strategies, and applications. These innovations have led to more stable training, higher-quality outputs, and improved alignment with conditional inputs. While the field has seen the rise of alternative architectures such as Diffusion Models for some applications, the adversarial framework of cGANs continues to be highly effective, especially in scenarios requiring fine-grained control, computational efficiency, and strong performance on specific, well-defined tasks.

These innovations have cemented cGANs as a versatile and powerful tool for image synthesis, image-to-image translation, and data augmentation.

Architectural Enhancements in cGANs

The following enhancements have pushed the performance of cGANs to new heights, making them more robust and applicable than ever:

- **Attention Mechanisms:** By allowing both the generator and discriminator to focus on the most relevant parts of an image or feature map, attention mechanisms enable the handling of complex, long-range dependencies. This is crucial for generating fine-grained details, and maintaining global consistency in scenes.
- **Projection Discriminator:** This technique elegantly integrates the conditional information into the discriminator's decision-making process via inner products. It allows the discriminator to not just ask, "*Is this real?*" but "*Is this real, and does it match the condition?*", significantly improving output coherence.
- **Multi-Scale and Progressive Training:** Methods like Progressive Growing of GANs (ProGAN) start by generating low-resolution images, and gradually increase the resolution. This stabilizes training, and allows the generation of remarkably high-quality, high-resolution outputs.
- **Contrastive Learning and Auxiliary Losses:** Incorporating self-supervised or contrastive learning (for example, using a Projection Head to maximize mutual information between related patches) helps the model learn more robust and diverse feature representations, directly combating mode collapse.

Benchmark cGAN Models

- **Pix2Pix:** A popular cGAN framework for image-to-image translation tasks, such as turning sketches into photorealistic images.
- **AttnGAN:** Utilizes attention mechanisms to generate high-quality images from textual descriptions, achieving fine-grained correspondence between text and image regions.
- **BigGAN:** Extends cGANs to large-scale datasets with advanced architectural enhancements, producing highly realistic and diverse images.

Advancements in cGAN Training

New techniques have been introduced to enhance training stability, diversity, and output quality:

- **Hybrid Loss Functions:** Combines adversarial loss with additional losses (for example, perceptual loss, cycle-consistency loss, and so on) to improve stability and realism.
- **Contrastive Learning in cGANs:** Uses contrastive loss to enforce better feature separation, ensuring that the generator captures diverse modes of data distribution.

Thus, by building on these advanced techniques and state-of-the-art innovations, Conditional GANs continue to push the boundaries of generative modeling. Their evolving capabilities enable breakthroughs in diverse fields, from creative industries to scientific research, solidifying their role as a cornerstone of controlled AI generation.

Case Study: Enhancing MRI Cancer Detection with Conditional GANs

Accurate cancer detection using MRI scans relies heavily on the availability of large and diverse datasets. However, medical imaging datasets have limited data availability and class imbalance. This limits the ability and reliability of diagnostic models in real-world clinical applications. To overcome these challenges, cGANs offered a promising solution by generating high-quality synthetic MRI images conditioned on tumor-specific attributes. In this case study, we explore how Zummit Infolabs, a software company, leveraged cGANs to generate condition-specific MRI scans as part of a project for a renowned hospital in Bengaluru, India, improving the accuracy and robustness of cancer detection models.

The Problem

MRI-based cancer detection often suffers from data scarcity and class imbalances, particularly for rare tumor types or specific grades of malignancy. This limitation affects the performance of diagnostic models, which require diverse and representative training datasets to generalize effectively.

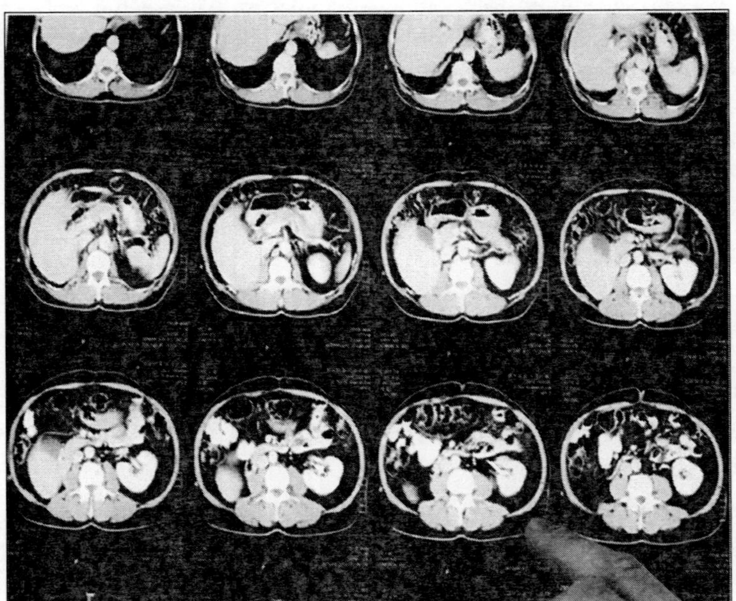

Figure 6.6: *MRI Scans are Used for Cancer Detection by Doctors*

Initially, traditional GANs were explored to generate synthetic MRI scans, but they failed to produce clinically meaningful and condition-specific images due to several challenges:

- **Lack of Control:** Standard GANs generate realistic images but do not allow conditioning on specific tumor attributes such as type, size, or location, making them unsuitable for targeted medical applications.
- **Mode Collapse:** The generator often produced limited variations, leading to repetitive outputs that lacked the subtle diversity required for medical diagnosis.
- **Training Instability:** Due to the high complexity of MRI data, traditional GANs struggled with training stability, resulting in unrealistic or low-resolution outputs.

Given with these shortcomings, the challenge was to augment datasets with high-quality, condition-specific synthetic MRI images that preserve subtle variations critical for accurate medical diagnosis. This necessitates a more structured generative approach, leading to the adoption of Conditional GANs (cGANs) to overcome these limitations.

Solution Approach

- **Conditional GANs** are employed to generate synthetic MRI images conditioned on tumor-specific attributes such as type (benign or malignant), size, and location.

  The generator is designed to produce realistic MRI scans that align with the given conditions, while the discriminator evaluates both the realism of the images, and their adherence to the specified conditions.

- **Data Augmentation for Imbalanced Datasets:**
  - Synthetic MRI images are generated for underrepresented classes, such as rare tumor types or specific grades of malignancy.
  - The augmented dataset provides the necessary diversity for training robust and generalizable cancer detection models.

Challenges:

- **Realism versus Specificity:** Generating MRI images that are not only realistic but also accurately reflect the specified conditions, such as tumor characteristics.
- **Training Stability:** Stabilizing the adversarial training process when dealing with high-dimensional MRI data, which can be computationally intensive.
- **Evaluation Metrics:** Establishing reliable evaluation criteria to measure the quality and utility of synthetic MRI images for diagnostic purposes.

Solution:

Generator and Discriminator Design:

- **Generator**: Combined noise vectors with one-hot encoded labels (for example, tumor type) and continuous variables (for example, tumor size and location) to generate synthetic MRI images.
- **Discriminator**: Evaluate the authenticity of the generated images, and check if they align with the specified conditions.

Regularization and Loss Functions:

- **Gradient Penalty**: Stabilized the training by enforcing smooth gradients in the discriminator.
- **Feature Matching**: Ensured that the generator learnt to produce diverse outputs by aligning feature distributions.
- **Integration with Detection Models**:
  - Synthetic MRI images were added to the training pipeline of diagnostic models to improve performance.
  - Models were fine-tuned using a combination of real and synthetic data to enhance generalization.

Outcome:

- **Augmented Dataset:** A significant increase in the volume and diversity of MRI data, particularly for rare tumor classes, leading to better-balanced datasets.
- **Enhanced Detection Accuracy:** Cancer detection models trained on augmented datasets showed improved accuracy and robustness, particularly for underrepresented conditions.

- **Visual Insights:** Synthetic MRI images exhibited realistic tumor characteristics, providing valuable training samples for both AI models and medical practitioners.

This case study highlights how Conditional GANs can address critical challenges in medical imaging by generating high-quality synthetic data, improving the performance of diagnostic models, and ultimately contributing to better patient outcomes.

Conclusion

In this chapter, we explored the architecture, working principles, and practical applications of Conditional GANs. By extending the traditional GAN framework with conditional inputs, cGANs enable controlled and targeted data generation, making them highly versatile across diverse domains. From generating class-specific images to augmenting datasets for underrepresented categories, cGANs demonstrate their utility in fields such as medical imaging, creative industries, and autonomous systems. We also examined the challenges associated with cGANs, including training instability, mode collapse, and difficulties in learning complex conditions. Practical solutions, such as label smoothing, feature matching, and regularization techniques, were discussed to address these issues effectively.

With a comprehensive understanding of cGANs, including hands-on implementation in TensorFlow and PyTorch, you are now well-equipped to leverage these models for solving real-world problems. In the next chapter, we will delve into CycleGANs, an advanced generative model designed for unpaired image-to-image translation. Building upon the foundational knowledge of GANs, we will explore how CycleGANs achieve transformations between domains, without requiring paired data, opening new possibilities for innovative applications.

Points to Remember

- Conditional GANs extend traditional GANs by incorporating conditional inputs, enabling controlled and targeted data generation.
- The generator combines noise vectors with conditional inputs to create outputs aligned with specified conditions.
- The discriminator evaluates both the authenticity of the generated samples, and their alignment with the conditions.
- Practical techniques such as label smoothing and feature matching enhance stability and diversity in cGAN training.
- cGANs are applied in areas such as medical imaging, data augmentation, image-to-image translation, and text-to-image synthesis.

Multiple Choice Questions

1. What is the primary advantage of using conditional inputs in cGANs?

    a. Increases training speed

    b. Reduces computational complexity

    c. Enhances the realism of generated samples

    d. Enables controlled and targeted generation

2. Which technique is commonly used to merge noise and conditional inputs in cGANs?
    a. Feature matching
    b. Gradient penalty
    c. Concatenation
    d. Normalization
3. What is a common challenge faced during cGAN training?
    a. Mode collapse
    b. Overfitting to the training data
    c. Limited diversity in conditions
    d. Excessive computational requirements
4. What role does the discriminator play in cGANs?
    a. Generates synthetic data conditioned on inputs
    b. Combines noise and labels for conditional inputs
    c. Evaluates authenticity and conditional alignment of inputs
    d. Normalizes activations in the network

Answers

1. d
2. c
3. a
4. c

Questions

1. How do conditional inputs enhance the generative capabilities of cGANs compared to traditional GANs?
2. What are the key architectural components of a cGAN, and how do they interact during training?
3. What strategies can be employed to prevent mode collapse in cGAN training?
4. Discuss the role of regularization techniques such as label smoothing in improving training stability.
5. What are some real-world applications of cGANs, and how do they benefit from conditional control?
6. How do conditional inputs affect the loss functions of the generator and discriminator?
7. Why is balancing diversity and specificity important in cGAN-generated outputs?
8. What are the primary differences between cGANs and other advanced GAN models?

9. How can monitoring the alignment between generated outputs and conditional inputs improve the training progress?
10. What future advancements could further improve the capabilities of cGANs?

Key Terms

- **Conditional Input:** Auxiliary data provided to both the generator and discriminator to guide the generative process.
- **Generator:** The component of a cGAN that creates synthetic data aligned with specified conditions.
- **Discriminator:** The component of a cGAN that evaluates both the authenticity of the data and its adherence to the conditions.
- **Concatenation:** A method of combining noise vectors and conditional inputs for the generator.
- **Label Smoothing:** A technique to prevent overfitting by slightly altering the target labels in the discriminator.
- **Mode Collapse:** A training issue where the generator produces limited variations in outputs.
- **Feature Matching:** A regularization technique that aligns feature distribution between the real and generated data.
- **Data Augmentation:** The use of synthetic data to expand and balance datasets.
- **Gradient Penalty:** A regularization technique that stabilizes cGAN training by enforcing smooth gradients in the discriminator.

Chapter 7
Cycle GANs

Introduction

Imagine being able to turn a daytime street photo into a nighttime one, or transform a sketch into a realistic image – all without ever showing matching examples of "*before*" and "*after*." That is the magic of Cycle-Consistent Generative Adversarial Networks or CycleGANs. These models can *translate* images from one world to another, and what makes them truly special is that they can learn these transformations without needing paired images. In this chapter, we will explore how CycleGANs make this possible in detail. You will discover the idea that allows an image to travel from one domain to another and back again, while still retaining its original meaning – a principle known as **cycle consistency**. Through practical exercises, you will build and train a CycleGAN step by step using **TensorFlow** and **PyTorch**. Thus, by the end of this chapter, you will not only master the core principles of CycleGANs but also understand their unique strengths, enabling you to create sophisticated models capable of learning complex mappings between unpaired image collections.

Structure

In this chapter, we will discuss the following topics:

- **Overview of CycleGANs and their Purpose**
  - The concept of cycle consistency
  - A real-world analogy: English to Chinese translator
  - Advantages of CycleGANs over paired data models
- **Key Differences between CycleGANs and Other GANs**
  - Training Methodology
  - The use of two generator-discriminator pairs
  - The role of cycle consistency loss
- **Data Preparation and Preprocessing**
  - Preprocessing techniques and data augmentation
  - Challenges in ensuring dataset diversity and quality
- **Architecture of CycleGANs**
  - Components of CycleGAN: Generators and Discriminators
  - Loss Functions
  - Role of the adversarial loss in training
  - The interplay between generators and discriminators
- **Implementing CycleGANs: Step-by-Step**
  - Key steps in implementing a CycleGAN
  - Example code snippets for building and training a CycleGAN
  - Visualizing translated outputs

- **Evaluating CycleGAN Performance**
- **Challenges and Limitations**
    - Common issues in training CycleGANs
    - The difficulty of generating high-resolution translations
    - Potential solutions, such as architectural modifications and improved loss functions
- **Applications of CycleGANs**
- **Ethical Considerations**
- **Case Study: Unpaired Image Translation with CycleGAN**

Overview of CycleGANs and Their Purpose

Unlike traditional approaches that require paired datasets for training, CycleGANs enable translation between two domains using unpaired datasets. For example, CycleGANs can convert images of horses to zebras, summer landscapes to winter scenes, or even Monet-style paintings to real-world photographs. This flexibility has made CycleGANs a valuable tool in domains such as art, medical imaging, and domain adaptation. The primary purpose of CycleGAN is to perform high-quality image translations, while ensuring that the transformations between domains maintain the original content and style characteristics.

At the heart of CycleGANs lies the idea of cycle consistency, which ensures that an image translated to another domain can be translated back to its original domain, without significant loss of information. This concept is a key differentiator from traditional GANs and conditional GANs (cGANs), where the focus is typically on single-direction translations with paired data.

The Concept of Cycle Consistency

The idea is simple yet powerful: If an image from domain A (for example, a horse) is translated to domain B (for example, a zebra), and then back to domain A, the resulting image should be identical or nearly identical to the original image. This principle is implemented through a specialized loss function called the cycle consistency loss. Let us break this down:

- **Forward Cycle Consistency**: Ensures that translating an image from domain A to B, and back to A results in an image similar to the original.
- **Backward Cycle Consistency**: Ensures that translating an image from domain B to A, and back to B results in an image similar to the original.

Thus, by enforcing these constraints, CycleGANs effectively align the distributions of the two domains, without paired data. This approach prevents the generators from making arbitrary or nonsensical transformations, ensuring meaningful and consistent translations.

A Real-World Analogy to Understand CycleGANs

Imagine you are a professional translator fluent in English and Chinese. You are given a book in English, and asked to translate it into Chinese. After completing the translation, another translator, who is also fluent in both languages, translates it back into English.

***Figure 7.1**: A Real-world Analogy, English to Chinese Translator*

If the final English version closely resembles the original book, it means the translation process preserved the essence of the content. However, if the book loses meaning or contains inconsistencies, the translators adjust their methods to improve accuracy.

This is exactly how CycleGANs work! They have two sets of generators to translate images from one domain to another, and then reconstruct them back – this is how it is different from other GANs.

- Translator A (Generator A) converts an image from English text to Chinese text.
- Translator B (Generator B) converts the translated text back into English.

If the reconstructed text does not match the original, the model improves its learning to ensure better translations.

Thus, CycleGANs are like professional translators who refine their skills by translating back and forth, until the meaning remains intact.

Understanding Paired vs Unpaired Datasets for Training Image Translation

Unlike standard GANs, CycleGANs do not require paired training data (that is, you do not need an exact English-Chinese sentence pair). Instead, they learn through this cycle consistency process.

The left side of the figure illustrates a paired dataset scenario. It features two images of the same landscape captured during different seasons–one in spring or summer, with lush green grass and a sunlit tree, and the other in winter, where snow blankets the ground, and the tree appears bare. Because both images depict the same location under different conditions, the dataset is structured and aligned, making it suitable for supervised learning techniques such as pix2pix. In this case, the model learns the precise transformation between summer and winter appearances by analyzing direct one-to-one mappings.

Figure 7.2: *Paired and Unpaired Datasets*

On the right side, a horse and a zebra are displayed side by side, representing an unpaired dataset. Unlike the left example, the two animals are not the same entity, meaning that there is no exact correspondence between a specific horse and its zebra equivalent. Instead, models like CycleGAN learn to translate between domains, without needing one-to-one mappings by enforcing cycle consistency—ensuring that a horse translated into a zebra, and then back into a horse remains recognizable. This allows CycleGAN to handle image-to-image translation tasks where paired data is unavailable, making it especially useful for artistic style transfer, domain adaptation, and other applications where collecting paired datasets is impractical.

Advantages of CycleGANs over Paired Data Models

Unlike traditional image-to-image translation models that require carefully curated datasets, CycleGANs operate effectively without the need for direct correspondences between source and target images. From artistic style transfer to medical imaging and domain adaptation, these models offer a practical solution for tasks that demand high-quality translations, while preserving essential image structures. Some of the key advantages are as follows:

- **Eliminating the Need for Paired Data:** Image-to-image translation models such as Pix2Pix require datasets with exact pairings (for example, a daytime photo and its corresponding nighttime version). Collecting such paired datasets is often labor-intensive, expensive, or even impossible for certain tasks. CycleGANs bypass this limitation by using unpaired datasets, where images from each domain are independent of the other.
- **Flexibility across Domains:** CycleGANs are versatile, and can handle a wide range of domain translation tasks, from artistic transformations to scientific applications. For instance:
  - **Artistic style transfer:** Converting photos into paintings or vice versa.
  - **Domain adaptation:** Translating synthetic images (for example, CGI) to real-world imagery.
  - **Medical imaging:** Converting CT scans to MRI scans.
- **Preservation of Content:** By enforcing cycle consistency, CycleGANs ensure that the core content of the image remains intact during translation. This makes the model particularly effective for tasks where maintaining structural integrity is critical, such as medical imaging or architectural transformations.
- **Simplicity in Implementation:** The architecture of CycleGANs is relatively straightforward, involving two generator-discriminator pairs, and a few key loss functions (adversarial loss

and cycle consistency loss). This simplicity makes CycleGANs accessible to developers and researchers, even those with limited experience in GANs.

- **Robustness to Diverse Datasets:** CycleGANs can handle diverse datasets with varying distribution, making them suitable for applications in fields like climate research, where the data often comes from different sources and conditions.
- **Scalability:** CycleGANs can be scaled to higher resolutions or more complex tasks by modifying their architecture or training strategies, making them a robust choice for evolving research and applications.

CycleGANs represent a significant leap forward in the field of image-to-image translation by enabling high-quality transformations. The concept of cycle consistency ensures that translations remain meaningful and reversible, while the model's inherent flexibility and scalability make it applicable to a wide range of real-world problems. Subsequent sections will dive deeper into the architecture, implementation, and applications of CycleGANs.

Key Differences between CycleGANs and Others

While traditional GANs and their variants such as conditional GANs (cGANs) have shown impressive results in generating data, CycleGANs stand out due to their unique capabilities and the implementation architecture. This section explores the key differences that set CycleGANs apart from other GAN models.

Training Methodology

CycleGAN works very differently compared to traditional GAN, DCGAN and cGAN in the way input data is provided, and the way training is done. As already discussed above, one of the most striking differences between CycleGANs and other GANs is their ability to work without paired datasets. In many real-world scenarios, obtaining paired data is impractical or impossible. For example, historical photographs cannot have paired modern-day equivalents.

CycleGANs address this limitation by using datasets, where images from two domains (for example, horses and zebras) are independent. The key to its success is the 'cycle' concept. It employs two generators:

- Generator G translates an image from Domain A (for example, a horse) to Domain B (a zebra).
- Generator F then translates that generated image back to Domain A (reconstructing the horse).

The model is then penalized if this cycled image is not similar to the original input. This cycle consistency loss acts as a powerful supervisory signal, allowing the model to learn the correct translation, without ever seeing an exact example of it. Thus, unlike other GANs that often rely on paired data or labels for their training, CycleGAN learns the underlying relationship between the two collections of images through this training cycle of translation and reconstruction.

The Use of Two Generator-Discriminator Pairs

Another critical distinction lies in the architecture of CycleGANs, which employs two generator-discriminator pairs, instead of one. This setup enables bi-directional translation, while maintaining the integrity of the original content.

Generators

- Translates images from domain X to domain Y.
- Translates images from domain Y to domain X.

Discriminators

- Distinguishes between real images from domain A and generated images from domain B translated back to A.
- Distinguishes between real images from domain B and generated images from domain A translated back to B.

This configuration ensures that the translation process is reversible, with each generator working collaboratively with its counterpart to achieve consistent results.

Advantages

- **Bidirectional Translation:** Enables learning mappings in both directions (for example, horse to zebra and zebra to horse) simultaneously.
- **Improved Consistency:** Ensures that translations remain coherent and reversible.
- **Flexibility:** Makes CycleGANs suitable for a variety of applications requiring bi-directional transformations.

The Role of Cycle Consistency Loss

The cycle consistency loss is the defining feature of CycleGANs and the key to their success in image-to-image translation. Unlike traditional GANs, which focus solely on generating realistic outputs, CycleGANs enforce a constraint that ensures the translation process is reversible and meaningful.

Understanding Cycle Consistency Loss in CycleGANs

Cycle consistency is composed of two components:

Forward Cycle Consistency:

- Ensures that an image x from domain A translates to domain B via Generator G, and then back to domain A via Generator F, resulting in an image close to the original.
- Mathematically expressed as: $F(G(x)) \approx x$
- This means that when an image is translated from A → B → A, the final image should be nearly identical to the original.

Backward Cycle Consistency:

- Ensures that an image y from domain B translates to domain A via Generator F, and then back to domain B via Generator G, resulting in an image close to the original.

  Mathematically expressed as: $G(F(y)) \approx y$
- This means that when an image is translated from B → A → B, the final image should be nearly identical to the original.

Mathematical Definition of Cycle Consistency Loss

The total Cycle Consistency Loss is defined as:

$$L_{cyc}(G, F) = E_{x \sim p_{data}(x)} [||F(G(x)) - x||_1] + E_{y \sim p_{data}(y)} [||G(F(y)) - y||_1]$$

Where:

- $E_{x \sim pdata(x)}$ represents the expected value over the data distribution of domain A.
- $E_{y \sim pdata(y)}$ represents the expected value over the data distribution of domain B.

- `G(x)` translates an image x from domain A to B.
- `F(G(x))` translates it back from B to A.
- `F(y)` translates an image y from domain B to A.
- `G(F(y))` translates it back from A to B.
- The L1 norm $\|\cdot\|_1$ is used as the loss function, which calculates the absolute difference between the original and the reconstructed images.

Impact on Training

- **Preserving Content:** Ensures that the translated image retains the core content of the original image.
- **Alignment of Domains:** Encourages the generators to learn mappings that align the distributions of the two domains.
- **Reduction of Artifacts:** Prevents arbitrary transformations that might degrade image quality or distort content.

Comparison with Adversarial Loss

While adversarial loss focuses on making the generated images indistinguishable from real images in the target domain, cycle consistency loss ensures that the transformation process is meaningful and reversible. Together, these two loss functions create a balanced training objective that promotes both realism and fidelity.

Feature	**Traditional GANs**	**CycleGANs**
Data Requirements	Paired datasets	Unpaired datasets
Architecture	Single generator - discriminator pair	Two generator - discriminator pairs
Key Loss Function	Adversarial loss	Adversarial loss + cycle consistency loss
Translation Direction	Single-directional	Bi-directional
Applications	Limited to paired data tasks	Broad, including unpaired tasks

Table 7.1: *Summary of Key Differences*

Thus, by addressing the challenges of data translation, and introducing innovative architectural and loss function designs, CycleGANs have revolutionized the field of image-to-image translation, opening new avenues for research and application. Subsequent sections will explore the working of CycleGANs, and their implementation in greater depth.

Data Preparation and Preprocessing

Before training a CycleGAN, it is crucial to ensure that the dataset is well-prepared and structured for effective learning. Proper data collection, organization, and augmentation techniques significantly impact the model's ability to learn meaningful transformations between domains. Preprocessing tasks such as resizing, normalizing, and handling imbalances also play a vital role in the training activity.

CycleGANs depend heavily on the quality and variety of the datasets used for training and introduces new challenges, such as maintaining domain diversity, alignment, and proper preprocessing. To train a CycleGAN, it is important to clearly define the two image domains between which translation will occur—such as photos of horses and zebras—each representing distinct visual characteristics the model can learn to map. These domains should be selected based on the goal of the application.

Datasets can be sourced from public datasets like ImageNet or COCO, scraped from the web using tools like Beautiful Soup or APIs, or generated synthetically using 3D rendering software. Regardless of the source, the datasets should be neatly organized in separate folders for each domain to simplify loading, and minimize errors during the training process.

Preprocessing Techniques and Data Augmentation

Preprocessing and data augmentation are critical in preparing datasets for CycleGAN training. These techniques improve the model's robustness and generalization capabilities, while ensuring that the data is suitable for the model architecture.

Image Resizing: CycleGANs typically operate on fixed input dimensions (for example, 128x128 or 256x256). All images should be resized to these dimensions to ensure consistency during training. Resizing can be achieved using tools like OpenCV or PIL in Python.

Normalization: Image pixel values are normalized to a specific range (for example, [-1, 1] or [0, 1]) to improve model convergence and stability. For instance, pixel values can be scaled using:

$$\text{Normalized Pixel} = \frac{\text{Pixel Value} - 127.5}{127.5}$$

Here 127.5 is the midpoint of the 0 to 255pixel range. Dividing by 127.5 scales the values to a range of [-1, 1], which is more suitable for training deep learning models.

The following table shows some sample calculations:

Pixel Value	Normalized Value
0	$\frac{0-127.5}{127.5} = -1$
127.5	$\frac{127.5-127.5}{127.5} = 0$
255	$\frac{255-127.5}{127.5} = 1$

Figure 7.3: *Data Normalization Preprocessing Technique*

Data Augmentation

Augmentation helps increase dataset diversity, and in turn helps prevent overfitting. Some of the common augmentation techniques include:

- **Random Cropping**: Extract random sub-regions of images.
- **Horizontal Flipping:** Flip images horizontally to create mirrored versions.
- **Color Jittering:** Adjust brightness, contrast, saturation, and hue.
- **Rotation and Scaling:** Apply small rotations or scaling transformations to simulate variations.

The following is a sample code for Data Augmentation:

```
from torchvision import datasets, transforms
# 3. Data augmentation + transformation
transform = transforms.Compose([
    transforms.Resize((160, 160)),
    transforms.RandomHorizontalFlip(),
    transforms.RandomRotation(15),
```

```
        transforms.ColorJitter(brightness=0.1, contrast=0.1),
        transforms.ToTensor(),
        transforms.Normalize([0.5], [0.5])
    ])
```

The preceding Python Code snippet demonstrates data augmentation using Torch vision's transforms module. Additionally, other libraries such as Augmentations and OpenCV can also be utilized for similar tasks. TensorFlow offers built-in augmentation capabilities through both **`tf.image`** and Keras' **`ImageDataGenerator`**, providing flexible options for preprocessing, and enhancing the training data.

Challenges in Ensuring Dataset Diversity and Quality

While unpaired datasets simplify data collection, they also introduce unique challenges that can impact model performance.

Limited Diversity: If the dataset lacks diversity, the model may fail to generalize well to unseen examples. For instance:

- A dataset of zebras containing only black-and-white striped zebras may struggle to translate to brown zebras or zebras in different environments.
- A dataset of horses limited to specific breeds or poses may result in translations that fail on other horse varieties.

To enhance diversity:

- Source images from multiple environments, perspectives, and lighting conditions.
- Include variations in texture, style, and other domain-specific characteristics.

Domain Gaps: Significant differences in image quality, resolution, or lighting conditions between the two domains can make it harder for the model to learn meaningful mappings. For example:

- Domain A might consist of high-resolution studio photographs.
- Domain B might include low-quality images with inconsistent lighting.

To address domain gaps:

- Normalize image quality by resizing and applying consistent preprocessing steps.
- Use domain adaptation techniques to bridge the gap between the datasets.

Data Labeling and Annotation Errors

Although unpaired datasets do not require explicit annotations, mislabeled or irrelevant images can introduce noise into the training process. For example:

- Including non-horse images in the horse domain can confuse the model.
- Irrelevant zebra images, such as abstract patterns resembling zebra stripes, may lead to incorrect mappings.

To mitigate these issues:

- Perform manual inspection of datasets or use automated filtering techniques to identify and remove outliers.
- Use clustering or feature extraction techniques to validate dataset consistency.

Scalability: Large-scale datasets increase the training time and computational requirements. For instance, training CycleGANs on high-resolution datasets (for example, 1024x1024) requires significant GPU memory and processing power. Balancing dataset size and quality is essential for efficient training.

Proper data preparation and preprocessing are foundational steps in the CycleGAN pipeline. Thus, by carefully gathering, preprocessing, and augmenting unpaired datasets, as well as addressing challenges such as domain gaps and diversity, practitioners can ensure that their CycleGAN models are well-equipped to produce high-quality translations.

Architecture of CycleGANs

The CycleGAN architecture is designed for image-to-image translation by employing a dual-generator framework. Its primary objective is to learn mappings between two domains, without requiring paired datasets. The architecture achieves this through the use of two generators and two discriminators, working collaboratively to ensure high-quality and consistent translations.

At its core, the CycleGAN architecture consists of:

1. **Two Generators:** Responsible for translating images between the two domains.
2. **Two Discriminators:** Evaluate the authenticity of the generated images in each domain.
3. **Loss Functions:** Ensure that the model learns to generate realistic and consistent outputs, incorporating adversarial loss and cycle consistency loss.

The interaction between these components enables CycleGANs to perform bidirectional translations, while preserving the structural and semantic integrity of the input images.

Components of CycleGAN

The innovative approach of CycleGAN, combined with adversarial training, allows it to generate high-quality, realistic transformations across a wide range of tasks. The architecture achieves this through the interplay of two generators and two discriminators, working collaboratively to enforce realism and consistency in the translations.

Generators

The CycleGAN model employs two generators:

- Generator G: Translates images from A to B (for example, horse to zebra).
- Generator F: Translates images from B to A (for example, zebra to horse).

Each generator is a neural network that uses convolutional layers, normalization layers, and non-linear activation functions to learn the mapping between the two domains. A common architecture for generators in CycleGANs is the ResNet-based generator, which consists of:

- **Downsampling Layers**: Extract features from the input image.
- **Residual Blocks:** Learn transformations while preserving essential content.
- **Up sampling Layers**: Reconstruct the image in the target domain.

Discriminators

The discriminators in CycleGANs are responsible for distinguishing real images from the generated images within each domain:

- **Discriminator D_A**: Distinguishes between real images from domain A, and fake images generated by F.
- **Discriminator D_B:** Distinguishes between real images from domain B, and fake images generated by G.

CycleGANs often use a PatchGAN discriminator, which evaluates image patches, rather than the entire image. This approach:

- Reduces computational complexity.
- Focuses on local features, which are critical for maintaining texture and style consistency.

Loss Functions

CycleGANs leverage multiple loss functions to achieve high-quality and consistent translations:

Adversarial Loss: Ensures that the generated images are indistinguishable from real images in the target domain. For generator G and discriminator D_B, the adversarial loss is:

$$L_{GAN}(G, D_B) = E_{y \sim p_{data}(y)} [\log D_B(y)] + E_{x \sim p_{data}(x)} [\log(1 - D_B(G(x)))]$$

Here, $D_B(y)$ is the probability assigned by the discriminator D_B that image y is real.

E represents the expectation (average value) over real images from the domain.

- **Cycle Consistency Loss:** Cycle Consistency Loss ensures that translations between domains are reversible. It is made up of two parts, the forward cycle consistency and the backward cycle consistency. The total cycle consistency loss is the sum of both these losses.
- **Forward Cycle Consistency:** Forward cycle consistency ensures that translating an image from domain A to domain B and back to domain A results in an image that closely resembles the original image from domain A.

  For example:

  - A photo of a sedan (domain A) is translated to an SUV-like image (domain B) using Generator G.
  - This SUV-like image is then translated back to the sedan domain using Generator F.
  - The final sedan image is compared with the original sedan image to calculate the forward cycle consistency loss.

  This process is mathematically expressed as:

$$L_{cyc}^{forward}(G,F)=E_{x \sim p_{data}(x)}[||F(G(x))-x||_1]$$

  where:

  - G: Generator for domain A to B.
  - F: Generator for domain B to A.
  - x: Image from domain A.
  - $\|\cdot\|_1$: loss function measuring the reconstruction error.
  - E Represents the expectation (average) over the data distribution of domain
- **Backward Cycle Consistency:** Similarly, backward cycle consistency ensures that translating an image from domain B to domain A and then back to domain B produces an image similar to the original image from domain B. This is defined as:

$$L_{cyc}^{backward}(G,F)=E_{y \sim p_{data}(y)}[\|G(F(y))-y\|1]$$

where:

- $F(y)$: Generator F translates an image y from domain B to domain A.
- $G(F(y))$: Generator G then translates the transformed image back from domain A to domain B.
- y: Image sampled from the dataset of domain B.
- E: The expectation operator averages the loss over the entire dataset

- **Total Cycle Consistency Loss:** The forward and backward cycle consistency losses are combined to form the total cycle consistency loss.

$$L_{cyc}(G, F) = L_{cyc}^{forward} + L_{cyc}^{backward}$$

This loss ensures that the generators learn mappings that are reversible, and maintain the content integrity of the images.

- **Identity Loss**: The identity loss is an additional constraint in CycleGANs that ensures that images already belonging to the target domain remain unchanged when passed through the generator. This prevents unnecessary modifications, and improves the stability of the model.

The formula for identity loss is:

$$L_{identity}(G) = E_{y \sim p_{data}(y)} [||G(y) - y||_1]$$

The total loss combines these components to guide the training process:

$$L_{total} = L_{GAN}(G, D_B) + L_{GAN}(F, D_A) + \lambda L_{cyc}(G, F)$$

where λ lambda is a weight parameter balancing the cycle consistency loss.

These losses play a crucial role in ensuring high-quality image translations in CycleGANs. Identity loss prevents unnecessary modifications to images already in the target domain, making transformations more natural. Cycle consistency loss enforces reversibility, ensuring that translations do not produce arbitrary changes. Adversarial loss ensures that generated images closely resemble real samples, improving realism. Together, these components contribute to the total loss function, which maintains a balance between realism, content preservation, and meaningful transformation.

Role of the Adversarial Loss in Training

Adversarial loss plays a salient role in CycleGAN training by ensuring that the generated images appear realistic and indistinguishable from real images in the target domain. This loss is based on the adversarial game between generators and discriminators, where the generators aim to produce high-quality translations, and the discriminators evaluate their authenticity.

Each generator in CycleGAN is paired with a corresponding discriminator which ensures that:

- Generator G translates images from domain A to domain B, while Discriminator D_B evaluates whether the generated images truly resemble those in domain B. The goal of G is to produce images that fool D_B, while D_B tries to distinguish between real and fake images.
- Similarly, Generator F translates images from domain B to domain A, and Discriminator D_A ensures that the translated images look like authentic domain A samples. Just like in the previous case, F attempts to generate convincing transformations, while D_A learns to detect any inconsistencies.

Through this adversarial process, the generators continuously improve their outputs, making them more realistic with each training step. The discriminators, in turn, become better at distinguishing between real and generated images, creating a feedback loop that drives the model towards more effective domain translation.

The total adversarial loss is a combination of the losses from both generator-discriminator pairs. This ensures that CycleGAN does not just generate visually convincing images but also maintains consistency in translating between the two domains. Therefore, by balancing the competition between generators and discriminators, adversarial loss enables CycleGANs to learn domain mappings without requiring paired datasets, making them highly effective for unpaired image-to-image translation tasks.

The Interplay between Generators and Discriminators

The effectiveness of CycleGANs comes from the continuous interaction between the generators and discriminators during training. This process follows a competitive framework where the generators attempt to create realistic images, while the discriminators work to distinguish between real and generated images. This adversarial relationship helps improve the quality of translations over time.

Training Dynamics

During training, each component plays a distinct role:

- **Discriminators' Role:** The discriminators assess the images produced by the generators, determining whether they belong to the real dataset or are artificially generated. If a generated image is too unrealistic, the discriminator forces the generator to refine its output.
- **Generators' Role:** The generators aim to deceive the discriminators by producing images that are as indistinguishable from real samples as possible. At the same time, they must maintain cycle consistency, ensuring that an image translated to another domain and back remains structurally similar to the original.

Balancing Realism and Consistency

For CycleGANs to generate high-quality transformations, there must be a balance between two competing objectives:

- Realism, ensured by the adversarial loss, which pushes the model to produce outputs that resemble real images.
- Consistency, enforced by cycle consistency loss, which ensures that transformations remain reversible and preserve content integrity.

A well-tuned balance between these losses prevents the model from focusing too much on one aspect at the expense of the other. If adversarial loss dominates, the model may generate highly realistic images that are inconsistent when mapped back to the original domain. If the cycle consistency loss is too strong, the transformations may become conservative, reducing the ability to generate meaningful domain shifts.

Avoiding Mode Collapse

A common issue in GAN-based models is mode collapse, where the generator produces limited variations of images instead of learning diverse transformations. Cycle consistency loss helps mitigate this by ensuring that generators do not simply map all inputs to a few fixed outputs. Instead, it encourages diverse and meaningful translations that preserve structural integrity across both domains.

Summary of the Working Mechanism

CycleGANs operate through a collaborative process where:

- Generators learn bidirectional mappings between two domains, while preserving content integrity.
- Discriminators provide constructive feedback to refine the realism of the generated images.
- Cycle consistency loss ensures that the transformations remain reversible and meaningful.

Thus, by leveraging this interplay, CycleGANs successfully perform image translation, achieving high-quality, coherent transformations even in scenarios where paired training data is unavailable.

Implementing CycleGANs: Step-by-Step

Building a CycleGAN requires careful implementation of multiple components, and training strategies to ensure correct implementation. Hence, by leveraging two generators, two discriminators, and cycle consistency loss, CycleGANs learn to transform images between two domains, while preserving key structural details. The following sections outline the step-by-step process for implementing a CycleGAN, from dataset preprocessing to training and visualization.

Key Steps in Implementing a CycleGAN

Implementing a CycleGAN involves several key steps, from preparing the dataset to building the model architecture, and training the model. The following is an outline of the process:

- **Data Preparation**
  - Collect and preprocess unpaired datasets for the two domains (for example, photos of horses and zebras).
  - Apply resizing, normalization, and data augmentation to improve training stability and model generalization.
- **Model Architecture**
  - **Define two generators**: One for translating images from domain A to domain B and another for translating images from domain B to domain A.
  - **Define two discriminators**: One for each domain, responsible for evaluating the authenticity of generated images.
- **Loss Functions**
  - Implement adversarial loss to ensure the generated images are realistic.
  - Add cycle consistency loss to maintain the integrity of the original content after translation.
  - Optionally, include identity loss to further stabilize the training process.
- **Training Loop**
  - Train the generators and discriminators iteratively.
  - Alternate updates between the generator and discriminator networks for stable adversarial training.
- **Visualization**
  - Save and visualize translated images during training to monitor progress and assess the quality of the outputs.

Example Code Snippets for Building a CycleGAN

The following is a simplified example using PyTorch for implementing a CycleGAN. The example focuses on defining the key components and training loop.

Defining the Generator

```
import torch
import torch.nn as nn

def generator_block(in_channels, out_channels, kernel_size, stride, padding):
    return nn.Sequential(
        nn.Conv2d(in_channels, out_channels, kernel_size, stride, padding),
        nn.InstanceNorm2d(out_channels),
        nn.ReLU(inplace=True)
    )

class Generator(nn.Module):
    def __init__(self):
        super(Generator, self).__init__()
        self.model = nn.Sequential(
            generator_block(3, 64, 7, 1, 3),
            generator_block(64, 128, 3, 2, 1),
            generator_block(128, 256, 3, 2, 1),
            *[ResidualBlock(256) for _ in range(9)],
            nn.ConvTranspose2d(256, 128, 3, 2, 1, output_padding=1),
            nn.ConvTranspose2d(128, 64, 3, 2, 1, output_padding=1),
            nn.Conv2d(64, 3, 7, 1, 3),
            nn.Tanh()
        )

    def forward(self, x):
        return self.model(x)

class ResidualBlock(nn.Module):
    def __init__(self, channels):
        super(ResidualBlock, self).__init__()
        self.block = nn.Sequential(
            nn.Conv2d(channels, channels, 3, 1, 1),
            nn.InstanceNorm2d(channels),
            nn.ReLU(inplace=True),
            nn.Conv2d(channels, channels, 3, 1, 1),
            nn.InstanceNorm2d(channels)
        )

    def forward(self, x):
        return x + self.block(x)
```

Defining the Discriminator

To build a discriminator for CycleGAN, follow a structure similar to the generator, but with a few key differences tailored to its purpose. While the generator transforms images from one domain to another, the discriminator acts as a binary classifier that determines whether a given image is real (from the dataset) or fake (generated).

Start by creating a series of convolutional blocks with increasing feature channels. These blocks should reduce the spatial dimensions progressively, while capturing finer texture details. Use a kernel size of 4, stride of 2, and padding of 1 for most layers to downsample effectively, and apply LeakyReLU activations instead of ReLU to allow small gradients for negative values. Use Instance Normalization (not BatchNorm) after each convolution except the first and last layers to maintain stable training.

Instead of outputting a single value, your final layer should produce a 2D map (using a 1-channel convolution) – this is known as a PatchGAN discriminator. Each value in the output map corresponds to the discriminator's prediction for a small patch in the input image, encouraging it to focus on local realism and texture.

This setup allows the discriminator to provide fine-grained feedback to the generator, helping it produce more detailed and realistic outputs. Design your discriminator as a standalone PyTorch module, just like the generator, and initialize one for each domain (for example, Discriminator A for domain A, Discriminator B for domain B) during training.

Visualizing Translated Outputs

Visualizing the translated images during training helps monitor the model's performance, and identify potential issues like mode collapse or training instability.

Saving Translated Outputs

```
import torchvision.transforms as transforms
from PIL import Image

def save_images(real_A, fake_B, reconstructed_A, epoch, i):
    transform = transforms.ToPILImage()
    real_A_img = transform(real_A.squeeze(0))
    fake_B_img = transform(fake_B.squeeze(0))
    reconstructed_A_img = transform(reconstructed_A.squeeze(0))

    real_A_img.save(f"output/real_A_epoch{epoch}_batch{i}.png")
    fake_B_img.save(f"output/fake_B_epoch{epoch}_batch{i}.png")
    reconstructed_A_img.save(f"output/reconstructed_A_epoch{epoch}_batch{i}.png")
```

Visualizing during Training

Use a library like Matplotlib to visualize the results:

```
import matplotlib.pyplot as plt

def plot_images(real_A, fake_B, reconstructed_A):
    images = [real_A, fake_B, reconstructed_A]
    titles = ["Real A", "Fake B", "Reconstructed A"]

    plt.figure(figsize=(10, 5))
    for i, img in enumerate(images):
        plt.subplot(1, 3, i + 1)
        plt.imshow(img.permute(1, 2, 0).detach().cpu().numpy())
        plt.title(titles[i])
        plt.axis("off")
    plt.show()
```

With these steps and tools, you can implement, train, and evaluate a CycleGAN model effectively, tailoring it to your specific application needs.

Evaluating CycleGAN Performance

Assessing the effectiveness of a CycleGAN model is crucial to ensure that it generates high-quality, realistic image translations, while preserving key structural details. Unlike traditional supervised models, CycleGANs operate in an unsupervised setting, making evaluation more challenging. A comprehensive assessment involves both quantitative metrics which measure aspects like image fidelity, domain alignment, and qualitative analysis that examine the perceptual realism of the generated images. Thus, by combining these approaches, researchers and practitioners can gain a deeper understanding of how well the model performs across different domains, and optimize it for better results.

Common Metrics

Frechet Inception Distance (FID): FID is a widely used metric to evaluate the quality of generated images by comparing their distribution to that of real images. It computes the Wasserstein distance between feature representations extracted from a pre-trained Inception network.

- **Formula:**

$$FID=||\mu_r - \mu_g||^2+Tr(\Sigma_r+\Sigma_g-2\sqrt{\Sigma_r\Sigma_g})$$

  Where:

  - μ_r and μ_g: The mean feature vectors of real and generated images, respectively. These are extracted from the Inception network at an intermediate layer, capturing high-level image features.
  - Σ_r and Σ_g: Covariance matrices of real and generated images, respectively.
- **Strengths:**
  - Captures both image quality and diversity.
  - Sensitive to artifacts in generated images.
- **Limitations:**
  - Requires sufficient samples for accurate estimation.
  - Depends on the choice of the pre-trained network.

Perceptual Loss: Perceptual loss measures the similarity between images based on feature representations extracted from a pre-trained network (for example, VGG). Unlike pixel-wise losses, it focuses on high-level semantic similarities.

- **Use Case**: Evaluates whether the generated images preserve content structure and style during translation.
- **Strengths**: Aligns better with human perception than simple pixel-wise losses.

Human Evaluation: This remains the gold standard for assessing the realism and relevance of generated images. Human judges are asked to compare real and generated images or rate the quality of translations based on specific criteria.

- **Criteria for Evaluation:**
  - **Realism**: How realistic does the image appear?
  - **Relevance**: Does the translation align with the target domain?
  - **Content Preservation**: Is the structure of the original image maintained?

Techniques for Qualitative and Quantitative Evaluation: Evaluating a CycleGAN involves both visual inspection and quantitative metrics, as traditional pixel-wise comparisons often fall short. Methods like cycle consistency checks, diversity analysis, and FID scores help assess realism and translation accuracy. Combining these approaches allows for better model refinement.

Visual Inspection: Visual examination of generated images remains the simplest method of evaluation. It helps assess whether structural integrity, such as poses and edges, is preserved, whether the output matches the style of the target domain, and whether the image is free from visual artifacts or distortions.

Cycle Consistency: This ensures the reversibility of translations, where a forward cycle ($G(F(A)) \approx A$) and a backward cycle ($F(G(B)) \approx B$) aim to reconstruct the original inputs. Inspecting these reconstructions provides insight into the consistency and stability of the translation process.

Output Diversity: Evaluating output diversity helps ensure the model captures variation within the target domain. This is done by generating results for a range of inputs and measuring differences across outputs using statistical methods such as computing feature-space standard deviations.

Quantitative Metrics: Quantitative evaluation includes comparing feature distributions of real and generated images using metrics like FID or KL divergence. In addition, reconstruction errors within the cycle, often measured using L1 or L2 losses, help quantify how accurately the model preserves content through translation.

Ablation Studies: Ablation studies systematically test the importance of model components by modifying or removing them and observing performance changes. For CycleGANs, this might include removing the cycle consistency loss, analyzing the role of identity loss, or comparing different architectural designs such as ResNet and U-Net.

Task-Specific Metrics: In domain-specific applications, tailored metrics offer deeper insight. For instance, style transfer tasks may use measures of style similarity, while in medical imaging, metrics like the Dice coefficient or Intersection over Union (IoU) help evaluate structural accuracy between input and output images.

Hybrid Evaluation: The most effective evaluation approach combines both quantitative metrics, such as FID or perceptual loss, and qualitative assessments like visual inspection or human judgment. This hybrid method ensures that the model performs well in both measurable accuracy and perceived image quality.

Challenges and Limitations

While CycleGANs have revolutionized unpaired image-to-image translation, they come with their own set of challenges and limitations. Understanding these issues, and exploring potential solutions is crucial for improving the performance and applicability of CycleGANs.

Common Issues in Training CycleGANs

Training CycleGANs often feels like balancing on a tightrope, because the model's two networks are learning in opposition while trying to maintain consistency across domains. This delicate setup makes the system prone to instability, repetition, and sensitivity to even small changes in configuration. Understanding these common issues is the first step toward building more reliable and higher-quality image translation models.

Training Instability

Training GAN-based models, including CycleGANs, is notoriously unstable due to the adversarial nature of their architecture. The generator and discriminator networks are engaged in a minimax game, where:

- The generator tries to produce outputs that can fool the discriminator.
- The discriminator tries to distinguish real images from the generated ones.

This adversarial interplay can lead to:

- **Vanishing Gradients:** When the discriminator becomes too strong, it may overpower the generator, leading to minimal gradient updates for the generator.
- **Exploding Gradients:** When the generator overpowers the discriminator, it may produce unrealistic images, causing the training process to diverge.

Mode Collapse

Mode collapse is a common problem where the generator produces limited variations of the output, regardless of the input diversity. For example:

- A CycleGAN trained to translate horses to zebras may consistently generate the same zebra pattern for all horse images.

Mode collapse reduces the diversity and generalizability of the model, limiting its practical utility.

Sensitivity to Hyperparameters

CycleGAN training is highly sensitive to hyperparameters, such as learning rates, loss function weights, and batch sizes. Poor choices can lead to suboptimal performance or failed training runs.

Difficulty of Generating High-Resolution Translations

Generating high-resolution images (for example, 1024×1024 or higher) is a significant challenge for CycleGANs due to:

- **Computational Complexity:** High-resolution images require more memory and computational power, making training slower and more resource-intensive.
- **Artifacts:** The model may struggle to maintain consistency in fine details, resulting in visible artifacts or distortions.
- **Gradient Vanishing in Deep Networks:** The deeper the network, the more likely gradients are to vanish, making it difficult to optimize high-resolution models effectively.

Potential Solutions

To address training instability and high-resolution challenges, several architectural improvements can be made:

- **Use of Attention Mechanisms:** Incorporating attention layers (for example, self-attention) helps the model focus on important regions of the image, improving detail preservation, and reducing artifacts.
- **Multi-Scale Architectures**: Multi-scale generators and discriminators process images at different resolutions, capturing both global structure and local details.
- **PatchGAN Discriminator:** The PatchGAN discriminator evaluates image patches, rather than the entire image, reducing computational complexity, and improving texture consistency.

Improved Loss Functions

Enhancing the loss functions can help stabilize training, and improve translation quality:

- **Least-Squares GAN Loss:** Replacing the standard adversarial loss with least-squares loss can prevent vanishing gradients, and improve convergence.
- **Wasserstein Loss:** Using Wasserstein loss with gradient penalty (WGAN-GP) improves training stability, and addresses mode collapse.
- **Perceptual Loss:** Adding perceptual loss ensures that high-level features are preserved during translation, reducing the risk of artifacts.

Advanced Training Techniques

- **Learning Rate Scheduling**: Gradual reduction of the learning rate during training helps avoid overfitting, and ensures smoother convergence.
- **Data Augmentation**: Applying extensive data augmentation (for example, cropping, flipping, and color jittering) improves the model's robustness to diverse input variations.
- **Instance Normalization:** Replacing batch normalization with instance normalization in the generator reduces style inconsistencies, especially for tasks like artistic style transfer.

Progressive Growing

Progressive growing is an effective approach for training high-resolution models. The model starts with low-resolution images, and gradually increases the resolution as training progresses. This method:

- Reduces computational requirements during early training.
- Allows the model to learn coarse features before focusing on finer details.

Regularization Techniques

Regularization helps prevent overfitting, and improves generalization:

- **Dropout:** Randomly dropping neurons during training prevents the model from over-relying on specific features.
- **Label Smoothing**: Using soft labels (for example, 0.9 for real and 0.1 for fake) reduces overconfidence in the discriminator, stabilizing training.

Thus, by addressing these issues, researchers and practitioners can unlock the full potential of CycleGANs, enabling their application to a broader range of tasks and industries.

Applications of CycleGANs

CycleGANs have found powerful applications across art, healthcare, computer vision, and much more. Their flexibility allows for a wide range of transformations that are not only visually compelling but also practically useful in both creative and industrial fields. Some of the important areas are explained as follows:

- **Artistic Style Transfer:** CycleGANs are popularly used for transforming images from one artistic style to another–such as converting a photograph into a painting in the style of Monet or Van Gogh. This enables artists and designers to generate stylistic content automatically, without needing original artworks and their photo counterparts as training data.

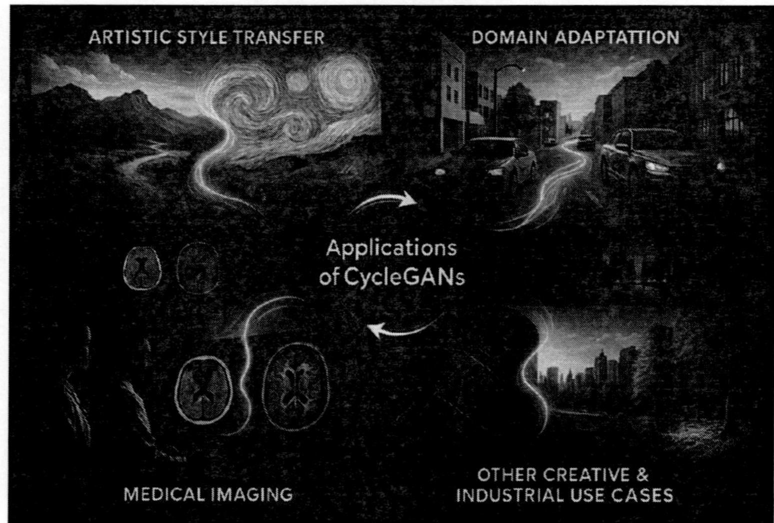

Figure 7.4*: Various Applications of CycleGAN*

- **Domain Adaptation:** In domain adaptation, CycleGANs are valuable for translating synthetic images–such as those from simulations–into realistic visuals. This is especially beneficial in fields like autonomous driving, where real-world data is limited, and adapting simulated environments can help train robust AI systems.
- **Medical Imaging:** CycleGANs contribute to healthcare by enabling translation between different medical imaging modalities such as converting CT scans into MRI images. This aids in comprehensive diagnosis, reduces the need for multiple costly scans, and improves the availability of multimodal data for research and analysis.
- **Other Creative and Industrial Use Cases:** Beyond art and medicine, CycleGANs are used in areas such as satellite-to-map translation, night-to-day image conversion, and even changing seasons or weather conditions in images. Their ability to generalize across visual domains makes them a powerful tool for content creation, simulation, and visual data enhancement.

Ethical Considerations

The rise of CycleGANs has enabled impressive advancements in image-to-image translation, but it also presents significant ethical concerns. These models can be misused to create misleading content such as deep fakes or fabricated evidence, posing risks in media, legal, and political domains. Additionally, if trained on biased or unrepresentative datasets, CycleGANs can reinforce harmful stereotypes and exclude marginalized groups, particularly in sensitive areas like healthcare or design. Privacy is another major concern, as models may use data without consent or enable de-anonymization of protected identities. Furthermore, the high computational demands of training CycleGANs contribute to environmental harm through large carbon footprints.

To ensure ethical use, developers should commit to transparency by labeling synthetic content and making models explainable. Careful dataset curation is essential to mitigate bias and protect privacy. Deployment should be limited to clearly beneficial use cases, with access controls to prevent misuse. Environmentally responsible training practices, such as optimizing model efficiency and using green energy, should be adopted. Collaboration with ethicists, regulators, and diverse communities can guide responsible innovation. Lastly, promoting public awareness and integrating ethics into AI education will foster a culture of accountability and informed use.

Case Study: Restaurant Menu Image Translation

Creating visually appealing restaurant menu images is a challenge, especially when dealing with raw photos captured in inconsistent lighting and cluttered backgrounds. Traditional editing methods are manual and time-consuming. This case study explores how CycleGANs can automate the transformation of raw food images into professional-grade menu visuals using unpaired datasets, enabling stylistic enhancement and background removal without explicit image pairs.

Problem: Enhancing Food Images for Delivery Platform

`Grxbxnxi-dot-com` (name changed), a food delivery platform, faced inconsistent and unprofessional food images submitted by restaurants, which negatively impacted customer experience. Manual enhancement was inefficient and unsustainable. To address this, a CycleGAN was designed to translate unprocessed food photos into stylized, clean menu images through unpaired image-to-image translation.

Solution: Designing a CycleGAN for Domain Adaptation

To tackle inconsistent and unprofessional food images in the application, a CycleGAN was used to automate background removal and style enhancement using unpaired image translation, producing high-quality, uniform visuals across listings.

Data Collection and Preparation

- **Domain A:** Unprocessed photos of dishes submitted by restaurants on the platform, including user-generated content and images captured in different lighting conditions.
- **Domain B:** Optimized, professional menu images with uniform backgrounds and lighting, reflecting the ideal presentation for food listings on the platform.
- **Preprocessing:** Images were resized to 256x256 pixels and normalized to [-1, 1] to ensure uniformity during training.
- **Data Augmentation:** Techniques such as random cropping, flipping, and color jittering, were applied to improve model robustness.

Model Architecture

- Two generators were implemented:
  - G_A→B: Translated raw food photos to stylized menu images.
  - G_B→A: Translated stylized menu images back to raw food photos.
- Two discriminators were used:
  - $\mathbf{D_A}$: Differentiated between real and fake images in domain A.
  - $\mathbf{D_B}$: Differentiated between real and fake images in domain B.
- The model used a ResNet-based architecture for the generators, with residual blocks to maintain content consistency during translation.

Loss Functions

- **Adversarial Loss**: Ensured that the translated images resembled real images in the target domain.
- **Cycle Consistency Loss:** Enforced that translations were reversible, preserving the original image content.
- **Identity Loss:** Stabilized the model by encouraging minimal changes for images already in the target domain.

Training

- The model was trained for 200 epochs using a batch size of 16 on a dataset of 5,000 images for each domain.
- The Adam optimizer was used with a learning rate of 0.0002 and beta values of (0.5, 0.999).
- Visual outputs were generated and saved after every 10 epochs to monitor progress.

Challenges: Consistency and Diversity in Translations

While the CycleGAN model effectively translated raw food images into professional menu visuals, several challenges arose during training. These included maintaining background consistency, ensuring stylistic diversity, and stabilizing adversarial learning. Addressing these issues involved refining the dataset, tuning loss functions, and applying regularization techniques to enhance image quality.

For background consistency, the model sometimes left traces or failed to isolate fine details like garnishes. This was improved by adding complex examples for example, transparent backgrounds) and applying perceptual loss. In terms of style, some outputs lacked variation or appeared overly processed. A style regularization term was added to balance uniformity and diversity. To prevent mode collapse and training instability, loss weights were adjusted, and learning rate decay was introduced after 100 epochs.

Outcome: Results and Insights for Future Applications

Visual Results

- The CycleGAN successfully translated raw food photos into stylized menu images with clean, professional backgrounds, and consistent color grading.
- The model preserved intricate details such as the texture of food and reflections on cutlery, while removing complex or cluttered backgrounds.
- Examples of translated outputs included:
    - A bowl of noodles with a messy kitchen background transformed into an image with a pristine white background.
    - A burger photo with uneven lighting adjusted to a vibrant, evenly lit presentation.

Quantitative Metrics

- FID Score: Improved from 52.3 (baseline) to 22.8, indicating high-quality outputs.
- User Study: In a blind test with 50 participants, 85% preferred the CycleGAN-generated menu images over raw photos for professional use.

Insights for Future Applications

- **Scalability:** The model can be extended to other domains such as e-commerce product photography or real estate listings, where background removal and styling are critical.
- **Customization:** By training on domain-specific datasets, the model can produce tailored outputs for different aesthetic preferences.
- **Integration:** The model can be integrated into photo-editing pipelines for restaurants, allowing real-time processing of new menu images.

This project demonstrates the practical value of CycleGANs in automating the transformation of raw food photos into polished, professional visuals, significantly reducing manual effort, and enhancing the visual appeal of restaurant menus.

Conclusion

In this chapter, we explored the architecture, working principles, and real-world applications of CycleGANs. Unlike traditional GANs and Conditional GANs (cGANs), CycleGANs enable unpaired image-to-image translation by learning transformations between domains, without requiring explicitly matched image pairs. We examined the key components of CycleGANs, including the dual-generator and dual-discriminator framework, and how cycle consistency loss ensures that translations remain meaningful and reversible. Additionally, we discussed the training challenges associated with CycleGANs, such as mode collapse, instability, and maintaining structural integrity in translations, along with techniques to address these issues, including perceptual loss, regularization, and adaptive learning rate scheduling.

With hands-on implementation in TensorFlow and PyTorch, you are now well-equipped to build and optimize CycleGAN models for a wide range of applications. In the next chapter, we will explore StyleGANs, an advanced generative model designed to generate high-resolution, photorealistic images with unprecedented control over fine-grained details. We will discuss its architecture, training methodology, and how it extends the capabilities of GANs for applications in face synthesis, texture generation, and creative AI.

Points to Remember

- CycleGANs enable unpaired image-to-image translation, eliminating the need for manually curated paired datasets.
- Two generators work in opposite directions, translating images between domains, while two discriminators ensure that generated images appear realistic.
- Cycle consistency loss enforces that translating an image back to its original domain preserves its structure and content.
- Adversarial loss ensures that generated images are indistinguishable from real images in the target domain.
- CycleGANs are widely used in style transfer, artistic transformations, domain adaptation, and medical imaging.

Multiple Choice Questions

1. What is the primary advantage of CycleGANs over traditional GANs?
    a. Faster training speed
    b. Ability to perform image-to-image translation without paired datasets
    c. Reduced computational requirements
    d. Improved latent space exploration
2. How does CycleGAN enforce structure preservation in image translations?
    a. By using paired training images
    b. By optimizing adversarial loss alone
    c. By incorporating cycle consistency loss
    d. By reducing the number of generator layers

3. What common issue can occur during CycleGAN training?
    a. Mode collapse
    b. Overfitting due to paired data
    c. Lack of latent space interpolation
    d. Weak discriminator performance
4. What role do discriminators play in CycleGANs?
    a. Translate images from one domain to another
    b. Ensure that the cycle consistency loss is minimized
    c. Distinguish real images from generated images in each domain
    d. Generate synthetic images conditioned on input labels

Answers

1. b
2. c
3. a
4. c

Questions

1. How does CycleGAN achieve image translation without paired datasets, and why is this advantageous?
2. What are the key architectural components of a CycleGAN, and how do they interact during training?
3. How does cycle consistency loss contribute to improving translation quality in CycleGANs?
4. What are the major challenges in training a CycleGAN, and how can they be mitigated?
5. How do CycleGANs compare with cGANs in terms of architecture and applications?
6. What role do adversarial and cycle consistency losses play in CycleGAN optimization?
7. Why is maintaining structural integrity in translated images critical for CycleGANs?
8. What are some real-world applications where CycleGANs have been successfully deployed?
9. How does using unpaired datasets impact the quality and generalization of CycleGAN translations?
10. What are the potential future advancements in CycleGANs that could enhance their capabilities?

Key Terms

- **Unpaired Image Translation:** The process of translating images between domains without paired training data.
- **Generator:** A neural network that transforms an image from one domain to another.
- **Discriminator:** A neural network that distinguishes between real and generated images in a domain.
- **Cycle Consistency Loss**: A constraint that ensures reversibility of image translations between two domains.
- **Mode Collapse:** A training issue where the generator produces repetitive outputs with limited diversity.
- **Style Transfer:** The process of applying visual characteristics from one domain to another.
- **Domain Adaptation:** The ability to transform images between different distributions, such as synthetic-to-real image conversion.
- **Perceptual Loss:** A loss function that helps preserve structural and content details in translated images.
- **Adversarial Loss**: A GAN-based loss that ensures generated images resemble the real samples in the target domain.
- **Regularization Techniques**: Methods used to stabilize GAN training, and improve the translation quality.

CHAPTER 8
Style GANs

Introduction

The evolution of Generative Adversarial Networks (GANs) has led to remarkable strides in how machines can create and imagine. Yet, for a long time, one question remained unsolved – how can we control *style* in generation? How can we guide a model, not just to produce something realistic, but to define *how* it looks? StyleGAN answers this question with elegance and precision. It opened a new era where creativity meets control, letting users fine-tune every nuance of generated content – from broad structure to subtle texture. In this chapter, you will explore how this innovation reshaped image synthesis, and redefined the standards of realism in AI-generated art.

The chapter will also guide you through hands-on exercises, gradually introducing the principles and mechanisms that make StyleGAN so distinctive. By the end, you will see how the concept of *style* became the missing link that brought personality and intentionality into generative models.

Structure

In this chapter, we will discuss the following topics:

- **Overview of StyleGAN and Its Purpose**
  - Evolution from traditional GANs to StyleGAN
  - Key innovations: Style-based generator architecture
  - Applications of StyleGAN in creative and industrial domains
- **Key Features of StyleGAN**
- **Style Manipulation in Generative Models**
  - Understanding latent spaces and their significance
  - The role of style in generating diverse outputs
- **Architecture Overview of StyleGAN**
  - Generator and discriminator
  - Role of the mapping network in style manipulation
  - Importance of Adaptive Instance Normalization
- **Working of StyleGAN**
  - High-Quality Images with Hierarchical Control
  - Understanding intermediate latent spaces for style manipulation
  - Interplay of noise, style injection, and latent spaces

- **Implementing StyleGAN: Step-by-Step**
  - Building the StyleGAN generator and discriminator
  - Code snippets for implementing key components
  - Training and Visualization
- **Evaluating StyleGAN Performance**
  - Common metrics: FID, perceptual loss, and visual quality assessments
  - Techniques for evaluating style consistency and diversity
  - Human evaluation as a qualitative benchmark
- **Challenges and Limitations**
- **Applications of StyleGAN**
- **Case Study: AI-Generated Indian Ethnic Wear Designs**

Overview of StyleGAN and Its Purpose

StyleGAN, developed by NVIDIA, represents a major breakthrough in the evolution of Generative Adversarial Networks (GANs). It introduces a new architecture that separates the process of image generation into multiple layers of detail – a feature that allows precise control over attributes such as facial expressions, texture, and lighting.

Unlike traditional GANs, which often lack flexibility and control, StyleGAN provides users with the ability to influence specific aspects of generated images, such as facial expressions, textures, or lighting conditions, without altering the overall structure. This innovation directly addresses two long-standing challenges in generative modeling:

- **Control over generation:** Allowing granular manipulation of image attributes at different levels.
- **Quality and consistency:** Producing images that are both realistic and diverse, with minimal artifacts.

With these capabilities, StyleGAN has become a go-to model for tasks in creative AI, powering applications across art, fashion, film, and industrial design – wherever realism and flexibility must coexist.

Analogy: The Hulk's Makeup Artist and StyleGAN

Imagine the makeup artist responsible for transforming Mark Ruffalo into the Hulk in the Marvel movies. The artist does not just apply random green paint; they carefully blend his original features (eyes, nose, facial structure, and so on) with the Hulk's monstrous look, while maintaining realism. Let us understand how this relates to StyleGAN:

- **Preserving Core Features:**
  - The makeup artist ensures that Ruffalo is still recognizable even as the Hulk.
  - StyleGAN keeps the identity of an image intact, while modifying certain features like age, expression, or artistic style.

***Figure 8.1**: Makeup Artist Analogy to Understand StyleGANs*

- **Style Transformation:**
  - The makeup artist can adjust the intensity of the transformation, making him look like a mildly angry Bruce Banner or a full-on raging Hulk.
  - StyleGAN allows controlled modifications, such as blending a real photo with a cartoon style or aging a person realistically.
- **High-Resolution Detail Enhancement:**
  - Hollywood makeup artists add realistic skin textures, lighting effects, and fine details to make the Hulk look believable.
  - StyleGAN progressively enhances details, starting with a rough image, and refining it into a high-quality, ultra-realistic final output.
- **Blending Two Identities (Style Mixing):**
  - In the movies, there is a balance between Ruffalo's human expressions and Hulk's monstrous features. The makeup artist ensures a smooth blend between the two styles.
  - StyleGAN can mix two different images or blend attributes, such as combining a real human face with an anime or artistic style.

Evolution from Traditional GANs to StyleGAN

To appreciate the significance of StyleGAN, it is essential to understand its evolution from traditional GANs. Early GAN architectures, such as those proposed by Goodfellow et al. in 2014, introduced the concept of adversarial training, where a generator and a discriminator compete to produce realistic outputs. However, these models faced several limitations:

- **Mode Collapse:** Traditional GANs often generated limited variations in output, repeatedly producing similar results.
- **Limited Control:** Early GANs provided no straightforward mechanism to influence specific attributes of the generated data.

- **Training Instability**: The adversarial training process was prone to instability, requiring significant tuning.

With the advent of DCGAN (Deep Convolutional GANs), convolutional neural networks were integrated into GAN architectures, improving their ability to generate high-resolution images. However, even DCGANs and later models such as CycleGAN or WGAN struggled to provide fine-grained control over the generation process.

StyleGAN addressed these challenges by introducing a **style-based generator architecture**, which separates the generation process into two distinct phases:

1. **Mapping Latent Space to Style Space:** A mapping network transforms input latent vectors into intermediate representations (styles) that define the attributes of the generated image.
2. **Style Injection:** Styles are applied at different layers of the generator, enabling independent control over coarse, middle, and fine features of the image.

This decoupling not only improved the quality of the generated images but also allowed for greater interpretability and manipulation, setting a new standard in generative modeling.

Key Innovations: Style-Based Generator Architecture

The core innovation of StyleGAN lies in its style-based generator architecture, which introduces several important features:

- **Mapping Network:** Instead of directly sampling from a latent space, StyleGAN uses a mapping network to transform latent vectors into intermediate styles. This mapping network ensures a disentangled representation, making it easier to control specific image attributes.
- **Adaptive Instance Normalization (AdaIN):** Styles are injected into the generator through these (AdaIN) layers, which adjust the mean and variance of feature maps at each layer. This allows for independent control over various levels of detail, such as:
    - **Coarse Features:** Global structure, such as the overall shape of a face.
    - **Middle Features**: Attributes like eye color or hairstyle.
    - **Fine Features:** Textures, skin details, and lighting.
- **Noise Injection:** StyleGAN adds stochastic noise at each layer to introduce fine-grained randomness, improving the naturalness and diversity of the generated images.
- **Progressive Growing**: StyleGAN refines the resolution of generated images incrementally during training, starting with low-resolution outputs, and gradually adding finer details. This ensures stability in training and high-quality results.

These innovations not only improve the fidelity and control of image generation but also open up new possibilities for creative and industrial applications.

Applications of StyleGAN in Creative and Industrial Domains

The flexibility and quality of StyleGAN have made it a valuable tool across various domains:

Creative Industries:

- **Art and Design:** Artists use StyleGAN to generate unique patterns, textures, and abstract art.
- **Fashion:** Designers create virtual prototypes of clothing and accessories, experimenting with styles and patterns.

- **Photography:** Photographers enhance their portfolios with synthetic yet photorealistic images, such as virtual backdrops.

Gaming and Entertainment:

- **Character Design:** StyleGAN helps game developers and animators generate diverse and realistic characters, saving time and resources.
- **Environment Generation:** The model is used to create lifelike environments, including landscapes and cityscapes, for virtual worlds.

Healthcare:

- **Data Augmentation:** StyleGAN generates synthetic medical images, such as MRIs or X-rays, to augment datasets for training diagnostic models.
- **Research**: It aids in studying latent representations, helping researchers understand patterns in medical imaging data.

Marketing and Advertising:

- **Content Creation:** StyleGAN generates personalized visual content for targeted advertising campaigns.
- **Customer Engagement:** Brands use the model to create virtual avatars or interactive experiences.

The versatility of StyleGAN demonstrates its potential to revolutionize creative workflows, and solve practical problems across industries, making it a cornerstone of modern generative AI.

Key Features of StyleGAN

StyleGAN revolutionizes image synthesis by reimagining the generation process as a collaborative, stylized workshop. Instead of a single, monolithic process, it uses a style-based generator that provides unprecedented control, much *like a fashion designer directing a team of specialists*. This architecture ensures training stability, and injects fine-grained details, resulting in highly customizable and photorealistic image generation by clearly separating high-level style from intricate content.

Differences from Previous GAN Models

StyleGAN introduces significant advancements over earlier GAN architectures such as DCGAN and CycleGAN, addressing key limitations, and enhancing the generation process. The key differences include:

- **Control and Manipulation:** Earlier GANs lacked intuitive control. StyleGAN, like a stylist giving specific instructions to tailors, allows for independent manipulation of attributes–from the overall silhouette (pose, shape, and so on) down to the finest embroidery (skin, hair and strands).
- **Disentangled Representations:** Unlike its predecessors, StyleGAN disentangles the latent space. The Mapping Network (the stylist) interprets a random customer request into a coherent set of style instructions (w), ensuring that changes correspond to meaningful variations, like switching from a "*French-style*" to a "*Japanese-style*" outfit, without altering the underlying garment structure.
- **Training Stability:** Traditional GANs often suffered from mode collapse and training instability. StyleGAN's progressive-growing and other architectural innovations significantly improve stability and convergence.
- **Higher Quality Outputs**: StyleGAN produces photorealistic images with fine-grained details, surpassing the visual fidelity of previous GANs, particularly in high-resolution tasks.

Style-Based Generator: The Fashion Boutique Workflow

The style-based generator is the cornerstone of StyleGAN, but let us understand by using the analogy of an efficient workflow of a luxury boutique (refer *Figure* 8.2).

Mapping Network: The Creative Stylist

- The process begins with a latent vector (z), which is like a customer's abstract wish (for example, "*I want a French-style outfit*"). The Mapping Network acts as the stylist, interpreting this request, and transforming it into a refined, intermediate set of style instructions (w). This step is crucial for disentangling the request into actionable, independent style commands for the design team.
- This intermediate space ensures that changes in 'w' correspond to meaningful variations in the output, such as structure or texture.

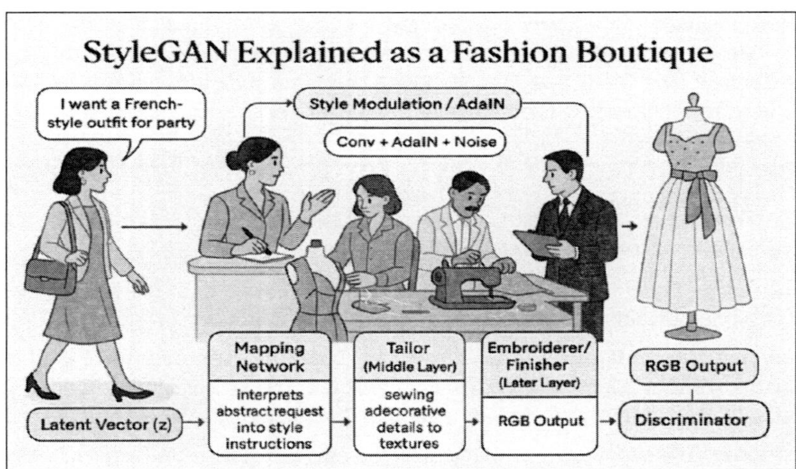

Figure 8.2: *Understanding the Concept of StyleGAN Features with an Analogy*

Style Injection: Directing the Design Team

The style instructions (w) are injected into the generator (the design workshop) through Adaptive Instance Normalization (AdaIN). This is the "*stylist*" giving direct, layer-specific guidance to the artisans:

- **Coarse Control (Early Layers/Pattern Cutter):** The stylist's instructions here affect the global structure of the image, such as pose, shape, or the overall cut of an outfit.
- **Middle and Fine Control (Later Layers/Embroiderer):** Instructions at these layers adjust finer details like texture, fabric color, or the decorative stitching on a garment.
- This process, often summarized as Conv + AdaIN + Noise, allows each part of the "*workshop*" to focus on its specialty, controlled by a unified creative vision.

Progressive Growing: Incremental Addition of Layers for Stability

Progressive growing, first introduced in earlier GAN architectures, is further refined in StyleGAN. This technique involves:

- **Incremental Layer Addition:** The generator and discriminator begin working on very low-resolution images (for example, 4×4 pixels), focusing only on the broadest shapes. Layers are progressively added to increase the resolution, allowing the model to learn coarse features first, before tackling fine details.

- **Stability in Training:** This step-by-step approach prevents the model from being overwhelmed, significantly reducing training instability and mode collapse, and ensuring that the final "*garment*" is well-constructed from the ground up.

Noise Injection: The Mark of Authentic Craftsmanship

To prevent generated images from looking too uniform and artificial, StyleGAN incorporates noise injection.

- **Role of Noise:** Random noise is added to each layer of the generator during the generation process. This noise does not alter global attributes but introduces subtle variations in fine details such as skin texture, hair strands, or background noise.
- **Improved Realism:** This noise is what gives each generated image its unique, authentic texture—like the subtle variations in fabric weave, the placement of individual freckles, or the stray strands of hair. It ensures that even with the same style instructions, no two outputs are exactly identical, enhancing the realism and diversity of the results.

Separation of Content and Style for Independent Manipulation

One of StyleGAN's most groundbreaking features is the ability to separate content and style, providing unparalleled control over the generation process.

- **Content versus Style:** Content refers to the structural aspects of the image, such as the pose or layout. Style pertains to the finer details, including color, texture, and lighting.
- **Independent Manipulation:** Users can modify content attributes (for example, changing a body shape) without affecting style (for example, fabric texture). Similarly, style attributes can be adjusted independently of content, enabling diverse outputs from the same base structure.
- **Applications:** This separation is particularly useful in creative industries, where users may want to experiment with different styles for a fixed composition, such as applying various artistic textures to the same portrait.

Architecture Overview of StyleGAN

StyleGAN's architecture introduces key innovations that prioritize disentangled control and high-fidelity output. It moves beyond a simple generator by splitting the process into two specialized networks: one that creates a structured style vector, and another that synthesizes the image based on that style. This separation allows for precise application of style variations at different hierarchical levels, while advanced training strategies ensure stability and realism.

Generator and Discriminator

The architecture consists of two neural networks in an adversarial setup, with the generator undergoing a fundamental redesign.

The Generator Component: The StyleGAN generator is decomposed into two distinct sub-networks:

- **The Mapping Network:** A feed-forward neural network that transforms the input latent code (z) into an intermediate latent space (w). This process disentangles the input, ensuring that directions in the 'w' space correspond to meaningful, independent visual attributes (for example, pose, lighting, texture, and so on).
- **The Synthesis Network:** This is the core image-creation network. It starts with a learned constant input, bypassing the need for a traditional input vector, and providing a stable

foundation. The style information from the 'w' vector is injected into the synthesis network at each convolutional layer via Adaptive Instance Normalization (AdaIN). This mechanism allows styles to control the visual features at different scales:

 - **Early Layers:** Govern coarse, high-level attributes (pose, shape, and so on).
 - **Middle Layers:** Control mid-level features (facial features, hair style, and so on).
 - **Later Layers:** Determine fine-grained details (color palette, micro-textures).

- **Noise Injection:** After AdaIN, per-pixel noise is added. This stochastic variation is essential for generating realistic, non-uniform details such as skin pores, hair strands, or background texture, preventing the outputs from appearing overly smooth or artificial.

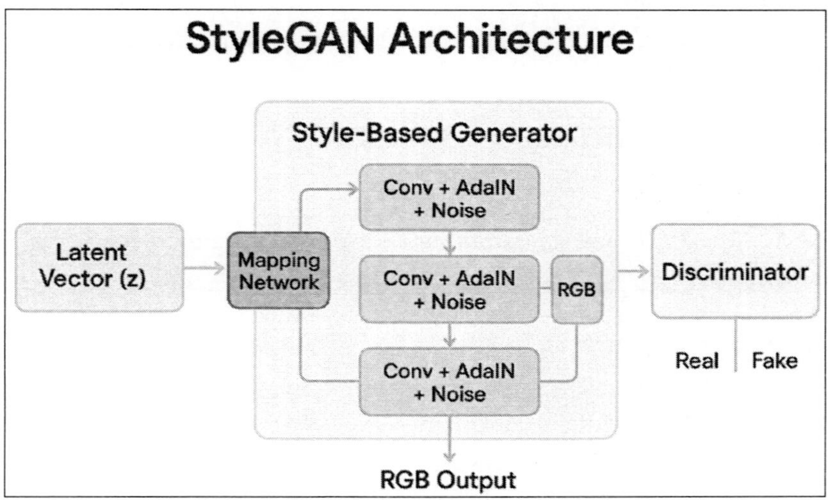

Figure 8.3: *StyleGAN Architectural Layers and Components*

- The final layer of the synthesis network uses a dedicated 1x1 convolution to produce the RGB Output, projecting the high-dimensional feature maps into a final, high-resolution color image.

The Discriminator Component

The discriminator acts as a critic, evaluating the realism of generated images, and providing the feedback necessary to guide the generator towards producing outputs indistinguishable from the real data.

- Its structure is typically a convolutional neural network, often designed with a progressively growing or residual architecture to effectively process images at increasing resolutions.
- To enhance training stability, and prevent overfitting, the discriminator commonly employs regularization techniques such as mini-batch standard deviation, which helps it learn features that are representative of the real data distribution as a whole, rather than memorizing individual training examples.

Together, the generator and discriminator engage in an adversarial game, where the generator strives to produce realistic images, while the discriminator aims to identify fake outputs.

Role of the Mapping Network in Style Manipulation

The mapping network is a critical innovation in StyleGAN that ensures disentangled and interpretable style representations. Its primary roles include:

Transformation of Latent Space:

- Traditional GANs directly sample from a latent space, z~N(0,1), which often results in entangled and unpredictable outputs.
- In StyleGAN, the mapping network transforms '*z*' into an intermediate latent space, '*w*', ensuring that changes in '*w*' correspond to meaningful variations in the generated image.

Improved Disentanglement:

- The mapping network allows better separation of features such as pose, texture, and lighting, making it easier to manipulate these attributes independently.

Flexibility in Style Application:

- By mapping the input into a style space, the network provides a robust foundation for style injection via AdaIN layers.

Importance of Adaptive Instance Normalization

Adaptive Instance Normalization (AdaIN) is a key component of StyleGAN that allows precise control over the style of generated images. It adjusts the mean and variance of feature maps in the generator, using a style vector from the mapping network, modifying visual features layer by layer.

AdaIN enables hierarchical style control—styles injected in early layers affect broad structures like face shape or pose, while styles in later layers refine details such as texture, lighting, and hair. This layered adjustment ensures consistent, realistic, and coherent image generation.

Thus, by enabling flexible and independent style manipulation, AdaIN allows StyleGAN to generate diverse outputs, while preserving the structural integrity of the content.

Loss Functions and Strategies for Stable Training

StyleGAN employs carefully designed loss functions and training strategies to achieve stability and high-quality outputs. The key aspects include:

Adversarial Loss:

- Like traditional GANs, StyleGAN uses an adversarial loss to optimize the generator and discriminator.
- This loss encourages the generator to produce outputs that are indistinguishable from the real data, while improving the discriminator's ability to detect fake images.

Perceptual Path Length Regularization:

- A new addition in StyleGAN is the perceptual path length regularization term, which ensures smoothness in the latent space.
- This regularization minimizes abrupt changes in the generated image when interpolating between latent vectors, improving interpretability and control.

R1 Regularization for the Discriminator:

- The discriminator is regularized using the R1 gradient penalty, which stabilizes training by penalizing large gradients with respect to the input.
- This technique reduces overfitting, and prevents mode collapse.

Implementing StyleGAN: Step-by-Step

Bringing StyleGAN to life requires a structured approach, from designing its core components to training it effectively. The process begins with constructing the foundational networks responsible for generating and evaluating images. By integrating the key functions and algorithms, developers can fine-tune the system for optimal performance. Training on extensive datasets demands efficient resource management and computational power to achieve high-quality results. Throughout the process, visualizing generated images, and tracking progress help refine the model, ensuring realistic and diverse outputs.

Building the StyleGAN Generator and Discriminator

The implementation of StyleGAN begins with constructing its core components: the generator and the discriminator. Both modules are central to the adversarial framework, and feature innovative architectural elements unique to StyleGAN.

Generator:

- The generator uses a design where a mapping network converts the input vector z into a refined version called w. This transformed representation is then applied to the generator through special layers that adjust style and details at different stages.
- The key stages in the generator are:
  - **Mapping Network**: Converts latent vectors into styles.
  - **Synthesis Network**: Uses styles to control various levels of details.
  - **Noise Injection**: Adds randomness to enhance diversity and fine-grained details.

Discriminator:

- The discriminator distinguishes between the real and generated images. It features a progressively growing architecture, matching the generator's resolution.
- **The following are the key discriminator features:**
  - Convolutional layers to extract image features.
  - Downsampling layers to process high-resolution inputs.
  - Binary classification output to determine real or fake.

Code Snippets for Implementing Key Components

The following are the simplified implementations of the key components in TensorFlow and PyTorch.

TensorFlow, Mapping Network Component:

```
import tensorflow as tf

def mapping_network(latent_dim, layers=8):
    model = tf.keras.Sequential()
    for _ in range(layers):
        model.add(tf.keras.layers.Dense(latent_dim, activation='relu'))
    return model

latent_dim = 512
mapping_net = mapping_network(latent_dim)
```

PyTorch, Mapping Network Component:

```
import torch
import torch.nn as nn

def mapping_network(latent_dim, layers=8):
    layers_list = []
```

```
        for _ in range(layers):
            layers_list.append(nn.Linear(latent_dim, latent_dim))
            layers_list.append(nn.ReLU())
        return nn.Sequential(*layers_list)

    latent_dim = 512
    mapping_net = mapping_network(latent_dim)
```

TensorFlow, AdaIN Layer:

```
    class AdaIN(tf.keras.layers.Layer):
        def call(self, inputs):
            content, style = inputs
            mean, variance = tf.nn.moments(content, axes=[1, 2], keepdims=True)
            normalized = (content - mean) / tf.sqrt(variance + 1e-8)
            return style[0] * normalized + style[1]
```

PyTorch, AdaIN Layer:

```
    class AdaIN(nn.Module):
        def forward(self, content, style):
            mean, std = content.mean([2, 3], keepdim=True), content.std([2, 3],
    keepdim=True)
            normalized = (content - mean) / (std + 1e-8)
            return style[0] * normalized + style[1]
```

TensorFlow, Progressive Growing:

```
    def progressive_block(input_shape):
        inputs = tf.keras.Input(shape=input_shape)
        x = tf.keras.layers.Conv2D(128, (3, 3), padding='same', activation='relu')
    (inputs)
        x = tf.keras.layers.UpSampling2D()(x)
        x = tf.keras.layers.Conv2D(64, (3, 3), padding='same', activation='relu')
    (x)
        return tf.keras.Model(inputs, x)
```

PyTorch, Progressive Growing:

```
    class ProgressiveBlock(nn.Module):
        def __init__(self, in_channels, out_channels):
            super(ProgressiveBlock, self).__init__()
            self.conv1 = nn.Conv2d(in_channels, out_channels, kernel_size=3,
    padding=1)
            self.conv2 = nn.Conv2d(out_channels, out_channels, kernel_size=3,
    padding=1)
            self.upsample = nn.Upsample(scale_factor=2, mode='nearest')

        def forward(self, x):
            x = self.conv1(x)
            x = torch.relu(x)
            x = self.upsample(x)
            x = self.conv2(x)
            return torch.relu(x)
```

Training and Visualization

Training StyleGAN is resource-intensive, requiring significant computational power and large-scale datasets. The key considerations include:

- **Dataset Preparation:**
  - Use high-quality, diverse datasets such as FFHQ (Flickr-Faces-HQ) for faces or LSUN for other image categories.
  - Ensure that images are pre-processed (cropped, resized, and so on) to maintain consistency.
- **Training Configuration:**
  - Utilize high-performance GPUs or TPUs to handle the computational load.
  - Set appropriate hyperparameters:
    - **Learning rate:** 0.001 for generator, 0.004 for discriminator.
    - **Batch size:** Typically, 16-32 for high-resolution images.
    - **Training steps:** Millions of iterations for convergence.
- **Optimizers and Loss Functions:**
  - StyleGAN uses non-saturating GAN loss with R1 regularization for stability.
  - Apply learning rate schedules for gradual optimization.

Visualizing Outputs and Monitoring Progress

Tracking the model's progress during training is crucial for ensuring high-quality results. By regularly saving outputs, logging key metrics, and analyzing performance, we can fine-tune the model, and detect issues early.

Output Visualization:

- Periodically save generated images during training to monitor progress.
- Use image grids to compare outputs at different resolutions.

TensorFlow Example:

```
import matplotlib.pyplot as plt

def visualize_images(images, rows, cols):
    fig, axs = plt.subplots(rows, cols, figsize=(10, 10))
    for i, ax in enumerate(axs.flatten()):
        ax.imshow(images[i])
        ax.axis('off')
    plt.show()
```

Logging Tools: Use TensorBoard for monitoring losses, visualizing generated images, and tracking metrics like FID (Fréchet Inception Distance).

TensorFlow Example:

```
import tensorflow as tf

log_dir = "logs/"
tensorboard_callback = tf.keras.callbacks.TensorBoard(log_dir=log_dir)
model.fit(dataset, epochs=10, callbacks=[tensorboard_callback])
```

PyTorch Visualization: Use libraries like Matplotlib or Weights and Biases (wandb) for logging and visual analysis.

```
import matplotlib.pyplot as plt
import torch

def show_images(images, rows, cols):
    fig, axs = plt.subplots(rows, cols, figsize=(10, 10))
```

```
    for i, ax in enumerate(axs.flatten()):
        img = images[i].detach().cpu().permute(1, 2, 0).numpy()
        ax.imshow(img)
        ax.axis('off')
    plt.show()
```

Regularly monitoring the training process helps identify problems such as mode collapse, poor convergence, or unstable outputs. Thus, by leveraging visualization tools and logging systems, we can fine-tune StyleGAN for better image quality and diversity.

Evaluating StyleGAN Performance

Evaluating a generative model involves measuring quality, diversity, and consistency. Analytical methods quantify detail and variation, while qualitative assessments, including human judgment, gauge realism. A balanced approach ensures high-fidelity images with coherent styles.

Common Metrics for StyleGAN Evaluation

Evaluating the performance of StyleGAN requires a combination of quantitative and qualitative methods. As a generative model, StyleGAN's outputs are judged on realism, diversity, and consistency. Several established metrics are commonly used to measure these aspects:

- **Fréchet Inception Distance (FID):**
  - **Definition:** FID measures the similarity between the distribution of real and generated images by comparing feature representations extracted from a pre-trained Inception Network.
  - **How it Works:** FID computes the mean and covariance of features from real and generated images, capturing both content similarity and diversity.
  - **Advantages:**
    - Sensitive to image quality and diversity.
    - Suitable for high-resolution images.
  - **Limitations:**
    - Depends on the choice of the pre-trained network.
    - May not fully capture subjective aspects of visual quality.
- **Perceptual Loss:**
  - **Definition:** Perceptual loss compares the high-level features of generated and real images, rather than pixel-wise differences.
  - **How it Works:** This metric evaluates discrepancies in feature maps extracted from a pre-trained neural network, emphasizing perceptual similarity over pixel accuracy.
  - **Use Case:** Useful for assessing visual fidelity, particularly when small distortions might not be noticeable to the human eye.
- **Inception Score (IS):**
  - **Definition:** IS evaluates the quality and diversity of generated images based on the confidence of predictions made by a pre-trained Inception Model.
  - **How it Works:** High-quality images result in confident predictions (low entropy) for specific classes, while diverse images span multiple classes.
  - **Advantages:**
    - Easy to compute.

        - Highlights diversity in generated outputs.
    - **Limitations:**
        - Assumes class labels in the pre-trained model align with the generated dataset.
- **Pixel-Level Metrics:**
    - While pixel-wise metrics such as Mean Squared Error (MSE) or Structural Similarity Index (SSIM) are sometimes used, they are less effective for generative models, as they fail to capture perceptual differences.

Evaluating Consistency and Diversity

- **Style Consistency:** StyleGAN's unique feature is its ability to manipulate styles independently of the content. Evaluating this requires:
    - **Latent Space Traversals:** By interpolating between latent vectors, the model's consistency in generating smooth transitions, and preserving structure is tested.
    - **Style Mixing:** Generating images by combining styles from different vectors at various layers, and assessing the consistency of the applied changes.
    - **Key Metric:** Measuring changes in specific attributes (for example, texture or lighting) while ensuring that the content remains stable.
- **Diversity:** A critical aspect of any generative model is its ability to produce diverse outputs. Techniques to evaluate diversity include:
    - **Feature Distribution Analysis:** Comparing the variance of features in generated images to those in real datasets.
    - **Pairwise Distance:** Calculating the pairwise distances between generated samples in the latent space to ensure a broad coverage of the latent manifold.
    - **Challenges:** Ensuring diversity without compromising quality can be difficult, as increasing diversity sometimes leads to artifacts.

Human Evaluation as a Qualitative Benchmark

Although quantitative metrics provide objective measures, human evaluation remains the gold standard for assessing the subjective quality of StyleGAN's outputs. The key aspects of human evaluation include:

- **Realism:**
    - Assessors rate the realism of generated images on a scale (for example, from 1 to 5), comparing them with real images.
    - **Example:** For facial image generation, human evaluators judge the believability of facial features, textures, and lighting.
- **Consistency and Style:**
    - Evaluators examine whether images maintain consistent styles across different outputs or when manipulating specific attributes.
    - **Example:** In a style-mixing test, assessors determine whether changes in style layers preserve global content, while modifying details.
- **Comparative Evaluation:**
    - Generated images are presented alongside real images or outputs from other models (for example, DCGAN or CycleGAN) for pairwise comparison.
    - **Focus:** Determining which images are more realistic or diverse.

- **Task-Specific Evaluation:** In industrial or creative applications, human evaluators assess images for specific criteria, such as usability in graphic design or consistency in medical imaging.
- **Crowdsourced Feedback:** Platforms like Amazon Mechanical Turk or user surveys can provide large-scale feedback on generated images, offering insights into their perceived quality and utility.

Combining Quantitative and Qualitative Approaches

To achieve a comprehensive evaluation of StyleGAN, it is essential to combine quantitative metrics with human judgment. For example:

- **FID and Human Evaluation:** While FID captures statistical differences, human evaluation ensures perceptual fidelity.
- **Latent Space Exploration and IS:** Testing latent space manipulation alongside Inception Score ensures that diversity is achieved without compromising quality.

Evaluation Challenges

- **Subjectivity:** Human evaluation is inherently subjective, and individual preferences can vary widely.
- **Metric Limitations:** No single metric captures all aspects of performance. For example, FID excels at measuring distribution alignment but may overlook perceptual qualities.
- **Trade-offs:** Models often face trade-offs between realism and diversity, requiring careful tuning and balanced evaluation metrics.

Challenges and Limitations of StyleGAN

Despite its capabilities, StyleGAN faces challenges in efficiency and accuracy. High computational demands make training resource-intensive, while artifacts and inconsistencies can affect the output quality. Additionally, handling diverse datasets remains a challenge, limiting the model's adaptability across different domains.

Computational Requirements and Resource Demands

StyleGAN's powerful architecture comes at the cost of high computational demands. Training the model requires significant resources, especially due to the large number of parameters, and the goal of generating high-resolution images. Running StyleGAN on consumer-grade hardware is often impractical, making high-end GPUs or TPUs essential.

The model's progressive growing and deep multi-layer structure also demand substantial memory. Generating images at resolutions like 1024×1024 can consume several gigabytes of GPU memory, creating accessibility challenges for developers and researchers with limited hardware.

Another concern is energy consumption. Training StyleGAN is energy-intensive, raising environmental concerns, particularly when models are trained at scale. While inference is less demanding than training, real-time applications still require significant computational power when scaled up.

To address these challenges, researchers are investigating optimizations like model pruning, quantization, and more efficient training algorithms. However, despite these efforts, the high resource requirements remain a major obstacle for broader adoption, particularly among smaller teams or independent developers.

Handling Artifacts and Image Inconsistencies

Despite its ability to generate photorealistic images, StyleGAN is not immune to artifacts and inconsistencies. These issues can manifest in various forms:

- **Visual Artifacts**: Generated images may exhibit distortions, particularly in fine details such as textures or complex patterns. For example:
    - Hairlines may appear blurred or unnaturally sharp.
    - Background elements might show repetitive or inconsistent patterns.
- **Structural Errors:** In some cases, StyleGAN fails to maintain consistent structural integrity, leading to abnormalities such as:
    - Asymmetric facial features.
    - Disproportionate or disconnected elements in objects.
- **Mode Collapse**: While StyleGAN improves upon traditional GANs, it can still suffer from mode collapse, where the generator produces a limited variety of outputs. This reduces the diversity of generated images, making the model less versatile.
- **Noise Interference**: The addition of stochastic noise for fine grained details can sometimes lead to unintended variations, creating unnatural or noisy features in the output.
- **Artifacts in High-Resolution Outputs**: As resolution increases, artifacts become more noticeable, requiring extensive post-processing to achieve production-level quality.

Researchers are addressing these issues through advanced regularization techniques, improved loss functions, and architectural modifications. For example, using perceptual loss metrics and fine-tuning noise injection can reduce visual artifacts, while enhancing output quality.

Limitations in Handling Diverse Datasets

While StyleGAN excels at generating realistic images for specific datasets, it struggles when applied to highly diverse or unbalanced datasets. The key limitations include:

- **Overfitting to Specific Domains:** StyleGAN performs exceptionally well on curated datasets with consistent features, such as faces or specific art styles. However, when trained on datasets with high variability, the model often overfits to dominant features, neglecting minority patterns.
- **Difficulty with Multimodal Distribution:** Diverse datasets containing multiple distribution (for example, animals, landscapes, and human portraits) pose challenges for StyleGAN. The model struggles to capture all modes effectively, leading to incomplete or biased representations.
- **Bias in Training Data:** StyleGAN inherits biases present in training datasets. For instance, a dataset with underrepresented demographic groups may result in outputs that fail to capture their features accurately. This limitation raises ethical concerns, particularly in applications involving human-related data.
- **Handling Complex Data:** Real-world datasets often contain noise, inconsistencies, and mislabeled data. StyleGAN's performance deteriorates when trained on such datasets, producing outputs that reflect the imperfections of the input data.
- **Generalization Issues:** StyleGAN is highly specialized for the dataset it is trained on, making it less effective for general-purpose generative tasks. A model trained on human faces, for example, may struggle to generate high-quality outputs when applied to entirely different domains.

To address these challenges, researchers are developing methods such as domain adaptation, transfer learning, and data augmentation. By enhancing the robustness of StyleGAN to diverse datasets, these approaches aim to expand its applicability across various fields.

Applications of StyleGAN

The ability to generate high-quality, diverse, and realistic images has opened new possibilities across multiple domains. From transforming creative workflows to enhancing scientific research, StyleGAN's impact extends far beyond image synthesis. Its capability to manipulate and refine visual content is driving innovation in unexpected ways, making it a valuable tool in fields that demand precision, realism, and adaptability.

Creative Industries: Artistic Content, Digital Portraits, and Design

StyleGAN has revolutionized the creative process, offering tools that empower artists, designers, and content creators to produce high-quality, innovative work. By providing control over various aspects of image generation, StyleGAN enables professionals in creative industries to explore new artistic directions, and automate time-intensive tasks.

Art and Visual Content Creation:

- Artists use StyleGAN to generate abstract art, patterns, and textures that might be difficult to create manually. For example, the model can create unique visual elements for digital paintings or installations.
- StyleGAN's ability to manipulate specific features allows creators to explore variations in style, color palettes, and composition, producing diverse artistic outputs from a single concept.

Digital Portraits:

- Photographers and graphic designers leverage StyleGAN to create photorealistic digital portraits. These images can be used in commercial projects, advertisements, or as virtual avatars.
- StyleGAN's ability to generate portraits with customizable attributes, such as age, gender, and expression, enables users to tailor images to specific project requirements.

Fashion and Product Design:

- Designers in the fashion industry use StyleGAN to prototype clothing patterns, accessories, and fabrics. The model's ability to blend styles, and generate realistic textures streamlines the design process.
- Product designers apply StyleGAN to create virtual prototypes for testing and presentation, saving both time and resources.

Gaming and Entertainment: Character and Environment Generation

The gaming and entertainment industries benefit immensely from StyleGAN's capabilities, as it simplifies and accelerates the creation of visually compelling characters and environments.

Character Design:

- Game developers use StyleGAN to create diverse characters with unique appearances, ranging from realistic humans to fantastical creatures. Thus, by controlling specific features like facial structure, clothing, or skin texture, developers can generate a vast array of character designs efficiently.

- In Virtual Reality (VR) and Augmented Reality (AR) applications, StyleGAN enables the creation of realistic avatars that enhance user immersion.

Environment and Landscape Generation:

- StyleGAN can generate detailed landscapes and environments for use in games, films, and virtual experiences. This includes urban settings, natural vistas, or even entirely fictional worlds.
- The model's ability to control granular details allows designers to experiment with various lighting conditions, textures, and layouts, ensuring visually stunning results.

Special Effects and Animation:

- In the film and animation industries, StyleGAN aids in generating high-quality assets for special effects, background art, and character animations. Its flexibility reduces the manual effort required for asset creation, while maintaining a high level of detail and realism.

Healthcare: Data Augmentation for Medical Imaging

In the healthcare domain, StyleGAN's capabilities extend beyond creative applications, providing practical solutions for augmenting medical datasets, and supporting research.

Synthetic Data Generation:

- StyleGAN generates synthetic medical images, such as MRIs, CT scans, or X-rays, which are vital for training machine learning models in medical diagnostics. These synthetic images help address the challenge of limited data availability in specialized medical fields.
- By creating diverse and realistic medical images, StyleGAN improves the robustness and generalizability of diagnostic models.

Data Augmentation:

- StyleGAN's ability to introduce controlled variations in images is used to augment the existing datasets, enhancing model performance, without the need for additional data collection.
- **For example**, variations in lighting, resolution, or anatomical features can be synthesized to simulate real-world scenarios, improving diagnostic accuracy.

Anonymization of Patient Data:

- StyleGAN can generate synthetic patient data that maintains the statistical properties of the original dataset, while removing identifiable information. This allows researchers to share and analyze data, without violating patient privacy regulations.

Research: Latent Spaces for Generative Processes

StyleGAN has become a powerful tool for researchers exploring generative processes and latent space representations, offering insights into the workings of deep learning models.

Latent Space Exploration:

- Researchers use StyleGAN to study the structure of latent spaces, which encode complex features and attributes. By understanding these spaces, researchers gain insight into how models represent and manipulate data.
- Latent space interpolation, where two points in the space are blended, reveals smooth transitions between features, helping researchers understand the relationship between high-level attributes.

Feature Disentanglement:

- StyleGAN's disentangled latent representations enable researchers to isolate specific attributes such as pose, texture, or color, and study their individual impact on the generated output.
- This understanding informs the development of more interpretable and controllable generative models.

Advancing Generative AI:

- StyleGAN serves as a foundation for advancing generative AI research, inspiring new architectures and applications. For example, researchers build upon StyleGAN's principles to create models capable of generating 3D objects or multimodal content.

Case Study: AI-Generated Indian Ethnic Designs

The rich heritage of Indian ethnic wear is characterized by intricate patterns, vibrant colors, and diverse regional styles. Designing these garments requires a deep understanding of tradition, craftsmanship, and evolving fashion trends. However, scaling the creation of unique, high-quality designs, while maintaining authenticity remains a challenge. Can AI help preserve this artistic legacy, while introducing new creative possibilities?

Problem: Bridging Tradition and AI in Fashion Design

Indian ethnic wear is deeply rooted in cultural heritage, with intricate patterns, rich fabrics, and diverse regional styles. Designing these garments manually requires immense effort, as traditional motifs, embroidery, and textile variations must be carefully incorporated. Scaling such designs, while preserving authenticity and creativity is a challenge. AI-driven generative models like StyleGAN provide a potential solution by enabling the automated creation of high-quality, diverse ethnic wear patterns and silhouettes, while allowing designers to refine and customize the outputs.

Solution Approach: Leveraging Style-Based Generator

StyleGAN's ability to manipulate different design attributes independently makes it an ideal tool for generating Indian ethnic wear. The model was trained to control key elements, allowing designers to fine-tune:

- **Fabric Patterns:** Generating intricate weaves, floral motifs, paisleys, and traditional embroidery styles like Zardozi and Phulkari.
- **Color Combinations:** Exploring vibrant palettes inspired by seasonal festivals and regional aesthetics.
- **Garment Structure:** Customizing drapes, silhouettes, and embellishments for sarees, lehengas, kurtas, and sherwanis.

Implementation Process

- **Dataset Preparation:** A dataset of high-resolution ethnic wear images, covering various traditional styles, was curated. Data preprocessing involved categorizing garments by type, embroidery patterns, and dominant color schemes for structured training.
- **Training the Model:** Progressive training ensured high-resolution outputs, and the mapping network was optimized to enable precise control over key design attributes.
- **Generating and Refining Designs:** Designers manipulated the latent space to explore variations in embroidery, border work, and textile textures. Style blending techniques allowed for hybrid designs, such as a fusion of Mughal-era motifs with contemporary silhouettes.

Challenges and Solutions

Deploying StyleGAN for fashion design required addressing several challenges:

- **Artifacts in Generated Designs:** Early iterations had inconsistencies in embroidery alignment and fabric draping. These were mitigated by refining the loss function and noise injection strategies.
- **Ensuring Design Diversity:** Preventing repetitive outputs was crucial for generating a wide range of ethnic styles. This was addressed by dataset augmentation and regularization techniques.
- **Practicality of Designs:** AI-generated designs were reviewed by textile and fashion experts to ensure feasibility in real-world production.

Outcome: AI-Enhanced Ethnic Fashion

StyleGAN successfully generated a variety of Indian ethnic wear designs, demonstrating its potential in modernizing and scaling traditional craftsmanship. The results included:

- **Diverse Garment Styles:** Sarees with intricate woven borders, lehengas with unique sequin patterns, and embroidered sherwanis.
- **Customizable Elements:** Designers could adjust sleeve lengths, embellishment intensity, or neckline styles independently.
- **Realistic Fabric Representations:** High-resolution outputs captured the fine details, making it easier for artisans to translate digital designs into real garments with improved realism.

Conclusion

In this chapter, we explored StyleGAN, an advanced generative model that significantly improves upon traditional GAN architectures by introducing a style-based generator. Unlike previous GAN variants such as DCGAN and CycleGAN, StyleGAN provides fine-grained control over style and content through its innovative mapping network, AdaIN normalization, and noise injection mechanisms. These features allow for high-resolution, photorealistic image generation with independent manipulation of different visual attributes.

We examined the key architectural components of StyleGAN, including progressive growing, which stabilizes training by incrementally adding layers, and style injection that enables nuanced control over image synthesis. Additionally, we discussed data preparation techniques, evaluation metrics, and the implementation of StyleGAN, covering both theoretical foundations and practical coding steps.

Thus, despite its powerful capabilities, StyleGAN faces challenges such as high computational requirements, potential artifacts, and dataset biases. However, its applications in art, gaming, healthcare, and research demonstrate its transformative potential in generative modeling.

With hands-on implementation in TensorFlow and PyTorch, you are now well-equipped to leverage StyleGAN for a range of creative and industrial applications. In the next chapter, we will look at special types of Variational Autoencoders, β-VAE and CVAE, to explore how probabilistic generative models offer an alternative approach to learning latent representations, and controlling feature disentanglement.

Points to Remember

- StyleGAN introduces a style-based generator that separates content and style, enabling fine-grained control over image synthesis.
- Progressive growing stabilizes training by adding layers incrementally.
- Adaptive Instance Normalization (AdaIN) allows direct manipulation of image features through latent space transformations.
- Noise injection enhances fine details, improving the realism of generated images.
- StyleGAN applications range from artistic image synthesis to medical data augmentation and gaming character generation.

Multiple Choice Questions

1. What is the primary advantage of StyleGAN over traditional GANs?
    a. Faster training speed
    b. The ability to generate unpaired image translations
    c. Lower computational cost
    d. Fine-grained control over image synthesis using style manipulation
2. How does StyleGAN achieve fine-grained control in image generation?
    a. Through direct pixel manipulation
    b. By incorporating a style-based mapping network
    c. Using adversarial loss alone
    d. By using conditional labels during training
3. What is the role of Adaptive Instance Normalization (AdaIN) in StyleGAN?
    a. It stabilizes the discriminator's learning process.
    b. It ensures progressive growth of the model.
    c. It enables style transfer by normalizing and injecting style vectors.
    d. It prevents overfitting during training.
4. Which of the following is a common challenge when training StyleGAN?
    a. Lack of latent space control
    b. High computational requirements and memory usage
    c. Inability to generate high-resolution images
    d. Limited applications outside artistic domains

Answers

1. d
2. b
3. c
4. b

Questions

1. How does StyleGAN's architecture differ from traditional GANs, and why is this beneficial for image generation?
2. What role does the mapping network play in StyleGAN, and how does it affect the generator's outputs?
3. How does AdaIN normalization contribute to style manipulation, and what are its advantages over batch normalization?
4. Why is progressive growing important in training StyleGAN, and how does it impact stability?
5. How does noise injection help in generating fine details in images?
6. What challenges arise in training large-scale StyleGAN models, and how can they be mitigated?
7. How can StyleGAN be adapted for domain-specific applications, such as medical imaging or gaming?
8. What evaluation metrics can be used to assess the quality and realism of StyleGAN-generated images?
9. What improvements could be made in future generative models beyond StyleGAN?

Key Terms

- **Style-Based Generator:** A generator that allows independent manipulation of content and style.
- **Mapping Network:** A latent space transformation network that injects learned style variations into the generator.
- **Adaptive Instance Normalization (AdaIN):** A normalization technique that enables fine control over style features.
- **Progressive Growing:** A training strategy where layers are added incrementally to stabilize learning.
- **Noise Injection:** A method for adding stochastic variation to enhance the fine details in generated images.
- **Latent Space Interpolation:** The ability to traverse the latent space to create smooth transitions between the generated outputs.
- **Perceptual Loss:** A loss function that assesses image quality based on feature similarity, rather than pixel differences.
- **Artifact Reduction:** Techniques used to minimize visual distortions in generated images.
- **High-Resolution Synthesis:** The ability to generate large-scale, realistic images with detailed textures.

CHAPTER 9
Variational Autoencoders Revisited: β-VAE and CVAE

Introduction

In this chapter, we revisit Variational Autoencoders (VAEs) and explore their advanced variants, β-VAE and Conditional VAE (CVAE), which address some of the limitations of traditional VAEs, and unlock new possibilities in generative modeling. By introducing a simple tuning knob that balances clarity and accuracy, β-VAE makes the AI's learned features more interpretable, and distinct. This makes it a powerful tool for finding patterns in data without supervision. On the other hand, CVAE adds a new capability, that is following instructions. By including guiding labels, it allows for controlled and specific generation of data.

We will dive into the design and core ideas behind these advanced models, including the role of the tuning knob in β-VAE, and the guided instructions in CVAE. Through practical code examples, we will demonstrate how to build, train, and use β-VAE and CVAE models, focusing on their real-world uses. These include learning clear data features, creating more training examples, and producing data based on specific requests. By the end of this chapter, you will gain a deeper understanding of these advanced VAEs, equipping you to leverage them for both research and practical applications.

Structure

In this chapter, we will discuss the following topics:

- **Introduction to Advanced Variational Autoencoders**
  - Limitations of Traditional VAEs
  - Motivation for Introducing β-VAE and CVAE
  - Real-World Analogy for Advanced VAEs
- **Comparison of β-VAE, CVAE, and Traditional VAEs**
- **Mathematical Foundations of β-VAE and CVAE**
  - Revisiting the Evidence Lower Bound Equation
  - Role of β in β-VAE: Trade-Off Between Reconstruction and Regularization
  - Conditional Latent Space in CVAE: Adding Labels to the Prior Distribution

- **Data Preparation and Preprocessing for β-VAE and CVAE**
  - Datasets Suitable for β-VAE and CVAE
  - Preprocessing for Conditional Labels in CVAE
- **Architecture of β-VAE and CVAE**
  - Architecture of β-VAE
  - Architecture of CVAE
- **Implementing β-VAE and CVAE: Step-by-Step**
  - Building a β-VAE
  - Building a CVAE
- **Evaluating the Performance of β-VAE and CVAE**
  - Metrics for Evaluating Disentanglement in β-VAE
  - Evaluating Conditional Accuracy in CVAE Outputs
  - Comparing Reconstruction Quality and Latent Space Organization
- **Challenges and Limitations of β-VAE and CVAE**
  - Trade-Offs in β-VAE
  - Data Dependency in CVAE
  - Generalization Issues and Computational Costs
- **Applications of β-VAE and CVAE**
  - β-VAE: Unlocking Interpretable Representations
  - CVAE: Conditioning for Controlled Outputs
- **Case Study: Translating Sketches into Realistic Images**

Introduction to Advanced VAEs

Building upon the foundational architecture of standard Variational Autoencoders, advanced variants such as β-VAE and Conditional VAE (CVAE) introduce critical innovations to enhance control and interpretability. The β-VAE modifies the core objective function by placing a hyperparameter, β, on the Kullback-Leibler (KL) divergence term. This explicitly regulates the trade-off between reconstruction fidelity and the disentanglement of the latent space, encouraging the model to learn statistically independent generative factors. In parallel, CVAE extends the framework by integrating conditional inputs, such as class labels or attributes, into both the encoder and decoder. This architectural shift enables directed data generation by conditioning the sampling process on specific user-defined contexts, thereby moving beyond unsupervised learning to facilitate targeted synthesis and data augmentation.

Recap of Variational Autoencoders

At their heart, VAEs are generative models that aim to learn a latent representation of data in a manner that enables both reconstruction and sampling. The architecture comprises two main components:

- **Encoder (Recognition Model):** Thismaps input data x into a latent space, producing a probabilistic distribution, q(z | x) over latent variables, z.
- **Decoder (Generative Model):** This maps latent variables, z back to the data space, generating a probabilistic distribution, p(x | z).

The objective of VAEs is to maximize the Evidence Lower Bound (ELBO), which balances reconstruction accuracy and latent space regularization. The ELBO is defined as:

$$L_{ELBO}=E_{q(z|x)}[\log p(x|z)]-KL(q(z|x)||p(z))$$

Where:

- The first term ensures that the reconstructed data is similar to the original input.
- The second term regularizes the latent space by minimizing the Kullback-Leibler (KL) divergence between the approximate posterior, $q(z \mid x)$ and a prior, $p(z)$, typically a standard Gaussian.

VAEs elegantly balance these two terms, producing coherent and meaningful generative results in many applications. However, as we will see, traditional VAEs face significant limitations in specific use cases.

Limitations of Traditional VAEs

While VAEs provide a robust framework for generative modeling, several shortcomings have emerged as researchers push the boundaries of what these models can achieve:

- **Latent Space Disentanglement:** The latent space learned by traditional VAEs often lacks interpretability. Features in the latent representation are entangled, making it difficult to manipulate specific aspects of the generated output. For example, in a VAE trained on facial images, varying a single latent dimension might unintentionally affect multiple facial features (for example, both hair color and expression).
- **Reconstruction versus Regularization Trade-off:** The ELBO objective inherently involves a trade-off between reconstruction quality and latent space regularization. In practice, VAEs often struggle to balance these terms effectively, leading to either poor reconstructions or a poorly structured latent space.
- **Conditional Modeling Limitations:** While VAEs can model complex distributions, they lack a straightforward mechanism to incorporate conditional dependencies. This limitation becomes apparent in tasks requiring targeted generation based on specific attributes, such as generating images conditioned on class labels.

These limitations highlight the need for advancements in VAE design to address issues of disentanglement, reconstruction quality, and conditional modeling. β-VAE and CVAE are two prominent extensions developed to overcome these challenges.

Motivation for Introducing β-VAE and CVAE

The innovations behind β-VAE and CVAE are driven by distinct but complementary motivations:

- **Disentangled Representations with β-VAE:** Traditional VAEs lack a mechanism to explicitly encourage disentanglement. β-VAE addresses this by modifying the ELBO objective with a β hyperparameter:

  $$L_{\beta\text{-}VAE}=E_{q(z|x)}[\log p(x|z)]-\beta\cdot KL(q(z|x)||p(z))$$

  By adjusting β, users can control the trade-off between reconstruction accuracy and latent space regularization. A higher β encourages a more disentangled latent space at the cost of reconstruction fidelity, making β-VAE particularly valuable for interpretability and downstream tasks such as feature manipulation.

- **Conditional Dependencies with CVAE:** Many real-world applications require the generation of data conditioned on specific attributes. For instance, generating handwritten digits conditioned on their labels or creating images based on textual descriptions. Traditional VAEs lack the capability to directly model such dependencies.

Conditional VAEs (CVAEs) extend the VAE framework by introducing conditional variables into both the encoder and decoder. This enables the model to learn conditional distributions q(z | x, c) and p(x | z, c), where c represents the conditioning information. Thus, by incorporating this additional information, CVAEs allow targeted and controlled generation.

Real-World Analogy for Advanced VAEs

β-VAE Analogy: Focused Financial Auditing: Imagine you are a financial auditor analyzing a company's expenses. A standard audit looks at all transactions, and records them with equal importance. However, if you are an investigative auditor, you might focus more on suspicious or high-value transactions, while reducing focus on less critical details.

***Figure 9.1**: Real-world Analogy for β-VAE with Financial Auditing Example*

In β-VAE, the β parameter acts like the audit severity level—increasing β forces the model to learn more structured and disentangled representations, similar to how an investigative audit highlights the most meaningful financial trends, while ignoring irrelevant noise.

- **Higher β** → More structured and interpretable financial reports but less detail in small transactions.
- **Lower β** → More detailed financial data but harder to interpret the key patterns.

CVAE Analogy: Customized Investment Portfolios

Imagine you are a financial advisor creating customized investment portfolios for clients. Instead of giving the same general advice to all, you tailor your recommendations based on the client's risk appetite, age, and financial goals.

Similarly, a CVAE generates data based on a specific condition (for example, a person's financial profile). The model learns to produce different latent representations depending on the input condition, just like a financial advisor generates different investment strategies based on client needs.

Figure 9.2: *Real-world Analogy of CVAE with Portfolio Management*

A CVAE can be trained to generate personalized trading signals conditioned on a trader's risk preference and market conditions. For example:

- **Aggressive traders** → CVAE suggests high-volatility, high-reward stocks.
- **Conservative traders** → CVAE suggests low-risk bonds or index funds.

Thus, by conditioning the generative model on market trends and investor profiles, CVAE can create synthetic financial data tailored to different risk profiles.

Comparison of β-VAE, CVAE, and Traditional VAEs

While the traditional VAE provides a strong baseline for encoding and decoding complex data distributions, advanced variants such as β-VAE and CVAE address specific limitations and extend the model's capabilities for more specialized tasks. This section delves into their comparative aspects, highlighting their differences, use cases, and challenges.

How β-VAE and CVAE Differ from Standard VAEs

β-VAE and CVAE differ from the standard VAE by introducing distinct architectural and objective modifications to the framework. So, let us look at the differences:

- **Traditional VAEs:** Standard VAEs optimize a trade-off between reconstruction loss and the Kullback-Leibler (KL) divergence to regularize the latent space. The loss function is defined as:

  $$L = E_{q(z|x)} [\log p(x|z)] - D_{KL}(q(z|x)||p(z))$$

  The balance between these terms ensures that the latent space is both informative and smooth. They aim for a general-purpose latent representation, without explicit separation.

- **β-VAE:** Introduces a scaling factor β to the KL divergence term in the loss function such as:

  $$L = E_{q(z|x)} [\log p(x|z)] - \beta \cdot D_{KL}(q(z|x)||p(z))$$

  Hence, by adjusting β, one can control the trade-off between disentanglement in the latent space and reconstruction fidelity. A higher β encourages more disentanglement but may sacrifice reconstruction quality. β-VAE prioritizes disentangling latent variables, which means that distinct factors of variation in the data are independently represented in the latent space.

- **CVAE:** This extends the standard VAE by incorporating conditional information into the latent variable distribution such as:

  `q(z | x, c), p(x | z, c)`

  This enables the model to generate outputs conditioned on specific attributes or labels such as c, making it particularly effective for tasks that require control over the generated data. It leverages conditional information to structure the latent space in a way that aligns with the given labels or attributes, enhancing controllability.

Use Cases for β-VAE and CVAE

The following are some of the common use cases for β-VAE:

- **Interpretable AI in Vision and Robotics:** In computer vision and robotics, β-VAE helps models learn distinct and manipulable attributes such as object shape, color, or pose, improving tasks such as robotic grasping and scene understanding.
- **Bias Detection and Fair AI:** In applications requiring fairness, such as hiring algorithms or credit scoring, β-VAE can separate bias-related features from meaningful ones, helping mitigate discrimination in decision-making.
- **Scientific Research and Discovery:** In genomics and material science, β-VAE can uncover hidden patterns by isolating complex factors, influencing gene expression or material properties, accelerating discoveries and insights.

The **Conditional VAE (CVAE)** is commonly used for specific tasks like **label-based generation** and **data augmentation**.

- **Image-to-Image Translation:** Used for tasks such as turning sketches into realistic images, or modifying attributes of an image (for example, adding glasses to a face).
- **Speech and Audio Generation:** Generates audio signals conditioned on specific speaker characteristics or other audio attributes.
- **Text-to-Image Generation:** Synthesizes images conditioned on textual descriptions, such as generating an image of "*a red sports car*" from a natural language prompt.
- **Domain-Specific Data Augmentation:** Augments datasets by generating synthetic examples conditioned on desired labels, improving downstream model performance.

Mathematical Foundations of β-VAE and CVAE

Why do β-VAE and CVAE matter? To truly grasp their power, we need to revisit the mathematical backbone that makes them work. At the heart of these models lies the ELBO equation, the foundation of Variational Inference, which balances reconstruction accuracy with latent space regularization. But what happens when we introduce a tuning factor, β, into this equation? The result is a model that trades off between faithful reconstructions and well-structured latent representations, unlocking disentangled feature learning.

Meanwhile, CVAE takes a different path. By injecting labels directly into the latent space, it transforms the VAE into a controlled generative powerhouse, allowing us to generate data tailored to specific conditions. But how does this actually work? Let us break it down.

Revisiting the ELBO Equation

To understand the mathematical foundations of β-VAE and CVAE, we must first return to a concept of standard Variational Autoencoders: The Evidence Lower Bound (ELBO).

The goal of a VAE is to train a model that can accurately reconstruct its input data, and generate new, realistic samples. This process relies on modeling the data's probability, p(x). However, direct computation of p(x) is often too difficult due to the complex integral over latent variables, z, such as:

$$p(x) = \int p(x|z)\ p(z)\ dz$$

To solve this, VAEs instead optimize a lower bound on log p(x), known as the ELBO. This is expressed as:

$$L_{ELBO} = E_{q(z|x)}\ [\log p(x|z)] - D_{KL}(q(z|x)||p(z))$$

Here:

- q(z | x) is the approximate posterior (encoder distribution).
- p(x | z) is the likelihood (decoder distribution).
- p(z) is the prior distribution over the latent variables, typically a standard normal distribution, N(0,I).
- D_{KL} is the Kullback-Leibler divergence, which measures the difference between the approximate posterior and the prior.

The ELBO has two key components:

- **Reconstruction Term:** Encourages q(z | x) to learn latent variables that can reconstruct the data accurately.
- **Regularization Term:** Penalizes deviations of q(z | x) from the prior p(z).

The balance between these terms is critical to the performance of the VAE, and β-VAEs introduce a scaling factor β to control this trade-off.

Role of β in β-VAE: Trade-off between Reconstruction and Regularization

The β-VAE modifies the standard ELBO by introducing a hyperparameter, β, which scales the regularization term:

$$L_{\beta\text{-VAE}} = E_{q(z|x)}\ [\log p(x|z)] - \beta D_{KL}(q(z|x)||p(z))$$

The parameter, β allows for explicit control over the trade-off between reconstruction quality and latent space disentanglement:

- **When β=1:** The model reduces to the standard VAE.
- **When β>1:** The model emphasizes regularization, encouraging disentangled latent spaces at the cost of reconstruction accuracy.
- **When β<1:** The model prioritizes reconstruction, which may lead to poor regularization and overfitting.

Intuition behind β-VAE

The disentanglement property of β-VAEs arises from the increased weight on the regularization term. By pushing q(z | x) closer to the prior p(z), the model learns to encode information about the data in a more structured manner. Disentangled representations are particularly useful in tasks such as generative modeling, where each dimension of the latent space corresponds to a distinct generative factor (for example, rotation, color, or shape).

Practical experiments with β-VAEs often involve tuning β to achieve a balance suited to the task at hand. For instance:

- A larger β is useful for generating interpretable latent spaces.
- A smaller β is preferable when high-quality reconstructions are paramount.

Conditional Latent Space in CVAE: Adding Labels to the Prior Distribution

The Conditional Variational Autoencoder (CVAE) extends the standard VAE by incorporating label information, y into both the encoder and the decoder, enabling the model to generate data conditioned on y.

The CVAE assumes a conditional generative process where the data, x is generated given a latent variable, z and a label, y:

$$p(x|y) = \int p(x|z,y)\ p(z|y)\ dz$$

To approximate this intractable marginal likelihood, CVAEs optimize a conditional variant of the ELBO:

$$L_{CVAE} = E_{q(z|x,y)}\ [\log p(x|z,y)] - D_{KL}(q(z|x,y)||p(z|y))$$

Here:

- q(z | x, y) is the approximate posterior, conditioned on both x and y.
- p(z | y) is the prior over latent variables, conditioned on y.
- p(x | z, y) is the likelihood, conditioned on both z and y.

Label Integration in CVAE

In CVAE, labels, y are used to guide the latent space. This label integration can be understood as adding structure to the prior distribution, p(z | y), allowing the model to learn conditional representations. For example:

- During encoding, an input image, x (example, a face) and its label, y (example, "smiling") are combined and passed through the encoder to estimate q(z | x, y).
- During decoding, the latent variable, z and a specific label, y (example, "not smiling") are used together to generate a modified version of the input via p(x | z, y), effectively changing the expression, while preserving the identity.

This conditional formulation enables CVAEs to perform tasks such as:

- **Controlled data generation** such as generating handwritten digits conditioned on digit labels.
- **Semi-supervised learning**, where the model leverages both labeled and unlabeled data for training.

Conditional Priors in CVAE

The choice of prior distribution p(z | y) is critical in CVAEs. A common assumption is that p(z | y) follows a Gaussian distribution, parameterized by a mean and variance dependent on y:

$$p(z|y) = \mathcal{N}(\mu_y,\ {}_y)$$

Thus, by conditioning the prior on y, CVAEs can learn disentangled latent spaces where each subspace corresponds to specific label-driven attributes. This structure enhances the interpretability of the latent space, and improves generative capabilities.

Practical Insights and Use Cases:

- **β-VAE** is widely used in unsupervised settings where interpretability and disentangled representations are desired, such as image generation and style transfer.
- **CVAE** excels in scenarios requiring controlled generation, such as data augmentation in classification tasks or domain-specific image synthesis.

Thus, by revisiting these advanced variants of VAEs, we can unlock the potential of generative models to address a broader spectrum of real-world challenges.

Data Preparation and Preprocessing for β-VAE and CVAE

Variational Autoencoders (VAEs), especially β-VAEs and Conditional VAEs (CVAEs), require careful data preparation to ensure effective training and meaningful results. This section explores datasets suitable for these models, preprocessing techniques for conditional labels in CVAEs, and strategies for promoting data diversity.

Datasets Suitable for β-VAE and CVAE

The choice of dataset plays a crucial role in the performance of generative models such as β-VAE and CVAE. The dataset must align with the objectives of the model, and should offer sufficient variability to explore and represent latent spaces effectively.

Commonly Used Datasets:

- **MNIST and Fashion-MNIST:**
  - Simple and lightweight datasets ideal for prototyping.
  - Contain grayscale images of handwritten digits (MNIST) or clothing items (Fashion-MNIST).
  - Useful for exploring disentangled representations in β-VAEs, and generating variations of a specific class in CVAEs.
- **CIFAR-10 and CIFAR-100:**
  - RGB image datasets of objects and animals.
  - These datasets are more complex, offering challenges for learning disentangled features, and generating high-quality outputs.
- **CelebA:**
  - A dataset of celebrity faces with multiple attribute labels.
  - Ideal for CVAEs due to their labeled attributes, such as gender, age, and hairstyle.
- **Custom Datasets:**
  - Domain-specific datasets can be created or curated for tasks such as medical imaging, product recommendation, or scientific research.
  - Custom datasets provide flexibility for targeting specific applications of β-VAE and CVAE.

Dataset Characteristics:

- **Labeled Data:** Essential for CVAE to incorporate conditional labels during training.
- **Diversity:** The dataset should represent a broad range of variations for meaningful latent representations.
- **Sufficient Size:** A larger dataset allows better generalization and disentanglement of latent factors.

Strategies for Ensuring Data Diversity

To achieve diversity, data augmentation is commonly used–ranging from basic techniques like rotation, flipping, and adding noise, to advanced methods like Cutout, Mix-up, and style transfer, which enhance variability in more sophisticated ways. Additionally, analyzing class distribution helps to identify imbalances, prompting either synthetic data creation or targeted sampling to address underrepresentation.

Other strategies include cluster-based sampling, where clustering algorithms such as k-means are used to ensure that the training data spans all identified clusters, enhancing representation. Unlabeled data can also be leveraged through semi-supervised learning—for instance, pretraining the VAE on unlabeled data to grasp general features, and then fine-tuning with labeled examples. When datasets are limited, domain adaptation techniques or transfer learning from richer datasets like ImageNet can inject diversity. Finally, diversity should be evaluated using metrics such as pairwise distance in feature space or entropy-based measures to quantify variation in the latent representations.

Preprocessing for Conditional Labels in CVAE

Conditional VAEs use labels to guide the generation process, enabling control over the output by conditioning on specific attributes. Preprocessing these labels ensures consistency and accuracy during training.

Encoding Labels:

- **One-Hot Encoding:**
  - Converts categorical labels into a binary matrix.
  - **Example:** For a dataset with three classes (dog, cat, bird), the labels are encoded as [1, 0, 0], [0, 1, 0], and [0, 0, 1], respectively.
  - Most commonly used for discrete attributes in CVAEs.
- **Embedding Representation:**
  - Embeds labels into continuous vector space using techniques such as word embeddings.
  - Useful when the dataset contains hierarchical or semantically rich labels.

Attribute Normalization:

- Ensures that numerical labels, such as age or temperature, are scaled to a range suitable for training.
- Techniques such as Min-Max scaling or Z-score normalization are effective.

Balancing Labels:

- In datasets with skewed label distributions, underrepresented classes might be ignored during training.
- Techniques such as oversampling, under sampling, or synthetic data generation can be applied to balance the dataset.

Augmenting Conditional Data:

- For datasets with limited labels, augmentation techniques such as rotation, flipping, and cropping can create diverse samples for each label.
- This ensures robustness in the conditional generation process.

Architecture of β-VAE and CVAE

What if we could take the traditional VAE, and make it smarter—more focused, more interpretable, and more controlled? β-VAE does just that by introducing a way to balance reconstruction quality with structured latent space learning. Meanwhile, CVAE takes this a step further, allowing us to guide the generative process with labels, enabling controlled outputs, rather than random sampling.

To truly appreciate these enhancements, we need to look under the hood. How does β-VAE modify the standard VAE architecture to enforce better disentanglement? And how does CVAE inject conditional information into the encoding-decoding process? Let us break it down.

Architecture of β-VAE

The β-VAE is a modified version of the standard Variational Autoencoder. While the standard VAE balances reconstruction accuracy and latent space regularization, β-VAE introduces a scaling factor, β, to modulate this tradeoff. This adjustment emphasizes disentanglement in the learned latent representations, making β-VAE particularly useful for unsupervised representation learning.

Adjustments to the Standard VAE Architecture:

- **Objective Function:** The β-VAE objective function introduces a β coefficient in the Evidence Lower Bound (ELBO):

  $$L = E_{q\varphi(z|x)}[\log p_\theta(x|z)] - \beta \cdot D_{KL}(q_\varphi(z|x)||p(z))$$

  Here, β controls the weight of the KL-divergence term, enabling a flexible tradeoff between reconstruction quality and latent space regularization.

- **Encoder-Decoder Design:**
  - The encoder maps the input data to a mean and variance vector, parameterizing the latent space distribution.
  - The decoder reconstructs the input from latent representations.
- **Latent Space:**
  - A higher β encourages sparsity and disentanglement, often leading to a latent space where distinct dimensions represent distinct generative factors.
- **Loss Implementation:**
  - The reconstruction loss remains a standard log-likelihood term.
  - The KL divergence term is multiplied by β to enforce stricter regularization or allow more freedom in the latent representation.
- **Training Challenges:**
  - High values of β may lead to underfitting, as the model prioritizes disentanglement excessively.
  - Low values of β may result in overfitting, reducing the generalization capability of the model.
- **Regularization Techniques:**
  - **Annealing β:** Gradually increasing β during training allows the model to learn reconstructions first, and disentanglement later.
  - **Dropout and Batch Normalization:** Regularization techniques in the encoder and decoder layers improve model robustness.

Architecture of CVAE

The Conditional Variational Autoencoder (CVAE) extends the VAE framework by incorporating conditional information into the generative process. CVAE is designed for tasks where outputs are conditioned on specific labels or attributes, enabling targeted data generation.

Integrating Labels into the Encoder and Decoder

- **Conditional Inputs:**
  - Both the encoder and decoder are conditioned on a label or auxiliary information, y.
  - The encoder maps the input, x and the label, y to the latent distribution.
  - The decoder reconstructs x from the latent representation, z and the label, y.
- **Modified Objective Function:** The CVAE optimizes a conditional ELBO:

$$L = E_{(z|x,y)}[\log p_\theta(x|z,y)] - D_{KL}(q_\varphi(z|x,y)||p(z|y))$$

  - A standard VAE is like a chef preparing random but plausible dishes without customer input, while a CVAE customizes meals based on specific orders, ensuring controlled, relevant, and high-quality outputs.
  - The CVAE objective function guarantees that the generated data is both accurate (tastes good), and follows a structured latent representation (recipe consistency).
- **Network Architecture:**
  - The encoder concatenates x and y before passing them through neural network layers to generate latent parameters.
  - The decoder receives z concatenated with y to conditionally reconstruct the input, x.
- **Advantages of Conditioning:**
  - Allows the generation of data samples corresponding to the specific labels.
  - Improves disentanglement by providing auxiliary information to the latent representation.

Visualizing the Conditional Latent Space

- **Latent Space Representation:**
  - CVAE enables visualizing how the latent space is influenced by the conditional label, y.
  - Samples from the latent space exhibit clear separation based on conditioning labels, aiding interpretability.
- **Latent Space Clustering:**
  - For tasks such as image generation, samples with the same label cluster together in latent space.
  - Visualization tools such as t-SNE or PCA can demonstrate the effectiveness of conditional encoding.
- **Generated Outputs:**
  - By sampling from different regions of the latent space, while fixing y, the CVAE generates outputs consistent with the given label.

The β-VAE and CVAE architectures represent significant advancements in the realm of variational autoencoders. While β-VAE focuses on disentangling latent representations to improve interpretability, CVAE leverages conditional information to enable targeted data generation. These models exemplify the flexibility and adaptability of VAEs for diverse applications, from unsupervised learning to conditional synthesis. Both architectures underline the importance of tailoring VAE designs to specific tasks, showcasing the potential of generative models in solving real-world problems.

Implementing β-VAE and CVAE: Step-by-Step

Now that we understand the concepts behind β-VAE and CVAE, it is time to bring them to life. But here is the catch—these advanced VAEs require precise modifications to their structure and loss functions to truly unlock their power. How do we introduce **β** into the loss function, without breaking reconstruction quality? How can we guide the generation process in CVAE to produce controlled outputs based on labels?

In this section, we will take a deep dive into the practical implementation of β-VAE and CVAE, carefully tweaking the key components to balance reconstruction accuracy, latent space regularization, and conditional generation. By the end, you will not only understand the mechanics but also be able to build and train these models yourself.

Building a β-VAE

The β-Variational Autoencoder (β-VAE) is an extension of the traditional VAE that introduces a β hyperparameter in the loss function to control the balance between reconstruction accuracy and latent space disentanglement. This encourages the model to learn structured and interpretable latent factors.

Define the Architecture:

- Similar to a standard VAE, a β-VAE consists of an encoder, decoder, and a latent space.
- The encoder maps the input data to a mean (μ) and variance (σ^2) in the latent space.
- The decoder reconstructs the input data from the latent representation.

Adjusting the Loss Function to Include β:

- The VAE loss function is a combination of reconstruction loss and KL divergence:

$$\mathcal{L}_{VAE} = E_{(z|x)}[-\log p_\theta(x|z)] + \beta \cdot D_{KL}(q_\varphi(z|x)||p(z))$$

- β allows for control over the trade-off between reconstruction fidelity and the disentanglement of latent representations.

Training on Datasets with Structured Latent Factors:

- Structured datasets, such as the dSprites dataset, are commonly used for β-VAE training as they have well-defined latent factors (for example, shape, scale, orientation, and so on).
- Data preprocessing includes normalization and resizing as required by the neural network.

Example Code for β-VAE:

```
import torch
import torch.nn as nn

# Encoder: maps input to latent space (mu and logvar)
class Encoder(nn.Module):
    def __init__(self, input_dim, latent_dim):
        super().__init__()
        self.fc = nn.Linear(input_dim, 256)
        self.mu = nn.Linear(256, latent_dim)
        self.logvar = nn.Linear(256, latent_dim)

    def forward(self, x):
        h = torch.relu(self.fc(x))
        return self.mu(h), self.logvar(h)

# Decoder: reconstructs input from latent vector z
class Decoder(nn.Module):
    def __init__(self, latent_dim, output_dim):
        super().__init__()
```

```
        self.fc = nn.Linear(latent_dim, 256)
        self.out = nn.Linear(256, output_dim)

    def forward(self, z):
        h = torch.relu(self.fc(z))
        return torch.sigmoid(self.out(h))

# β-VAE Loss: reconstruction + β-weighted KL divergence
def beta_vae_loss(x, x_hat, mu, logvar, beta=4):
    recon_loss = nn.functional.binary_cross_entropy(x_hat, x, reduction='sum')
    kl_loss = -0.5 * torch.sum(1 + logvar - mu**2 - logvar.exp())
    return recon_loss + beta * kl_loss

# Latent sampling using reparameterization trick
def reparameterize(mu, logvar):
    std = torch.exp(0.5 * logvar)
    eps = torch.randn_like(std)
    return mu + eps * std
```

The minimal β-VAE implementation in PyTorch consists of an Encoder, a Decoder, a reparameterization function, and a custom loss that balances reconstruction and latent regularization. The Encoder maps the input data into a latent space by producing a mean (μ) and log variance (logvar), which are then used to sample latent vectors using the reparameterization trick. The Decoder reconstructs the input from these sampled vectors. The custom loss combines binary cross-entropy for reconstruction fidelity and a KL divergence term that is scaled by a tunable β coefficient. This β term controls the degree of disentanglement in the learned latent representations. Higher values of β promote independence among latent factors, making the model better at capturing structured, interpretable variations in data—an essential trait for generative tasks that demand clarity and control.

Building a CVAE

A Conditional Variational Autoencoder (CVAE) extends the VAE by conditioning both the encoder and decoder on additional label information. This allows the model to generate outputs conditioned on specific attributes or categories.

Conditioning the Encoder and Decoder:

- Input data is concatenated with label information.
- The encoder learns a latent representation conditioned on the input, and its label.
- The decoder reconstructs the input data conditioned on both the latent representation and the label.

Training and Sampling Conditioned Outputs:

- During training, labels are appended to the input data for both the encoder and decoder.
- For sampling, the latent vector is combined with the desired label information to generate conditioned outputs.

Example Code for CVAE:

```
import torch
import torch.nn as nn

# Conditional VAE: conditions both encoder and decoder on label
class CVAE(nn.Module):
    def __init__(self, input_dim, latent_dim, label_dim):
```

```
            super().__init__()
            self.encoder = nn.Linear(input_dim + label_dim, 256)
            self.mu = nn.Linear(256, latent_dim)
            self.logvar = nn.Linear(256, latent_dim)
            self.decoder = nn.Linear(latent_dim + label_dim, 256)
            self.out = nn.Linear(256, input_dim)

        def encode(self, x, y):
            xy = torch.cat([x, y], dim=-1)
            h = torch.relu(self.encoder(xy))
            return self.mu(h), self.logvar(h)

        def decode(self, z, y):
            zy = torch.cat([z, y], dim=-1)
            h = torch.relu(self.decoder(zy))
            return torch.sigmoid(self.out(h))

        def forward(self, x, y):
            mu, logvar = self.encode(x, y)
            std = torch.exp(0.5 * logvar)
            z = mu + std * torch.randn_like(std)
            return self.decode(z, y), mu, logvar

    def vae_loss(x, x_hat, mu, logvar, beta=1):
        recon = nn.functional.binary_cross_entropy(x_hat, x, reduction='sum')
        kl = -0.5 * torch.sum(1 + logvar - mu.pow(2) - logvar.exp())
        return recon + beta * kl
```

Both β-VAE and CVAE are extensions of the standard Variational Autoencoder (VAE) architecture, designed for different goals: β-VAE for learning abstract, disentangled representations, and CVAE for controlled, label-driven generation. Training β-VAE involves adjusting the β hyperparameter to balance reconstruction and regularization, while CVAE depends on proper one-hot encoding of labels to condition the latent space effectively.

Evaluating the Performance of β-VAE and CVAE

Evaluating the performance of Beta Variational Autoencoders (β-VAE) and Conditional Variational Autoencoders (CVAE) requires tailored approaches, as these models have unique objectives. In this section, we will explore the key metrics and methodologies to evaluate these models effectively.

Metrics for Evaluating Disentanglement in β-VAE

β-VAE has the capability to represent distinct generative factors of data in separate dimensions of the latent space. Several metrics and techniques have been developed to quantify this aspect:

Mutual Information Gap (MIG)

MIG measures the gap in mutual information between the most informative latent variable and the next most informative one for each generative factor. Higher MIG scores indicate better disentanglement.

Calculation Steps:

- Compute the mutual information between each latent dimension, and each ground truth factor.

- Calculate the difference between the highest and the second-highest mutual information scores for each factor.
- Average these differences across all factors.

Disentanglement, Completeness, and Informativeness (DCI):

- **Disentanglement:** Measures how uniquely each latent variable is associated with a specific generative factor.
- **Completeness:** Assesses whether all generative factors are captured by the latent variables.
- **Informativeness:** Quantifies the predictive power of latent variables for reconstructing the data.

Beta-TCVAE Metric

A variation of Total Correlation (TC) measures how well β-VAE balances disentanglement and reconstruction. Low TC values indicate minimal redundancy among latent variables, which is desirable for disentanglement.

Latent Traversals:

- Visualizing the effect of varying individual latent dimensions, while keeping others fixed.
- Qualitatively evaluate disentanglement by observing interpretable changes in generated outputs.

FactorVAE Score: This metric employs a classifier to predict generative factors from latent representations. A higher score indicates better alignment between the latent dimensions and the generative factors.

Downstream Task Performance: Evaluate the usefulness of disentangled representations by training a classifier or regressor on a downstream task. Better disentanglement often correlates with improved performance.

Evaluating Conditional Accuracy in CVAE Outputs

CVAE is designed to generate data conditioned on specific input variables. Its performance depends on how accurately it generates outputs aligned with the given conditions.

Conditional Accuracy:

- Measures how often the generated outputs conform to the specified conditions.
- **Example:** For a CVAE generating faces conditioned on "smile", the model's accuracy can be computed as the percentage of generated images, correctly classified as "smiling face" by a pre-trained classifier.

Negative Log-Likelihood (NLL):

- Assesses how well the model captures the conditional data distribution.
- Lower NLL values indicate better performance in modeling conditional relationships.

Kullback-Leibler (KL) Divergence:

- Quantifies the divergence between the approximate posterior and the prior distribution for the latent variables.
- While regular KL divergence evaluates the overall performance, "*per-condition* KL *divergence*" can assess the quality of conditional representations.

Mode Coverage:

- Ensures that the CVAE generates diverse outputs spanning all possible conditions.
- This can be evaluated using metrics such as Inception Score (IS) or the number of unique modes captured by the model.

Conditional Diversity Score:

- Measures the diversity of generated outputs for a fixed condition.
- Higher scores reflect better modeling of variability within the conditioned data distribution.

Visual Inspection:

- Visualize generated samples for various conditions to qualitatively evaluate adherence to conditions and output diversity.

Comparing Reconstruction Quality and Latent Space Organization

Both β-VAE and CVAE aim to balance reconstruction quality with latent space organization. The following metrics and analyses are commonly used:

Reconstruction Loss: Measures the fidelity of reconstructed data relative to the input data. Typically computed using Mean Squared Error (MSE) or Binary Cross-Entropy (BCE), depending on the data type.

Latent Space Visualization:

- Techniques such as t-SNE or UMAP are used to project the latent space into 2D or 3D for visual inspection.
- For β-VAE, disentangled latent spaces should show clear clustering of data points based on generative factors.
- For CVAE, clusters should align with the conditioning variables.

Reconstruction versus Regularization Trade-Off:

- β-VAE often increases the β coefficient to encourage disentanglement, but this can harm reconstruction quality. The trade-off can be assessed by plotting disentanglement metrics (for example, MIG) against reconstruction loss.
- In CVAE, the trade-off involves preserving conditional accuracy, while maintaining high reconstruction quality.

Interpolation in Latent Space:

- Evaluate the smoothness of the latent space by interpolating between two latent vectors, and generating corresponding outputs.
- Smooth transitions indicate well-structured latent spaces, a desirable property for both β-VAE and CVAE.

Fréchet Inception Distance (FID): Measures the similarity between the distributions of generated and real data. Lower FID scores indicate better reconstruction and generative quality.

Structural Similarity Index (SSIM): Evaluates the similarity between original and reconstructed images, focusing on perceptual quality.

Latent Space Arithmetic: Perform arithmetic operations in the latent space to assess interpretability. For instance, subtracting and adding latent vectors should yield meaningful transformations (for example, removing a smile from a face).

Log-Likelihood of Held-Out Data: Measures the ability of the model to generalize to unseen data. Higher log-likelihood values indicate better latent space organization.

Thus, by leveraging the preceding metrics and evaluation techniques, researchers and practitioners can effectively assess and compare the performance of β-VAE and CVAE models. These insights enable informed decisions about model design and optimization, based on specific application requirements.

Challenges and Limitations of β-VAE and CVAE

Variational Autoencoders (VAEs) and their variants, such as β-VAE and Conditional VAE (CVAE), have brought substantial advancements in generative modeling. However, these models are not without their challenges and limitations. Understanding these hurdles is crucial for researchers and practitioners aiming to improve the applicability and robustness of these models.

Trade-offs in β-VAE

One of the hallmark features of β-VAE is its ability to enforce disentangled representations, thanks to the adjustable β parameter that scales the Kullback-Leibler (KL) divergence term in the loss function. However, this flexibility introduces a critical trade-off between reconstruction quality and disentanglement.

The Disentanglement-Reconstruction Trade-off

- **Reconstruction Loss:** A lower reconstruction loss ensures the generated data remains close to the original input, preserving fine details. However, prioritizing reconstruction often leads to entangled latent spaces, where individual latent dimensions fail to correspond to interpretable features.
- **Disentanglement:** Higher β values encourage disentanglement, where each latent dimension captures distinct, meaningful features of the data. Unfortunately, this comes at the expense of reconstruction fidelity, as the model sacrifices data-specific details to minimize KL divergence.

Tuning β: A Double-Edged Sword

The choice of β is pivotal but non-trivial. High β values promote disentangled latent representations but often lead to blurry reconstructions, especially in complex datasets such as natural images. Conversely, low β values yield high-quality reconstructions but fail to achieve meaningful disentanglement.

Application-Specific Challenges:

- **Sensitive Applications:** In fields such as medical imaging, poor reconstruction fidelity can lead to misinterpretations.
- **Interpretability:** While disentanglement is appealing for downstream tasks, its practical utility depends on whether the disentangled features align with meaningful attributes in the data.

Addressing this trade-off requires novel techniques, such as dynamic β-scheduling, which adjusts β during training, or hybrid loss functions that better balance the competing objectives.

Data Dependency in CVAE

Conditional Variational Autoencoders (CVAE) extend the standard VAE by incorporating label information, enabling label-conditioned generation. While this framework offers enhanced control over the generative process, it is highly dependent on the quality and distribution of the labeled data.

Challenges in Label-Conditioned Generation:

- **Imbalanced Datasets:** When labels are unevenly distributed, the CVAE may overfit dominant classes, producing biased samples for minority classes. This imbalance undermines the diversity of generated samples.
- **Noisy Labels:** Labels with errors or inconsistencies introduce ambiguity into the generative process, affecting both the quality and fidelity of the generated data.
- **Sparse Labels:** In domains with limited annotated data, such as medical or rare datasets, the CVAE struggles to learn robust label-conditioned representations.

Generalization across Labels

Even with clean, balanced datasets, CVAEs often struggle with generalization. This limitation manifests in:

- **Overfitting:** The model memorizes specific label-conditioned patterns, rather than generalizing across the label space.
- **Inter-class Relationships:** CVAEs rarely capture nuanced relationships between labels, resulting in a lack of diversity and coherence in generated data.

Label Conditioning and Latent Space Alignment

Aligning the latent space with labels is another non-trivial challenge. Poor alignment can:

- Produce noisy or unrealistic outputs for certain labels.
- Lead to mode collapse, where the generative process produces only a subset of possible outcomes for a given label.

Potential solutions include augmenting data, employing adversarial regularization, or using semi-supervised techniques to reduce dependency on extensive labeled datasets.

Generalization Issues and Computational Costs

Both β-VAE and CVAE face broader issues related to generalization and the computational demands of training and inference.

Generalization Challenges:

- **Domain Shift:** When trained on a specific dataset, these models often fail to generalize to unseen distributions. For example, a β-VAE trained on synthetic cartoon-style faces may struggle to generate realistic, photographic portraits.
- **Representation Gaps:** Latent representations, even when disentangled or label-aligned, may not capture all relevant features, limiting the utility of generated outputs.
- **Scaling to Complex Data:** While effective for simple datasets such as MNIST or CIFAR-10, these models struggle with high-dimensional data, such as videos or 3D shapes.

Computational Costs

Training and deploying VAEs come with significant computational overheads:

- **Training Time:** Both β-VAE and CVAE require iterative optimization of complex loss functions, often demanding high-performance GPUs for acceptable training times.
- **Memory Requirements:** Handling large datasets or high-dimensional data increases memory usage, particularly for CVAE, which must account for additional label information.

- **Inference Speed:** Generating samples or reconstructing data in real-time can be computationally expensive, limiting the practicality of these models in resource-constrained environments, such as mobile or edge devices.

Mitigation Strategies

To address these challenges, researchers are exploring:

- **Efficient Architectures:** Lightweight neural network architectures reduce training and inference costs.
- **Transfer Learning:** Pre-trained models fine-tuned on specific tasks can save time and computational resources.
- **Approximation Techniques:** Techniques such as quantization or pruning reduce model size without significantly sacrificing performance.

Despite their transformative potential, β-VAE and CVAE face significant challenges related to trade-offs in performance, data dependency, and computational feasibility. Addressing these limitations requires careful design choices, innovative regularization techniques, and domain-specific adaptations. By understanding these hurdles, researchers and practitioners can develop more robust and efficient generative models, paving the way for broader applications and deeper insights into data generation and representation learning.

Applications of β-VAE and CVAE

VAEs are powerful tools for learning latent representations in a wide range of tasks. Both the variants, β-VAE and CVAE, extend their capabilities by introducing constraints and conditions, making them particularly valuable for specialized applications. In this section, we explore the unique applications of β-VAE and CVAE, emphasizing their contributions to fields such as representation learning, data augmentation, and controlled content generation.

β-VAE: Unlocking Interpretable Representations

β-VAE excels in learning interpretable features from the raw data, particularly in unsupervised scenarios. The disentangled latent representations it produces allow for the separation of meaningful factors of variation in the data. For example:

- In computer vision, β-VAE can learn to disentangle attributes such as object shape, size, and color in image datasets, enabling researchers to study these factors independently.
- In healthcare, β-VAE can analyze the patient data to uncover latent variables corresponding to distinct clinical features, aiding in diagnosis and treatment planning.

The structured latent space of β-VAE makes it a valuable tool for downstream machine learning tasks. Once trained, the latent variables can be used as input features for tasks such as classification or clustering. For instance:

- In robotics, β-VAE representations can simplify control policies by isolating factors such as object position and orientation.
- In Natural Language Processing (NLP), β-VAE can be employed to extract disentangled features from the textual data, facilitating tasks such as sentiment analysis or topic modeling.

CVAE: Conditioning for Controlled Outputs

Conditional Variational Autoencoders (CVAE) extend the VAE framework by incorporating conditional inputs into the encoding and decoding processes. This capability allows the model to generate outputs controlled by specific input labels, making CVAE particularly useful for tasks requiring explicit control over the generated data.

Image-to-Image Translation Tasks

CVAE is widely used in image-to-image translation, where the goal is to transform an image from one domain to another, while preserving its content. Examples include:

- Converting sketches to realistic images by conditioning the model on specific object categories.
- Translating between weather conditions, such as changing a sunny scene to a rainy one, by conditioning on the desired weather type.
- Generating facial expressions or attributes by providing labels such as "*smile*" or "*glasses*."

Data Augmentation in Supervised Learning

In supervised learning, the scarcity of labeled data often limits the model performance. CVAE addresses this issue by generating diverse labeled samples to augment the training dataset.

Applications include:

- Expanding medical datasets by generating synthetic X-ray or MRI images labeled with specific conditions, improving diagnostic models.
- Enhancing datasets for autonomous vehicles by creating labeled variations of road scenes, such as different lighting or traffic conditions.

Controlled Content Generation for Specific Domains

CVAE's ability to generate data conditioned on specific attributes makes it invaluable for creative and domain-specific applications. For instance:

- In fashion design, CVAE can generate clothing designs conditioned on parameters such as style, color, or season.
- In personalized education, CVAE can create tailored educational content, such as math problems with controlled difficulty levels.
- In gaming, CVAE can design environments or characters with attributes specified by game designers.

Both β-VAE and CVAE are pivotal advancements in the VAE family, addressing key challenges in representation learning and content generation. β-VAE provides interpretable and disentangled representations ideal for unsupervised tasks and downstream applications, while CVAE enables precise control over generated content through conditioning. Together, these models bridge the gap between understanding complex data and generating creative solutions, driving innovation across diverse domains such as healthcare, autonomous systems, and creative industries.

Case Study: Translating Sketches to Images

Turning a simple sketch into a realistic image is more than just filling in details—it requires understanding the underlying structure, textures, and shading. However, traditional generative models struggle to separate these features, often producing entangled representations that limit control. In this case study, we explore how β-VAE and CVAE can work together to learn disentangled and interpretable representations, enabling precise and condition-guided image translation.

Problem: Enhancing Image Translation by Learning Disentangled and Interpretable Representations

A digital design studio needed to transform the basic architectural sketches into photorealistic renderings, but encountered a critical limitation with the existing AI tools. Their designers required independent control over specific visual attributes—wanting to adjust shading, texture, and material finishes separately, without affecting other elements.

Figure 9.3: *Generating Realistic Images from Sketches for a Designer Studio*

Traditional image translation systems consistently failed because they treated all the features as entangled, causing unwanted changes across the entire image when modifying any single parameter. When designers attempted to modify one attribute (for example, "*make the walls brick instead of wood*"), the system would unpredictably alter other elements like window shapes or roof angles.

The key challenge in image translation is generating realistic outputs, while maintaining control over specific visual attributes. Traditional Variational Autoencoders struggle with this because they tend to entangle different features in the latent space, making it difficult to isolate and manipulate individual aspects of an image. This limitation hinders applications such as our sketch-to-image translation, where details such as shading, texture, and color need to be controlled independently.

Solution Approach: Using β-VAE for Disentanglement and CVAE for Controlled Generation

We designed and implemented a dual-VAE framework in two steps that combines the strengths of the two specialized VAE models.

Step 1: β-VAE for Disentangled Representations

The β parameter controls the trade-off between reconstruction accuracy and latent space regularization. A higher β encourages the model to focus on structured representations, ensuring that distinct latent variables correspond to different visual features such as texture, shape, or lighting.

- **Dataset Preparation:** A dataset of hand-drawn sketches and corresponding real images is used for training. These images are preprocessed and normalized for consistency.

- **Model Architecture:** The encoder extracts meaningful latent representations, while the decoder reconstructs images from the latent space. The key addition is a modified loss function that increases the emphasis on disentanglement.
- **Training Objective:** The β-VAE loss function includes a KL divergence term weighted by β, allowing fine-tuning of latent space structure. By adjusting β, we achieve a balance between capturing details, and enforcing interpretability.

Step 2: CVAE for Controlled Generation

CVAE extends VAEs by conditioning both the encoder and decoder on additional information, such as object type, shading intensity, or color preferences. This enables more structured image translations, where a user can specify attributes, and generate controlled outputs.

- **Conditioning Mechanism:** Sketches are paired with attribute labels indicating features such as stroke thickness, shading level, or object category. These labels are incorporated into both the encoder and decoder.
- **Model Architecture:** CVAE modifies the standard VAE by concatenating these labels with the latent space representation, ensuring that the generated outputs align with the given conditions.
- **Training Objective:** The loss function ensures that the generated images match their intended attributes, preventing inconsistencies during translation.

Outcome: Translating Sketches into Realistic Images

Our approach, leveraging a combined β-VAE and CVAE framework, produced significantly better results than traditional models. We successfully transformed simple sketches into highly realistic images by solving the core issue of entangled representations. The key improvements were:

- **Precise Control:** β-VAE's disentangled latent space allowed for independent adjustment of specific features (for example, shading, line style, and so on) without affecting others.
- **Conditional Accuracy:** CVAE ensured the final output faithfully adhered to both the original sketch and any additional guidance (for example, "*make it look metallic*").
- **Overall Quality:** This synergy resulted in more realistic, detailed, and user-controllable image synthesis.

This case study demonstrates how combining β-VAE and CVAE enables interpretable and controlled sketch-to-image translation. These models empower applications in digital art, automated design, and scientific visualization, where precision in generative modeling is crucial.

Conclusion

In this chapter, we explored the advanced VAEs, focusing on β-VAE and Conditional VAE, and their innovations beyond traditional VAEs. β-VAE introduces a β-term in the loss function to improve latent space disentanglement, making it effective for structured and interpretable representation learning. Meanwhile, CVAE extends VAEs by incorporating conditional inputs, allowing for controlled and guided generation, making it ideal for supervised generative tasks.

We examined their mathematical foundations, particularly how β affects the Evidence Lower Bound (ELBO) equation, and how CVAE integrates labels into the latent space. Through architectural adjustments and step-by-step implementations, we demonstrated how these models can be built and optimized. We also discussed evaluation metrics, highlighting the trade-offs between reconstruction quality, latent space organization, and conditional accuracy.

Despite their advantages, β-VAEs and CVAEs face challenges, such as balancing reconstruction fidelity with disentanglement, ensuring label diversity, and managing computational complexity. However, their applications in representation learning, image-to-image translation, data augmentation, and controlled content generation make them powerful tools in modern generative modeling.

With a solid understanding of β-VAE and CVAE, you are now prepared to explore the next frontier in generative models. In the next chapter, we will delve into Diffusion Models, an exciting class of deep generative models that iteratively refine images from noise, achieving state-of-the-art results in high-fidelity image synthesis and denoising applications.

Points to Remember

- β-VAE modifies the VAE framework by introducing a β-weighted KL divergence term, improving the disentanglement of latent representations.
- CVAE enhances VAEs by incorporating conditional inputs, allowing for label-guided generation.
- Cycle consistency in β-VAE ensures a structured and interpretable latent space, aiding in representation learning.
- Conditional sampling in CVAE allows for domain-specific generation, making it useful for image-to-image translation and supervised tasks.
- The β parameter acts as a crucial trade-off knob: higher values promote cleaner disentanglement but can lead to blurrier reconstructions, requiring careful tuning for a specific task.
- CVAE leverages explicit labels, showcasing two powerful but distinct paths toward achieving controllability in generative models.
- The key challenges include balancing reconstruction and disentanglement (β-VAE) and data dependency for meaningful label-driven generation (CVAE).

Multiple Choice Questions

1. What is the primary goal of β-VAE?
   a. Reducing computational complexity
   b. Enhancing conditional sampling
   c. Removing the need for KL divergence
   d. Improving latent space disentanglement
2. How does CVAE differ from standard VAEs?
   a. It uses additional layers in the decoder.
   b. It conditions the encoder and decoder with label information.
   c. It removes the latent space regularization.
   d. It replaces the ELBO equation.
3. What is the main trade-off in β-VAE training?
   a. Higher reconstruction fidelity versus better disentanglement.
   b. Increased latent space smoothness versus reduced interpretability.
   c. Faster training speed versus lower accuracy.
   d. Increased dataset requirements versus reduced generalization.

4. Which real-world application benefits most from CVAE?
    a. Unsupervised anomaly detection
    b. Self-supervised learning
    c. Image-to-image translation
    d. Noise reduction in diffusion models

Answers

1. d
2. b
3. a
4. c

Questions

1. How does β-VAE improve disentanglement, and why is this useful in representation learning?
2. What are the key differences in mathematical formulation between β-VAE, CVAE, and traditional VAEs?
3. How does conditional sampling in CVAE enable better generative control?
4. What are some real-world applications of β-VAE in unsupervised learning and CVAE in supervised generative tasks?
5. How does the β parameter impact the KL-divergence term, and what are its effects on reconstruction and latent space organization?
6. What are the computational challenges of training β-VAE and CVAE, and how can they be optimized?
7. How can β-VAE principles be integrated with GANs or Diffusion Models to enhance generative quality?
8. Why is balancing disentanglement and reconstruction fidelity a crucial challenge in β-VAE?
9. How can label conditioning in CVAE be improved for better generalization?
10. What future research directions could further improve β-VAE and CVAE for generative modeling?

Key Terms

- **Variational Autoencoder (VAE):** A generative model that learns probabilistic latent space representations.
- **β-VAE:** A modified VAE that enhances disentanglement by controlling the KL-divergence term with a β factor.
- **Conditional VAE (CVAE):** A VAE variant that conditions both the encoder and decoder with label information for guided generation.
- **Evidence Lower Bound (ELBO):** The function optimized during VAE training to balance reconstruction loss and KL divergence.

- **Latent Space Disentanglement:** The process of structuring latent representations so that each dimension captures independent generative factors.
- **Conditional Sampling:** A method in CVAE that enables the generation of samples based on specified labels.
- **KL-Divergence:** A measure of the difference between the learned latent space distribution and a prior distribution.
- **Reconstruction versus Regularization Trade-Off:** The balance between preserving input details, and enforcing structured latent space constraints in VAEs.
- **Data Augmentation in CVAE:** The use of CVAE-generated samples to enhance supervised learning datasets.
- **Hybrid VAEs:** Advanced architectures that combine **β-VAE and CVAE** principles with other generative models.

CHAPTER 10
Diffusion Models

Introduction

Diffusion models represent a new paradigm in generative modeling, leveraging principles of stochastic processes and probabilistic frameworks to create high-quality synthetic data. Rooted in the mathematical foundations of noise processes and denoising algorithms, diffusion models offer a unique approach to generating data by progressively adding and removing noise. This innovative methodology allows for exceptional control over the generative process, resulting in outputs that are not only diverse but also highly realistic.

In this chapter, we explore the core concepts and mechanisms behind diffusion models, including their forward and reverse diffusion processes, the role of noise, and the time-conditional probabilistic framework that underpins their operation. We will delve into the mathematical principles that guide their training and generation, such as stochastic differential equations and variational inference, while also highlighting their key differences from traditional models like GANs and VAEs.

Through practical examples and step-by-step implementations in TensorFlow and PyTorch, you will learn how to build and train diffusion models, understand their unique strengths, and apply them to tasks such as image generation and restoration. Hence, by the end of this chapter, you will have a solid understanding of diffusion models, empowering you to leverage their capabilities for both research and real-world applications.

Structure

In this chapter, we will discuss the following topics:

- **Introduction to Diffusion Models**
  - Evolution from traditional generative models to diffusion models
  - Applications of diffusion models in creative and industrial domains
- **Key Concepts in Diffusion Models**
  - Understanding the diffusion process: Forward and reverse steps
  - Role of noise in training and generation
  - Probabilistic framework of diffusion models
- **Comparison with Other Generative Models**
- **Mathematical Foundations of Diffusion Models**
  - Stochastic processes and their role in diffusion models
  - Variational inference and the ELBO in diffusion training
  - Reverse diffusion process for image generation
- **Data Preparation and Preprocessing**
- **Architecture of Diffusion Models**
  - **Components of a diffusion model:** Encoder, decoder, and noise schedule.

  - **Key innovations:** Time-conditional networks and noise scheduling.
  - **Visualization** of the forward and reverse diffusion processes.
- **Implementing Diffusion Models: Step-by-Step**
  - Building the forward and reverse diffusion processes.
  - Example code snippets for implementing the key components.
  - Visualizing generated outputs at different time steps.
- **Evaluating Diffusion Model Performance**
  - **Common metrics:** FID, inception score, and visual quality assessment.
  - Evaluating diversity and fidelity of the generated images.
  - Comparing diffusion model performance to GANs and VAEs.
- **Challenges and Limitations**
- **Applications of Diffusion Models**
- **Case Study:**
  - **Case Study 1:** In painting and Image Restoration for a restaurant photo
  - **Case Study 2:** Low-Light Video Processing

Introduction to Diffusion Models

Diffusion models represent a transformative approach to generative modeling, leveraging the concept of gradual data refinement to synthesize high-quality outputs. These models simulate a process of iterative noise removal, mimicking natural phenomena like heat diffusion, to generate data samples. By capturing the underlying structure of data distributions through a progressive denoising process, diffusion models have emerged as powerful tools in both creative and industrial applications.

Diffusion models operate by incrementally transforming random noise into structured data. They achieve this through a two-phase process:

- **Forward Diffusion:** Noise is systematically added to the data over several time steps, creating a noisy representation.
- **Reverse Diffusion:** A model learns to reconstruct the original data by reversing this process, step by step, removing noise to reveal the desired structure.

The primary purpose of diffusion models is to generate realistic and diverse samples across various modalities, such as images, audio, and text. Unlike earlier generative models, diffusion models excel in capturing fine-grained details, and handling complex data distribution, making them versatile and robust. Thus, let us understand this with a simple analogy.

Figure 10.1: *Real-World Analogy – The Cat Sculpture and Diffusion*

Imagine you have a beautiful cat sculpture sitting perfectly on a pedestal – smooth, detailed, and complete. Now, picture slowly striking it with tiny taps of a hammer, adding cracks and chips each time. With every strike, the sculpture loses a bit of its shape and detail, until it eventually becomes a pile of scattered fragments – **completely noisy and unrecognizable**.

That is what happens in the forward diffusion process – the model gradually adds noise to an image until all the structure is lost.

Now imagine doing the reverse: you start with those random fragments and, with careful precision, reassemble them piece by piece, reversing the damage until the sculpture is perfectly whole again.

That is what diffusion models do during the denoising (reverse) process – they learn how to reconstruct the original image from the pure noise.

- **Training Phase (Adding Noise):** Just as the cat sculpture is slowly chipped away with gentle hammer strikes, real images are gradually corrupted with noise, until all the structure is lost.
- **Generation Phase (Removing Noise):** Like carefully restoring the broken sculpture piece by piece, the AI learns to reverse the damage – bringing order back from randomness, and reconstructing the original image.

Evolution from Traditional Generative Models to Diffusion Models

The journey of generative modeling has seen significant milestones:

- **Autoregressive Models:** These models such as PixelCNN and WaveNet, generate data sequentially, predicting the next element based on previous ones. While effective, they often suffer from slow generation times and difficulty in capturing global dependencies.
- **Variational Autoencoders (VAEs):** VAEs introduced probabilistic frameworks for generative modeling, offering a balance between quality and computational efficiency. However, they sometimes produce blurry outputs due to their reliance on approximate inference.
- **Generative Adversarial Networks (GANs):** GANs revolutionized generative modeling by introducing adversarial training, leading to sharp and realistic outputs. Despite their success, GANs face challenges like mode collapse and unstable training dynamics.

Diffusion models address many of these limitations. Their iterative refinement process ensures high-quality outputs, and their training does not rely on adversarial setups, avoiding the instability common in GANs. This evolution positions diffusion models as a promising alternative in the generative landscape.

Applications of Diffusion Models in Creative and Industrial Domains

Diffusion models have found applications in diverse areas such as:

Creative Domains:

- **Image Synthesis:** Tools like DALL•E 2 and Stable Diffusion use diffusion models to create detailed and imaginative images from textual descriptions, enabling artists and designers to explore new creative avenues.
- **Video Generation:** By extending their capabilities, diffusion models are being used to generate realistic videos, opening possibilities for film, animation, and virtual reality content creation.
- **Music Composition:** Diffusion-based approaches in audio modeling have enabled the generation of harmonious compositions and realistic soundscapes.

Industrial Domains:

- **Drug Discovery:** In pharmaceuticals, diffusion models assist in generating molecular structures with the desired properties, accelerating the discovery of potential drug candidates.
- **Data Augmentation:** Diffusion models generate synthetic data to enhance training datasets for machine learning applications, improving model performance in scenarios with limited real-world data.
- **Defect Detection:** In manufacturing, diffusion models are used to generate high-resolution images of defective and non-defective products for quality control systems.

The versatility and efficacy of diffusion models continue to inspire new research and applications, cementing their place as a cornerstone of modern generative AI.

Key Concepts in Diffusion Models

At the first glance, the idea of generating realistic images from pure noise might seem like magic. How does a model take scattered randomness, and reconstruct meaningful patterns? The answer lies in a carefully orchestrated two-step process–one that mirrors the way nature itself handles disorder and order.

The secret ingredient? Noise. By strategically introducing, and then removing it, diffusion models learn to recreate structured images from what appears to be a chaos! But this is not just a simple before-and-after transformation–it is a probabilistic journey, where each step brings the model closer to understanding how data can emerge from randomness.

To truly grasp how diffusion models work, we must uncover three fundamental ideas: How the diffusion process operates in both directions, why noise is more than just a disruptor, and how probability governs every step of the reconstruction.

Understanding the Diffusion Process

Diffusion models are rooted in the idea of progressively transforming data into noise, and then learning to reverse this process. This bidirectional transformation involves two key phases:

Forward Process (Noising):

- In the forward process, data is gradually corrupted by the addition of Gaussian noise over multiple steps. The goal is to transform the data into pure noise in a controlled manner.
- Mathematically, given a data sample, $\mathbf{x}_0$, the forward process generates a sequence of noisy samples, $\mathbf{x}_1, \mathbf{x}_2, \ldots, \mathbf{x}_t$, where **T** is the total number of steps.

Reverse Process (Denoising):

- The reverse process involves learning a model to predict and remove the noise added during the forward process. This allows the recovery of data from noisy representations.
- The reverse steps are modeled probabilistically, and the goal is to approximate the conditional distribution $\mathbf{p}(\mathbf{x}_{t-1} \mid \mathbf{x}_t)$ using a neural network.
- Starting from pure noise, $\mathbf{x}_t$, the reverse process generates progressively less noisy samples such as $\mathbf{x}_{t-1}, \mathbf{x}_{t-2}, \ldots, \mathbf{x}_0$, ultimately recovering the original data distribution.

The iterative forward and reverse processes form the foundation of diffusion models, making them powerful tools for generative tasks.

Role of Noise in Training and Generation

Noise plays a central role in the functioning of diffusion models. Understanding its significance is critical to appreciating how these models work:

Noise as a Learning Signal:

- During the forward process, noise is systematically added to the data, creating a training dataset with varying levels of corruption.
- The model is trained to predict the added noise at each step. This prediction is necessary for reversing the corruption, and recovering the original data.

Controlled Degradation and Reconstruction: The noise schedules β_t to control how quickly the data transitions into noise. Proper scheduling ensures a smooth transformation, and allows the reverse process to effectively reconstruct the data.

Improved Sample Diversity: Noise introduces stochasticity into the generation process, which helps produce diverse outputs. By sampling different noise vectors ϵ during inference, the model generates varied outputs from the same underlying data distribution.

Probabilistic Denoising: The addition of noise transforms deterministic data into probabilistic distribution. The reverse process then learns to denoise these distribution, which adds robustness and flexibility to the model's generative capabilities.

Overall, noise is not just a disruptive element but a vital component that enables learning, and ensures high-quality data generation.

Probabilistic Framework of Diffusion Models

Diffusion models operate within a probabilistic framework, leveraging principles from probability and statistical modeling to perform generative tasks. This framework is central to understanding their theoretical underpinnings:

- **Markov Chains in Diffusion:** Both the forward and reverse processes are modeled as Markov Chains, where the next state depends only on the current state.

  The forward process transitions from $\mathbf{x}_{t-1}$ to $\mathbf{x}_t$ via a known conditional probability distribution, $\mathbf{q}(\mathbf{x}_t \mid \mathbf{x}_{t-1})$.

The reverse process is modeled by $\mathbf{p}(\mathbf{x}_{t-1} \mid \mathbf{x}_t)$, which the model learns to approximate.

- **Variational Inference:** Training a diffusion model involves minimizing the difference between the true data distribution, and the model's learned distribution. This is achieved using variational inference techniques.

  The training objective is derived from the Evidence Lower Bound (ELBO), which quantifies how well the model approximates the data distribution.

- **Learned Noise Estimation:** A neural network is trained to estimate the noise $\boldsymbol{\epsilon}$ added at each step $\mathbf{t}$, enabling the computation of $\mathbf{p}(\mathbf{x}_{t-1} \mid \mathbf{x}_t)$.

  This estimation transforms the problem of data generation into a sequence of denoising tasks.

- **Likelihood-based Generative Modeling:** Unlike GANs, which rely on adversarial training, diffusion models explicitly maximize the likelihood of the data. This probabilistic approach makes them more stable during training, and less prone to issues such as mode collapse.

The probabilistic nature of diffusion models is what sets them apart, allowing for rigorous theoretical grounding and effective practical implementation.

Diffusion models represent a fascinating intersection of noise, probability, and iterative learning. By understanding the forward and reverse processes, appreciating the role of noise, and delving into the probabilistic framework, one gains a comprehensive view of how these models operate. This foundational knowledge sets the stage for exploring advanced topics such as noise schedules, sampling strategies, and applications in various domains.

Comparison with Other Generative Models

Diffusion models have emerged as a powerful alternative to GANs and VAEs, offering distinct methods for data generation. Unlike GANs, which rely on an adversarial game between the generator and discriminator, diffusion models use a forward process to add noise and a learned reverse process to denoise and recover data. This leads to better mode coverage and architectural simplicity, avoiding GANs' common issues such as mode collapse and training instability.

Compared to VAEs, diffusion models bypass latent space encoding, and work directly in the data space. While VAEs often produce blurry outputs due to Gaussian assumptions, diffusion models iteratively refine noise into sharp, detailed images. Their training minimizes a noise prediction loss, instead of optimizing an ELBO.

Diffusion models excel in producing high-fidelity, diverse outputs with more stable training and broad applicability–from in painting to text-to-image generation. However, they are computationally intensive, require longer training times, and involve larger model sizes, making them less ideal for real-time or resource-limited applications. Despite these challenges, their ability to generate high-quality data often places them ahead in tasks demanding realism and variety.

Mathematical Foundations of Diffusion Models

Diffusion models are a class of generative models that have gained significant attention for their ability to generate high-quality images and other complex data. Their foundations lie in the principles of stochastic processes, variational inference, and reverse diffusion processes. In this section, we explore these topics in detail, elucidating the mathematical underpinnings of diffusion models.

Stochastic Processes and Their Role in Diffusion Models

At the heart of diffusion models lies the concept of stochastic processes. A stochastic process is a collection of random variables indexed by time or another parameter, describing how a system evolves over time under the influence of randomness. In the context of diffusion models, these processes are used to model the gradual corruption of data, and its subsequent reconstruction.

Forward Diffusion Process

The forward diffusion process involves gradually adding noise to a data sample over a series of steps. Mathematically, this can be described as:

$$x_t = \sqrt{\alpha_t} x_{t-1} + \sqrt{1 - x_t} \epsilon, \quad \epsilon \sim \mathcal{N}(0, I)$$

where:

- $\mathbf{x}_t$ is the noisy version of the data at time, **t**.
- α_t is a variance schedule that controls the noise addition.
- ϵ is the Gaussian noise.

The forward process transforms clean data into a distribution that approximates pure noise as 't' approaches infinity. This transition can be seen as a Markov process, where each step depends only on the previous state.

Reverse Diffusion Process

The reverse diffusion process aims to invert the forward process, reconstructing the original data from noise. This requires learning a parameterized function $p\theta(x_{t-1} \mid x_t)$ which predicts the previous step, given the current noisy data. This reverse process is central to data generation, and involves approximating the true data distribution.

Variational Inference and ELBO in Diffusion Training

Training a diffusion model involves learning the reverse process parameters such that the reconstructed data distribution matches the original data distribution. Variational Inference provides a framework for this by optimizing the Evidence Lower Bound (ELBO).

The Evidence Lower Bound (ELBO)

The ELBO is a measure of how well the learned distribution approximates the true data distribution. For diffusion models, it can be expressed as:

$$E_{LBO} = E_q \left[\log p(x_0) - \sum_{t=1}^{T} KL(q(x_t \mid x_{t-1}) \| p_\theta(x_t \mid x_{t-1})) \right]$$

Here:

- $\mathbf{q(x_t \mid x_{t-1})}$ represents the forward process distribution.
- $\mathbf{p\theta(x_t \mid x_{t-1})}$ represents the reverse process distribution.
- **KL** denotes the Kullback-Leibler divergence, which quantifies the difference between two probability distributions.

Thus, by minimizing the KL divergence term, the model learns to accurately reverse the diffusion process.

Noise Prediction and Simplification

In practice, diffusion models often simplify the training objective by directly predicting the noise added in the forward process. This reformulation replaces the KL divergence with a Mean Squared Error (MSE) loss:

$$L_t = E_{\varepsilon,\, x_0,\, t} [\ || \varepsilon - \varepsilon_\theta(x_t, t)||^2\ ]$$

where ϵ_θ is the predicted noise. This approach is computationally efficient, and aligns well with the forward process definition.

Reverse Diffusion Process for Image Generation

Once the reverse diffusion process is learned, it can be used for image generation by sequentially denoising a sample of pure noise. This process involves the following steps:

- **Initialization:** Start with a sample, $\mathbf{x}_t$ drawn from a Gaussian distribution, **N(0, I)**.
- **Iterative Denoising:** For each step, **t**, predict the noise, $\boldsymbol{\epsilon\theta}(\mathbf{x}_t, \mathbf{t})$ and compute $\mathbf{x}_{t-1}$ using the learned reverse process:

  $$x_{t-1} = f(x_t, \epsilon\theta(x_t, t), t) + \sigma_t * z$$

  where **z** is optional noise drawn from **N(0, I)** for added stochasticity, and $\boldsymbol{\sigma_t}$ controls its scale.
- **Final Output**: After iterating through all steps, $\mathbf{x}_0$ is the generated sample.

Connection to Score-Based Models

Diffusion models share a close relationship with score-based generative models, which estimate the gradient of the data distribution–known as the score function. By leveraging stochastic differential equations (SDEs), these models unify diffusion processes with score-based approaches, providing a continuous perspective on generation.

Practical Implications and Advances

Diffusion models have demonstrated state-of-the-art performance in image generation, outperforming traditional methods like GANs in quality and diversity. Their mathematical foundation enables precise control over the generation process, allowing for various extensions:

- **Conditional Diffusion Models:** Incorporating class labels or other conditioning information to guide generation.
- **Efficient Sampling:** Reducing the number of diffusion steps, without compromising quality through techniques like adaptive variance schedules.

The mathematical foundations of diffusion models, encompassing stochastic processes, variational inference, and reverse diffusion, provide a robust framework for generative modeling. By combining these principles, diffusion models offer a powerful and versatile approach to generating high-quality data across various domains.

Data Preparation and Preprocessing

Before a diffusion model can learn to generate realistic images, it must first be trained on high-quality, well-structured data. But the raw data is rarely perfect–it comes in different formats, varying resolutions, and sometimes, with noise that can interfere with learning. How do we ensure that the model sees clean, consistent, and meaningful patterns? The answer lies in **careful data preparation**.

From organizing datasets to applying sophisticated pre-processing techniques, every step in this phase is crucial. Without it, even the most powerful models will struggle to learn effectively. But preparing data is not always straightforward. What happens when datasets are inconsistent? How do we deal with missing values, distortions, or outliers? In the next section, we dive into the intricate world of dataset curation and preprocessing—the foundation that shapes the success of diffusion models.

Preparing Datasets for Training Diffusion Models

Training diffusion models starts with carefully curated datasets tailored to the task—be it image synthesis, audio generation, or text-based applications. For visual tasks, datasets such as CIFAR-10 or ImageNet are common, while audio-based models may rely on datasets such as LibriSpeech. Selecting a dataset that aligns with the model's objective is the first critical step.

Once selected, the dataset must go through several key stages. Raw data should be collected from reliable sources, ensuring enough diversity for the model to generalize effectively. If the model is conditional, proper annotation becomes vital—such as labeling images or pairing them with captions. Cleaning the dataset by removing corrupted, mislabelled, or duplicate samples is essential for maintaining quality. Partitioning the dataset into training, validation, and test sets—typically in an 80:10:10 ratio—helps in evaluating model performance. Lastly, balancing the dataset across classes is crucial to avoid bias, especially when the model is expected to generate category-specific outputs.

Preprocessing Techniques to Normalize and Augment Data

Preprocessing is vital for preparing data in a format suitable for training diffusion models. It reduces computational load, stabilizes training, and improves the overall performance. For image datasets, normalization scales pixel values to a standard range—such as [0, 1] or [-1, 1]—ensuring consistency across samples. This is particularly important for diffusion models, where noise is added and removed over many time steps. Common normalization methods include min-max scaling, standardization, and z-score normalization to unify data distribution.

Beyond normalization, data augmentation plays a key role in improving generalization. It expands the dataset by generating altered versions of the existing samples. For images, techniques include random flipping, rotation, cropping, scaling, and color jittering. In text, augmentation may involve paraphrasing or back-translation, while audio data can be modified using pitch shifts or added background noise. In multimodal settings, such as models that process both images and text, preprocessing must ensure cross-modality consistency—for example, using tokenization for text and resizing for images—so that all inputs align with the model's architecture.

Challenges in Handling Diverse Datasets

Working with large and varied datasets strengthens diffusion models but introduces notable challenges. Data imbalance is a key issue—when certain classes dominate, and models may become biased. For instance, a dataset with more urban than natural scenes can cause overfitting. To counter this, techniques like oversampling, undersampling, or using class weights during training are helpful.

Noisy or corrupted data also pose problems, as mislabelled or low-quality samples can degrade performance. Automated filtering and noise-tolerant training methods can reduce their impact. Scalability becomes a concern with high-resolution images or long sequences, requiring efficient data pipelines and memory-friendly preprocessing. In cases of domain mismatch, where the training data differs from the target application, fine-tuning on domain-specific samples or applying domain adaptation techniques is essential. Lastly, ethical and legal issues must be addressed by ensuring that datasets comply with privacy laws, and avoid copyrighted material. Managing these challenges is crucial for building reliable and generalizable diffusion models.

Architecture of Diffusion Models

Diffusion models represent a significant breakthrough in generative modeling, excelling in producing high-quality samples for a variety of data types, including images, audio, and text. At their core, diffusion models operate by progressively transforming data into noise, and then learning to reverse this process. This approach enables the generation of realistic and diverse samples from a latent noise space. In the following paragraphs, we explore the architecture and components that make diffusion models effective, along with the key innovations that have driven their success.

Components of a Diffusion Model

Diffusion models revolve around a pair of complementary mechanisms that transform data into noise and then learn to reconstruct it. Their architecture is built around predictable noising, a learned denoising network, and a noise schedule that binds the two directions together. These components act as the model's scaffolding, shaping how information is destroyed and recovered during training and generation.

Forward Process (Diffusion Process)

The forward process is a fixed procedure that systematically adds noise to the input data across a series of time steps. Unlike a trainable encoder that compresses data into a compact latent code, this process uses a predefined noising schedule to gradually corrupt the data, until it becomes indistinguishable from pure Gaussian noise.

- **Noise Schedule:** This schedule controls the amount of noise added at each timestep. It is a crucial design choice that balances the preservation of the data structure with the introduction of stochasticity, guiding the transformation from an ordered data to random noise.
    - **Linear vs. Exponential Schedules:** Linear schedules increase the noise variance gradually, while exponential schedules can concentrate the corruption into fewer, more aggressive steps.
    - **Learned Schedules:** Recent advancements explore making the noise schedule a learnable parameter to optimize the diffusion process dynamically.
- **Mathematical Representation:** Given an input 'x', the forward process can be expressed as:

  $$q(x_t \mid x_{t-1}) = N(x_t ; \text{sqrt}(1 - \beta_t) * x_{t-1}, \beta_t * I)$$

  Where:
    - $q(x_t \mid x_{t-1})$ represents the probability distribution of x_t given x_{t-1}.
    - N(...) denotes a normal (Gaussian) distribution.
    - $\text{sqrt}(1 - \beta_t) * x_{t-1}$ is the mean of the distribution, which scales the previous step x_{t-1}.
    - $\beta_t * I$ is the variance, where β_t is a noise variance term, and I is the identity matrix.

Reverse Process (Denoising Process)

The reverse process is a learned neural network that systematically reverses the forward diffusion. It starts from pure Gaussian noise and iteratively denoises it over multiple time steps to reconstruct a coherent data sample. This process is trained to approximate the true reverse of the forward diffusion.

- **Denoising Network:** A time-conditional neural network (typically a U-Net) is trained to predict either the noise component ϵ or the denoised data, x_0 at each timestep. The most common approach is to predict the noise ε using a parameterized network εθ, which is trained to minimize the difference between the predicted and actual noise added during the forward process.

- **Mathematical Representation:** The reverse process is expressed as:

$$p_\theta(x_{t-1} \mid x_t) = N(x_{t-1} ; \mu_\theta(x_t, t), \Sigma_\theta(x_t, t))$$

Where:

  - $p_\theta(x_{t-1} \mid x_t)$ represents the probability distribution of x_{t-1} given x_t.
  - N(...) denotes a normal (Gaussian) distribution.
  - $\mu_\theta(x_t, t)$ is the predicted mean, which depends on x_t and time step, t.
  - $\Sigma_\theta(x_t, t)$ is the predicted variance, also dependent on x_t and t.

Noise Schedule: The noise schedule is a critical component that governs both the forward and reverse processes. It determines how much noise is added at each time step during the forward process, and consequently guides the denoising during the reverse process.

- **Role in Training and Generation:** A well-designed noise schedule ensures stable training convergence, and high-quality sample generation.
- **Schedule Types:**
  - **Linear Schedules:** Gradually increase noise variance β_t linearly across time steps.
  - **Exponential/Cosine Schedules:** Non-linear schedules that can provide better performance.
  - **Learned Schedules:** Recent approaches make the noise schedule a learnable parameter.

Key Innovations

- **Time-Conditional Networks:** A major innovation in diffusion models is the use of time-conditional neural networks. These networks incorporate the timestep, t as an additional input, allowing the model to learn time-specific denoising patterns.
  - **Implementation:** Timestep embeddings are concatenated or added to the input features at each step. These embeddings are typically sinusoidal, similar to positional encodings in transformers.
  - **Advantage:** Time-conditional networks improve the model's ability to handle diverse noise levels, and achieve better reconstruction accuracy.
- **Noise Scheduling:** Carefully designed noise schedules are critical for diffusion models. Innovations in this area include:
  - **Cosine Noise Schedules:** These schedules adjust the noise variance to follow a cosine function, ensuring smooth transitions between time steps.
  - **Adaptive Noise Scheduling:** Adaptive schedules dynamically adjust noise addition based on the data and the model's performance, reducing unnecessary distortions.

Visualization of Forward and Reverse Diffusion

- **Forward Diffusion:** The forward diffusion process progressively corrupts the data by adding noise at each timestep. This process can be visualized as a sequence of images (in the case of image data) where the original image becomes increasingly noisy. At the final timestep, the data resembles pure Gaussian noise.

  Example: Consider an image of a cat. Over several time steps, the image becomes blurry, and then indistinguishable as random noise dominates.

- **Reverse Diffusion:** The reverse diffusion process reconstructs the original data from noise. Starting from Gaussian noise, the decoder generates intermediate reconstructions that gradually gain structure and detail.

  Example: Starting with random noise, the reverse process might first outline the cat's shape, then refine the texture, and finally, restore the fine details.

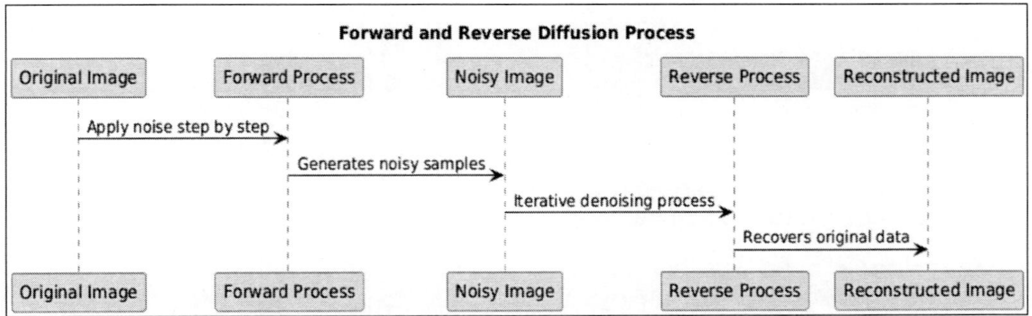

***Figure 10.2**: Forward Noise Addition and Reverse Denoising in Diffusion Models*

These visualizations not only clarify the mechanics but also highlight the intuitive appeal of diffusion models as generative frameworks.

The architecture of diffusion models is built upon a robust framework of incremental noise addition and removal, supported by innovative techniques such as time-conditional networks, and advanced noise scheduling. These components work in tandem to enable high-fidelity generation across various data modalities. Visualizing the forward and reverse processes further underscores the elegance of this approach, making diffusion models a powerful tool in the generative modeling landscape.

Implementing Diffusion Models: Step-by-Step

Diffusion models have emerged as powerful tools for generative modeling, producing high-quality images and other data types. This section provides a detailed guide to implementing diffusion models step-by-step, covering essential concepts such as building forward and reverse diffusion processes, training on large-scale datasets, and visualizing outputs at different stages.

Building the Forward and Reverse Diffusion Processes

The core idea behind diffusion models is to iteratively corrupt data through a forward process, and then learn to reverse this corruption. Let us explore each step:

Forward Diffusion Process

In the forward process, noise is gradually added to a data point, x_0, transforming it into a completely noisy distribution, x_T. This is achieved through a Markov Chain.

The forward process can be described mathematically as:

```
xₜ = √(αₜ) * xₜ₋₁ + √(1 - αₜ) * ϵ, where ϵ ~ N(0, I)
```

where:

- $\mathbf{x_t}$: Intermediate data at time step. t.
- $\boldsymbol{\alpha_t}$: A noise scheduling parameter.
- $\boldsymbol{\epsilon}$: Gaussian noise.

Key Implementation: Use predefined schedules for $\boldsymbol{\alpha_t}$, such as linear or cosine schedules, to determine how noise increases.

Code Snippet:

```
import numpy as np

def forward_diffusion(x0, t, alpha_schedule):
    alpha_t = alpha_schedule[t]
    noise = np.random.normal(size=x0.shape)
    xt = np.sqrt(alpha_t) * x0 + np.sqrt(1 - alpha_t) * noise
    return xt

# Example: Linear schedule
def linear_alpha_schedule(T):
    return np.linspace(0.0001, 0.02, T)

T = 1000  # Total diffusion steps
alpha_schedule = linear_alpha_schedule(T)
```

Reverse Diffusion Process

The reverse process is the generative step, where the model learns to denoise data iteratively, starting from pure noise. The process can be modeled as:

$$x_{t-1} = (1 / \sqrt{\alpha_t}) * (x_t - \sqrt{(1 - \alpha_t)} * \epsilon\theta(x_t, t)) + \sqrt{\beta_t} * z, \text{ where } z \sim N(0, I)$$

where $\boldsymbol{\epsilon\theta}$ is the learned noise prediction model, and $\boldsymbol{\beta_t}$ controls the noise level.

Code Snippet:

```
def reverse_diffusion(xt, t, alpha_schedule, noise_model):
    alpha_t = alpha_schedule[t]
    beta_t = 1 - alpha_t
    predicted_noise = noise_model(xt, t)
    z = np.random.normal(size=xt.shape) if t > 0 else 0
    xt_prev = (xt - np.sqrt(1 - alpha_t) * predicted_noise) / np.sqrt(alpha_t)
+ np.sqrt(beta_t) * z
    return xt_prev
```

Visualizing Generated Outputs at Different Time Steps

One of the key advantages of diffusion models is their ability to generate intermediate outputs during the reverse diffusion process. Visualizing these outputs helps in understanding the denoising process.

Code Snippet:

```
import matplotlib.pyplot as plt

# Visualize intermediate steps
x_t = np.random.normal(size=(1, 64, 64, 3))  # Start with pure noise
for t in reversed(range(0, T, T // 10)):
    x_t = reverse_diffusion(x_t, t, alpha_schedule, noise_model)
    plt.imshow((x_t[0] + 1) / 2)  # Rescale to [0, 1] for display
    plt.title(f"Step {t}")
    plt.show()
```

Thus, by following this step-by-step approach, you can implement a diffusion model from scratch, train it on large-scale datasets, and visualize its generative process. This foundation sets the stage for further experimentation with advanced diffusion techniques.

Evaluating Diffusion Model Performance

The performance of diffusion models, like any generative model, must be systematically evaluated to ensure their efficacy in generating high-quality, diverse, and meaningful outputs. This section delves into the metrics and methodologies commonly used to assess the performance of diffusion models, comparing their effectiveness to GANs (Generative Adversarial Networks) and VAEs (Variational Autoencoders).

Common Metrics: FID, Inception Score, and Visual Quality Assessment

Frechet Inception Distance (FID):

- FID measures the similarity between the distribution of generated images and real images. It does so by computing the Wasserstein-2 distance between the feature representations of both sets, typically extracted from the intermediate layers of a pre-trained Inception Network.
- Lower FID scores indicate better performance, as they reflect that the generated images are closer to real images in terms of both fidelity and diversity.
- For diffusion models, FID often captures their ability to generate high-quality and realistic outputs. As diffusion models inherently follow a noise-to-data transformation, FID is well-suited to evaluate their progression.

Inception Score (IS):

- IS evaluates the diversity and quality of generated images by analyzing their classification confidence scores using a pre-trained Inception Network.
- High-quality images yield confident and meaningful class predictions, while diverse images span across multiple distinct classes. Thus, higher IS scores indicate better performance.
- While useful, IS has limitations, such as its reliance on the pretrained classifier's domain, and its inability to account for mode collapse fully.

Visual Quality Assessment:

- Human judgment remains crucial for evaluating the perceptual quality of generated images. This involves subjective assessments where evaluators rate the realism and aesthetics of samples.
- Despite its subjectivity, human evaluation often reveals insights that automated metrics cannot, particularly in identifying subtle artifacts or contextual mismatches.

Evaluating Diversity and Fidelity of Generated Images

Diffusion models aim to strike a balance between diversity and fidelity. Achieving diversity ensures that the model does not produce monotonous outputs, while fidelity ensures that the generated outputs are indistinguishable from the real data.

Diversity Assessment:

- The diversity of generated images can be quantified by measuring the spread of features in the latent space or by calculating metrics like the total variance of generated samples.

- FID also indirectly captures diversity by assessing the overall distribution of generated images against real images. A high degree of overlap indicates good diversity.
- Techniques such as coverage metrics evaluate the percentage of real data features covered by the generated dataset, ensuring that the model avoids mode collapse.

Fidelity Assessment:

- Fidelity ensures that the generated images are of high quality, and resemble real-world samples. Pixel-level similarities such as Mean Squared Error (MSE) or Structural Similarity Index Measure (SSIM) can be used, though these are less common in generative model evaluation.
- Metrics like FID and IS inherently include fidelity as part of their computation.

Balancing Diversity and Fidelity:

- This is one challenge is achieving high diversity, without sacrificing fidelity. Diffusion models often excel in this balance due to their iterative denoising process, which allows for controlled generation.
- Adjusting hyperparameters such as the number of diffusion steps or noise levels can impact this trade-off, requiring careful tuning during model training and inference.

Comparing Diffusion Model Performance to GANs and VAEs

When compared to GANs, diffusion models show clear strengths in generating high-quality, stable images, without the adversarial instability or mode collapse that GANs often suffer from. They are more robust during training, and consistently produce diverse outputs. However, diffusion models are computationally heavier due to their iterative denoising process, making them slower during both training and inference. Despite this, they generally achieve better performance on standard benchmarks, with lower Fréchet Inception Distance (FID) scores, indicating superior image realism and variety.

Against VAEs, diffusion models again demonstrate stronger image fidelity, avoiding the blurriness that VAEs often exhibit due to Gaussian assumptions in their latent space. Since diffusion models operate directly in the data space, without relying on fixed latent structures, they allow for more flexible and detailed generation. That said, like with GANs, diffusion models are significantly slower than VAEs, and require more computational power. Still, they tend to outperform VAEs across evaluation metrics such as FID and Inception Score (IS), offering more realistic and visually convincing outputs.

In human evaluations, diffusion models consistently produce more natural and artifact-free images compared to both GANs and VAEs. This is attributed to their gradual noise refinement, which allows for finer control over image generation. While GANs remain useful for real-time applications due to their speed, and VAEs for tasks requiring interpretable latent spaces, diffusion models are rapidly becoming the preferred choice for applications demanding the highest quality and diversity in generative outputs. Their performance, though resource-intensive, makes them a standout in the current landscape of generative models.

Challenges and Limitations of Diffusion Models

Diffusion models have emerged as powerful tools in generative modeling, offering remarkable capabilities in applications such as image synthesis, text-to-image generation, and beyond. However, like any technology, they come with their own set of challenges and limitations. Understanding these aspects is crucial for advancing the field, and optimizing the use of these models in practical applications. In this section, we delve into three significant challenges: the computational demands of training diffusion models, addressing instability in the reverse diffusion process, and the limitations in generating diverse outputs.

Computational Demands of Training Diffusion Models

Diffusion models, while powerful, are notoriously demanding in terms of computational resources. Their training involves repeatedly adding and removing noise over hundreds or even thousands of steps, leading to intense processing requirements. This iterative process results in high memory usage, extended training times, and a reliance on expensive GPUs or TPUs—barriers that make diffusion models less accessible to those without significant hardware infrastructure. For high-resolution tasks, the memory footprint grows even further, and training can stretch across days or weeks, making energy consumption an another growing concern.

To mitigate these challenges, researchers are innovating on multiple fronts. Approaches such as reducing the number of diffusion steps through accelerated sampling, designing more efficient architectures, and using model compression techniques (like pruning or quantization) are being explored to ease the computational load. Despite these advances, achieving efficiency without compromising image quality remains one of the field's key battles.

Addressing Instability in the Reverse Diffusion Process

The reverse diffusion process is the linchpin of generation in diffusion models, yet it is also a fragile dance of precision. Each denoising step relies heavily on the accuracy of the last, making the system vulnerable to even slight errors. These errors can compound, resulting in visual artifacts or output degradation. The model's sensitivity to noise prediction, especially in later stages, adds to the instability. Designing the noise schedule—dictating how noise is added and removed—is a subtle craft; missteps here can lead to poor convergence or instability, particularly when generating high-resolution images where every small error becomes glaring.

To counter these issues, researchers are experimenting with improved noise schedules that adapt based on model feedback, hybrid architectures that combine diffusion with GAN-like stability, and alternative loss functions that are more tolerant of prediction variance. Another promising strategy is progressive denoising, where low-resolution outputs are first generated, and then refined in stages, reducing the chance of instability in a single sweep. These innovations aim to steady the reverse process, and ensure that the model does not lose its way as it turns noise into order.

Limitations in Generating Diverse Outputs

Diffusion models, while celebrated for their realism and fidelity, often stumble when it comes to generating diverse outputs—a limitation that stings in applications where variety matters. Like GANs, they can fall prey to mode collapse, generating repetitive outputs, rather than sampling the full creative spectrum of the data. The culprit often lies in the training data itself—if the data is biased or narrow in scope, the model mirrors those blind spots. Overfitting only deepens the rut, trapping the model in familiar patterns, and stifling originality.

This loss of diversity is not just a data problem—it is also baked into the architecture. The noise injection-removal cycle, if not finely tuned, can smother subtle or rare patterns, ironing out the quirks that give data its richness. Balancing signal and noise becomes a delicate high-wire act, and missing the mark means flattening the generative landscape. To revive variety, researchers are arming diffusion models with enhanced data augmentation, model ensembles, and smart exploration techniques that dig deeper into the latent space. Regularization terms are also used like guiding hands and nudging models to reach beyond the obvious.

Ultimately, while diffusion models are evolving fast, these challenges such as diversity, computational heft, and stability must be faced head-on. Solving them is not just a matter of efficiency, but of unleashing the full expressive power of generative AI. With every tweak in architecture, loss function, or training pipeline, the models inch closer to mastering not just realism, but the full spectrum of imagination.

Applications of Diffusion Models

Diffusion models have rapidly emerged as a transformative technology in artificial intelligence, offering innovative solutions across diverse fields. Their ability to generate, enhance, and manipulate data has made them indispensable in several domains. In the following paragraphs, we explore their applications in creative industries, healthcare, research, and industrial use cases.

Creative Industries

The creative industries are among the most impacted by diffusion models. These models have revolutionized the way artists, designers, and creators approach their work. Some key applications include:

- **Art Generation and Style Transfer:** Diffusion models can generate stunning artwork by learning and mimicking specific artistic styles. They enable the creation of novel pieces of art, blending styles or creating entirely new ones. Artists can use these tools as inspiration or for generating pieces in bulk for commercial use.
- **Photorealistic Image Synthesis:** Creating lifelike images from textual descriptions is a hallmark of diffusion models. For example, platforms like DALL-E leverage these models to produce photorealistic visuals based on user prompts. This has significant implications for advertising, where custom visuals can be generated on demand.
- **Design Prototyping:** In industrial and graphic design, diffusion models streamline prototyping by generating realistic mockups. Designers can visualize multiple iterations of a product or layout quickly, significantly reducing development cycles.
- **Video and Animation:** Beyond static images, diffusion models are being extended to video synthesis, enabling the generation of seamless animations and special effects. This technology is already being adopted in filmmaking and gaming industries to create immersive experiences.

Healthcare: Data Augmentation for Medical Imaging

The healthcare sector has embraced diffusion models to address critical challenges in medical imaging and diagnostics. The key applications include:

- **Data Augmentation:** Medical imaging often suffers from a scarcity of labeled data, especially for rare conditions. Diffusion models augment the existing datasets by generating synthetic but realistic medical images, enhancing the training of machine learning models.
- **Anomaly Detection:** By modeling normal data distributions, diffusion models help identify anomalies in medical scans, such as tumors or fractures. This is particularly valuable in radiology and pathology, where early detection is crucial.
- **Improved Diagnosis:** These models enable enhanced visualization of medical images by denoising or sharpening them. For instance, low-resolution or noisy MRI scans can be refined to reveal critical details, aiding more accurate diagnosis.
- **Simulation and Training:** Medical professionals can use synthetic images generated by diffusion models for training purposes. These simulations expose trainees to a wider variety of cases, preparing them for real-world scenarios.

Research

In the research community, diffusion models provide a powerful framework for understanding and modeling generative processes. Some noteworthy applications include:

- **Modeling Complex Systems:** Diffusion models simulate intricate systems, such as weather patterns, stock market behaviors, or protein folding. Their probabilistic foundation enables accurate predictions of system dynamics.
- **Exploration of Data Manifolds:** Researchers use diffusion models to explore and visualize high-dimensional data manifolds. This helps in uncovering latent structures in datasets, leading to deeper insights and novel discoveries.
- **Scientific Visualization:** Diffusion models can generate visual representations of abstract scientific concepts, such as quantum states or fluid dynamics, making them more comprehensible.
- **Understanding Bias in Generative Models:** Studying diffusion models allows researchers to analyze and mitigate biases in generative systems, ensuring fairer AI solutions.

Image Restoration and Super-Resolution

Diffusion models are also finding significant applications in industrial contexts, particularly in enhancing and restoring visual data. These include:

- **Image Restoration:** Diffusion models excel at repairing degraded images. Whether it is removing noise, restoring color, or fixing artifacts, these models provide unparalleled results. This technology is widely used in fields like surveillance and historical archiving.
- **Super-Resolution:** Industries require high-resolution images for tasks such as quality control or satellite imaging. Diffusion models upscale low-resolution images, while preserving intricate details, making them valuable in manufacturing, geospatial analysis, and much more.
- **Quality Assurance in Manufacturing:** Thus, by analyzing product images, diffusion models identify defects and inconsistencies with high accuracy. This streamlines quality control processes, reducing costs and improving reliability.
- **Entertainment and Media:** Beyond restoration, diffusion models enhance old footage for modern viewing. Film restoration projects have adopted these techniques to bring classics into the high-definition era.

The versatility of diffusion models positions them as a cornerstone of innovation across industries. Thus, from enabling creative expression to solving critical healthcare challenges and advancing scientific understanding, their impact is profound. As the technology matures, we can expect even broader adoption and integration into everyday applications, reshaping how we generate and interpret data in the modern world.

Case Study 1: In Painting and Image Restoration for a Restaurant

Imagine capturing a breath-taking landscape, only to see it ruined by heavy distortion and noise. What if we could magically restore every lost detail, bringing the scene back to life with perfect clarity? This is the challenge researchers face when generating high-quality images from noisy data. The solution lies in a ground-breaking AI approach—one that does not just enhance images but learns to recreate them from near chaos. But how does it work? What obstacles must be overcome? And just how realistic can these generated images become?

Problem: Restoring High-Quality, Photorealistic Images from Incomplete or Noisy Inputs

Restoring old photographs is a challenging yet rewarding task, particularly when these images hold sentimental or historical value. In this project, the goal was to restore and improve the quality of old photos of a restaurant, many of which were either black and white, partially damaged, or both. These photographs represented a significant part of the restaurant's history and cultural identity. The primary challenge was to restore these images to their former glory, while ensuring photorealistic quality, and preserving their historical essence. Traditional approaches struggled with handling the dual challenges of in painting damaged regions and colorizing black-and-white images, often producing results that lacked visual coherence and authenticity.

Solution Approach: Implementing a Diffusion Model to Restore and Enhance Old Photos

Diffusion models provided a robust solution to this complex problem by leveraging their iterative denoising capabilities to reconstruct missing regions and enhance image quality. The key steps in implementing the solution were:

- **Preprocessing the Dataset:**
    - A curated dataset was created by scanning the old restaurant photographs, and categorizing them based on their level of damage, and whether they were black and white, or partially colored.
    - Synthetic data augmentation techniques were used to introduce additional noise and damage patterns, enabling the model to learn a wide range of restoration scenarios.
- **Training the Forward Diffusion Process:**
    - Gaussian noise was gradually added to clean, high-quality images during training to simulate the degradation process.
    - The model was trained to reverse this process, reconstructing clean images from noisy or incomplete inputs.
- **Reverse Diffusion for Restoration:**
    - The diffusion model was conditioned on available image content to guide the restoration process.
    - For black-and-white images, an additional colorization module was integrated, using learned priors from the dataset to generate realistic colors.
- **Fine-Tuning for Historical Context:**
    - The model was fine-tuned using a subset of photographs with known historical and visual details, ensuring that restored images retained their authenticity and period-specific aesthetics.

Challenges

Several challenges arose during the project:

- **Reconstructing Damaged Regions:** Many images had extensive damage, such as large missing sections or heavy scratches. The model needed to learn how to extrapolate plausible details, while maintaining coherence with the surrounding areas.
- **Colorizing Black-and-White Photos:** Restoring realistic colors required leveraging

contextual information from the dataset. For instance, the model needed to infer the original colors of furniture, decor, and dishes typical of the era.

- **Ensuring Visual Consistency:** Restored areas needed to blend seamlessly with the undamaged parts of the images, avoiding artifacts or abrupt transitions.
- **Balancing Computation and Quality:** High-quality restoration demanded a significant number of reverse diffusion steps, which required careful optimization to balance computational efficiency and output quality.

Outcome

The project yielded impressive results, breathing new life into the old photographs of the restaurant. The key outcomes included:

- **Photorealistic Restoration:** The restored images featured high-quality details, with damaged regions seamlessly reconstructed and black-and-white photos colorized convincingly.
- **Preservation of Historical Integrity:** By incorporating period-specific details, the restored images retained their cultural and historical significance, ensuring that they were authentic representations of the restaurant's past.
- **Broad Applicability:** The methodology demonstrated robustness across diverse images, from slightly damaged photos to severely degraded ones. This adaptability made it a valuable tool for other restoration projects.
- **Enhanced Engagement:** The restored photographs were displayed in the restaurant, attracting attention from patrons, and sparking conversations about its rich history. These images also became valuable assets for marketing and social media campaigns.

This project highlights the transformative potential of diffusion models in in painting and restoring old photographs. By combining advanced machine learning techniques with a focus on historical and visual integrity, the project successfully revived treasured memories, and preserved the legacy of the restaurant. Future enhancements could include integrating user feedback for iterative improvements, and extending the approach to other types of historical artifacts.

Case Study 2: Low-Light Video Enhancement Using Diffusion Models

Imagine recording a memorable night at a concert or a candlelit dinner, only to find the video bathed in murky shadows, stripped of detail and color. What if AI could illuminate that scene—not just brighten it, but recover what the human eye barely caught? This is the challenge researchers face when enhancing videos captured in low-light environments. The solution lies in a revolutionary approach—one that does not merely denoise or sharpen, but learns to reconstruct light, detail, and motion from obscured reality. But how does this alchemy work? What hurdles must be overcome? And how true-to-life can these illuminated videos become?

Problem: Enhancing Visibility and Restoring Clarity in Low-Light Video Recordings

Low-light video enhancement is a notoriously difficult task, complicated by sensor noise, motion blur, and the severe lack of exposure. In this project, the aim was to restore clarity and natural colors to surveillance footage captured in poorly lit environments. These videos were crucial for nighttime security monitoring at a transportation hub, but their darkness and noise rendered them nearly unusable. Traditional video enhancement methods struggled with retaining temporal consistency, and failed to recover fine details, often amplifying artifacts instead of reducing them. The goal was to develop an AI-driven system capable of enhancing such videos, without compromising temporal fluidity or generating artificial-looking frames.

Solution Approach: Implementing a Diffusion Model for Frame-by-Frame and Temporal Restoration

Diffusion models emerged as a powerful solution, enabling both spatial and temporal restoration through iterative denoising. By learning the complex distribution of natural images, these models could effectively hallucinate realistic details even in extreme low-light conditions. The implementation involved several key steps:

- **Preprocessing the Video Dataset:** Raw night-time surveillance videos were split into individual frames and labeled based on luminance levels and noise severity. To simulate more extreme conditions and improve robustness, synthetic low-light degradation (including shot noise, motion blur, and underexposure) was applied to clean video clips.
- **Training the Forward Diffusion Process:** Clean video frames were gradually corrupted with Gaussian noise over time steps to teach the model the degradation process. A temporal embedding mechanism was introduced to preserve motion continuity across frames during training.
- **Reverse Diffusion for Enhancement:** The model was conditioned not only on spatial pixel data but also on temporal neighbors—past and future frames—using attention-based fusion. This allowed the model to maintain coherence in motion while reconstructing light and color. An auxiliary brightness estimation network was added to guide exposure correction during sampling.
- **Temporal Fine-Tuning:** A small batch of manually annotated video sequences was used for fine-tuning, ensuring the model did not produce flickering artifacts, and preserved object boundaries consistently across frames.

Challenges

Several formidable obstacles surfaced during the process:

- **Temporal Consistency in Motion:** Maintaining smooth motion without flicker was difficult, especially in scenes with fast movement. Without temporal conditioning, the model sometimes enhanced frames inconsistently.
- **Noise vs. Detail Trade-off:** In extremely dark regions, the model struggled to distinguish noise from actual features. Fine-tuning the denoising strength was crucial to avoid over smoothing.
- **Color Hallucination:** In areas with near-zero light, the model occasionally introduced unrealistic colors. Training on a wide variety of low-light scenarios helped reduce this issue.
- **Real-Time Constraints:** The diffusion process, inherently iterative, was computationally expensive. A lightweight distillation technique was later applied to accelerate inference for near real-time usage.

Outcome

The final model demonstrated remarkable improvements in low-light video quality across a variety of scenes:

- **Enhanced Visibility and Realism:** Videos showed significantly better brightness, color accuracy, and fine detail recovery. Street signs, faces, and moving objects that were once indiscernible became visible.

- **Temporal Stability:** Flickering artifacts were minimized, and motion appeared smooth and natural. The model preserved scene continuity across frame sequences.
- **Practical Deployment:** The enhanced videos proved valuable in real-world scenarios, helping security personnel identify individuals and events previously lost in the darkness.
- **Broad Impact:** This technology can be extended to smartphone camera apps and autonomous driving datasets, where reliable low-light video perception is critical.

This case study highlights the power of diffusion models in video enhancement. By treating light itself as a generative process—recovered step-by-step from noise—diffusion models do more than brighten a frame; they resurrect moments nearly lost to the dark. With further optimizations in speed and model size, these systems may soon become standard in every low-light imaging pipeline, from cinematic editing to real-time surveillance and beyond.

Conclusion

In this chapter, we explored Diffusion Models, a powerful class of generative models that have revolutionized high-quality image synthesis. Unlike GANs and VAEs, diffusion models generate images through an iterative denoising process, gradually refining random noise into coherent, high-resolution outputs. Their probabilistic framework and stochastic processes enable them to capture fine details, and produce photorealistic images, making them ideal for applications in art, medical imaging, super-resolution, and scientific research.

We examined the core concepts of diffusion models, including the forward and reverse diffusion processes, the role of noise, and the mathematical foundations that govern their training. Additionally, we compared them with other generative models, highlighting their strengths in image diversity and realism, while also addressing their computational challenges.

With hands-on implementation and performance evaluation techniques, you are now equipped to apply diffusion models in real-world scenarios. In the next chapter, we will explore Data Augmentation with Generative Models, discussing how generative approaches like GANs, VAEs, and Diffusion Models can be leveraged to enhance datasets for machine learning applications.

Points to Remember

- Diffusion models generate images by progressively denoising random noise, following a probabilistic approach.
- The forward diffusion process gradually adds noise to an image, while the reverse diffusion process reconstructs the image by learning to remove noise step by step.
- Diffusion models outperform GANs in generating high-quality, diverse, and photorealistic images, but they require more computational resources.
- Common evaluation metrics for diffusion models include FID (Fréchet Inception Distance), Inception Score, and qualitative visual assessments.
- Diffusion models are widely applied in creative industries, healthcare, scientific research, and industrial applications.

Multiple Choice Questions

1. What is the primary advantage of diffusion models over GANs?

    a. Faster training times

    b. More stable training and higher-quality image generation

   c. Lower computational requirements

   d. Direct latent space interpolation

2. What is the purpose of the forward diffusion process in diffusion models?

   a. To incrementally add noise to data, making it unrecognizable

   b. To generate images directly from a noise distribution

   c. To improve adversarial training stability

   d. To optimize image embeddings

3. Which component is responsible for generating images in a diffusion model?

   a. Discriminator

   b. Variational Autoencoder

   c. Reverse diffusion process

   d. Fully connected layers

4. What is a major challenge of training diffusion models?

   a. Mode collapse

   b. High computational cost due to iterative denoising

   c. Lack of image diversity

   d. Limited applicability to image tasks

Answers

1. b
2. a
3. c
4. b

Questions

1. How do diffusion models differ from GANs and VAEs in their approach to image generation?
2. What are the main advantages of using diffusion models for high-resolution image synthesis?
3. How does the forward diffusion process contribute to learning in a diffusion model?
4. What challenges arise in training diffusion models, and how can they be addressed?
5. How do noise scheduling and time-conditioning improve the effectiveness of diffusion models?
6. What are some real-world applications where diffusion models have shown significant advantages?
7. How does the ELBO (Evidence Lower Bound) contribute to training diffusion models?
8. Why do diffusion models require more computational power compared to GANs?

9. What future advancements could make diffusion models more efficient and accessible?
10. How can diffusion models be combined with other generative techniques to improve performance?

Key Terms

- **Diffusion Process:** The gradual transformation of structured data into noise and vice versa.
- **Forward Diffusion:** The step-by-step process of adding noise to an image.
- **Reverse Diffusion:** The process of reconstructing an image by removing noise in small steps.
- **Probabilistic Framework:** The mathematical approach diffusion models use to generate data.
- **Noise Scheduling:** The method of controlling the amount of noise added or removed at each step.
- **Fréchet Inception Distance (FID):** A metric for evaluating the realism of generated images.
- **Inception Score:** A measure of both image quality and diversity in generative models.
- **Computational Complexity:** The high resource requirement of diffusion models due to iterative generation.
- **Stochastic Process:** A mathematical process governing the random nature of noise addition and removal.
- **ELBO (Evidence Lower Bound):** A probabilistic approach used to optimize diffusion models.

CHAPTER 11
Data Augmentation with Generative Models

Introduction

Data augmentation is a cornerstone of modern machine learning, enhancing model performance by increasing dataset diversity and mitigating overfitting. While traditional techniques like flipping, cropping, and rotation have been widely used, they often fall short in addressing more complex data needs. Generative models, such as GANs, VAEs, and diffusion models, offer a transformative approach to data augmentation by creating entirely new samples that closely mimic the underlying data distribution.

In this chapter, we explore the role of generative models in data augmentation, examining how they overcome the limitations of conventional methods, and enable the creation of diverse, high-quality datasets. From generating synthetic medical images to augmenting imbalanced text datasets, these models have revolutionized data preparation across domains. We will delve into the mechanisms of generative augmentation, discuss their applications, and provide practical examples using TensorFlow and PyTorch. By the end of this chapter, you will have a comprehensive understanding of how generative models can be leveraged to enhance dataset quality, and improve the robustness of your machine learning models.

Structure

In this chapter, we will discuss the following topics:

- **Introduction to Data Augmentation**
  - Challenges with Traditional Data Augmentation Techniques
  - Role of Generative Models in Data Augmentation
  - Benefits of Data Augmentation with Generative Models
- **Applications of Data Augmentation with Generative Models**
- **Mathematical Foundations of Data Augmentation**
  - Probabilistic Frameworks for Generating Diverse Data
  - Exploring Latent Spaces for Targeted Augmentation
  - Loss Functions and Optimization Techniques
- **Data Preparation and Dataset Requirements**
- **Using GANs for Data Augmentation**
  - Overview of GAN-based Augmentation Techniques
  - Challenges in Training for Realistic Data Generation
- **Using VAEs for Data Augmentation**
  - Overview of VAE-based Augmentation Techniques
  - Conditional VAEs for Class-specific Data Augmentation

- **Using Diffusion Models for Data Augmentation**
  - o Overview of Diffusion-based Augmentation Techniques
  - o Training Diffusion Models for Generating Diverse and High-quality Samples
- **Implementing Data Augmentation with Generative Models: Step-by-Step**
  - o Setting up a Generative Model for Data Augmentation
  - o Example Code Snippets for Augmenting Image, Text, and Audio Datasets
- Evaluating the Effectiveness of Augmentation
- Challenges and Limitations
- **Case Study:** Medical Imaging Data Augmentation

Introduction to Data Augmentation

Data augmentation is a foundational technique in machine learning that involves artificially expanding the size and diversity of a dataset by applying transformations or generating synthetic data. By exposing a model to more varied data during training, data augmentation enhances its generalization ability, reduces overfitting, and improves overall performance.

As machine learning tasks become increasingly complex and data-hungry, the importance of effective data augmentation techniques has grown significantly.

At its core, data augmentation aims to address a fundamental challenge in machine learning: The need for large, high-quality datasets. In many real-world scenarios, collecting and labeling data is time-consuming, expensive, or impractical. For example, medical imaging datasets often require domain experts to annotate, while rare-event datasets (like fraud detection) inherently suffer from data scarcity. By synthetically expanding datasets, data augmentation provides an efficient and cost-effective solution.

Traditional data augmentation techniques involve applying transformations such as rotation, flipping, cropping, scaling, and adding noise to the existing data. These methods are simple yet effective in increasing dataset variability. For instance, flipping an image horizontally can simulate a different perspective, while adding Gaussian noise to audio data can mimic real-world distortions. These transformations allow models to learn robust features that generalize well to the unseen data.

Figure 11.1: *A Single Image of a Cat Augmented to Get Multiple Images*

The importance of data augmentation extends beyond increasing dataset size. It plays a pivotal role in improving model robustness by exposing the model to diverse scenarios and edge cases. Furthermore, data augmentation can help mitigate biases in datasets by artificially balancing underrepresented classes. For example, in an imbalanced classification task, generating more samples for minority classes can significantly improve model fairness and accuracy.

Challenges with Traditional Data Augmentation Techniques

Despite their utility, traditional data augmentation techniques have limitations. These methods rely on predefined rules and transformations, which may not always capture the true complexity or diversity of real-world data. The key challenges include:

- **Limited Diversity:** While flipping, rotating, and scaling are effective, they often fail to create entirely new patterns or scenarios. For example, rotating an image of a cat does not generate a new cat; it only introduces minor variations of the same sample.
- **Domain-Specific Limitations:** In specialized fields like medical imaging or Natural Language Processing (NLP), traditional augmentation methods may not adequately mimic real-world variations. For instance, duplicating and rotating X-rays might not introduce meaningful diversity to a medical dataset.
- **Overfitting to Augmented Patterns:** Models may inadvertently overfit to the artificial patterns introduced by simple augmentation techniques, especially when these patterns deviate from natural data distribution.
- **Bias Reinforcement:** Traditional augmentation techniques can inadvertently reinforce biases present in the dataset. For example, augmenting an imbalanced dataset, without addressing its inherent biases may increase the problem, rather than solving it.

Role of Generative Models in Data Augmentation

Generative models, such as Generative Adversarial Networks (GANs) and Variational Autoencoders (VAEs), offer a sophisticated approach to data augmentation. Unlike traditional methods that manipulate the existing data, generative models create entirely new data samples by learning the underlying distribution of the original dataset. This capability addresses many of the challenges associated with traditional augmentation techniques.

- **Increased Diversity and Realism:** Generative models excel at producing highly diverse and realistic samples. For example, a GAN trained on images of human faces can generate entirely new faces that are indistinguishable from the real ones. This ability is particularly valuable in fields like autonomous driving, where synthetic images of various driving scenarios can enhance model robustness.
- **Domain-Specific Applications:** In domains like medical imaging, generative models can create synthetic samples that mimic rare conditions, aiding in the training of diagnostic models. For instance, VAEs have been used to generate synthetic MRI scans with varying degrees of anomalies, enabling models to detect rare diseases with greater accuracy.
- **Addressing Data Scarcity:** Generative models are particularly useful in scenarios with limited data. By learning the distribution of a small dataset, these models can generate a virtually unlimited number of new samples, effectively addressing data scarcity. This is crucial in applications like fraud detection, where labeled data is inherently rare.
- **Balancing Imbalanced Datasets:** Generative models can help balance datasets by generating synthetic samples for underrepresented classes. For example, a GAN trained on a dataset with

imbalanced class distributions can produce additional samples for minority classes, improving model performance and fairness.

- **Advanced Augmentation for NLP and Audio**: While traditional augmentation methods for NLP and audio are limited, generative models can create entirely new text or audio samples. Language models like GPT can generate diverse textual data, while generative audio models can synthesize realistic speech or environmental sounds.
- In summary, generative models represent a paradigm shift in data augmentation. Thus, by creating diverse, realistic, and domain-specific data, they overcome the limitations of traditional techniques, and enable more effective training of machine learning models.

As we explore the practical applications of generative models for data augmentation in subsequent sections, their transformative potential will become even more evident. Let us understand the concept of Data Augmentation with a real world analogy.

Real-world Analogy: Expanding a Fashion Model's Portfolio

Imagine a fashion model who is auditioning for a major casting opportunity. She only has 10 professional photos in her portfolio, but the casting manager requests 50 different shots showcasing various looks, poses, and styles.

Figure 11.2: *A Fashion Model Using Editing Techniques to Increase Her Portfolio*

Since scheduling another full professional photoshoot is expensive and time-consuming, her team gets creative using manual augmentation techniques:

- **Cropping and Resizing:** They take the original images, and create close-up shots, waist-up shots, and full-length images.
- **Flipping and Rotating:** They mirror some pictures to show her from different angles, adding variety.
- **Changing Backgrounds:** Using basic editing, they replace studio backdrops with different settings (for example, an outdoor scene, a runway, and so on).
- **Altering Colors and Filters:** Adjusting brightness, contrast, and tones to create different moods in the images.

- **Adding Accessories and Makeup Changes:** Using minimal touch-ups like changing hairstyles or adding a jacket to simulate a different outfit.

Thus, by applying these modifications, the model's team successfully expands her portfolio to 50 unique-looking images, enhancing variety, without changing her core identity.

How This Relates to Data Augmentation in Machine Learning

Similarly, in machine learning, when we have a small dataset (just like the model's 10 pictures), we create variations manually or with transformations (cropping, flipping, color changes, and so on.) to increase diversity. This ensures the model learns more effectively, without needing massive new data collection.

Benefits of Data Augmentation with Generative Models

Data augmentation using generative models has transformed the way machine learning practitioners address the challenges of data scarcity and quality. By creating synthetic data samples that closely resemble real-world data, generative models enable the development of more robust and accurate machine learning systems. The following are the key benefits of leveraging generative models for data augmentation.

Improving Model Performance by Addressing Data Scarcity

Data scarcity is a common challenge in machine learning, particularly in specialized domains such as medical imaging, satellite imagery, and niche industries where collecting large datasets is expensive, time-consuming, or logistically challenging. Generative models, such as GANs and VAEs, offer a powerful solution by synthesizing realistic data samples. For instance, in medical imaging, GANs can create high-resolution images of CT scans or MRIs, allowing models to train on diverse data, without requiring additional patients or imaging sessions. This approach not only expands the dataset but also ensures that rare or underrepresented categories are adequately captured.

A practical example comes from the field of autonomous driving. By using GANs to generate synthetic road conditions, such as varying weather, lighting, and traffic scenarios, developers can train models to perform well in diverse real-world conditions, even if the original dataset was limited. This augmented data helps fill gaps in the original dataset, leading to improved generalization and performance across unseen scenarios.

Enhancing Diversity and Robustness in Datasets

One of the core strengths of generative models is their ability to increase the diversity of datasets. Traditional augmentation techniques, such as flipping or rotating images, often produce variations that are predictable and limited. Generative models, however, can create entirely new samples that exhibit nuanced variations, such as subtle changes in texture, style, or background. This diversity helps models learn to recognize the underlying patterns in data, rather than memorizing the specific examples.

For instance, in natural language processing, large language models like GPT can generate synthetic text that expands the diversity of training datasets. By providing additional sentence structures, tones, and vocabulary, these models enhance a system's ability to understand language in various contexts. Similarly, in computer vision tasks, CycleGANs can transform images from one domain to another (for example, converting horse images to zebras), creating datasets with domain-specific diversity that traditional methods cannot achieve.

Diverse data also helps models perform well in edge cases, which are often overlooked in smaller datasets. Consider a facial recognition system being trained for global use: generating synthetic faces with varied ethnicities, lighting conditions, and accessories (for example, glasses, hats, and so on) ensures robustness across different real-world scenarios.

Reducing Overfitting in Machine Learning Models

Overfitting occurs when a model learns to memorize the training data, rather than generalizing from it. This is especially problematic in datasets with limited examples, where the model struggles to differentiate between noise and meaningful patterns. Generative models help alleviate this issue by providing additional synthetic data, effectively increasing the size of the dataset, and introducing variability.

For example, when training a Convolutional Neural Network (CNN) for image classification, incorporating synthetic data generated by a VAE ensures that the model encounters more varied examples during training. This reduces the likelihood of the model over-relying on specific features in the original dataset. Additionally, GANs can generate data that closely matches the statistical distribution of the original data, while introducing slight variations, further promoting generalization.

Beyond images, generative models have shown promise in other domains. In financial modeling, GANs can synthesize realistic time-series data, capturing trends and anomalies without duplicating the existing data. This prevents overfitting, while ensuring that the model learns to identify the underlying patterns, making predictions more reliable in the unseen data.

In essence, reducing overfitting not only improves the accuracy of machine learning models but also enhances their reliability in production environments where the test data distribution may differ from the training data.

The benefits of data augmentation with generative models extend far beyond the capabilities of traditional methods. By addressing data scarcity, enhancing dataset diversity, and reducing overfitting, generative models empower machine learning practitioners to build robust, high-performing systems across diverse applications. Thus, whether it is synthesizing images, text, or time-series data, these models provide a flexible and powerful solution for overcoming some of the most pressing challenges in modern AI.

Applications of Data Augmentation with Generative Models

Data augmentation is a powerful technique to improve the performance of Machine Learning (ML) models by artificially increasing the size and diversity of the training datasets. Generative models such as GANs (Generative Adversarial Networks) and VAEs (Variational Autoencoders), play a transformative role in augmenting data. These models can synthesize highly realistic data samples across domains, addressing the challenges of limited and imbalanced datasets. The following are several applications where generative models excel in data augmentation:

Healthcare: Augmenting Medical Imaging Datasets

The healthcare domain is often constrained by the availability of labeled medical imaging datasets due to patient confidentiality, and the high cost of annotation by experts. Generative models provide a solution by synthesizing realistic medical images, enabling researchers to:

- **Expand Small Datasets:** GANs can create high-resolution synthetic images for rare conditions, such as specific types of cancer or neurological disorders, where acquiring real samples is challenging.
- **Enhance Diversity:** By generating variations of the existing images, generative models ensure that neural networks learn from diverse representations, reducing overfitting.

- **Simulate Edge Cases:** In medical imaging, identifying anomalies or rare pathologies is critical. Generative models can simulate these edge cases, ensuring robust training for anomaly detection systems.

For example, GANs have been used to synthesize MRI scans for training brain tumor detection models. Similarly, synthetic chest X-rays generated by conditional GANs (cGANs) have been leveraged to improve pneumonia detection.

Natural Language Processing (NLP): Text Generation

In NLP, class imbalances often hinder the performance of language models. For instance, datasets may lack sufficient examples of rare intents or uncommon linguistic patterns.

Generative models can help by:

- **Creating Synthetic Sentences:** Models like GPT or VAEs can generate meaningful text samples for underrepresented classes, ensuring a balanced dataset.
- **Data Augmentation for Sentiment Analysis:** By generating diverse text samples with specific sentiments, generative models enhance training for sentiment classification tasks.
- **Low-Resource Language Support:** Generative models can synthesize text in low-resource languages, expanding the applicability of NLP systems globally.

For example, in customer support chatbots, GANs have been used to generate synthetic user queries, especially for rare intents, improving the model's ability to handle diverse scenarios.

Computer Vision: Generating Diverse Training Samples

In computer vision, the success of deep learning models often depends on large and diverse datasets. Generative models have become a game-changer in this field by:

- **Augmenting Object Detection Datasets:** GANs can generate new images with realistic objects in varying poses, lighting conditions, and backgrounds.
- **Domain Adaptation:** When labeled data from a specific domain is scarce, generative models can synthesize domain-specific images. For instance, converting synthetic CAD images into photo-realistic images for object detection tasks.
- **Style Transfer:** Using models such as CycleGANs, the existing datasets can be augmented by altering their style (for example, converting day images to night images).

One practical example is autonomous driving, where GANs have been employed to create diverse street scenes, such as foggy or rainy conditions, to improve model performance in adverse weather scenarios.

Other Domains: Speech Synthesis and Time-Series

Generative models have applications beyond healthcare, NLP, and computer vision. In various other domains, they continue to demonstrate their versatility:

- **Speech Synthesis:** In speech processing, generative models like WaveGAN can synthesize audio samples for speaker recognition or accent classification tasks. They help create balanced datasets, particularly for accents or languages with limited resources.
- **Time-Series Data Augmentation:** For financial modeling, energy forecasting, or IoT applications, generative models can produce synthetic time-series data, mimicking real-world patterns, while introducing controlled variations.

For instance, VAEs have been used to generate synthetic sensor data in predictive maintenance applications, enabling robust training for fault detection systems. Similarly, in financial modeling,

GANs have been utilized to augment time-series datasets, ensuring better risk modeling and anomaly detection.

The Transformative Impact of Generative Models

The ability of generative models to produce synthetic yet realistic data has made them indispensable in the realm of data augmentation. By addressing challenges such as data scarcity, class imbalance, and diversity, these models empower machine learning systems to perform better across industries, paving the way for more accurate and robust AI solutions.

Comparison of Generative Models for Augmentation

Generative models have revolutionized the field of data augmentation, offering unparalleled capabilities for synthesizing realistic and diverse datasets. Unlike traditional augmentation methods that rely on transformations of the existing data, generative models can create entirely new samples, significantly enriching datasets, and improving model performance. This section explores how various generative models contribute to data augmentation, highlighting their unique strengths, and comparing their effectiveness.

GANs for Augmenting Image Datasets

Generative Adversarial Networks (GANs) have emerged as a powerful tool for augmenting image datasets. By leveraging the adversarial training process between a generator and a discriminator, GANs can produce highly realistic images. For instance, they have been used to augment datasets in medical imaging, where labeled data is often scarce. They can generate high-resolution synthetic MRI scans, X-rays, or histopathological images, enabling models to train on diverse samples that mimic real-world conditions.

GAN-based augmentation is especially effective in addressing class imbalance in datasets. By generating new samples of underrepresented classes, GANs help to ensure that models are not biased towards overrepresented categories. Furthermore, GANs can create domain-specific variations, such as different lighting conditions, textures or occlusions, making the model more robust to real-world scenarios.

VAEs for Creating Realistic but Diverse Data Samples

Variational Autoencoders (VAEs) offer a probabilistic approach to data augmentation. Unlike GANs, VAEs encode input data into a latent space and then decode it to reconstruct the original data. This process allows for controlled generation of new samples by manipulating the latent space. VAEs are particularly valuable for tasks requiring diverse but realistic data.

For example, in handwriting recognition, VAEs can generate new handwritten samples by interpolating between latent vectors of existing characters. This results in a smooth transition of styles while preserving the core features of the data. Additionally, VAEs are effective in generating structured data, such as time-series data for financial modeling or anomaly detection. Their probabilistic nature ensures that the generated samples are not only realistic but also diverse, covering a wide range of potential variations.

Diffusion Models for Data Augmentation

Diffusion models represent a relatively recent advancement in generative modeling, showing immense potential for data augmentation. These models work by iteratively refining noise into meaningful data through a series of learned transformations. Diffusion models excel at producing high-quality samples, often surpassing GANs in terms of fidelity and diversity.

One notable application of diffusion models is in augmenting datasets for image-to-image translation tasks. For example, they can be used to create realistic weather variations in outdoor images, such as adding fog, rain, or snow. In medical imaging, diffusion models can generate synthetic scans with varying pathologies, helping to train models for diagnostic tasks.

Moreover, diffusion models are inherently stable during training, avoiding common pitfalls like mode collapse seen in GANs. Their ability to produce a broader range of samples with fine-grained details makes them a promising choice for applications requiring high-quality augmented data.

Differences between Generative Models and Traditional Augmentation Methods

Traditional data augmentation methods rely on applying predefined transformations to existing data. These transformations, such as rotation, flipping, scaling, or cropping, are simple yet effective for improving model robustness. However, they are inherently limited by the diversity of the original dataset. For instance, augmenting an image of a cat by flipping it horizontally does not introduce any fundamentally new information to the dataset.

Generative models, on the other hand, overcome these limitations by synthesizing entirely new data points. While traditional methods are deterministic, generative models offer stochasticity, enabling the creation of a virtually unlimited number of unique samples. For example, a GAN trained on a dataset of human faces can generate new faces with different poses, expressions, and attributes, significantly expanding the dataset's diversity.

Another key difference lies in the level of control offered by generative models. VAEs, for instance, allow users to interpolate in the latent space, generating samples with specific attributes or characteristics. Diffusion models enable fine-grained control over the level of detail in the generated data, making them suitable for applications requiring high precision.

In summary, while traditional augmentation methods are indispensable for basic transformations, generative models provide a sophisticated approach to augmenting data with greater diversity and realism. By leveraging the strengths of GANs, VAEs, and diffusion models, practitioners can create datasets that better reflect the complexities of real-world scenarios, ultimately leading to more robust and accurate machine learning models.

Mathematical Foundations of Data Augmentation

Generative data augmentation leverages mathematical principles to synthesize diverse and realistic data, enhancing the training of machine learning models. This section delves into the probabilistic frameworks, latent spaces, and optimization techniques that underpin this transformative capability, enabling data enrichment beyond traditional augmentation methods.

Probabilistic Frameworks for Generating Diverse Data

At the heart of generative data augmentation lies the probabilistic modeling of data distributions. Generative models, such as Variational Autoencoders (VAEs) and Generative Adversarial Networks (GANs), aim to learn the underlying data distribution, denoted as $\mathbf{P(x)}$, from which real-world samples are drawn. These models approximate this distribution to generate synthetic data, represented as $\tilde{\mathbf{x}}$, that appears indistinguishable from the original data.

In a probabilistic framework, the generative process involves a latent variable $\mathbf{z}$, sampled from a prior distribution $\mathbf{P(z)}$ (commonly Gaussian or Uniform). The model then transforms $\mathbf{z}$ into observable data $\mathbf{x}$ through a generative mapping $\mathbf{G(z)}$. This mapping is expressed as:

$$P(x)=\int\delta(x-G(z))P(z)dz$$

where **G** is a neural network that learns to generate realistic samples by capturing the essential characteristics of the original data.

This probabilistic formulation ensures that the generated data aligns with the variability and richness of the original dataset. Models like VAEs explicitly maximize the Evidence Lower Bound (ELBO) to optimize this generative process, balancing data fidelity and diversity.

Exploring Latent Spaces for Targeted Augmentation

Latent spaces are compact, multidimensional representations of data learned by generative models. In the context of augmentation, these spaces serve as the playground for generating diverse data samples. The latent space structure reflects meaningful data attributes, enabling targeted modifications.

For example, consider a latent space, **Z** trained on facial images. Each point in **Z** represents a unique combination of facial features, such as age, expression, or pose. By interpolating or sampling within specific regions of **Z**, practitioners can generate data tailored to specific tasks, such as augmenting underrepresented demographics in a dataset.

Mathematically, targeted augmentation is achieved by controlling the latent vector, **z**. For instance:

- Sampling **z** from specific regions of **Z** ensures the generation of samples with desired properties.
- Conditional models, such as **Conditional GANs (cGANs)**, extend this by incorporating a conditioning variable **c** into the generative process, where **G(z, c)** produces data **x** conditioned on **c**:

x = G(z | c), where c represents class labels or attributes.

This ability to navigate and manipulate latent spaces enables practitioners to create highly customized and task-specific datasets.

Loss Functions and Optimization Techniques

The effectiveness of generative data augmentation hinges on the design of loss functions and optimization strategies tailored to the augmentation task. Loss functions guide the learning of generative models, ensuring that synthetic data aligns with the real data distribution, while maintaining sufficient diversity.

Adversarial Loss

In GANs, the generator and discriminator engage in a minimax game, defined by:

$$\min_G \max_D E_{x\sim Pdata(x)}[\log D(x)] + E_{z\sim P(z)}[\log(1 - D(G(z)))]$$

This loss ensures that the generator produces data indistinguishable from real samples, while the discriminator distinguishes between the real and synthetic data.

Reconstruction Loss

For VAEs, the reconstruction loss quantifies how well the generated data matches the original input. It measures the difference between the reconstructed sample, **x'** and the original input, **x**:

$$L_{recon} = || x - x' ||^2$$

KL Divergence

VAEs also employ a Kullback-Leibler divergence term to regularize the latent space:

$$L_{KL} = D_{KL}[Q(z|x) || P(z)]$$

This regularization ensures that the latent space maintains a smooth and interpretable structure, facilitating targeted sampling.

Wasserstein Loss

To address issues such as mode collapse in GANs, Wasserstein GANs (WGANs) replace the adversarial loss with the Wasserstein distance:

$$L_{WGAN} = E_{x} \sim P_{data} [D(x)] - E_{z} \sim_{P(z)}\} [D(G(z))]$$

This loss provides a smoother gradient landscape, stabilizing training, and promoting diversity in generated samples.

Optimization Techniques

Training generative models for data augmentation involves advanced optimization techniques:

- **Learning Rate Scheduling:** Adaptive learning rates mitigate instability during training.
- **Gradient Penalty:** In WGAN-GP, a gradient penalty term enforces Lipschitz continuity:

  $$L_{GP} = \lambda E_{\hat{x} \sim P(\hat{x})}[(\|\nabla D(\hat{x})\|_2 - 1)^2]$$

- **Batch Normalization:** Stabilizes training by normalizing intermediate activations.

Therefore, by designing and optimizing these components, generative models achieve robust and meaningful augmentation, empowering machine learning pipelines with richer, more balanced datasets.

Data Preparation and Dataset Requirements

Data preparation is a critical step when using generative models for data augmentation. Proper preparation ensures that the generative models operate effectively, and generate realistic, high-quality augmented data. This section covers the necessary steps for preparing raw datasets, preprocessing techniques to ensure compatibility, and addressing class imbalances through targeted augmentation.

Preparing Raw Datasets for Augmentation

Before applying generative models to augment data, raw datasets must be organized and cleaned. This involves:

- **Data Cleaning:** Remove inconsistencies such as duplicate entries, outliers, or corrupted samples. For example, in an image dataset, ensure that all files are valid image formats, and correctly labeled.
- **Label Verification:** Verify the accuracy of labels in supervised datasets. Incorrect or ambiguous labels can propagate errors through augmented data.
- **Dataset Splitting:** Split the dataset into training, validation, and test sets. Augmentation is typically applied only to the training set to avoid data leakage.
- **File Organization:** Maintain a clear directory structure to distinguish the original data from the augmented data. This can help in tracking the origin of samples, and understanding their influence on model performance.

By ensuring that the raw dataset is well-prepared, you set a strong foundation for effective augmentation with generative models.

Preprocessing Techniques to Ensure Compatibility with Generative Models

Generative models often have specific requirements for input data, and preprocessing ensures that these requirements are met. The key preprocessing techniques include:

- **Normalization:** Scale the numerical data to a consistent range, such as [0, 1] or [-1, 1], to match the input requirements of models like GANs or VAEs. For instance, image pixel values are typically normalized to [0, 1] in deep learning pipelines.
- **Resizing:** Resize images to the dimensions required by the model. For example, most GAN architectures expect square images of sizes like 64×64 or 128×128 pixels.
- **Data Augmentation Preprocessing:** Apply basic augmentation methods such as cropping, flipping, or rotation to increase the initial data diversity. This creates a richer starting point for generative models to learn robust patterns.
- **Data Encoding:** For non-image datasets, encode categorical features into numerical representations. Text data may require tokenization or embedding techniques to ensure compatibility with text-based generative models.
- **Handling Missing Data:** Fill the missing values using imputation methods or remove incomplete samples, depending on the dataset's characteristics.

Preprocessing ensures that generative models receive clean, consistent, and appropriately formatted data, which improves the quality of generated samples.

Fixing Class Imbalance with Targeted Augmentation

Class imbalance is a common challenge in machine learning where certain categories are underrepresented in the dataset. Generative models can be leveraged to address this imbalance effectively:

- **Synthetic Sample Generation:** Use generative models to create additional samples for minority classes. For instance, in a medical imaging dataset, GANs can generate synthetic X-rays for rare conditions to balance the dataset.
- **Conditional Generative Models:** Utilize conditional GANs (cGANs) or class-conditional VAEs to generate data specific to a target class. These models take the class label as input, ensuring that augmented samples belong to the desired category.
- **Oversampling Minority Classes:** Combine generative approaches with oversampling techniques. For example, create synthetic data for minority classes, and then apply traditional oversampling methods such as SMOTE (Synthetic Minority Oversampling Technique).
- **Data Diversity:** Focus on generating diverse variations within the minority class to avoid overfitting. For instance, vary attributes like lighting, orientation, or texture in generated images.

Addressing class imbalances with targeted augmentation improves model performance by ensuring that all categories are adequately represented. This leads to better generalization and more reliable predictions.

Thus, effective data preparation and preprocessing are essential for leveraging generative models in data augmentation. By cleaning and organizing raw datasets, applying preprocessing techniques, and addressing class imbalances, you can maximize the potential of generative models to enhance data diversity and quality. These steps lay the groundwork for more robust and accurate machine learning models, ensuring that the augmented data contributes meaningfully to the overall training process.

Using GANs for Data Augmentation

Generative Adversarial Networks (GANs) have revolutionized the way we generate synthetic data for augmentation purposes. By leveraging their ability to create highly realistic samples, GANs are particularly effective in scenarios where the labeled data is scarce or hard to acquire. From enhancing datasets in computer vision tasks to generating synthetic medical images, GANs provide an invaluable tool for improving model performance and robustness.

Overview of GAN-based Augmentation Techniques

GAN-based data augmentation techniques rely on the adversarial process between the generator and the discriminator. The generator creates synthetic data samples that resemble the real dataset, while the discriminator evaluates their authenticity. Over time, the generator learns to produce highly realistic data. Here are some key techniques used in GAN-based augmentation:

- **Unconditional GANs:** Generate random samples from the dataset's distribution, useful for general augmentation tasks.
- **Conditional GANs (cGANs):** Incorporate label information to generate class-specific data, making them ideal for multi-class datasets.
- **CycleGANs and StyleGANs:** Used for domain-specific augmentation, such as style transfer or image-to-image translation.
- **Data Balancing:** Address class imbalances by generating additional samples for underrepresented classes.
- **Domain Adaptation**: Use GANs to generate data in a new domain, while preserving the original dataset's features.

Challenges in Training for Realistic Data Generation

When working with GANs, we face some common challenges in training models for realistic data generation. By applying techniques discussed in the previous chapters, we can overcome many of these challenges to a great extent. However, a solid understanding of these challenges is essential for effective data augmentation.

- **Mode Collapse:** The generator produces limited variations, reducing data diversity. Techniques like minibatch discrimination can mitigate this.
- **Training Instability:** Balancing the generator and discriminator is challenging. Improper tuning of learning rates or loss functions can lead to poor results.
- **Vanishing Gradients:** In early training, the generator may struggle to improve due to negligible gradients from the discriminator.
- **Resource Intensity:** GANs often require extensive computational resources for realistic outputs.
- **Evaluation Metrics:** Assessing GAN performance remains non-trivial. Metrics like Frechet Inception Distance (FID) help but are computationally expensive.

Thus, by addressing these challenges through innovative techniques and proper parameter tuning, GANs can significantly enhance the effectiveness of data augmentation.

Using VAEs for Data Augmentation

Variational Autoencoders (VAEs) provide a powerful framework for generating new data samples by learning the underlying latent representation of a dataset. Unlike traditional augmentation methods, which rely on geometric transformations or noise addition, VAEs generate entirely new and realistic samples based on the learned distribution of the input data. This makes them particularly valuable for tasks where data scarcity or class imbalance is a significant challenge.

Overview of VAE-Based Augmentation Techniques

VAEs use a probabilistic approach to encode the input data into a latent space, and then decode it back into the original data space. This encoding-decoding process enables the model to learn a compressed representation of the data, while capturing its inherent variability. By sampling from the learned latent distribution, VAEs can generate novel data points that are consistent with the original dataset's structure.

Key Techniques in VAE-Based Augmentation:

- **Latent Space Sampling:** The encoder maps the input data into a latent space represented by a mean and variance. Sampling from this distribution allows the generation of new data points.
- **Interpolation in Latent Space:** By interpolating between two latent points, the decoder can generate intermediate data samples, which are particularly useful for creating smooth transitions between classes.
- **Noise Addition:** Adding controlled noise to the latent representations during sampling enhances the diversity of the generated data, preventing overfitting, and improving model robustness.

These techniques ensure that the augmented data is not only realistic but also diverse, addressing the limitations of traditional methods.

Conditional VAEs for Class-Specific Data Augmentation

Conditional Variational Autoencoders (CVAEs) extend the VAE framework by incorporating class-specific information into the latent space. By conditioning the generation process on class labels, CVAEs allow precise control over the type of data being synthesized. This is particularly useful for addressing class imbalance in datasets.

How CVAEs Work:

- **Input Conditioning:** The encoder receives both the input data and its corresponding class label. This ensures that the latent representation captures both the features of the data, and its class-specific characteristics.
- **Latent Space Conditioning:** During sampling, class labels are provided alongside the latent vectors, guiding the decoder to generate samples specific to the desired class.
- **Enhanced Diversity:** By varying the latent vector, while keeping the class label fixed, CVAEs can produce a wide range of samples within the same class.

Applications of CVAEs in Augmentation:

- **Balancing Imbalanced Datasets:** CVAEs can generate additional samples for underrepresented classes, ensuring that the dataset is balanced, and the model does not exhibit bias.
- **Synthetic Data Creation for Rare Events:** In domains like medical imaging or fraud detection, CVAEs can synthesize rare but critical cases, enabling better model training.
- **Domain-Specific Augmentation:** By conditioning on specific attributes, CVAEs can create data tailored to specific requirements, such as generating images with particular features (for example, smiling faces or specific tumor types).

Using Diffusion Models for Data Augmentation

Diffusion models have recently emerged as a powerful tool in generative modeling, capable of producing high-quality and diverse samples across various domains. By leveraging the principles of iterative noise addition and removal, these models provide a novel approach to data augmentation, addressing key challenges such as overfitting and data scarcity in machine learning tasks. Their flexibility makes them ideal for generating new, realistic data points, particularly in fields where the labeled data is expensive or hard to acquire.

Overview of Diffusion-Based Augmentation Techniques

Diffusion-based augmentation techniques involve two key phases: noise addition and denoising. During the noise addition phase, random noise is progressively added to the input data through a defined number of steps. This process transforms the original data into a noise-like distribution. In the subsequent denoising phase, the model learns to reverse this process, reconstructing the original data from noise. The ability to interpolate between these steps enables the creation of novel data points that share similar characteristics with the original dataset, while introducing controlled variations.

Unlike traditional augmentation methods, such as rotation or cropping, diffusion models enable more sophisticated transformations. For example, they can generate entirely new data samples, while maintaining the underlying distribution's semantics. This is particularly advantageous in domains like medical imaging, where generating plausible variations of rare disease cases is critical for robust model training. Additionally, diffusion models can create highly realistic synthetic data in natural language processing and computer vision tasks.

Training Diffusion Models for Generating Diverse and High-Quality Samples

Training a diffusion model for data augmentation typically involves the following steps:

- **Data Preparation:** Collect a high-quality dataset representative of the target distribution. Preprocessing is essential to normalize the data, and ensure consistency across samples.
- **Noise Schedule Design:** Define the noise schedule that controls how noise is added at each step. A common approach is to use a linear or cosine schedule to balance the trade-off between computational efficiency and sample quality.
- **Model Architecture Selection:** Choose an architecture suitable for the task. U-Net-based architectures are popular in diffusion models, especially for image synthesis. For text data, transformer-based architectures adapted to noise modeling are commonly used.
- **Loss Function Optimization:** Employ a loss function, such as the mean squared error (MSE), to measure the difference between predicted and target denoised samples. Advanced techniques might incorporate perceptual losses to enhance the fidelity of the generated samples.
- **Training Process:** Train the model by iteratively applying noise to the input data, and teaching the model to predict the noise at each step. This training requires significant computational resources but results in a highly capable generative model.
- **Inference for Augmentation:** During inference, the trained diffusion model generates new data samples by starting with pure noise, and iteratively denoising it to create the realistic synthetic data.

The outcome is a model capable of generating diverse samples that enrich the dataset, helping machine learning models generalize better to the unseen data.

Implementing Data Augmentation with Generative Models: Step-by-Step

Data augmentation using generative models involves leveraging their ability to create synthetic yet realistic data samples that can enhance the diversity and size of the training datasets. This process improves the robustness and generalization capabilities of machine learning models. So, let us delve into the steps required to implement data augmentation with generative models, complemented by code snippets and evaluation techniques.

Setting Up a Generative Model for Data Augmentation

The first step is selecting an appropriate generative model based on the task and data modality. Generative Adversarial Networks (GANs) are widely used for image synthesis, while Variational Autoencoders (VAEs) and autoregressive models are suitable for text and audio data. The key considerations include:

- **Dataset Preparation:** Ensures that the dataset is clean, labeled, and preprocessed.
- **Model Selection:** Choose a model architecture tailored to the data type (for example, StyleGAN for images or GPT-based models for text).
- **Hyperparameter Tuning:** Set parameters such as learning rates, batch sizes, and epochs to achieve optimal performance.

The following is an example of setting up a GAN for image data augmentation using TensorFlow:

```
import tensorflow as tf
from tensorflow.keras import layers

# Define the generator model
def build_generator():
    model = tf.keras.Sequential([
        layers.Dense(256, activation='relu', input_dim=100),
        layers.BatchNormalization(),
        layers.LeakyReLU(),
        layers.Dense(512, activation='relu'),
        layers.BatchNormalization(),
        layers.LeakyReLU(),
        layers.Dense(28 * 28 * 1, activation='tanh'),
        layers.Reshape((28, 28, 1))
    ])
    return model

# Define the discriminator model
def build_discriminator():
    model = tf.keras.Sequential([
        layers.Flatten(input_shape=(28, 28, 1)),
        layers.Dense(512, activation='relu'),
        layers.LeakyReLU(),
        layers.Dense(256, activation='relu'),
        layers.LeakyReLU(),
        layers.Dense(1, activation='sigmoid')
    ])
    return model
```

```
# Instantiate models
generator = build_generator()
discriminator = build_discriminator()
```

This setup initializes the generator and discriminator. The next steps involve training the GAN, and generating synthetic data for augmentation.

Example Code Snippets for Augmenting Image, Text, and Audio Datasets

Image Augmentation with GANs: Once the GAN is trained, it can generate new image samples.

```
import numpy as np

# Generate random noise
noise = np.random.normal(0, 1, (10, 100))

# Generate synthetic images
synthetic_images = generator.predict(noise)

# Visualize generated images
import matplotlib.pyplot as plt

for i in range(10):
    plt.subplot(2, 5, i + 1)
    plt.imshow(synthetic_images[i].reshape(28, 28), cmap='gray')
    plt.axis('off')
plt.show()
```

Text Augmentation with VAEs: VAEs can encode the textual data into latent representations, and decode them into variations.

```
from transformers import AutoTokenizer, AutoModelForSeq2SeqLM

# Load a pre-trained VAE model
tokenizer = AutoTokenizer.from_pretrained("t5-small")
model = AutoModelForSeq2SeqLM.from_pretrained("t5-small")

# Input text
texts = ["The weather is sunny.", "I love playing football."]
inputs = tokenizer(texts, return_tensors="pt", padding=True, truncation=True)

# Generate augmented text
outputs = model.generate(inputs['input_ids'], max_length=20, num_return_
sequences=3, do_sample=True)
augmented_texts = [tokenizer.decode(output, skip_special_tokens=True) for
output in outputs]
print(augmented_texts)
```

Audio Augmentation with Generative Models: WaveNet or similar models can synthesize the audio data.

```
import torchaudio
import torch
from torchaudio.models import WaveRNN

# Initialize a WaveRNN model
model = WaveRNN()
```

```
# Generate synthetic audio waveform
latent_vector = torch.randn(1, 128)
synthetic_waveform = model(latent_vector)

# Save the waveform as an audio file
torchaudio.save("synthetic_audio.wav", synthetic_waveform, sample_rate=16000)
```

Evaluating the Effectiveness of Augmentation

The effectiveness of data augmentation plays a pivotal role in ensuring that the augmented dataset not only enhances model performance but also maintains relevance and diversity in the generated samples. Proper evaluation ensures that the augmented data does not introduce noise, bias, or redundancy, and truly enriches the training dataset for better generalization.

Metrics for Assessing Augmented Dataset Quality and Diversity

- **Inception Score (IS):** Evaluates quality and diversity of the generated images using a pre-trained classifier like the Inception network. Higher scores indicate better image quality and class variety.
- **Frechet Inception Distance (FID):** Measures similarity between real and generated datasets by comparing their feature distributions. Lower FID values imply better alignment.
- **Perceptual Hashing:** Detects similarity between original and augmented images. Lower similarity implies higher diversity.
- **Diversity Metrics (for example, Shannon Entropy)**: Quantifies variability in categorical or **continuous data, useful for text or tabular datasets.**
- **Human Evaluation:** Domain experts manually assess the realism and relevance of augmented samples, especially in fields like medical imaging.

Analyzing the Impact of Augmentation on Model Accuracy and Robustness

- **Accuracy Improvements:** Compare model metrics (accuracy, precision, recall, F1-score) on original vs. augmented datasets to assess predictive improvement.
- **Out-of-Distribution (OOD) Testing:** Test models on novel inputs (for example, altered lighting or noise) to evaluate generalization from augmentation.
- **Adversarial Robustness:** Check performance under adversarial attacks to see if augmented data improves resistance to model deception.
- **Cross-Validation:** Use k-fold cross-validation to ensure improvements are consistent across different data splits.
- **Learning Curves:** Analyze training vs. validation performance to assess if augmentation reduces overfitting, and speeds up convergence.

Comparing Generative Augmentation to Traditional Techniques

Quality of Data: Traditional methods (for example, flips, rotations, and so on) create simple variations, while generative models (for example, GANs) produce entirely new, diverse data samples.

Example: A GAN can generate cars with different shapes and colors, unlike rotation-based augmentation that only alters angle.

- **Scalability and Customization:** Generative models like GANs/VAEs can be tuned for specific domains (for example, generating rare disease samples in medical imaging).
- **Performance Impact:** Generative augmentation often boosts model performance by adding realistic variability, improving tasks like object detection.
- **Flexibility:** Generative techniques support various data types–text, audio, tabular–unlike traditional methods, which are mostly image-specific.
- **Computational Cost:** Traditional methods are lightweight, while generative models require more resources but offer greater long-term value.
- **Low-Data Scenarios:** In data-scarce environments, generative models help by creating high-quality synthetic data, enhancing model training.

Challenges and Limitations

While generative models have revolutionized data augmentation, they also come with their own set of challenges and limitations. Understanding these is crucial to effectively harnessing their potential while mitigating risks and inefficiencies.

Balancing Quality and Diversity in Augmented Data

One of the primary challenges is finding the right balance between the quality and diversity of generated data. High-quality samples that lack sufficient diversity can lead to overfitting, where the model becomes too attuned to specific patterns and fails to generalize effectively. On the other hand, overly diverse samples might include unrealistic or irrelevant data points, which can confuse the model and degrade its performance. Achieving this balance often requires careful tuning of the generative model, such as adjusting the latent space sampling or implementing advanced regularization techniques.

For instance, in medical imaging, generating synthetic images with high fidelity is critical, but it is equally important that the variations introduced by the generative model align with real-world anomalies. A misstep here could lead to diagnostic errors or unreliable insights in clinical applications.

Computational Demands of Data Augmentation

Generative data augmentation often comes with significant computational requirements. Training GANs, VAEs, or diffusion models to generate high-quality samples is resource-intensive, requiring powerful GPUs or TPUs and considerable time. This computational demand becomes particularly challenging in scenarios where real-time or near-real-time data augmentation is necessary, such as online learning systems or edge-device deployments.

Moreover, the iterative nature of fine-tuning these models to specific datasets adds to the computational overhead. Smaller organizations or individual researchers with limited access to high-performance computing resources may find it difficult to adopt generative augmentation methods at scale.

Addressing Domain-Specific Challenges and Biases

Generative models, while powerful, can unintentionally amplify biases present in the original datasets. For instance, if certain demographics or geographic features are overrepresented, the generated data may reflect and reinforce these imbalances, leading to unfair predictions and biased outcomes in downstream applications.

Specialized domains pose additional challenges. In areas like autonomous driving, generative models must capture subtle but critical details–such as road conditions under different weather types–to produce realistic and reliable data. Inaccurate generation in such contexts can compromise model performance and safety.

To mitigate these risks, applying domain expertise, tailored architectures, and robust validation methods are essential. Techniques such as domain adaptation, adversarial training, and fairness-aware sampling are gaining traction to improve the relevance and fairness of augmented data. Ultimately, unlocking the full value of generative augmentation requires balancing quality, diversity, computational efficiency, and ethical considerations.

Case Study: Medical Imaging Data Augmentation

A leading medical research institution partnered with our team to develop an AI-driven solution for detecting cancer from MRI scans. The goal was to create a tool that could assist radiologists by providing a rapid and accurate initial assessment. This case study details our approach to overcoming a fundamental obstacle in medical AI: the critical shortage of reliable training data, and how we leveraged advanced generative models to build a more robust and generalizable diagnostic system.

Problem: Class Imbalance in MRI Cancer Dataset

The project's primary challenge was a fundamental data scarcity, which manifested in two critical ways:

- **Overall Data Volume:** The total number of high-quality, expert-annotated MRI scans was limited, constraining the model's ability to learn the full spectrum of anatomical variations.
- **Severe Class Imbalance:** This scarcity was acutely worse for the "`cancer`" class. Confirmed malignant cases were drastically outnumbered by benign or healthy examples.

This combination of a small dataset and a pronounced class imbalance created a high risk of developing a model that was both inaccurate and biased. The model could easily learn to take the shortcut of always predicting "`no cancer`," leading to dangerously high false-negative rates, and failing its core diagnostic purpose.

Solution Approach: Using GANs and VAEs to Generate Synthetic Medical Images

Generative models such as Variational Autoencoders (VAEs) and Generative Adversarial Networks (GANs) offered a powerful solution to our dual challenges of data scarcity and class imbalance by creating synthetic, clinically valid medical images.

- **Using GANs for Realistic Image Synthesis:** GANs, through the adversarial training of a generator and a discriminator, can produce highly realistic medical images. In our project, this capability was harnessed to generate synthetic MRI slices that displayed the specific textural and structural hallmarks of malignant tumors, directly augmenting the critically small set of positive cancer cases.
- **Leveraging VAEs for Diverse Sample Generation:** VAEs provided a different advantage such as control. By encoding images into a structured latent space, we could interpolate between data points or slightly vary the latent codes to generate nuanced variations of a single tumorous scan. This allowed us to create a diverse set of synthetic cancer images that

retained pathological truth but introduced valuable variations in size, shape, and positioning, thereby increasing the dataset's robustness.

- **Combining GANs and VAEs:** We also explored architectures that combine the strengths of both, such as VAE-GANs. These models leverage the VAE's structured latent space for meaningful representation and the GAN's discriminator to refine the output, resulting in synthetic MRIs that were both highly realistic and diagnostically relevant.

Challenges: Ensuring Clinical Validity of Augmented Samples

While generative models can produce visually realistic images, ensuring their clinical validity remains a significant challenge. The key concerns include:

- **Preserving Diagnostic Features:** The synthetic images must accurately reflect the diagnostic features critical for identifying conditions. For instance, a synthetic tumor should exhibit the same texture, size, and contrast as real tumors.
- **Avoiding Artifacts:** Generative models can sometimes produce artifacts or unrealistic patterns, which could mislead machine learning models or clinicians.
- **Regulatory Compliance:** In medical applications, generated data must comply with strict regulations like GDPR or HIPAA, ensuring patient data privacy, and ethical use of synthetic samples.
- **Validation with Experts:** Collaboration with medical professionals is necessary to validate the synthetic data. Domain experts can review the images to ensure that they meet the required clinical standards before integrating them into the training pipeline.

Outcome: Improved Performance of Models in Medical Diagnosis

By augmenting the dataset with high-quality synthetic samples, the models trained on these datasets showed significant improvements in performance. The key outcomes include:

- **Enhanced Model Accuracy:** The model trained on the augmented dataset achieved superior accuracy, particularly in identifying malignant cases. This was evident in its improved ability to distinguish between aggressive cancer and benign hyperplasia.
- **Improved Recall for Cancer Detection:** The recall metric, which measures the model's ability to correctly identify actual positive cases, showed a noticeable increase. This was critical for ensuring that true cancers were not missed, directly reducing the risk of false negatives.
- **Robustness to Data Variations:** The synthetic data, which incorporated realistic anatomical variations, made the model more robust to differences in patient anatomy and imaging noise, improving its generalizability across different clinical settings.
- **Reduced Data Collection Costs:** Generative models reduced the dependency on expensive and time-consuming manual data collection efforts, allowing researchers to focus resources on model development and validation.

Conclusion

In this chapter, we explored how generative models enhance data augmentation by addressing the key challenges such as data scarcity, class imbalance, and model overfitting. Traditional augmentation techniques, while effective in certain scenarios, are often limited in their ability to generate truly diverse and realistic data. Generative models such as GANs, VAEs, and Diffusion Models provide a more advanced approach by learning complex data distributions, and producing synthetic samples that closely resemble the real data.

We examined various applications of generative data augmentation across multiple domains, including healthcare, NLP, computer vision, and speech synthesis, demonstrating its potential to improve model robustness and generalization. Additionally, we covered the mathematical foundations behind generative data augmentation, along with practical implementation techniques, including GAN-based image augmentation, VAE-based text generation, and diffusion-based augmentation.

While generative data augmentation provides numerous advantages, challenges such as balancing quality and diversity, computational costs, and domain-specific biases must be carefully managed. Through case studies and hands-on implementation, you are now equipped to apply generative models for enhancing datasets, and improving ML model performance in real-world applications.

In the next chapter, we will explore Generative Models in NLP, focusing on how models such as GPT, BERT, VAEs, and diffusion-based text generators are revolutionizing text generation, augmentation, and language understanding.

Points to Remember

- Generative models can create synthetic training samples, helping to overcome data scarcity and class imbalance.
- GANs, VAEs, and Diffusion Models each offer unique advantages for data augmentation, depending on the use case.
- Augmenting data with generative models improves model robustness, generalization, and diversity, while reducing overfitting.
- Applications span multiple domains, including medical imaging, NLP, computer vision, and speech synthesis.
- Challenges include computational costs, balancing quality and diversity, and domain-specific biases in the augmented data.

Multiple Choice Questions

1. What is a key advantage of using generative models for data augmentation?
   a. Reduces dataset size
   b. Speeds up model inference
   c. Eliminates the need for training data
   d. Generates new, realistic data samples
2. Which generative model is commonly used for augmenting image datasets?
   a. GANs
   b. Transformers
   c. RNNs
   d. Decision Trees
3. What is a challenge in using generative models for data augmentation?
   a. Limited dataset diversity
   b. High computational requirements
   c. Lack of data generation capabilities
   d. Poor performance on structured datasets

4. Why is cycle consistency loss important in CycleGANs for data augmentation?
    a. Ensures high-resolution image generation
    b. Prevents overfitting in the model
    c. Ensures that translations between domains are reversible
    d. Eliminates the need for training a discriminator

Answers

1. d
2. a
3. b
4. c

Questions

1. How do generative models enhance data augmentation compared to traditional augmentation methods?
2. What are the key differences between GANs, VAEs, and Diffusion Models for data augmentation?
3. How does generative augmentation help in addressing class imbalance in machine learning?
4. What are the challenges of using generative models for data augmentation, and how can they be mitigated?
5. In which domains do generative augmentation techniques provide the most significant benefits?
6. How does GAN-based augmentation compare to VAE-based augmentation in terms of sample diversity and realism?
7. What role does latent space manipulation play in targeted data augmentation?
8. How do diffusion models differ from GANs and VAEs for generating synthetic datasets?
9. What are some ethical concerns surrounding generative data augmentation?
10. What are the potential future advancements in generative data augmentation techniques?

Key Terms

- **Generative Data Augmentation:** The use of generative models to create synthetic training data.
- **Generative Adversarial Networks (GANs):** A generative model that learns to produce realistic images or data.
- **Variational Autoencoders (VAEs):** A probabilistic model used for generating diverse but realistic data.
- **Diffusion Models:** A type of generative model that gradually transforms noise into structured data.
- **Latent Space:** The internal representation learned by generative models that enables data synthesis.

- **Cycle Consistency Loss:** A loss function ensuring that translated images can be mapped back to their original domain.
- **Overfitting:** A problem where a model learns to memorize training data rather than generalize.
- **Class Imbalance:** A dataset issue where some classes are underrepresented, affecting model performance.
- **Active Learning:** A technique where models actively select data for augmentation and training.
- **Domain Adaptation:** The ability to use generative models to bridge gaps between different data distributions.

CHAPTER 12
Generative Models in Natural Language Processing

Introduction

Generative models have revolutionized Natural Language Processing (NLP) by enabling machines to generate coherent, context-aware, and creative text. These models build upon strong mathematical and computational foundations, leveraging advancements in probability theory, deep learning, and attention mechanisms to understand and replicate the nuances of human language. Unlike traditional NLP models that focus on classification or extraction, generative models are designed to create, translate, and summarize text with remarkable fluency and accuracy.

In this chapter, we explore the principles and techniques behind generative models in NLP, from foundational concepts like language modeling and embeddings to state-of-the-art transformer architectures. Practical examples using TensorFlow and PyTorch will provide hands-on experience, helping you to fine-tune and deploy generative models for real-world applications.

Structure

In this chapter, we will discuss the following topics:

- **Introduction to Generative Models in NLP**
  - Evolution of generative models: From rule-based to deep learning approaches
  - Applications of generative models
  - A Master Storyteller: Understanding through a Real-World Analogy
- **Key Concepts in NLP Generative Models**
  - Understanding language modeling: Probabilistic foundations
  - Text Representation: Embeddings and Tokenization
  - Role of attention mechanisms in NLP generative models
- **Comparison of Generative Models for NLP**
  - Traditional language models vs. modern generative approaches
  - Overview of Transformer-based models: GPT, BERT, and T5
  - Advantages of generative models over discriminative models in NLP
- **Mathematical Foundations of NLP Generative Models**
  - Probability distributions in text modeling
  - Masked Language Models (MLM) vs. causal models

    - Loss functions and optimization strategies for NLP generative models
- **Data Preparation and Preprocessing for NLP**
- **Transformer Architecture for Generative NLP**
- **Working of NLP Generative Models**
    - Training objectives: Next-word prediction and masked token prediction
    - Fine-tuning pre-trained models for specific NLP tasks
    - Handling context and coherence in text generation
- **Implementing Generative NLP Models: Step-by-Step**
    - Fine-tuning GPT for text generation tasks
    - Training a T5 model for summarization and translation
    - Practical examples and code snippets using TensorFlow and PyTorch
- **Evaluating Generative NLP Models**
- **Challenges and Limitations**
- **Case Study: Fine-Tuning GPT for Text Summarization**
- **Future Directions**

Introduction to Generative Models in NLP

By learning patterns from vast amounts of text data, Generative models generate coherent, contextually relevant, and creative text outputs, opening up new possibilities in areas like conversational AI, content generation, and machine translation.

At the heart of generative NLP lies the ability to predict and produce new data based on learned patterns. Unlike discriminative models, which classify inputs into predefined categories, generative models focus on understanding the underlying probability distribution of the data. This enables them to predict the next word in a sentence, generate entire paragraphs, or even create novel text that mimics human writing.

One key feature of generative NLP models is their adaptability. They can be trained on diverse corpora, ranging from literary classics to real-time social media feeds, to learn language patterns, grammar rules, and even stylistic nuances. The significance of generative models extends to applications like machine translation, where the ability to generate contextually accurate sentences in a target language is crucial, and text summarization, where models distill key information from large texts.

Evolution of NLP Generative Models: From Rule-Based to Deep Learning Approaches

The journey of generative models in NLP began with rule-based systems, which relied on handcrafted rules and templates to process language. While effective in specific, well-defined scenarios, these systems lacked the flexibility to adapt to the nuances and complexities of natural language. For instance, early chatbots were heavily scripted, unable to respond creatively or handle unexpected inputs.

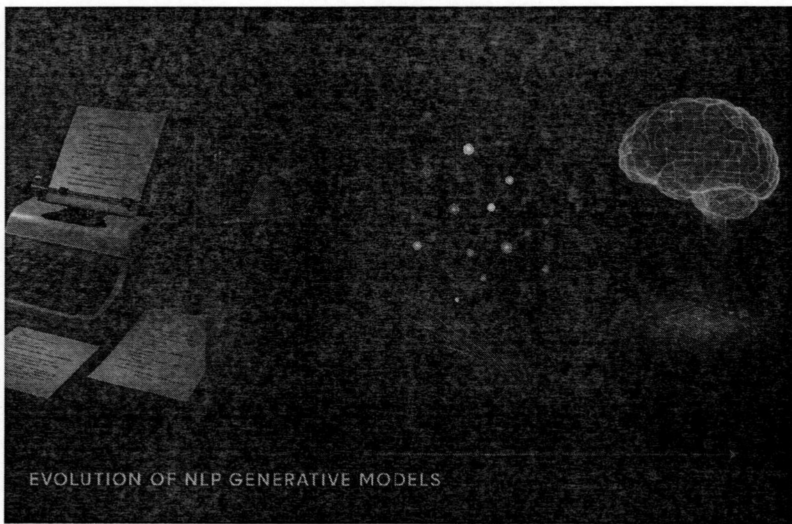

Figure 12.1: *From Textbooks to Neural Networks, the Transformative Journey*

The advent of statistical methods in the 1990s marked a significant shift. Probabilistic models, such as Hidden Markov Models (HMMs) and n-grams, brought statistical rigor to language modeling, enabling the prediction of word sequences based on likelihoods derived from training data. These methods laid the foundation for more sophisticated approaches but were still limited by their reliance on shallow feature representations and fixed-context windows.

Deep learning marked a paradigm shift in generative NLP. Neural network architectures, starting with Recurrent Neural Networks (RNNs), provided the capacity to model long-range dependencies and complex patterns in text. RNNs, and later their enhanced variants such as Long Short-Term Memory (LSTM) networks and Gated Recurrent Units (GRUs), became the backbone of many early generative NLP models. These architectures were particularly effective for tasks like sequence-to-sequence modeling, which underpins applications such as machine translation and text summarization.

In recent years, attention mechanisms and transformers have further revolutionized the field. Transformers, introduced through the seminal "*Attention is All You Need*" paper, enabled parallel processing of text data, significantly improving training efficiency and model scalability. Models like OpenAI's GPT series and Google's BERT as well as T5 have leveraged transformers to achieve the state-of-the-art performance across a wide range of NLP tasks. The self-attention mechanism in transformers allows models to capture intricate relationships between words in a sentence, regardless of their distance, leading to outputs that are both coherent and contextually accurate.

Applications of Generative Models in Text Processing, Creation, and Understanding

Generative models have found diverse applications in NLP, pushing the boundaries of what AI can achieve in text-based tasks. Some of the most impactful areas include:

- **Conversational AI:** Generative models underpin advanced conversational agents like chatbots and virtual assistants. Unlike rule-based bots, which follow predefined scripts, generative models enable systems to engage in dynamic, context-aware conversations. Examples include Gemini, ChatGPT, which can answer questions, provide recommendations, and even engage in creative storytelling.

- **Text Completion and Autocompletion:** Modern text editors and messaging applications frequently employ generative models to suggest completions for partially typed sentences. For instance, tools such as Gmail's Smart Compose leverage these models to provide contextually relevant suggestions, streamlining communication.
- **Content Generation:** One of the most visible applications of generative models is automated content creation. Advanced Models can write articles, generate videos, or create social media posts that are almost indistinguishable from human-authored content. These capabilities have profound implications for industries like journalism, marketing, and entertainment.
- **Information Retrieval and Question Answering (QA Systems):** Generative models have enhanced information retrieval by allowing systems to generate precise and context-aware answers rather than just retrieving documents. LLM Models demonstrate this shift from "*searching*" to "*understanding and responding*".
- **Code Generation and Programming Assistance:** LLMs such as Claude, OpenCode, and Gemini Code Assist can generate, explain, and debug code in multiple programming languages. This extends generative NLP beyond natural language to structured languages such as Python, Java, and SQL.
- **Sentiment Analysis and Personalization:** By generating responses tailored to a user's emotional tone or preferences, generative models enhance user engagement. Applications in customer service and recommendation systems highlight the potential for highly personalized interactions.
- **Creative Writing and Art:** Beyond functional applications, generative models inspire creativity. Writers and artists use these models as collaborative tools to brainstorm ideas, generate creative content, and explore new artistic directions. Projects like AI-generated screenplays and novels illustrate the intersection of technology and art.

A Master Storyteller: Understanding Generative Models in NLP through a Real-World Analogy

The Campfire Storyteller Analogy

***Figure 12.2**: Real-world Analogy with Storyteller*

Imagine sitting around a campfire with a group of friends. There is one person in the group—a master storyteller—who has spent years listening to countless folktales, myths, and legends. They have absorbed the structures of these stories, the rhythm of the sentences, and the way characters develop over time.

Now, someone gives the storyteller a prompt:

"Once upon a time, in a kingdom beyond the mountains, a young warrior discovered a hidden cave..."

The storyteller does not just recall a specific story from memory. Instead, they generate an entirely new tale by drawing from their vast experience. They take into account elements they have learned—like how stories usually have a hero, a challenge, and a resolution—and create something original on the spot, ensuring that it feels natural and engaging.

This process is exactly how generative NLP models work.

How This Relates to Generative NLP Models

A generative NLP model or an LLM, functions just like the storyteller:

- Training (Learning Stories)
  - The storyteller has listened to and internalized thousands of stories over time.
  - Similarly, an NLP model is trained on massive amounts of text data, absorbing grammar, context, storytelling techniques, and even cultural nuances.
- Generating Content (Creating New Stories)
  - When given a prompt, the storyteller does not copy a specific story but generates something new and coherent, inspired by past experiences.
  - An NLP model, when given a text prompt, does not retrieve pre-written text. Instead, it generates new sentences dynamically, predicting what should come next based on learned patterns.
- Understanding Context (Keeping the Story Sensible)
  - A good storyteller ensures that the plot remains consistent. If the protagonist is a warrior, they will not suddenly turn into a scientist in the middle of the story.
  - Generative models use context windows and attention mechanisms (like in Transformer models) to maintain coherence, ensuring that generated responses stay on topic.
- Creativity Adaptation (Different Styles, Different Stories)
  - If you ask the storyteller for a scary ghost story instead of a fantasy tale, they will change their tone, pacing, and vocabulary.
  - Similarly, generative models adjust their style and tone based on input. If you prompt a model with "Write a poem about the ocean," it will generate something poetic and lyrical, rather than factual and dry.

Key Concepts in NLP Generative Models

Generative models in Natural Language Processing (NLP) have revolutionized how we interact with machines. From composing poetry to writing code, these models are reshaping human-computer interaction. This section delves into foundational concepts, highlighting how language modeling, embeddings, and attention mechanisms underpin these advancements.

Understanding Language Modeling: Probabilistic Foundations

Language modeling lies at the heart of NLP generative models. It involves predicting the next word or sequence of words in a text based on the preceding context. At its core, this relies on probabilistic foundations: assigning probabilities to sequences of words.

Mathematically, a language model aims to estimate the probability distribution such as:

$P(w_1, w_2, \ldots, w_n)$, where w_i represents the words in a sentence. Using the chain rule of probability, this can be decomposed as:

$$P(w_1, w_2, \ldots, w_n) = P(w1)P(w2|w1)P(w3|w1,w2)\ldots P(wn|w1,w2,\ldots,wn-1)$$

Generative NLP models leverage this formulation, training neural networks to predict:

$$P(wi+1|w1,w2,\ldots,wi)$$

thus generating coherent and contextually relevant text. The transition from statistical **n-gram** models to deep learning-based models, such as **Transformers**, has drastically improved the quality of text generation by incorporating long-range dependencies and richer contextual understanding.

Text Representation: Embeddings and Tokenization

The representation of text plays a critical role in generative NLP models. Early approaches such as one-hot encoding, suffered from high dimensionality and lack of semantic meaning. Modern techniques have addressed these issues, enabling models to understand and generate human-like text.

- **Word Embeddings:** Methods like Word2Vec and GloVe map words into dense vector spaces, capturing semantic relationships. For example, the vectors for "*king*" and "*queen*" exhibit similar structures, differing primarily along the "*gender*" axis.
- **Contextual Embeddings:** Unlike static embeddings, contextual embeddings (for example, ELMo, BERT) generate word representations that vary based on the surrounding text. For instance, the word "*bank*" would have different embeddings in "*river bank*" versus "*bank account.*"
- **Tokenization**: Tokenization is the preprocessing step where text is broken down into smaller units (tokens). Subword tokenization methods such as Byte Pair Encoding (BPE) and WordPiece, are particularly useful in generative models, as they balance vocabulary size and representation granularity.

By combining these techniques, generative models effectively transform text into input that neural networks can process and understand, forming the foundation for tasks like translation, summarization, and creative writing.

Role of Attention Mechanisms in NLP Generative Models

Attention mechanisms have revolutionized generative NLP, particularly with the advent of Transformer architectures. The attention mechanism allows models to focus on relevant parts of the input, while generating output, overcoming the limitations of traditional sequence models such as RNNs and LSTMs.

In the context of generative models, the scaled dot-product attention mechanism is a cornerstone. It computes the relevance of one word to another by:

$$\text{Attention}(Q, K, V) = \text{softmax}\left(\frac{QK^T}{\sqrt{d_k}}\right) V$$

Here:

- Q, K, and V represent the query, key, and value matrices derived from the input embeddings.
- d_k is the dimension of the key vectors, and scaling by sqrt (d_k) prevents large dot-product values from dominating the Softmax computation.

Multi-head attention, an extension of this mechanism, enables the model to attend to multiple aspects of the input simultaneously. In generative tasks like text completion or translation, attention ensures that each generated token considers the most relevant parts of the input, and previously generated tokens.

Transformers, powered by attention, replaced the sequential processing of RNNs with parallel processing, making training on large datasets feasible. This innovation paved the way for state-of-the-art generative models, such as GPT and T5, which excel at producing fluent, coherent, and contextually appropriate text.

Through probabilistic language modeling, advanced text representations, and powerful attention mechanisms, NLP generative models continue to push the boundaries of what machines can achieve in understanding and generating human language.

Comparison of Generative Models for NLP

The evolution of generative models in natural language processing represents a paradigm shift in how machines understand and generate human language. Unlike traditional models that relied on rule-based approaches or basic statistical methods, modern generative models have harnessed the power of deep learning to revolutionize NLP. This section explores the differences between traditional language models and modern generative approaches, dives into key Transformer-based architectures, and highlights the advantages of generative models over their discriminative counterparts.

Traditional Language Models vs. Modern Generative Approaches

Traditional language models, such as n-grams and Hidden Markov Models (HMMs), operate by calculating probabilities over sequences of words. They are limited by their dependency on fixed-length contexts and their reliance on handcrafted features. For instance, an n-gram model only considers a fixed window of prior words, making it incapable of capturing long-range dependencies in text. While these models laid the foundation for computational linguistics, their simplicity is a double-edged sword: they are computationally efficient but lack the nuance needed for complex tasks.

Modern generative approaches, powered by deep learning, fundamentally change how language modeling is performed. Recurrent Neural Networks (RNNs) and their variants, such as Long Short-Term Memory (LSTM) networks, marked the first significant improvement by allowing models to learn sequential dependencies. However, the real revolution came with Transformer-based architectures, which overcome the inherent limitations of RNNs and LSTMs by enabling parallelization and leveraging self-attention mechanisms to model context across entire sequences.

Overview of Transformer Models: GPT, BERT, and T5

The introduction of Transformer models by Vaswani et al. in 2017 reshaped the NLP landscape. Transformers rely on a self-attention mechanism to assign varying levels of importance to different words in a sentence, capturing intricate patterns of meaning and dependency.

- **Generative Pre-Trained Transformer (GPT):** GPT models are autoregressive in nature, meaning that they generate text by predicting the next word in a sequence based on previous words. This approach is ideal for tasks such as text completion, story generation, and summarization. In fact, GPT's ability to learn contextual information across a vast corpora has made it a cornerstone of generative NLP.

- **Bidirectional Encoder Representations from Transformers (BERT):** While primarily a discriminative model, BERT laid the groundwork for understanding bidirectional context–essential for tasks like question answering and sentiment analysis. Though not generative in its original form, BERT's masked language modeling pre-training has inspired hybrid approaches that blend generative and discriminative features.
- **Text-to-Text Transfer Transformer (T5):** T5 reframes all NLP tasks as a text-to-text problem. Hence, whether it is summarization, translation, or sentiment analysis, the input and output are always text, simplifying the architecture and enabling multitask learning. T5 demonstrates how generative models can unify various NLP tasks under a single framework, delivering impressive results across benchmarks.

Advantages of Generative Models over Discriminative Models in NLP

- **Flexibility across Tasks:** Generative models can handle a wide range of tasks–from generating coherent text to translating languages–without requiring task-specific architectures. This versatility stems from their ability to model the entire data distribution, rather than focusing solely on specific labels or outputs.
- **Rich Contextual Understanding:** Modern generative models, especially those based on Transformers, excel at capturing long-range dependencies and nuanced relationships between words. This capability results in more coherent and contextually relevant outputs, particularly in creative applications like storytelling or dialogue generation.
- **Reduced Dependency on Large Labeled Datasets:** Generative models pre-trained on large unlabeled corpora can fine-tune effectively on smaller, task-specific datasets. This reduces the need for extensive labeled data, a significant advantage in domains where labeled data is scarce or expensive to obtain.
- **Multilingual and Cross-Domain Capabilities:** Pre-trained generative models can often perform well across multiple languages and domains, without extensive retraining. For example, models like GPT and T5 have demonstrated impressive zero-shot and few-shot learning abilities, allowing them to generalize to new tasks with minimal additional data.
- **Creative Output:** Unlike discriminative models, which focus on classification or regression tasks, generative models are inherently designed to produce new content. This opens up possibilities for applications such as creative writing, automatic code generation, and art generation.
- **Integration with Conversational AI:** Generative models have become the backbone of conversational agents, providing more human-like and engaging interactions. ChatGPT, for example, uses generative principles to simulate conversational depth and coherence that surpasses traditional rule-based or discriminative approaches.

While generative models have their challenges, such as computational demands and susceptibility to generating plausible but incorrect information, their advantages make them indispensable in advancing the state-of-the-art in NLP. The ongoing evolution of Transformer-based architectures and the rise of hybrid models promise even greater breakthroughs in the years to come.

Mathematical Foundations of NLP Generative Models

Generative models in Natural Language Processing rely on mathematical principles to capture the complexity and richness of human language. These models aim to predict or generate coherent sequences of text by understanding patterns in data. To achieve this, they leverage foundational concepts in probability theory, optimization, and statistical modeling.

Probability Distribution in Text Modeling

At the heart of NLP generative models lies the concept of probability distributions over text sequences. Given a sequence of words or tokens, a generative model estimates the likelihood of the sequence occurring. For example, consider a sequence of words such as $w_1, w_2, \ldots, w_T$. A language model assigns a probability $P(w_1, w_2, \ldots, w_T)$, which can be decomposed using the chain rule of probability:

$$P(w_1, w_2, \ldots, w_T) = \prod_{t=1}^{T} P(wt \mid w_1, w_2, \ldots, wt-1)$$

This formulation enables models to predict the next word in a sequence based on the context provided by preceding words. Capturing this conditional probability is crucial for generating coherent and contextually relevant text.

Modern NLP generative models often use discrete probability distributions over vocabulary tokens. Techniques like Softmax normalization ensure that the probabilities sum to one, making them valid probability distribution. Additionally, models incorporate embeddings to represent words or subwords in continuous vector spaces, enabling richer semantic understanding.

Language Modeling Objectives: Masked Language Models (MLM) vs. Causal Models

Two primary approaches dominate the landscape of generative language models: Masked Language Models (MLM) and causal models. Each employs distinct objectives and architectures to achieve generative capabilities:

Masked Language Models (MLM): MLMs predict missing or masked tokens in a sequence. For instance, given a sentence with a masked token, such as "The weather is [MASK] today," the model predicts the most likely word to fill the blank. This bidirectional context analysis allows MLMs to consider information from both preceding and succeeding tokens. A notable example is BERT (Bidirectional Encoder Representations from Transformers), which uses the MLM objective for pretraining.

The loss function for MLM is typically based on cross-entropy, calculated over the masked tokens:

$$L_{MLM} = -\frac{1}{N} \sum_{i=1}^{N} \log P(w_i^{true} \mid \text{context})$$

Here, N represents the number of masked tokens, and w_i(true) is the true token at position i.

Causal Models: Causal models predict the next token in a sequence based solely on preceding tokens. For example, given the input "*The cat sat on the*," the model predicts "*mat*." This unidirectional approach is ideal for autoregressive generation tasks, where text is generated sequentially from left to right. Examples include GPT (Generative Pre-trained Transformer) and its variants.

The loss function for causal models is also based on cross-entropy, but it considers all tokens in the sequence:

$$L_{causal} = -\frac{1}{T}\sum_{t=1}^{T} \log P(wt \mid w_1, w_2, \ldots, wt-1)$$

Causal models are particularly effective for tasks such as text completion, summarization, and conversational agents.

Loss Functions and Optimization Strategies for NLP Generative Models

Loss functions play a pivotal role in training NLP generative models by quantifying the error between predicted and true distribution. Cross-entropy loss is the most commonly used metric, as it directly measures the divergence between the predicted probability distribution and the ground truth:

$$L = -\sum_i y_i \log \hat{y}_i$$

Here, y_i represents the true probability distribution (typically one-hot encoded), and is the predicted probability distribution over the vocabulary. Minimizing cross-entropy encourages the model to assign higher probabilities to correct tokens.

To optimize the loss function, generative models rely on Stochastic Gradient Descent (SGD) and its variants. Popular optimization algorithms include:

- **Adam:** Adaptive Moment Estimation combines the benefits of momentum and adaptive learning rates, making it particularly effective for NLP tasks with large datasets.
- **RMSprop:** Focuses on adjusting learning rates based on recent gradients, helping to stabilize training.
- **Adafactor:** A variant of Adam that reduces memory usage, making it suitable for large-scale transformer models.

Regularization techniques, such as dropout and weight decay, further enhance model robustness by preventing overfitting. Additionally, techniques like gradient clipping mitigate issues such as exploding gradients, which are common in deep neural networks.

The interplay between probability distributions, language modeling objectives, and loss functions underpins the success of generative NLP models. These mathematical foundations enable models to understand and generate human-like text, opening doors to innovative applications in translation, summarization, and content creation.

Data Preparation and Preprocessing for NLP

Preprocessing is the cornerstone of every successful NLP pipeline. The quality and structure of data significantly impact the performance of generative models. This section explores the essential steps involved in preparing and preprocessing data for NLP tasks, ensuring the foundation for building robust generative models.

Collecting and Curating Textual Datasets

The first step in any NLP project is gathering relevant datasets. These datasets can come from various sources, including:

- **Publicly Available Datasets:** Platforms such as Kaggle, Hugging Face Datasets, and government repositories offer vast collections of textual data.

- **Web Scraping**: Tools like BeautifulSoup and Scrapy enable the extraction of domain-specific text from websites.
- **Custom Data Collection:** Businesses often generate proprietary datasets through customer interactions, logs, or surveys.

After collection, curation ensures that the datasets are relevant, diverse, and clean. Curation involves:

- **Filtering Unnecessary Data:** Removing duplicates, boilerplate text, or irrelevant content.
- **Balancing the Dataset:** Ensuring representation across classes, topics, or languages.
- **Removing Sensitive Information:** Stripping Personally Identifiable Information (PII) to comply with data protection regulations.

Tokenization Techniques: Subword Units, BPE, and SentencePiece

Tokenization is a fundamental step in transforming text into a format consumable by machine learning models. While traditional word-based tokenization works for many tasks, modern techniques like subword tokenization are crucial for generative models. They help manage vocabulary size, handle rare words, and maintain semantic continuity.

- **Subword Units**
  - Subword tokenization splits words into smaller meaningful chunks, such as prefixes, suffixes, or stems.
  - **Example**: The word, "*unbelievable*" can be tokenized into "*un-*", "*believe*", and "*-able.*"
  - Subwords reduce out-of-vocabulary (OOV) issues, and improve model generalization.
- **Byte Pair Encoding (BPE)**
  - BPE is a data compression technique adapted for NLP to iteratively merge the most frequent pairs of characters into subwords.
  - **Example**: Starting with "*l*", "*o*", "*v*", "*e*", and merging frequently observed pairs results in "*lo*" and eventually "*love.*"
  - Widely used in models like GPT and OpenAI's Codex.
- **SentencePiece**
  - SentencePiece is an unsupervised text tokenizer and detokenizer that supports subword segmentation, and treats text as a continuous stream of characters.
  - It enables seamless processing of languages without whitespace (for example, Chinese, Japanese).
  - **Example**: "神話的世界" (Japanese for "*world of myths*") can be tokenized into meaningful subword units directly.

Preprocessing for Diverse and Multilingual Datasets

Preprocessing plays a vital role when generative models are applied to diverse datasets spanning multiple languages, dialects, or domains. In such cases, text normalization becomes the first critical step—standardizing input by converting into lowercase, removing punctuation, or harmonizing Unicode characters. For instance, variations like "*Café*" and "*Cafe*" are normalized to a single form: "*cafe*".

Different languages present unique preprocessing challenges. French uses diacritics, German has compound words, and many languages follow distinct grammatical rules. Language-specific libraries such as spaCy and NLTK provide tools tailored to these needs, enabling precise cleaning. When working with multilingual datasets, it becomes essential to perform accurate language detection and tagging. Utilities like langid.py and fastText help identify the language of each text snippet, while transliteration or translation techniques may be employed for cross-lingual tasks, especially when aligning input-output pairs in different languages.

Although generative models do not always require stopword removal, doing so can reduce noise, and applying lemmatization helps unify various word forms into their root. For example, "*running*", "*ran*", and "*runs*" can all be reduced to "*run*", improving consistency across training samples. Encoding text into numerical formats–such as word embeddings or one-hot vectors–is another crucial step. It's important to ensure that the encoding method used during training aligns with the decoding mechanism at inference time to maintain model fidelity.

To boost robustness, data augmentation techniques such as synonym replacement, paraphrasing, or back-translation can be used. A sentence translated from English to French and back might yield subtle variations that enrich the training data. Ultimately, effective preprocessing–from gathering diverse corpora to applying advanced tokenization methods like Byte Pair Encoding (BPE) or SentencePiece–lays the foundation for powerful generative NLP systems. Such pipelines empower models to handle complex multilingual contexts, paving the way for breakthroughs in translation, conversational AI, and automated content creation.

Transformer Architecture for Generative NLP

Transformer Architecture has revolutionized Natural Language Processing (NLP) by enabling powerful generative capabilities. Introduced in the seminal paper, *Attention Is All You Need*, the Transformer employs self-attention mechanisms to handle long-range dependencies in text, overcoming the limitations of Recurrent Neural Networks (RNNs) and Convolutional Neural Networks (CNNs). Its scalability and efficiency make it the backbone of modern generative models like GPT, BERT, and T5.

At its core, the Transformer is designed around the concept of attention. The attention mechanism assigns varying levels of importance to different words in a sentence, allowing the model to focus on the most relevant parts of the input. This is achieved through the scaled dot-product attention, which computes weights for each token by considering its relationships with all other tokens in the sequence.

The Transformer consists of two main components:

- **Encoder:** The encoder processes the input text, creating a sequence of contextualized embeddings. Each encoder layer includes multi-head self-attention and feed-forward neural networks, with residual connections and layer normalization to facilitate stable training.
- **Decoder:** The decoder generates the output sequence step-by-step. Each decoder layer incorporates multi-head self-attention, encoder-decoder attention (to focus on the input), and a feed-forward network. The decoder uses masking to ensure that predictions are conditioned only on previously generated tokens.

This encoder-decoder setup allows Transformers to excel in tasks like machine translation, where the input and output sequences are distinct.

Differences between Encoder-Only, Decoder-Only, and Encoder-Decoder Models

The flexibility of the Transformer Architecture has led to variations tailored to different tasks:

- **Encoder-Only Models:**
  - Focus exclusively on processing input sequences to generate contextual representations.

  - Examples include BERT and RoBERTa, which are designed for understanding tasks like text classification and question answering.
  - These models use bidirectional self-attention, enabling them to consider both preceding, and following tokens in a sequence.
- **Decoder-Only Models:**
  - Focus solely on generating sequences from scratch.
  - Examples include GPT models, which are optimized for autoregressive text generation tasks such as story writing and summarization.
  - These models employ causal masking to ensure that predictions depend only on previous tokens.
- **Encoder-Decoder Models:**
  - Combine both components, making them suitable for tasks that involve transforming one sequence into another, such as translation or summarization.
  - Examples include T5 and BART, which leverage both input context (encoder) and sequential generation capabilities (decoder).

Each variation is suited to specific NLP tasks, and their strengths can be combined in hybrid approaches.

Time and Memory Complexities of Transformer-Based Generative Models

The Transformer's self-attention mechanism, while powerful, has significant computational requirements. The main challenge lies in the quadratic time and memory complexity relative to the sequence length:

- **Time Complexity:** In self-attention, every token attends to every other token in the sequence. This results in a complexity of $\mathbf{O(n^2d)}$, where n is the sequence length and d is the dimensionality of the token embeddings. For long sequences, this can lead to substantial computational overhead.
- **Memory Complexity:** The need to store the attention weights for all token pairs also results in $O(n^2)$ memory usage. This makes Transformers resource-intensive for tasks involving lengthy texts or batch processing.

To address these challenges, several optimizations and alternative architectures have been proposed:

- **Efficient Attention Mechanisms:**
  - Sparse Attention: Focuses on a subset of token pairs, reducing computational cost.
  - Longformer and BigBird: Introduce sliding window and global attention mechanisms to handle long sequences efficiently.
- **Low-Rank Approximations:**
  - Methods like Linformer approximate the attention matrix, reducing its rank to lower memory usage.
- **Memory-Enhanced Models:**
  - Models such as Reformer use locality-sensitive hashing to approximate attention, enabling processing of extremely long sequences with linear complexity.

Despite these complexities, the Transformer's ability to scale and its state-of-the-art performance on generative tasks have made it a cornerstone of NLP research and application. The evolution of

Transformer-based models continues to drive innovation, with new techniques emerging to balance performance and efficiency for diverse NLP tasks.

Working of NLP Generative Models

Natural Language Processing (NLP) generative models are designed to produce coherent, contextually relevant text by learning patterns from massive datasets. These models leverage advanced neural architectures, such as transformers, to understand linguistic nuances, semantics, and syntax. By predicting sequences of words, phrases, or even entire paragraphs, they achieve remarkable fluency and relevance in text generation. So, let us explore how these models function through their key components and methodologies.

Training Objectives: Next-word Prediction and Masked Token Prediction

NLP generative models are primarily trained using two fundamental objectives: next-word prediction and masked token prediction. These objectives form the basis of tasks such as language modeling and bidirectional understanding.

- **Next-word Prediction:** In next-word prediction, the model's goal is to predict the most likely subsequent word, given a sequence of preceding words. This training objective is commonly used in autoregressive models such as GPT (Generative Pre-trained Transformer). For instance, given the input sequence, "The sun rises in the", the model predicts "east" as the next word. Through repeated exposure to extensive text data, the model learns to generate coherent sentences by optimizing for likelihood.

  Example:

  - **Input**: "*She walked into the room and saw a*"
  - **Output**: "*cat sitting on the table.*"

- **Masked Token Prediction**: Masked token prediction involves predicting a missing word or token within a sentence. This technique is employed by bidirectional models like BERT (Bidirectional Encoder Representations from Transformers). Instead of processing the text sequentially, these models analyze the context both before and after the masked token, enabling a deeper understanding of sentence semantics.

  Example:

  - **Input**: "*The [MASK] was delicious after a long day.*"
  - **Output**: "*meal*"

By combining these objectives, models develop robust capabilities to handle a variety of downstream NLP tasks, including text generation, summarization, and translation.

Fine-tuning Pre-trained Models for Specific NLP Tasks

Pre-trained generative models are like a Swiss army knife for NLP, offering a versatile foundation that can be adapted for specific tasks. Fine-tuning involves taking a pre-trained model and retraining it on a smaller, domain-specific dataset to enhance its performance for a particular use case. Modern fine-tuning heavily leverages Parameter-Efficient Fine-Tuning (PEFT) methods, such as LoRA (Low-Rank Adaptation) and QLoRA (Quantized LoRA), which achieve high performance by updating only a small subset of the model's parameters. This approach is efficient and cost-effective because it avoids training models from scratch.

- **Domain-specific Fine-tuning**: Fine-tuning allows models to adapt to specific industries or domains. For example, a generative model pre-trained on general English text can be fine-tuned on medical literature using LoRA to efficiently specialize it for healthcare applications, without altering its entire architecture.

  Example Application: A pre-trained GPT model can be adapted with QLoRA for legal documents, enabling it to draft contracts or summarize case law effectively with minimal computational overhead.

- **Task-specific Fine-tuning**: Generative models can be fine-tuned for tasks such as:
  - **Summarization**: Condensing articles into concise summaries.
  - **Dialogue Generation:** Powering chatbots to provide human-like responses.
  - **Question Answering**: Generating accurate answers based on context.

  Example: Fine-tuning BERT for summarizing news articles enables it to produce concise and relevant summaries, tailored for busy readers.

- **Transfer Learning Advantage:** Fine-tuning leverages the transfer learning paradigm, where a model trained on one task or dataset transfers its knowledge to another. Techniques like LoRA and QLoRA enhance this by drastically reducing the data, storage, and computational requirements for adapting models to specialized tasks, making advanced AI more accessible.

Handling Context and Coherence in Text Generation

One of the most challenging aspects of text generation is ensuring that the output is contextually appropriate and coherent over extended sequences. Generative models use advanced mechanisms to maintain context and fluency:

- **Attention Mechanism:** The introduction of attention mechanisms, particularly in transformer-based models, revolutionized NLP. Attention allows models to focus on relevant parts of the input text, while generating output. For example, when generating a response to a query, the model can "attend" to the key parts of the question to ensure an accurate and relevant response.

  Example:

  - **Input**: "*The book, written by the famous author John Doe, explores themes of science and philosophy.*"
  - **Attention**: Focus on "*themes of science and philosophy*" when generating related output.

- **Context Windows:** Generative models like GPT use context windows to process input. These windows define the maximum number of tokens (words or subwords) that can be considered at once. Larger windows enable better context understanding but require more computational resources. Thus, by processing text in chunks, the model ensures that the generated content aligns with the context.

- **Beam Search and Sampling Strategies:** During text generation, models rely on decoding strategies such as beam search and nucleus sampling to optimize coherence and diversity.
  - Beam Search explores multiple possible outputs simultaneously, selecting the most probable sequences.
  - Nucleus Sampling adjusts randomness in predictions, ensuring creativity without sacrificing relevance.

  Example:

  - **Input**: "*Describe the benefits of renewable energy.*"

  - **Output**: "*Renewable energy reduces greenhouse gas emissions, promotes energy security, and supports sustainable development.*"
- **Long-range Dependencies**: Models like GPT-5 and T5 (Text-to-Text Transfer Transformer) address long-range dependencies, ensuring that the generated text remains consistent over extended outputs. This capability is crucial for applications like story generation and document drafting.

So, by balancing these techniques, generative NLP models produce text that is not only coherent and contextually relevant but also tailored to specific applications and user requirements. Their ability to generate human-like language opens up vast possibilities in industries ranging from customer support to creative writing.

Implementing Generative NLP Models: Step-by-Step

Generative NLP models have revolutionized the way we approach tasks like text generation, summarization, and translation. In this section, we will walk through the step-by-step implementation of two popular generative models–GPT (Generative Pre-trained Transformer) and T5 (Text-to-Text Transfer Transformer). These models, powered by advanced transformer architectures, have set benchmarks in natural language processing. By fine-tuning them for specific tasks, you can achieve remarkable results with relatively small datasets. In the following paragraphs, we explore the nuances of fine-tuning GPT for text generation, and training T5 for summarization and translation, accompanied by practical examples and code snippets using TensorFlow and PyTorch.

Fine-tuning GPT for Text Generation Tasks

Fine-tuning a pre-trained GPT model involves adapting it to a specific task or domain. Here is how you can do it step-by-step:

1. **Dataset Preparation:** Start with a domain-specific or task-specific dataset. For instance, if you want the GPT model to generate product descriptions, collect a dataset of the existing product descriptions.
2. **Preprocessing:** Tokenize your text using the tokenizer associated with the GPT model. Ensure that your dataset is split into training and validation sets.
3. **Model Loading:** Load a pre-trained GPT model, such as Mistral7b or GPT-Neo, using a framework like Hugging Face Transformers. This provides access to pre-trained weights, saving computational resources.
4. **Fine-tuning:** Use a language modeling objective to fine-tune the model. This involves training the model to predict the next word in a sequence, optimizing for cross-entropy loss.
5. **Evaluation and Validation:** Evaluate the model's performance on the validation set to monitor overfitting or underfitting. Use metrics such as perplexity or BLEU scores.
6. **Deployment:** Once satisfied with the results, deploy the fine-tuned model for inference. This could involve integrating it into a web app or API for real-world usage.

Training a T5 Model for Summarization and Translation

The T5 model frames all NLP tasks as a text-to-text problem. Summarization is treated as generating a summary text from an input text, and translation is treated as generating text in the target language from a source language input. Here are the steps to train T5:

1. **Dataset Selection:** Choose an appropriate dataset for the task. For summarization, you might use the CNN/DailyMail dataset. For translation, you can use datasets like WMT (for example, WMT 2014 English-German).
2. **Preprocessing:** Preprocess your data to fit the text-to-text format. Add task-specific prefixes like "*summarize:*" or "*translate English to French:*" at the start of your inputs.
3. **Model Loading:** Load a pre-trained T5 model, such as T5-Small or T5-Large, depending on your resource constraints.
4. **Fine-tuning:** Fine-tune the model on the specific task using a sequence-to-sequence learning objective. This involves optimizing the likelihood of the target sequence given the input sequence.
5. **Evaluation:** Evaluate the model using metrics such as ROUGE for summarization and BLEU for translation.
6. **Inference:** Use the trained model for inference by providing inputs with task-specific prefixes.

Practical Examples and Code Snippets Using TensorFlow and PyTorch

Combining the power of frameworks like TensorFlow and PyTorch with Hugging Face Transformers makes it easier to implement generative NLP models. Here is a practical example of Fine-tuning GPT for Text Generation Tasks:

```
from transformers import AutoTokenizer, AutoModelForCausalLM, Trainer,
TrainingArguments
from datasets import load_dataset

model_name = "mistralai/Mistral-7B-v0.1"
tokenizer = AutoTokenizer.from_pretrained(model_name, use_fast=True)
tokenizer.pad_token = tokenizer.eos_token
model = AutoModelForCausalLM.from_pretrained(model_name)

dataset = load_dataset("text", data_files={"train": "train.txt", "validation":
"valid.txt"})
tokenize = lambda x: tokenizer(x["text"], truncation=True, padding="max_
length", max_length=512)
data = dataset.map(tokenize, batched=True, remove_columns=["text"])

args = TrainingArguments("mistral-finetuned", num_train_epochs=3, per_device_
train_batch_size=2, per_device_eval_batch_size=2, evaluation_strategy="epoch",
save_strategy="epoch", gradient_accumulation_steps=4, logging_dir="logs",
fp16=True)

Trainer(model=model, args=args, train_dataset=data["train"], eval_dataset
=data["validation"]).train()
model.save_pretrained("mistral-finetuned"); tokenizer.save_pretrained
("mistral-finetuned")
```

Training a T5 Model for Summarization and Translation

The following Python Code uses the Hugging Face Transformers library to perform text summarization using the pre-trained T5-small model. It begins by loading the tokenizer and model designed for the T5 architecture. The input text is prepended with the task-specific prefix "*summarize:*"–a format T5 expects to understand what task to perform. The tokenizer converts the input string into token IDs compatible with the model. These IDs are then passed to the model's generate method, which uses beam search (with 4 beams) and early stopping to generate a concise summary with a maximum length of 20 tokens. Finally, the generated token IDs are decoded back into human-readable text, and printed without special tokens.

```
from transformers import T5Tokenizer, T5ForConditionalGeneration

# Load the tokenizer and model
tokenizer = T5Tokenizer.from_pretrained("t5-small")
model = T5ForConditionalGeneration.from_pretrained("t5-small")

# Example input text
input_text = "summarize: The quick brown fox jumps over the lazy dog."
input_ids = tokenizer(input_text, return_tensors="pt").input_ids

# Generate summary
outputs = model.generate(input_ids, max_length=20, num_beams=4,
early_stopping=True)
print(tokenizer.decode(outputs[0], skip_special_tokens=True))
```

Experimenting with Learning Rates

Adjust learning rates dynamically using learning rate schedulers.

```
from torch.optim.lr_scheduler import StepLR
optimizer = torch.optim.Adam(model.parameters(), lr=1e-4)
scheduler = StepLR(optimizer, step_size=1, gamma=0.9)

#Saving and Loading Models
torch.save(model.state_dict(), "t5_finetuned.pt")
```

These examples demonstrate the flexibility and power of generative models for diverse NLP tasks. By following these steps and adapting the code, you can build robust systems for real-world applications.

Evaluating Generative NLP Models

Evaluation is a critical aspect of generative NLP models, as it determines their ability to generate coherent, relevant, and high-quality text. Unlike traditional NLP tasks, where evaluation can often be straightforward (for example, accuracy for classification), assessing generative models requires specialized metrics and methodologies to address the subjective nature of text generation. This section explores key evaluation metrics, the inherent challenges, and comparative approaches to understanding model performance across tasks.

Metrics for Text Quality: Perplexity, BLEU, ROUGE, and Human Evaluation

Evaluating the quality of generated text requires both quantitative and qualitative approaches. The following metrics are widely used:

- **Perplexity:** This is a statistical measure commonly used to evaluate language models. It indicates how well a probability model predicts a sample. Lower perplexity implies that the model assigns higher probabilities to the correct sequence of words, thus producing more coherent and fluent text. However, perplexity alone is not sufficient to capture semantic quality or relevance.

- **BLEU (Bilingual Evaluation Understudy):** A precision-based metric that compares the n-grams in the generated text to reference texts. It is used for tasks like machine translation. While BLEU provides insights into lexical overlap, it is often criticized for its inability to measure semantic similarity or handle paraphrased text effectively.
- **ROUGE (Recall-Oriented Understudy for Gisting Evaluation):** ROUGE focuses on recall. and is primarily used for summarization tasks. It measures the overlap of n-grams, word sequences, and longest common subsequences between the generated text and reference summaries. ROUGE complements BLEU by emphasizing the ability to capture the essential content.
- **Human Evaluation:** Human evaluation remains the gold standard for assessing the quality of generated text. Human judges assess attributes like coherence, relevance, fluency, and creativity. While reliable, this approach is resource-intensive and prone to variability across evaluators.

Challenges in Evaluating Coherence, Relevance, and Diversity of Generated Text

Generative NLP models aim to produce text that is not only grammatically correct but also contextually appropriate and diverse. Evaluating these presents several challenges:

- **Coherence:** Models often struggle to maintain coherence over long-form text. Evaluating coherence requires understanding the logical flow and consistency of ideas, which automated metrics fail to capture effectively.
- **Relevance:** Relevance measures how well the generated text aligns with the input prompt or task requirements. This is particularly important in tasks like dialogue generation, where responses must be contextually appropriate. Automated metrics such as BLEU and ROUGE often fail to measure contextual relevance accurately.
- **Diversity:** Generative models sometimes produce repetitive or overly generic text, sacrificing diversity for higher precision or recall. Metrics to evaluate diversity, such as distinct-n, have been proposed but require careful interpretation.
- **Semantic Quality:** Lexical overlap-based metrics cannot assess whether the generated text conveys the same meaning as the reference. This limitation becomes apparent in tasks involving paraphrasing or creative text generation.

Comparative Analysis of Model Performance across Tasks

Different tasks in generative NLP require tailored evaluation approaches due to the diversity in output characteristics and goals. Let us consider some examples:

- **Machine Translation:** In machine translation, BLEU and ROUGE are commonly used to evaluate the alignment of generated translations with reference texts. However, human evaluations are often needed to judge subtle nuances, idiomatic expressions, and cultural context.
- **Summarization:** Summarization tasks rely heavily on ROUGE for evaluation. However, modern approaches often incorporate semantic evaluation metrics like BERTScore, which uses pre-trained transformer models to compute similarity based on contextual embeddings.
- **Dialogue Generation:** Dialogue models require multi-dimensional evaluation criteria, including relevance, coherence, engagement, and persona consistency. Metrics like METEOR and self-BLEU are used alongside human evaluation to assess conversational quality.

- **Creative Text Generation:** Tasks like story generation or poetry writing necessitate a balance between coherence, creativity, and diversity. Human judgment is indispensable in these cases, but automated metrics such as novelty scores and distinct-n provide supplementary insights.

Challenges and Limitations in Generative NLP

Generative models in natural language processing have revolutionized the field, enabling capabilities like text completion, machine translation, and content creation. However, their advancements are not without challenges. These limitations, though often nuanced, are critical to address for achieving sustainable and ethical development in NLP technologies. In the following paragraph, we delve into some of the most pressing challenges and limitations associated with generative NLP.

Managing Large-Scale Datasets and High Computational Requirements

One of the primary challenges in developing and deploying generative NLP models is the sheer scale of data and computational power required. Models like GPT or BERT are typically trained on terabytes of text data, necessitating extensive preprocessing, storage, and management. Training these models requires high-end hardware such as GPUs or TPUs, and often spans weeks or even months. This reliance on significant resources makes generative NLP inaccessible to smaller organizations or independent developers, leading to a disparity in who can create and benefit from these technologies. Furthermore, the environmental cost associated with the energy consumption of training and fine-tuning such models raises concerns about their long-term sustainability.

Addressing Biases and Ethical Considerations in Generated Text

Generative NLP models are trained on massive datasets scraped from the internet, which include biases, stereotypes, and other problematic content. These biases can manifest in the generated text, potentially reinforcing harmful narratives or excluding marginalized groups. A model may generate gendered or racially biased language, perpetuating inequities present in the training data. Beyond biases, ethical concerns such as misinformation, malicious content generation, and privacy violations are also significant risks. Ensuring ethical use of generative NLP requires rigorous auditing of the training data, implementing fairness-aware algorithms, and building mechanisms to detect and prevent harmful outputs.

Limitations in Handling Low-Resource Languages and Rare Vocabulary

Despite the advancements in generative NLP, there remains a significant gap in performance when it comes to low-resource languages and rare vocabulary. Many widely used datasets and pre-trained models prioritize high-resource languages like English, Chinese, or Spanish, while languages with fewer available text resources are often neglected. This leads to subpar performance in translation, summarization, or text generation tasks for these languages. Additionally, rare words, domain-specific terminology, and neologisms are often not adequately captured, resulting in unnatural or incorrect outputs. Addressing these issues requires specialized training approaches, such as few-shot or zero-shot learning, along with the curation of more diverse and representative datasets.

Case Study: Fine-Tuning GPT for Text Summarization

In this case study, we explore the practical implementation of fine-tuning a generative model–specifically GPT–for the task of abstractive text summarization. The aim is to distill lengthy and complex documents into concise, meaningful summaries that retain the necessary information, while eliminating redundancies. This process highlights the transformative power of generative models in solving real-world natural language processing challenges.

Problem: Summarizing Lengthy Documents into Concise, Meaningful Text

Summarizing extensive documents poses a significant challenge in fields like legal, healthcare, journalism, and academia. Manually condensing pages of text into brief summaries is labor-intensive and prone to human errors. Automated summarization tools, while useful, often struggle with maintaining coherence, relevance, and fluency. Abstractive summarization, which generates new sentences instead of merely extracting the existing ones, is a particularly demanding task. It requires an advanced understanding of context, syntax, and semantics–skills that generative models like GPT are uniquely positioned to handle.

Solution Approach: Fine-Tuning a Generative Model for Abstractive Summarization

Fine-tuning GPT for abstractive summarization involves the following steps:

- **Dataset Preparation:** The process begins with curating a high-quality dataset consisting of document-summary pairs. Commonly used datasets include CNN/DailyMail for news summarization or PubMed for scientific articles. Preprocessing ensures that text is tokenized and formatted correctly for the model.
- **Pre-trained Model Selection:** OpenAI's GPT is chosen due to its robust language modeling capabilities. Its ability to understand complex sentence structures, and generate human-like text makes it ideal for summarization tasks.
- **Fine-Tuning Process:** The pre-trained model is fine-tuned on the curated dataset using supervised learning. The objective is to minimize the cross-entropy loss between the model's predictions and the target summaries. Key hyperparameters, such as learning rate, batch size, and maximum sequence length, are optimized for performance.
- **Inference and Evaluation:** After fine-tuning, the model generates summaries for new, unseen documents. The output is evaluated using metrics such as ROUGE (Recall-Oriented Understudy for Gisting Evaluation) and BLEU (Bilingual Evaluation Understudy) to assess quality, relevance, and fluency.

Challenges: Ensuring Coherence and Relevance in Summaries

Despite its strengths, fine-tuning GPT for summarization is not without challenges:

- **Balancing Precision and Recall:** The model may struggle to include all the key points without overloading the summary with unnecessary details.
- **Avoiding Repetition:** Generative models often repeat phrases or ideas in summaries, reducing their coherence and readability.

- **Maintaining Context:** Long input sequences can cause the model to lose track of context, especially when summarizing very lengthy documents.
- **Bias in Summarization:** The model might reflect biases present in the training data, leading to skewed or incomplete summaries.

Outcome: Examples of Generated Summaries with Evaluation Results

After fine-tuning, the model's performance is tested on real-world documents. The following are some examples of its outputs, along with their evaluations:

Example 1:

Input Document: A five-page scientific article discussing the benefits and risks of a new pharmaceutical drug.

Generated Summary: "*The study highlights significant benefits of Drug X in reducing symptoms of Condition Y. However, it cautions against potential side effects, including Z and W, and emphasizes the need for further clinical trials.*"

Evaluation: ROUGE-L score of 0.82, indicating a high overlap with human-written summaries.

Example 2:

Input Document: A 10-page legal document outlining the terms and conditions of a merger agreement.

Generated Summary: "*The agreement stipulates that Company A will acquire Company B for $5 billion, subject to regulatory approval. Key conditions include compliance with antitrust laws, and securing shareholder approval.*"

Evaluation: BLEU score of 0.79, reflecting strong grammatical accuracy and contextual relevance.

Example 3:

Input Document: A 15-page research paper on climate change and its economic impact.

Generated Summary: "*The paper analyzes the economic repercussions of climate change, focusing on agriculture and energy sectors. It proposes policy interventions to mitigate long-term risks.*"

Evaluation: ROUGE-2 score of 0.68, indicating room for improvement in capturing specific details. These results demonstrate the model's ability to generate coherent, concise, and contextually relevant summaries. While the scores vary depending on the document's complexity and domain, the fine-tuned GPT consistently produces summaries that are comparable to human efforts.

Fine-tuning GPT for text summarization showcases the versatility of generative models in NLP. By addressing challenges such as coherence and relevance, these models can significantly enhance productivity and efficiency across various industries. However, continuous advancements in training techniques and evaluation metrics are essential to achieve human-like performance in abstractive summarization tasks.

Future Directions

As generative models continue to evolve, the field of Natural Language Processing (NLP) is poised for groundbreaking advancements. These developments are not only shaping how machines understand and generate language but also unlocking new possibilities by integrating diverse modalities and addressing critical challenges. In the following section, we explore some key future directions that will likely define the next decade of generative NLP research and applications.

Advancements in Multi-Modal Generative Models Combining Text, Image, and Audio

One of the most promising areas in NLP is the convergence of text, image, and audio generation. Multi-modal generative models like DALL-E, Sora and Veo have demonstrated the potential to produce coherent and contextually accurate content across modalities. By combining language understanding with visual and auditory cues, these models open up a myriad of applications.

For instance:

- **Creative Content Generation:** Multi-modal systems can generate synchronized audio and visual narratives from textual prompts, revolutionizing storytelling, game design, and animation.
- **Accessibility Enhancements:** By synthesizing audio descriptions for visual content and vice versa, these models can create inclusive experiences for people with disabilities.
- **Educational Tools:** Interactive tools powered by multi-modal models can transform learning by offering immersive experiences, such as virtual tutors that explain concepts visually and verbally.

Future research will focus on improving the alignment of modalities, ensuring consistency and reducing biases in the generated content. Techniques such as cross-modal attention mechanisms and shared latent space representation are pivotal to achieving these goals.

Research Trends in Real-Time Generative NLP Applications

Generative NLP models have traditionally been computationally intensive, posing challenges for real-time applications. However, recent innovations in model optimization and inference techniques are paving the way for real-time generative systems. These advancements include:

- **Efficient Architectures:** Lighter transformer models, such as DistilBERT and MobileBERT, are being adapted for generative tasks, enabling faster response times without significant sacrifices in accuracy.
- **Edge Deployment:** Deploying generative NLP models on edge devices, such as smartphones or IoT devices, ensures low-latency responses for applications like real-time translation or conversational agents.
- **Streaming Models:** Streaming transformers that generate outputs token by token, rather than processing entire sequences, are another key area of development. These models enhance user experiences in real-time chatbots, gaming, and live transcription.

Moreover, with the growing demand for seamless human-computer interaction, applications like real-time sentiment analysis, adaptive storytelling, and dynamic query generation are expected to benefit immensely from these trends. The focus will be on balancing computational efficiency with output quality to deliver responsive systems.

Scaling Generative Models for Low-Resource Languages and High-Resolution Tasks

While major breakthroughs in generative NLP have predominantly benefited high-resource languages, the majority of the world's languages remain underrepresented. Addressing this disparity is a pressing need, particularly as generative models gain traction in global applications. The key strategies to scale generative models for low-resource languages include:

- **Transfer Learning:** Leveraging pre-trained models on high-resource languages, and fine-tuning them for low-resource scenarios can drastically reduce the data requirements.

- **Data Augmentation:** Techniques like back-translation and synthetic data generation help create robust training datasets for low-resource languages, improving model performance.
- **Community Collaboration:** Open initiatives such as Masakhane and AI4Bharat are fostering collaborations to develop NLP tools for African and Indian languages, respectively. Such efforts emphasize inclusivity and community-driven innovation.

The future of generative models in NLP is marked by opportunities and challenges. Advancements in multi-modal generative models, real-time applications, and scaling for low-resource languages will not only expand the reach of these technologies but also address pressing issues of inclusivity and accessibility. By fostering innovation and collaboration, the next wave of generative NLP is set to transform industries and redefine how humans interact with technology.

Conclusion

In this chapter, we explored the role of generative models in NLP, their evolution from rule-based approaches to deep learning-based architectures, and their applications across diverse text-processing tasks. We examined the key concepts such as language modeling, text representation, and attention mechanisms, which form the foundation of modern NLP generative models. The comparison between traditional statistical models and transformer-based generative approaches highlighted the advantages of self-attention and deep contextual embeddings, which enable state-of-the-art models like GPT, BERT, and T5 to generate high-quality, coherent text.

We also discussed various applications of NLP generative models, including text generation, machine translation, summarization, conversational AI, and Text-to-Speech (TTS), emphasizing their growing importance in AI-driven communication systems. The mathematical foundations of generative models were covered, explaining probability distribution, loss functions, and optimization techniques that drive these models. Furthermore, we explored data preprocessing techniques, including tokenization and dataset preparation, which are crucial for training effective NLP models.

With hands-on implementation of GPT and T5 models for tasks like text generation and summarization, you are now well-equipped with the knowledge to fine-tune and deploy generative NLP models in practical applications. In the next chapter, we will focus on Model Evaluation and Optimization, where we will explore different metrics, evaluation challenges, and techniques to fine-tune generative models for improved performance.

Points to Remember

- Generative models in NLP create coherent and meaningful text using deep learning architectures.
- Transformer-based models like GPT, BERT, and T5 outperform traditional language models due to their self-attention mechanisms and deep contextual learning.
- Applications of generative models include text generation, summarization, translation, and conversational AI.
- Mathematical foundations such as probability distribution, language modeling objectives, and loss functions drive generative NLP models.
- Preprocessing techniques such as tokenization, subword modeling, and multilingual dataset handling are essential for training robust models.

Multiple Choice Questions

1. What is the primary advantage of transformer-based models over traditional language models?
    a. They require less training data.
    b. They use self-attention for better contextual understanding.
    c. They rely only on rule-based approaches.
    d. They do not require fine-tuning.
2. Which generative NLP model is best suited for text summarization tasks?
    a. CNN
    b. RNN
    c. T5
    d. Naïve Bayes
3. Which key mechanism allows GPT to generate coherent text?
    a. Recurrent connections
    b. Sequence labeling
    c. Rule-based tokenization
    d. Attention mechanisms
4. Which evaluation metric is commonly used to measure the quality of machine translation and summarization models?
    a. BLEU
    b. Perplexity
    c. Precision-Recall
    d. Mean Squared Error

Answers

1. b
2. c
3. d
4. a

Questions

1. How do transformer-based generative models improve upon traditional NLP models?
2. What are the main components of an NLP generative model, and how do they work together?
3. How does attention contribute to better text generation in models like GPT and T5?

4. What are the challenges of evaluating generative NLP models, and which metrics are most effective?
5. How do generative models handle multilingual text processing, and what preprocessing steps are necessary?
6. What role does tokenization play in preparing textual data for NLP models?
7. What are the ethical concerns related to generative NLP models, such as biases and misinformation?
8. How do loss functions like cross-entropy impact the training of generative NLP models?
9. What are the limitations of current generative NLP models in handling low-resource languages?
10. What future advancements in generative NLP could further improve text coherence, diversity, and contextual understanding?

Key Terms

- **Language Modeling**: Predicting the probability of a sequence of words in a given context.
- **Transformer Architecture**: A deep learning model that uses **self-attention** to generate contextual representations of text.
- **Generative Model**: A model that generates new text, rather than simply classifying the existing text.
- **Tokenization**: The process of breaking text into smaller units (tokens) for model training.
- **Perplexity**: A metric used to evaluate the fluency of a language model's generated text.
- **BLEU Score:** A widely used evaluation metric for machine translation and summarization.
- **Attention Mechanism:** A technique in neural networks that helps models focus on important parts of input sequences.
- **Fine-Tuning**: Adapting a pre-trained model to a specific NLP task by training it further on task-specific data.
- **Multimodal Generative Models:** Generative models that combine **text, image, and audio** to create richer outputs.
- **Ethical AI in NLP:** Ensuring fairness, transparency, and safety in the deployment of generative text models.

Chapter 13
Model Evaluation and Optimization

Introduction

Model evaluation and optimization are essential components of the machine learning lifecycle, ensuring that generative models perform effectively and efficiently in real-world applications. While building a generative model such as GANs or VAEs is a significant achievement, it is the rigorous process of evaluation and optimization that transforms these models into practical, high-performing solutions. From measuring the quality of generated outputs to fine-tuning hyperparameters and improving stability during training, evaluation and optimization are critical for achieving state-of-the-art results.

In this chapter, we delve into the principles and techniques behind evaluating and optimizing generative models. We explore key metrics as well as strategies for assessing the diversity, fidelity, and coherence of generated outputs. Additionally, we examine optimization methods and architectural enhancements to address generative model challenges. Through practical examples and step-by-step implementations, you will learn how to evaluate your models effectively and apply optimization techniques to improve their performance. By the end of this chapter, you will have the knowledge and tools to maximize the potential of your generative models, ensuring they meet the demands of real-world applications.

Structure

In this chapter, we will cover the following topics:

- **Introduction to Model Evaluation and Optimization**
    - Importance of Evaluation and Optimization in Machine Learning Models
    - Techniques for Improving Model Performance
    - Analogy: A Chess Grandmaster Preparing for the World Chess Championship
- **Key Metrics for Evaluating Generative Models**
    - Quantitative Metrics - FID, IS, Perplexity
    - Qualitative Metrics - Human Evaluation, Visual Inspection
    - Task-Specific Metrics
- **Challenges in Evaluating Generative Models**
- **Optimization Techniques for Generative Models**
    - Hyperparameter Tuning
    - Architectural Enhancements
    - Loss Function Improvements

- **Training Stability and Convergence**
  - Identifying and Addressing Instability in Training
  - Techniques to Improve Convergence Speed
  - Monitoring Training Progress with Loss Curves and Metrics
- **Tools for Model Evaluation and Optimization**
- **Data-Centric Optimization Approaches**
- **Implementing Evaluation and Optimization**
  - Setting Up Evaluation Pipelines for Generative Models
  - Tuning Hyperparameters
  - Visualizing Evaluation Results and Model Improvements
- **Case Study: Improving a GAN for Image Synthesis**
- **Future Directions**

Introduction to Model Evaluation and Optimization

Evaluating and optimizing machine learning models is a crucial step in the development lifecycle, bridging the gap between theoretical understanding and real-world applicability. For generative models, this process is particularly nuanced due to the complexity of their outputs, which are often evaluated for qualities such as realism, diversity, and relevance. Effective evaluation and optimization not only ensure the reliability of the models but also make them more adaptable to diverse use cases in industries ranging from healthcare to creative arts.

Importance of Evaluation and Optimization in Machine Learning Models

In machine learning, evaluation serves as a mirror, reflecting how well a model aligns with its intended purpose. Without rigorous evaluation, the effectiveness of a model remains ambiguous, which can lead to low performance. Optimization plays a key role in fine-tuning parameters to improve output quality while minimizing computational costs.

For instance, a generative adversarial network (GAN) designed for creating photorealistic images must be evaluated for the authenticity of the images it generates. Similarly, an NLP model such as a Variational Autoencoder (VAE) tasked with generating coherent text must be scrutinized for syntactical correctness and contextual relevance. Optimization ensures that these models perform well across such parameters without overfitting or underperforming.

Challenges in Evaluating Generative Models Compared to Discriminative Models

Unlike discriminative models, which output clear labels or predictions, generative models produce data distributions or samples. This difference introduces several challenges:

- **Subjectivity in Evaluation:** The output of generative models often requires human interpretation. For example, the "*quality*" of a generated image or text might vary depending on individual perspectives, making quantitative evaluation difficult.
- **Metrics Complexity:** Discriminative models can be evaluated using metrics such as accuracy, precision, or recall. Generative models, however, require more nuanced metrics such as

Inception Score (IS), FID, or BLEU score. They measure specific aspects, such as diversity or fidelity, but may not fully capture the quality of the output.

- **Lack of Ground Truth:** In many scenarios, there is no definitive "*correct*" answer for generative outputs. For instance, a model generating creative writing does not have a specific reference to compare against, unlike a classifier predicting labels.
- **Mode Collapse:** Generative models such as GANs can face issues where they fail to cover the full diversity of the data distribution. Evaluating whether the model captures all modes is a challenge in itself.

Techniques for Improving Model Performance

Improving the performance of generative models involves a combination of algorithmic enhancements, training strategies, and robust evaluation methods. Below are some key techniques:

- **Loss Function Engineering:** Customizing loss functions to align better with the intended output quality is a common practice. For example:
  - Wasserstein Loss improves GAN stability and alleviates mode collapse.
  - Perceptual Loss ensures high-quality visual features in image generation.
- **Regularization:** Applying techniques such as Dropout or L1/L2 regularization helps prevent overfitting, ensuring the model generalizes well to unseen data.
- **Hyperparameter Tuning:** Systematic tuning of learning rates, batch sizes, and other hyperparameters using methods such as grid search or Bayesian optimization can significantly enhance performance.
- **Advanced Training Techniques:** Methods such as transfer learning, curriculum learning, or reinforcement learning can improve training efficiency and output quality. For instance:
  - Progressive Growing of GANs helps train complex models by starting with low-resolution outputs and gradually increasing resolution.
  - Using pre-trained embeddings such as Word2Vec or BERT enhances generative models.
- **Evaluation Metrics Optimization:** Selecting the right combination of metrics for the task is critical. For text generation, a mix of BLEU, ROUGE, and human evaluation might be necessary to ensure both precision and creativity.
- **Ensemble Models:** Combining multiple generative models into an ensemble can improve output diversity and mitigate individual model shortcomings. For example, an ensemble of VAEs and GANs might balance image diversity with sharpness.
- **Domain-Specific Optimizations:** Tailoring the architecture or training process to the domain's requirements is often beneficial. In NLP, this might involve fine-tuning on domain-specific corpora, while in image synthesis, it might mean incorporating style-specific layers.

Analogy: A Chess Grandmaster Preparing for the World Chess Championship

Imagine a chess grandmaster preparing for the World Championship. The process they follow to refine their game is similar to model evaluation and optimization in machine learning.

***Figure 13.1**: Real-World Analogy with Chess Grandmaster Preparation*

- **Training the Grandmaster (Model Training)**
  - A chess player does not become a world champion overnight. They start by learning openings, tactics, and endgames–just like a machine learning model begins by training on data.
  - The grandmaster plays many practice games (training phase) to understand different positions and strategies.
  - The model is trained on historical data to recognize patterns and make accurate predictions.
- **Evaluating Performance in Training Games (Model Evaluation)**
  - Before entering the championship, the grandmaster evaluates their performance through practice games, simulations, and engine analysis.
  - They play against strong opponents, analyzing their wins and losses (validation/testing phase).
  - A machine learning model, similarly, is tested on unseen data to measure accuracy, loss, and generalization.

  Metrics Comparison:
  - Win/Loss ratio in chess ≈ Accuracy & Loss in machine learning.
  - Blunder rate (mistakes made) ≈ Error rate in predictions.
  - Time management ≈ Inference speed of a model.
- **Optimizing Openings, Strategies, and Endgames (Hyperparameter Tuning)**

  A grandmaster does not just play random moves; they refine their strategy by:
  - Adjusting opening repertoires based on opponent tendencies (such as tuning hyperparameters in ML).
  - Reviewing their mistakes and finding better moves (gradient descent improving model weights).

  - Preparing surprise novelties (innovative strategies) to counter unexpected plays (similar to data augmentation or ensemble learning in ML).
  - If they play too conservatively, they may not seize opportunities (underfitting), but if they take too many risks, they may blunder (overfitting). Balancing between the two is key.
- **Facing Different Opponents (Generalization)**
  - A grandmaster must adapt to different opponents with unique styles—some aggressive, some positional.
  - If they memorize only one kind of opening without flexibility, they might struggle against an unexpected strategy (overfitting to training data).
  - They must generalize their skills to handle multiple styles and game situations (ensuring the model performs well on unseen data).
- **Continuous Learning Even After the Championship (Model Deployment and Continuous Improvement)**
  - Even after winning, the grandmaster continues to improve by analyzing new games, adapting to evolving chess trends, and refining their preparation.
  - Similarly, machine learning models need updates, retraining, and fine-tuning as new data becomes available.

Final Thought

A chess grandmaster preparing for the World Chess Championship follows a structured process of training, evaluation, optimization, and adaptation—mirroring how machine learning models are built, tested, optimized, and deployed.

Key Metrics for Evaluating Generative Models

Evaluating generative models is critical to ensuring their quality, applicability, and effectiveness in real-world scenarios. Unlike traditional machine learning models that focus on accuracy or loss, generative models require more nuanced evaluation methods because their outputs are creative, often subjective, and context-dependent.

Figure 13.2: *Generative Models Require More Nuanced Evaluation Methods*

Evaluation metrics for generative models fall into three broad categories: quantitative metrics, qualitative metrics, and task-specific metrics, each addressing different aspects of model performance.

Quantitative Metrics - FID, IS, Perplexity

Quantitative metrics provide mathematical measurements of the similarity between generated and real data. These metrics are objective and computationally efficient, making them widely used for benchmarking.

- **Fréchet Inception Distance (FID):** The FID score is a popular metric for evaluating image-generating models such as GANs. It compares the statistical distribution of features from real and generated images using the Inception network. A lower FID score indicates that the generated data is closer to the real data in terms of feature similarity. FID has become the gold standard in many image synthesis tasks because it captures both the quality and diversity of generated images.
- **Inception Score (IS):** The Inception Score evaluates the quality and diversity of generated images. It measures how confidently a classifier (usually the Inception network) can identify objects in the generated images. High IS values indicate that the generated images are both diverse and meaningful. However, IS has limitations, such as being less sensitive to mode collapse and not comparing generated images directly to real ones.
- **Perplexity for Text Models:** Perplexity is a standard metric for evaluating generative models in NLP, such as language models. It measures how well the model predicts a sequence of words. A lower perplexity score indicates that the model assigns higher probabilities to the observed sequences, suggesting better performance. Despite its popularity, perplexity does not always correlate perfectly with human judgment of text quality, as it focuses solely on the likelihood of sequences.

Qualitative Metrics

Qualitative evaluation involves subjective analysis of the outputs generated by the model. These methods often complement quantitative metrics and provide insights into the model's creativity and applicability in real-world tasks.

- **Human Evaluation:** Human evaluation is one of the most reliable methods for assessing the quality of generative models. For example, in NLP, humans may rate text based on coherence, fluency, and relevance. In creative applications such as image synthesis, humans assess visual quality and realism. Although subjective and time-consuming, human evaluation provides invaluable insights that quantitative metrics might overlook.
- **Visual Inspection for Image Models:** For image generative models, visual inspection remains an essential step. Researchers and practitioners manually examine generated images to identify artifacts, assess style consistency, and ensure diversity. While this approach does not scale well, it is particularly useful during early development or for niche applications where automated metrics are insufficient.

Task-Specific Metrics

Task-specific metrics measure how well the generated data aligns with the requirements of a particular application. In NLP, these metrics are crucial for evaluating the relevance and coherence of generated text.

- **Bilingual Evaluation Understudy (BLEU):** BLEU is a precision-based metric widely used for evaluating machine translation models. It calculates how many n-grams in the generated text match the reference text. Higher BLEU scores indicate better alignment with the reference text. However, BLEU has limitations, such as sensitivity to exact matches and inability to capture synonyms or contextual variations.
- **Recall-Oriented Understudy for Gisting Evaluation (ROUGE):** ROUGE focuses on recall and

is commonly used for summarization tasks. It evaluates the overlap between n-grams in the generated summary and the reference summary. ROUGE-L, a variant, considers the longest common subsequence to assess sentence-level coherence. While ROUGE is useful, it may not capture deeper semantic similarities.

- **Other Metrics:** Depending on the task, other metrics such as METEOR, CIDEr, or SPICE might be used. For example, METEOR emphasizes semantic similarity in translation, while CIDEr is optimized for image captioning. Each metric provides a unique perspective on generative model performance, making it crucial to choose the right one based on the application.
- **Balancing Metrics:** In practice, a combination of metrics is often used to evaluate generative models comprehensively. For instance, quantitative metrics such as FID or perplexity provide an objective baseline, while qualitative assessments such as human evaluation add context and depth. Task-specific metrics ensure that the model aligns with application-specific goals, creating a balanced evaluation framework. By leveraging these diverse metrics, practitioners can gain a holistic understanding of their model's capabilities and limitations, driving continuous improvement and innovation.

Challenges in Evaluating Generative Models

Evaluating generative models remains a complex task, as the criteria for judging their outputs often depend on the specific use case and subjective human judgment. Unlike traditional machine learning models, generative models produce outputs that must balance creativity, fidelity, and diversity. This chapter delves into the core challenges faced when assessing these models and offers insights into mitigating these issues.

Measuring Diversity and Fidelity in Generated Outputs

Diversity and fidelity are two critical dimensions for evaluating the performance of generative models. Diversity ensures that the generated outputs are varied and not repetitive, while fidelity measures how closely the outputs resemble the true data distribution.

For example, in the case of image generation, diversity would mean generating multiple distinct images of a cat, while fidelity would mean that the generated images look photorealistic. The balance between these two often defines the success of a generative model. However, measuring them quantitatively is challenging. Metrics such as FID and IS are commonly used, but they have limitations. FID, for instance, is sensitive to noise in the data and may not accurately reflect perceptual similarity.

In NLP, measuring diversity can involve examining n-gram overlaps, while fidelity might require evaluating how closely generated text aligns with human-written content. BLEU, ROUGE, and perplexity scores are widely used, but they often fail to capture nuanced aspects such as creativity or coherence. Hence, incorporating human evaluations alongside automated metrics is a standard practice, albeit resource-intensive.

Addressing Mode Collapse and Overfitting

Mode collapse and overfitting are persistent challenges in training generative models. Mode collapse occurs when a model generates outputs that lack variety, essentially producing similar or identical results for different inputs. This is particularly detrimental in applications such as text generation, where varied responses are essential for a natural conversational experience.

Overfitting, on the other hand, happens when the model memorizes the training data instead of learning the underlying data distribution. This leads to outputs that fail to generalize to new inputs, reducing the practical usability of the model. In NLP, this can manifest as a chatbot regurgitating exact phrases from its training corpus instead of generating contextually relevant responses.

To address these issues, techniques such as regularization, dropout, and data augmentation are frequently employed. Additionally, advanced training techniques such as Wasserstein GANs or Variational Autoencoders (VAEs) with disentangled representations help mitigate these problems by better capturing the data's latent structure. Periodic monitoring of loss curves and qualitative evaluation of generated samples also help identify and address these issues early in the training process.

Biases in Evaluation Datasets and Their Impact on Results

Evaluation datasets play a pivotal role in determining the perceived performance of a generative model. However, biases in these datasets can lead to misleading results and unintended consequences. For instance, datasets used to train and evaluate language models often reflect societal biases present in the text. If these biases are not addressed, the generated outputs may perpetuate stereotypes or exclude underrepresented groups.

Consider an NLP model trained on news articles predominantly authored by a specific demographic. When generating content, the model may inadvertently favor that demographic's perspectives, leading to biased outputs. This can undermine the inclusivity and fairness of the system, particularly in applications such as automated content creation or conversational agents.

Mitigating these biases involves curating diverse and representative datasets and employing techniques such as adversarial training or bias correction during post-processing. Transparency in reporting model performance on different subsets of data is also necessary to highlight any disparities and foster trust among users.

Moreover, the lack of standardized benchmarks for certain applications adds to the complexity of evaluation. Developing comprehensive, unbiased, and domain-specific benchmarks can significantly improve the reliability of model assessments, and ensure generative models are more equitable and effective in real-world scenarios.

Optimization Techniques for Generative Models

Optimization techniques are pivotal in achieving the best performance from generative models such as GANs and VAEs. These techniques ensure that the models converge faster, generate high-quality outputs, and maintain stability during training. By fine-tuning hyperparameters, improving loss functions, and adopting advanced architectural and regularization methods, practitioners can overcome common challenges such as mode collapse in GANs or posterior collapse in VAEs.

Hyperparameter Tuning

Hyperparameter tuning involves systematically adjusting key parameters to find the optimal configuration for a generative model. Critical hyperparameters include:

- **Learning Rate Adjustments**: The learning rate determines how quickly the model updates its parameters during training. A learning rate that is too high can lead to divergence, while one that is too low may result in slow convergence. Techniques such as learning rate schedulers and cyclical learning rates can dynamically adjust the rate during training, leading to more efficient optimization.
- **Batch Size Optimization**: The size of the training batch significantly impacts model performance. Smaller batch sizes often add noise to the gradient estimates, which can help escape local minima but may result in unstable training. Larger batch sizes provide more stable gradients but demand greater computational resources. Finding a balance is crucial, and techniques such as mixed precision training can help manage resource constraints.

- **Weight Initialization Strategies**: Proper initialization of weights can prevent issues such as vanishing or exploding gradients, ensuring smooth gradients for backpropagation. Popular strategies include Xavier initialization for shallow networks and He initialization for deeper networks.

Architectural Enhancements

Generative models can benefit from architectural modifications that promote stability and improve their ability to learn complex data distributions. Key enhancements include:

- **Adding Regularization Techniques**: Regularization methods such as Dropout and Weight Decay help prevent overfitting and improve generalization. Dropout randomly drops units from the network during training, forcing the model to learn redundant representations. Weight Decay penalizes large weights, encouraging simpler and more robust models.
- **Using Advanced Optimizers**: Optimizers play a crucial role in the training dynamics of generative models. Advanced optimizers such as AdamW and RMSProp improve stability and convergence rates. AdamW, for example, decouples weight decay from gradient updates, which is particularly beneficial for GANs where training can be unstable.

Loss Function Improvements

The choice of loss function directly impacts the quality of outputs from generative models. For GANs and VAEs, specialized loss functions address specific challenges and enhance performance:

- **Wasserstein Loss for GANs**: Unlike the traditional binary cross-entropy loss, Wasserstein loss addresses mode collapse by providing a smoother and more informative gradient signal. It works by minimizing the Wasserstein distance (Earth Mover's Distance) between the real and generated data distributions. This loss, combined with techniques such as gradient penalty, significantly stabilizes GAN training.
- **Modified ELBO for VAEs**: The Evidence Lower Bound (ELBO) is the standard objective function for VAEs, balancing reconstruction accuracy with latent space regularization. Modified versions of ELBO, such as β-ELBO, allow weighting of the regularization term (β), giving more control over the trade-off between reconstruction quality and latent representation disentanglement.

Thus, by employing these optimization techniques, practitioners can effectively address the inherent challenges in training generative models and achieve superior results, whether generating realistic images with GANs or learning meaningful latent representations with VAEs. Coupling these techniques with domain-specific insights ensures that models are both efficient and robust in real-world applications.

Training Stability and Convergence

Training stability and convergence are critical challenges when working with generative models, particularly in Natural Language Processing (NLP). Achieving stable training ensures that the model generates coherent and meaningful outputs, while convergence determines how quickly the model reaches optimal performance. Understanding and addressing instability issues, leveraging techniques to speed up convergence, and effectively monitoring progress are essential for building robust NLP generative models.

Identifying and Addressing Instability in Training

Instability in training arises from several factors, including poorly chosen hyperparameters, vanishing or exploding gradients, and imbalanced updates between components of the model (for example, generator and discriminator in GANs or encoder and decoder in sequence models).

Symptoms of instability include erratic loss curves, inability to generate meaningful outputs, and failure to converge.

To address instability:

- **Adjust Learning Rates**: Start with smaller learning rates and gradually increase or decrease using techniques such as learning rate schedules or adaptive optimizers such as Adam or RMSprop.
- **Gradient Clipping**: To prevent exploding gradients, limit the magnitude of gradients during backpropagation.
- **Model Architecture**: Carefully design components, such as using attention mechanisms in transformers or layer normalization to stabilize updates.

For instance, training transformers for text generation can become unstable when the dataset is too complex or poorly preprocessed. Tokenization, removal of noise, and ensuring balanced datasets can significantly improve training stability.

Techniques to Improve Convergence Speed

Improving convergence speed allows models to reach satisfactory performance in fewer training iterations, saving computational resources. Techniques to accelerate convergence include:

- **Warm-Up Learning Rates**: Begin training with a smaller learning rate and gradually increase it over a few initial epochs. This prevents the model from taking overly large steps that might destabilize training.
- **Pretraining and Fine-Tuning**: Utilize pretrained models such as BERT, GPT, or T5 and fine-tune them for specific tasks. Pretraining on massive corpora helps models develop strong representations, reducing the time required for task-specific convergence.
- **Batch Normalization and Layer Normalization**: Normalization layers stabilize training dynamics by standardizing intermediate activations.
- **Curriculum Learning**: Train the model on simpler tasks or datasets before progressing to more complex examples. This incremental approach helps the model converge faster.
- **Regularization**: Techniques such as dropout, weight decay, and label smoothing prevent overfitting and stabilize training.

For example, using a pretrained GPT model and fine-tuning it on a dataset such as WikiText can achieve better results with fewer iterations compared to training from scratch.

Monitoring Training Progress with Loss Curves and Metrics

Effective monitoring during training helps detect issues early and assess convergence. Key metrics and visualizations include:

- **Loss Curves**: Plotting loss values for the training and validation datasets over time is essential. Diverging curves or a stagnant validation loss might indicate overfitting, underfitting, or instability.
- **Perplexity**: Commonly used in NLP, perplexity measures how well the model predicts a sequence of words. Lower perplexity indicates better performance.
- **BLEU and ROUGE Scores**: For generative tasks such as translation or summarization, these scores quantify output quality by comparing generated text with references.

- **Visualization of Outputs**: Periodically sampling generated text during training provides qualitative insights into the model's progress.

Practical tools such as TensorBoard can simplify the process of tracking these metrics and visualizing loss curves in real time. For instance, while training a sequence-to-sequence model, sudden spikes in loss may suggest that the optimizer is stuck in poor local minima or gradients have become unstable. Implementing gradient clipping and adjusting the learning rate schedule can help resolve these issues.

Example: Case Study on Fine-Tuning GPT for Text Summarization

Consider a case where GPT is fine-tuned on a summarization dataset. Initially, the loss curve fluctuates due to noisy gradients, and the outputs are incoherent. By applying gradient clipping and adopting a warm-up learning rate schedule, training stabilizes, and the loss decreases smoothly. Monitoring BLEU scores reveals consistent improvement, and sampling summaries every 1000 steps shows progressively better results. These observations illustrate how addressing stability and convergence holistically impacts model performance.

Hence, by focusing on these principles, practitioners can mitigate instability, enhance convergence speed, and build generative NLP models that are both reliable and efficient.

Tools for Model Evaluation and Optimization

The evaluation and optimization of generative models, especially in Natural Language Processing (NLP), are pivotal to ensuring high-quality outputs and robust performance. This process involves using tools and techniques to measure, visualize, and improve the performance of models systematically. Here, we delve into some essential frameworks, libraries, and tools that facilitate evaluation and optimization.

Frameworks and Libraries for Evaluation

Frameworks and libraries are the backbone of model evaluation, offering pre-built functions and metrics to streamline the process:

- **TensorFlow**: TensorFlow is a versatile library that includes modules such as tf.keras.metrics to evaluate models on metrics such as BLEU, perplexity, and ROUGE, which are crucial for assessing text generation quality in NLP tasks.
- **PyTorch**: PyTorch's simplicity and flexibility make it ideal for custom evaluation pipelines. The torchmetrics library, an extension of PyTorch, provides ready-to-use metrics for tasks such as text classification and translation.
- **Scikit-learn**: Although not exclusive to NLP, Scikit-learn offers essential tools for evaluating components such as feature extraction and intermediate classification models. Metrics such as F1-score, precision, recall, and confusion matrices are widely used in NLP evaluation.

Therefore, by combining these libraries, developers can build custom evaluation pipelines that align with their model's specific requirements.

Visualization: TensorBoard, Matplotlib, and Seaborn

Visualization plays a vital role in interpreting and improving generative models. Observing trends, loss curves, and performance metrics visually allows researchers to gain actionable insights.

- **TensorBoard**: TensorBoard integrates seamlessly with TensorFlow to provide a dashboard for tracking model training and evaluation. It visualizes metrics such as loss, accuracy, and even embeddings, offering an intuitive way to debug and optimize generative models.

- **Matplotlib**: As a general-purpose plotting library, Matplotlib is indispensable for creating static, interactive, and animated visualizations of training dynamics. For example, plotting loss curves or word distribution histograms gives insights into model behavior.
- **Seaborn**: Built on Matplotlib, Seaborn is tailored for statistical visualizations. It can be used to plot heatmaps of confusion matrices or pair plots for feature analysis, aiding in understanding patterns within the data.

Combining these tools ensures that every aspect of model behavior, from training dynamics to evaluation metrics, is thoroughly analyzed and visualized.

Automated Hyperparameter Tuning

Hyperparameter tuning is critical in optimizing NLP models to achieve better performance. Manual tuning is often time-intensive and prone to errors. Automated tools such as Optuna and Ray Tune address this challenge effectively:

- **Optuna:**
    - Optuna is an automatic hyperparameter optimization framework that enables users to define search spaces for parameters such as learning rate, batch size, or dropout rate.
    - Its ease of integration with both TensorFlow and PyTorch makes it a popular choice for NLP practitioners.
    - Features such as pruning—where suboptimal trials are terminated early—significantly reduce computation time.
- **Ray Tune:**
    - Ray Tune is a scalable hyperparameter tuning library that supports distributed computing.
    - With built-in schedulers and search algorithms, it can handle complex search spaces and execute trials across multiple GPUs or nodes.
    - Ray Tune's integration with popular frameworks allows seamless experimentation, making it suitable for large-scale NLP projects.

By leveraging these tools, researchers and developers can systematically explore hyperparameter configurations, ultimately leading to models that perform better with fewer resources.

The ecosystem of tools for model evaluation and optimization in NLP is vast and continually evolving. From foundational libraries such as TensorFlow and PyTorch to advanced visualization tools and hyperparameter tuning frameworks, these resources provide a robust foundation for developing high-quality generative models. By combining these tools effectively, NLP practitioners can ensure their models meet performance and efficiency standards, paving the way for state-of-the-art applications in language generation, translation, and beyond.

Data-Centric Optimization Approaches

In natural language processing (NLP), the effectiveness of generative models is often determined not just by the architecture of the model but by the quality and richness of the data they are trained on. Data-centric optimization focuses on refining datasets to enhance model performance. This approach recognizes that even state-of-the-art algorithms can underperform if the training data is poorly curated, unbalanced, or lacks diversity. Ensuring high-quality, diverse, and well-preprocessed datasets is pivotal for creating robust generative NLP models.

Ensuring Dataset Diversity and Quality for Better Training

Dataset diversity and quality are fundamental to developing generative NLP models that generalize effectively across various tasks and domains. A diverse dataset should include examples from different linguistic styles, contexts, and formats to ensure that the model can handle real-world variability. For instance, a text generation model trained on datasets representing formal, colloquial, and domain-specific language will better capture the intricacies of human communication.

Quality control measures such as deduplication, error correction, and the removal of ambiguous or misleading samples are equally important. Poor-quality data, including irrelevant or contradictory samples, can confuse the model during training, leading to degraded performance. Leveraging human-in-the-loop methods and automated tools for dataset curation ensures that the training data meets the necessary standards for optimal model performance.

Data Augmentation Strategies to Address Imbalances

Data augmentation techniques help mitigate the challenges of imbalanced datasets, where certain classes or linguistic features may dominate the training data. For example, in a dataset designed for text-to-text generation, some sentence structures or topics might be underrepresented. This imbalance can lead to a model that performs poorly on less frequent patterns or topics.

Common data augmentation strategies in NLP include:

- **Back-translation**: Translating a sentence into another language and back to create paraphrased examples.
- **Synonym replacement**: Substituting words with their synonyms while retaining the original sentence meaning.
- **Random word dropout or swapping**: Modifying sentence structures slightly to introduce variability.
- **Paraphrasing using pre-trained models**: Employing existing NLP models, such as GPT or T5, to generate paraphrases for underrepresented samples in the dataset.

These strategies not only enhance diversity but also help the model become more robust to variations in input data, making it better suited to handle edge cases in downstream applications.

Preprocessing Techniques to Standardize Inputs

Preprocessing is a critical step in preparing data for training generative NLP models. Standardizing inputs ensures that models receive consistent and interpretable data, reducing the risk of training instabilities. Key preprocessing techniques include:

- **Tokenization**: Splitting text into tokens such as words, subwords, or characters. Advanced tokenization methods, such as byte pair encoding (BPE) or WordPiece, ensure efficient representation of rare and common words alike.
- **Lowercasing and punctuation handling**: Uniformly formatting text to avoid inconsistencies caused by capitalization or varying punctuation styles.
- **Stopword removal or retention**: Depending on the task, removing or keeping stopwords can influence the quality of the generated text. For summarization, for instance, retaining stopwords ensures grammatical fluency.
- **Normalization**: Converting text to a standard format, such as replacing contractions (for example, "*don't*" with "*do not*") or normalizing numbers and dates.
- **Noise removal**: Eliminating special characters, excessive whitespace, or irrelevant metadata, such as HTML tags in scraped web data.

Modern frameworks also emphasize dynamic preprocessing pipelines that adapt to specific tasks. For example, in dialogue generation tasks, context-specific preprocessing such as identifying speaker turns or handling interruptions is crucial for accurate model training.

Thus, by focusing on data-centric optimization approaches, practitioners can maximize the effectiveness of generative NLP models, ensuring that they are not just technically advanced but also well-grounded in diverse, high-quality, and preprocessed datasets.

Implementing Evaluation and Optimization

Evaluation and optimization are critical steps in building generative models. While creating a model that generates impressive outputs is an achievement, ensuring the model's reliability, scalability, and efficiency requires systematic evaluation and iterative optimization. This section provides a step-by-step guide to setting up evaluation pipelines, tuning hyperparameters, and visualizing improvements to refine generative models effectively.

Setting Up Evaluation Pipelines for Generative Models

An effective evaluation pipeline serves as the backbone of understanding how well a generative model performs. The key components of such a pipeline include quantitative metrics, qualitative analysis, and benchmarking against baseline models.

- **Define Evaluation Metrics:**
    - **Quantitative Metrics:** For generative models, metrics such as Fréchet Inception Distance (FID), Inception Score (IS), and perplexity are commonly used. These metrics help measure the diversity and quality of the generated samples.
    - **Task-Specific Metrics:** For text generation models, BLEU, ROUGE, and METEOR scores are used to evaluate the alignment of generated text with ground-truth references.
    - **Adversarial Robustness:** Testing the model's ability to withstand adversarial inputs ensures robustness.
- **Establish Baseline Models:**
    - Compare the model's outputs against simpler generative models (for example, standard VAEs or unoptimized GANs).
    - Use baseline results as benchmarks for performance improvements.
- **Automate Evaluation Pipelines:**
    - Use frameworks such as TensorFlow Model Analysis or PyTorch Lightning's built-in logging utilities.
    - Automate the evaluation process to ensure consistency across experiments, especially when experimenting with different architectures or datasets.
- **Incorporate Qualitative Analysis:**
    - Visual inspection of generated images or manual review of generated text is crucial. For example, in image generation, artifacts or mode collapse issues are often spotted visually.
    - Human-in-the-loop evaluations can also provide insights into subjective quality aspects, such as coherence or creativity in generated outputs.

Tuning Hyperparameters

Optimization often starts with adjusting hyperparameters that directly impact the generative model's performance. Examples of key hyperparameters and their tuning include:

- **Learning Rate and Optimizer Selection:**
  - The choice of optimizer (for example, Adam, RMSprop) and its parameters, such as learning rate, play a significant role in stability and convergence.
  - For instance, in GANs, a lower learning rate for the generator compared to the discriminator can stabilize training.
- **Batch Size:**
  - Larger batch sizes can improve gradient estimates but require more computational resources.
  - Smaller batches might introduce noise but can generalize better in some cases. Experimenting with different batch sizes helps balance performance and training speed.
- **Latent Space Dimensions:**
  - The size of the latent vector impacts the diversity of generated samples. A higher dimension often captures more variability, while a smaller dimension might lead to over-simplified outputs.
- **Regularization Techniques:**
  - Regularization methods such as Dropout, Gradient Penalty (in WGAN-GP), or spectral normalization can help improve training stability and prevent overfitting.
  - For VAEs, adjusting the β hyperparameter in β-VAEs balances the trade-off between reconstruction quality and disentanglement.
- **Loss Function Adjustments:**
  - Modify loss functions based on training observations. For example, replacing binary cross-entropy with Wasserstein loss in GANs can improve convergence.
  - Monitor losses for both the generator and discriminator (in GANs) to detect imbalances.
- **Experimentation Tools:**
  - Use grid search or random search for coarse hyperparameter tuning.
  - Employ advanced methods such as Bayesian Optimization (for example, with the Optuna library) for fine-grained control.

Visualizing Evaluation Results and Model Improvements

Visualization is an indispensable tool for interpreting and communicating the performance of generative models. Some practical approaches include:

Loss Curves:

- Plot generator and discriminator loss curves for GANs to monitor adversarial training dynamics.
- For VAEs, visualize reconstruction loss and KL divergence to understand the balance between the encoder and decoder.

Sample Outputs: Regularly generate and save sample outputs during training. For example:

- In image generation tasks, display a grid of generated images at various epochs.
- In text generation tasks, log generated sequences alongside ground truth to evaluate coherence and fluency.

Metric Trends: Track quantitative metrics (for example, FID, IS, BLEU) over training epochs. Plotting these trends helps identify when the model overfits or stagnates.

Dimensionality Reduction for Latent Space Analysis: Use techniques such as t-SNE or PCA to visualize the latent space. Cluster patterns in the latent space often correlate with the diversity of generated outputs.

Dashboarding: Leverage tools such as TensorBoard, Weights & Biases, or custom Streamlit dashboards for interactive visualization. These platforms enable dynamic tracking and comparison of multiple experiments.

Heatmaps and Attention Maps:

- For text-based models, visualize attention mechanisms to understand which parts of the input the model focuses on.
- For image-based tasks, Grad-CAM visualizations can highlight areas influencing the model's decisions.

Iterative Improvement and Monitoring

Evaluation and optimization are iterative. By systematically monitoring metrics, visualizing trends, and refining hyperparameters, generative models can achieve state-of-the-art performance while avoiding common pitfalls such as mode collapse or overfitting. Combining automated pipelines, advanced tuning techniques, and visual insights forms a robust approach to mastering evaluation and optimization for generative models.

Case Study: Improving a GAN for Image Synthesis

Generative Adversarial Networks (GANs) have revolutionized the field of image synthesis by enabling the creation of realistic and diverse images. However, training GANs effectively remains a significant challenge due to issues such as mode collapse and poor output quality. This case study delves into an approach to improve GAN training outcomes by addressing these critical challenges.

Problem: Mode Collapse and Poor Output Quality

Mode collapse, where the generator produces limited variations of data, is one of the most notorious challenges in GAN training. This issue undermines the diversity of generated images, which is crucial for applications such as art generation, data augmentation, and virtual reality. Moreover, poor output quality resulting from training instability or suboptimal loss functions can lead to unrealistic or blurry images, making the model less effective for real-world use cases.

In this case study, the problem was to enhance both the diversity and the fidelity of images generated by a GAN while maintaining stable training dynamics. The focus was to overcome the limitations of traditional GANs and achieve outputs suitable for practical applications.

Solution Approach: Hyperparameter Tuning, Advanced Loss Functions, and Improved Regularization

The solution involved a multi-pronged approach:

- **Hyperparameter Tuning:**
  - **Learning Rate Adjustment**: The learning rates for the generator and discriminator were decoupled, allowing for better synchronization between the two components. Smaller learning rates were found to improve stability without sacrificing convergence speed.

  - **Batch Size Optimization**: Batch sizes were varied to balance memory constraints with the stability of gradient updates. Larger batch sizes helped in reducing noise in the gradients.
- **Advanced Loss Functions**:
  - The standard binary cross-entropy loss was replaced with the Wasserstein loss with gradient penalty (WGAN-GP). This modification addressed issues of vanishing gradients and provided more meaningful loss signals, improving training stability and output quality.
  - Experiments were also conducted with Least Squares GAN (LSGAN) loss, which reduced the gap between real and fake data distributions by penalizing the discrepancy more smoothly.
- **Improved Regularization Techniques:**
  - **Spectral Normalization**: Applied to the discriminator to ensure Lipschitz continuity, leading to more stable and reliable training.
  - **Dropout**: Introduced in the generator to prevent overfitting and encourage more diverse outputs during training.
  - **Label Smoothing**: Implemented for the discriminator's targets to mitigate overconfidence and prevent the discriminator from overpowering the generator.
- **Architectural Enhancements:**
  - Added residual connections in the generator network to improve gradient flow.
  - Incorporated instance normalization layers instead of batch normalization for better style consistency in the outputs.

Challenges: Balancing Diversity and Fidelity in Generated Images

The key challenge was to strike a balance between generating diverse and high-fidelity images. While the advanced loss functions and regularization techniques improved individual aspects, combining these changes without destabilizing training required careful experimentation.

- **Mode Collapse**: Despite implementing WGAN-GP, some residual issues with mode collapse persisted, especially when training with limited data. To address this, additional noise injection and minibatch discrimination were explored.
- **Hyperparameter Sensitivity**: The success of the training heavily depended on fine-tuning hyperparameters, which required extensive experimentation and computational resources.
- **Evaluation Metrics**: Choosing the right evaluation metrics, such as Fréchet Inception Distance (FID) and Inception Score (IS), to assess improvements was critical but added complexity to the validation process.

Outcome: Enhanced Visual Quality and Diversity of Generated Outputs

The enhanced GAN model demonstrated significant improvements in both the visual quality and diversity of its generated outputs. Key outcomes included:

- **Improved Diversity**: The addition of minibatch discrimination and regularization techniques reduced the incidence of mode collapse, enabling the generator to produce a wider range of images.
- **Higher Fidelity**: The use of advanced loss functions and spectral normalization resulted in

sharper, more realistic images. The outputs were evaluated using FID scores, which showed a marked reduction compared to the baseline model.

- **Stable Training Dynamics**: The architectural and hyperparameter adjustments minimized instances of oscillatory or diverging loss curves, ensuring smoother training processes.

This case study highlights the importance of a holistic approach to GAN training, combining innovations in loss functions, regularization, and hyperparameter optimization. These techniques are not only effective in improving GAN performance but also provide valuable insights for future research and practical applications in image synthesis.

Future Directions

The field of generative models in natural language processing (NLP) is evolving at a breakneck pace, driven by the ever-increasing demand for sophisticated AI applications. As the technology matures, researchers and practitioners are exploring new frontiers to enhance model performance, usability, and ethical alignment. This section delves into three key areas shaping the future of generative models: advancements in evaluation metrics, techniques for real-time optimization, and trends in automated model evaluation and optimization.

Advancements in Evaluation Metrics for Generative Models

The effectiveness of generative models heavily relies on how well they are evaluated. Traditional evaluation methods such as BLEU, ROUGE, and perplexity often fall short in capturing the nuances of human-like text generation. Future advancements are expected to focus on:

- **Human-Centric Metrics**: Researchers are developing metrics that align better with human judgment. For instance, metrics such as BERTScore leverage pre-trained transformer models to assess the semantic similarity between generated and reference texts, offering a more nuanced evaluation than traditional n-gram overlap metrics.
- **Task-Specific Metrics**: Domain-specific applications demand tailored evaluation metrics. For example, in conversational AI, metrics such as Contextual Appropriateness and Emotional Intelligence are emerging to assess dialogue quality.
- **Dynamic Metrics**: Real-time feedback mechanisms, where metrics evolve during training, are gaining traction. These metrics adapt based on the model's learning trajectory, ensuring continuous alignment with task requirements.

The integration of these advanced metrics into generative NLP pipelines will significantly improve the interpretability and trustworthiness of model outputs.

Techniques for Real-Time Optimization During Model Training

Real-time optimization during training is becoming a critical focus area to enhance the efficiency and accuracy of generative models. Current research and innovation efforts are centered around:

- **Dynamic Learning Rates**: Techniques such as learning rate schedules and adaptive optimizers, such as AdamW, are being extended with real-time adjustments based on training performance. This minimizes overfitting and accelerates convergence.
- **Gradient Noise Injection**: By adding controlled noise to gradients during optimization, models can escape local minima and achieve better generalization. This technique is particularly useful in large-scale generative models.
- **Federated Learning**: Distributed training methods, including federated learning, enable real-time updates across decentralized data sources while maintaining user privacy. This is especially relevant for applications such as personalized generative models for mobile devices.

- **Neural Architecture Search (NAS)**: Automated tools for exploring optimal neural network architectures during training are gaining momentum. NAS techniques help identify the best-performing configurations dynamically, reducing manual trial-and-error processes.

Real-time optimization not only reduces training time but also improves the adaptability of models to diverse datasets and tasks, paving the way for more robust generative AI systems.

Trends in Automated Evaluation and Optimization

Automation is revolutionizing the evaluation and optimization of generative models. With the increasing complexity of NLP tasks, manual methods are becoming infeasible. Emerging trends include:

- **AI-Assisted Evaluation**: Tools leveraging AI for model evaluation are on the rise. These systems use machine learning algorithms to benchmark model performance, eliminating human bias and reducing evaluation time.
- **Continuous Integration of Feedback Loops**: Automated systems now incorporate real-time user feedback into model evaluation cycles. This is particularly valuable in applications such as chatbots, where user interactions provide critical data for improving response quality.
- **Hyperparameter Optimization (HPO)**: Automated HPO methods such as Bayesian optimization and gradient-free search are increasingly employed to fine-tune generative models. These methods explore vast hyperparameter spaces efficiently, ensuring optimal configurations for specific tasks.
- **Model Compression and Pruning**: Automation tools for compressing and pruning generative models are making them more resource-efficient without compromising performance. Techniques such as knowledge distillation and quantization are integrated into automated pipelines to optimize model deployment.
- **Explainability and Fairness Modules**: Automated evaluation frameworks are incorporating modules to assess explainability and fairness. This ensures that generative models are not only performant but also ethical and transparent in their decision-making processes.

These trends highlight the increasing reliance on automation to handle the growing complexity and demands of NLP applications, ensuring scalability and efficiency in real-world deployments.

The future of generative models in NLP is undoubtedly exciting, with continuous advancements in evaluation metrics, real-time optimization techniques, and automated processes driving innovation. These developments will not only enhance model performance but also address key challenges such as ethical considerations, scalability, and adaptability, ensuring that generative NLP systems remain at the forefront of AI evolution.

Conclusion

In this chapter, we explored model evaluation and optimization techniques for generative models, highlighting the importance of robust assessment methods to ensure high-quality outputs. Unlike discriminative models, generative models present unique challenges in evaluation due to the subjective nature of image and text generation. We examined quantitative metrics such as Fréchet Inception Distance (FID) and Inception Score (IS), as well as qualitative evaluation methods including human assessment and visual inspection.

To optimize generative models, we discussed hyperparameter tuning, architectural improvements, and loss function refinements, which play a crucial role in enhancing model stability and output diversity. Additionally, we explored strategies to address common challenges such as mode collapse, training instability, and overfitting, ensuring that generative models produce high-quality, diverse, and realistic outputs.

With hands-on implementations and case studies, you are now equipped to evaluate and refine generative models effectively. In the next chapter, we will focus on deploying generative models, covering key aspects such as model inference, optimization for real-time applications, and integration into production systems to bring generative AI to real-world applications.

Points to Remember

- Generative model evaluation differs from discriminative models and often requires a combination of quantitative and qualitative metrics.
- FID and Inception Score (IS) are widely used for assessing image quality and diversity, while BLEU and ROUGE are common for text-based models.
- Challenges in evaluation include measuring fidelity and diversity, handling mode collapse, and ensuring unbiased dataset representation.
- Optimization techniques such as hyperparameter tuning, regularization, and loss function modifications improve training stability and model performance.
- Visualization tools such as TensorBoard and Matplotlib help monitor model progress and identify areas for improvement.

Multiple Choice Questions

1. Which metric is commonly used to evaluate the quality of images generated by GANs?
   a. BLEU
   b. Perplexity
   c. Fréchet Inception Distance (FID)
   d. Mean Squared Error (MSE)
2. What is a common challenge when evaluating generative models?
   a. Lack of available training data
   b. The difficulty in objectively measuring output quality
   c. The need for paired input-output samples
   d. Limited computational requirements
3. Which technique helps address mode collapse in GANs?
   a. Using larger batch sizes
   b. Increasing the number of discriminator layers
   c. Applying dropout to the generator
   d. Adjusting the learning rate dynamically
4. What role does hyperparameter tuning play in optimizing generative models?
   a. It helps find the best model configuration for stable training and quality outputs.
   b. It reduces the computational complexity of training.
   c. It ensures that only real samples are used for training.
   d. It prevents the model from generating diverse samples.

Answers

1. c
2. b
3. d
4. a

Questions

1. Why is it difficult to evaluate generative models compared to discriminative models?
2. What are the advantages of using FID over traditional pixel-wise metrics for evaluating image quality?
3. How can mode collapse impact the diversity of generated outputs, and what are potential solutions?
4. What are some key hyperparameters that significantly affect the training of generative models?
5. How can data augmentation improve the evaluation and optimization of generative models?
6. What role do visualization tools such as TensorBoard play in monitoring model performance?
7. Why is balancing fidelity and diversity important when optimizing generative models?
8. What are the differences between Wasserstein loss and traditional adversarial loss in GAN training?
9. How does automated hyperparameter tuning improve the efficiency of model optimization?
10. What trends in generative model evaluation are expected to evolve in the future?

Key Terms

- **Fréchet Inception Distance (FID):** A metric for evaluating image quality and diversity in generative models.
- **Inception Score (IS):** A metric measuring the diversity and realism of generated images.
- **Perplexity:** A measure of uncertainty in text-based generative models.
- **Mode Collapse:** A phenomenon in GANs where the generator produces limited variations of outputs.
- **Regularization:** Techniques such as dropout and weight decay used to improve model stability.
- **Wasserstein Loss:** A loss function used in WGANs to improve training stability and reduce mode collapse.
- **Hyperparameter Tuning:** The process of optimizing parameters such as learning rate, batch size, and weight initialization.
- **Data Augmentation:** Enhancing training datasets with transformations to improve model generalization.
- **TensorBoard:** A tool for visualizing training progress and model performance.
- **Automated Optimization:** Using frameworks such as **Optuna and Ray Tune** to automate hyperparameter search.

CHAPTER 14
Deployment of Generative Models

Introduction

Deploying generative models is the critical step that bridges the gap between research and real-world applications, enabling their transformative potential to reach end-users. While training and optimizing models such as GANs, VAEs, and diffusion models is challenging in itself, deploying these models presents unique hurdles such as ensuring scalability, reducing latency, and meeting diverse hardware requirements. Effective deployment strategies are essential for integrating generative models into production systems, powering applications ranging from content creation and recommendation engines to real-time AI assistants.

In this chapter, we explore the end-to-end process of deploying generative models, covering everything from model optimization techniques such as quantization and pruning to platform-specific deployment on cloud and edge devices. We discuss how to build APIs and microservices to serve generative models at scale, optimize inference performance, and monitor deployed models for reliability and security. Through practical examples and real-world case studies, this chapter provides the tools and strategies you need to successfully deploy generative models, ensuring they deliver high-quality results efficiently and effectively in production environments.

Structure

In this chapter, we will cover the following topics:

- **Introduction to Deployment of Generative Models**
  - Importance of Deploying Generative Models for Real-World Applications
  - Overview of Deployment Workflows and Tools
- **Generative Models for Deployment**
  - Preparation Activities
  - Deployment Platforms and Environments
  - APIs and Microservices for Generative Models
- **Inference Optimization**
- **Monitoring and Maintaining Deployed Models**
  - Practical Tip: Build a Monitoring Checklist
- **Tools and Frameworks for Model Deployment**
  - Deployment Frameworks: TensorFlow Serving, TorchServe, and NVIDIA Triton
  - Containerization with Docker and Orchestration with Kubernetes
  - Using CI/CD Pipelines for Automating Model Updates

- **Scaling Generative Models in Production**
  - Scaling for High User Demand and Large-Scale Inference
  - Load Balancing and Fault Tolerance for Generative Model APIs
  - Cost-Efficient Strategies for Scaling in Cloud Environments
- **Implementing Deployment of a Generative Model: Step-by-Step**
  - Deploying the Model on a Cloud Platform and Testing the API
  - Monitoring Usage and Optimizing for Production
- **Challenges and Limitations in Deployment**
- **Case Study: Deploying a StyleGAN Model for Image Generation**

Introduction to Deployment of Generative Models

Deploying generative models represents a critical phase in the lifecycle of artificial intelligence systems. While training and fine-tuning these models often receive significant attention, the deployment process bridges the gap between theoretical advancements and practical, real-world applications. This chapter delves into the importance, challenges, and workflows associated with deploying generative models, ensuring they are ready for operational use across diverse industries.

Importance of Deploying Generative Models for Real-World Applications

The deployment of generative models transforms theoretical capabilities into actionable solutions, enabling applications that range from personalized content generation to advanced data augmentation. Key reasons for deploying generative models include:

- **Real-World Utility**: Generative models power applications such as image synthesis, language translation, and virtual assistants, providing immense value in sectors such as healthcare, entertainment, and e-commerce.
- **Scalability and Accessibility**: Deployment ensures that models are not confined to research environments but are accessible to end-users and systems at scale. For instance, language models such as GPT are integrated into tools used by millions of people daily.
- **Feedback and Continuous Improvement**: Deployed models generate real-world data, offering valuable feedback to refine and improve the system iteratively. This feedback loop is critical for maintaining relevance and accuracy.
- **Economic Impact**: Deployed generative models can streamline workflows, reduce operational costs, and open up new revenue streams, making them indispensable for businesses seeking a competitive advantage.

Challenges in Deploying Generative Models Compared to Other ML Models

While deployment is a common aspect of machine learning, generative models pose unique challenges due to their complexity and high computational demands. These challenges include:

- **Model Complexity**: Generative models, such as GANs and VAEs, often have intricate architectures with multiple components (for example, generator and discriminator in GANs) that require precise coordination during inference.
- **Resource Intensity**: Generative models typically demand significant computational resources, including high-performance GPUs or TPUs, to deliver real-time performance.

- **Latency Constraints**: Applications such as real-time video synthesis or interactive AI-powered tools necessitate low-latency inference, which can be challenging to achieve with large models.
- **Deployment Environment Variability**: Generative models must be optimized for diverse environments, such as cloud servers, edge devices, and mobile applications, each with distinct constraints.
- **Security and Ethical Considerations**: Deployed generative models can inadvertently generate biased, inappropriate, or harmful content, necessitating robust monitoring and safeguards.
- **Model Updates and Maintenance**: Continuous monitoring, retraining, and updating deployed models are essential to ensure they remain effective and aligned with user expectations.

Overview of Deployment Workflows and Tools

Successfully deploying generative models involves a well-defined workflow supported by specialized tools and frameworks. Key aspects include:

- **Model Optimization:**
  - **Quantization**: Reducing model precision (for example, from FP32 to INT8) to improve inference speed and reduce resource consumption.
  - **Pruning**: Removing redundant parameters to create a lightweight model without significant loss in accuracy.
  - **Knowledge Distillation**: Training a smaller model (student) to mimic the behavior of a larger model (teacher).
- **Containerization and Orchestration:**
  - **Docker**: Packaging the model, dependencies, and environment into a container for consistent deployment.
  - **Kubernetes**: Orchestrating containers for scalable and reliable deployment in production.
- **Serving Frameworks:**
  - **TensorFlow Serving**: A high-performance framework for serving TensorFlow models.
  - **TorchServe**: A flexible tool for deploying PyTorch models.
  - **ONNX Runtime**: A cross-platform engine optimized for running models converted to ONNX format.
- **API Integration:**
  - Models are exposed via REST or gRPC APIs, allowing seamless integration with applications.
  - Frameworks such as FastAPI and Flask are popular choices for creating lightweight API layers.
- **Monitoring and Logging:**
  - Tools such as Prometheus and Grafana enable real-time monitoring of model performance and system health.
  - Logging frameworks capture inference errors, latencies, and user feedback for continuous improvement.
- **Edge Deployment:**
  - Optimized deployment to edge devices such as smartphones, IoT devices, or embedded systems using libraries such as TensorFlow Lite and PyTorch Mobile.

  - Balancing computational efficiency with performance to meet real-world constraints.
- **Testing and Validation:**
  - Rigorous testing ensures models perform reliably under diverse scenarios and workloads.
  - Techniques include A/B testing, load testing, and simulation of real-world conditions.

In the upcoming sections, we will explore each of these aspects in greater detail, providing actionable insights and best practices to navigate the complex landscape of deploying generative models effectively.

Generative Models for Deployment

Generative models, with their immense potential, are increasingly used in real-world applications ranging from image synthesis to text generation. However, deploying these models in production requires careful preparation to ensure they are efficient, scalable, and capable of performing well in varied environments. This chapter delves into key strategies for optimizing generative models for deployment.

Preparation Activities

Deploying generative models presents challenges such as large model size, high computational demands, and diverse deployment formats. Optimizing models is essential for smooth operation in real-world environments. Models such as GANs, VAEs, or large language models can be computationally expensive and memory-intensive, making them difficult to deploy on devices with limited resources.

Optimizing Model Size for Deployment

Optimizing model size is essential to ensure smooth operation in real-world settings. Some of the primary techniques include:

- **Quantization:** Quantization involves reducing the precision of the weights and activations in a model. Instead of using 32-bit floating-point numbers, models can be converted to 16-bit or even 8-bit integers. This significantly reduces the memory footprint and computational load without drastically affecting performance. For example, TensorFlow and PyTorch provide tools such as TensorFlow Lite and PyTorch's quantization utilities to implement this technique seamlessly.
- **Pruning:** Model pruning removes unnecessary weights and neurons that do not contribute significantly to the model's output. By identifying and eliminating these components, the model's size can be reduced, leading to faster inference times and lower memory usage. Structured and unstructured pruning methods can be applied, depending on the requirements.
- **Model Compression:** Compression techniques such as knowledge distillation and low-rank approximation can further reduce the size of generative models. Knowledge distillation involves training a smaller model (the student) to mimic the behavior of a larger model (the teacher). This enables the deployment of lightweight models that retain the functionality of their larger counterparts.

Handling Computational Requirements for Resource-Constrained Environments

Deploying generative models on edge devices, mobile phones, or embedded systems poses significant challenges due to limited computational resources. Effective strategies to address these challenges include:

- **Edge-Specific Optimization:** Edge deployment requires fine-tuning models to operate efficiently on specific hardware, such as ARM processors or GPUs. Frameworks such as TensorFlow Lite and ONNX Runtime enable developers to tailor models for edge devices.
- **Efficient Architecture Design:** Using model architectures designed for efficiency, such as MobileNet or EfficientNet, can help reduce computational requirements. These architectures are specifically optimized for low-power devices while maintaining accuracy.
- **Hardware Acceleration:** Utilizing hardware accelerators such as Tensor Processing Units (TPUs), NVIDIA Jetson devices, or Neural Processing Units (NPUs) can significantly boost performance in resource-constrained environments. Hardware-aware neural architecture search (NAS) can also be employed to design models that take full advantage of the available hardware.

Exporting Models to Deployment-Ready Formats

Once a generative model is optimized, it must be exported to a format compatible with the target environment. Common formats include:

- **ONNX (Open Neural Network Exchange):** ONNX is a versatile format supported by various frameworks such as PyTorch, TensorFlow, and Keras. It enables seamless interoperability and allows models to run on multiple platforms, including mobile and web.
- **TensorFlow Lite:** TensorFlow Lite is a lightweight version of TensorFlow specifically designed for mobile and embedded devices. It supports quantized models and provides APIs for integrating models into Android and iOS applications.
- **TorchScript:** TorchScript is PyTorch's format for serializing models. It enables deployment in production environments where the Python runtime is unavailable. TorchScript models can be run in C++ environments, making them suitable for high-performance applications.
- **Custom Deployment Pipelines:** In some cases, it may be necessary to create custom pipelines for deployment, especially when working with unique hardware or proprietary systems. This involves exporting the model in a raw format and using specialized tools to integrate it into the target platform.

Preparing generative models for deployment is a multi-faceted process involving optimization, resource management, and format conversion. By adopting techniques such as quantization, pruning, and compression, developers can ensure their models are lightweight and efficient. Tailoring models to the computational constraints of the target environment and exporting them to deployment-ready formats further facilitates smooth integration. These strategies ensure that generative models are not only powerful in functionality but also practical for real-world use cases.

Deployment Platforms and Environments

Deploying generative models effectively requires a thorough understanding of the available platforms and environments. These platforms cater to different use cases, ranging from high-performance cloud solutions to resource-constrained edge devices. Each option presents unique advantages, challenges, and considerations, depending on the application and audience.

Generative models can be deployed across three primary platforms: cloud, edge, and on-premises. Cloud platforms offer scalable and powerful infrastructure, making them ideal for demanding workloads such as training large language models or performing high-volume inference. Edge devices, such as Raspberry Pi and Jetson Nano, prioritize low-latency, on-device processing, particularly useful in applications such as IoT and mobile apps. On-premises deployment provides control over data privacy and security, appealing to industries with stringent compliance requirements.

Deploying on Cloud Services

Cloud platforms such as AWS, Google Cloud, and Microsoft Azure are popular choices for deploying generative models. These platforms provide managed services that simplify model deployment and scaling:

- **Amazon Web Services (AWS):** AWS offers services such as SageMaker for model training and deployment, Lambda for serverless execution, and EC2 instances optimized for machine learning tasks. AWS also supports Elastic Inference, which can reduce inference costs by attaching GPU acceleration to EC2 instances.
- **Google Cloud:** Google AI Platform and Vertex AI provide a robust ecosystem for deploying generative models. With TensorFlow Extended (TFX) integration, users can create end-to-end pipelines for model serving, monitoring, and versioning. Google's TPUs (Tensor Processing Units) are a significant advantage for large-scale training and inference.
- **Microsoft Azure:** Azure Machine Learning (Azure ML) facilitates model deployment through its MLOps integration. Azure also provides support for containerized deployments using Docker and Kubernetes, making it suitable for microservices architectures.

Deploying on Edge Devices

Deploying generative models on edge devices has gained traction with the growth of IoT and mobile applications. Edge deployment emphasizes minimal latency, reduced bandwidth usage, and offline capabilities.

- **Raspberry Pi:** Lightweight models such as TFLite can be deployed on Raspberry Pi for applications such as real-time object detection or voice synthesis. Its GPIO (General-Purpose Input/Output) pins enable integration with hardware sensors, making it ideal for embedded systems.
- **Jetson Nano:** NVIDIA's Jetson Nano provides superior GPU performance, suitable for running slightly more complex models such as YOLOv5 or EfficientDet. Its CUDA-enabled architecture supports TensorRT, enhancing inference speed.
- **Mobile Devices:** Mobile-focused frameworks such as TensorFlow Lite and Core ML allow seamless deployment on Android and iOS devices. These models optimize inference speed and energy consumption, catering to applications such as augmented reality and speech-to-text.

Comparison of Deployment Platforms for Generative Models

Selecting the right deployment platform involves balancing these factors to meet specific business or technical goals. For example, a healthcare application might prioritize data privacy and opt for on-premises deployment, while an e-commerce platform might favor the scalability of cloud services to handle varying traffic loads.

Feature	Cloud	Edge	On-Premises
Scalability	High; elastic scaling with demand	Limited by hardware constraints	Moderate; dependent on in-house resources
Latency	May involve network delays	Low; on-device inference	Moderate; depends on local network speed
Cost	Pay-as-you-go; can be expensive at scale	Upfront cost for hardware; low recurring cost	High initial investment and maintenance cost

Data Privacy	Dependent on provider's compliance	High; data stays on-device	Very high; complete control over data
Use Case Examples	SaaS, large-scale ML services	IoT, mobile apps, remote locations	Banking, healthcare, regulated industries

Table 14.1: *Deployment Platforms Comparison*

By understanding these platforms' characteristics and capabilities, developers can make informed decisions about where and how to deploy their generative models effectively. The choice of platform can significantly impact model performance, user experience, and overall project success.

APIs and Microservices for Generative Models

Generative models have evolved from academic concepts into practical tools used across industries. To make these models accessible and integrate them into larger systems, APIs and microservices play a pivotal role. By exposing generative models through APIs, developers can enable seamless integration into web or mobile applications while maintaining scalability and efficiency. This section explores building APIs for generative models, integrating them into applications, and best practices for microservices.

Creating APIs for generative models allows developers to interact with these models over the web, enabling use cases such as image generation, text completion, and data augmentation. Frameworks such as **FastAPI** and **Flask** provide powerful tools to build APIs quickly and efficiently.

Both frameworks allow rapid development and testing, with deployment options to scale for production.

Integrating Generative Models with Web or Mobile Applications

Once an API is built, it can be consumed by web or mobile applications to deliver generative model capabilities to end-users. This integration involves:

Frontend-Backend Communication:

- Use HTTP requests to send input data (for example, image prompts, text queries) to the API and retrieve the generated outputs.
- For mobile apps, libraries such as **Retrofit** (Android) and **Alamofire** (iOS) can streamline API requests.

Real-Time Interactions:

- Leverage WebSockets for low-latency applications such as real-time chatbots or image editing tools.
- Combine APIs with streaming services such as Kafka to handle continuous data flows.

Deployment on the Cloud:

- Use platforms such as AWS Lambda, Azure Functions, or Google Cloud Run to deploy APIs, ensuring automatic scaling and fault tolerance.
- Containerization with Docker enables consistent deployments across environments.

Example Workflow:

- A user uploads an image via a web app.
- The frontend sends the image to an API hosted on AWS Lambda.
- The API processes the image using a StyleGAN model and returns the stylized output.

Best Practices for Scalable and Efficient Microservices

Deploying generative models at scale demands efficient microservices, especially for high-traffic applications. Asynchronous frameworks such as FastAPI and libraries such as `aiohttp` and `asyncio` enable non-blocking request handling, boosting performance. Load balancing—via NGINX or AWS ELB—helps distribute traffic, prevent bottlenecks, and maintain availability.

To speed up inference, apply model quantization with tools such as TensorFlow Lite or ONNX, and cache repeated responses for faster delivery. Use Prometheus and Grafana to monitor service health and metrics, and adopt structured logging with Loguru or Python's built-in logging module.

Automate deployments using CI/CD pipelines (for example, GitHub Actions, Jenkins) for rapid updates and rollbacks. Secure APIs through OAuth2 or API keys, and sanitize inputs to prevent attacks.

Microservices power the real-world deployment of generative models, enabling seamless integration into apps and services. With efficient architecture, proper tooling, and security-first design, these systems can scale reliably—unlocking the full potential of generative AI.

Inference Optimization

Optimizing inference is a critical step in deploying generative models, especially when real-time or near-real-time performance is required. The focus lies in reducing latency and improving inference speed to ensure that models deliver predictions efficiently without sacrificing accuracy. This chapter explores key techniques for optimizing inference, including software-level strategies and hardware accelerations, ensuring generative models operate effectively in production environments.

Reducing Latency and Improving Inference Speed

Latency, or the delay between receiving an input and producing an output, is one of the most significant bottlenecks in deploying generative models. Reducing latency is crucial for applications such as conversational AI, autonomous vehicles, and real-time image generation. Here are some common strategies:

- **Model Quantization:** Converting model weights from high-precision (for example, 32-bit floating point) to lower precision (for example, 8-bit integer) reduces computational overhead without significantly compromising accuracy. Quantization can dramatically reduce the size of the model and improve execution speed.
- **Pruning:** Removing less significant weights and neurons from a model reduces complexity and speeds up inference. Techniques such as structured pruning, which remove entire layers or channels, can simplify model architecture.
- **Knowledge Distillation:** Transferring knowledge from a large, complex model (teacher) to a smaller, simpler model (student) reduces inference time. The student model mimics the teacher's behavior while being computationally less intensive.
- **Early Exit Mechanisms:** Incorporating intermediate classifiers into deep networks allows early predictions, reducing computation when high confidence is achieved at earlier stages.

Techniques such as Batching, Caching, and Asynchronous Processing

Optimization at the system level can further enhance inference performance. These methods focus on managing requests, data, and computations efficiently:

- **Batching:**
    - Combining multiple inference requests into a single batch for processing increases the

utilization of hardware resources. This is particularly effective for hardware accelerators such as GPUs and TPUs.

  - Frameworks such as TensorFlow Serving and NVIDIA TensorRT support batching, allowing multiple inputs to be processed simultaneously.

- **Caching:**
  - Reusing results from previously processed inputs can significantly reduce inference time for repetitive tasks. For instance, embeddings generated for frequent queries in a search engine can be cached.
  - Caching can be implemented at various levels, such as database query caching, in-memory caching (for example, Redis), or application-layer caching.
- **Asynchronous Processing:**
  - Instead of processing each request synchronously, asynchronous frameworks allow requests to be queued and processed in parallel. This approach improves throughput by leveraging multi-threading or multi-processing.
  - Asynchronous APIs in frameworks such as FastAPI or libraries such as asyncio in Python facilitate this optimization.

Leveraging Hardware Acceleration: GPUs, TPUs, and FPGAs

Modern hardware accelerators play a pivotal role in achieving high-speed inference. Choosing the right hardware and optimizing model execution for it can significantly improve performance:

- **Graphics Processing Units (GPUs):**
  - GPUs are well-suited for parallelizable tasks, such as matrix multiplications in deep learning. Frameworks such as CUDA and cuDNN provide optimized libraries for GPU-accelerated inference.
  - NVIDIA TensorRT is a popular tool for optimizing models for GPU inference, offering features such as quantization, layer fusion, and kernel auto-tuning.
- **Tensor Processing Units (TPUs):**
  - Developed by Google, TPUs are specialized hardware designed for tensor computations. They provide high throughput for both training and inference tasks, especially in TensorFlow-based applications.
  - TPUs are ideal for large-scale deployments where high efficiency is required, such as in recommendation systems and large language models.
- **Field-Programmable Gate Arrays (FPGAs):**
  - FPGAs allow custom hardware configurations tailored to specific workloads. They offer low latency and high energy efficiency, making them suitable for edge devices.
  - Frameworks such as OpenVINO and Vitis AI enable developers to deploy optimized models on FPGAs.

Balancing Trade-Offs between Accuracy and Speed

While optimizing inference, it is essential to strike a balance between speed and accuracy. Over-optimization may lead to reduced model fidelity, negatively affecting user experience in critical applications. Techniques such as adaptive precision and progressive inference allow dynamic adjustments based on the desired trade-off.

Practical Example: Optimizing Inference for an NLP Application

Consider a chatbot powered by a transformer-based model. Inference optimization involves:

- Quantizing the model to 8-bit precision using TensorFlow Lite.
- Implementing batching for handling multiple user queries concurrently.
- Caching embeddings for frequently asked questions.
- Deploying the model on NVIDIA GPUs with TensorRT optimization.

Thus, by combining these techniques, latency can be reduced from 500 milliseconds to under 100 milliseconds, enhancing user satisfaction.

Inference optimization is a multidisciplinary challenge requiring an understanding of model architecture, system-level engineering, and hardware capabilities. By employing techniques such as batching, caching, and leveraging accelerators such as GPUs, TPUs, and FPGAs, developers can achieve significant improvements in speed and efficiency, paving the way for deploying generative models at scale.

Monitoring and Maintaining Deployed Models

The deployment of a generative model is not the end of its lifecycle but rather the beginning of a critical phase: monitoring and maintaining the model in a production environment. Without continuous oversight, even the best-performing models can degrade over time, rendering their predictions inaccurate or biased. Effective monitoring ensures that the model delivers reliable and secure outputs, while adapting to the evolving data landscape.

Setting Up Monitoring for Model Performance and Usage Metrics

Monitoring a deployed generative model involves tracking key performance indicators (KPIs) and usage metrics to ensure that the model operates as intended. This includes:

- **Performance Metrics**: Continuously measure metrics such as accuracy, precision, recall, or BLEU scores (for text generation). For image generation, monitor metrics such as Fréchet Inception Distance (FID) or Inception Score (IS). Regular updates on these metrics provide insights into whether the model's output quality remains consistent.
- **Latency and Throughput**: Track response times and the number of requests processed per second. Low latency and high throughput are critical for maintaining a seamless user experience in real-time applications such as chatbots or image synthesis platforms.
- **User Interaction Metrics**: For applications that involve user interaction, collect data on usage patterns, such as the frequency of certain requests or user feedback on generated outputs. Metrics such as click-through rates or satisfaction scores can be pivotal in identifying areas of improvement.
- **Error Monitoring**: Set up alerts for exceptions, failed requests, or unusual spikes in errors. Logging systems such as ELK Stack or cloud services such as AWS CloudWatch and Google Cloud Monitoring can facilitate real-time error detection.

Handling Drift in Generative Outputs and Retraining Requirements

Model drift occurs when the statistical properties of the input data change over time, leading to degradation in model performance. This can be particularly problematic for generative models, as they often rely on implicit assumptions about the underlying data distribution. Addressing drift involves:

- **Detecting Drift**: Utilize tools such as Kolmogorov-Smirnov tests or population stability indexes to identify changes in data distribution. For generative models, visual inspection of outputs–such as comparing recently generated samples to historical benchmarks–can also highlight drift.
- **Feedback Loops**: Implement mechanisms to gather feedback from users. For instance, in a generative chatbot, user ratings on the relevance or quality of responses can help identify patterns of degradation.
- **Retraining and Fine-Tuning**: Schedule periodic retraining of the model using up-to-date datasets. Transfer learning or fine-tuning techniques can be employed to adapt the existing model to new data without needing a complete retrain from scratch.
- **Automated Pipelines**: Develop automated pipelines for data ingestion, retraining, and redeployment. MLOps tools such as Kubeflow or MLflow can streamline this process, ensuring minimal downtime during updates.

Ensuring Security and Access Control for Deployed Models

Security is paramount when deploying generative models, particularly when sensitive or proprietary data is involved. A breach or misuse can have severe consequences, both financially and reputationally. Key considerations include:

1. **Authentication and Authorization**: Implement robust authentication mechanisms (for example, OAuth or API keys) to ensure that only authorized users can access the model. Role-based access control (RBAC) can further restrict access based on user roles.
2. **Encryption**: Secure data at rest and in transit using strong encryption protocols such as TLS/SSL for communication and AES-256 for storage. This prevents unauthorized access or tampering.
3. **Adversarial Defense**: Protect the model from adversarial attacks designed to manipulate its outputs. Techniques such as input sanitization, robust training methods, and anomaly detection can mitigate these risks.
4. **Audit Logging**: Maintain detailed logs of all interactions with the model, including API calls, input data, and generated outputs. These logs can be invaluable for forensic analysis in the event of a security incident.
5. **Compliance**: Ensure that the deployment adheres to relevant legal and regulatory requirements, such as GDPR for data privacy or HIPAA for healthcare applications. Regular audits and compliance checks can prevent legal issues.

Practical Tip: Build a Monitoring Checklist

To ensure deployed generative models remain reliable, efficient, and secure, it is essential to monitor key metrics, respond to changes in data or performance, and implement strong security measures. The following checklist summarizes practical actions and considerations for maintaining models effectively in production environments.

1. Performance Monitoring
    - Track output quality metrics: Accuracy, BLEU score (text), FID/IS (images)
    - Monitor latency and throughput to ensure responsiveness
    - Collect user interaction data: clicks, ratings, feedback

   - Set up error alerts for failed requests or unusual spikes
2. Drift Detection and Retraining
   - Detect data drift using statistical tests (KS test, PSI)
   - Monitor concept drift in input-output relationships
   - Implement feedback loops to gather user insights
   - Schedule periodic retraining or fine-tuning with updated datasets
   - Automate pipelines using MLOps tools (Kubeflow, MLflow) for minimal downtime
3. Security and Access Control
   - Enforce authentication and authorization (OAuth, API keys, RBAC)
   - Apply encryption for data in transit (TLS/SSL) and at rest (AES-256)
   - Implement adversarial defenses and input sanitization
   - Maintain audit logs of all API calls and generated outputs
   - Conduct regular **compliance checks** (GDPR, HIPAA, and so on)

Monitoring and maintaining deployed generative models is an ongoing process that ensures their performance, security, and reliability in production environments. By setting up robust monitoring systems, proactively handling drift, and implementing stringent security measures, organizations can maximize the value of their generative AI systems while minimizing risks. This lifecycle approach not only enhances user trust but also ensures the long-term sustainability of AI deployments.

Tools and Frameworks for Model Deployment

In the ever-evolving field of artificial intelligence, deploying models efficiently and reliably is as crucial as developing them. While training and refining models garner much attention, model deployment ensures their real-world usability and scalability. This chapter explores essential tools and frameworks that streamline the deployment process, emphasizing the role of deployment frameworks, containerization, orchestration, and automation through CI/CD pipelines.

Deployment Frameworks: TF Serving, TorchServe, and NVIDIA Triton

Deployment frameworks act as intermediaries between trained models and end-users, offering a structured way to serve predictions with low latency and high throughput. Three of the most prominent frameworks are:

- **TensorFlow Serving**: Specifically designed for TensorFlow models, TensorFlow Serving enables efficient deployment of machine learning models in production environments. It supports advanced features such as versioning, load balancing, and GPU acceleration, ensuring seamless integration into diverse production setups. TensorFlow Serving's REST and gRPC APIs make it accessible for various applications, from web services to mobile apps.
- **TorchServe**: Developed by PyTorch, TorchServe simplifies the process of deploying PyTorch models at scale. It provides features such as multi-model serving, logging, metrics, and customizable inference handlers. TorchServe is highly flexible, allowing developers to extend its functionality to suit custom requirements, making it an excellent choice for real-time inference and batch processing.
- **NVIDIA Triton**: Designed to cater to high-performance AI workflows, NVIDIA Triton Inference Server supports multiple frameworks, including TensorFlow, PyTorch, and ONNX. It leverages NVIDIA GPUs for accelerated inference and offers features such as dynamic batching, model

ensembles, and multi-model serving. Triton is particularly well-suited for enterprise-grade AI solutions that require robust performance and scalability.

Framework	Supported Models	Key Features	Best Use Cases
TensorFlow Serving	TensorFlow	Versioning, GPU acceleration, REST/gRPC APIs	Production TensorFlow models, low-latency inference
TorchServe	PyTorch	Multi-model serving, logging, metrics, custom inference handlers	Real-time PyTorch inference, batch processing, flexible deployments
NVIDIA Triton	TensorFlow, PyTorch, ONNX	Dynamic batching, model ensembles, multi-GPU support	High-performance AI workloads, enterprise-scale inference

***Figure 14.1**: Comparison of AI Workflow Deployment Frameworks*

Containerization with Docker and Orchestration with Kubernetes

Model deployment often involves complex environments with multiple dependencies. Containerization and orchestration are powerful tools to address these challenges:

- **Containerization with Docker:**
  - Docker packages applications, including ML models and their dependencies, into lightweight, portable containers. This ensures consistency across development, testing, and production environments.
  - By isolating each model's runtime environment, Docker minimizes conflicts and simplifies scaling.
  - With Docker images, developers can version and update their deployments seamlessly, ensuring quick rollback in case of issues.
- **Orchestration with Kubernetes:**
  - Kubernetes takes containerization a step further by managing the deployment, scaling, and operation of containers in a distributed environment.
  - It automates critical tasks such as load balancing, resource allocation, and health monitoring of containers.
  - For machine learning, Kubernetes can manage multiple model deployments, ensuring high availability and fault tolerance. Integrations with tools such as Kubeflow further enhance its capabilities, allowing seamless end-to-end workflows for ML applications.

Using CI/CD Pipelines for Automating Model Updates

Continuous Integration (CI) and Continuous Deployment (CD) pipelines are integral to modern software development practices, and their adoption in ML model deployment ensures faster and more reliable updates:

- **CI/CD for Machine Learning:**
  - CI/CD pipelines automate the process of integrating, testing, and deploying models. This minimizes manual intervention, reduces errors, and ensures a streamlined workflow.
  - These pipelines can include automated checks for model performance metrics, ensuring only the best-performing models are deployed.

- **Automating Model Updates:**
  - With CI/CD, updating a model becomes as simple as committing new code or retrained models to a repository.
  - Tools such as Jenkins, GitHub Actions, and GitLab CI/CD integrate seamlessly with deployment frameworks, enabling end-to-end automation.
  - CI/CD pipelines can also monitor deployed models for drift, triggering retraining workflows when performance deteriorates.
- **Version Control and Rollbacks:**
  - Version control ensures that every deployed model and its associated configurations are tracked. If issues arise, rolling back to a previous version is straightforward.
  - This practice improves reliability, and instills confidence in production systems.

Effective model deployment is a multifaceted process requiring robust tools and frameworks. From the flexibility of TensorFlow Serving and TorchServe to the high-performance capabilities of NVIDIA Triton, deployment frameworks are indispensable for serving models at scale. Docker and Kubernetes simplify the management of complex environments, while CI/CD pipelines automate updates, ensuring models stay relevant and performant. Together, these technologies enable seamless transitions from development to production, empowering organizations to derive maximum value from their AI solutions.

Scaling Generative Models in Production

The deployment of generative models in production environments brings exciting opportunities and unique challenges. These models, ranging from Variational Autoencoders (VAEs) to Generative Adversarial Networks (GANs) and Large Language Models (LLMs), are increasingly being used in applications such as personalized recommendations, content creation, and real-time translations. However, scaling these models to meet high user demand while ensuring cost efficiency, reliability, and performance is a multifaceted task. In this chapter, we explore key strategies and considerations for scaling generative models effectively in production environments.

Scaling for High User Demand and Large-Scale Inference

Generative models are often computationally intensive, requiring substantial processing power for both training and inference. When scaling for high user demand, the following approaches are essential:

- **Model Optimization for Inference:**
  - Techniques such as quantization, pruning, and knowledge distillation can significantly reduce the computational load of models, enabling faster inference with lower resource usage.
  - Precomputing and caching common outputs can help reduce latency for frequently requested results.
- **Dynamic Scaling:**
  - Implement autoscaling mechanisms to adapt to fluctuating user demands. Tools such as Kubernetes can dynamically adjust the number of pods or instances based on traffic patterns.
  - Serverless computing platforms such as AWS Lambda or Google Cloud Functions can also help manage short bursts of high traffic efficiently.

- **Accelerated Hardware:**
  - Employ GPUs or TPUs specifically optimized for the type of generative model being deployed. For example, NVIDIA's TensorRT library can optimize inference for deep learning models.
  - Consider hardware accelerators such as FPGAs or edge devices for decentralized, low-latency inference.
- **Sharding and Parallelism:**
  - Split large models into shards to distribute computation across multiple machines. This approach, known as model parallelism, is especially useful for LLMs that cannot fit entirely in the memory of a single device.
  - Use data parallelism to process multiple inference requests simultaneously across different nodes.

Approach	Description	Best For
Quantization & Pruning	Reduces model size and speeds up inference	Edge deployment, low-latency apps
Dynamic Autoscaling	Adjusts compute resources based on traffic	Cloud-based, variable workloads
Model Parallelism	Splits computation across devices	Large LLMs or image generators
Caching & Precomputation	Stores frequent outputs	Repetitive generation tasks
GPU/TPU Acceleration	Uses optimized hardware for deep inference	Enterprise-grade deployments

***Figure 14.2**: Comparison of AI Scaling Approaches for High Demand*

Load Balancing and Fault Tolerance for Generative Model APIs

Ensuring that generative model APIs are resilient and perform reliably under varying loads requires robust load balancing and fault tolerance mechanisms. Key strategies include:

- **Load Balancing:**
  - Utilize load balancers such as NGINX, HAProxy, or cloud-native solutions (for example, AWS Elastic Load Balancing) to distribute requests across multiple servers evenly.
  - Implement request routing based on the type of request (for example, image generation vs. text generation) to optimize resource allocation.
- **Redundancy and Failover:**
  - Deploy multiple instances of generative models in different availability zones to ensure availability in case of regional outages.
  - Implement failover mechanisms that automatically redirect traffic to backup instances during server failures.
- **Health Monitoring and Self-Healing:**
  - Use monitoring tools such as Prometheus, Grafana, or Datadog to track system health and performance metrics.

    - Automate self-healing processes to restart or replace unhealthy instances, minimizing downtime.
- **Throttling and Rate Limiting:**
    - Protect APIs from being overwhelmed by implementing rate-limiting policies. This ensures fair usage and prevents abuse by malicious actors.
    - Use token-based authentication or API keys to manage user access and prioritize premium users if necessary.

Cost-Efficient Strategies for Scaling in Cloud

While cloud platforms provide scalable infrastructure, cost management is crucial to prevent budget overruns. Here are strategies to achieve cost-efficient scaling:

- **Optimizing Resource Allocation:**
    - Choose appropriate instance types based on the computational needs of the model. Spot instances or preemptible VMs can offer significant cost savings for non-critical workloads.
    - Use autoscaling to dynamically allocate resources during peak hours and scale down during off-peak times.
- **Using Managed Services:**
    - Leverage managed machine learning services such as AWS SageMaker, Google AI Platform, or Azure ML, which provide optimized environments for deploying generative models.
    - These platforms often include integrated scaling and monitoring tools, reducing the overhead of managing infrastructure.
- **Model Compression and Efficiency:**
    - Use lightweight model architectures or reduced-precision computations to decrease hardware requirements without compromising accuracy.
    - Fine-tune pre-trained models instead of training from scratch to save both time and resources.
- **Hybrid and Multi-Cloud Strategies:**
    - Implement hybrid deployments where frequently accessed models run on-premises while less-used models are hosted in the cloud.
    - Use multi-cloud strategies to optimize costs by selecting the most cost-effective provider for specific workloads.
- **Monitoring and Cost Analysis:**
    - Continuously monitor resource usage with cloud-native tools such as AWS Cost Explorer or Google Cloud's Billing Reports.
    - Analyze cost-performance trade-offs to identify areas for further optimization, such as rightsizing instances or modifying model architectures.

In conclusion, scaling generative models for production is a complex yet rewarding endeavor. It requires balancing user demands, cost constraints, and system reliability. By adopting advanced optimization techniques, leveraging cloud-native tools, and implementing robust fault tolerance mechanisms, organizations can ensure that their generative models operate efficiently and effectively at scale.

Implementing Deployment of a Generative Model: Step-by-Step

Deploying a generative model into production involves more than just training and saving the model. It requires careful preparation, robust infrastructure, and ongoing monitoring to ensure optimal performance in a real-world environment. Whether you are deploying a GAN for image synthesis or a VAE for anomaly detection, the steps outlined below will help you navigate the process effectively.

Preparing a Generative Model for Deployment

Before deploying a generative model, ensure that it is optimized for inference. This includes:

- **Selecting the Appropriate Model Format:** Convert the trained model into a format suitable for deployment, such as TensorFlow SavedModel, ONNX, or TFLite, depending on the target platform.
- **Optimizing the Model:** Use techniques such as quantization, pruning, and model compression to reduce latency and memory usage without significant loss in performance.
- **Validating the Model:** Conduct extensive testing on unseen validation datasets to confirm the model's accuracy and reliability.

For example, in a GAN, ensure the generator produces high-quality outputs under varied latent space inputs, and validate the discriminator's consistency in evaluating synthetic data.

Step	Description	Example Tools
1. Model Preparation	Optimize and validate the trained model for inference	TensorFlow Lite, ONNX Runtime, PyTorch FX
2. Containerization	Package model and dependencies for portability	Docker, Podman
3. Cloud Deployment	Host model on scalable infrastructure	AWS, GCP, Azure
4. API Integration	Expose endpoints for inference requests	FastAPI, Flask, Uvicorn
5. Testing & Validation	Verify model performance in production	Postman, Locust, Grafana

Figure 14.3: *Overview of Deployment Steps for Generative Models*

Deploying the Model on a Cloud Platform and Testing the API

Cloud platforms such as AWS, Google Cloud Platform (GCP), and Azure provide scalable solutions for deploying generative models. The steps include:

- **Choosing a Deployment Service:** Options include AWS Elastic Beanstalk, GCP App Engine, or Azure App Service for web apps. For serverless solutions, consider AWS Lambda or Google Cloud Functions.

- **Containerization:** Package the API and model in a container using Docker to ensure consistency across environments. A sample Dockerfile might look like this:

```
# Use the official Python 3.11 slim image as the base image
FROM python:3.11-slim

# Set the working directory inside the container to /app
WORKDIR /app

# Copy the requirements.txt file into the working directory
COPY requirements.txt .

# Install the Python dependencies listed in requirements.txt
RUN pip install --no-cache-dir -r requirements.txt

# Copy the rest of the application code into the working directory
COPY . .

# Expose port 8000 to the outside world
EXPOSE 8000

# Run the Uvicorn server to serve the application
CMD ["uvicorn", "app:app", "--host", "0.0.0.0", "--port", "8000"]
```

- **Pushing the Container to a Registry:** Use Docker Hub, AWS Elastic Container Registry (ECR), or GCP Container Registry to store the container image.
- **Deploying the Container:** Deploy the container to the cloud service. For instance, with AWS Elastic Beanstalk:
    - Upload the container image.
    - Configure environment variables and network settings.
    - Launch the application.
- **Testing the Deployment:** Access the deployed API using its public URL and verify its functionality.

Testing the API

- Use tools such as Postman or curl to verify inference responses and latency.
- Integrate logging and metrics (via Prometheus or Datadog) to track usage.
- Simulate concurrent users with Locust or JMeter to evaluate scalability.
- Set up alerts for response failures or high latency using cloud-native monitoring (for example, AWS CloudWatch or GCP Monitoring).

Monitoring Usage and Optimizing for Production

Once the model is live, monitoring its usage and performance is critical for ensuring reliability and scalability. Key practices include:

- **Logging and Metrics:** Use logging tools such as ELK Stack or Amazon CloudWatch to monitor API calls, errors, and system performance. Implement metrics such as response time, memory usage, and throughput.
- **Alerting:** Set up alerts for anomalies, such as high error rates or unexpected spikes in latency.
- **Feedback Loop:** Collect user feedback and use it to retrain or fine-tune the model periodically. For instance, update a VAE to better capture emerging patterns in anomaly detection.

- **Scaling:** Leverage autoscaling features provided by cloud platforms to handle increased traffic.
- **Optimizing for Cost:** Use serverless platforms or spot instances to reduce costs without compromising performance.

Deploying a generative model involves careful planning and execution. By following the steps outlined above, you can ensure your model is production-ready, accessible, and efficient. The process–from preparing the model to monitoring its performance–lays the foundation for creating AI-driven applications that provide real-world value.

Challenges and Limitations in Deployment

Deploying generative models in real-world systems is powerful but challenging. One major hurdle lies in ensuring model performance on low-resource devices such as smartphones or edge platforms. Generative models such as GANs and VAEs demand heavy compute and memory, which can strain limited hardware. To tackle this, developers use optimization techniques such as quantization, pruning, and knowledge distillation to reduce model size and inference time without compromising accuracy. Architectures such as MobileNet, EfficientNet, and TinyGANs are designed specifically for such environments, enabling responsive AI even on modest devices.

Summary: Key Challenges and Mitigation Strategies

Category	Challenge	Impact	Mitigation Strategies / Tools
Technical	High computational and memory demands on low-resource devices	Slower inference, limited deployment scope	Model compression, quantization, pruning, TinyGAN, EfficientNet
Ethical	Misuse (deepfakes, misinformation)	Reputational and societal harm	Watermarking, content moderation, user consent, bias testing
Regulatory	Compliance with data privacy and industry laws	Legal and financial risks	GDPR, HIPAA, anonymization, audit logs, explainability tools
Operational	Model drift or performance decay	Reduced accuracy over time	Continuous monitoring, retraining pipelines, feedback loops

Figure 14.4: *Challenges in AI Model Deployments*

Beyond technical constraints, ethical challenges loom large. Generative models can be misused to create deepfakes or spread misinformation. Developers must embed safeguards such as invisible watermarks, content authenticity checks, and moderation systems. Ethical deployment also involves clear user consent, transparency, and training on diverse, unbiased data to avoid reinforcing stereotypes. For example, deploying a text-to-speech model in customer service should involve measures to prevent impersonation and inform users that they are interacting with AI.

Regulatory compliance is another critical dimension, especially in sensitive sectors such as healthcare or finance. Developers must align with data protection laws such as GDPR or CCPA, ensuring user consent and anonymized training data. Industry-specific standards such as HIPAA or FDA guidelines demand strict security and transparency in model usage. By navigating this complex terrain–technical, ethical, and legal–developers not only ensure safe and responsible deployments but also lay the foundation for trusted, scalable generative AI solutions.

Case Study: Deploying a StyleGAN Model for Image Generation

This case study examines the deployment of a StyleGAN model for generating high-resolution images. It explores the challenge of producing realistic images efficiently, the solution of training the model in TensorFlow or PyTorch, and the deployment strategy using a REST API with Docker and GPU acceleration. It also outlines the outcomes, such as scalable real-time image generation, and the challenges, including computational resource management, latency optimization, and maintaining image quality. This highlights the practical aspects of deploying generative AI in production environments.

Problem: Serving a StyleGAN Model for User-Generated Content on a Web Application

Generative models have transformed the way content is created and shared, enabling applications such as personalized avatars, artistic renderings, and product visualizations. However, deploying such models in a web application presents unique challenges, particularly when serving a StyleGAN model for real-time user-generated content.

The specific problem in this case study revolves around enabling users to generate high-quality, StyleGAN-based images directly from a web application. Users should be able to upload a set of preferences or input images and receive generated results within seconds. Ensuring a seamless user experience requires addressing key concerns such as latency, scalability, and model optimization for deployment.

Solution Approach: Optimizing the Model for Deployment and Integrating with an API

To meet the demands of the application, a comprehensive deployment strategy was implemented:

- **Model Optimization:** The pre-trained StyleGAN model was optimized for deployment by reducing its computational complexity without compromising output quality. Techniques such as model pruning and quantization were employed.
  - **Pruning:** Redundant connections in the neural network were eliminated, reducing the model size.
  - **Quantization:** We converted the model to use lower precision arithmetic (for example, INT8) to minimize computational load, particularly beneficial when deploying on CPUs or edge devices.
- **Infrastructure Setup:**
  - The optimized StyleGAN model was deployed on a cloud-based server using NVIDIA GPUs to leverage high-speed inference capabilities.
  - Docker containers were utilized to package the application for consistent deployment across different environments. This modular setup allowed for rapid updates and scaling.
- **API Integration:** A FastAPI-based backend was implemented to manage user requests. The workflow involved the following steps:
  - **User Input:** Users uploaded preferences or seed vectors through a web interface.
  - **Model Inference:** The API triggered the StyleGAN model for inference, generating images based on the input.

  - **Response Handling:** The generated images were returned as downloadable files or directly displayed on the web application.
- **Front-End Optimization:**
  - The web application was designed using React.js to provide a dynamic and responsive user experience.
  - Lazy loading techniques and asynchronous API calls were used to enhance performance, ensuring users did not experience noticeable delays during interactions.

Challenges: Reducing Latency and Ensuring Consistent Performance

Deploying a StyleGAN model introduced several challenges, which were tackled through innovative solutions:

- **Reducing Latency:**
  - **Batch Processing:** User requests were aggregated and processed in batches when possible, reducing overhead associated with frequent model loading and unloading.
  - **Caching:** Intermediate results, such as generated latent vectors, were cached to prevent redundant computations.
- **Ensuring Consistent Performance:**
  - **Load Balancing:** Traffic spikes were managed using a load balancer that distributed requests across multiple server instances.
  - **Autoscaling:** Cloud-based resources were configured to scale dynamically based on user demand, ensuring consistent performance during peak hours.
- **Managing Model Size and Dependencies:** The StyleGAN model required substantial memory and compute resources. A custom runtime environment was created, ensuring all dependencies were optimized for minimal resource usage. TensorRT was employed to further accelerate inference.
- **Monitoring and Maintenance:** Real-time monitoring tools such as Prometheus and Grafana were integrated to track system performance, enabling rapid identification and resolution of bottlenecks or failures.

Outcome: Insights into Deploying Generative Models for End-User Applications

The deployment of the StyleGAN model in a web application demonstrated the feasibility of serving high-quality, generative AI models to end-users. Key outcomes of the project included:

- **Enhanced User Engagement:** The application received overwhelmingly positive feedback for its ability to generate realistic, personalized images. This feature became a unique selling point, driving user engagement and retention.
- **Scalable and Reliable Architecture:** The optimized deployment pipeline ensured the system could handle thousands of concurrent users without significant latency or downtime.
- **Technical Learnings:**
  - The importance of model optimization for deployment was underscored, highlighting techniques such as pruning, quantization, and batch processing.
  - API design and integration played a crucial role in delivering a seamless user experience.

  - Real-time monitoring tools were invaluable for maintaining system health and preemptively addressing issues.
- **Future Directions:**
  - Incorporating user feedback, plans were made to enhance the model's functionality, including adding features such as image editing and multi-style blending.
  - Experimentation with edge deployment was initiated, aiming to bring StyleGAN's capabilities closer to users on devices such as smartphones and tablets.

This case study provides a blueprint for deploying generative AI models such as StyleGAN in real-world applications. It highlights the interplay between model optimization, infrastructure setup, API integration, and user-centric design in creating a scalable and efficient solution. By addressing challenges such as latency and performance, this project exemplifies how advanced AI models can be transformed into practical tools for end-users, paving the way for broader adoption of generative AI technologies.

Conclusion

In this chapter, we explored the end-to-end process of deploying generative models, covering key aspects such as model optimization, deployment platforms, API integration, inference optimization, and scaling strategies. Unlike traditional machine learning models, deploying generative models presents unique challenges due to their computational complexity, large model sizes, and real-time performance constraints.

We discussed various optimization techniques such as quantization, pruning, and model compression, which help in reducing the model footprint for deployment on edge devices, mobile platforms, and cloud services. The chapter also highlighted the importance of building scalable APIs and microservices, ensuring efficient inference with techniques such as batching, caching, and hardware acceleration, and monitoring model performance post-deployment.

Additionally, we covered deployment frameworks such as TensorFlow Serving, TorchServe, NVIDIA Triton, and best practices for using Docker, Kubernetes, and CI/CD pipelines to manage model updates efficiently. The case study on deploying a StyleGAN model provided practical insights into optimizing model performance, reducing latency, and handling deployment challenges in real-world applications.

By understanding the tools, workflows, and best practices for deploying generative models, you are now equipped to bring your AI-driven applications into production. In the next chapter, we will explore the ethical considerations and future directions of generative models, discussing challenges such as bias, misuse, regulatory concerns, and responsible AI practices for deploying these models at scale.

Points to Remember

- Deploying generative models presents unique challenges, including high computational costs, large model sizes, and real-time inference requirements.
- Optimization techniques such as quantization, pruning, and compression help reduce model size and improve efficiency for deployment on edge devices and mobile platforms.
- Generative models can be deployed using cloud services (AWS, Google Cloud, Azure), on-premises servers, or edge devices.
- APIs and microservices allow models to be integrated into applications using frameworks such as FastAPI and Flask.

- Inference optimization techniques such as batching, caching, and hardware acceleration enhance the performance of deployed models.
- Monitoring and maintenance are crucial to ensure model reliability, track performance, detect drift, and retrain models when necessary.
- Deployment frameworks such as TensorFlow Serving, TorchServe, and NVIDIA Triton streamline the process of serving generative models in production environments.

Multiple Choice Questions

1. What is the primary challenge of deploying generative models compared to traditional ML models?
    a. Higher computational and memory demands
    b. Smaller dataset requirements
    c. Lower latency requirements
    d. Simpler model architectures
2. Which technique helps reduce the size of a generative model for efficient deployment?
    a. Increasing the number of layers
    b. Data augmentation
    c. Quantization and pruning
    d. Increasing batch size
3. Which of the following is NOT a common deployment platform for generative models?
    a. Cloud services such as AWS and Google Cloud
    b. Edge devices such as Raspberry Pi and Jetson Nano
    c. On-premises servers
    d. Manual execution on a local Jupyter Notebook
4. What is the purpose of using TensorFlow Serving or TorchServe in model deployment?
    a. Enhancing model training speed
    b. Generating synthetic datasets
    c. Improving adversarial loss calculations
    d. Serving models efficiently as APIs in production

Answers

1. a
2. c
3. d
4. d

Questions

1. What are the major challenges in deploying generative models, and how do they differ from deploying traditional ML models?
2. How do quantization, pruning, and compression help in optimizing generative models for deployment?
3. What are the advantages and trade-offs of deploying generative models on cloud platforms versus edge devices?
4. How can inference optimization techniques such as batching, caching, and hardware acceleration improve model performance?
5. What role do APIs and microservices play in integrating generative models into real-world applications?
6. Why is monitoring deployed models crucial, and how can drift in generative outputs be detected and handled?
7. What are some real-world applications of generative models that require scalable deployment solutions?
8. How can deployment frameworks such as TensorFlow Serving, TorchServe, and NVIDIA Triton simplify the model serving process?
9. What are the key considerations when deploying generative models in resource-constrained environments?
10. What challenges arise when deploying generative models in applications where real-time inference is required?

Key Terms

- **Quantization:** A technique to reduce model size by lowering precision (for example, converting 32-bit floats to 8-bit integers).
- **Pruning:** Removing redundant weights from a model to optimize performance and reduce memory usage.
- **Compression:** Reducing the overall model footprint to enable deployment on low-resource devices.
- **Inference Optimization:** Techniques such as batching, caching, and hardware acceleration to speed up predictions.
- **Edge Deployment:** Running AI models on local devices such as **Raspberry Pi, Jetson Nano, and mobile hardware** instead of cloud servers.
- **APIs and Microservices:** Systems that expose generative models as RESTful or gRPC services for seamless integration into applications.
- **TensorFlow Serving/TorchServe:** Frameworks designed to efficiently serve deep learning models in production.
- **Kubernetes:** An orchestration tool for managing model deployment and scaling across cloud environments.
- **CI/CD Pipelines:** Automated workflows for continuously deploying and updating machine learning models.
- **Model Drift:** The degradation of model performance over time due to changes in data distributions.

CHAPTER 15
Ethical Considerations and Future Directions

Introduction

As generative models continue to revolutionize industries with their ability to create realistic images, text, video, and audio, they also raise significant ethical challenges and societal implications. The potential for misuse–ranging from deepfakes to biased outputs–underscores the importance of responsible development and deployment of these powerful tools. Generative models, while offering immense benefits, require thoughtful consideration of fairness, transparency, and accountability to ensure they contribute positively to society.

In this chapter, we delve into the ethical considerations surrounding generative models, exploring issues such as bias, misinformation, intellectual property concerns, and privacy risks. We discuss strategies to mitigate these challenges, including the adoption of fairness guidelines, dataset auditing, and transparency in AI design. Additionally, we look toward the future of generative AI, examining emerging trends, advancements in multimodal generation, and efforts to align AI with human values. By the end of this chapter, you will gain a deeper understanding of the ethical landscape in generative AI and be equipped to navigate the complexities of developing and deploying these models responsibly.

Structure

In this chapter, we will discuss the following topics:

- **Introduction to Ethics in Generative AI**
  - Importance of Responsible AI Development and Deployment
  - Balancing Innovation with Ethical Accountability
- **Ethical Challenges in Generative Models**
  - Bias in Training Data
  - Misuse of Generated Content
  - Copyright and Intellectual Property Issues
  - Privacy Concerns
- **Strategies for Ethical Implementation of Generative Models**
- **Ethical Frameworks and Guidelines**
  - Overview of AI Ethics Guidelines
  - Best Practices for Ethical AI Development and Deployment
  - Incorporating Human Oversight in Generative AI Systems

- **Evaluating the Ethical Impact of Generative Models**
  - Tools for Auditing Fairness, Bias, and Transparency in Models
  - Role of Interdisciplinary Collaboration in Ethical Evaluation
- **Future Directions in Generative AI**
- **Challenges in the Future of Generative AI**
- **Case Study: Responsible AI Implementation in Smart Glasses Project**

Introduction to Ethics in Generative AI

As generative AI continues to revolutionize industries, from creative arts to scientific research, the ethical considerations surrounding its development and deployment become increasingly critical. These models have the power to generate remarkably realistic content, but their potential for misuse, bias amplification, and unintended consequences raises important questions. Addressing these ethical challenges is not only a moral imperative but also essential for fostering public trust and sustainable innovation in the AI field.

Generative AI introduces unique ethical challenges that stem from its ability to create content indistinguishable from human-generated material. Key challenges include:

- **Deepfakes and Misinformation:** Generative models can produce deepfake videos, images, and audio clips that mimic real individuals. These can be weaponized to spread misinformation, disrupt elections, or damage reputations. Detecting such fabrications becomes increasingly difficult as the technology advances.
- **Bias and Stereotyping:** Generative models often inherit biases from their training data, leading to the perpetuation of stereotypes and systemic inequities. For example, a generative model might overrepresent certain demographic groups while underrepresenting others, reinforcing harmful societal narratives.
- **Intellectual Property Concerns:** The use of copyrighted materials in training data raises questions about intellectual property (IP) rights. Generative AI can inadvertently create content that closely resembles existing works, leading to disputes over originality and ownership.
- **Privacy Violations:** Models trained on publicly available data may inadvertently expose sensitive or personal information. This poses risks for individuals whose data was used without explicit consent.
- **Environmental Impact:** Training and deploying large generative models consume significant computational resources, contributing to carbon emissions. Balancing technological progress with environmental sustainability is a pressing challenge.
- **Unregulated Use:** The accessibility of powerful generative models to individuals and organizations without clear regulations can lead to unethical applications, such as creating harmful content or enabling malicious activities.

***Figure 15.1**: Ethical and Responsible AI Aspects in Generative AI*

Importance of Responsible AI Development and Deployment

Developing and deploying generative AI responsibly is paramount to ensuring that its benefits outweigh the risks. Responsible AI development includes:

- **Transparency and Explainability:** Developers must prioritize transparency by documenting how models are trained, the data used, and the intended applications. Explainability tools can help users understand model outputs, fostering trust and accountability.
- **Bias Mitigation:** Implementing techniques to detect and mitigate bias during model training is critical. This includes diversifying datasets, using fairness algorithms, and conducting thorough audits to identify potential disparities in model behavior.
- **User Awareness and Consent:** Organizations should educate users about the capabilities and limitations of generative AI systems. For example, platforms hosting generative AI tools should clearly label AI-generated content to prevent deception.
- **Ethical Guidelines and Governance:** Establishing comprehensive ethical guidelines and governance frameworks helps developers adhere to best practices. Regulatory bodies and organizations can collaborate to create standards that balance innovation with ethical accountability.
- **Sustainability Efforts:** Reducing the environmental footprint of generative AI is crucial. This can be achieved through energy-efficient training methods, model optimization, and investing in renewable energy sources for data centers.
- **Collaboration and Multidisciplinary Input:** Addressing ethical concerns requires collaboration among technologists, ethicists, policymakers, and sociologists. A multidisciplinary approach ensures that diverse perspectives are considered in decision-making.

Balancing Innovation with Ethical Accountability

While innovation drives progress, ethical accountability ensures that advancements are aligned with societal values. Striking this balance involves:

- **Innovation with Caution:** Organizations must innovate responsibly, recognizing the broader implications of their technologies. For instance, releasing powerful generative models should be accompanied by safeguards to prevent misuse.

- **Ethics by Design:** Incorporating ethical considerations into the design and development process from the outset helps preempt potential issues. This includes conducting ethical impact assessments and integrating feedback from diverse stakeholders.
- **Proactive Regulation:** Governments and regulatory bodies should work proactively to establish clear policies for generative AI. These policies should encourage innovation while setting boundaries to prevent harmful applications.
- **Public Engagement:** Engaging with the public to understand their concerns and expectations can guide the ethical deployment of generative AI. Transparency initiatives and open dialogue foster trust and accountability.
- **Continuous Monitoring and Iteration:** Ethical challenges evolve as generative AI advances. Continuous monitoring, coupled with iterative improvements, ensures that systems remain aligned with ethical standards.

Generative AI holds immense potential to transform society positively, but its ethical implications cannot be ignored. By addressing these challenges with a commitment to responsible development and deployment, we can harness the power of generative AI while safeguarding individual rights and societal values.

Ethical Challenges in Generative Models

The rapid advancement of generative models has opened up incredible opportunities across diverse domains, from art creation to data augmentation. However, this growth has brought ethical challenges that cannot be overlooked. These challenges span biases in training data, misuse of generated content, intellectual property issues, and privacy concerns, which require careful consideration and proactive solutions.

Bias in Training Data

Generative models rely heavily on the quality and diversity of their training data. If the datasets used for training are biased, the generated outputs will reflect and potentially amplify those biases.

- **Sources of Bias in Datasets:** Bias in datasets can originate from various sources. Historical data often carries the prejudices and inequalities of the society in which it was collected. For example, datasets used to train image generation models might lack diversity in race, gender, or age, leading to outputs that underrepresent certain groups or reinforce stereotypes. Similarly, text-based datasets may perpetuate biases inherent in the language, tone, and content of the material.
- **Impact on Fairness and Inclusivity of Generated Outputs:** When biased datasets are used, the generated outputs can lack fairness and inclusivity. For instance, a generative model trained on biased hiring data might create outputs that favor certain demographics while marginalizing others. These biases can perpetuate systemic inequalities and erode trust in AI systems. Addressing this challenge requires rigorous auditing of training data, balanced representation, and methods such as adversarial training to mitigate bias.

Misuse of Generated Content

Generative models have immense potential, but their capabilities also raise concerns about misuse. Malicious actors can exploit these technologies to produce harmful content with far-reaching consequences.

- **Deepfakes and the Spread of Misinformation:** One of the most notorious misuses of generative models is the creation of deepfakes—synthetic media that convincingly mimic real people's voices or appearances. These deepfakes can be weaponized for spreading misinformation, political propaganda, or personal attacks. The ease of creating such content challenges the integrity of information and undermines public trust.

- **Challenges in Detecting and Preventing Malicious Applications:** Detecting and mitigating the misuse of generative content is a persistent challenge. While detection tools have improved, they often lag behind increasingly sophisticated generative techniques. Developing robust detection algorithms, combined with legal and ethical guidelines, is crucial to preventing the malicious use of these models. Collaborative efforts between technologists, policymakers, and researchers are needed to establish accountability frameworks.

Copyright and Intellectual Property Issues

Generative models pose unique challenges in the realm of copyright and intellectual property. The ownership and use of generated content often blur legal and ethical lines.

- **Ownership of Generated Content:** Determining the ownership of AI-generated content is a complex issue. For instance, if a generative model creates a piece of art, who holds the copyright–the model's creator, the user who prompted the model, or no one at all? This ambiguity can lead to disputes, especially in commercial applications.
- **Legal Challenges in Training on Copyrighted Data:** Training generative models often involves using vast amounts of data, some of which may be copyrighted. The legality of this practice depends on jurisdiction, with varying interpretations of "fair use" and copyright exceptions. Lawsuits and controversies surrounding unauthorized use of copyrighted material highlight the need for clear regulations and transparent practices.

Privacy Concerns

Privacy is another critical issue in the ethical landscape of generative models. Sensitive data used during training or in real-world applications can expose individuals to risks.

- **Risks of Exposing Sensitive Data During Training:** Generative models trained on sensitive or personal data can inadvertently memorize and reproduce such information, posing significant privacy risks. For instance, a text generation model might reproduce private emails or confidential documents present in its training data. This raises concerns about the security of proprietary or personal information.
- **Protecting User Data in Real-World Applications:** Real-world applications of generative models often involve handling user data, such as personalized text generation or image synthesis. Ensuring robust data protection measures, including encryption, anonymization, and secure storage, is essential. Additionally, organizations must comply with data privacy regulations such as GDPR and CCPA to avoid legal and ethical violations.

Challenge	Ethical Risk	Examples	Mitigation Strategies
Bias in Training Data	Reinforces stereotypes and systemic inequalities	Underrepresentation of gender/race in generated images	Data auditing, balanced datasets, fairness metrics
Misuse of Generated Content	Misinformation and reputational harm	Deepfakes, fake news, voice impersonation	Detection algorithms, content watermarking, policy regulation
Intellectual Property	Copyright infringement, unclear ownership	Training on copyrighted images, music	Licensing frameworks, dataset transparency, model documentation
Privacy Concerns	Leakage of personal/sensitive data	Model reproduces private text or faces	Data anonymization, consent-based training, encryption compliance

***Figure 15.2**: Key Ethical Challenges in Generative AI*

While generative models hold transformative potential, their ethical implications must be addressed to ensure responsible usage. Mitigating bias, preventing misuse, resolving intellectual property disputes, and safeguarding privacy are crucial for building trustworthy AI systems. Researchers, developers, and policymakers must collaborate to create frameworks that balance innovation with accountability, paving the way for ethical and equitable generative technologies.

Strategies for Ethical Implementation of Generative Models

The rapid advancement of generative models has unlocked a world of possibilities, from creating realistic images to crafting natural-sounding text. However, with great power comes great responsibility. Ensuring ethical implementation of these models is not just a technical challenge but a societal necessity. In the following paragraphs, we explore key strategies for fostering ethical practices in the development and deployment of generative models.

Ensuring Fairness and Reducing Bias in Training Datasets

Generative models learn patterns and representations from the data they are trained on, making the choice of datasets a critical factor in their ethical deployment. If training datasets reflect societal biases, the models are likely to reproduce and amplify these biases, leading to unfair or discriminatory outcomes.

To ensure fairness:

- **Diverse Data Collection:** Use datasets that are representative of different demographics, geographic regions, and cultural backgrounds.
- **Bias Audits:** Regularly evaluate datasets for inherent biases using tools such as fairness metrics or algorithmic audits.
- **Data Preprocessing:** Apply preprocessing techniques such as re-weighting, resampling, or augmentation to mitigate identified biases.
- **Human Oversight:** Involve domain experts to review the data selection and labeling process, ensuring that diverse perspectives are accounted for.

Therefore, implementing these measures can help create generative models that produce equitable outcomes across various user groups.

Developing Detection Mechanisms for Harmful or Unethical Outputs

Generative models, while powerful, have the potential to produce harmful, misleading, or unethical outputs if not carefully monitored. This includes generating fake news, deepfakes, or offensive content. To address this risk, detection mechanisms must be integrated into the model lifecycle.

Key approaches include:

- **Content Filtering:** Implement post-processing steps to identify and block harmful outputs before they reach end users.
- **Ethical Benchmarks:** Develop specific evaluation criteria that measure the ethicality of generated outputs.
- **Adversarial Testing:** Simulate potential misuse scenarios to identify vulnerabilities and strengthen safeguards.

- **Feedback Loops:** Enable user reporting mechanisms that allow harmful outputs to be flagged and investigated.

Detection mechanisms not only minimize harm but also reinforce trust in generative AI systems among users and stakeholders.

Adhering to Legal and Regulatory Guidelines for AI Development

The development of generative models must align with existing laws and regulations to ensure compliance and accountability. This is particularly important in industries such as healthcare, finance, and defense, where ethical lapses can have severe consequences.

Strategies for legal adherence include:

- **Understanding Jurisdictional Laws:** Familiarize with local and international regulations governing AI development, such as GDPR for data protection or the EU AI Act for ethical AI deployment.
- **Data Privacy Measures:** Implement strict protocols for handling sensitive user data, ensuring that privacy rights are upheld.
- **Licensing and Attribution:** Respect intellectual property rights by attributing the sources of training data and obtaining necessary licenses where required.
- **Ethical AI Frameworks:** Adopt industry standards and frameworks, such as the IEEE Global Initiative on Ethics of Autonomous and Intelligent Systems, to guide development practices.

Thus, by adhering to these guidelines, organizations can mitigate legal risks and build generative models that align with societal norms and expectations.

Promoting Transparency and Explainability in Generative Models

Transparency and explainability are critical for fostering user trust and enabling accountability in generative AI systems. Black-box models, while effective, can lead to skepticism and reluctance among users and regulators.

Ways to promote transparency and explainability include:

- **Model Interpretability Tools:** Utilize tools such as SHAP (SHapley Additive exPlanations) or LIME (Local Interpretable Model-agnostic Explanations) to provide insights into model decisions.
- **Clear Documentation:** Maintain comprehensive documentation detailing model architecture, training data, and evaluation metrics.
- **Explainable Interfaces:** Design user interfaces that offer explanations for generated outputs, such as highlighting the key factors influencing the results.
- **Open Practices:** Share model code and training processes with the research community to encourage collaboration and scrutiny.

Transparency initiatives not only enhance user confidence but also pave the way for ethical advancements in AI technology.

Ethical implementation of generative models is a multifaceted challenge that requires collaboration across disciplines, from data scientists to policymakers. By ensuring fairness, detecting harmful outputs, adhering to legal standards, and promoting transparency, we can harness the transformative potential of generative AI while minimizing its risks. In doing so, we pave the way for AI systems that not only perform effectively but also align with societal values and ethical principles.

Ethical Frameworks and Guidelines

The rapid advancements in artificial intelligence (AI) bring unparalleled opportunities for innovation across various domains. However, the increasing complexity and pervasive influence of AI systems necessitate a robust ethical framework to ensure their responsible use. This chapter delves into essential ethical frameworks and guidelines, offering insights into the principles, best practices, and strategies for integrating ethics into the development and deployment of generative AI systems.

Overview of AI Ethics Guidelines

The global community recognizes the importance of ethical considerations in AI. Organizations and governments worldwide have introduced various guidelines and regulatory frameworks aimed at ensuring transparency, fairness, and accountability in AI systems. Prominent examples include:

- **EU AI Act:** The European Union's AI Act is a comprehensive regulatory framework designed to manage risks associated with AI technologies. It categorizes AI systems based on risk levels—ranging from minimal to high-risk applications—and enforces stringent requirements for high-risk systems. Key principles include human oversight, robustness, security, and privacy.
- **IEEE Standards:** The IEEE's Global Initiative on Ethics of Autonomous and Intelligent Systems focuses on fostering ethical AI by developing practical standards. Notable standards include IEEE 7010 (Assessing the Impact of AI on Human Well-Being) and IEEE 7001 (Transparency of Autonomous Systems). These guidelines emphasize ethical design, operational transparency, and the alignment of AI systems with human values.
- **UNESCO AI Ethics Recommendation:** UNESCO's framework emphasizes the need for inclusivity, sustainability, and the protection of human rights. It highlights the societal and environmental implications of AI and advocates for international cooperation in promoting ethical AI practices.
- **U.S. Blueprint for an AI Bill of Rights:** Published by the White House, this framework outlines five principles to protect individuals in the age of AI: safe and effective systems, protection from algorithmic discrimination, data privacy, user control, and transparency.

Best Practices for Ethical AI Development and Deployment

To align AI systems with ethical guidelines, developers and organizations must adopt best practices that foster trust and minimize harm. These practices include:

- **Transparency and Explainability:** Generative AI systems should operate transparently, with clear documentation and understandable decision-making processes. Explainability allows stakeholders to understand how models generate outputs, fostering trust and enabling accountability.
- **Bias Mitigation:** Addressing bias is critical for ensuring fairness. This involves curating diverse datasets, employing fairness-aware algorithms, and continuously monitoring models for unintended biases during deployment.
- **Privacy Preservation:** Ethical AI systems prioritize user privacy by implementing robust data protection measures such as encryption, anonymization, and federated learning. These practices ensure compliance with regulations such as GDPR and maintain user trust.

- **Robustness and Security:** AI models must be resilient against adversarial attacks and unexpected inputs. Employing rigorous testing protocols and maintaining up-to-date security measures are essential for safeguarding against vulnerabilities.
- **Stakeholder Engagement:** Engaging with diverse stakeholders, including ethicists, legal experts, and end-users, ensures that generative AI systems address societal needs and values. Participatory design approaches enhance inclusivity and reduce risks of ethical oversights.
- **Lifecycle Monitoring:** Ethical AI development does not end at deployment. Continuous monitoring and regular updates are necessary to adapt to evolving ethical standards, technological advancements, and societal expectations.

Incorporating Human Oversight in Generative AI Systems

Human oversight remains a cornerstone of ethical AI, especially in generative systems capable of producing complex and high-impact outputs. Integrating human oversight involves:

- **Human-in-the-Loop (HITL):** HITL frameworks ensure human involvement at critical stages of the AI lifecycle, such as model training, validation, and decision-making. For instance, moderators may review content generated by AI to prevent misinformation or harmful outputs.
- **Augmented Decision-Making:** Instead of replacing human judgment, generative AI systems can augment decision-making processes by providing insights, suggestions, or predictions. Human operators retain ultimate control, ensuring accountability and contextual awareness.
- **Ethical Review Boards:** Establishing dedicated boards to oversee AI development can help organizations proactively identify and address ethical concerns. These boards typically include ethicists, domain experts, and community representatives.
- **Transparency Tools:** Providing tools that enable end-users to understand AI outputs empowers them to make informed decisions. Examples include model explainability dashboards and provenance tracking for generated content.
- **Clear Escalation Pathways:** AI systems should have predefined mechanisms for escalating issues to human operators when uncertainties or ethical dilemmas arise. This ensures critical decisions are subjected to human judgment.

Case Study: Ethical Oversight in Content Generation

A practical example of ethical oversight can be seen in content moderation systems employed by social media platforms. These systems leverage generative AI models to detect and filter harmful content. However, final decisions–such as flagging or removing posts–are often made by human moderators. This approach balances efficiency with accountability, ensuring that nuanced or context-sensitive issues are addressed appropriately.

The Path Forward

As generative AI continues to transform industries, its ethical implications demand careful consideration. Developers, policymakers, and organizations must collaborate to establish and uphold ethical standards. By embracing transparency, fairness, and human oversight, we can unlock the full potential of generative AI while safeguarding societal values.

Evaluating the Ethical Impact of Generative Models

The rapid advancements in generative models have reshaped artificial intelligence, providing unprecedented capabilities in image synthesis, text generation, and more. However, these innovations also come with ethical challenges that need careful consideration. Evaluating the ethical impact of generative models ensures that their deployment aligns with societal values and minimizes harm. This chapter explores the frameworks, tools, and collaborative approaches essential for ethical evaluation in generative AI.

Tools for Auditing Fairness, Bias, and Transparency in Models

Technological tools are essential in operationalizing ethical principles and ensuring that generative models are fair, unbiased, and transparent. These tools assist in identifying and mitigating risks associated with the deployment of AI systems.

- **Fairness Auditing Tools:**
  - **AI Fairness 360**: Developed by IBM, this toolkit provides metrics to detect and mitigate bias in datasets and models. It supports various fairness definitions and offers algorithms to address identified issues.
  - **Fairlearn**: An open-source tool by Microsoft, Fairlearn helps quantify and reduce disparities in AI model performance across demographic groups.
- **Bias Detection Tools:**
  - **Facets**: Google's Facets is a visualization tool that helps in exploring and understanding datasets. By identifying imbalances or outliers in the data, it ensures the training data's representativeness.
  - **What-If Tool**: Integrated with TensorBoard, this tool allows users to experiment with models and visualize how changes in inputs affect predictions. It helps uncover biases embedded in models.
- **Transparency and Explainability Tools:**
  - **LIME (Local Interpretable Model-agnostic Explanations)**: LIME provides interpretable explanations for model predictions, making it easier to understand how generative models produce outputs.
  - **SHAP (SHapley Additive exPlanations)**: SHAP explains the output of machine learning models by attributing the contribution of each feature to the prediction. This is particularly useful for complex models such as GANs or VAEs.
- **Ethical Risk Mitigation Platforms**: Platforms such as HolisticAI and Weights & Biases provide end-to-end solutions for monitoring, auditing, and managing AI models to ensure ethical compliance throughout their lifecycle.

Using these tools, developers and organizations can systematically address ethical concerns and build trust in generative AI systems.

Role of Interdisciplinary Collaboration in Ethical Evaluation

Addressing ethical challenges in generative AI requires input from multiple disciplines. Ethical evaluation is not merely a technical exercise; it involves understanding societal, cultural, and philosophical dimensions.

- **Diversity in Expertise:**
  - Collaboration between data scientists, ethicists, sociologists, and legal experts enriches

the evaluation process. For example, ethicists can identify potential moral dilemmas, while sociologists provide insights into societal impact.

- Industry-academia partnerships often foster innovative solutions by combining theoretical rigor with practical experience.

- **Stakeholder Involvement:**
  - Ethical evaluations must include feedback from end-users and affected communities. Engaging stakeholders ensures that diverse perspectives are considered and that ethical blind spots are minimized.
  - For instance, when designing generative models for healthcare applications, consultations with medical professionals and patient advocacy groups are critical.
- **Policy and Regulatory Guidance**: Collaboration with policymakers and regulators ensures compliance with laws and guidelines. For example, the European Union's AI Act provides specific requirements for high-risk AI systems, which can guide the ethical evaluation of generative models.
- **Interdisciplinary Training**: Building cross-disciplinary teams equipped with ethical training can enhance the understanding and resolution of ethical issues. Training programs can include workshops on responsible AI, bias detection, and legal compliance.

Interdisciplinary collaboration fosters a holistic approach to ethical evaluation, ensuring that generative models are not only technically sound but also socially responsible.

As generative models continue to transform industries, evaluating their ethical impact becomes an essential responsibility. Frameworks provide structured guidance, tools enable the practical application of ethical principles, and interdisciplinary collaboration ensures diverse perspectives are accounted for. By embracing these approaches, the AI community can harness the power of generative models responsibly and equitably, contributing to a more inclusive and trustworthy AI ecosystem.

Future Directions in Generative AI

Generative AI has evolved at an extraordinary pace over the past decade, driving innovation across industries from healthcare to entertainment. As we look to the future, the development of generative models promises even greater breakthroughs, particularly in terms of their quality, efficiency, interpretability, and alignment with human values. This chapter explores key areas where generative AI is expected to advance, highlighting the trends and challenges that will shape its trajectory in the coming years.

Advancements in Generative Model Architectures: Toward Higher Quality and Efficiency

The architectural foundations of generative models have undergone a significant transformation, from basic autoencoders and GANs to cutting-edge transformers and diffusion models. Future advancements will likely focus on:

- **Efficient Training Techniques**: Current generative models require vast computational resources, often limiting accessibility. Future research aims to optimize training algorithms, reduce hardware dependency, and enhance model scalability without compromising performance.
- **Enhanced Data Utilization**: Semi-supervised and unsupervised learning approaches will gain prominence, enabling models to learn from minimal labeled data. This is especially critical in domains with scarce or sensitive datasets, such as medical imaging.
- **Increased Resolution and Fidelity**: Models such as StyleGAN3 and advanced diffusion models

have set benchmarks for high-quality image generation. Future developments will push boundaries to achieve near-photorealistic outputs for diverse modalities, including video synthesis.

- **Real-Time Applications**: Efficient architectures will pave the way for real-time generative applications, such as live content generation in Virtual Reality (VR) and Augmented Reality (AR), enabling seamless user experiences.

Trends in Multimodal Generative Models Combining Text, Image, and Audio

Generative AI is increasingly moving toward multimodal capabilities, where models integrate information across different data types. This trend represents a leap toward creating AI systems that understand and generate content in a human-like manner.

- **Unified Multimodal Architectures**: Future models will seamlessly combine modalities such as text, image, audio, and video within a single framework. Projects such as DALL-E and CLIP have laid the groundwork, and next-generation models will refine this integration for more cohesive outputs.
- **Cross-Modal Understanding**: These models will improve in their ability to infer relationships between modalities, such as generating detailed visualizations from textual prompts or synthesizing music that complements a given video.
- **Accessibility and Personalization**: Multimodal generative models will drive personalized applications, such as creating custom audiobooks with user-selected voice tones or generating adaptive visuals based on user preferences.
- **Interactive AI Systems**: The convergence of multimodal AI with conversational agents will result in interactive systems capable of holding context-rich, dynamic interactions across various modalities. This will revolutionize areas such as education, gaming, and healthcare.

Increasing Interpretability and Control in Generative Models

A longstanding challenge in generative AI is the opacity of its decision-making processes. Addressing this issue is critical for building trust and ensuring responsible use of generative technologies.

- **Explainable Generative AI**: Techniques such as attention visualization and latent space disentanglement will improve interpretability, allowing users to understand how specific outputs are generated.
- **Fine-Grained Control**: Models will offer users greater control over the generation process, enabling adjustments in style, tone, or content attributes. For instance, users could specify the artistic style of generated images or the sentiment of generated text.
- **Ethical Safeguards**: Incorporating interpretability into generative AI systems will help mitigate risks of misuse, such as generating deceptive content, by enabling robust validation mechanisms.

Research on Aligning Generative Models with Human Values and Intentions

Ensuring that generative AI aligns with human values and intentions is paramount for its ethical and societal acceptance. Future research will delve deeper into:

- **Bias Mitigation**: Models will undergo rigorous training to identify and eliminate biases in their outputs, ensuring fairness and inclusivity across different demographic groups.

- **Alignment Mechanisms**: Techniques such as Reinforcement Learning with Human Feedback (RLHF) will be further refined to ensure that AI-generated content aligns with the user's intended goals and ethical considerations.
- **Value-Sensitive Design**: Future frameworks will integrate societal values into the design of generative AI systems, ensuring that they prioritize human welfare and environmental sustainability.
- **Regulatory Compliance**: As generative models impact sensitive domains such as finance and law, compliance with global regulations will become an integral aspect of AI development. This will involve collaboration between researchers, policymakers, and industry stakeholders.

Generative AI stands on the brink of transformative advancements that promise to redefine how we interact with technology. As we progress, the focus will shift toward creating models that are not only more powerful but also more accessible, interpretable, and aligned with human needs. By addressing challenges such as bias, resource inefficiency, and lack of control, generative AI will unlock unprecedented possibilities across industries, fostering a future where AI systems work seamlessly with humans to achieve shared goals.

Challenges in the Future of Generative AI

As generative AI reshapes industries from medicine to media, its rapid evolution brings a cascade of challenges. Scaling these models comes at a cost–training massive architectures such as GPT-4 demands extraordinary computational power, specialized hardware, and energy-intensive infrastructure. This not only limits access but also raises environmental concerns and strains global energy resources. Simultaneously, the need for vast, diverse datasets introduces privacy and security risks. Solutions such as algorithmic efficiency, model compression, distributed training, and renewable energy are emerging, but a sustainable future demands their widespread adoption.

Beyond technical hurdles, societal risks are mounting. AI-generated misinformation threatens to blur reality, while automation sparks fears of job displacement. If left unchecked, generative AI could erode cultural diversity, replacing authentic human expression with homogenized machine output. Combating this requires more than clever code–it needs robust content verification tools, inclusive training datasets, policies that anticipate abuse, and large-scale educational efforts to equip people for a shifting job landscape. Regulation and public engagement are crucial to steer this transformative power toward collective benefit.

Perhaps, the most profound challenge lies in AI's emergent behaviors–unexpected reasoning, autonomy, or self-improvement–raising ethical dilemmas no one fully anticipated. When an AI system makes a harmful decision, who bears the blame? Bias in training data can amplify inequality, while opaque decision-making undermines trust. To counter this, developers must adopt ethical frameworks, enforce bias audits, prioritize transparency, and build human-in-the-loop systems. The path forward is not easy, but with shared responsibility, we can shape generative AI into a tool that amplifies human potential rather than replacing it.

Case Study: Responsible AI Implementation in Smart Glasses Project

The advent of AI-powered smart glasses has opened new possibilities for empowering visually impaired individuals, providing them with tools to navigate the world with greater independence. However, implementing such innovative solutions necessitates careful consideration of ethical challenges to ensure the technology benefits users without compromising privacy, safety, or inclusivity.

Problem

The visually impaired community faces significant barriers in everyday life, ranging from reading printed materials and recognizing currency to identifying objects, faces, and environmental obstacles. While traditional assistive devices address some of these needs, they often lack real-time capabilities and context-aware functionality. AI smart glasses aim to fill this gap, but their implementation raises ethical concerns. These include safeguarding user data, avoiding biases in detection algorithms, ensuring accessibility, and maintaining compliance with diverse regulatory standards.

Solution Approach: Developing Detection Algorithms and Ethical Guidelines

To address these challenges, a comprehensive solution was designed, encompassing both technological and ethical dimensions:

- **Advanced Detection Algorithms:**
    - **Object Detection**: The smart glasses incorporate state-of-the-art models such as YOLOv8 or EfficientDet, optimized for on-device inference to identify objects, text, and obstacles in real time.
    - **Face Recognition**: AI algorithms enable face detection and recognition while ensuring consent mechanisms are integrated to respect privacy.
    - **Currency Identification**: Trained models classify denominations of currencies, supporting users in financial transactions.
- **Ethical Guidelines:**
    - **Privacy by Design**: Implementing local data processing on the device to minimize reliance on cloud-based services, thereby reducing exposure to potential data breaches.
    - **Bias Mitigation**: Regular audits of training datasets to ensure inclusivity, avoiding biases related to ethnicity, gender, or environmental conditions.
    - **Transparency and Consent**: Developing features that seek explicit user consent for functionalities such as face recognition, ensuring the technology is not invasive.
    - **User-Centric Design**: Engaging visually impaired individuals throughout the development process to align the product with their needs and preferences.

Challenges: Balancing Innovation with Compliance

The development and deployment of AI smart glasses for the visually impaired posed several challenges:

- **Regulatory Compliance:**
    - Navigating privacy laws such as GDPR in Europe and similar frameworks in other regions requires a robust framework for data handling and user consent.
    - Ensuring adherence to accessibility standards, such as WCAG, to provide equitable experiences for all users.
- **Technological Hurdles:**
    - Achieving high performance for detection algorithms on lightweight, wearable devices without compromising accuracy or speed.
    - Managing edge-case scenarios such as poorly lit environments, occluded objects, or diverse currency designs.

- **Ethical Considerations:**
  - Balancing innovation with user trust, particularly in features such as face recognition, which can potentially be misused.
  - Addressing the digital divide to ensure the solution remains affordable and accessible for a wider demographic.

Outcome: Insights into Addressing Ethical Risks While Leveraging Generative Potential

The project yielded valuable lessons and impactful outcomes:

- **Ethical Deployment Framework:**
  - Developed a set of actionable ethical principles tailored for AI applications in assistive technologies, emphasizing transparency, inclusivity, and accountability.
  - Established partnerships with regulators and advocacy groups to ensure alignment with societal expectations and legal standards.
- **Innovative Product Design:**
  - Created AI-powered smart glasses that seamlessly combine functionality and ethical considerations, offering real-time object detection, obstacle avoidance, and contextual audio feedback.
  - Reduced the device's reliance on internet connectivity, enhancing user privacy and operational reliability in low-connectivity regions.
- **Empowering the Visually Impaired:**
  - Enabled users to perform tasks such as reading signs, identifying faces, and navigating unfamiliar spaces independently, fostering inclusivity and societal participation.
  - Received positive feedback from pilot users, highlighting the importance of a user-centric approach in technology development.

This case study underscores the importance of ethical foresight in developing AI technologies. While innovation drives progress, ensuring trust and inclusivity paves the way for transformative, sustainable impacts on society.

Summary and Call to Action

Generative AI stands as a transformative force in technology, reshaping industries and redefining creativity. As we conclude this journey through the intricate world of generative models, it is crucial to reflect on the ethical challenges, future opportunities, and the role we all play in shaping a responsible AI-driven world.

Summary of Key Ethical Challenges and Future Opportunities

The rise of generative AI has brought unparalleled potential to innovate across various domains, from healthcare and education to art and entertainment. However, this rapid advancement has also introduced significant ethical dilemmas. Among these are the risks of misinformation, bias amplification, and the misuse of AI for malicious purposes. Generative models, for instance, can create highly realistic synthetic content that blurs the line between reality and fabrication, raising concerns about deepfakes and their societal implications.

Another pressing ethical issue is the environmental cost of training large-scale models. Generative AI often relies on computationally expensive processes, resulting in substantial energy consumption. Striking a balance between innovation and sustainability remains a critical challenge for the AI community.

Despite these challenges, the future of generative AI holds immense promise. Applications such as personalized medicine, adaptive learning systems, and creative collaboration tools have the potential to revolutionize how we live and work. The emergence of tools such as GPT, StyleGAN, and diffusion models demonstrates that generative AI can empower individuals and industries to achieve remarkable outcomes. By focusing on transparency, inclusivity, and ethical development, we can unlock these opportunities responsibly.

Importance of Interdisciplinary Efforts in Shaping the Future of Generative AI

The complexity of generative AI requires a collaborative approach that spans multiple disciplines. Developers, researchers, ethicists, policymakers, and end-users must work together to ensure AI technologies are designed and deployed responsibly. For example, incorporating insights from sociology and psychology can help address the societal impacts of AI, while contributions from environmental scientists can guide sustainable AI practices.

Interdisciplinary efforts can also foster innovation by integrating diverse perspectives. The development of generative AI tools that cater to underrepresented languages and cultures is a testament to how inclusivity enriches technological progress. Furthermore, partnerships between academia, industry, and government can establish robust frameworks for AI governance, ensuring accountability and fairness in the deployment of generative technologies.

Encouraging Readers to Adopt Responsible AI Practices

As pioneers, enthusiasts, and stakeholders in the AI landscape, each of us holds the power to influence its trajectory. By adopting responsible AI practices, we can mitigate risks and amplify the benefits of generative AI. Here are a few actionable steps for readers:

- **Prioritize Ethical Design:** Incorporate fairness, transparency, and accountability into AI models from the outset. Utilize tools and frameworks that help detect and mitigate biases.
- **Advocate for Sustainability:** Opt for energy-efficient algorithms, explore model compression techniques, and support initiatives aimed at reducing the environmental impact of AI.
- **Foster Public Awareness:** Educate end-users about the capabilities and limitations of generative AI. Transparent communication can help build trust and demystify the technology.
- **Engage in Continuous Learning:** Stay informed about the evolving landscape of AI ethics, standards, and best practices. Actively participate in discussions and communities focused on responsible AI.
- **Collaborate across Disciplines:** Work with professionals from diverse fields to address complex challenges and create holistic solutions.

A Vision for the Future

Imagine a world where generative AI harmonizes with human creativity, enabling solutions to global challenges while upholding ethical values. This vision is achievable if we collectively commit to responsibility and inclusivity. By leveraging the insights gained in this book and applying them thoughtfully, readers can contribute to a future where AI enhances lives while respecting humanity's core principles.

In closing, generative AI is not just a technological advancement; it is a testament to human ingenuity. Let us harness its power wisely, ensuring that it becomes a force for good. Whether you are an AI researcher, developer, or enthusiast, your role in this journey is invaluable. Together, we can shape a future where generative AI serves as a tool for progress, equity, and creativity.

Call to Action

The journey does not end here. Continue exploring, questioning, and innovating. Share your knowledge, engage with the community, and lead by example. Let us build an AI-driven world that reflects the best of humanity–a world where technology and ethics coexist seamlessly.

The future of generative AI is in your hands. Make it count.

Conclusion

In this chapter, we explored the ethical challenges and responsibilities surrounding generative AI. As these models continue to advance, their potential for bias, misuse, privacy risks, and legal concerns must be carefully addressed. We examined issues such as biased training data, deepfakes, intellectual property concerns, and privacy violations, along with strategies to promote fairness, transparency, and accountability in AI development. Additionally, we discussed ethical frameworks, regulatory guidelines, and evaluation methodologies that can help ensure responsible AI deployment.

Looking ahead, the future of generative AI presents both exciting opportunities and pressing challenges. While advancements in model architectures, multimodal learning, and interpretability are improving AI's capabilities, concerns around scalability, societal impact, and emergent ethical dilemmas remain critical areas of focus. By fostering interdisciplinary collaboration, regulatory alignment, and responsible innovation, we can ensure that generative AI technologies align with human values and ethical principles.

With this foundational understanding of AI ethics, you are now better equipped to develop and deploy generative models responsibly. In the next chapter, we will explore Large Language Models (LLMs), diving into their architecture, capabilities, and impact on the field of artificial intelligence.

Points to Remember

- Ethical considerations in generative AI include bias, misuse, copyright concerns, and privacy risks.
- Bias in training data can lead to unfair or discriminatory outputs, affecting inclusivity and representation.
- Deepfake technology and misinformation pose significant societal risks, requiring effective detection and regulation.
- Intellectual property issues arise when AI is trained on copyrighted content, leading to legal and ownership disputes.
- Privacy concerns must be addressed by ensuring user data protection during model training and deployment.
- Ethical AI development involves bias mitigation, regulatory compliance, transparency, and explainability.
- Future advancements in generative AI will focus on interpretability, multimodal capabilities, and ethical alignment.

Multiple Choice Questions

1. What is one of the primary ethical challenges in generative AI?
    a. Model efficiency
    b. Training dataset size
    c. Bias and fairness in generated outputs
    d. Speed of content generation
2. Why is bias in training data a critical issue in generative AI?
    a. It increases model accuracy.
    b. It can lead to unfair and discriminatory outputs.
    c. It improves generalization across domains.
    d. It ensures more diverse content generation.
3. What is a major risk associated with deepfake technology?
    a. Misinformation and identity fraud
    b. Increased training time
    c. Lack of available datasets
    d. Higher computational costs
4. What role do AI ethics guidelines play in generative model development?
    a. They define the model architecture.
    b. They ensure responsible AI deployment.
    c. They increase training speed.
    d. They improve GPU efficiency.
5. Which strategy helps in mitigating bias in generative AI models?
    a. Using smaller datasets
    b. Ignoring data augmentation
    c. Ensuring diverse and representative training data
    d. Removing fairness constraints from the model

Answers

1. c
2. b
3. a
4. b
5. c

Questions

1. What are the major ethical risks associated with generative AI, and how can they be mitigated?
2. How can AI developers reduce bias in generative models while maintaining performance?
3. What are some legal challenges related to AI-generated content, and how can they be addressed?
4. How do privacy concerns impact the adoption of generative AI in industries such as healthcare and finance?
5. What role do regulatory frameworks play in ensuring ethical AI development?
6. How can generative AI models be designed to balance innovation and ethical accountability?
7. What are the societal risks posed by deepfake technology, and how can they be minimized?
8. Why is transparency important in generative AI, and what techniques can enhance explainability?
9. How can interdisciplinary collaboration improve the ethical implementation of AI models?
10. What future advancements in generative AI could help address current ethical concerns?

Key Terms

- **Bias in AI**: The presence of systematic errors in model outputs due to skewed or unbalanced training data.
- **Deepfake**: AI-generated synthetic media used for face-swapping, often raising concerns about misinformation and identity fraud.
- **Intellectual Property in AI**: Legal challenges surrounding ownership of AI-generated content and the use of copyrighted materials in training data.
- **Privacy in AI**: Ensuring that user data remains protected and anonymized during training and inference.
- **Transparency and Explainability**: Techniques that allow AI models to provide interpretable and understandable decisions.
- **Regulatory Compliance**: Adherence to laws and guidelines governing AI ethics, such as the **EU AI Act** and **IEEE standards**.
- **Fairness in AI**: Strategies to ensure that generative models do not reinforce discrimination or societal biases.
- **Multimodal Generative Models**: AI models that combine text, image, and audio generation for richer outputs.
- **AI Safety**: Research efforts focused on aligning AI behavior with human values to prevent harmful or unintended consequences.
- **Future AI Research**: Ongoing studies in improving **scalability, interpretability,** and **ethical alignment** of generative models.

CHAPTER 16
Introduction to Large Language Models

Introduction

Large Language Models (LLMs) have revolutionized natural language processing by achieving unprecedented levels of fluency, coherence, and understanding in tasks ranging from text generation to translation and summarization. Built upon advanced mathematical and computational principles, these models leverage vast amounts of data and state-of-the-art architectures to analyze and generate human-like language. By scaling up parameters, training on massive datasets, and employing innovative techniques such as attention mechanisms, LLMs have set new benchmarks across industries.

In this chapter, we explore the evolution, architecture, and capabilities of LLMs, from foundational models to cutting-edge advancements. We will delve into their underlying principles, including pre-training, fine-tuning, and the mechanics of attention, which enable these models to capture intricate language patterns. Practical examples will demonstrate how LLMs can be fine-tuned and applied to real-world tasks. By the end of this chapter, you will have a comprehensive understanding of LLMs, their strengths, and how to leverage them for a wide array of natural language processing applications.

Structure

In this chapter, we will cover the following topics:

- **Introduction to Large Language Models (LLMs)**
  - Evolution from Traditional NLP Models to Modern LLMs
  - Applications of LLMs across Industries
- **Key Concepts Behind LLMs**
  - Understanding Pre-Training and Fine-Tuning in LLMs
  - Tokenization Techniques: Subword Units, BPE, and SentencePiece
  - Attention Mechanisms and Their Role in LLMs
- **Evolution of Language Models**
  - From n-grams to RNNs and Transformers
  - Key Milestones in the Evolution of LLMs
  - How LLMs Differ from Earlier Models in Terms of Scale and Capability
- **Architecture of LLMs**
  - Overview of the Transformer Architecture
  - Encoder versus Decoder Structures in LLMs
  - Importance of Scaling: Parameters, Training Data, and Compute Power

- **Training LLMs**
    - Pre-Training Objectives: Masked Language Modeling, Causal Language Modeling
    - Fine-Tuning for Specific Tasks: Transfer Learning in LLMs
    - Challenges in Training Large-Scale Models: Data, Compute, and Optimization
- **Applications of Large Language Models**
    - **Text Generation**: Storytelling, Content Creation, and Chatbots
    - **Summarization**: Extractive and Abstractive Approaches
    - **Machine Translation**: Real-Time and High-Accuracy Translation Systems
    - **Code Generation**: Assisting Developers with Coding and Debugging
    - **Other Applications**: Sentiment Analysis, Question Answering, and Knowledge Extraction
- **Evaluating Large Language Models**
    - **Metrics for LLM Evaluation**: Perplexity, BLEU, ROUGE, and Accuracy
    - **Human Evaluation**: Measuring Coherence, Relevance, and Fluency
    - Addressing Biases and Limitations in LLM-Generated Content
- **Challenges and Limitations of LLMs**
    - **Ethical Concerns**: Bias, Misinformation, and Hallucinations
    - High Computational Requirements and Environmental Impact
    - Challenges in Handling Multilingual and Low-Resource Languages
- **Implementing and Using LLMs**
    - **Accessing Pre-Trained Models**: OpenAI, Hugging Face, and Other Frameworks
    - Fine-Tuning LLMS for Domain-Specific Tasks
    - Practical Examples Using TensorFlow, PyTorch, or APIs
- **Case Study: Fine-Tuning BERT for a Specific Task**
- **Future Directions in Large Language Models**

Introduction to Large Language Models (LLMs)

In recent years, Artificial Intelligence has been transformed by the rise of Large Language Models (LLMs) – systems capable of understanding and generating human-like text with unprecedented fluency. These models have redefined natural language processing (NLP), enabling applications that range from conversational assistants to creative writing and automated reasoning.

LLMs are deep neural networks trained on massive text corpora to learn language patterns, context, and relationships. Unlike earlier NLP systems, which were designed for narrow, task-specific purposes, LLMs are highly generalized – allowing a single model to perform multiple tasks such as summarization, translation, and question answering.

Their impact is visible across research and industry alike, with leading organizations such as OpenAI, Google, and Metadeveloping landmark models such as GPT, BERT, and PaLM. Each has demonstrated new levels of linguistic competence and adaptability.

This chapter explores the foundations, evolution, architectures, training methods, applications, and challenges of large language models. It provides the conceptual groundwork for understanding the next chapter, which focuses specifically on the Generative Pre-trained Transformer (GPT) – one of the most influential LLM families to date.

Evolution from Traditional NLP Models to Modern LLMs

The journey from traditional NLP models to modern LLMs has been marked by significant technological advancements. Early NLP systems relied on rule-based approaches and statistical models, which required extensive feature engineering and lacked generalization capabilities. These systems often struggled with complex tasks due to their limited understanding of language structure and context.

The introduction of neural networks, particularly Recurrent Neural Networks (RNNs) and Long Short-Term Memory networks (LSTMs), brought a new wave of progress. These models could capture sequential dependencies in text, enabling better performance on tasks such as language modeling and sentiment analysis. However, they still faced challenges with long-term dependencies and scalability.

The game-changer came with the development of the Transformer architecture in 2017. By replacing recurrence with an attention-based mechanism, Transformers could process entire sequences in parallel and model long-distance dependencies more effectively. This innovation unlocked the potential for large-scale pretraining on massive text corpora, giving rise to models such as BERT and GPT, which demonstrated how general language knowledge could be transferred across diverse tasks through fine-tuning.

Today, LLMs have scaled to unprecedented levels, with models containing billions or even trillions of parameters. This scale enables them to learn intricate patterns in language, perform zero-shot and few-shot learning, and generalize across domains with minimal additional training.

Applications of LLMs across Industries

Large Language Models have found applications in virtually every industry, transforming the way organizations operate and innovate. Below are some notable use cases across different sectors:

- **Healthcare:** In the medical field, LLMs assist in analyzing patient records, generating clinical summaries, and even providing diagnostic support. LLMs are used to create conversational agents for patient interaction, improving accessibility to medical advice and reducing the workload on healthcare professionals.
- **Education:** In education, LLMs power intelligent tutoring systems that offer personalized learning experiences. They can generate explanations, summarize study material, and even assist in language learning by providing real-time feedback. Tools such as Duolingo have integrated LLMs to enhance user engagement.
- **Customer Support:** LLMs are widely used to build chatbots and virtual assistants that provide efficient and accurate customer support. These systems can handle queries, process complaints, and guide users through troubleshooting, significantly reducing response times and operational costs for businesses.
- **Content Creation:** From drafting articles and reports to generating creative content such as poetry and scripts, LLMs have become invaluable tools for content creators. Platforms such as Jasper and Copy.ai utilize these models to assist marketers and writers in producing high-quality content efficiently.
- **Finance:** In the financial sector, LLMs analyze market trends, generate financial reports, and detect fraudulent activities. They are also used in algorithmic trading to process large volumes of textual data, such as news articles and analyst reports, to inform investment decisions.
- **Legal Industry:** Law firms use LLMs to analyze legal documents, extract key information, and assist with drafting contracts. This reduces the time spent on routine tasks, allowing legal professionals to focus on more complex matters.

- **Entertainment:** LLMs contribute to the entertainment industry by generating scripts, creating dialogue for video games, and even composing music lyrics. They enhance storytelling by providing ideas and suggestions that align with creative goals.
- **Scientific Research:** Researchers use LLMs to generate literature reviews, analyze research papers, and even draft grant proposals. These models facilitate faster knowledge discovery and dissemination, accelerating scientific progress.

As LLMs continue to evolve, their applications will expand further, unlocking new possibilities and reshaping industries in ways we are only beginning to imagine. The following sections of this chapter will delve deeper into the technical foundations of LLMs, their architectures, and the challenges and ethical considerations associated with their use.

Key Concepts Behind LLMs

Large Language Models (LLMs) represent a significant milestone in the field of artificial intelligence and natural language processing (NLP). These models have revolutionized the way machines understand and generate human language by leveraging massive datasets and advanced architectures. At their core, LLMs are built on foundational concepts such as pre-training, fine-tuning, tokenization, and attention mechanisms, each playing a vital role in their remarkable capabilities. Let us dive into these key concepts to gain a deeper understanding of how LLMs work.

Understanding Pre-Training and Fine-Tuning in LLMs

Pre-training is the first phase in the development of an LLM. During this stage, the model is exposed to a vast corpus of text data, often encompassing books, articles, websites, and other textual sources. The goal is to teach the model to predict the next word in a sequence (language modeling) or fill in missing words (masked language modeling). This process enables the model to learn:

- **Linguistic Structures:** Understanding grammar, syntax, and semantic relationships between words.
- **World Knowledge:** Absorbing factual information and contextual relationships from the training data.
- **Token Representations:** Encoding textual data into dense, meaningful vectors that capture context.

For example, in causal-language modeling, pre-training involves autoregressive modeling where the task is to predict the next word in a sequence based on previous words. In contrast, masked language models such as BERT, where certain words in a sentence are masked, the model is trained to predict based on the context provided by unmasked words.

Fine-tuning follows pre-training and tailors the model for specific tasks, such as sentiment analysis, machine translation, or question answering. During fine-tuning, the pre-trained model is updated using task-specific datasets, often much smaller than the pre-training corpus. Fine-tuning allows the model to:

- Adapt its general knowledge to specialized domains.
- Optimize for task-specific metrics such as accuracy or F1 score.
- Learn nuances specific to the target dataset, improving performance on the given task.

An important benefit of this two-stage training process is the reusability of pre-trained models across various domains, reducing computational costs and improving efficiency.

Tokenization Techniques: Subword Units, BPE, and SentencePiece

Tokenization is the process of breaking down text into smaller units, called tokens, which are then input into the model. LLMs rely on advanced tokenization techniques to handle the diverse and complex nature of human languages.

Subword Units

Subword tokenization strikes a balance between word-level and character-level tokenization. Instead of splitting text into full words or individual characters, subword tokenization divides text into meaningful units such as prefixes, suffixes, or root words. This method is especially effective for:

- Handling rare or unseen words by breaking them into familiar components.
- Reducing the vocabulary size while retaining the ability to encode complex language patterns.

Byte Pair Encoding (BPE)

BPE is a widely used tokenization algorithm in LLMs. It starts by treating each character as a token and iteratively merging the most frequent pairs of tokens to form subword units. This approach offers several advantages:

- Combines frequently co-occurring characters or words to create meaningful tokens.
- Balances vocabulary size and representation power, enabling efficient training.

For instance, the word "*unbelievable*" may be tokenized into subword units such as "*un*," "*believ*," and "*able*." This allows the model to understand and generate words it has not explicitly encountered during training.

SentencePiece: SentencePiece is another popular tokenization technique, often used in models such as BERT. It treats text as a sequence of Unicode characters and applies algorithms such as unigram language modeling or BPE to tokenize the text. Key benefits include:

- Language-agnostic design, suitable for multilingual models.
- Ability to handle input without requiring spaces between words (useful for languages such as Chinese or Japanese).

SentencePiece also introduces flexibility by allowing the user to define the desired vocabulary size, making it adaptable to various computational and linguistic requirements.

Attention Mechanisms and Their Role in LLMs

Attention mechanisms are the cornerstone of modern LLM architectures, such as the Transformer model. Introduced in the seminal paper "Attention Is All You Need," attention mechanisms enable models to focus on the most relevant parts of the input when making predictions.

How Attention Works: The attention mechanism assigns a weight to each word in a sequence based on its relevance to the current word being processed. For example, in a sentence such as "*The cat sat on the mat*," the word "*cat*" would receive higher attention weights when predicting words such as "*sat*" or "*mat*" than less related words. This allows the model to:

- Capture long-range dependencies between words in a sequence.
- Understand the context more effectively than previous architectures, such as RNNs or LSTMs.

Types of Attention in LLMs

- **Self-Attention:** Used within a single sequence to determine relationships between words in the same input. Self-attention computes a weighted sum of all words in the sequence, enabling context-aware representations.
- **Cross-Attention:** Used in tasks such as translation, where the model aligns words between two sequences (for example, source and target languages).

Scaled Dot-Product Attention

A key component of attention mechanisms is scaled dot-product attention, which involves:

- Computing query, key, and value vectors for each token.
- Using the dot product of queries and keys to compute attention scores.
- Scaling the scores and applying a softmax function to ensure they sum to one.

This process allows the model to dynamically focus on different parts of the input sequence, improving its ability to understand and generate language.

Multi-Head Attention

LLMs employ multi-head attention to enhance their representational power. By projecting queries, keys, and values into multiple subspaces, multi-head attention allows the model to capture diverse linguistic patterns and relationships in parallel. This leads to more robust and contextually aware predictions.

The success of LLMs lies in their ability to combine pre-training, fine-tuning, advanced tokenization techniques, and powerful attention mechanisms. Together, these concepts enable LLMs to process, understand, and generate human language with unprecedented accuracy and fluency. As research continues, these foundational principles will likely evolve, unlocking new possibilities for LLMs in AI applications.

Evolution of Language Models

Language models have come a long way from their humble beginnings to the cutting-edge systems that power today's applications. These advancements reflect a combination of theoretical breakthroughs and practical innovations, making language models increasingly effective at understanding and generating human-like text. Let us explore this fascinating journey from simple n-gram models to the revolutionary large language models (LLMs).

From n-grams to RNNs and Transformers

The journey of language modeling began with n-grams, statistical models that relied on probabilities to predict the next word based on a fixed sequence of preceding words. For instance, given a sentence fragment, an n-gram model calculates the likelihood of a word appearing next by analyzing its frequency in a large corpus. While n-grams were straightforward and computationally efficient, they suffered from limitations such as a fixed context window and data sparsity.

To address these issues, researchers turned to Recurrent Neural Networks (RNNs). Unlike n-grams, RNNs introduced the concept of recurrence, enabling them to consider arbitrarily long contexts. By maintaining a hidden state that evolves over time, RNNs could capture dependencies in sequential data, making them ideal for tasks such as text generation and sentiment analysis. However, traditional RNNs struggled with vanishing gradients, limiting their ability to model long-range dependencies.

The introduction of Long Short-Term Memory (LSTM) networks and Gated Recurrent Units (GRUs) marked a significant improvement. These architectures incorporated gates to regulate the flow of information, allowing them to retain relevant context over longer sequences. Despite their advantages, RNN-based models were computationally expensive and challenging to parallelize, which constrained their scalability.

Transformers revolutionized language modeling by addressing these limitations. Introduced in the seminal paper "*Attention Is All You Need*," Transformers replaced sequential processing with self-attention mechanisms, enabling them to process entire sequences simultaneously. This architectural shift allowed for better handling of long-range dependencies and significantly improved training efficiency. Transformers laid the foundation for today's state-of-the-art models.

Key Milestones in the Evolution of LLMs

The evolution of language models is punctuated by key milestones that reflect both incremental improvements and paradigm shifts. Among the most notable are:

- **Bidirectional Encoder Representations from Transformers (BERT)**: BERT introduced a bidirectional approach, allowing it to consider both past and future context simultaneously. This made BERT particularly effective for tasks requiring nuanced understanding, such as question answering and sentiment analysis. Its "masked language modeling" objective further enhanced its contextual representations.
- **Generative Pre-trained Transformer (GPT)**: OpenAI's GPT series demonstrated the power of large-scale pre-training on diverse text corpora. By fine-tuning the pre-trained model on specific tasks, GPT set new benchmarks in natural language understanding and generation. GPT-5, with its trillions of parameters, showcased unprecedented versatility across applications ranging from conversational agents to creative writing.
- **T5 and FLAN-T5**: The Text-to-Text Transfer Transformer (T5) unified various NLP tasks under a single framework by treating all tasks as text generation problems. This versatility was further refined in FLAN-T5, which focused on instruction-tuning to align outputs more closely with user intent.
- **Google's LaMDA and PaLM**: LaMDA focused on conversational AI, fine-tuned to generate coherent and contextually appropriate dialogue. PaLM, with its focus on scalability and multilingual capabilities, pushed the envelope of what LLMs can achieve.

Each milestone represents a step toward building models that are not only more powerful but also more aligned with human needs.

How LLMs Differ from Earlier Models in Terms of Scale and Capability

Large Language Models (LLMs) differ fundamentally from earlier generations of language models in their scale, training approach, and versatility. These differences have transformed how AI systems learn and use language.

- **Scale**: LLMs operate at an unprecedented scale, with billions to trillions of parameters. This scale enables them to capture intricate patterns and nuanced relationships in data, resulting in more coherent and contextually appropriate outputs. The availability of massive datasets and advanced computational infrastructure has been instrumental in this leap.
- **Training Paradigms**: LLMs employ unsupervised or semi-supervised pre-training on diverse corpora, allowing them to develop a broad understanding of language before fine-tuning on specific tasks. This transfer learning approach contrasts sharply with earlier models, which were typically trained from scratch for individual tasks.

- **Contextual Understanding**: Earlier models, such as n-grams and RNNs, were constrained by fixed context windows, whereas LLMs leverage mechanisms such as self-attention to model long-range dependencies effectively. This enables LLMs to generate coherent responses in tasks requiring deep contextual understanding, such as summarization and creative writing.
- **Generative Capabilities**: LLMs excel at generating human-like text, thanks to their ability to model intricate relationships between words and phrases. Unlike earlier models, which often produced repetitive or shallow outputs, LLMs can create diverse and contextually rich content.
- **Multitasking and Few-Shot Learning**: LLMs can perform a wide range of tasks without explicit re-training, thanks to their multitasking abilities. Few-shot and zero-shot learning capabilities enable them to generalize effectively, even with minimal task-specific examples.
- **Applications and Impact**: The versatility of LLMs extends across domains such as healthcare, education, and entertainment. From powering virtual assistants to aiding medical research, LLMs are transforming industries at an unprecedented pace.

The evolution of language models reflects a journey from rule-based systems to highly adaptive, data-driven architectures. As research continues, the potential for further breakthroughs remains vast, promising even more sophisticated and capable systems in the future.

Architecture of LLMs

Large Language Models (LLMs) have revolutionized the field of artificial intelligence by demonstrating remarkable abilities in understanding and generating human-like text. These models are built upon the foundation of deep learning and natural language processing, leveraging the power of the Transformer architecture. This section delves into the key components that make LLMs so powerful, focusing on their architecture, the distinction between encoder and decoder structures, and the critical role of scaling in achieving their unprecedented capabilities.

Overview of the Transformer Architecture

The Transformer architecture, introduced by Vaswani et al. in 2017, is the cornerstone of modern LLMs. It replaces the recurrent structures of previous models with a self-attention mechanism, enabling the parallelization of computations and capturing long-range dependencies in text. At its core, the Transformer consists of:

- **Self-Attention Mechanism**: This mechanism computes the importance of each token in the input sequence relative to every other token, allowing the model to understand context effectively. It uses the key, query, and value vectors to determine attention scores.
- **Multi-Head Attention**: Instead of a single attention mechanism, multiple attention heads are used to capture different aspects of the input, providing richer contextual understanding.
- **Feedforward Neural Networks**: After the self-attention layers, the data passes through fully connected feedforward networks, which apply non-linear transformations to enhance the model's representational power.
- **Positional Encoding**: Since Transformers process input sequences in parallel, positional encodings are added to the input embeddings to provide information about the order of tokens.

The combination of these components allows Transformers to process input data efficiently and accurately, making them ideal for LLMs.

Encoder versus Decoder Structures in LLMs

LLMs can be broadly classified based on their reliance on the encoder, decoder, or both components of the Transformer architecture:

- **Encoder-Only Models**: These models, such as BERT (Bidirectional Encoder Representations from Transformers), are designed for understanding tasks such as text classification, sentiment analysis, and question answering. The encoder processes the entire input sequence bidirectionally, considering context from both preceding and succeeding tokens.
- **Decoder-Only Models**: Models such as GPT (Generative Pre-trained Transformer) use only the decoder component. They excel at generative tasks, including text completion, summarization, and story generation. Decoders focus on autoregressive generation, where each token is predicted based on preceding tokens.
- **Encoder-Decoder Models**: Combining both components, models such as T5 (Text-to-Text Transfer Transformer) and BART (Bidirectional and Auto-Regressive Transformers) are versatile and capable of handling a wide range of NLP tasks. The encoder reads the input sequence to generate a representation, which is then passed to the decoder to produce the output sequence.

The choice of architecture depends on the intended application, with encoder-only models excelling in comprehension tasks and decoder-only models dominating generative tasks. Encoder-decoder models strike a balance by supporting both capabilities.

Importance of Scaling: Parameters, Training Data, and Compute Power

Scaling has been instrumental in the evolution of LLMs, significantly influencing their performance and capabilities. Three critical factors drive this scaling:

- **Parameters**: Increasing the number of parameters enhances a model's ability to capture complex patterns and subtle relationships in language. Larger parameter counts allow LLMs to represent more nuanced associations between words, concepts, and contexts, leading to smoother, more coherent text generation. As models scale from millions to hundreds of billions of parameters, their ability to generalize and reason across domains improves dramatically.
- **Training Data**: The quality and quantity of training data play a pivotal role in shaping the knowledge and generalization abilities of LLMs. Massive datasets, often comprising terabytes of text from diverse sources, are used to train these models. This extensive data exposure equips LLMs with broad linguistic and domain knowledge.
- **Compute Power**: Training large models requires immense computational resources. High-performance hardware, such as GPUs and TPUs, accelerates the training process by handling parallel computations. Distributed computing frameworks further enhance scalability, allowing researchers to train LLMs on clusters of machines.

The interplay of these factors—parameters, data, and compute—creates a virtuous cycle where scaling one component drives improvements in others. This has led to breakthroughs in LLM capabilities, enabling them to perform tasks such as translation, summarization, and even complex reasoning with remarkable proficiency.

The architecture of Large Language Models, grounded in the Transformer framework, exemplifies the synergy of innovative design and scaling. The careful orchestration of encoder and decoder components, combined with advancements in training techniques and computational resources, has propelled LLMs to the forefront of AI. Understanding these architectural nuances not only sheds light on their current capabilities but also sets the stage for future advancements in the field of artificial intelligence.

Training LLMs

Training Large Language Models (LLMs) is a complex, multi-phase process designed to give machines a broad understanding of language before specializing them for particular tasks. This process typically involves two stages: pre-training and fine-tuning.

Pre-Training Objectives

Pre-training is the foundational phase in training LLMs. It focuses on equipping the model with general linguistic knowledge by leveraging massive datasets. Two primary objectives govern this phase:

- **Masked Language Modeling (MLM):** Masked language modeling is a self-supervised learning technique popularized by models such as BERT. During training, random tokens in a sentence are masked, and the model is tasked with predicting these masked tokens based on the context provided by the surrounding words. For instance, given the sentence "*The cat sat on the* [MASK]," the model learns to predict the word "*mat*."

  MLM has proven effective in helping models capture bidirectional context, which is critical for understanding the nuanced relationships between words in a sentence. This approach enables the model to grasp both syntactic and semantic information.

- **Causal Language Modeling (CLM):** Common in generative architectures, this objective trains the model to predict the next word in a sequence based only on prior tokens. This unidirectional learning aligns naturally with text generation, storytelling, and conversational tasks.

  While CLM captures the unidirectional dependencies between tokens, it excels in generating coherent and contextually relevant text. The combination of MLM and CLM in hybrid models, such as T5, allows for both understanding and generation capabilities.

Fine-Tuning for Specific Tasks

Fine-tuning tailors pre-trained LLMs to perform specialized tasks by adapting them to task-specific datasets. This process relies on the transfer learning paradigm, where the knowledge acquired during pre-training is transferred to downstream tasks. Fine-tuning typically involves:

- **Task-Specific Objectives:** The model is optimized for a specific task, such as sentiment analysis, machine translation, or question answering. For instance, a fine-tuned model can summarize text or generate creative content based on user prompts.
- **Supervised Learning:** Fine-tuning often involves supervised learning, where labeled datasets guide the model's adjustments. A labeled dataset for sentiment analysis might include sentences tagged as positive, neutral, or negative.
- **Domain Adaptation:** Fine-tuning enables LLMs to adapt to specialized domains such as healthcare, law, or finance. For example, a general-purpose language model can be fine-tuned using legal documents to assist with legal research and contract analysis.
- **Few-Shot and Zero-Shot Learning:** Recent advancements in fine-tuning have reduced the dependency on large labeled datasets. Techniques such as few-shot and zero-shot learning allow LLMs to perform tasks with minimal or no task-specific training data, further broadening their applicability.

Challenges in Training Large-Scale Models

Training LLMs at scale presents several challenges that necessitate careful consideration of data, compute resources, and optimization strategies. These challenges include:

- **Data:**
  - **Quantity and Quality:** The effectiveness of an LLM largely depends on the size and quality of its training data. Ensuring diversity, inclusivity, and the lack of bias in datasets is critical to prevent the propagation of harmful stereotypes.
  - **Data Curation:** Collecting and preprocessing vast amounts of text data from diverse sources, such as books, websites, and social media, is a daunting task. Noise and redundancy in the data can affect the model's performance.
  - **Ethical Considerations:** Issues related to copyright infringement, data privacy, and ethical usage are significant concerns during data collection.
- **Compute Resources:**
  - **Hardware Requirements:** Training LLMs demands immense computational power, typically provided by GPUs or TPUs. The costs of hardware infrastructure can be prohibitive, limiting accessibility for smaller organizations.
  - **Energy Consumption:** Training large-scale models consumes substantial energy, raising concerns about environmental sustainability.
  - **Scalability:** Efficient parallelization and distributed training are essential to handle the enormous size of LLMs, often requiring sophisticated frameworks and infrastructure.
- **Optimization Challenges:**
  - **Gradient Descent Instabilities:** Large models often face issues such as exploding or vanishing gradients, which can hinder effective training. Techniques such as gradient clipping and layer normalization are commonly employed to address these challenges.
  - **Hyperparameter Tuning:** Determining optimal hyperparameters, such as learning rates and batch sizes, is critical yet time-consuming. Automated methods such as Bayesian optimization are sometimes used to streamline this process.
  - **Overfitting:** Despite their size, LLMs are prone to overfitting when fine-tuned on small datasets. Regularization techniques and dropout layers help mitigate this risk.

Training large language models is a multifaceted process that balances sophisticated pre-training objectives with targeted fine-tuning for specific applications. While advancements in technology continue to address many challenges, issues related to data quality, computational requirements, and optimization persist. Understanding these aspects not only demystifies the process of training LLMs but also highlights the collaborative efforts needed to push the boundaries of what these models can achieve in diverse domains.

Applications of Large Language Models

Large Language Models (LLMs) are transforming the way humans interact with technology. These models, powered by advanced neural networks and immense datasets, are capable of understanding, generating, and refining natural language at an unprecedented scale. From revolutionizing industries to empowering individuals, the applications of LLMs are as diverse as they are impactful. Below, we explore some of the key areas where LLMs are making significant contributions.

Text Generation: Storytelling, Content Creation, and Chatbots

One of the most prominent applications of LLMs is text generation. By leveraging their deep understanding of language patterns, LLMs can produce coherent and contextually relevant text for various purposes. In storytelling, they can craft engaging narratives for novels, screenplays, or interactive experiences, offering a tool for writers and content creators to generate ideas or complete drafts.

In the realm of content creation, businesses use LLMs to generate articles, blogs, marketing copy, and social media posts. These models can adapt to specific tones, styles, and audiences, enabling marketers to produce large volumes of tailored content efficiently.

Chatbots powered by LLMs have redefined customer service and virtual assistance. These chatbots not only answer user queries but also engage in meaningful conversations, simulating human-like interactions. Industries such as e-commerce, healthcare, and education are increasingly adopting LLM-powered chatbots to enhance user experiences and reduce operational costs.

Summarization: Extractive and Abstractive Approaches

Summarization is another critical application of LLMs, addressing the growing need to process vast amounts of information quickly. Using extractive methods, LLMs identify the most relevant sentences or phrases from a document and present them as a concise summary. This approach is particularly useful in scenarios such as legal or academic research, where precision is paramount.

Abstractive summarization, on the other hand, involves generating a summary that rephrases the content while retaining its core meaning. This approach is more challenging but provides a human-like summary that captures the essence of the original text. Applications include summarizing news articles, scientific papers, and even meeting transcripts, helping professionals stay informed without spending hours reading detailed documents.

Machine Translation: Real-Time and High-Accuracy Translation Systems

Machine translation has been a cornerstone of natural language processing, and LLMs have elevated its accuracy and usability. By understanding the context and nuances of languages, LLMs can provide real-time translations that go beyond word-for-word substitution. This capability is invaluable in bridging communication gaps in multilingual environments.

For businesses, real-time translation enables global collaboration, allowing teams across different regions to communicate seamlessly. In customer-facing applications, translation tools powered by LLMs enhance user accessibility by supporting multiple languages. Furthermore, sectors such as tourism, international trade, and education benefit greatly from high-accuracy translation systems, fostering cross-cultural interactions.

Code Generation: Assisting Developers with Coding and Debugging

LLMs are proving to be indispensable tools for software developers. By understanding programming languages and development frameworks, these models can generate code snippets, suggest optimizations, and even debug errors. Platforms such as GitHub Copilot and OpenAI Codex exemplify how LLMs can streamline the development process, making coding faster and more efficient.

For beginners, LLMs act as virtual mentors, guiding them through coding exercises and helping them understand complex concepts. For experienced developers, they serve as productivity enhancers, reducing the time spent on repetitive coding tasks or troubleshooting. As a result, LLMs are reshaping software development workflows, enabling teams to focus on innovative problem-solving rather than mundane tasks.

Other Applications: Sentiment Analysis, Question Answering, and Knowledge Extraction

Beyond the highlighted areas, LLMs are being applied to a wide range of tasks that require language understanding and reasoning. Sentiment analysis is one such area where businesses use LLMs to gauge public opinion, monitor brand sentiment, and analyze customer feedback. This application helps organizations make informed decisions and tailor their strategies based on real-time insights.

Question answering systems, powered by LLMs, are transforming how users access information. Whether through voice assistants, search engines, or customer support platforms, these systems provide precise and contextually appropriate answers, often with references to reliable sources.

Knowledge extraction is another transformative application. LLMs can parse large volumes of unstructured data to extract meaningful information, creating structured datasets that can drive analytics and decision-making. Industries such as healthcare, finance, and legal services leverage this capability to uncover valuable insights from medical records, financial reports, and legal documents.

Evaluating LLMs

Evaluating the performance of LLMs is both an art and a science. These models, while capable of generating human-like text, require rigorous evaluation to ensure they meet quality standards for their intended applications. Evaluation encompasses both automated metrics and human judgment, each contributing unique insights into the model's capabilities, limitations, and areas for improvement. A thorough evaluation strategy not only measures the accuracy and fluency of LLMs but also considers ethical implications, such as biases and societal impacts.

Metrics for LLM Evaluation: Perplexity, BLEU, ROUGE, and Accuracy

- **Perplexity:** Perplexity is a standard metric for evaluating language models. It measures how well a model predicts a sample of text, essentially reflecting the model's confidence in its predictions. Lower perplexity indicates a better-performing model. For example, if a model predicts the next word in a sentence with high certainty, the perplexity score will be low. While perplexity is useful for comparing models during training, it does not directly correlate with human-perceived quality.
- **BLEU (Bilingual Evaluation Understudy):** BLEU is commonly used to evaluate text generation tasks such as machine translation. It measures the overlap between generated text and reference text using n-grams. For instance, a BLEU score of 0.85 suggests that the model's output closely matches the human-provided reference. Despite its widespread use, BLEU can be overly rigid, as it penalizes valid paraphrases that differ in wording but retain the same meaning.
- **ROUGE (Recall-Oriented Understudy for Gisting Evaluation):** ROUGE focuses on recall and is widely used in summarization tasks. It evaluates the overlap of n-grams, word sequences,

or word pairs between the generated summary and a reference summary. Metrics such as ROUGE-1 and ROUGE-L measure unigrams and longest common subsequences, respectively. ROUGE is effective for summarization but may not fully capture the nuances of semantic similarity.

Accuracy

Accuracy measures the correctness of the output in tasks with definitive answers, such as question answering or classification. For example, in an LLM designed to answer trivia questions, accuracy evaluates whether the model's responses are factually correct. While accuracy is straightforward to compute, it may not capture the subtleties of natural language generation, such as fluency and coherence.

Human Evaluation: Measuring Coherence, Relevance, and Fluency

Automated metrics provide valuable insights, but human evaluation remains critical for assessing qualitative aspects of LLM performance. Human evaluators measure attributes such as coherence, relevance, and fluency, which are difficult to quantify with automated methods.

- **Coherence:** Coherence refers to the logical consistency and flow of generated text. For instance, an LLM-generated paragraph describing a scientific phenomenon should maintain logical connections between sentences. Evaluators judge whether the content makes sense as a whole, avoiding contradictions or disjointed ideas.
- **Relevance:** Relevance measures how well the generated text aligns with the input prompt or task requirements. For example, if a model is tasked with generating a marketing pitch, evaluators assess whether the output effectively targets the intended audience and adheres to the specified topic.
- **Fluency:** Fluency evaluates the grammatical correctness and naturalness of the generated text. A fluent response mimics human writing, avoiding awkward phrasing or grammatical errors. For example, an LLM outputting, "*The cat is sleeping on the mat*," is considered fluent, while "*Cat sleep mat on*," is not.

Human evaluation can be conducted using structured rating scales or through comparative analysis, where evaluators rank multiple model outputs. While subjective, human evaluation captures the qualitative richness of language that automated metrics often miss.

Addressing Biases and Limitations in LLM-Generated Content

LLMs are not immune to biases and limitations, as they learn patterns from the data they are trained on. Addressing these challenges is crucial for building fair and responsible AI systems.

- **Understanding Biases:** Biases in LLMs can manifest in various forms, such as gender stereotypes, racial prejudices, or cultural insensitivities. For example, an LLM trained on imbalanced datasets may generate content that disproportionately favors one demographic over others. To identify and mitigate biases, researchers analyze model outputs for discriminatory patterns and retrain models on more balanced datasets.
- **Mitigation Strategies:** Techniques such as adversarial training, data augmentation, and fairness-aware algorithms help reduce biases. For instance, adversarial training involves exposing the model to biased examples and teaching it to produce neutral responses. Similarly, data augmentation enriches the training dataset with diverse examples to reduce skewness.

- **Ethical Implications:** LLM-generated content can have far-reaching societal impacts. For example, biased job descriptions generated by an LLM may perpetuate workplace inequalities. Addressing such issues requires not only technical solutions but also robust ethical guidelines. Organizations often establish AI ethics committees to oversee the deployment of LLMs and ensure they align with societal values.

Limitations

LLMs face inherent limitations, such as:

- **Lack of Domain Knowledge:** While proficient in general language tasks, LLMs may struggle with domain-specific expertise.
- **Tendency to Hallucinate:** LLMs sometimes generate plausible-sounding but factually incorrect information.
- **Inability to Reason:** Despite advancements, LLMs cannot yet perform complex reasoning tasks akin to human cognition.

Addressing these limitations involves combining LLMs with external knowledge sources, improving training methodologies, and continuously monitoring model behavior.

In conclusion, evaluating LLMs requires a multi-faceted approach that combines quantitative metrics with qualitative human judgment. While metrics such as perplexity, BLEU, and ROUGE offer objective measurements, human evaluation ensures the assessment of nuanced aspects such as coherence and fluency. Moreover, addressing biases and limitations is essential for building ethical and reliable language models, paving the way for more responsible AI applications.

Challenges and Limitations of LLMs

Large Language Models (LLMs) represent one of the most transformative advancements in artificial intelligence. Despite their groundbreaking achievements, they are not without significant challenges and limitations. As these models become increasingly integrated into society and industry, understanding their drawbacks is crucial for responsible deployment and future innovation.

Concerns: Bias, Misinformation, and Hallucinations

LLMs are trained on vast datasets that include information from across the internet, including both credible and non-credible sources. This expansive training introduces the potential for these models to reproduce and even amplify biases present in the training data. For example, an LLM might inadvertently generate text that reflects gender, racial, or cultural stereotypes, perpetuating societal inequalities.

Misinformation is another pressing concern. LLMs can generate content that appears factual but is entirely fabricated, leading to what is known as hallucination in AI. These hallucinations can range from minor inaccuracies to dangerously misleading information, posing significant risks in applications such as medical advice, financial decision-making, and legal consultations. For instance, a hallucinated response suggesting incorrect drug dosages could have dire consequences in healthcare.

Addressing these ethical concerns requires a multifaceted approach. Developers must implement rigorous data curation processes, integrate ethical guidelines into model design, and establish robust content moderation mechanisms. However, achieving a truly unbiased and trustworthy LLM remains a formidable challenge.

High Computational Requirements and Environmental Impact

The development and deployment of LLMs require immense computational resources. Training state-of-the-art models involves running large-scale computations across hundreds or thousands of GPUs or TPUs for weeks or months. This process consumes enormous amounts of electricity, contributing to significant carbon emissions. For instance, training a single large model has been reported to have a carbon footprint comparable to the lifetime emissions of several cars.

In addition to training, the inference phase–when the model is used to generate responses–also demands substantial computational power, especially when serving millions of users simultaneously. This high resource requirement makes LLMs expensive to develop, deploy, and maintain, limiting their accessibility to large organizations and well-funded institutions.

Mitigating the environmental impact of LLMs involves exploring more efficient model architectures, optimizing hardware utilization, and investing in renewable energy sources for data centers. Techniques such as model distillation and quantization can also reduce the computational demands of LLMs, making them more sustainable without compromising performance.

Challenges in Handling Multilingual and Low-Resource Languages

Despite their impressive capabilities, LLMs struggle to handle multilingual tasks effectively, particularly for low-resource languages. High-resource languages such as English dominate the training data, resulting in models that perform exceptionally well in these languages but significantly underperform in others. This imbalance exacerbates the digital divide and limits the applicability of LLMs in global contexts.

Low-resource languages, which lack extensive digital corpora, pose a unique challenge. LLMs trained on limited data for these languages often generate less accurate, less coherent, or even irrelevant outputs. This can alienate communities that could benefit from AI-driven applications in education, healthcare, and governance.

Efforts to address this limitation include curating diverse and inclusive datasets, leveraging transfer learning techniques, and employing multilingual pretraining methods. Additionally, community-driven initiatives that involve native speakers in data collection and model evaluation can play a pivotal role in improving LLM performance for underrepresented languages.

Towards Addressing These Challenges

The challenges and limitations of LLMs underscore the importance of adopting a balanced perspective. While their capabilities are remarkable, their shortcomings necessitate careful consideration. Ethical concerns must be addressed through transparency, fairness, and accountability in AI development. The environmental impact demands innovative solutions for energy-efficient AI. Finally, bridging the linguistic divide requires concerted efforts to make AI inclusive and accessible to all.

By recognizing and addressing these challenges, researchers, developers, and policymakers can ensure that LLMs are developed and deployed responsibly, paving the way for AI that benefits humanity as a whole.

Implementing and Using LLMs

Large Language Models (LLMs) are revolutionizing the AI landscape by providing powerful tools for understanding and generating human-like text. With their vast potential for applications ranging from customer service automation to creative writing and medical diagnosis, LLMs have become indispensable in modern AI solutions. Implementing and leveraging these models effectively requires an understanding of pre-trained models, fine-tuning techniques, and practical use cases.

Accessing Pre-Trained Models: OpenAI, Hugging Face, and Other Frameworks

Pre-trained models form the backbone of most LLM implementations. These models, trained on vast amounts of text data, offer a robust starting point for a variety of applications. Notable frameworks and platforms that provide access to pre-trained LLMs include:

- **OpenAI**: OpenAI offers APIs that allow developers to interact with powerful LLMs. Using these APIs, you can easily integrate text generation, summarization, translation, and other functionalities into your applications. OpenAI's API ecosystem ensures scalability and reliability for production use cases.
- **Hugging Face**: Hugging Face's Transformers library is a treasure trove for developers working with LLMs. It provides pre-trained models from various architectures, including BERT, GPT, and T5. With support for fine-tuning and inference, Hugging Face enables rapid prototyping and deployment across diverse tasks.
- **Other Frameworks**: Google's TensorFlow Hub, PyTorch Hub, and EleutherAI's GPT-Neo are additional resources for accessing pre-trained LLMs. These platforms support a range of use cases and allow seamless integration with existing ML pipelines.

Fine-tuning LLMs for Domain-Specific Tasks

While pre-trained models are versatile, they often need fine-tuning to excel in specific domains or tasks. Fine-tuning involves adapting the model's weights by training it on a smaller, task-specific dataset. The steps for fine-tuning typically include:

- **Dataset Preparation**: Curate a high-quality dataset that aligns with your domain or task. For instance, if you are fine-tuning an LLM for legal document summarization, ensure the dataset consists of annotated legal texts.
- **Model Selection**: Choose a pre-trained model that best suits your requirements. For example, use BERT for token-level tasks such as named entity recognition or GPT-4 for text generation.
- **Fine-Tuning Process**: Utilize frameworks such as Hugging Face's Trainer API or PyTorch's custom training loops. The training involves setting appropriate hyperparameters, such as learning rates, batch sizes, and epochs.
- **Validation and Evaluation**: Monitor the model's performance using metrics such as BLEU, ROUGE, or accuracy. Use validation datasets to avoid overfitting.
- **Deployment**: Deploy the fine-tuned model using APIs or save it in an optimized format, such as ONNX, for inference.

Practical Examples Using TensorFlow, PyTorch, or APIs

Let us explore practical implementations using different frameworks:

Example 1: Using Hugging Face Transformers with PyTorch

```
from transformers import T5ForConditionalGeneration, T5Tokenizer

# Load pre-trained T5 model and tokenizer
model_name = "t5-small"
model = T5ForConditionalGeneration.from_pretrained(model_name)
tokenizer = T5Tokenizer.from_pretrained(model_name)

# Input text
input_text = "Large language models can perform multiple NLP tasks with
minimal task-specific data."
input_ids = tokenizer("summarize: " + input_text, return_tensors="pt").
input_ids

# Generate summary
outputs = model.generate(input_ids, max_length=20, num_beams=2)
summary = tokenizer.decode(outputs[0], skip_special_tokens=True)

print("Summary:", summary)
```

This example demonstrates text generation using T5. Similar workflows can be extended to fine-tuning tasks with additional configurations.

Example 2: Fine-tuning a BERT Model with TensorFlow

```
from transformers import TFBertForSequenceClassification, BertTokenizer
import tensorflow as tf

# Load pre-trained model and tokenizer
model_name = "bert-base-uncased"
model = TFBertForSequenceClassification.from_pretrained(model_name,
num_labels=2)
tokenizer = BertTokenizer.from_pretrained(model_name)

# Prepare data
texts = ["This movie was fantastic!", "I did not like this film."]
labels = [1, 0]
inputs = tokenizer(texts, padding=True, truncation=True, return_tensors="tf")

# Convert labels to tensor
targets = tf.convert_to_tensor(labels)

# Fine-tuning
model.compile(optimizer=tf.keras.optimizers.Adam(learning_rate=5e-5),
              loss=tf.keras.losses.SparseCategoricalCrossentropy
(from_logits=True),
              metrics=["accuracy"])

history = model.fit(inputs.data, targets, epochs=3, batch_size=2)
```

This example fine-tunes BERT for binary sentiment classification. TensorFlow simplifies the process with built-in optimization and loss handling.

Example 3: Using OpenAI API

```
import openai

# Set API key
openai.api_key = "your-api-key"

# Query the model
response = openai.Completion.create(
    engine="text-davinci-003",
    prompt="Explain how to fine-tune a language model for legal text
summarization.",
    max_tokens=100
)

# Print the response
print(response.choices[0].text.strip())
```

This example illustrates how to interact with OpenAI's API for text completion. The simplicity of the API makes it suitable for rapid integration.

Implementing and using LLMs effectively requires leveraging pre-trained models, understanding fine-tuning techniques, and applying them to real-world problems. Frameworks such as OpenAI, Hugging Face, TensorFlow, and PyTorch offer robust tools to harness the capabilities of LLMs, enabling developers to create innovative solutions across various domains. With the right approach, these models can be fine-tuned and deployed to meet specific needs, unlocking the full potential of generative AI.

Case Study: Fine-Tuning BERT for a Specific Task

The ability to fine-tune LLMs such as BERT has transformed how we approach task-specific natural language processing applications. This case study explores the process of adapting BERT for sentiment analysis, where the goal is to determine the sentiment of a text, such as reviews or social media posts. It highlights the methods, challenges, and outcomes of fine-tuning BERT to achieve high performance on a domain-specific task.

Problem: Adapting LLM for Sentiment Analysis

Sentiment analysis is crucial for understanding customer feedback, brand reputation, and public opinion. While general-purpose models such as BERT are pre-trained on massive text corpora and understand language patterns, they lack domain-specific capability for tasks such as classifying nuanced sentiments without fine-tuning. The challenge is to adapt BERT to a sentiment analysis dataset and achieve reliable performance across diverse linguistic contexts.

For this case study, the dataset consists of product reviews, each labeled as positive, negative, or neutral, requiring the model to interpret subtle emotional cues and generalize well across varying expressions of sentiment.

Solution Approach: Preprocessing Data, Setting Up Fine-Tuning, and Evaluating Outputs

Fine-tuning BERT for sentiment analysis involves several key steps:

Data Collection and Preprocessing

The first step is to gather a dataset of labeled text samples. For this task, we use a dataset of product reviews, each annotated with a sentiment label ("*positive*," "*negative*," or "*neutral*"). Preprocessing includes:

- **Cleaning the Data:** Removing irrelevant metadata, special characters, and excessive whitespace.
- **Tokenization:** Using BERT's WordPiece tokenizer to convert text into input tokens.
- **Balancing Classes:** Ensuring that the dataset has a balanced representation of all sentiment classes to avoid model bias.

Fine-Tuning the Model

Fine-tuning involves adapting the pretrained BERT model on the sentiment dataset. Key aspects include:

- **Setting Up the Training Environment:** Using frameworks such as Hugging Face Transformers to load `bert-base-uncased`.
- **Configuring Hyperparameters:** Adjusting parameters such as the learning rate, batch size, and number of training epochs to optimize performance.
- **Using a Classification Head:** Adding a fully connected layer on top of BERT's pooled output to predict sentiment classes.
- **Supervised Learning:** Training the model with labeled input-output pairs to minimize the cross-entropy loss.

For this case study, we used a learning rate of 5e-5, a batch size of 16, and trained the model for three epochs.

Evaluating Outputs

Evaluation involves testing the fine-tuned model on a separate validation dataset. Metrics such as accuracy, precision, recall, and F1-score are used to gauge performance. Additionally, qualitative evaluation helps identify specific cases where the model struggles, such as handling ambiguous or sarcastic text.

Challenges: Managing Biases and Ensuring Accurate Predictions

Despite the structured fine-tuning process, several challenges arise:

Bias in Training Data

- **Issue:** The model's performance heavily depends on the quality of the training data. If the dataset is skewed towards a particular sentiment or contains biased language, the model's predictions will reflect these biases.
- **Mitigation:** Conducting thorough exploratory data analysis (EDA) to identify and address biases in the dataset.

Handling Sarcasm and Context

- **Issue:** Sarcasm and context-dependent sentiments pose significant challenges, as they often require deep contextual understanding beyond surface-level text.

- **Mitigation:** Augmenting the dataset with examples of sarcasm and nuanced sentiments, and using advanced loss functions to focus on hard-to-classify samples.

Overfitting

- **Issue:** Overfitting occurs when the model performs well on the training data but poorly on unseen data.
- **Mitigation:** Regularization techniques such as dropout, early stopping, and reducing the number of training epochs are employed to prevent overfitting.

Outcome: Results and Insights from Fine-Tuning

The fine-tuned BERT model achieved notable improvements in sentiment classification accuracy, with the following metrics on the validation dataset:

- **Accuracy:** 91.2%
- **Precision:** 89.8%
- **Recall:** 90.5%
- **F1-Score:** 90.1%

Key Insights:

- **Improved Understanding of Nuances:** Fine-tuning enabled the model to better interpret subtle linguistic cues, such as implied sentiments and context-dependent meanings.
- **Generalization:** Despite being fine-tuned on a specific dataset, the model demonstrated robust performance on diverse test samples.
- **Limitations:** Challenges such as handling sarcasm and extreme class imbalance still require further innovation in training strategies and dataset design.

In conclusion, this case study highlights the potential of fine-tuning BERT for domain-specific applications. By carefully preprocessing data, configuring training, and addressing challenges, we can adapt general-purpose LLMs to deliver precise and meaningful results for tasks such as sentiment analysis.

Future Directions in Large Language Models

Large Language Models (LLMs) are at the forefront of advancements in artificial intelligence, driving innovations across industries. As these models continue to grow in scale and capability, their impact is expected to permeate even more aspects of technology and society. However, their evolution is accompanied by challenges that researchers and practitioners aim to address. This chapter explores the future directions of LLMs, focusing on scaling trends, multimodal advancements, and efforts to align these models with human values.

Trends in Scaling LLMs Further: Efficiency and Interpretability

The remarkable success of LLMs has largely been driven by scaling–increasing the number of parameters and the size of training datasets. However, the era of blind scaling is coming to an end due to limitations in computational resources, environmental concerns, and diminishing returns on model performance. Future trends are focused on scaling LLMs efficiently while maintaining or even improving their capabilities.

- **Parameter Efficiency:** Research is shifting towards optimizing model architectures to deliver better performance without increasing the number of parameters excessively. Techniques such as sparsity-based training, weight-sharing, and quantization are gaining traction, allowing models to operate with fewer resources.

- **Model Compression:** Knowledge distillation and pruning are increasingly used to create smaller, more efficient versions of large models without compromising much on performance. These approaches are critical for deploying LLMs on edge devices and resource-constrained environments.
- **Interpretability:** Another major focus is making LLMs more interpretable. Researchers are developing tools and methods to analyze how LLMs process and generate information. The goal is to create models that can not only produce accurate outputs but also provide insights into the decision-making process, enhancing trust and usability.

Research on Multimodal Models Combining Text, Image, and Audio

The next frontier for LLMs lies in multimodal capabilities–the ability to process and generate content across different data modalities such as text, images, and audio. This research area is rapidly evolving, with significant progress being made toward building more holistic and versatile AI systems.

- **Unified Architectures:** New architectures such as CLIP and Flamingo demonstrate the potential for unifying multiple modalities under a single framework. These models can understand and generate content that integrates text with images, enabling applications in fields such as graphic design, content creation, and education.
- **Applications:** Multimodal models have transformative potential in real-world scenarios. For instance, they can be used in accessibility tools for visually impaired individuals, combining text-to-speech and image recognition. In healthcare, they can assist in medical imaging analysis integrated with patient records.
- **Challenges:** Despite these advancements, there are significant challenges. Training multimodal models requires even larger and more diverse datasets, raising ethical and logistical concerns. Additionally, ensuring the coherence and accuracy of outputs across modalities remains an open problem.

Efforts to Align LLMs with Human Values and Minimize Risks

As LLMs become increasingly powerful, aligning them with human values and minimizing potential risks is a pressing concern. Misaligned AI systems can perpetuate biases, generate harmful content, and pose ethical dilemmas. Efforts are underway to address these challenges and create AI systems that serve humanity responsibly.

- **Bias Mitigation:** Researchers are actively working on identifying and mitigating biases in LLMs. This involves curating more diverse training datasets, applying fairness-aware algorithms, and continuously monitoring outputs to detect and rectify unintended biases.
- **Robustness and Safety:** Ensuring the robustness of LLMs is crucial for their safe deployment. Techniques such as adversarial training and reinforcement learning from human feedback (RLHF) are being employed to make models less prone to generating misleading or harmful outputs.
- **Regulatory Frameworks:** The development of ethical and legal frameworks for the deployment of LLMs is gaining momentum. Policymakers, AI researchers, and industry leaders are collaborating to establish guidelines that govern the responsible use of these technologies.

- **Human-AI Collaboration:** The future of LLMs also involves fostering collaboration between humans and AI. Tools that allow humans to guide and refine AI outputs in real time are being developed, ensuring that these models act as effective assistants rather than autonomous agents.

The future of LLMs is marked by exciting possibilities and significant challenges. Scaling efficiency, multimodal integration, and ethical alignment are pivotal areas shaping their evolution. By addressing these challenges head-on, researchers and practitioners can harness the full potential of LLMs to create transformative technologies that align with human values and serve society effectively. This journey requires a collaborative effort across disciplines, ensuring that the benefits of LLMs are maximized while minimizing their risks.

Conclusion

In this chapter, we explored the fundamentals, architecture, training, and applications of Large Language Models (LLMs) and their significance in modern artificial intelligence. We examined how LLMs evolved from traditional NLP models, highlighting key advancements such as transformer-based architectures, pre-training and fine-tuning strategies, and the impact of attention mechanisms in improving language understanding and generation.

We also discussed the practical applications of LLMs, ranging from text generation and summarization to machine translation and code generation, demonstrating their versatility across multiple domains. Additionally, we covered evaluation techniques, ethical considerations, and challenges in training and deploying large-scale models, including issues such as bias, misinformation, computational demands, and multilingual limitations.

With hands-on implementation insights and real-world case studies, you are now equipped to leverage, fine-tune, and evaluate LLMs for various NLP tasks. In the next chapter, we will dive deeper into Generative Pre-trained Transformers (GPT), one of the most impactful advancements in LLMs, to understand its training methodology, architecture, and applications in modern AI.

Points to Remember

- LLMs are transformer-based models that leverage large-scale training on diverse datasets for natural language understanding and generation.
- Pre-training and fine-tuning enable LLMs to generalize well across tasks while being adaptable to specific applications.
- Tokenization techniques such as BPE, SentencePiece, and WordPiece help handle large vocabularies efficiently.
- Evaluation of LLMs involves perplexity, BLEU, ROUGE, and human assessments to measure coherence and relevance.
- LLMs face challenges such as bias, hallucinations, ethical concerns, and high computational requirements, which researchers continue to address.

Multiple Choice Questions

1. What is the primary advantage of transformer-based LLMs over traditional NLP models?
   a. Reduced training time
   b. Ability to process large amounts of text in parallel
   c. No requirement for labeled data
   d. Lower memory consumption

2. What is the role of fine-tuning in LLMs?
    a. Reducing model size
    b. Making the model more efficient in training
    c. Adapting a pre-trained model to specific tasks
    d. Improving tokenization techniques
3. Which mechanism allows LLMs to understand word relationships across long sequences?
    a. Convolutional layers
    b. Recurrent connections
    c. Attention mechanism
    d. Hidden Markov models
4. What are some common applications of LLMs?
    a. Weather prediction
    b. Machine translation, text generation, and summarization
    c. Data encryption
    d. Image classification
5. Which evaluation metric is commonly used for assessing text generation quality in LLMs?
    a. Perplexity
    b. IoU (Intersection over Union)
    c. Mean Squared Error (MSE)
    d. BLEU score

Answers

1. b
2. c
3. c
4. b
5. d

Questions

1. How do Large Language Models (LLMs) differ from traditional NLP models in terms of architecture and performance?
2. What are the advantages and challenges of pre-training and fine-tuning in LLMs?
3. How does tokenization impact the efficiency and effectiveness of LLMs?
4. Discuss the role of attention mechanisms in transformer-based language models.
5. What are some ethical concerns associated with deploying LLMs in real-world applications?

6. How can LLMs be fine-tuned for domain-specific tasks, and what factors should be considered?
7. What strategies can be used to evaluate the quality and coherence of text generated by LLMs?
8. How do computational requirements and energy consumption affect the scalability of LLMs?
9. What are the key differences between encoder-only, decoder-only, and encoder-decoder architectures in LLMs?
10. How does GPT differ from other transformer-based models, such as BERT, in terms of training objectives and applications?

Key Terms

- **Large Language Model (LLM)**: A deep learning model trained on vast amounts of text data to perform natural language tasks.
- **Transformer Architecture**: The backbone of LLMs, utilizing self-attention mechanisms for parallel processing.
- **Pre-training**: Initial training of an LLM on a large corpus before fine-tuning for specific tasks.
- **Fine-tuning**: Adapting a pre-trained model to specialized domains or applications.
- **Tokenization**: The process of splitting text into meaningful units (tokens) for model processing.
- **Attention Mechanism**: A key component in transformers that allows models to focus on relevant words in a sequence.
- **Perplexity**: A metric used to evaluate how well an LLM predicts the next word in a sequence.
- **Bias and Misinformation**: Ethical concerns in LLMs where models can generate inaccurate or skewed content.
- **Human Evaluation**: Assessing the quality of LLM-generated text based on coherence, fluency, and relevance.
- **Generative Pre-trained Transformer (GPT)**: A specific class of LLMs designed for autoregressive text generation.

Chapter 17
Generative Pre-Trained Transformers

Introduction

Generative Pre-trained Transformers (GPT) represent a transformative leap in natural language processing, redefining how machines generate, understand, and interact with human language. Built on the foundational principles of generative modeling and the groundbreaking Transformer architecture, GPT models excel at a wide range of tasks, including text generation, summarization, translation, and conversational AI. By leveraging vast amounts of data and an autoregressive training approach, GPT models are capable of producing coherent, contextually relevant, and human-like text.

In this chapter, we delve into the inner workings of GPT, exploring its architecture, training objectives, and evolution from GPT-1 to state-of-the-art versions such as GPT-5. We will examine the principles behind pre-training on massive datasets and fine-tuning for specific applications, along with the challenges and advantages of using GPT models. Through practical examples and step-by-step guidance, this chapter equips you with the knowledge to understand, implement, and utilize GPT for real-world tasks. By the end of this chapter, you will appreciate the transformative power of GPT and its role in advancing AI-driven language generation.

Structure

In this chapter, we will cover the following topics:

- **Introduction to Generative Pre-Trained Transformers (GPT)**
    - Significance of GPT in NLP
    - Evolution of GPT: From GPT-1 to GPT-5
    - Applications of GPT across Industries
- **Key Concepts in GPT**
    - Understanding Pre-Training and Key Concepts in GPT
    - Causal Language Modeling: The Autoregressive Approach
    - Tokenization Techniques: Byte Pair Encoding (BPE) and Other Methods
- **Architecture of GPT**
    - The Transformer Architecture: Encoder versus Decoder
    - Components of GPT: Self-Attention, Positional Embeddings, and Feedforward Layers
    - Importance of Scaling Parameters for Performance
- **Training GPT Models**
    - Pre-Training Objectives: Next-Token Prediction and Context Modeling
    - Fine-Tuning GPT for Specific Tasks and Domains

- Challenges in Training GPT: Data, Compute, and Optimization
- **Applications of GPT**
- **Advantages and Limitations of GPT**
  - Strengths: Scalability, Coherence, and Versatility Across Tasks
  - Limitations: Bias, Hallucinations, and Contextual Inconsistencies
  - Ethical Concerns: Addressing Misuse, Biases, and Misinformation
- **Evaluating GPT Models**
  - Metrics for Evaluation: Perplexity, BLEU, ROUGE, and Human Judgment
  - Assessing Quality, Coherence, and Diversity of Outputs
  - Addressing Biases and Ensuring Fair Evaluation
- **Implementing GPT: Step-by-Step**
  - Accessing Pre-Trained GPT Models via APIs or Frameworks such as Hugging Face
  - Fine-Tuning GPT for Specific Use Cases
  - Practical Examples Using TensorFlow or PyTorch
- **Case Study: Building a Conversational AI System with GPT**
- **Future Directions for GPT**

Introduction to Generative Pre-Trained Transformers

Building upon the foundations of Large Language Models (LLMs) discussed earlier, Generative Pre-trained Transformers (GPT) represent the most influential family of models driving today's AI revolution. Developed by OpenAI, GPT integrates three powerful principles into a single framework:

- **Generative Modeling:** Learning to predict and generate text rather than merely classify it.
- **Pre-training on Massive Corpora:** Acquiring broad linguistic and world knowledge through unsupervised learning.
- **Transformer Architecture:** Leveraging self-attention and positional embeddings to understand contextual relationships.

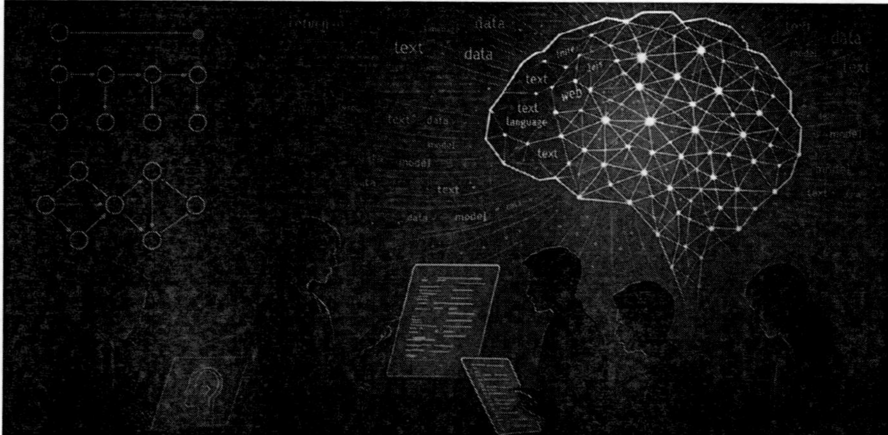

Figure 17.1: *Generative Models Pre-Training on Massive Corpora*

By combining these ideas, GPT models excel at producing coherent, context-aware, and human-like text. They have redefined how machines understand and generate language, forming the backbone of modern applications in dialogue systems, code generation, summarization, and creative writing.

Significance of GPT in NLP

Generative Pre-trained Transformers (GPT) mark a paradigm shift in natural language processing by redefining what a language model can do. Unlike earlier NLP systems that were designed for specific tasks such as translation or summarization, GPT models are trained to learn language itself at scale. Through exposure to vast datasets spanning books, articles, web content, and code, they internalize not only linguistic structures but also reasoning patterns and factual knowledge.

What sets GPT apart is its integration of three transformative capabilities:

- **Generative Fluency**: GPT produces text that is coherent, context-aware, and stylistically adaptive across domains.
- **Emergent Reasoning**: At scale, GPT demonstrates general reasoning and problem-solving abilities beyond explicit training data.
- **Interactive Adaptability**: Users can guide GPT's behavior through prompting, eliminating the need for retraining for every new task.

Together, these traits elevate GPT from a task-specific model to a general-purpose reasoning system—capable of writing essays, summarizing legal documents, generating code, or conducting dialogues within a single unified framework. This versatility positions GPT as the cornerstone of modern foundation models, bridging language understanding, generation, and interactive intelligence.

Evolution of GPT: From GPT-1 to GPT-5 and More

The evolution of GPT reflects the progressive advancements in model architecture, training techniques, and computational power. Here is a closer look at each iteration:

- **GPT-1**: Introduced in 2018, GPT-1 marked the beginning of the transformer-based pre-training era. With 117 million parameters, it showcased the potential of unsupervised pre-training for NLP tasks. Although limited in scope, GPT-1 laid the groundwork for its successors by demonstrating that pre-training on large text corpora could significantly enhance performance.
- **GPT-2**: Released in 2019, GPT-2 was a substantial upgrade with 1.5 billion parameters. It gained widespread attention for its ability to generate coherent and contextually relevant text. OpenAI initially hesitated to release GPT-2 publicly due to concerns about potential misuse, highlighting the ethical implications of advanced language models.
- **GPT-3**: Launched in 2020, GPT-3 featured a staggering 175 billion parameters, representing a quantum leap in scale and capabilities. GPT-3 became a game-changer, powering a myriad of applications such as chatbots, virtual assistants, and content generation tools. Its ability to perform zero-shot and few-shot learning demonstrated unprecedented adaptability, requiring minimal input to generate accurate and relevant outputs.
- **GPT-4**: The latest iteration, GPT-4, builds upon the strengths of its predecessors with enhanced reasoning capabilities, reduced biases, and improved multilingual support. GPT-4's advancements include better handling of complex queries, a more nuanced understanding of context, and a significant reduction in generating harmful or misleading content. These improvements have expanded its utility across even more sophisticated applications, such as legal document analysis, medical diagnostics, and creative writing.

- **GPT-4 Turbo**: GPT-4 Turbo builds upon GPT-4's capabilities, offering a more efficient and scalable solution for developers. With an extended context window and improved function calling, it enables more sophisticated interactions while maintaining cost-effectiveness.
- **GPT-5:** GPT-5 moves beyond text and images to unified multimodal intelligence, combining reasoning, planning, and interaction. It embodies the latest lessons in scaling, alignment, and efficiency, and hints at the future of agentic AI systems that can operate autonomously while collaborating with humans across tasks and modalities.

The journey from GPT-1 to GPT-5 underscores the rapid pace of innovation in AI, fueled by increased computational resources, larger datasets, and refined architectural designs. In future versions of GPT, we can expect these systems to become even more nuanced, capable, and deeply integrated into the fabric of problem-solving and creative expression.

Applications of GPT Across Industries

Generative Pre-trained Transformers (GPT) extend the capabilities of earlier language models by enabling context-aware reasoning, dialogue, and creativity at scale. Rather than performing isolated tasks, GPT models serve as adaptive tools that can be tailored through prompting and fine-tuning to meet diverse industry needs.

- **Healthcare:** GPT assists clinicians by generating clinical summaries, analyzing patient notes, and explaining medical terminology in accessible language. Fine-tuned medical versions support diagnosis assistance and patient triage, while conversational agents enhance accessibility to healthcare guidance.
- **Education:** GPT powers intelligent tutoring systems that personalize learning experiences. It can explain complex subjects interactively, generate quizzes or lesson plans, and provide real-time feedback—making it a dynamic supplement to traditional teaching methods.
- **Customer Support:** GPT-driven assistants can handle complex, multi-turn conversations, adapting tone and intent dynamically. Unlike rule-based bots, they learn context over longer interactions, offering human-like support experiences that scale across languages and platforms.
- **Content Creation and Media:** GPT automates creative and editorial tasks—writing articles, marketing copy, scripts, and even code—while maintaining brand voice or narrative coherence. Advanced models such as GPT-4 and GPT-5 incorporate multimodal inputs, expanding creativity across text, image, and video production.
- **Finance:** GPT streamlines financial analysis by generating reports, interpreting regulatory documents, and summarizing market data. Its language understanding aids in fraud detection and client communication, reducing manual review time in high-volume operations.
- **Legal and Compliance:** Legal professionals use GPT to draft, summarize, and cross-reference legal documents efficiently. Its capacity to interpret lengthy contracts and legislation accelerates compliance workflows and reduces human error.
- **Gaming and Interactive Media:** GPT models enable dynamic storytelling, procedural dialogue, and responsive non-player characters (NPCs). This creates immersive gaming environments where narratives evolve in real time based on player interaction.

Through scalable reasoning and adaptability, GPT has evolved from a text generator into a universal cognitive engine—one that supports creativity, decision-making, and automation across industries. As newer versions integrate multimodal and agentic capabilities, GPT continues to redefine how humans and machines collaborate in professional and creative domains.

Key Concepts in GPT

Generative Pre-trained Transformers (GPT) build upon the Transformer foundation to achieve state-of-the-art language understanding and generation. Unlike encoder-decoder or bidirectional models, GPT employs a decoder-only architecture optimized for *autoregressive text generation*—predicting each new token based on all preceding ones.

At the core of this design is causal self-attention, which restricts attention to earlier tokens, ensuring coherence and a natural flow of thought. This principle underpins GPT's ability to generate contextually consistent, human-like text across a wide variety of domains.

Understanding Pre-training key concepts in GPT

GPT is built on two primary phases of learning in its process: pre-training and fine-tuning. These phases are further broken into key concepts designed to equip the model with general knowledge and specific task-related expertise, respectively.

- **Pre-training**: Conducted on massive, unlabeled text corpora, this phase teaches the model to predict the next token given its context. Through this objective, GPT captures deep semantic and syntactic patterns without task-specific supervision.
- **Fine-tuning**: After pre-training, the model can be refined for specialized objectives. Techniques such as supervised fine-tuning and Reinforcement Learning from Human Feedback (RLHF) align GPT's behavior with user intent, improving factual reliability, tone, and ethical compliance.
- **Modern Extensions**: Recent versions of GPT extend beyond text to incorporate multimodal reasoning, integrating visual and auditory understanding. Additionally, agentic capabilities such as function calling and retrieval-augmented generation (RAG) enable GPT to interact with external tools, access up-to-date information, and perform complex reasoning in real-world applications.

Causal Language Modeling: Autoregressive Approach

The defining principle behind GPT's generative power is causal language modeling—an autoregressive training approach where each token prediction depends solely on previous context. This unidirectional structure allows GPT to produce coherent, temporally consistent text and mirror human-like reasoning patterns. When combined with in-context learning, it enables GPT to adapt flexibly to new tasks, write code, summarize documents, and maintain long-range coherence in dialogue or narratives.

Tokenization Techniques

Tokenization plays a crucial role in GPT's ability to process language efficiently across diverse domains. Rather than using traditional word or character segmentation, GPT employs subword-based tokenization, most notably Byte Pair Encoding (BPE), which balances vocabulary compactness and linguistic expressiveness.

- **Byte Pair Encoding (BPE):** BPE begins with a base vocabulary of individual characters and iteratively merges the most frequent adjacent pairs into new tokens until the desired vocabulary size is reached. This approach allows GPT to:
    - Represent rare or compound words using familiar subword units, minimizing out-of-vocabulary issues.
    - Maintain contextual meaning while keeping the vocabulary manageable.

   - Improve efficiency by reducing sequence length compared with character-level methods.
- **Variants and Evolution:** Successive GPT models have refined tokenization strategies. GPT-2 popularized standard BPE, while GPT-3 and GPT-4 adopted optimized variants such as tiktoken, which handle Unicode text more robustly and support multiple languages and domains. Alternative subword methods, such as WordPiece or SentencePiece, follow similar principles but differ in merge algorithms and handling of raw text; GPT can adapt these when domain requirements demand a different tokenization strategy.
- **Significance:** By adopting scalable subword tokenization, GPT achieves a fine-grained yet computationally efficient representation of text, enabling consistent performance across languages, programming code, and specialized vocabularies. This foundation supports the model's broader strengths in contextual understanding, coherence, and reasoning.

Architecture of GPT

Generative Pre-trained Transformer (GPT) models are built upon the Transformer framework but streamline it into a decoder-only architecture optimized for text generation. While Chapter 16 introduced the Transformer's general encoder–decoder structure, GPT narrows its focus exclusively to the decoder stack, aligning its design with the autoregressive objective of predicting the next token in a sequence.

Recap of Transformer Architecture

The Transformer comprises two main components – an encoder that processes input sequences bidirectionally, and a decoder that generates outputs sequentially. GPT simplifies this design by discarding the encoder entirely, relying only on the decoder.

Each decoder layer in GPT uses causal self-attention, which ensures that the model can attend only to previous tokens, not future ones. This unidirectional processing mirrors the natural left-to-right flow of language and is fundamental to GPT's ability to generate coherent, contextually consistent text.

The diagram illustrates the step-by-step flow of information through GPT:

1. **Input Tokens**: The text is tokenized into discrete units that the model can process.
2. **Decoder Stack:** A series of transformer decoder layers, each refining contextual understanding.
3. **Self-Attention (Causal):** Each token attends only to previous tokens, preserving temporal order and ensuring that future information is masked during training.
4. **Positional Embeddings:** Encodes the position of each token, enabling the model to retain the sequential structure of language.

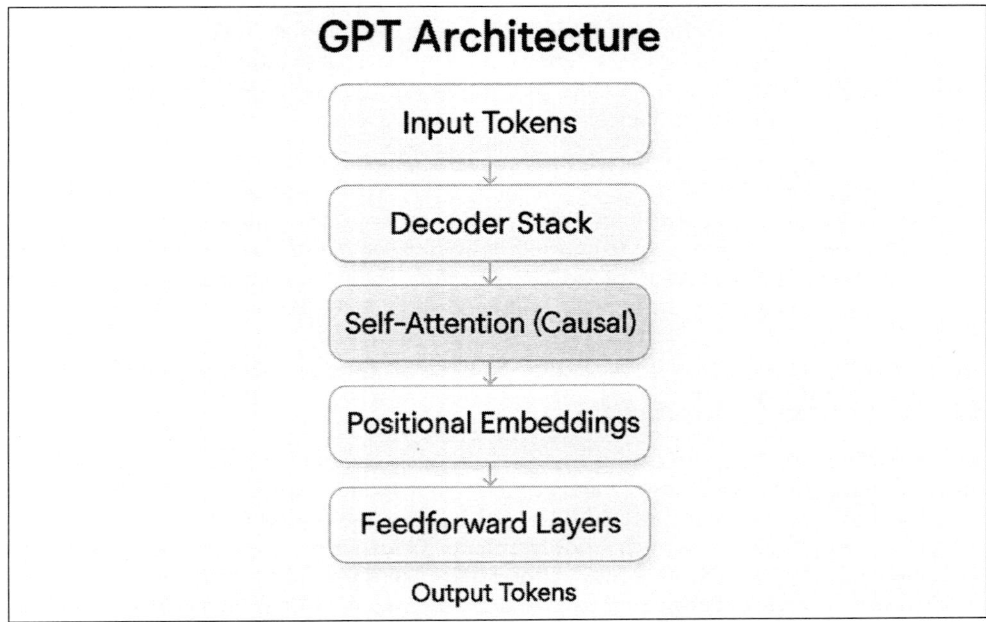

Figure 17.2: *Key Components in the GPT Architecture*

5. **Feedforward Layers:** Non-linear transformations that enrich the representation before producing the next predicted token.
6. **Output Tokens**: The generated text, produced one token at a time, based on the accumulated context.

This flow shows how GPT transforms input tokens into coherent outputs using causal attention and positional information to maintain sequence order.

Components of GPT

GPT's architecture is composed of a stack of identical decoder layers, each containing three core components: causal self-attention, positional embeddings, and feedforward layers.

- **Causal Self-Attention:** Enables the model to capture long-range dependencies while ensuring that predictions are based only on prior context. This mechanism is central to GPT's generative capability, allowing it to build text token by token with continuity and logical flow.
- **Positional Embeddings:** Since the model processes all tokens in parallel, it lacks inherent awareness of order. Positional embeddings encode this order so the model understands sequence relationships. Modern versions of GPT (for example, GPT-4 Turbo, GPT-5) use advanced forms such as rotary embeddings or ALiBi to support extended context windows.
- **Feedforward Layers:** Fully connected layers within each decoder block perform non-linear transformations, enhancing representational richness. They allow the model to abstract linguistic features and integrate them into coherent output predictions.

Importance of Scaling Parameters for Performance

- Scaling remains one of the defining principles of GPT's architecture. As model parameters, data size, and compute resources grow, GPT's performance scales predictably, giving rise to emergent behaviors such as few-shot and zero-shot learning. Larger models exhibit improved reasoning, contextual understanding, and even cross-domain generalization.

- Scaling also enables multimodal reasoning in recent iterations–integrating text, code, and visual data into unified workflows. Innovations such as sparse attention, mixture-of-experts (MoE) routing, and parameter-efficient fine-tuning (LoRA, QLoRA) further extend GPT's performance without linear increases in computational cost.

GPT's architecture exemplifies the principle of focused simplicity. By retaining only the decoder stack and aligning it with a causal attention mechanism, GPT transforms the general-purpose Transformer into a generative powerhouse. The architecture diagram underscores this streamlined process–progressing from token input to autoregressive output through a carefully layered structure of attention, embeddings, and feedforward computation. Scaling this design has propelled GPT models from basic language generators to the foundation of modern AI systems capable of reasoning, creation, and interaction.

Training GPT Models

Training Generative Pre-trained Transformer (GPT) models is a multi-phase process that extends the general training principles of large language models but applies them specifically to the decoder-only, autoregressive architecture of GPT. The process includes pre-training on vast, unlabeled datasets to acquire general language understanding, followed by fine-tuning or alignment to specialize the model for tasks or user interaction styles. This two-stage design allows GPT models to generalize widely while adapting precisely to domain-specific or instruction-driven needs.

Pre-Training Objectives

At the core of GPT's training lies causal language modeling, also known as next-token prediction. During pre-training, the model learns to predict the next word or token in a sequence based solely on preceding context. For example, given the text "*The cat sat on the __*", GPT must predict "*mat*." This simple objective, when applied to trillions of tokens from diverse sources (books, web text, articles, and code), enables the model to internalize grammar, semantics, factual patterns, and reasoning structures.

GPT's transformer-based causal attention architecture supports this process by attending to every prior token simultaneously, rather than processing text sequentially like RNNs. This parallelism allows GPT to model long-range dependencies efficiently, capturing nuanced relationships between words and ideas. Modern pre-training also integrates additional refinements:

- **Scaling laws:** model size, dataset size, and compute increase predictably improve performance.
- **Data curation and deduplication:** prevent overfitting to repeated content.
- **Curriculum scheduling:** orders training data from simple to complex tasks to accelerate convergence.

Together, these strategies allow GPT models to acquire broad linguistic competence during unsupervised pre-training.

Fine-Tuning GPT for Specific Tasks and Domains

Fine-tuning adapts the pre-trained model to specific tasks or user behaviors through targeted training on smaller, curated datasets. Unlike the general fine-tuning techniques discussed in the previous chapter, GPT's fine-tuning often centers on instruction and alignment, rather than pure task optimization. Common fine-tuning and adaptation approaches include:

- **Instruction Tuning:** Training on datasets of human-written prompts and responses so the model can follow natural instructions effectively.

- **Reinforcement Learning from Human Feedback (RLHF):** A feedback-driven approach that aligns model outputs with human preferences, reducing harmful or irrelevant responses.
- **Parameter-Efficient Fine-Tuning (PEFT):** Methods such as LoRA, QLoRA, and adapters enable domain specialization without retraining the full model.
- **Domain Specialization:** Applying GPT to areas such as medicine, law, or finance by using domain-specific corpora. For example, a healthcare-tuned GPT trained on clinical notes can generate concise patient summaries or draft medical reports.

Fine-tuning must balance specialization and generalization. Overfitting to small datasets can reduce GPT's broad reasoning ability, so techniques such as early stopping, dropout regularization, and careful validation are essential.

Challenges in Training GPT

Training GPT models remains a resource-intensive and technically complex endeavor, driven by three main factors:

- **Data Requirements:** GPT demands massive and diverse datasets to generalize across topics and writing styles. Ensuring data quality, diversity, and fairness is critical, as imbalanced or biased data can propagate unwanted patterns into model outputs. Data preprocessing typically involves deduplication, filtering of low-quality text, and balancing linguistic representation.
- **Compute Demands:** Large-scale GPT models, containing billions or trillions of parameters, require weeks of training on GPU or TPU clusters. Distributed training frameworks (for example, Megatron-LM, DeepSpeed) and optimizations such as mixed-precision training, gradient checkpointing, and pipeline parallelism are used to manage memory and computation efficiently.

  Environmental sustainability has also become a consideration, motivating research into more energy-efficient architectures and fine-tuning strategies.
- **Optimization and Stability:** Training stability is a persistent challenge due to the immense number of parameters. Techniques such as gradient clipping, adaptive optimizers (Adam, AdamW), and learning-rate warmup are vital to achieving convergence. Recent innovations—such as ZeRO redundancy optimizers, sparse activation, and mixture-of-experts (MoE) models—help distribute training load while maintaining accuracy.

Training GPT involves combining large-scale unsupervised learning with precise post-training alignment. Through causal language modeling, the model learns the statistical and structural foundations of language. Subsequent fine-tuning and alignment ensure that GPT behaves safely, helpfully, and contextually across domains.

Although the process demands extensive data and computation, advancements in distributed optimization, parameter-efficient tuning, and human-feedback alignment continue to make training GPT models more scalable, ethical, and effective.

Applications of GPT

Generative Pre-trained Transformers (GPT) have revolutionized the way artificial intelligence processes, generates, and interacts with language. Beyond their general language modeling capabilities, GPT models demonstrate unique strengths in autonomous reasoning, interactive dialogue, and cross-domain creativity. Modern iterations such as GPT-4, GPT-4 Turbo, and GPT-5 extend these capabilities beyond text into multimodal reasoning, code generation, and agentic task orchestration, marking a pivotal shift from language models to general-purpose AI systems.

Text Generation: Creative Writing, Content Creation, and Storytelling

GPT has redefined content generation through its mastery of coherent, stylistically adaptive, and context-sensitive writing. Unlike traditional LLMs that rely heavily on templates or narrow prompts, GPT can interpret nuanced instructions and adapt tone, structure, and emotion dynamically. From creative writing (poems, narratives, screenplays) to marketing content and technical documentation, GPT acts as a collaborative partner rather than a static generator. Its understanding of rhythm, narrative flow, and stylistic variation allows writers to maintain creative intent while accelerating the drafting process. GPT-powered tools are now integrated into publishing workflows, ad copy systems, and entertainment scripting, blending machine precision with human imagination.

Code Generation: Assisting Developers

Among GPT's most transformative contributions is its ability to understand and generate code. Specialized derivatives such as Codex, GPT-Engineer, and newer multimodal GPT variants can translate natural language descriptions into executable programs, explain algorithms, and debug code efficiently. By combining linguistic reasoning with programming syntax, GPT supports a wide range of developer tasks:

- Generating or refactoring code across multiple programming languages.
- Explaining complex logic to improve accessibility for non-programmers.
- Integrating with development environments (for example, GitHub Copilot) to provide real-time code suggestions and context-aware debugging.

The evolution toward agentic GPT systems enables autonomous software assistants that can plan, write, test, and deploy code in iterative loops–paving the way for self-managing development pipelines.

Summarization: Generating Meaningful Summaries

While many LLMs can summarize text, GPT stands out for its abstractive summarization and retrieval-augmented generation (RAG) capabilities. By referencing external documents or databases, GPT produces fact-grounded, contextually aware summaries rather than surface-level compressions. Key applications include:

- Summarizing complex research papers, contracts, or policy briefs with high factual accuracy.
- Synthesizing multi-document inputs into unified, concise narratives.
- Extracting actionable insights from large corpora such as medical records or legal databases.

This ability to merge reasoning with retrieval marks GPT as a knowledge distiller rather than a mere compressor of information.

Conversational AI: Chatbots and Virtual Assistants

GPT set a new benchmark for human-like conversational systems. Its autoregressive decoding and context retention allow for natural, multi-turn dialogues that maintain tone and memory over long interactions. Applications span:

- Customer support and onboarding assistants that adapt to user intent.
- Educational tutors capable of personalized, Socratic-style engagement.

- Personal productivity agents that can execute tasks such as scheduling, writing emails, or generating reports.

Modern GPT systems (for example, GPT-4 Turbo and GPT-5) also feature tool use and function calling, enabling them to interface with APIs, perform searches, or retrieve live data – transforming chatbots into interactive AI collaborators rather than static responders.

Other Applications

Beyond core language and coding tasks, GPT models demonstrate adaptability across emerging domains:

- **Translation and Multilingual Communication**: GPT's expansive multilingual training enables accurate, context-sensitive translation and cross-lingual reasoning.
- **Sentiment and Intent Analysis**: GPT can infer emotions and motivations from text, supporting brand management, HR analytics, and user-experience research.
- **Research and Discovery**: GPT assists in generating hypotheses, drafting literature reviews, and even simulating experimental reasoning.
- **Legal, Financial, and Medical Workflows**: Through fine-tuning and retrieval augmentation, GPT supports specialized use cases such as contract drafting, financial forecasting, and medical note summarization while maintaining domain-specific precision.

The Transformative Potential of GPT

Beyond core language and coding tasks, GPT models demonstrate adaptability across emerging domains:

- **Translation and Multilingual Communication**: GPT's expansive multilingual training enables accurate, context-sensitive translation and cross-lingual reasoning.
- **Sentiment and Intent Analysis**: GPT can infer emotions and motivations from text, supporting brand management, HR analytics, and user-experience research.
- **Research and Discovery**: GPT assists in generating hypotheses, drafting literature reviews, and even simulating experimental reasoning.
- **Legal, Financial, and Medical Workflows**: Through fine-tuning and retrieval augmentation, GPT supports specialized use cases such as contract drafting, financial forecasting, and medical note summarization while maintaining domain-specific precision.

Advantages and Limitations of GPT

Generative Pre-trained Transformers (GPT) mark a major leap in Natural Language Processing (NLP). Building on the transformer decoder architecture, GPT combines large-scale pre-training, causal attention, and alignment strategies to generate coherent, human-like text across contexts. Its strengths–scalability, coherence, and versatility–have made it indispensable across industries, while its limitations highlight the need for responsible deployment and continual refinement.

Strengths: Scalability, Coherence, and Versatility

- **Scalability**: GPT models scale predictably with data, compute, and parameters, a relationship formalized through scaling laws. Larger GPT versions (for example, GPT-3 → GPT-4 → GPT-5) exhibit emergent abilities such as few-shot reasoning, multimodal comprehension, and contextual learning without task-specific retraining. Their decoder-only causal architecture efficiently leverages massive datasets, making GPT adaptable to both general and specialized domains–from medical text generation to financial forecasting–through fine-tuning or parameter-efficient techniques such as LoRA and QLoRA.

- **Coherence**: GPT's causal self-attention enables exceptional contextual coherence. Each token attends to all prior tokens, ensuring logical flow and continuity. This makes GPT especially strong in conversational AI, narrative generation, and long-form content. Modern versions extend context windows from thousands to hundreds of thousands of tokens, allowing GPT to sustain topic continuity across entire documents or lengthy conversations—something earlier LLMs struggled to achieve.
- **Versatility**: Pre-training on diverse multimodal and multilingual datasets grants GPT broad adaptability. It performs zero-shot, one-shot, and few-shot learning, reducing the dependence on labeled data. GPT's instruction-following fine-tuning and function-calling capabilities empower it to handle creative writing, data analysis, code generation, and even reasoning with external tools—making it a foundation model rather than a single-task system.

Limitations: Bias, Hallucinations, and Inconsistencies

- **Bias**: GPT inherits social, cultural, and linguistic biases from its training data. These may surface as stereotypes or imbalances in representation. To mitigate such effects, OpenAI and others employ Reinforcement Learning from Human Feedback (RLHF), Constitutional AI, and bias audits. Though these methods reduce harmful outputs, complete elimination remains a challenge, underscoring the importance of transparency and responsible use.
- **Hallucinations**: Because GPT is optimized for linguistic plausibility rather than factual accuracy, it can generate convincing but incorrect statements—so-called *hallucinations*. Mitigation strategies include Retrieval-Augmented Generation (RAG) and tool-integrated prompting, which ground responses in verified data sources. Still, when disconnected from external knowledge, GPT may over-confidently fabricate information, limiting reliability in domains requiring precision, such as law or medicine.
- **Contextual Inconsistencies**: Despite large context windows, maintaining long-term narrative or conversational memory remains difficult. GPT may lose track of earlier details in extended sessions, leading to contradictions or repetition. Newer architectures (for example, GPT-4 Turbo, GPT-5) employ context compression and persistent memory modules to improve long-range coherence, but perfect recall remains an open research frontier.

Ethical Concerns: Misuse, Biases, and Misinformation

- **Misuse:** GPT's ability to generate high-quality text and media introduces risks of spam, deepfakes, phishing, and misinformation. Responsible deployment requires multilayer safeguards: content moderation, watermarking of AI-generated material, API usage limits, and organizational governance frameworks. OpenAI's monitoring and policy enforcement systems exemplify best practices for mitigating misuse at scale.
- **Bias and Fairness:** Even with RLHF and alignment, GPT outputs can reflect training-set biases. Ethical design includes dataset transparency, bias testing, and diverse annotator participation. Continuous audits and user feedback loops are critical to improving fairness across global applications.
- **Misinformation:** GPT can inadvertently amplify false or outdated information. Hybrid models that integrate RAG pipelines or live-data tools help ground responses in verifiable facts. Educating users about model limits and promoting transparency about output reliability are equally important to preserve trust.

GPT combines architectural efficiency with scalable intelligence, enabling coherent and versatile performance across tasks. Its strengths—emergent reasoning, adaptability, and human-like fluency—make it a cornerstone of modern AI applications. Yet, challenges such as bias, hallucination, and ethical misuse highlight the need for continuous oversight and technical innovation.

With advances in alignment, retrieval grounding, and multimodal integration, GPT is steadily evolving toward systems that are not only more powerful but also safer, more transparent, and aligned with human values.

Evaluating GPT Models

Evaluating GPT models requires a nuanced approach that goes beyond conventional accuracy metrics. Unlike traditional NLP systems designed for fixed tasks, GPT models perform a broad spectrum of generative, reasoning, and interactive functions. Their evaluation, therefore, involves measuring quality, coherence, factual accuracy, safety, and fairness, often combining both automated and human-centric methods.

Metrics for Evaluation

- **Perplexity:** Perplexity remains a foundational metric for assessing GPT's ability to predict language sequences. Lower perplexity indicates stronger linguistic fluency. However, for models such as GPT-4 or GPT-5, which generate open-ended and context-rich outputs, perplexity alone fails to capture creativity, factual accuracy, or alignment quality. It is thus used mainly as a diagnostic metric during pre-training rather than a holistic performance measure.
- **BLEU and ROUGE:** BLEU (for translation) and ROUGE (for summarization) provide structural comparisons between generated and reference texts. While useful for benchmarking narrow tasks, these metrics are limited for evaluating GPT's open-domain generation, where semantic richness and contextual adaptability matter more than word overlap. Consequently, newer frameworks rely on embedding-based similarity measures (for example, BERTScore, MoverScore) that assess semantic rather than lexical alignment.
- **Human Judgment:** Human evaluation remains the gold standard for GPT assessment. Human raters evaluate fluency, coherence, helpfulness, factual correctness, and emotional tone–dimensions that automated scores cannot fully capture. OpenAI, Anthropic, and others employ large-scale human preference modeling to guide fine-tuning (as in RLHF and Constitutional AI). To ensure consistency, structured rubrics and inter-rater reliability checks are typically used.
- **Emerging Benchmarks:** Beyond traditional metrics, specialized GPT evaluation suites have emerged, including:
    - **MT-Bench**: Assesses dialogue and reasoning quality through multi-turn interactions.
    - **TruthfulQA**: Tests factual accuracy and resistance to falsehoods.
    - **Holistic Evaluation of Language Models (HELM)**: Measures robustness, efficiency, fairness, and calibration across diverse tasks.
    - **OpenAI Evals**: A framework for continuous testing of task performance, bias, and safety in deployed GPT systems.

These benchmarks better reflect GPT's multifaceted capabilities and evolving real-world applications.

Assessing Quality, Coherence, and Diversity of Outputs

- **Quality Assessment:** GPT's output quality is evaluated through a combination of automated metrics and human scoring. Automated tools track syntactic fluency and semantic consistency, while human raters assess contextual appropriateness and factual grounding. Increasingly, GPT models are evaluated with pairwise human preference tests, comparing outputs across prompts to measure perceived helpfulness and truthfulness.

- **Coherence Analysis:** Coherence refers to the logical and thematic consistency of generated text. GPT's large context windows and causal attention enhance coherence, but performance may degrade in very long conversations. Tools such as topic-flow tracking and entity consistency metrics evaluate whether GPT maintains narrative and referential continuity across extended sequences.
- **Diversity Measurement:** A key evaluation axis for GPT is output diversity—the ability to produce varied yet relevant responses. Metrics such as Self-BLEU, distinct-n, and entropy-based diversity quantify lexical and structural variety. In practice, tuning decoding parameters such as temperature and nucleus sampling (top-p) helps balance creativity and determinism, a tradeoff central to GPT's generative performance.

Addressing Biases and Ensuring Fair Evaluation

- **Identifying Biases:** Because GPT is trained on large-scale web data, it may internalize and reproduce social, cultural, or linguistic biases. Evaluating fairness involves analyzing outputs across demographic and contextual variations using differential treatment analysis and bias benchmarks such as RealToxicityPrompts or StereoSet.
- **Bias Mitigation:** Modern GPT systems employ multiple layers of bias control—data filtering, RLHF, adversarial testing, and constitutional guidance. Post-training moderation layers and reinforcement with human feedback further align responses to ethical and inclusive norms.
- **Ensuring Fair Evaluation:** Fair model assessment requires diverse, representative test datasets that include multiple languages, cultures, and dialects. Evaluation teams composed of raters from varied backgrounds help mitigate subjective bias. In multimodal GPT models, fairness also extends to how images, code, or audio inputs are interpreted and described, ensuring equitable performance across modalities.

Evaluating GPT models is a multifaceted process that combines automated metrics, human judgment, and fairness considerations. Metrics such as perplexity, BLEU, and ROUGE provide valuable insights into structural and linguistic performance, while human evaluators offer a deeper understanding of contextual and semantic nuances. Addressing biases and ensuring fair evaluation practices are essential for deploying GPT models that are not only effective but also ethical and inclusive. By adopting comprehensive evaluation strategies, developers and researchers can better align GPT models with the diverse needs of real-world applications.

Implementing GPT: Step-by-Step

Generative Pre-trained Transformers (GPT) are among the most transformative advancements in artificial intelligence, enabling a wide range of applications from chatbots to creative writing. In this section, we will explore the practical implementation of GPT, from accessing pre-trained models to fine-tuning them for specific use cases. This section focuses on practical strategies for deploying GPT—covering API usage, open-source implementations, fine-tuning, and real-world applications.

Accessing GPT Models via APIs or Frameworks

One of the easiest ways to begin working with GPT is by utilizing pre-trained models available through APIs or open-source frameworks. Pre-trained GPT models, such as OpenAI's GPT-4, come with billions of parameters trained on massive datasets, making them versatile for various natural language processing tasks. Here is how you can get started:

1. **Using OpenAI API**: OpenAI provides a simple-to-use API that allows developers to access GPT models such as GPT-4 Turbo or GPT-5. After signing up and obtaining an API key, you can interact with the model by sending prompts and receiving responses.

Example code snippet:

```
import openai
openai.api_key = "your_api_key_here"

response = openai.ChatCompletion.create(
    model="gpt-4-turbo",
    messages=[
        {"role": "system", "content": "You are a helpful assistant."},
        {"role": "user", "content": "What is the capital of France?"}
    ]
)

print(response['choices'][0]['message']['content'])
```

This code demonstrates how to send a query to the GPT model and retrieve its response.

2. **Using Hugging Face Transformers Library**: Hugging Face's Transformers library provides access to both GPT-family models and open-source alternatives such as **GPT-Neo**, **GPT-J**, **LLaMA-3**, and **Mistral**. These can be fine-tuned locally or used directly for inference.

Install the library using pip:

```
pip install transformers
```

3. **Load a pre-trained model:**

```
from transformers import AutoTokenizer, AutoModelForCausalLM

tokenizer = AutoTokenizer.from_pretrained("gpt2")
model = AutoModelForCausalLM.from_pretrained("gpt2")

input_text = "Once upon a time in a distant galaxy"
input_ids = tokenizer(input_text, return_tensors="pt").input_ids

output = model.generate(input_ids, max_length=50, num_return_sequences=1)
print(tokenizer.decode(output[0], skip_special_tokens=True))
```

This snippet demonstrates how to load a pre-trained GPT model and generate coherent continuations from a given text prompt.

Fine-Tuning GPT for Specific Use Cases

While pre-trained models are powerful, fine-tuning enables them to excel at domain-specific tasks. Fine-tuning involves training the model on a smaller, specialized dataset, allowing it to better understand context and nuances relevant to a particular application.

Dataset Preparation: Ensure your dataset is formatted correctly. For text-based tasks, it is often stored in JSON or plain text format. Hugging Face's Datasets library can help you preprocess and load datasets efficiently:

```
from datasets import load_dataset

dataset = load_dataset("imdb")
print(dataset["train"][0])
```

Fine-tuning with Hugging Face:

Hugging Face's Trainer API simplifies the fine-tuning process:

```
from transformers import AutoTokenizer, AutoModelForCausalLM, Trainer,
TrainingArguments
```

```
tokenizer = AutoTokenizer.from_pretrained("gpt2")
model = AutoModelForCausalLM.from_pretrained("gpt2")

tokenized_dataset = dataset.map(lambda x: tokenizer(x["text"], truncation
=True, padding=True), batched=True)

training_args = TrainingArguments(
    output_dir="./results",
    num_train_epochs=3,
    per_device_train_batch_size=8,
    save_steps=10_000,
    save_total_limit=2,
    logging_dir="./logs",
)

trainer = Trainer(
    model=model,
    args=training_args,
    train_dataset=tokenized_dataset["train"],
    eval_dataset=tokenized_dataset["test"]
)

trainer.train()
```

Customizing for Your Application: Depending on the use case, adjust hyperparameters, learning rates, and datasets. For example, fine-tune GPT for sentiment analysis, chatbot development, or generating domain-specific content.

Practical Examples Using TensorFlow or PyTorch

Python's popular deep learning frameworks—**PyTorch** and **TensorFlow**—make it easy to implement, experiment with, and fine-tune GPT models. The following example demonstrates a basic fine-tuning setup using the Hugging Face Transformers library with PyTorch.

Using PyTorch:

```
# Fine-tune a GPT model on a custom dataset:
import torch
from transformers import AutoTokenizer, AutoModelForCausalLM

# Load a pre-trained GPT model (GPT-2 shown here; can be replaced with
"EleutherAI/gpt-neo-125M" or "microsoft/phi-2")
tokenizer = AutoTokenizer.from_pretrained("gpt2")
model = AutoModelForCausalLM.from_pretrained("gpt2")

# Ensure the model is in training mode
model.train()

# Encode input text into tensor format
input_text = "Fine-tuning GPT models for domain adaptation"
input_ids = tokenizer(input_text, return_tensors="pt").input_ids

# Forward pass: the model returns loss when labels are provided
(self-supervised objective)
outputs = model(input_ids=input_ids, labels=input_ids)

# Extract and print the training loss
```

```
loss = outputs.loss
print(f"Training loss: {loss.item():.4f}")
```

This short script demonstrates the **core mechanism** of GPT fine-tuning.

- It loads a pre-trained GPT model and tokenizer using Hugging Face's transformers library.
- The same input text is used as both the prompt and target–mimicking GPT's causal language modeling objective (predicting the next token).
- The model returns a loss value, which quantifies how well it predicts the next token sequence.
- In a real fine-tuning setup, you would then use an optimizer (such as AdamW) and perform multiple training steps to minimize this loss across a dataset.

This example does not update model weights but provides the foundation for understanding how GPT learns from data–the essential building block of fine-tuning custom GPT models for domain-specific tasks.

Using TensorFlow:

Generate text using a pre-trained model:

```
import tensorflow as tf
from transformers import TFGPT2LMHeadModel, GPT2Tokenizer

# Load the pre-trained GPT-2 tokenizer and TensorFlow model
tokenizer = GPT2Tokenizer.from_pretrained("gpt2")
model = TFGPT2LMHeadModel.from_pretrained("gpt2")

# Input text
input_text = "Fine-tuning GPT models"

# Tokenize the input text into tensor format
inputs = tokenizer(input_text, return_tensors="tf")

# Perform a forward pass
# In self-supervised learning, labels are the same as inputs
outputs = model(inputs["input_ids"], labels=inputs["input_ids"])

# Extract and print the loss
loss = outputs.loss
print(f"Training loss: {loss.numpy():.4f}")
```

This TensorFlow script performs the same operation as the PyTorch version but uses TensorFlow's computation graph.

- **Model and Tokenizer Loading**
  - It loads the TFGPT2LMHeadModel and corresponding tokenizer from Hugging Face's Transformers library.
  - The GPT-2 model is pre-trained for *causal language modeling*, meaning it predicts the next token given previous ones.
- **Tokenization**
  - The input text ("*Fine-tuning GPT models*") is converted into numerical token IDs that GPT-2 can process.
- **Forward Pass and Loss Computation**
  - The same tensor is passed as both **`input_ids`** and **`labels`**, mimicking GPT's self-supervised setup.

  - The model outputs a loss that represents how well GPT predicts the next token in the sequence.
- **Output**
  - The script prints the computed loss value, which reflects the model's prediction quality on that small input.
  - Like before, this example does not perform optimization (no gradient updates), but it shows the core training mechanism that fine-tuning builds upon.

Applications in Real-World Scenarios:

- Build a text summarizer using GPT to condense articles into concise summaries.
- Develop a conversational chatbot that can assist customers in real-time.
- Generate creative content, such as poems, stories, or marketing slogans, tailored to specific needs.

By following these steps, you can effectively implement GPT models for a variety of tasks, from experimentation to production-grade applications. Leveraging APIs, frameworks, and practical coding techniques ensures a smooth workflow for unlocking the immense potential of GPT technology.

Case Study: Building a Conversational AI System with GPT

Conversational AI has revolutionized the way businesses interact with customers, enabling personalized, real-time assistance at scale. In this case study, we will explore how to build a customer support chatbot using GPT, focusing on problem identification, solution design, and implementation challenges, and examining the final outcome through examples and insights.

Problem: Creating a Chatbot for Customer Support

Businesses often face challenges in managing customer queries effectively, especially during high-demand periods. Customers expect quick, accurate, and context-aware responses. Traditional rule-based chatbots often fail to deliver satisfying experiences due to their inability to handle complex queries or adapt to conversational contexts. The goal of this project is to create a chatbot that not only answers customer questions but also understands the nuances of dialogue, providing human-like interaction and improving overall customer satisfaction.

Solution Approach: Fine-tuning GPT for Dialogue Generation and Contextual Understanding

To address the problem, we decided to leverage a pre-trained GPT model. The solution involves fine-tuning GPT on a domain-specific dataset to enhance its contextual understanding and dialogue generation capabilities. The following steps outline the approach:

- **Dataset Preparation**: We collected a large dataset of customer support interactions, including FAQs, email transcripts, and live chat logs. The dataset was preprocessed to remove sensitive information and was labeled for training purposes.
- **Fine-Tuning GPT**: Using a pre-trained GPT model, we fine-tuned it on the prepared dataset. Fine-tuning involved supervised learning techniques to align the model's outputs with the tone and style of customer support communication.

- **Context Management**: To ensure coherent and context-aware responses, we implemented context windows. This allowed the chatbot to remember and reference previous messages in a conversation.
- **Validation and Testing**: The fine-tuned model was rigorously tested using both automated evaluation metrics, such as BLEU and perplexity, and human evaluation for quality assurance. Feedback from test users was incorporated to further refine the model.
- **Integration**: The final chatbot was integrated with existing customer support platforms via APIs, enabling seamless deployment across multiple communication channels, including web chat, mobile apps, and email.

Challenges: Ensuring Relevance and Avoiding Inappropriate Responses

Building a conversational AI system comes with its own set of challenges:

- **Relevance of Responses**: One of the primary challenges was ensuring that the chatbot's responses were accurate and contextually relevant. In some cases, the model generated plausible but incorrect answers, which required additional post-processing rules.
- **Avoiding Inappropriate Outputs**: Pre-trained models can inadvertently generate inappropriate or biased content due to the nature of their training data. Mitigating this required careful dataset curation and the use of filtering mechanisms to detect and suppress undesired outputs.
- **Handling Ambiguity**: Customers often ask ambiguous or open-ended questions. Ensuring that the chatbot could request clarification or provide meaningful responses required extensive scenario testing.
- **Scalability**: Training and deploying a fine-tuned GPT model on customer queries while maintaining low latency was computationally intensive. This required optimizing the model and leveraging cloud infrastructure for scalability.

Outcome: Examples of Conversations and Insights into Building Robust Systems

The final chatbot demonstrated significant improvements in customer interaction quality. Below are examples of how the system performed in real-world scenarios:

Example 1: Resolving a Billing Query

Customer: "*I was charged twice for my subscription. Can you help?*"

Chatbot: "*I understand your concern. Let me check that for you. Could you please provide your subscription ID?*"

Customer: "It's 4872."

Chatbot: "*Thank you! I see that there was indeed a duplicate charge. I have initiated a refund for the extra payment. You should receive it within 5-7 business days. Is there anything else I can assist you with?*"

Example 2: Providing Product Information

Customer: "*What are the features of your premium plan?*"

Chatbot: "*Our premium plan includes unlimited access to all features, priority customer support, and additional storage. Would you like me to send you a detailed brochure?*"

The chatbot's ability to handle diverse queries showcased its contextual understanding and adaptability. The following insights were gathered:

- **Importance of Domain-Specific Fine-Tuning**: Fine-tuning the model on domain-specific datasets significantly improved its relevance and accuracy in customer support contexts.
- **Continuous Monitoring and Updates**: Regular monitoring and iterative updates were essential to address new types of queries and improve response quality.
- **Human-in-the-Loop Systems**: Integrating human agents for complex or sensitive queries ensured a fallback mechanism, enhancing customer satisfaction.
- **Bias Mitigation**: Ongoing efforts in bias detection and removal were critical to maintaining ethical standards in customer interactions.

In conclusion, building a customer support chatbot using GPT demonstrates the potential of conversational AI to transform customer engagement. Despite challenges, the outcome highlighted the importance of careful planning, fine-tuning, and continuous optimization to create robust systems that deliver meaningful and human-like interactions.

Future Directions for GPT

Generative Pre-trained Transformers (GPT) have reshaped artificial intelligence by enabling machines to generate and understand human language with remarkable fluency. As these systems evolve, the next phase of development will focus not only on scaling but also on efficiency, multimodality, and interpretability. This essay explores how future iterations of GPT – potentially including models such as GPT-5 and beyond – are expected to advance in scope, capability, and responsibility.

Advancements in Scaling GPT Models

Scaling has underpinned GPT's success, with larger architectures consistently delivering stronger reasoning and language capabilities. Yet, expanding model size introduces challenges in computation, cost, and sustainability. Future progress will depend on smarter, not just larger, models.

- **Architectural Innovation:** Next-generation GPTs may adopt hybrid or Mixture-of-Experts (MoE) designs that dynamically activate only subsets of parameters, preserving performance while reducing compute demands.
- **Training Optimization:** Sparse training, model distillation, and parameter-efficient fine-tuning (PEFT) approaches such as LoRA can improve efficiency and accessibility.
- **Distributed Frameworks:** Advances in distributed GPU and TPU infrastructures will make large-scale GPT training feasible for broader research communities, democratizing innovation in generative AI.

Evolving Toward Multimodal and Agentic GPT Systems

The next stage in GPT's evolution lies in seamless multimodal intelligence – the ability to process and generate across text, images, audio, and other sensory inputs. Unlike traditional text-only models, emerging GPT architectures are designed to reason over multiple data streams simultaneously, enhancing contextual understanding and creativity.

- **Unified Multimodal Architectures:** Future GPT models are expected to merge transformer-based modules for language, vision, and audio into a cohesive framework. Integrating components such as Vision Transformers (ViTs) or audio encoders enables GPT to describe, interpret, and generate content across modalities – for example, summarizing videos, analyzing medical imagery, or narrating visual scenes with natural speech.

- **Agentic Capabilities:** Beyond perception, multimodal GPTs are beginning to act – not merely predict. New architectures incorporate *function calling*, *retrieval-augmented generation* (RAG), and *tool use*, allowing GPT to execute reasoning chains, query external systems, and take context-aware actions. This shift marks a transition from passive text generation to active task completion.
- **Applications and Challenges:** These multimodal, agentic systems hold transformative potential across domains such as healthcare, creative industries, and education. However, ensuring coherence and alignment between modalities remains a key challenge. GPT must learn to maintain semantic consistency – for instance, aligning textual and visual elements in a narrative – while adhering to ethical and factual constraints.

Reducing Biases and Improving Interpretability

As GPT systems continue to expand their influence across industries, addressing ethical concerns such as bias, fairness, and interpretability is increasingly vital. The challenge lies not only in minimizing harmful outputs but also in ensuring that GPT's reasoning processes are transparent and aligned with human values.

- **Bias Mitigation Strategies:** Reducing bias begins at the data level. Future GPT development will rely on curated, demographically balanced datasets and advanced techniques such as *adversarial debiasing* and *synthetic data augmentation* to counteract representation gaps. Beyond data curation, integrating *reinforcement learning from human feedback (RLHF)* and *Direct Preference Optimization* (DPO) allows GPT models to internalize fairness constraints during fine-tuning rather than relying solely on post hoc filtering.
- **Measuring and Auditing Fairness:** Researchers are establishing standardized fairness and safety benchmarks to evaluate GPT behavior systematically. These metrics enable continuous auditing and guide interventions that promote equitable treatment across linguistic, cultural, and demographic contexts.
- **Improving Interpretability and Transparency:** Understanding how GPT arrives at specific outputs remains a central research focus. Emerging *explainable* AI (XAI) tools and visualization methods aim to illuminate GPT's internal reasoning, showing how particular inputs influence generated responses. Techniques such as *attention heatmaps* and *attribution tracking* provide valuable insights into decision pathways, fostering trust and accountability in model outputs.
- **Ethical and Governance Frameworks:** Alongside technical measures, the future of GPT development will depend on robust governance. Organizations are increasingly adopting *ethical AI frameworks* emphasizing transparency, accountability, and inclusivity. Collaboration among researchers, policymakers, and industry stakeholders will be essential to ensure that GPT advances responsibly and in alignment with societal values.

The trajectory of GPT is not defined solely by scale or capability but by the integrity of its design. As advancements in debiasing, interpretability, and governance converge, GPT systems will evolve into more equitable, comprehensible, and trustworthy collaborators–reshaping the relationship between humans and intelligent machines.

Conclusion

In this chapter, we explored the architecture, working principles, and real-world applications of Generative Pre-trained Transformers (GPT), a breakthrough in natural language processing (NLP). We examined the evolution of GPT models, from GPT-1 to GPT-5, and how they have transformed various industries, from content generation and conversational AI to code generation and knowledge retrieval.

We discussed the core concepts behind GPT, including pre-training and fine-tuning, causal language modeling, and tokenization techniques such as Byte Pair Encoding (BPE). The Transformer architecture was analyzed in depth, covering self-attention mechanisms, positional embeddings, and scaling strategies that enhance GPT's ability to generate coherent and contextually relevant text.

Additionally, we explored the challenges in training GPT models, such as computational requirements, biases, and hallucinations, and discussed methods for evaluating their performance using metrics such as perplexity, BLEU, and ROUGE. The implementation section provided hands-on guidance on accessing and fine-tuning pre-trained GPT models using APIs and deep learning frameworks such as Hugging Face, TensorFlow, and PyTorch.

Finally, we examined a case study on building a Conversational AI system with GPT, highlighting the potential of GPT-powered chatbots for customer support, dialogue generation, and virtual assistance. Despite its strengths in scalability, coherence, and adaptability, GPT also has limitations, including bias, misinformation, and contextual inconsistencies, which must be carefully managed.

With a comprehensive understanding of GPT and its applications, you are now equipped to build and fine-tune GPT models for real-world NLP tasks. In the next chapter, we will explore LangChain, a powerful framework for building AI-powered applications that integrate large language models (LLMs) with external knowledge sources, APIs, and retrieval-augmented generation (RAG) techniques to enhance reasoning and contextual awareness.

Points to Remember

- GPT models use a Transformer-based architecture that employs self-attention, positional embeddings, and feedforward networks to generate text in an autoregressive manner.
- Pre-training and fine-tuning are crucial in GPT's training pipeline, allowing models to learn general language representations and later specialize in specific tasks.
- Causal language modeling ensures that GPT predicts the next token sequentially, making it ideal for generative tasks.
- Applications of GPT span multiple industries, including text generation, code generation, summarization, conversational AI, and sentiment analysis.
- Evaluating GPT outputs requires a mix of quantitative metrics (perplexity, BLEU, ROUGE) and qualitative assessments (human evaluation, coherence analysis, and bias detection).
- Despite its strengths, GPT has limitations, such as bias, hallucination, and contextual inconsistencies, which need careful monitoring and mitigation strategies.
- Byte Pair Encoding (BPE) is a commonly used tokenization technique in GPT, enabling efficient handling of rare and compound words.
- The performance of GPT improves with scale—larger models, more data, and greater compute lead to significantly better language understanding and generation.
- Fine-tuning GPT on domain-specific data allows it to adapt to specialized tasks such as legal document analysis, medical reporting, or customer support.
- Ethical considerations around GPT include preventing misuse, addressing representational bias, and reducing the spread of misinformation.

Multiple-Choice Questions

1. What is the primary training objective of GPT models?
    a. Masked language modeling
    b. Causal language modeling

   c. Reinforcement learning
   d. Contrastive learning
2. Which technique is commonly used for tokenization in GPT models?
   a. Word2Vec
   b. Convolutional tokenization
   c. Byte Pair Encoding (BPE)
   d. Fast Fourier Transform
3. Which of the following is a major advantage of GPT over traditional NLP models?
   a. Requires less training data
   b. Can generate coherent and contextually rich text without predefined templates
   c. Uses rule-based methods for text generation
   d. Does not require pre-training
4. What is a key limitation of GPT models?
   a. They do not support text generation
   b. They always produce factually accurate outputs
   c. They can generate biased or misleading content
   d. They require explicitly labeled paired datasets for training
5. Which evaluation metric is commonly used to measure the coherence of GPT-generated text?
   a. SSIM
   b. Mean Squared Error
   c. IoU
   d. BLEU
6. What type of architecture forms the backbone of GPT models?
   a. Transformer
   b. Recurrent Neural Network
   c. Convolutional Neural Network
   d. Support Vector Machine

Answers

1. b
2. c
3. b
4. c
5. d
6. a

Questions

1. How does GPT differ from traditional NLP models in terms of architecture and training approach?
2. What are the advantages of using causal language modeling for text generation?
3. How do pre-training and fine-tuning contribute to GPT's performance across different tasks?
4. What are some real-world applications of GPT, and how has it transformed industries such as content creation and AI assistants?
5. How can bias and hallucinations in GPT-generated content be mitigated?
6. Why is tokenization important in GPT models, and how does Byte Pair Encoding (BPE) improve efficiency?
7. What are the main evaluation metrics for assessing GPT's text generation quality?
8. How does GPT compare with other transformer-based models such as BERT and T5?
9. What are the computational challenges in training large-scale GPT models?
10. How can GPT be integrated with external tools and APIs to enhance its capabilities?

Key Terms

- **Generative Pre-trained Transformer (GPT)**: A Transformer-based NLP model designed for text generation using **causal language modeling**.
- **Pre-training**: The initial phase of GPT training, where the model learns general language patterns from large-scale text corpora.
- **Fine-tuning**: A subsequent training phase where GPT is specialized for specific tasks, such as **summarization, translation, or question answering**.
- **Self-Attention**: A mechanism in Transformers that allows GPT to **analyze relationships between words** in a sequence, regardless of their position.
- **Byte Pair Encoding (BPE)**: A **tokenization technique** that breaks words into subword units, improving efficiency and handling rare words.
- **Perplexity**: A metric for evaluating **language model fluency**, measuring how well the model predicts a given text sequence.
- **BLEU and ROUGE Scores**: Evaluation metrics for measuring **the quality of generated text** by comparing it with reference texts.
- **Hallucination**: A phenomenon where GPT generates **factually incorrect or misleading** content.
- **Bias in NLP**: The tendency of GPT models to generate responses that reflect **societal biases** present in the training data.
- **Conversational AI**: The use of GPT for building **chatbots and AI assistants** capable of natural, human-like interactions.

CHAPTER 18
Langchain: Building AI-Powered Applications

Introduction

Langchain is a cutting-edge framework designed to simplify the development of AI-powered applications by seamlessly integrating large language models (LLMs) with external tools and data sources. As generative AI continues to evolve, Langchain empowers developers to build sophisticated applications that leverage the full potential of LLMs, combining the creativity of text generation with structured workflows and real-world data integration. Whether it is creating dynamic chatbots, knowledge retrieval systems, or automated workflows, Langchain provides a modular approach to orchestrating complex AI tasks.

In this chapter, we dive into the foundational principles and architecture of Langchain, exploring its key components such as prompt templates, memory, chains, and agents. We will discuss how Langchain enables interaction with external data sources, such as vector databases and APIs, to create robust and context-aware applications. Through practical examples and hands-on implementations, you will learn how to harness Langchain to build intelligent, scalable, and efficient AI solutions tailored to various domains. By the end of this chapter, you will have the skills to design and deploy AI-powered applications that seamlessly combine the power of LLMs with structured workflows and data-driven intelligence.

Structure

In this chapter, we will cover the following topics:

- **Introduction to Langchain**
    - Why Langchain is Essential for Working with LLMs and Generative Models
    - Applications of Langchain in Industries and Real-World Scenarios
- **Key Concepts in Langchain**
    - Understanding the Modular Design of Langchain
    - Core Components: Prompt Templates, Memory, and Chains
    - Integrating External Data Sources with Langchain
- **Langchain Architecture and Components**
    - Langchain Architecture
    - Components: Prompt Templates, Memory, Chains, Agents
- **Data Integration with Langchain**
    - Connecting Langchain to APIs, Databases, and External Tools

Introduction to Langchain

The exponential growth in generative AI technologies has spurred a new era of applications powered by Large Language Models (LLMs). While these models have demonstrated incredible capabilities, their integration into real-world applications often requires a structured and efficient approach. Enter Langchain, a powerful framework designed to simplify the development of AI-powered applications by leveraging the strengths of LLMs. Langchain bridges the gap between raw model capabilities and practical implementations, providing developers with tools to create robust, scalable, and intelligent solutions seamlessly.

Langchain is an open-source framework specifically tailored for building applications that utilize language models. At its core, Langchain enables developers to chain together multiple components, including prompts, memory, APIs, and user interfaces, to create cohesive AI workflows. Its modular architecture allows for customization, extensibility, and the seamless integration of LLMs into complex pipelines.

Key features of Langchain include:

- **Prompt Engineering:** Provides a structured way to craft, optimize, and reuse prompts for specific tasks.
- **Memory Integration:** Supports both short-term and long-term memory, enabling applications to maintain context across interactions.
- **API Integration:** Facilitates connections to external APIs, databases, and other tools, enhancing the functionality of applications.
- **Tool Management:** Allows developers to design tools that the language model can interact with, such as calculators, search engines, or domain-specific APIs.

By simplifying the intricacies of working with LLMs, Langchain accelerates the development process, making it accessible even to teams with limited AI expertise.

Why Langchain Is Essential for Working with LLMs and Generative Models

Generative AI models, while highly advanced, often present challenges in terms of usability and scalability. These include difficulties in:

- **Context Management:** Maintaining conversation history or data context over extended interactions.
- **Dynamic Workflow Design:** Creating flexible and interactive systems that adapt based on user input or external events.
- **Integration Complexity:** Combining multiple AI and non-AI components into a unified application.

Langchain addresses these challenges by offering a comprehensive toolkit for orchestrating workflows. For instance, developers can:

- Design multi-step reasoning processes using sequential chains.
- Incorporate external data sources such as vector databases for contextual retrieval.
- Enable applications to interact with real-world tools, APIs, and systems effortlessly.

In essence, Langchain transforms LLMs from standalone models into integral components of intelligent systems. This transformation not only enhances the utility of generative models but also allows businesses to create tailored solutions that align with specific needs.

Applications of Langchain in Industries and Real-World Scenarios

The versatility of Langchain makes it a game-changer across various industries. Its ability to integrate LLMs with external tools and workflows has paved the way for innovative applications. Below are some real-world scenarios demonstrating its potential:

- **Customer Support and Chatbots:** Langchain enables the creation of advanced conversational agents that not only answer customer queries but also integrate with CRM systems to fetch personalized information. For example, an e-commerce chatbot built with Langchain can handle product recommendations, order tracking, and issue resolution seamlessly.
- **Knowledge Management and Document Summarization:** Businesses can use Langchain to build tools for summarizing long documents, generating insights, or retrieving specific information from vast knowledge bases. These applications are particularly valuable in industries such as legal, healthcare, and finance.
- **Educational Platforms:** With Langchain, educational apps can leverage LLMs to provide personalized learning experiences. These include creating dynamic quizzes, offering real-time explanations, or tailoring content based on a student's progress.
- **Content Creation and Editing:** Langchain's prompt management capabilities are ideal for applications in content generation. From drafting blog posts to editing and rephrasing content, the framework can streamline creative workflows for writers and marketers.
- **Healthcare Assistance:** In healthcare, Langchain can power virtual assistants capable of answering patient questions, scheduling appointments, or providing preliminary diagnoses based on symptoms. When integrated with medical databases, these assistants become even more robust.

- **Financial Analysis and Reporting:** Langchain facilitates the development of AI tools that automate financial report generation, analyze market trends, or provide investment recommendations by integrating with financial APIs and data sources.

By addressing both general-purpose and domain-specific needs, Langchain positions itself as an essential framework for developing next-generation AI solutions. Its adaptability ensures that businesses across diverse sectors can unlock the full potential of LLMs and generative models.

Key Concepts in Langchain

Langchain is a powerful framework for developing applications that utilize large language models (LLMs). It provides developers with a structured way to integrate LLM capabilities into their workflows, enabling more intelligent and context-aware solutions. The framework's modular design makes it versatile, allowing for seamless integration with external data sources and adaptability to various application needs. Below, we delve into the foundational aspects of Langchain.

Understanding the Modular Design of Langchain

Langchain's modular design is one of its most compelling features. This design philosophy divides the framework into independent yet interconnected components, each catering to specific functionalities. By organizing the framework in this way, developers can focus on individual elements of their application without being overwhelmed by the complexity of the entire system.

For instance, you can work on prompt engineering independently of memory management or chain construction. This modularity also ensures reusability, as components can be adapted or replaced without significant disruptions to the overall application. Such flexibility is crucial in scenarios where rapid prototyping or iterative development is required.

Another advantage of this design is scalability. As the application grows, you can incorporate new components or expand existing ones without rewriting significant portions of the codebase. For example, adding a new external data source to enhance the LLM's capabilities involves integrating a data retrieval module without altering the core logic.

Core Components: Prompt Templates, Memory, and Chains

Langchain's core components form the backbone of its functionality. Each component is tailored to address specific challenges faced when working with LLMs.

Prompt Templates in Langchain are pre-defined structures or blueprints that guide the interaction between the user and the LLM. They ensure that the input provided to the LLM is clear, concise, and aligned with the intended task. By defining prompts systematically, developers can minimize ambiguities and improve the model's performance.

For example, a prompt template for a customer support chatbot might look like this:

"*You are an AI assistant for customer support. Respond politely and concisely to the user's query.* `Query: {user_query}`"

This ensures consistency in the model's responses, irrespective of the query's complexity.

Memory in Langchain plays a pivotal role in maintaining context during multi-turn conversations. Unlike traditional LLM interactions, where each query is treated as independent, Langchain's memory component enables the model to retain information across exchanges. This creates a more natural and human-like interaction experience.

Langchain supports different types of memory, such as short-term memory for retaining context within a session and long-term memory for persisting information across sessions. For instance, a virtual tutor application can use memory to remember a student's progress and provide tailored recommendations in future sessions.

Chains in Langchain link various operations or components to perform complex tasks. A chain could be as simple as a single prompt-response flow or as intricate as a multi-step process involving data retrieval, computation, and interaction with the LLM.

For example, a document summarization chain might include the following steps:

- Retrieve a document from an external source.
- Break the document into manageable chunks.
- Generate summaries for each chunk using the LLM.
- Combine the summaries into a coherent final output.

Chains allow developers to build workflows that extend beyond simple text generation, making Langchain suitable for real-world applications such as report generation, data analysis, and automated decision-making.

Integrating External Data Sources with Langchain

One of Langchain's strengths is its ability to seamlessly integrate external data sources. This feature allows developers to enhance the LLM's responses with up-to-date and contextually relevant information. Commonly integrated data sources include:

- **APIs**: Langchain can interact with APIs to fetch real-time information. For example, a weather bot can use weather APIs to provide accurate forecasts.
- **Databases**: Integration with databases allows Langchain to retrieve and manipulate structured data. This is particularly useful for applications such as inventory management or personalized user experiences.
- **Document Repositories**: Langchain can connect to document repositories to fetch unstructured data, such as articles or research papers, which can then be summarized or analyzed by the LLM.

The process of integrating external data sources involves creating a data retrieval module that interfaces with the desired source. This module can preprocess the data before passing it to the LLM. For instance, if the external data is in JSON format, the module can extract relevant fields and format the content as a prompt for the LLM.

By enabling external data integration, Langchain transcends the limitations of standalone LLMs, offering richer and more context-aware solutions. This capability is particularly valuable in dynamic environments where the information landscape is constantly evolving, such as financial analysis, e-commerce, and news aggregation.

Langchain's modular design, robust core components, and ability to integrate external data sources make it an indispensable tool for developers leveraging LLMs. Whether building conversational agents, data-driven applications, or intelligent automation workflows, Langchain provides the tools and flexibility to innovate and excel.

Langchain Architecture and Components

Langchain has emerged as a critical framework for orchestrating large language models (LLMs) effectively, enabling developers to build complex applications by integrating modular components. At its core, Langchain is designed to simplify the interaction with LLMs, ensuring flexibility, reusability, and scalability. This section explores the fundamental building blocks of Langchain's architecture, including its key components: Prompt Templates, Memory, Chains, and Agents. Each of these components plays a vital role in creating robust LLM-based applications, offering an efficient way to handle natural language processing workflows.

Langchain Architecture

The architecture of Langchain revolves around the seamless integration of LLMs with structured workflows. By modularizing the various aspects of LLM interactions, Langchain provides developers with the tools to:

- Generate dynamic and reusable prompts.
- Maintain contextual understanding across conversations.
- Sequence multiple operations to create comprehensive workflows.
- Enable intelligent decision-making through agent-based systems.

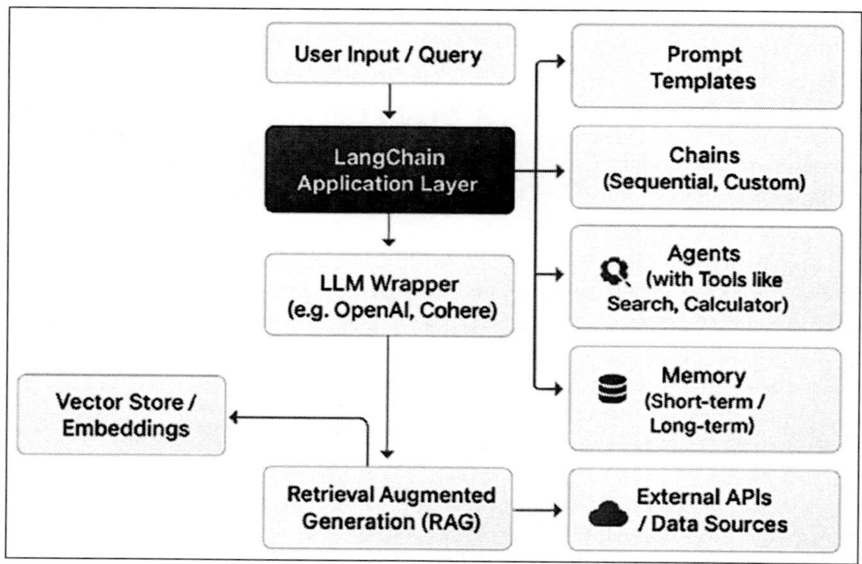

***Figure 18.1**: LangChain Overview*

This modular design allows developers to build applications that scale from simple chatbots to intricate multi-step pipelines involving external APIs, databases, and logic-based decision-making.

Components: Prompt Templates, Memory, Chains, Agents

LangChain organizes its capabilities into modular components that work together to build sophisticated LLM-driven applications. These components provide structure for everything from crafting prompts to maintaining context, orchestrating multi-step workflows, and enabling autonomous decision-making. Each module handles a distinct part of the reasoning pipeline, creating a flexible foundation for scalable AI systems.

Prompt Templates: Building Dynamic and Reusable Prompts

Prompts are the cornerstone of effective LLM utilization, dictating the quality and relevance of model responses. Langchain's **Prompt Templates** module provides a systematic way to construct prompts that are dynamic, reusable, and tailored to specific tasks. Key features include:

- **Parameterized Prompts**: Developers can define placeholders within prompts, enabling customization at runtime. For instance, a customer support application can generate responses dynamically based on user queries and contextual data.
- **Template Libraries**: Langchain supports storing and managing collections of prompts for various use cases, ensuring consistency across applications.
- **Dynamic Formatting**: With integrated formatting tools, Langchain allows developers to include variables, external data, or computed values seamlessly within prompts.

Example:

```
from langchain.prompts import PromptTemplate

template = "Translate the following text to {language}: {text}"
prompt = PromptTemplate(template=template, input_variables=["language",
"text"])
formatted_prompt = prompt.format(language="French", text="Hello, how are
you?")
print(formatted_prompt)
# Output: Translate the following text to French: Hello, how are you?
```

Memory: Maintaining Context Across Interactions

In conversational AI and multi-step workflows, maintaining context is critical to delivering coherent and relevant responses. Langchain's **Memory** module addresses this by enabling state persistence across interactions. This ensures that the model can recall past interactions and use them effectively to inform future outputs.

- **Types of Memory:**
  - **Short-Term Memory**: Keeps track of recent exchanges within a single session.
  - **Long-Term Memory**: Stores information persistently across sessions to build a richer context over time.
- **Use Cases:**
  - Personalized assistants that remember user preferences.
  - Multi-turn dialogues that require reference to prior messages.
  - Continuous task execution where context accumulation is essential.

Example:

```
from langchain.memory import ConversationBufferMemory

memory = ConversationBufferMemory()
memory.save_context({"input": "What's the weather?"}, {"output":
"It's sunny."})
context = memory.load_memory_variables()
print(context)
# Output: {'history': 'Human: What's the weather?\nAI: It's sunny.'}
```

Chains: Sequencing Multiple Operations to Build Complex Workflows

Chains in Langchain enable the sequencing of multiple operations, allowing developers to build pipelines that involve diverse tasks such as data retrieval, processing, and output generation. Chains can be simple or complex, integrating multiple LLM invocations, memory modules, and external API calls.

- **Single-Task Chains**: Perform a single operation, such as text summarization.
- **Multi-Task Chains**: Combine several tasks, such as retrieving data from a database, generating a response, and formatting the output.
- **Custom Chains**: Developers can design bespoke chains tailored to specific application needs.

Example:

```
from langchain.chains import SimpleSequentialChain
from langchain.prompts import PromptTemplate
from langchain.llms import OpenAI

llm = OpenAI(model="text-davinci-003")

first_prompt = PromptTemplate(template="Summarize this: {text}",
input_variables=["text"])
second_prompt = PromptTemplate(template="Translate to French: {summary}",
input_variables=["summary"])

chain = SimpleSequentialChain(chains=[first_prompt, second_prompt], llm=llm)
result = chain.run({"text": "The quick brown fox jumps over the lazy dog."})
print(result)
```

Agents: Enabling Decision-Making and Multi-Step Processes

Agents are the most sophisticated components in Langchain's architecture, designed to handle decision-making and orchestrate multi-step processes autonomously. By integrating tools such as APIs, databases, and logic-based reasoning, agents can execute complex workflows that go beyond single-task operations.

- **Tool-Enabled Agents**: Equipped with access to APIs, they can fetch external data and make informed decisions.
- **Reactive Agents**: Adapt dynamically to user inputs, selecting appropriate actions based on context.
- **Planning Agents**: Capable of devising and executing step-by-step plans for achieving specified objectives.

Example:

```
from langchain.agents import initialize_agent, Tool
from langchain.llms import OpenAI

llm = OpenAI(model="text-davinci-003")
tools = [Tool(name="WeatherAPI", func=get_weather, description="Fetch weather
info")]

agent = initialize_agent(tools, llm, agent_type="zero-shot-react-description")
response = agent.run("What's the weather in Paris?")
print(response)
```

Langchain's architecture, with its robust components such as Prompt Templates, Memory, Chains, and Agents, empowers developers to build sophisticated applications that leverage the full potential of large language models. By providing modularity, reusability, and extensibility, Langchain enables the creation of scalable and intelligent systems that meet diverse application needs.

Data Integration with Langchain

In the modern landscape of AI-powered applications, data integration is a cornerstone of building robust and intelligent systems. Langchain, a versatile framework for developing applications powered by large language models (LLMs), offers powerful tools for seamless data integration. By connecting to APIs, databases, and external tools, Langchain empowers developers to build dynamic and data-rich applications. This section explores how Langchain facilitates these integrations and provides practical insights into its capabilities.

Connecting Langchain to APIs, Databases, and External Tools

Langchain simplifies the process of integrating with APIs, databases, and various external tools, enabling applications to leverage diverse data sources. This is particularly crucial in scenarios where LLMs need real-time or contextually rich data to enhance their responses.

API Integration

Langchain supports connecting to APIs using its built-in modules, allowing developers to fetch data in real time. For example, consider an application that provides weather forecasts or stock market updates. By integrating with APIs such as OpenWeatherMap or Alpha Vantage, Langchain can dynamically retrieve relevant data and incorporate it into the model's responses. Here is an example:

```
from langchain.chains import APIChain
from langchain.llms import OpenAI

llm = OpenAI(temperature=0)
api_chain = APIChain.from_api_url(
    llm=llm,
    api_url="https://api.example.com/data",
    headers={"Authorization": "Bearer YOUR_API_KEY"}
)
response = api_chain.run("Get the latest data for user queries.")
print(response)
```

Database Connectivity

Langchain also enables seamless interaction with databases, making it easier to query structured data. Whether it is SQL-based relational databases or NoSQL systems, Langchain can fetch data efficiently. For instance, a customer service chatbot could use Langchain to query a customer database and provide personalized responses.

```
from langchain.chains import SQLDatabaseChain
from langchain.llms import OpenAI
from langchain.sql_database import SQLDatabase

llm = OpenAI()
sql_db = SQLDatabase.from_uri("sqlite:///example.db")
chain = SQLDatabaseChain(llm=llm, database=sql_db)
response = chain.run("What is the latest order for customer ID 123?")
print(response)
```

External Tool Integration

Langchain's extensibility allows developers to connect with tools such as Slack, Google Sheets, and Zapier, automating workflows and bridging the gap between LLM capabilities and business operations. For example, a Langchain application could send automated reports to a Slack channel or update a Google Sheet based on user inputs.

Using Vector DB for Document Retrieval and RAG

Vector databases play a critical role in document retrieval and retrieval-augmented generation (RAG), two essential components for building intelligent applications. Langchain provides native support for integrating with vector databases, enabling efficient storage and retrieval of embeddings.

Document Embedding and Storage

By embedding documents into vector spaces, Langchain allows applications to perform similarity searches. This is especially useful for building knowledge retrieval systems, where the most relevant documents can be identified based on their semantic similarity to a query. Popular vector databases such as Pinecone, Weaviate, or FAISS can be integrated with Langchain.

```
from langchain.vectorstores import FAISS
from langchain.embeddings import OpenAIEmbeddings

embeddings = OpenAIEmbeddings()
vectorstore = FAISS.load_local("faiss_index")

# Add documents to the vector store
documents = ["Document 1 content", "Document 2 content"]
vectorstore.add_texts(documents)

# Perform a similarity search
query = "What is the summary of Document 1?"
results = vectorstore.similarity_search(query)
print(results)
```

Retrieval-Augmented Generation (RAG)

Langchain's RAG capabilities enhance LLM performance by retrieving relevant context for queries. Instead of relying solely on the model's training data, RAG combines retrieved documents with generative capabilities, resulting in more accurate and contextually aware outputs. Here is how it works in Langchain:

1. **Retrieve:** Relevant documents are retrieved from a vector database.
2. **Combine:** Retrieved documents are combined with the user query.
3. **Generate:** An LLM generates a response based on the combined input.

```
from langchain.chains import RetrievalQA
from langchain.llms import OpenAI
from langchain.vectorstores import FAISS

llm = OpenAI()
retriever = FAISS.load_local("faiss_index").as_retriever()
qa_chain = RetrievalQA(llm=llm, retriever=retriever)
```

```
response = qa_chain.run("Explain the content of Document 1.")
print(response)
```

Unstructured and Structured Data in Langchain

Langchain excels at managing both unstructured and structured data, offering flexibility for diverse application scenarios.

Working with Unstructured Data

Unstructured data, such as free-form text, images, or audio, can be integrated into Langchain applications by leveraging appropriate preprocessing and embeddings. For instance, text embeddings can be generated using OpenAI's models, while images can be processed using tools such as CLIP.

```
from langchain.embeddings import OpenAIEmbeddings
from langchain.vectorstores import FAISS

text_data = ["This is a sample paragraph.", "Another piece of text content."]
embeddings = OpenAIEmbeddings()
vectorstore = FAISS.load_local("faiss_index")
vectorstore.add_texts(text_data)

query = "What is discussed in the sample paragraph?"
results = vectorstore.similarity_search(query)
print(results)
```

Working with Structured Data

Structured data, such as rows in a database or JSON responses, can be directly utilized in Langchain workflows. This makes it easy to process and transform data for downstream tasks. For example, a chatbot could parse JSON API responses to provide real-time information.

```
import json
from langchain.chains import LLMChain
from langchain.prompts import PromptTemplate

json_data = {"temperature": 25, "humidity": 60}
formatted_data = json.dumps(json_data)
prompt = PromptTemplate(template="The current weather data: {data}")
chain = LLMChain(llm=OpenAI(), prompt=prompt)
response = chain.run({"data": formatted_data})
print(response)
```

Langchain's ability to handle both types of data makes it a valuable framework for building intelligent, data-driven applications across industries.

Data integration with Langchain unlocks the potential to build smarter and more effective applications. By connecting to APIs, databases, and external tools, leveraging vector databases for RAG, and handling both structured and unstructured data, developers can create powerful solutions tailored to diverse use cases. Langchain's versatility ensures that it remains a go-to choice for applications powered by LLMs and other AI technologies.

Applications of Langchain

Langchain is an innovative framework that has opened up exciting possibilities for the development and deployment of advanced language-based applications. By integrating multiple components such as Large Language Models (LLMs), memory, and tools, Langchain provides a seamless environment for building versatile and intelligent solutions. Below, we explore some of the primary applications of Langchain that are reshaping the landscape of AI-powered solutions.

Conversational AI: Building Chatbots and Assistants

One of the most prominent applications of Langchain is in Conversational AI, where it enables the creation of context-aware chatbots and virtual assistants. Unlike traditional bots, which are often limited to handling static and predefined queries, Langchain-powered chatbots leverage advanced LLMs to maintain context over multiple interactions. This capability allows for fluid, human-like conversations that adapt to user input dynamically.

For instance, a Langchain-based virtual assistant in a customer service application can recall details from previous interactions, understand complex queries, and provide accurate solutions tailored to the user's needs. Similarly, healthcare bots can use contextual memory to manage patient records and deliver personalized recommendations, significantly enhancing the user experience and operational efficiency.

Knowledge Management: Summarization and Search

Langchain excels in applications involving knowledge management by enabling efficient summarization and intelligent search capabilities across vast datasets. This is particularly valuable for industries dealing with extensive documentation, such as legal, healthcare, and education.

For example, legal professionals can utilize Langchain to summarize lengthy contracts, identify critical clauses, and search for specific legal precedents within a database. Similarly, researchers can quickly extract key findings from a collection of academic papers, enabling faster decision-making and insights.

Incorporating Langchain into knowledge management systems transforms the way organizations handle information, making it more accessible and actionable.

Automated Workflows

Langchain's ability to integrate various tools and APIs makes it a powerful solution for automating workflows that require multiple steps. By chaining together tasks, Langchain creates intelligent pipelines capable of handling complex processes without human intervention.

For example, consider an e-commerce platform that uses Langchain to streamline customer support. The workflow might involve identifying the customer's issue through natural language input, retrieving the relevant order details from a database, generating an appropriate response, and even triggering a refund or replacement process automatically. This level of automation reduces response times, minimizes errors, and improves customer satisfaction.

In enterprise environments, Langchain can be used to automate reporting and analytics workflows by integrating data extraction, transformation, visualization, and summarization tasks into a cohesive process.

Content Generation and Recommendations

Langchain has unlocked new possibilities for creativity by enabling advanced content generation and personalized recommendation systems. Writers, marketers, and developers can leverage Langchain to produce engaging and original content tailored to specific audiences.

For instance, Langchain can be used to generate personalized marketing copy, design interactive storytelling experiences, or even compose music and poetry. The ability to include user preferences and contextual data ensures that the output is highly relevant and engaging.

In recommendation systems, Langchain enhances user experiences by providing suggestions that align with individual preferences. For example, a video streaming platform can use Langchain to recommend movies or shows based on a user's viewing history and current trends. Similarly, an online learning platform can offer tailored course recommendations based on a learner's progress and interests.

The creative and personalized applications of Langchain are helping organizations stand out in competitive markets by delivering unique and highly engaging experiences to their users.

Langchain's versatility and advanced capabilities make it a game-changer for developing a wide range of applications. From enhancing Conversational AI to transforming knowledge management, automating workflows, and driving creative innovation, Langchain provides the tools needed to build intelligent and impactful solutions. As adoption continues to grow, the potential applications of Langchain are limited only by imagination and creativity.

Implementing Langchain: Step-by-Step

Langchain is a powerful framework designed to simplify the development of applications that leverage large language models (LLMs). By offering modular components such as chains, memory, and prompt templates, Langchain enables developers to create context-aware, dynamic, and multi-step AI-powered workflows. This section provides a comprehensive, step-by-step guide to implementing Langchain in Python, with practical examples to illustrate its utility in real-world applications.

Setting up Langchain in Python

To get started with Langchain, you first need to set up your Python environment and install the required libraries. Langchain can be installed using pip, and it works seamlessly with popular LLM APIs such as OpenAI's GPT and Hugging Face Transformers.

```
# Install Langchain
pip install langchain openai

# Optional: Install additional libraries for integrations
pip install tiktoken huggingface_hub
```

After installation, configure your API keys for the LLM provider you intend to use. For example, if you are using OpenAI's GPT models:

```
import os
from langchain.llms import OpenAI

# Set your OpenAI API key
os.environ["OPENAI_API_KEY"] = "your-api-key"

# Initialize the LLM
llm = OpenAI(model_name="text-davinci-003")
```

This setup ensures that your environment is ready for further development using Langchain.

Creating and Using Prompt Templates for Dynamic Responses

Langchain provides a flexible way to define and use prompt templates. These templates allow you to dynamically customize your prompts based on user inputs or specific tasks.

For example, you can create a simple template for generating product descriptions:

```
from langchain.prompts import PromptTemplate

# Define the prompt template
prompt = PromptTemplate(
    input_variables=["product_name", "audience"],
    template="Write a compelling description for {product_name} targeted at
{audience}."
)

# Use the template
prompt_text = prompt.format(product_name="Smart Glasses", audience="tech
enthusiasts")
print(prompt_text)

# Pass the prompt to the LLM
response = llm(prompt_text)
print(response)
```

This approach ensures that your application can generate contextually relevant outputs based on user-provided inputs, making it highly adaptable.

Building Chains for Complex Multi-Step Operations

Chains in Langchain allow you to combine multiple steps into a cohesive workflow. For instance, you might need to perform sentiment analysis on a product review and then generate a response based on the detected sentiment.

Here is how to build a chain for this scenario:

```
from langchain.chains import LLMChain
from langchain.prompts import PromptTemplate

# Step 1: Define a prompt for sentiment analysis
sentiment_prompt = PromptTemplate(
    input_variables=["review"],
    template="Analyze the sentiment of this review: {review}"
)

# Step 2: Define a prompt for response generation
response_prompt = PromptTemplate(
    input_variables=["sentiment"],
    template="Write a reply to a review with {sentiment} sentiment."
)

# Step 3: Create chains
sentiment_chain = LLMChain(llm=llm, prompt=sentiment_prompt)
response_chain = LLMChain(llm=llm, prompt=response_prompt)
```

```
# Execute the chains
review = "The product is amazing! It exceeded all my expectations."
sentiment = sentiment_chain.run(review)
response = response_chain.run(sentiment)

print("Detected Sentiment:", sentiment)
print("Generated Response:", response)
```

By chaining these operations, Langchain simplifies the implementation of workflows involving multiple steps, each dependent on the output of the previous step.

Integrating Memory for Context-Aware Applications

Memory in Langchain enables your applications to retain context over multiple interactions, making it particularly useful for conversational AI. Langchain provides various memory classes, such as **`BufferMemory`** and **`ConversationBufferMemory`**, to store and manage conversation history.

Here is an example of integrating memory into a chatbot application:

```
from langchain.chains import ConversationChain
from langchain.memory import ConversationBufferMemory

# Initialize memory
memory = ConversationBufferMemory()

# Create a conversation chain
conversation = ConversationChain(llm=llm, memory=memory)

# Simulate a conversation
print(conversation.run("What is Langchain?"))
print(conversation.run("How does it handle memory?"))

# Retrieve the memory
print("Conversation History:")
print(memory.buffer)
```

With memory integration, the chatbot remembers previous interactions, enhancing the user experience by providing coherent and contextually aware responses.

Practical Examples of End-to-End AI Applications

Langchain's flexibility allows you to build a variety of end-to-end applications. Here is an example of a customer support chatbot that uses chains, memory, and prompt templates to handle user queries dynamically:

```
# Import required components
from langchain.chains import ConversationChain
from langchain.prompts import PromptTemplate
from langchain.memory import ConversationBufferMemory

# Define the prompt template
support_prompt = PromptTemplate(
    input_variables=["query", "history"],
    template=(
        "You are a customer support agent. Use the conversation history:\n"
        "{history}\n"
        "Respond to the following query:\n"
        "{query}"
```

```
    )
)

# Initialize memory and the chain
memory = ConversationBufferMemory()
customer_support_chain = ConversationChain(
    llm=llm, prompt=support_prompt, memory=memory
)

# Simulate a support conversation
print(customer_support_chain.run("I need help with my order."))
print(customer_support_chain.run("Can you check the status of my shipment?"))

# Display conversation history
print("Support Conversation History:")
print(memory.buffer)
```

This example demonstrates how Langchain can be used to create sophisticated applications that adapt dynamically to user needs, combining modular components such as chains, prompts, and memory for a seamless experience.

By leveraging Langchain, developers can build robust, context-aware, and efficient applications that integrate seamlessly with large language models. Whether you are building a chatbot, automating workflows, or creating a knowledge assistant, Langchain provides the tools to bring your ideas to life.

Optimizing Langchain Applications

Langchain, a powerful framework for building AI-powered applications, enables developers to integrate large language models (LLMs) into workflows seamlessly. While Langchain provides immense flexibility, optimizing its applications is essential for efficiency, cost management, and ensuring a smooth user experience. In this chapter, we delve into best practices and strategies to design efficient chains, manage computational overhead, and debug prompts effectively.

Best Practices for Efficient Chains and Workflows

Efficient chain design is the foundation of a robust Langchain application. Poorly constructed workflows can lead to unnecessary computations, increased latency, and inflated costs. Here are some best practices to ensure optimized chain performance:

- **Understand Your Use Case:** Clearly define the objectives of your application. Focus on designing chains that only include the necessary components for the task, avoiding redundant steps.
- **Minimalist Chain Construction:** Use the minimum number of steps required to achieve the desired output. For example, instead of chaining multiple LLM calls, consolidate tasks where possible by leveraging the model's multitasking capabilities.
- **Preprocessing and Postprocessing:** Incorporate preprocessing steps to clean and prepare input data. Similarly, use lightweight postprocessing to filter or structure model outputs efficiently. This reduces the burden on LLMs, which can be computationally expensive.
- **Reusability:** Modularize your chain components. Reusable modules reduce development time and enhance consistency across different parts of the application.
- **Efficient Memory Management:** Use Langchain's memory modules judiciously. While memory can provide context persistence, it is crucial to avoid unnecessary storage of irrelevant data, as this can slow down subsequent interactions.

- **Conditional Execution:** Implement conditional logic in chains to bypass unnecessary steps based on the input context. This prevents execution of irrelevant computations and improves response times.

Managing Latency and Computational Overhead

Managing latency and computational overhead in Langchain apps is crucial for speed and efficiency. Choose lightweight models such as GPT-3.5-turbo for simple tasks, and batch or asynchronously process requests to reduce delays. Cache repeated responses to avoid redundant LLM calls, and use rate limiting to stay within usage quotas. Monitor system resources–CPU, GPU, and memory–to detect bottlenecks, and keep prompts clear and concise to minimize processing time.

Debugging and Optimizing Prompts and Responses

The quality of prompts and their corresponding responses play a pivotal role in the effectiveness of Langchain applications. Debugging and optimizing prompts ensure that the model delivers accurate and relevant outputs:

- **Iterative Prompt Design:** Start with a simple prompt and iteratively refine it based on the model's responses. Use examples to guide the model's behavior effectively.
- **Prompt Templates:** Leverage Langchain's prompt templates to standardize input formatting. Consistent prompts reduce variability in model outputs.
- **Test with Diverse Inputs:** Validate prompts with a variety of test cases, including edge cases, to ensure robustness across different scenarios.
- **Analyze Failure Points:** Identify patterns in suboptimal responses to pinpoint areas for prompt improvement. For example, if the model misunderstands a specific question type, refine the prompt to clarify intent.
- **Use Temperature and Top-k Sampling:** Fine-tune generation parameters such as temperature and top-k to balance creativity and precision. Lowering the temperature reduces randomness, leading to more deterministic outputs.
- **Incorporate Feedback:** Implement a feedback loop where user inputs help refine prompts. Use tools such as Langchain's memory modules to dynamically adjust prompts based on prior interactions.
- **Error Logging:** Maintain detailed logs of model interactions, including prompts, parameters, and responses. Analyzing logs helps uncover systemic issues and areas for optimization.
- **Tool Integration Testing:** If your chain incorporates tools (for example, databases, APIs), ensure the prompts are correctly passing and receiving data. Misaligned tool integrations can lead to cascading errors.

Optimizing Langchain applications requires a holistic approach that balances efficient design, resource management, and robust debugging practices. By adhering to the strategies outlined above, developers can enhance the performance, reliability, and scalability of their applications. With careful planning and continuous improvement, Langchain can unlock the full potential of large language models in a wide range of real-world applications.

Challenges and Limitations of Langchain

LangChain is a powerful tool for building applications on top of large language models (LLMs), but it is not without its share of challenges. Developers often wrestle with ambiguous responses, scalability issues, and unreliable integrations with external data sources. These obstacles, if left unchecked, can lead to poor user experiences and bloated systems. Addressing them head-on is essential for building robust, production-grade AI applications.

One major hurdle is the unpredictability of LLM responses. Since these models operate on probability rather than hard logic, outputs can be vague, verbose, or off-topic. To combat this, developers use strategies such as prompt engineering, validation layers, fallback mechanisms, and fine-tuning models with domain-specific data. For example, in legal document summarization, vague prompts may cause the model to skip critical terminology—this can be mitigated by combining structured prompts with a fine-tuned legal dataset.

Scalability and reliability form the next battleground. As usage scales, latency from multiple LLM queries, resource overhead, and integration with slow or unstable APIs become bottlenecks. Solutions include asynchronous processing, caching, model compression, and robust error handling. In a customer support chatbot, for instance, caching frequent queries and deploying fallback APIs ensures smooth performance even during peak traffic. Ultimately, building reliable LangChain systems requires not just clever coding but also architectural foresight and continuous optimization.

Case Study: Building a Knowledge Retrieval System

Knowledge retrieval systems are critical in modern applications where large volumes of information must be accessed, summarized, and queried efficiently. This case study explores the design and implementation of a scalable knowledge retrieval system leveraging Langchain, a framework tailored for integrating language models with external knowledge sources, and vector databases for efficient document retrieval. By addressing challenges such as accuracy and ambiguity in responses, this system demonstrates how cutting-edge AI tools can transform information processing workflows.

Problem: Summarizing and Answering Queries on a Large Document Repository

Organizations across industries face a common challenge: managing and extracting actionable insights from vast document repositories. Whether it is legal firms sifting through contracts, research institutions analyzing scientific papers, or customer support teams answering queries from extensive knowledge bases, the ability to provide concise and accurate responses is crucial. Traditional keyword-based search systems often fall short, as they lack the contextual understanding needed to interpret queries effectively.

In this scenario, we aim to:

- Summarize key points from a repository of documents.
- Provide accurate, contextually relevant answers to user queries.
- Ensure scalability as the document repository grows.

Solution Approach: Using Langchain with Vector Databases for Document Retrieval

To tackle the problem, we designed a system that integrates Langchain with a vector database. The solution follows a modular approach:

- **Document Preprocessing**
  - Documents are ingested and preprocessed to remove irrelevant data, standardize formats, and tokenize content.

    - Preprocessed documents are embedded into vector representations using a language model such as OpenAI's embeddings or Sentence Transformers.
- **Vector Database Integration**
    - A vector database (for example, Pinecone, Weaviate, or FAISS) is employed to store document embeddings.
    - This allows for efficient similarity-based searches, where user queries can be matched with relevant document sections.
- **Langchain Workflow**
    - Langchain serves as the orchestration layer, enabling seamless interaction between the vector database and the language model.
    - It uses chains to retrieve relevant document embeddings based on the query and passes them to the language model for summarization or answering.
- **Query Handling and Summarization**
    - The system processes user queries by finding the top-k similar document embeddings.
    - Relevant content is fed to the language model, which generates summarized responses or directly answers the query.
- **User Interface**
    - A simple web-based interface allows users to submit queries and view results.
    - Features such as query history and response ranking enhance usability.

Challenges: Ensuring Accuracy and Handling Ambiguous Queries

While the solution is robust, several challenges were encountered during development:

- **Accuracy in Retrieval**
    - Ensuring the vector embeddings capture the semantic nuances of documents was critical. Fine-tuning the embedding model and adjusting similarity thresholds were necessary to improve retrieval accuracy.
- **Handling Ambiguous Queries**
    - Ambiguous or overly broad queries posed a significant hurdle. For instance, a query such as "What are the benefits?" without additional context required iterative refinement to provide meaningful responses.
    - Incorporating query clarification mechanisms, such as follow-up prompts, helped address this challenge.
- **Scalability**
    - As the document repository grew, so did the demand for storage and retrieval efficiency. Optimizing database indexing and adopting distributed computing techniques ensured the system remained performant.
- **Latency**
    - Query latency was another concern, particularly for real-time applications. Caching frequently accessed results and using optimized inference pipelines helped reduce response times.

Outcome: An Efficient Knowledge Retrieval Application

The final system successfully addressed the outlined problems, delivering significant benefits:

- **Enhanced User Experience**
  - Users received concise and accurate responses to their queries, reducing the time spent searching for information manually.
  - Summaries were contextually relevant, improving decision-making processes across various use cases.
- **Scalability**
  - The integration of a vector database ensured seamless scaling as the document repository expanded.
  - Load testing confirmed the system could handle concurrent queries with minimal performance degradation.
- **Adaptability**
  - The modular architecture allowed for easy updates, such as integrating new embedding models or fine-tuning existing ones to cater to domain-specific needs.
- **Business Impact**
  - Organizations reported increased productivity and efficiency. For instance, a legal firm using the system reduced contract analysis times by 40%, while a customer support team improved response accuracy by 35%.

Future Enhancements

The system lays the groundwork for future improvements, including:

- **Multi-modal Retrieval**: Incorporating other data types such as images or videos alongside text.
- **Feedback Loops**: Leveraging user feedback to refine model responses and improve accuracy.
- **Domain Adaptation**: Fine-tuning the language model and embeddings for specific industries such as healthcare or finance.
- **Real-time Collaboration**: Enabling multiple users to interact with the system simultaneously, enhancing teamwork.

By leveraging Langchain and vector databases, this case study underscores the potential of combining generative AI with retrieval-augmented techniques to create transformative solutions for knowledge management.

Future Directions for Langchain

LangChain stands at the frontier of AI development, poised to evolve alongside advances in multimodal models and real-time applications. Its modular design allows seamless integration with technologies such as CLIP, DALL·E, and Whisper, enabling the creation of applications that not only understand and generate text but also respond with images, audio, and video. Such capabilities could revolutionize industries such as education, healthcare, and entertainment—where context-rich, multi-sensory communication is key.

The framework is also moving toward real-time use cases, such as live customer support, transcription, and sentiment tracking during streaming events. By leveraging event-driven architectures and edge computing, LangChain can power low-latency systems even in connectivity-constrained environments such as autonomous vehicles or IoT setups. These enhancements promise to extend LangChain's utility into new domains where immediacy and responsiveness are non-negotiable.

Automation remains a core focus, with research exploring how LangChain can self-orchestrate tasks, learn from interactions, and personalize user experiences without constant human oversight. However, challenges such as model interoperability, latency, and ethical automation must be tackled. With thoughtful innovation, LangChain is well-positioned to become a foundational tool for next-gen AI systems—flexible, adaptive, and deeply embedded in the way intelligent software will be built.

Conclusion

In this chapter, we explored Langchain, a powerful framework for building AI-powered applications that leverage large language models (LLMs) effectively. Langchain simplifies LLM orchestration by providing modular components such as prompt templates, memory, chains, and agents, enabling developers to create scalable, context-aware, and dynamic applications.

We discussed Langchain's architecture, including its ability to integrate with APIs, databases, and vector stores for retrieval-augmented generation (RAG) and knowledge management. By exploring real-world applications, such as conversational AI, document retrieval, and automated workflows, we demonstrated how Langchain can enhance efficiency and intelligence in AI-driven solutions.

Furthermore, we examined best practices for optimizing Langchain applications, addressing scalability, performance, and debugging challenges, and ensuring the reliability of external data integrations. The case study on knowledge retrieval systems illustrated Langchain's potential in managing and querying large datasets efficiently.

With hands-on experience in setting up and implementing Langchain in Python, you are now equipped to build sophisticated AI-powered applications. In the next chapter, we will dive into Retrieval-Augmented Generation (RAG)—an advanced technique that enhances LLM performance by retrieving and integrating external knowledge into AI responses, significantly improving accuracy and contextual relevance.

Points to Remember

- Langchain provides a modular framework for building AI-powered applications that interact with large language models (LLMs).
- Key components include prompt templates (for structured inputs), memory (to maintain context), chains (to sequence tasks), and agents (for decision-making workflows).
- Data integration is a critical feature of Langchain, allowing interaction with APIs, vector databases, and structured/unstructured data.
- Applications of Langchain span conversational AI, knowledge retrieval, automation, and creative AI workflows.
- Optimization techniques include efficient prompt design, managing latency, and debugging Langchain workflows.
- Challenges include handling LLM ambiguity, ensuring scalability, and integrating external data reliably.

Multiple Choice Questions

1. What is the primary purpose of Langchain?
   a. Managing and orchestrating interactions with LLMs
   b. Training deep learning models from scratch
   c. Replacing databases with AI-generated responses
   d. Building low-level neural network layers
2. Which of the following is a core component of Langchain?
   a. Backpropagation
   b. Prompt templates
   c. Weight initialization
   d. Loss functions
3. What does Langchain's memory module enable?
   a. Storing model weights for future fine-tuning
   b. Caching API requests for performance improvements
   c. Maintaining conversational context across multiple interactions
   d. Reducing the computational cost of training LLMs
4. Which feature of Langchain is used to sequence multiple tasks into a logical workflow?
   a. Chains
   b. Agents
   c. Embeddings
   d. Data augmentation

Answers

1. a
2. b
3. c
4. a

Questions

1. How does Langchain simplify LLM orchestration, and why is it useful for building AI-powered applications?
2. What are the key components of Langchain, and how do they contribute to efficient AI interactions?
3. How does Langchain integrate with external data sources, and why is this important for real-world applications?

4. What are the advantages of using vector databases with Langchain for knowledge retrieval?
5. How can Langchain agents be used to enable multi-step decision-making in AI workflows?
6. What are the challenges in integrating external APIs and databases with Langchain, and how can they be mitigated?
7. How does memory in Langchain help improve AI-generated responses, particularly in conversational AI?
8. What are some best practices for optimizing Langchain applications for performance and reliability?
9. How does Langchain compare to other AI frameworks, and when should it be preferred?
10. What are the potential future advancements in Langchain, particularly for real-time and multimodal AI applications?

Key Terms

- **Langchain**: A framework for building AI-powered applications that interact with LLMs.
- **Prompt Templates**: Predefined structures for LLM inputs, ensuring consistency in responses.
- **Memory**: A module that helps retain context across interactions in a conversation or workflow.
- **Chains**: A mechanism for sequencing multiple tasks, enabling complex AI-powered workflows.
- **Agents**: Decision-making components that allow multi-step reasoning and adaptive responses.
- **Vector Database**: A specialized database for storing and retrieving high-dimensional embeddings.
- **Retrieval-Augmented Generation (RAG)**: A technique for enhancing LLM responses by retrieving external knowledge.
- **LLM Orchestration**: The process of managing and optimizing interactions with large language models.
- **Scalability**: The ability of Langchain applications to handle large datasets and complex workflows efficiently.
- **Debugging AI Workflows**: Identifying and resolving issues in prompt execution, data retrieval, and LLM-generated outputs.

CHAPTER 19
Prompt Engineering, RAG, and Fine-Tuning

Introduction

The evolution of large language models has opened up new possibilities across industries, from natural language understanding to complex decision-making systems. While pre-trained models provide a strong foundation, real-world applications often demand more control, precision, and adaptability. This chapter focuses on three advanced techniques—Prompt Engineering, Retrieval-Augmented Generation (RAG), and Fine-Tuning—that extend the capabilities of LLMs beyond their out-of-the-box potential.

These methods address key challenges such as improving factual accuracy, handling domain-specific queries, and refining model outputs to meet application-specific needs. Together, they form a powerful toolkit for building intelligent, responsive, and context-aware AI systems.

Structure

In this chapter, we will cover the following topics:

- **Introduction to Advanced LLM Techniques**
- **Overview of Key Methods to Enhance LLM Performance**
- **Key Concepts in RAG**
    - How RAG Bridges Retrieval Systems and Generative Models
    - Role of Retrievers (Dense versus Sparse: FAISS, BM25) and Generators (GPT, T5)
    - Fusion of Retrieved Knowledge with Generative Outputs
- **Architecture of RAG**
    - Step-by-Step Pipeline: Retriever Setup + Generator Integration
    - Handling Multi-Hop Retrieval and Contextual Dependencies
    - Practical Examples: FAQ Systems, Document QA
- **Applications and Challenges of RAG**
    - Use Cases: Knowledge Management, Conversational AI, Research Assistance
    - Limitations
- **Fundamentals of Prompt Engineering**
    - How LLMs Interpret Prompts: Zero-Shot, Few-Shot, Chain-of-Thought
    - Balancing Specificity and Flexibility in Design
- **Advanced Prompt Techniques**
    - Instruction Design, Example Selection, and Iterative Refinement

  - Dynamic Prompting and Template-Based Approaches
- **Fine-Tuning Large Language Models**
- **Applications and Evaluation**
  - Text Generation, QA, Conversational AI, Code Generation

Introduction to Advanced LLM Techniques

Modern large language models (LLMs) have revolutionized artificial intelligence with their ability to generate human-like text, answer complex questions, and even assist in creative tasks. However, their performance can be significantly enhanced through advanced techniques that address key limitations, such as factual inaccuracies, lack of domain-specific knowledge, and inconsistent outputs.

This chapter explores three critical methods for optimizing LLM performance:

- **Prompt Engineering**: The art and deliberate design of clear, structured instructions to shape model behavior. Well-crafted prompts help guide tone, reasoning, and relevance—improving outcomes without retraining the model.
- **Retrieval-Augmented Generation (RAG)**: A hybrid approach that lets models access external knowledge before generating a response. By grounding answers in real data, RAG improves factual accuracy and keeps information current.
- **Fine-Tuning**: The process of refining a pre-trained model on domain-specific data, enhancing its precision and style within specialized contexts such as law, healthcare, or technical writing.

By combining these approaches, developers can create AI systems that are not only more accurate and reliable but also adaptable to diverse real-world applications—from customer support chatbots to research assistants and automated content generation.

In the following sections, we will explore each technique in depth, examining its architecture, best practices, and practical implementations.

Overview of Key Methods to Enhance LLM Performance

Despite their impressive generative capabilities, LLMs face constraints such as limited domain sensitivity, static pretraining, and uneven reasoning consistency. To mitigate these, a combination of techniques has evolved—each improving how models interpret prompts, access knowledge, or adapt to specific tasks.

Prompt Engineering

Prompt engineering is the process of designing effective inputs to help a language model understand exactly what you want it to do. In simple terms, it is about "*talking to the model the right way*." By carefully choosing words, structure, and examples in a prompt, users can guide the model's reasoning, tone, and level of detail. Common techniques include few-shot prompting (showing examples of correct answers), chain-of-thought prompting (encouraging the model to explain its reasoning step-by-step), and template-based prompts (using consistent formats for tasks).

These methods allow users to improve accuracy and clarity without retraining the model itself. Prompt engineering is especially useful for tasks such as writing summaries, building chatbots, or generating reports, where clear communication between the user and the AI makes a big difference.

Retrieval-Augmented Generation

Retrieval-Augmented Generation, or RAG, is a method that helps language models find and use real-world information before answering a question.

Normally, models rely only on what they learned during training, which means they can sometimes produce outdated or incorrect facts. RAG fixes this by adding a retrieval step – it first searches for relevant documents or data from an external source (such as a database or website) and then uses that information to generate a response.

This approach reduces hallucinations (false or made-up answers) and keeps outputs more factual and up-to-date. RAG is very effective in areas such as research assistance, question answering, and domain-specific writing, where accuracy and current information are essential.

Fine-Tuning

Fine-tuning is the process of teaching an existing model new skills or domain-specific knowledge by training it on specialized data. While prompt engineering and RAG work from the outside, fine-tuning changes how the model itself behaves internally.

For example, a general LLM can be fine-tuned with medical data to better understand clinical terms, or with legal documents to produce accurate summaries of court cases. This allows the model to speak the language of a specific field more naturally.

Fine-tuning takes more time and computing power than prompt design or RAG, but it delivers deep customization and consistency. It is especially helpful when tasks require strong expertise or a particular tone that cannot be easily achieved through prompts alone.

A Real-World Analogy to Understand These Concepts Better

Imagine a highly skilled chef who can cook a wide range of dishes. When you give the chef a very specific request– such as "*Make a mildly spiced, creamy mushroom pasta with no garlic*"–you are guiding their output through precise instructions, much like prompt engineering. The chefs skills remain the same, but the clarity of your request helps them deliver exactly what you want. Sometimes, the chef might not remember a rare recipe or wants to ensure it is made with the latest twist, so they consult a cookbook or look up a recipe online before cooking. This is like Retrieval-Augmented Generation (RAG), where external information is pulled in to enhance the output.

Figure 19.1: *The Master Chef Analogy for LLM Enhancement Techniques*

Now, if the chef starts working in a Japanese restaurant and undergoes dedicated training to master Japanese cuisine, their style and knowledge shift to match that domain. This is fine-tuning–retraining the chef to specialize in a new kind of cooking so they can perform expertly even without detailed instructions or external references.

Importance of Combining These Techniques for Accuracy, Relevance, and Adaptability

The true power of modern AI systems emerges when combining retrieval-augmented generation, prompt engineering, and fine-tuning into an integrated framework. RAG provides the factual foundation by accessing current, verifiable knowledge, while prompt engineering shapes how this information is processed and presented, and fine-tuning optimizes the model's underlying capabilities for specific domains. This triad approach creates AI systems that are simultaneously accurate (grounded in retrieved evidence), relevant (tailored through precise prompting), and adaptable (specialized via fine-tuning). For instance, a medical AI assistant might use RAG to access the latest research, employ carefully engineered prompts to structure clinical recommendations, and leverage fine-tuning to understand complex medical terminology - resulting in outputs that are more trustworthy and actionable than any single technique could produce alone. The combination also future-proofs systems, as each component addresses different aspects of model limitations: RAG overcomes knowledge cutoffs, prompt engineering adjusts to new tasks without retraining, and fine-tuning provides deep domain mastery where needed. This layered approach represents the cutting edge of practical AI deployment across industries where precision and reliability are paramount.

Key Concepts in RAG

At the heart of Retrieval-Augmented Generation lies a powerful synergy between information retrieval and generative AI, combining the precision of search systems with the fluency of language models. RAG fundamentally transforms how LLMs access and utilize knowledge by introducing a dynamic two-stage process: first, retrieving relevant information from external sources, then synthesizing it into coherent, context-aware responses. This architecture hinges on three core components–the retriever that fetches pertinent data, the generator that produces natural language outputs, and the fusion mechanism that intelligently blends these capabilities. Unlike traditional LLMs limited by their parametric memory, RAG-equipped models can tap into constantly updated knowledge bases while maintaining the linguistic sophistication of large neural networks. Understanding these foundational elements–from the technical distinctions between dense and sparse retrievers to the art of knowledge integration–is essential for building AI systems that are both knowledgeable and articulate, capable of delivering responses that are as factually grounded as they are naturally expressed.

How RAG Bridges Retrieval Systems and Generative Models

Retrieval-Augmented Generation (RAG) fundamentally redefines how large language models (LLMs) access and apply knowledge by seamlessly integrating the precision of information retrieval with the creativity of generative AI. Traditional LLMs rely solely on their pre-trained parametric memory, which can lead to outdated, generic, or hallucinated responses. RAG overcomes this limitation by introducing a dynamic two-phase process:

1. **Intelligent Retrieval**: Before generating text, the system consults an external knowledge base (documents, databases, or APIs) to fetch the most relevant, up-to-date information using specialized search algorithms.

2. **Context-Aware Generation**: The retrieved evidence is then fed into the generative model as contextual grounding, enabling it to produce responses that are factually accurate, domain-specific, and citation-ready.

This hybrid approach effectively closes the "*knowledge gap*" in pure generative models by:

- Adding memory through retrieval, so the model can access accurate information while still writing fluently.
- Separating knowledge from reasoning, meaning facts are stored in databases, while the model focuses on understanding and generating text.
- Enabling real-time updates–new information can be added to the knowledge base without retraining the model.

Example: When asked "*What were the main outcomes of the recent U.S. presidential election?*", a RAG system first retrieves trusted news articles or official results, then generates a clear summary with accurate names, dates, and vote counts–details a standard LLM might miss or get wrong.

By connecting generative models to verifiable sources, RAG creates AI systems that are both knowledge-rich and linguistically sophisticated, making it indispensable for applications where accuracy is non-negotiable.

Role of Retrievers (FAISS, BM25) and Generators (GPT, LLaMA)

RAG systems rely on two specialized components working together–the retriever, which fetches relevant information, and the generator, which transforms that data into coherent responses.

Retrievers: Precision Search Engines

Retrievers act as the "*fact-checkers*" of the system, scanning external knowledge bases to find the most useful passages. They come in two main types:

- **Dense Retrievers** (for example, FAISS, vector databases)
  - Encode text into numerical embeddings, capturing semantic meaning
  - Excel at finding conceptually related content (for example, "canine" and "dog")
  - Require more computational resources but deliver nuanced results
- **Sparse Retrievers** (for example, BM25)
  - Use keyword matching and traditional search algorithms
  - Better for exact term lookup (for example, finding "2023 Tesla Model Y specifications")
  - Faster and more lightweight than dense methods

Practical Consideration: Many advanced systems combine both–using sparse retrieval for initial filtering, then dense retrieval for re-ranking.

Generators: The Storytellers

Once retrievers deliver the facts, generators (such as GPT-5 or Llama) take over to:

- Combine the retrieved passages into clear, natural sentences
- Keep the tone and flow consistent throughout the response
- Fill in logical gaps while staying true to the original information

Key Innovation: Modern RAG systems use cross-attention mechanisms, allowing the generator to dynamically weight which retrieved facts are most relevant mid-response.

Fusion of Retrieved Knowledge with Generative Outputs

The real strength of RAG is how it combines retrieved information with the model's natural writing ability, turning raw facts into clear and meaningful answers. This fusion happens through sophisticated architectural techniques that ensure the model remains grounded in evidence while maintaining natural language flow.

Key Fusion Mechanisms

- **Contextual Embedding Injection**
  - Retrieved documents are encoded alongside the original prompt as additional context tokens.
  - The generator attends to both the query *and* retrieved passages simultaneously via cross-attention layers.
- **Dynamic Relevance Weighting**
  - The model's attention mechanism automatically picks the most relevant snippets from the retrieved information.
  - Example: For "Explain quantum computing to a 5-year-old," technical details get lower weights than simple analogies.
- **Iterative Refinement**
  - Advanced systems perform multiple retrieval-generation cycles: Initial draft → Identify knowledge gaps → Secondary retrieval → Final output

Challenge	**Modern Solution**
Information overload	Top-k passage filtering + diversity sampling
Context window limitations	Hierarchical or recursive retrieval
Fact-generator mismatch	Contrastive learning to align representations

Table 19.1: *Challenges and Solutions*

Real-World Example: When answering "*What caused the 2023 Silicon Valley Bank collapse?*", a RAG system:

1. Retrieves relevant sources such as FDIC reports, news articles, and analyst commentaries.
2. Uses attention mechanisms to focus on key points such as regulatory failures rather than less relevant market trends.
3. Produces a response that combines direct quotes (for example, "*The FDIC cited...*") with clear, synthesized explanations.

Architecture of RAG

The RAG pipeline operates through a carefully orchestrated sequence where a retriever module first queries a vector database (such as FAISS or Pinecone) to fetch relevant documents, which are then passed to a generator model (such as GPT or T5) to synthesize coherent, context-aware responses.

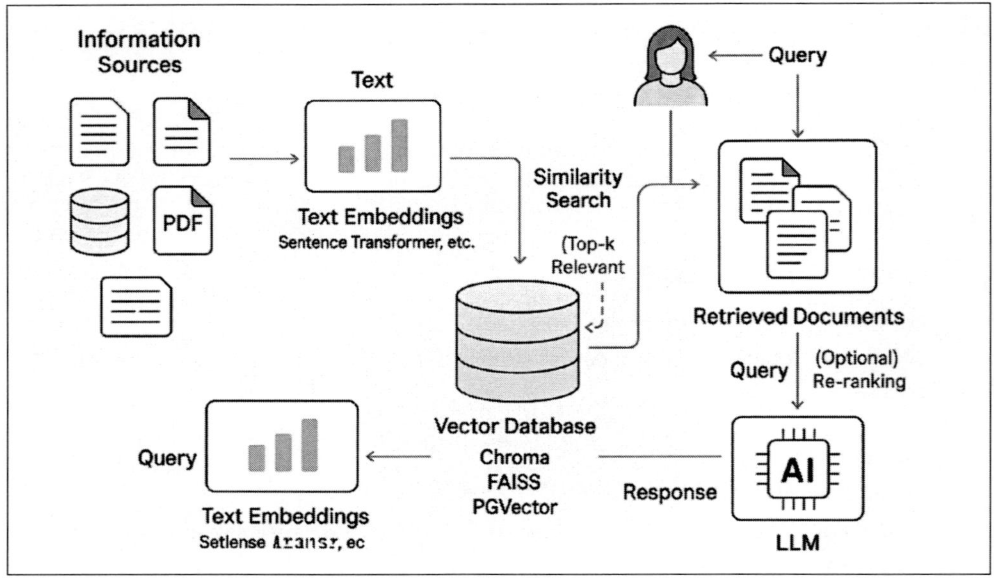

Figure 19.2: *Retrieval Augmented Generation Architectural Flow*

This end-to-end system handles challenges such as multi-hop retrieval—where answering complex queries requires chaining multiple searches—and contextual dependencies by dynamically refining retrieved knowledge before generation. Practical implementations, such as FAQ chatbots or document-based question answering, demonstrate RAG's versatility: for instance, a customer support system might index product manuals in a vector store, retrieve the most relevant sections using semantic search, and generate precise, citation-backed answers—all while maintaining conversational fluency. This modular yet integrated architecture makes RAG scalable for real-world deployments where accuracy and adaptability are critical.

Step-by-Step Pipeline: Retriever Setup (for example, FAISS, Pinecone) + Generator Integration

1. **Document Processing and Indexing**
   - **Data Preparation**: Clean and normalize source documents (PDFs, HTML, DB records)
   - **Chunking**: Split content into logical segments (for example, 512-token passages with overlap)
   - **Embedding Generation**: Convert text to vectors using embedding models (for example, BERT, SBERT)
   - **Vector Database Setup**: Index embeddings in FAISS/Pinecone/Weaviate with metadata storage
2. **Query-Time Retrieval**
   - **Query Embedding**: Encode user input into the same vector space as documents
   - **Semantic Search**: Find top-k nearest neighbors (for example, cosine similarity search)
   - **Optional Re-ranking**: Apply cross-encoder models (for example, MiniLM) to refine passage relevance

3. **Generation and Synthesis**
   - **Context Augmentation**: Prepend retrieved passages to the query (formatted as "`Document 1: ...\nDocument 2: ...\nQuestion: ...`")
   - **Prompt Engineering**: Use instructions such as "*Answer using* ONLY *the following context...*" to constrain hallucinations
   - **Confidence Calibration**: Output confidence scores or citation links to retrieved sources
4. **Deployment Optimizations**
   - **Caching**: Store frequent query embeddings to reduce compute costs
   - **Hybrid Search**: Combine semantic + keyword search (BM25) for better recall
   - **Feedback Loops**: Log user thumbs-up/down to improve retrieval rankings

```
# Pseudocode for basic RAG pipeline
retriever = FAISS.load_index("legal_docs.index")
generator = HuggingFacePipeline("t5-large")

def rag_answer(question):
    query_embed = embed_model.encode(question)
    retrieved = retriever.search(query_embed, top_k=3)
    context = "\n".join([doc.text for doc in retrieved])
    prompt = f"Context: {context}\nQuestion: {question}\nAnswer:"
        return generator(prompt)
```

This pipeline powers applications like:

- FAQ Bots: Instant answers from product manuals
- Research Assistants: Paper summarization with citations
- Enterprise Search: Connecting queries to internal wikis

Handling Multi-Hop Retrieval and Contextual Dependencies

Unlike simple queries that can be answered with a single document lookup, multi-hop retrieval requires the system to perform sequential searches–connecting information across multiple sources to arrive at a complete answer. This mirrors human reasoning, where we often "chain" facts together (for example, answering "*What was the CEO's response to the 2023 product recall?*" might require first finding the recall notice, then locating the CEO's subsequent press statement).

Implementation Strategies

- **Iterative Retrieval-Generation**

  Step 1: Retrieve initial documents based on the original query

  Step 2: Generate sub-questions from gaps in knowledge (for example, "*What was the date of the recall?*")

  Step 3: Execute follow-up searches using sub-questions

  Step 4: Synthesize all retrieved content into a final answer

- **Graph-Based Reasoning**
  - Build a knowledge graph during indexing linking related entities (products → recalls → statements)

    - Traverse connections at query time using graph algorithms
- **Hybrid Retrieval**
    - Combine vector search (for semantic matches) with SQL queries (for structured data joins)

Example Workflow:

```
# Multi-hop pseudocode
def multi_hop_qa(question):
    # First hop
    docs1 = retriever.search(question)
    identified_gaps = analyze_missing_info(docs1)

    # Second hop
    sub_questions = generate_followups(identified_gaps)
    docs2 = [retriever.search(q) for q in sub_questions]
    return generator(question, docs1 + docs2)
```

Handling Contextual Dependencies

- **Conversational State**: Maintain dialogue history as additional retrieval context
- **Temporal Filtering**: Prioritize recent documents for time-sensitive queries
- **Contradiction Resolution**: Detect conflicting retrieved facts and prompt for clarification

Real-World Application

A financial analyst's query, "*How did Microsoft's Azure growth impact their* Q1 *earnings*?" would trigger:

- (1) Retrieval of Azure revenue reports → (2) Follow-up search for earnings calls → (3) Cross-referencing of growth rates

Practical Examples: FAQ systems, Document QA

RAG shines in real-world applications where accuracy and traceability matter. Here is how it transforms two common use cases:

FAQ Systems with Dynamic Knowledge

Problem: Static FAQ bots fail when questions require:

- Answers drawn from multiple documents (for example, "*What is the return policy for refurbished items?*" needing both *Terms of Service* and *Refurbishment Guidelines*)
- Real-time updates (for example, holiday shipping deadlines)

RAG Solution:

- **Indexing Phase:**
    - Embed all FAQ pages, product manuals, and policy PDFs into a vector DB
    - Tag documents by freshness/priority (for example, Shipping Policies_2024-07)
- **Query Flow:**

```
# Example: Handling a layered FAQ query
query = "Can I return opened software if the seal was broken during delivery?"

# Parallel retrieval from multiple knowledge slices
policy_snippets = vector_search(query, filter="category=returns")
```

```
delivery_snippets = vector_search("broken seal", filter="category=shipping")

# Generate verified answer
Returns Policy Context: {policy_snippets}
Shipping Context: {delivery_snippets}
Question: {query}
```

- **Answer step-by-step:**

  Output: "Yes, *if delivery damage is verified* (Section 3.2), *opened software can...*"

Document QA for Technical Domains

In technical fields, engineers often waste a lot of time searching through long manuals–sometimes 300 pages or more–just to find simple information such as "*What is the max RPM for Model X at high altitude*?" This slows down work and leads to frustration, especially when the data is hidden in tables or specific sections.

An optimized RAG system can solve this by first organizing the manual: it pulls out tables and important sections, tags them with helpful labels such as "*Operating Limits*" or "*Altitude Info*," and then uses both keyword and AI-based search to find the best matches. When a user asks a question, the system searches smartly and then gives a precise answer using the actual numbers and units from the document, such as: "2,850 RPM (Page 47, Table 6-2)".

Key Implementation Lessons:

- **FAQ Systems**: Use metadata filtering for policy version control
- **Document QA**: Leverage layout-aware chunking (for example, keeping captions with figures)
- **Both**: Add citation tracing ([*Source: Warranty Doc v12.3*]) to build trust

Applications and Challenges of RAG

RAG systems unlock significant potential across industries–knowledge management platforms use them to provide accurate, sourced answers from internal wikis; conversational AI benefits from context-aware responses grounded in up-to-date policies or product details; and research assistance tools use RAG to synthesize insights from vast academic corpora with citations. However, these systems face key challenges, including computational overhead from real-time retrieval and generation, latency in multi-hop queries, and occasional inconsistencies where the generator may misinterpret or overlook retrieved evidence. Additionally, maintaining data freshness requires continuous knowledge base updates, while evaluation complexity grows when assessing both retrieval relevance and generative quality. Despite these hurdles, RAG's ability to combine dynamic knowledge with fluent generation makes it indispensable for applications demanding both precision and adaptability.

Use Cases: Knowledge Management, Conversational AI, Research Assistance

RAG's ability to dynamically integrate external knowledge with generative AI makes it invaluable across several key applications:

- **Knowledge Management**
  - **Enterprise wikis and intranets**: Employees query internal documents (meeting notes, project briefs, HR Policies) and get compiled answers with source links

- **Example:**
  - "*Summarize key decisions from last quarter's leadership offsite*" → RAG pulls relevant meeting minutes and generates a bulleted recap
  - "*What is the leave policy for parental leave?*" → RAG retrieves HR policy sections and provides a clear summary

- Conversational AI
  - **Customer support**: Chatbots reference up-to-date policy documents (for example, "*What is the warranty coverage for my device?*")
  - **Personalization**: Dialogue systems recall past interactions (retrieved from user history) for context continuity
- **Research Assistance**
  - **Academic/scientific**: "*Compare neural architecture search methods in recent arXiv papers*" → RAG fetches and summarizes 2023-24 studies
  - **Legal/medical**: Queries cross-reference verified sources (case law, drug databases) with citations
- **Emerging Applications:**
  - **Education**: Tutoring bots that explain concepts using approved textbooks
  - **Due diligence**: Analyzing contracts by retrieving similar clauses from past agreements

Limitations

While RAG offers significant advantages, it also introduces unique challenges that impact real-world deployment:

1. **Computational Overhead**
   - **Latency**: Real-time retrieval (vector search → re-ranking → generation) adds 300-800ms versus pure LLM inference
   - **Infrastructure costs**: Maintaining vector databases (FAISS/Pinecone) + running large generators requires scalable GPU/CPU resources
   - **Example**: A customer support bot handling 10K queries/day may need 5x more servers than a prompt-only system
2. **Retrieval-Generator Consistency Issues**
   - **Knowledge Neglect**: Generators sometimes ignore retrieved content (studies show 15-30% of outputs are not properly grounded in provided context)
   - **Citation Fidelity**: Models may hallucinate sources or misattribute facts to wrong documents
   - **Contradiction Risk**: Retrieved evidence might conflict with parametric knowledge (for example, old manual versus updated generator training)

Challenge	**Solution**
High latency	Hybrid caching (memoize frequent queries)
Knowledge neglect	Forced attention mechanisms (for example, RAG-Fidelity)
Citation inaccuracies	Post-hoc fact verification modules

Table 19.2: *Mitigation Strategies*

Real-World Impact

A healthcare RAG system might retrieve correct dosage guidelines but generate "*take twice daily*" instead of the source's "2.5*mg every* 12 *hours*"–highlighting why human-in-the-loop validation remains critical for high-stakes domains.

Fundamentals of Prompt Engineering

As mentioned earlier, Prompt engineering is the strategic design of inputs to guide large language models (LLMs) toward desired outputs by making use of their inherent capabilities in specific ways. At its core, it involves understanding how LLMs process different prompt structures: zero-shot prompts (direct instructions such as "*Summarize this article in one sentence*"), few-shot prompts (providing examples to demonstrate the task, for example, showing 2-3 summarized sentences before asking for a new one), and chain-of-thought prompts (explicitly requesting step-by-step reasoning, such as "*First, identify the key points, then condense them*"). Effective prompt design balances specificity (clear constraints, for example, "*Answer in 50 words or less*") with flexibility (allowing creativity when needed, for example, "*Suggest 3 analogies for...*"), while accounting for model quirks such as token sensitivity or instruction bias. Mastering these fundamentals enables precise control over outputs–whether generating code, analyzing data, or powering conversational agents–without modifying the underlying model.

How LLMs Interpret Prompts: Zero-Shot, Few-Shot, Chain-of-Thought

The effectiveness of a large language model's output hinges on how prompts structure tasks. LLMs interpret inputs differently based on their design:

Zero-shot prompting is when you give the model a direct instruction or question, and it has to generate an answer without being shown any examples first. The model relies entirely on what it has learned during training to figure out the correct response.

- **Key Idea**: The model is "on its own" and must use its internal knowledge to complete the task.
- **Why it Works**: For simple or clear tasks, the model already knows enough to respond correctly.
- **Example**:
  Prompt: "*List three healthy snacks a student can eat between classes.*"
  Output: "*1. Apple slices 2. Almonds 3. Bananas*"

Best for: Simple, well-defined tasks where the instruction is unambiguous.

Few-shot prompting is when you give the model a few examples in the prompt to show it the pattern, format, or reasoning style you want it to follow. These examples guide the model in producing the desired type of output.

- **Key Idea**: The model does not just rely on its pre-trained knowledge; it learns the format or approach from the examples.
- **Why it Works**: Some tasks require a specific structure, tone, or reasoning style that the model might not get right without seeing examples.
- **Example**:
  Prompt:

  Q: Write a 2-sentence book review for "Harry Potter". A: "Harry Potter is an exciting story of friendship and bravery. The magical world keeps readers hooked from start to finish."

Q: Write a 2-sentence book review for "Charlotte's Web". A: ""The Da Vinci Code is an exciting thriller full of puzzles and secret codes. The story keeps readers guessing as Robert Langdon uncovers hidden truths throughout Europe."

Q: Write a 2-sentence book review for "The Hunger Games". A: ___

Output: "The Hunger Games is a thrilling story of survival and courage. Katniss's journey in a dystopian world keeps readers on the edge of their seats."

Best for: Tasks requiring specific formats (for example, tables, structured responses) or nuanced reasoning.

Chain-of-Thought prompting asks the model to think step by step, explaining its reasoning before giving the final answer. This is especially useful for multi-step problems or logical reasoning.

- **Key Idea**: The model breaks down a problem into smaller steps and solves each in sequence.
- Why it works: Makes complex problems easier to follow and reduces errors.
- **Example**:
  Prompt: "A *student has 12 science chapters to revise in 3 days. How many chapters should they study each day? Solve step by step.*"
  Output:
  - Total chapters = 12
  - Number of days = 3
  - Chapters per day = 12 : 3 = 4

Best for: Math, logic puzzles, or multi-factorial reasoning where transparency is critical.

Why It Matters

- Zero-shot is fast but may lack precision.
- Few-shot improves accuracy but requires careful example selection.
- Chain of Thought unlocks complex reasoning but increases verbosity.

Balancing Specificity and Flexibility in Design

Crafting effective prompts requires walking a tightrope between precision (constraining outputs for accuracy) and adaptability (allowing creative or nuanced responses). Striking this balance is critical—overly rigid prompts may produce forced or incomplete answers, while vague prompts risk irrelevant or hallucinated content. Key principles are:

Precision Through Constraints

- **Structured Outputs:**
  - **Weak**: "*Tell me about Paris.*" → Unfocused essay
  - **Strong**: "List 3 cultural landmarks in Paris with 1-sentence descriptions." → Actionable response
- **Format Control**: "*Summarize the article in 3 bullet points. Each bullet must start with an emoji* (🎨, 📜, 🔍)."

Strategic Open-Endedness

- **When Exploring Ideas or Brainstorming**: "*Propose 5 innovative uses for blockchain in healthcare—prioritize feasibility.*"

- **Avoid False Specificity**: "*Write a 200-word Shakespearean sonnet about AI*" may fail if the model cannot count tokens accurately.

Contextual Flexibility

- **For creative tasks**: "*Write a sci-fi dialogue where:*
    - *Characters debate AI ethics*
    - *Use casual language*
    - *Keep endings open for sequels*"
- **For technical tasks**: "*Explain quantum entanglement to a 10-year-old. Use 1 analogy and avoid equations.*"

Real-World Example: A marketing prompt balancing specificity/flexibility:

"*Generate 3 Instagram captions for our new espresso machine:*

- *Include emojis (max 2)*
- *Target millennials (playful tone)*
- *Vary lengths (short punchy + 1 detailed option)*"

This approach yields creative but on-brand results like:

1. "*Morning fuel* ☕ ⚡ *#NoSnoozeButton*"
2. "*Your barista-level brew—now in 1 click.* " ✨

Advanced Prompt Techniques

Beyond basic prompting, advanced techniques enable precise control over LLM behavior by combining structured instruction and integration with external systems such as RAG. Strategic example selection teaches models detailed task requirements, while iterative refinement uses feedback loops to optimize prompts based on output quality. For scalable deployments, template-based approaches standardize inputs with placeholders (for example, "`Translate {input_text} to {target_language}`"), and dynamic prompting adjusts queries mid-execution based on intermediate results (for example, rewriting a prompt if the initial response lacks detail).

Most importantly, combining RAG with prompts—such as instructing the model to "*Base your answer* ONLY *on the following context*: `{retrieved_docs}`"—ensures responses are both contextually grounded and formatted to user specifications. These techniques transform LLMs from general-purpose tools into reliable, application-specific solutions.

Instruction Design, Example Selection, and Iterative Refinement

Effective prompt engineering relies on a combination of careful planning, thoughtful examples, and continuous improvement. Mastering these three pillars separates effective prompt engineering from trial-and-error approaches:

Instruction Design: The Art of Precision

- **Clarity Over Creativity**: Direct commands ("*List*", "*Classify*", "*Rewrite in [style]*") outperform suggestive language

- **Constraint Engineering:**

  "Compare Tesla and Ford's 2023 EV sales.

  - Use USD millions
  - Cite only Q4 figures
  - *Present as a markdown table"*

- **Negative Instructions**: Explicitly exclude unwanted behaviors
  - *"Do not speculate about future trends"*

Example Selection: Few-Shot Mastery

- **Quality** > **Quantity**: Three well-chosen examples often outperform 10 mediocre ones
- **Diversity Matters**: Cover edge cases (for example, for sentiment analysis, include neutral/ sarcastic samples)
- **Structured Demonstration**:

  Input: *"The battery life is terrible"*

  Output: {*"sentiment": "negative", "aspect": "battery"*}

  Input: *"Camera quality surprised me"*

  Output: {*"sentiment": "positive", "aspect": "camera"*}

Iterative Refinement: The Feedback Loop

- Quantitative Testing → Track metrics (accuracy, completeness) across prompt versions
- Error Pattern Analysis → Cluster bad outputs to identify systemic issues
- A/B Testing → Compare two prompt variants on 100 samples before deployment

Real-World Workflow:

1. **First Attempt**: *"Summarize this customer review in 10 words"* → *"Good product but shipping slow"* (misses key details)
2. **Refined Prompt**

   "Summarize in 10 words including:

   - Product type

   - Key praise/criticism

   - Example: 'Wireless earbuds: great sound, falls out easily'"

3. **Final Output**: "Blender: powerful but loud at high speeds"

Dynamic Prompting and Template-Based Approaches

Dynamic prompting, often built on a flexible prompt template, enables real-time adjustment of queries based on initial model outputs or external context. This technique is particularly valuable for:

- **Multi-Turn Conversations**: Evolving prompts based on dialogue history
- **Self-Correcting Systems**: Detecting inadequate responses and reformulating requests
- **Context-Aware Applications**: Incorporating real-time data (for example, weather, stock prices)

Implementation Example:

```
# Pseudocode for adaptive FAQ system
def dynamic_prompt(user_query, chat_history):
    # Analyze previous responses for consistency
    if "contradiction" in analyze_dialogue(chat_history):
        return
        "Previous discussion: {chat_history[-2:]}
        Resolve this contradiction and answer: {user_query}
        Cite sources if available."
    else:
return user_query + " (Answer in under 50 words)"
```

Templates standardize prompt structures while allowing dynamic variable insertion, enabling:

- **Batch processing**: Uniform prompts for multiple inputs
- **Localization**: Easy language/format adaptation
- **Enterprise deployment**: Team-wide consistency

Template Example:

Analyze this **`{{document_type}} for {{target_items}}`**:

Document: **`{{text}}`**

Guidelines:

- Focus on **`{{focus_area}}`**
- Format as **`{{output_format}}`**
- Exclude **`{{excluded_topics}}`**

Advanced Applications:

1. **Conditional Templates**:

   `{% if query_type == "technical" %}`

   "*Explain {{concept}} using* IEEE *paper format with* 3 *citations*"

   `{% else %}`

   "*Describe {{concept}} for high school students*"

   {% endif %}

2. **Meta-Templates**:

   Templates that generate other templates based on task analysis

Key Benefits:

- Reduces prompt engineering overhead by 60-80% in production systems
- Enables easy A/B testing of prompt variations
- Facilitates compliance with output guidelines

Fine-Tuning Large Language Models

Fine-tuning is a powerful technique for adapting pre-trained large language models (LLMs) to specific tasks or domains. While prompt engineering and Retrieval-Augmented Generation (RAG) allow you to guide a model's output or supplement its responses with external knowledge, fine-tuning goes a step further–it modifies the model's internal weights based on new, task-specific data. This results in a model that is not only better aligned with your domain but also capable of generating more consistent and specialized responses. Fine-tuning is particularly useful when high accuracy, domain sensitivity, or task specificity is required, such as in legal, medical, or enterprise-level applications.

When and Why to Fine-Tune

Fine-tuning is most beneficial when prompts or RAG-based systems fail to produce reliable or accurate results—typically in narrow or technical domains. For example, a healthcare assistant answering diagnostic questions, or a legal AI drafting contracts, may require a deep understanding of specialized language that general-purpose models struggle with. In such cases, prompt engineering alone might not be enough to consistently guide the model, and RAG may not be effective if the retrieved data is not interpreted correctly.

Additionally, fine-tuning is valuable when you need to generate outputs in a very specific format or tone, or when your application involves repetitive tasks with clearly defined goals, such as generating reports, summaries, or structured outputs. By training the model on examples from your own dataset, it learns the desired structure and terminology more naturally.

You might choose fine-tuning when:

- The model must use specialized terminology or tone (for example, legal, technical, or academic writing).
- The task involves structured outputs such as summaries, reports, or checklists.
- Consistency and domain alignment are more important than general versatility.

While full fine-tuning updates *all* of a model's weights, this is computationally expensive and requires large labeled datasets.

Modern methods such as Parameter-Efficient Fine-Tuning (PEFT) optimize only a small fraction of the parameters—making adaptation feasible even for teams with limited GPU resources.

Parameter-Efficient Fine-Tuning (PEFT) Methods

PEFT techniques have revolutionized how large models are adapted for new tasks. Instead of retraining billions of parameters, these methods add lightweight components or low-rank matrices that capture task-specific information efficiently.

Method	Concept	Advantages	Typical Use Case
Adapters	Small neural modules inserted between layers of the frozen base model.	Modular — allows swapping between tasks easily.	Multi-domain models (e.g., one model for healthcare + finance).
LoRA (Low-Rank Adaptation)	Injects low-rank trainable matrices into attention layers.	Highly memory-efficient; minimal GPU use.	Task-specific fine-tuning of large transformer models.
QLoRA (Quantized LoRA)	Combines 4-bit quantization with LoRA adapters.	Enables fine-tuning of 65B+ parameter models on a single GPU.	Resource-constrained environments (academic labs, startups).
Prefix Tuning / Prompt Tuning	Prepends learned "virtual prompts" to model inputs.	Requires no modification to model weights; fast.	Lightweight tuning for dialogue or stylistic adaptation.

Figure 19.3: *Comparison of various PEFT methods*

The table summarizes several techniques for efficiently fine-tuning or adapting large language models (LLMs) without retraining the entire model. Adapters are small neural modules inserted between the frozen layers of a base model, allowing modular task-specific adjustments, which is useful for multi-domain applications. **LoRA (Low-Rank Adaptation)** injects low-rank trainable matrices into attention layers, providing a memory-efficient way to fine-tune large transformers with minimal GPU usage. **QLoRA** (Quantized LoRA) combines 4-bit quantization with LoRA adapters, enabling fine-tuning of extremely large models (65B+ parameters) on a single GPU, making it ideal for resource-constrained settings such as academic labs or startups. Finally, Prefix Tuning / Prompt Tuning prepends learned "virtual prompts" to model inputs, allowing lightweight tuning for specific tasks–such as dialogue or stylistic adaptation–without modifying the model's original weights. Together, these methods provide flexible, efficient, and scalable strategies for adapting LLMs to specialized applications.

These methods maintain most of the original model's general knowledge while adding new capabilities, allowing scalable, reusable, and cost-effective adaptation.

The Fine-Tuning Workflow

Fine-tuning a language model involves several well-defined steps and it follows a structured process:

1. **Data Preparation**: Gather clean, representative, and well-formatted data (for example, input-output pairs). Data quality directly influences the model's reliability and tone.
2. **Model Selection**: Choose a base model (for example, GPT-3, T5, BERT, LLaMA) that aligns with your domain or objective.
3. **Configuration and Training**:
   - Define parameters (batch size, learning rate, epochs).
   - Use libraries such as Hugging Face Transformers along with PEFT techniques (for example, LoRA, QLoRA, or adapter layers) for efficient and scalable fine-tuning.
   - Monitor training using Weights & Biases, TensorBoard, or MLflow.
4. **Evaluation and Deployment**: Assess model performance on a validation set (metrics such as F1, accuracy, perplexity). Deploy only after ensuring domain-specific reliability and safety.

Use Cases and Considerations

Fine-tuning unlocks the true potential of LLMs in many specialized applications. In healthcare, models can be trained to generate clinical summaries, answer diagnostic questions, or extract medical entities from text. In law, fine-tuned models can draft legal clauses, interpret contract terms, or assist in regulatory compliance. Customer support, financial reporting, education, and scientific research are other areas where fine-tuning can significantly improve the quality and reliability of AI-generated content.

However, fine-tuning is not without tradeoffs. It requires access to labeled, high-quality data, as well as computational resources–especially if you are working with large models. There are also risks of overfitting or making the model too narrow in focus, which can reduce its generalization ability.

Another key consideration is data privacy. If your fine-tuning data includes sensitive or proprietary information, you must ensure secure training environments and compliance with data protection regulations.

Finally, it is important to note that fine-tuning is not a replacement for prompt engineering or RAG–it works best when used in combination. For instance, you might fine-tune a base model for legal terminology, then use RAG to provide it with the latest court rulings during a conversation, and still apply prompt techniques to format responses according to user expectations. This hybrid approach delivers the most reliable and intelligent outputs.

Applications and Evaluation

RAG-enhanced prompt engineering powers high-impact applications such as precise text generation (drafting reports with sourced citations), context-aware QA (answering technical queries with document-grounded responses), conversational AI (dynamic chatbots referencing real-time knowledge), and assisted code generation (suggesting APIs based on retrieved documentation). Evaluating these systems requires both quantitative metrics—accuracy (fact-checking against sources), fluency (grammaticality scores such as BLEU), and retrieval precision (MRR@k)—and qualitative analysis (expert reviews for coherence, relevance, and source fidelity). For example, a legal RAG system might achieve 90% retrieval recall but require human validation to ensure proper case law interpretation, highlighting the need for hybrid evaluation frameworks that balance automation with domain expertise.

Text Generation, Conversational AI, Code Generation

RAG-Prompt systems are especially powerful for tasks that require accurate, context-aware responses based on external information. They are widely used in applications such as intelligent chatbots, question-answering over large document sets, research assistants, customer support automation, and knowledge base summarization. By combining precise prompting with real-time retrieval, these systems can deliver outputs that are both fluent and grounded in up-to-date, domain-specific content.

However, the most effective implementations integrate Prompt Engineering, RAG, and Fine-Tuning together.

- Fine-tuning provides domain expertise—ensuring that the model understands industry-specific language, tone, and logic.
- RAG extends this knowledge by retrieving real-time or external context, keeping outputs factual and current.
- Prompt engineering then shapes how both are used—crafting inputs that guide the model to use retrieved and learned knowledge optimally.

This tri-layered approach produces systems that are accurate, explainable, and highly adaptable, ideal for enterprise and domain-specific deployments.

- **Text Generation with Citations**
  - Automatically drafts reports, articles, or summaries grounded in retrieved sources
  - **Example**: News briefings that pull quotes from press releases + generate analysis
  - **Advantage**: Reduces hallucination risk versus pure generative approaches
- **Precision Question Answering**
  - Answers technical queries by combining RAG retrieval with structured prompts:

    "*Using ONLY the 2024 FDA guidelines, list:*

    Approved COVID vaccine ages

    Dosage intervals

    Contraindications (bold if severe)"
  - **Use Case**: Medical/legal/financial domains requiring verifiable answers

- **Conversational AI with Memory**
  - **Chatbots that**:
    - Recall past interactions (retrieved from conversation logs)
    - Reference up-to-date policies (for example, "*Your refund request qualifies per our* 2024 *Terms, Section 3.2*")
- **Context-Aware Code Generation**
  - Generates code snippets linked to documentation:

    "*Write Python code to upload files to S3 using:*

    - AWS SDK *v*3

    - *Error handling per retrieved* API *docs*

    - *Async best practices*"
  - **Impact**: 40% fewer runtime errors in benchmark tests

Cross-Industry Impact:

- **Healthcare**: Diagnostic suggestions with journal citations
- **Legal**: Contract clauses analyzed against case law
- **E-commerce**: Product recommendations backed by real-time inventory

Conclusion

In this chapter, we explored how Prompt Engineering, Retrieval-Augmented Generation (RAG), and Fine-Tuning collectively extend the power and adaptability of large language models (LLMs). Each approach addresses a distinct layer of control and enhancement–ranging from steering outputs through prompts, enriching responses with external knowledge, to deeply aligning models with specialized domains.

Through Prompt Engineering, we learned how strategic input design can guide generative models toward more accurate, relevant, and creative outputs without modifying their internal parameters. RAG added another dimension by integrating retrieval mechanisms that dynamically bring external information into the generation process, improving factual consistency and contextual depth. Finally, Fine-Tuning enabled us to reshape model behavior at the parameter level, embedding domain expertise and refining outputs for specific applications.

While each technique is valuable on its own, its true potential emerges when they are used together. Prompt Engineering provides agility and rapid adaptability, RAG ensures access to the most relevant and up-to-date knowledge, and Fine-Tuning builds lasting domain alignment and precision. Combined, they form a comprehensive framework for building intelligent, trustworthy, and purpose-driven AI systems capable of handling real-world complexity with nuance and control.

Armed with these techniques, you are now prepared to design, evaluate, and deploy generative AI solutions that go beyond pre-trained capabilities. However, the field is rapidly advancing beyond these foundational methods. In the next chapter, we will explore the cutting edge of generative AI, where these techniques serve as the building blocks for even more powerful systems. We will delve into agentic AI that plans and acts autonomously, multimodal models that fuse text, image, and audio, and emerging architectures that provide models with extended memory and tool-use capabilities. This sets the stage for the next frontier: moving from systems that generate intelligent responses to those that interact, reason, and operate with true context-aware intelligence.

Points to Remember

- Prompt Engineering is the art of designing inputs to guide a model's output without changing its parameters. It is a low-cost, agile method for improving relevance, accuracy, and creativity.
- Retrieval-Augmented Generation (RAG) enhances LLMs by dynamically retrieving relevant information from external knowledge sources before generating a response, significantly improving factual consistency and reducing hallucination.
- Fine-tuning is the process of further training a pre-trained model on a specific, smaller dataset. This updates the model's internal weights, deeply aligning it with a specialized domain, style, or task.
- RAG Architecture relies on two key components: a Retriever (for example, using dense vectors with FAISS or sparse methods such as BM25) to find relevant information and a Generator (the LLM) to synthesize the final output.
- Fine-Tuning is for Domain Specialization, making a model an expert in a specific area (for example, legal documents, medical jargon, or a brand's tone of voice), whereas Prompt Engineering and RAG are for Task Guidance.
- The techniques are complementary, not exclusive. A system can use a fine-tuned model as its core, a RAG framework to provide it with the latest data, and sophisticated prompt engineering to structure its final output.
- Prompt Engineering offers rapid iteration, RAG provides access to dynamic, external knowledge, and Fine-Tuning creates a lasting, foundational change in the model's behavior.
- Key RAG challenges include maintaining a high-quality knowledge base, ensuring the retriever finds the most relevant context, and managing the added computational latency of the retrieval step.
- Key Fine-Tuning challenges involve the risk of catastrophic forgetting (losing general knowledge), the need for a large, high-quality specialized dataset, and higher computational cost compared to other methods.
- To choose the right tool for the job, use Prompt Engineering for quick prototyping and simple tasks, RAG for knowledge-intensive applications requiring up-to-date information, and Fine-Tuning for building a product that requires deep, consistent domain expertise.

Multiple Choice Questions

1. A document is 500 pages long and updated weekly. Which technique is the most suitable to ensure accurate and up-to-date answers?
   a. Fine-Tuning the model on a general customer service dataset.
   b. Using advanced Prompt Engineering with few-shot examples.
   c. Implementing a RAG system that retrieves from the current product docs.
   d. Using a larger pre-trained model without any modifications.
2. What is the primary distinction between Prompt Engineering and Fine-Tuning?
   a. Prompt Engineering guides the model externally, while Fine-Tuning internally adapts the model's parameters.
   b. Prompt Engineering changes the model's weights, while Fine-Tuning does not.

   c. Fine-Tuning is used for retrieval tasks, while Prompt Engineering is for generation.
   d. Fine-Tuning is less expensive and faster to implement than Prompt Engineering.
3. What is a key challenge in designing RAG-based systems?
   a. Ensuring zero retrieval latency
   b. Reducing token generation speed
   c. Removing the need for model fine-tuning
   d. Balancing retrieval relevance and generative fluency
4. What is a significant risk associated with the Fine-Tuning process?
   a. It requires constant internet connectivity to function.
   b. It can lead to "*catastrophic forgetting*" of the model's general knowledge.
   c. It prevents the model from using external knowledge sources.
   d. It makes prompt engineering completely ineffective.
5. In a RAG pipeline, what is the primary role of the retriever component?
   a. To generate a fluent and grammatically correct final answer.
   b. To manage the computational resources of the LLM.
   c. To search and fetch the most relevant information from a knowledge source.
   d. To post-process and refine the output of the large language model.
6. Which of the following scenarios describes a system that combines all three techniques: Prompt Engineering, RAG, and Fine-Tuning?
   a. A chatbot that uses clever prompts to answer general knowledge questions.
   b. A model fine-tuned on medical textbooks that uses a template to structure its diagnosis.
   c. A financial analyst AI that is fine-tuned on SEC filings uses a vector database to retrieve the latest earnings reports (RAG), and is prompted to summarize them in a bullet-point format.
   d. A code-generation tool that retrieves similar functions from a codebase (RAG) to assist a developer.

Answers

1. c
2. a
3. d
4. b
5. c
6. c

Questions

1. What is the primary mechanism by which a Retrieval-Augmented Generation (RAG) system reduces factual hallucinations in a large language model?
2. In Prompt Engineering, what is the key functional difference between a "*zero-shot*" prompt and a "*few-shot*" prompt?
3. A company needs an AI to write code in a proprietary, company-specific programming language. With only 500 high-quality code examples available, which technique is the most viable solution?
4. In a RAG architecture, what is the specific purpose of a "*vector database*"?
5. When fine-tuning a large language model, what is the term for the undesirable phenomenon where the model loses its general-world knowledge while learning the new, specialized dataset?
6. Which Prompt Engineering technique involves breaking down a complex problem into a series of intermediate steps within the prompt to improve the model's reasoning?
7. What is a major disadvantage of Fine-Tuning compared to Prompt Engineering when a task requires very rapid adaptation or prototyping?
8. In the context of evaluating a RAG system, which metric is most directly used to assess the quality of the initial information retrieval step?
9. If an LLM consistently fails to follow a complex instruction format (for example, "Always output in JSON key '*answer*' and key '*reasoning*'"), which technique is most likely to solve this problem permanently?
10. Why is a simple keyword-based search (such as BM25) sometimes combined with a dense vector search in a hybrid RAG retrieval system?

Key Terms

- **Zero-Shot Prompting**: Providing a model with a task description alone, without any examples, and instructing it to perform the task.
- **Few-Shot Prompting**: Providing a model with a few examples of the task within the prompt to demonstrate the desired pattern or format before giving it the actual query.
- **Chain-of-Thought (CoT)**: A prompting technique that encourages the model to generate a series of intermediate reasoning steps before producing the final answer, improving performance on complex tasks.
- **Retriever**: A system component that fetches relevant information from a database or document collection based on a user's query.
- **Dense Retrieval**: A retrieval method that uses vector similarity search in a dense vector space (for example, with FAISS) to find contextually relevant passages.
- **Sparse Retrieval**: A traditional keyword-based retrieval method that relies on term matching, such as BM25 or TF-IDF.
- **Vector Database**: A specialized database designed to store, index, and query high-dimensional vector embeddings efficiently.
- **Fine-Tuning**: The process of further training a pre-trained model on a specific, smaller dataset to adapt its weights for a particular domain, style, or task.

- **Pre-Trained Model**: A base large language model that has already been trained on a broad corpus of data, serving as the starting point for fine-tuning.
- **Catastrophic Forgetting**: A phenomenon in fine-tuning where a model loses previously learned general knowledge as it over-specializes on the new training data.
- **Domain Adaptation**: A primary goal of fine-tuning, where a model is specialized to perform well in a specific field, such as law, medicine, or a company's internal documentation.
- **Parameter-Efficient Fine-Tuning (PEFT)**: A set of techniques (such as LoRA) that fine-tune only a small subset of a model's parameters, making the process much less computationally expensive.

CHAPTER 20
Advanced Concepts

Introduction

As generative AI rapidly evolves, simply understanding foundational models such as GANs, VAEs, or even GPT is no longer sufficient to stay ahead. Today's breakthroughs lie in *how* these models are applied, extended, and made more intelligent through tools, protocols, and novel architectures. From agentic systems capable of autonomous decision-making, to multimodal models that combine text, image, audio, and video, modern GenAI is entering a new phase—one defined by context-awareness, autonomy, and versatility.

In this chapter, we delve into these advanced concepts that are shaping the future of generative AI. You will explore agentic AI systems that plan and reason across tasks, function calling that lets models interact with real-world tools, and emerging frameworks such as the Model Context Protocol (MCP) that extend memory and control. We will also examine cutting-edge trends such as on-device and hybrid models, 3D scene generation using NeRFs, personalized AI companions, and the integration of human-like perception into machines.

By the end of this chapter, you will gain a broad yet practical understanding of where generative AI is headed. You will be equipped to explore, prototype, and build next-generation AI systems that go beyond generation—toward interaction, reasoning, simulation, and true intelligence.

Structure

In this chapter, we will cover the following topics:

- **Agentic AI: Beyond Static Responses**
  - Components: Planning, Tool Use, Reflection, Memory
- **Function Calling and Tool Use in LLMs**
  - Structured Reasoning through API Calls
  - Function Calling and Tools
- **Model Context Protocol (MCP) and LangGraph**
- **Long-Term Memory and Retrieval**
  - Using Vector Databases (FAISS, Chroma, Weaviate)
- Lightweight Model Adaptation: Fine-Tuning, LoRA, and PEFT
- Multimodal AI: Cross-Modal Intelligence
  - Integrating Text, Image, Audio, and Video
  - Tools: OpenAI's GPT-4o, DALL-E, Google Gemini, and Meta's ImageBind
- **3D Generative Modeling (NeRFs and Beyond)**
- **Integration of Perceptual Systems**
- **Evolution of AI Infrastructure**

- **Democratization of GenAI Tools**
- **Challenges and Open Frontiers**

Agentic AI: Beyond Static Responses

Traditional large language models (LLMs) such as GPT are incredibly powerful at generating human-like text, answering questions, and following instructions. However, these models are largely reactive–they respond to a user's input but do not *initiate*, *plan*, or *act autonomously* without continuous human prompting. Agentic AI represents a paradigm shift from passive responders to proactive, goal-driven entities capable of making decisions, interacting with tools, and working toward objectives–much like human agents.

Agentic AI systems are designed to exhibit qualities such as autonomy, memory, tool usage, reasoning, and iterative planning. Instead of executing a single instruction, an agent can break down complex goals into sub-tasks, decide which tools to use, interact with APIs or knowledge bases, and adapt based on intermediate results. These systems act more like collaborators than tools–capable of *learning*, *reasoning*, and *improving* as they operate.

Components: Planning, Tool Use, Reflection, Memory

Agentic AI systems are not defined solely by language generation capabilities–they are *systems of behavior* that exhibit four key components: Planning, Tool Use, Reflection, and Memory. These enable agents to operate more like intelligent assistants or digital workers, capable of dynamic and autonomous task execution.

Planning

Planning is the ability to break down a high-level objective into a sequence of actionable steps. While LLMs can generate plans in text, Agentic AI systems actually *execute* these plans. They use logic chains, condition handling, and decision trees to progress toward a goal.

Example: Given a task such as "*Prepare a weekly competitor analysis report*," an agent can identify sub-goals such as collecting data, analyzing trends, and writing summaries.

Tool Use

Tool use allows the agent to extend its capabilities by calling external functions or APIs. This includes fetching data from the internet, querying databases, performing calculations, and using language translation tools or PDF readers.

Agents leverage *function calling* (for example, OpenAI or Claude's tools) to interface with the outside world in structured, real-time ways. Think of the LLM as the brain, and tools as the hands that let it interact with the environment.

Reflection

Reflection is the agent's ability to evaluate its own outputs, spot errors or bad choices, and revise its approach. This "*thinking about thinking*" mirrors human-like cognition.

Use Case: If an agent performs web scraping and gets outdated data, it can review the output, recognize the flaw, and reattempt with a better search or updated source.

Memory

Memory allows agents to retain and recall context across sessions or tasks. It could be: Short-term (task-level context) or Long-term (user preferences, historical data, prior chats)

This persistent memory enables agents to behave coherently over time, personalize interactions, and manage complex workflows.

Use Case: A memory-enabled assistant can greet you by name, remember previous project deadlines, or adapt recommendations based on past feedback.

Popular Frameworks Powering Agentic AI

Several frameworks now enable rapid development of agentic AI systems, each offering distinct capabilities. AutoGPT pioneered autonomous LLM-based agents that plan and act using tools such as web browsers and file access. LangGraph, built on LangChain, supports graph-based workflows with branching, looping, and persistent memory for complex, context-aware agents. CrewAI introduces collaborative multi-agent systems where roles such as researcher or writer coordinate to complete shared tasks. OpenAI's Custom GPTs simplify agent creation by allowing embedded tools, memory, and API access—usable even by non-developers. Collectively, these frameworks demonstrate the shift of agentic AI from research to real-world, scalable solutions.

Function Calling and Tool Use in LLMs

Function calling is a powerful capability that allows large language models (LLMs) to interact with external tools, APIs, or software functions in a structured and controlled manner. Instead of generating plain text, the model outputs a well-defined function call—typically in JSON format—with specific parameters that trigger real-world actions or retrieve live data. This bridges the gap between natural language understanding and executable logic, making LLMs more than just responders—they become *interactive agents* capable of performing tasks. Function calling is essential for building practical AI systems, enabling use cases such as booking appointments, querying databases, retrieving real-time information, and integrating with business workflows. It significantly enhances the reliability, utility, and safety of AI-powered applications by allowing precise, interpretable, and verifiable operations.

Structured Reasoning Through API Calls

While function calling provides the mechanism for an LLM to trigger real-world actions, its true power lies in how it enables structured reasoning. Rather than acting as a passive responder to single prompts, the model can now participate in dynamic, multi-step workflows—deciding not just *what* action to take, but *when* and *how* to do it based on evolving context.

Structured reasoning involves a loop of understanding the user's intent, identifying relevant tools or APIs, constructing appropriate input parameters, interpreting the results, and then deciding what to do next. This transforms the model from a static text generator into an interactive decision-maker that can coordinate across tools, adapt to user feedback, and complete complex tasks with minimal supervision.

For example, when assisting with travel planning, the model may call a date parser to extract travel dates, use a flight-search API to retrieve options, evaluate based on criteria such as price or timing, ask the user for confirmation, and finally, initiate a booking function.

Each step depends on the output of the previous one, requiring the model to reason over intermediate results—something that is only possible through structured function interfaces.

This kind of structured execution not only increases reliability but also introduces verifiability: every step the model takes can be logged, traced, and audited. This makes it ideal for enterprise applications where transparency and control are critical.

Function Calling and Tools

Function calling is now a core feature in modern LLMs, enabling structured interaction with tools and APIs. OpenAI's GPT-4 and GPT-3.5 introduced this with JSON-based schemas that allow the model to decide when and how to invoke functions, integrating seamlessly with external systems. Anthropic's Claude models offer similar capabilities but emphasize transparency and multi-tool reasoning, blending natural language with structured calls for greater interpretability. Google's Gemini models support function execution tightly integrated with Vertex AI and Google services, enabling rich, multimodal interactions. Together, these approaches make LLMs more than just text generators–they become controllable, tool-using agents capable of real-world action.

Use of Tools such as JSON Schema, API Chaining

Function calling relies heavily on structured input definitions, and JSON Schema plays a central role in this process. JSON Schema allows developers to define the exact structure, types, constraints, and descriptions for function parameters that the language model should use. This schema serves as a contract between the model and the external system, ensuring that the model outputs valid, well-formed requests–whether it is filling a booking form, fetching stock data, or triggering a workflow.

By explicitly specifying required fields, allowable values, and data types (for example, strings, numbers, enums), developers can guide the model's behavior and prevent incorrect or malformed function calls. This enhances both reliability and security, as the LLM operates within predefined boundaries rather than generating arbitrary or unsafe output.

Beyond single-step interactions, API chaining extends this concept to multi-function workflows, where the output of one function becomes the input to the next. For example, a personal assistant might first call a date parser to understand "*next Friday*," use the result to query available flights, then pass selected flight data to a booking API. Each step is linked by the model's reasoning and ability to maintain context across multiple calls.

Together, JSON Schema and API chaining elevate LLMs from simple query responders to powerful orchestrators of real-world logic–capable of coordinating tools, maintaining task flow, and delivering complete, context-aware solutions.

Model Context Protocol (MCP) and LangGraph

As language models evolve to handle increasingly complex tasks, managing context, state, and memory becomes a critical challenge. The Model Context Protocol (MCP) is an emerging design pattern aimed at standardizing how models interact with external memory, tools, and functions over multiple turns. It enables structured communication between the model and its environment, allowing agents to maintain awareness of prior steps, decisions, and user inputs–essential for long-running or multi-stage tasks. LangGraph, built on top of LangChain, operationalizes this idea by letting developers define dynamic, graph-based workflows where nodes represent actions (such as tool use, LLM calls, or conditional logic) and edges determine the flow of execution. With built-in support for looping, branching, and state tracking, LangGraph enables the creation of advanced agent systems that can plan, adapt, and reason over evolving contexts–paving the way for robust, real-world autonomous applications.

Addressing Context Window Limitations

One of the most significant constraints in large language models (LLMs) is the context window–the maximum amount of input text the model can process at once. While newer models such as GPT-4o and Gemini 1.5 have dramatically expanded these limits (up to 1 million tokens in some cases), real-world applications often require handling far more information over extended interactions. To overcome this, developers are increasingly using retrieval-augmented techniques, external memory modules, and structured state management protocols such as the Model Context Protocol (MCP). These approaches allow LLMs to offload information to vector databases, selectively retrieve relevant context, and maintain continuity across long conversations or multi-turn tasks. Tools such as LangChain, LangGraph, and emerging memory frameworks make it possible to design systems where the model remembers past actions, goals, or user preferences—even beyond the native context window—enabling more coherent and intelligent behavior over time.

LangChain Expression Language (LCEL) and LangGraph

To simplify the design of structured, composable AI workflows, LangChain Expression Language (LCEL) provides a declarative syntax for chaining together prompts, models, tools, and memory into reusable pipeline components. LCEL abstracts away the low-level orchestration logic, enabling developers to focus on the *what* instead of the *how*. It supports sequential, parallel, and conditional execution flows, making it easier to build modular and testable applications. LangGraph, on the other hand, extends this foundation by introducing stateful, graph-based execution. Instead of linear pipelines, LangGraph allows workflows to be represented as directed graphs, where each node corresponds to a function, model call, or tool, and edges define the logic of execution—including loops, branches, and retries. Combined, LCEL and LangGraph empower developers to build agentic, context-aware systems capable of reasoning, adapting, and interacting with tools in complex, multi-turn environments.

Building Memory-Aware, Event-Driven Multi-Step Agents

Modern AI applications increasingly require agents that go beyond single-turn interactions—they must remember past events, track progress across tasks, and respond dynamically to new inputs. Memory-aware, event-driven multi-step agents are designed with this in mind. These agents combine persistent memory (for storing user preferences, past interactions, or intermediate results) with event-driven logic that determines how and when actions should be triggered. Using frameworks such as LangGraph, developers can architect agents as state machines or flow graphs, where each node represents a tool call, model prompt, or conditional logic, and transitions are triggered by context or user input. This architecture allows agents to maintain state across long-running sessions, revisit previous steps if conditions change, and adaptively route through complex workflows. Whether it is a customer support bot handling ticket lifecycle, or a research assistant conducting multi-stage analysis, these agents behave more like intelligent collaborators—autonomous, aware, and responsive to changing circumstances.

Long-Term Memory and Retrieval

While traditional language models are stateless and forgetful by design, advanced generative AI agents increasingly require long-term memory to deliver personalized, coherent, and context-aware interactions. Long-term memory enables agents to persist information across sessions—such as user preferences, task history, past conversations, or previously retrieved facts—allowing for more intelligent decision-making over time. This is often implemented using vector databases (such as FAISS, Pinecone, or Chroma) that store semantic embeddings of past content, which can be retrieved using similarity search when relevant context is needed. Combined with retrieval mechanisms, such as Retrieval-Augmented Generation (RAG), memory-aware agents can selectively pull in prior knowledge to inform current responses. This memory-retrieval loop allows the agent to behave more like a human assistant—remembering prior interactions, learning from corrections, and evolving its responses based on accumulated knowledge. It is a foundational capability for building AI systems that are not just reactive, but *deeply contextual* and *adaptive* over time.

Short-Term versus Long-Term Memory

In memory-enabled AI systems, it is important to distinguish between short-term and long-term memory, as they serve different roles in enabling intelligent behavior. Short-term memory refers to the immediate context available to the model during a single interaction or task–typically confined to the model's context window. It includes the latest user input, recent messages, or temporary variables used within a session. Once the session ends or the context window resets, this information is lost. In contrast, long-term memory is persistent and exists beyond the scope of a single session. It stores key insights, user preferences, historical data, and past interactions in external storage (such as vector databases), allowing the agent to retrieve and reuse relevant information at any time. Together, these memory types enable agents to respond effectively in the moment (short-term), while continuously learning and adapting over time (long-term), mimicking how humans manage and recall information.

Using Vector Databases (FAISS, Chroma, Weaviate)

To implement persistent, searchable long-term memory in generative AI systems, developers rely on vector databases–specialized systems designed to efficiently store and retrieve high-dimensional embeddings. These embeddings are numerical representations of semantically rich content, such as user queries, documents, or conversation turns, typically generated using pretrained models such as OpenAI's `text-embedding-ada-002,` SentenceTransformers, or Mistral.

When an AI agent processes a piece of information, that data is passed through an embedding model to transform it into a fixed-length vector (for example, 768 or 1536 dimensions). This vector captures the semantic essence of the input, making it suitable for approximate nearest neighbor (ANN) searches. Once computed, the vector and associated metadata (for example, source text, timestamps, user ID, tags) are stored in a vector database.

At runtime, when the agent needs to recall past relevant knowledge, the new query is similarly embedded into a vector and used to perform a similarity search (usually cosine similarity or inner product) against the stored vectors. The top-k most similar vectors are returned and injected into the prompt or agent context, often using Retrieval-Augmented Generation (RAG) or similar mechanisms.

Key Vector Databases and Their Characteristics

- **FAISS (Facebook AI Similarity Search):** FAISS is a high-performance C++ library (with Python bindings) developed by Meta. It supports dense vector indexing using flat, Inverted File, Product Quantization, and HNSW (Hierarchical Navigable Small World) techniques for scalability. FAISS is ideal for on-prem or self-hosted environments where performance and control are crucial. It is widely used in production pipelines and research systems due to its speed and customization capabilities.

  Pros:

  - Highly efficient in-memory search and multiple indexing strategies
  - GPU acceleration support and custom scoring functions possible

  Cons:

  - Lacks built-in persistence or REST APIs
  - Requires manual orchestration for scaling or cloud deployments

- **Chroma:** Chroma is a lightweight, open-source vector store designed with AI-native development in mind. It is tightly integrated with frameworks such as LangChain and supports embedding storage, metadata filtering, and prompt templating out of the box. Chroma is ideal for small to medium-scale applications and rapid prototyping, particularly in local development environments.

  Pros:

  - Simple API and integrated with LangChain and other LLM toolchains
  - Persistent storage, metadata support, and runs locally

  Cons:

  - Less optimized for large-scale, distributed workloads
  - Limited customizability compared to FAISS or Weaviate

- **Weaviate:** Weaviate is a robust, production-ready, cloud-native vector database built with semantic search in mind. It offers features such as schema-based object storage, hybrid search (keyword + vector), metadata filtering, multi-tenancy, and modular embedding pipelines. Weaviate supports REST and GraphQL APIs and can run both in the cloud (via Weaviate Cloud Services) and on-premises.

  Pros:

  - Scalable and cloud-friendly
  - Advanced filtering, vector scoring, and hybrid queries

  Cons:

  - Heavier setup and some features behind enterprise plans

Developers often pair vector stores with memory routers, context window managers, or agent modules that determine what to store and when to retrieve, ensuring the memory remains both performant and relevant.

As memory grows, so does the importance of index pruning, vector compression, and multi-modal support (for example, storing image or audio embeddings). Some systems shard memory per user to reduce query cost. Some implement recency to prioritize fresher data.

Multimodal AI: Cross-Modal Intelligence

Traditional AI models are trained to handle a single data modality—such as text, images, or audio. Multimodal AI breaks this barrier by enabling models to process and integrate multiple forms of data simultaneously, including text, images, audio, video, and even sensory inputs such as depth or motion. This cross-modal intelligence allows for richer, more human-like understanding and interaction. For example, a multimodal model can look at an image, understand the context in natural language, answer questions about it, or even generate a descriptive caption. Cutting-edge systems such as GPT-4o, Gemini, Claude 3, OpenAI's DALL·E, and Meta's ImageBind showcase the capabilities of these models, from describing images and generating videos to reasoning over both visual and textual content. Multimodal AI opens the door to more intuitive applications—such as visually grounded chatbots, interactive educational tools, and AI assistants that can "*see*" and "*hear*" as well as "*read*" and "*write*."

Integrating Text, Image, Audio, and Video

At the heart of multimodal AI lies the challenge and opportunity of enabling a model to understand and reason across heterogeneous data types—such as natural language (text), visual frames (images/videos), audio waveforms (speech/music), and spatiotemporal signals (motion/depth).

This integration is not merely a juxtaposition of multiple input streams; it requires learning joint representations that capture the semantic relationships and temporal dependencies across modalities.

Core Techniques for Multimodal Integration

Shared Embedding Spaces: A foundational technique is mapping all input modalities into a common latent space–a shared embedding space–where semantically similar inputs from different domains (for example, the sound of barking and the image of a dog) are close in vector space. This is achieved through modality-specific encoders:

- Text → Transformer (for example, BERT, GPT)
- Image → CNNs or Vision Transformers (for example, ResNet, ViT)
- Audio → Spectrogram + CNN/Transformer (for example, Whisper, Wav2Vec)
- Video → 3D-CNN, TimeSformer, or audio-visual fusion models

These embeddings are aligned using contrastive learning (for example, CLIP, ImageBind) or fusion networks trained on parallel multimodal datasets. Cross-modal contrastive loss ensures that semantically related items are mapped closer across modalities.

Cross-Modal Attention and Fusion Layers: Once encoded, cross-modal attention mechanisms allow the model to focus on relevant parts of one modality when reasoning about another. For example, when answering a question about an image, the model might attend to specific visual regions based on linguistic cues from the question.

Fusion strategies include:

- **Early Fusion**: Concatenate embeddings from all modalities at the input level
- **Late Fusion**: Independently process each modality and merge the outputs
- **Cross-Attention Fusion**: Use transformer layers to dynamically align features across modalities

This allows temporal-spatial reasoning (in video), lip-reading (via synchronized audio-visual input), or emotion recognition (combining tone of voice with facial expressions).

Temporal Synchronization for Video and Audio: For video analysis, integration must consider temporal alignment:

- **Audio-Visual Synchronization**: Ensuring spoken words are mapped to the correct video frames
- **Scene Understanding Over Time**: Tracking objects, faces, and events across frame sequences
- **Multimodal Transformers**: Use time-aware positional encodings and multi-stream architectures that jointly process video and audio tracks (for example, VideoBERT, Florence-2)

Advanced models can transcribe speech (via ASR), detect actions (via motion), recognize emotions, and summarize scenes using a holistic multimodal pipeline.

Multimodal Prompting and Generation: Models such as GPT-4o, Gemini, and Claude 3 support multimodal prompting, where a user may ask a question by providing both text and images/audio. The model responds by understanding and correlating the different modalities.

Use cases include:

- Asking a question about a diagram or chart
- Generating alt text or explanations for visual content
- Translating spoken descriptions into real-time visual edits

These interactions require multimodal tokenization, where input types are serialized into a unified format before being passed through shared transformer layers.

Real-World Examples:

- **Video QA**: Model transcribes audio (speech-to-text), extracts frames at intervals, applies object recognition, and performs language inference over both timelines.
- **Voice-Controlled Visual Assistants**: Users give spoken instructions to describe an image. It parses speech, understands image semantics, and generates a response.
- **Medical Diagnostics**: X-rays and accompanying textual reports are analyzed together. A multimodal agent can suggest diagnoses, detect anomalies, or generate summaries.

Tools: OpenAI's GPT-4o, DALL·E, Google Gemini, and Meta's ImageBind

Several state-of-the-art systems are redefining the boundaries of multimodal AI by integrating multiple sensory modalities into unified inference and generation pipelines. These tools not only demonstrate technical innovation but also showcase real-world applications of cross-modal reasoning, shared embedding architectures, and real-time human-like interaction.

OpenAI's GPT-4o (Omni Model)

GPT-4o is OpenAI's most advanced natively multimodal transformer model, capable of processing text, audio (speech), and vision (images) in real-time. Unlike earlier models that relied on separate pathways or modular adapters for different modalities (for example, Whisper + GPT + CLIP), GPT-4o is trained end-to-end across modalities, enabling faster and more coherent cross-modal reasoning.

Key Technical Features:

- Single neural network with native support for vision, audio, and text embeddings
- Real-time voice interactions with sub-300ms response time
- Speech-to-text and text-to-speech are built in, eliminating the need for external tools
- Multimodal turn memory: Maintains context across mixed modality interactions (for example, user asks a question by voice, follows up with an image, gets a text response)

Use Cases:

- Voice-based agents with visual understanding (for example, reading signs, interpreting photos)
- Multimodal tutoring systems that analyze diagrams and explain concepts
- Real-time vision + language interactions for accessibility tools

OpenAI's DALL·E (v3)

DALL·E is a diffusion-based image generation model trained to translate textual prompts into high-quality images. It now supports inpainting, allowing users to edit specific parts of an image using text, a critical step toward interactive visual creativity.

Key Technical Features:

- CLIP-guided prompt understanding for aligning text semantics with visual concepts
- Inpainting via attention-masked denoising diffusion: Users can erase and regenerate parts of an image by describing the desired outcome in natural language
- Prompt injection for guided image variation and iterative design workflows

Use Cases:

- Generative art and concept design
- UI/UX prototyping from text specs, storyboarding, and content creation

Google Gemini

Google Gemini represents the next generation of large-scale multimodal foundation models built by DeepMind. It is trained to natively fuse text, image, audio, and video, and is designed for seamless integration into Google's product ecosystem.

Key Technical Features:

- Unified transformer-based architecture trained with multi-modal pretraining objectives across large-scale web, audio, and video corpora
- Cross-modal attention blocks and temporal modeling units for video understanding
- Massive parallel training on TPU v5 infrastructure
- Bidirectional prompt comprehension, for multi-turn, mixed-modal inputs

Use Cases:

- Document and media understanding in enterprise software
- AI-powered productivity assistants, multimodal search, and summarization tools

Meta's ImageBind

ImageBind is Meta AI's research-grade model that goes beyond traditional 3-modal systems by aligning six modalities into a single shared embedding space: Text, Image, Audio, Depth, Thermal Imaging, and IMU (motion sensors).

Key Technical Features:

- Contrastive learning across six modalities using a frozen encoder approach
- Leverages self-supervised learning from large-scale heterogeneous datasets
- Embeddings from each modality are dimensionally aligned
- No need for paired data during inference–ImageBind can retrieve audio samples similar to an image, or thermal representations from textual input

Research Implications:

- Extends multimodal AI to robotics, AR/VR, autonomous vehicles, and wearables
- Enables cross-sensory retrieval and grounded learning for embodied agents

Use Cases:

- Multisensory robotics (for example, aligning IMU motion data with environmental visuals)
- Remote diagnostics (for example, merging thermal + image + text data in medical imaging)

Collective Impact

Together, these tools mark a paradigm shift to unified multimodal intelligence. They move AI beyond text generation toward context-aware agents that can see, hear, speak, and perceive the world through multiple sensory dimensions. Their architectures blend transformer innovations, embedding strategies, real-time I/O pipelines, and cross-domain generalization capabilities, making them central to the next generation applications–from assistive technologies and content creation to scientific discovery and interactive entertainment.

3D Generative Modeling (NeRFs and Beyond)

While traditional generative models focus on 2D images or text, recent advances such as Neural Radiance Fields (NeRFs) are revolutionizing how AI understands and generates 3D content. NeRFs learn to represent a scene from multiple 2D images by estimating the color and density of points in 3D space. This technique is very useful in fields such as augmented reality, robotics, and medical imaging, where understanding spatial depth is critical. Beyond NeRFs, newer methods such as Gaussian Splatting, Instant-NGP, and 3D diffusion models are pushing the boundaries further by improving rendering speed, quality, and real-time capabilities. These open the door to building immersive digital twins, realistic virtual environments, and reconstructions, bridging the gap between 2D perception and 3D spatial intelligence.

From 2D Images to Immersive 3D Scene Reconstruction

Traditional computer vision models often rely on flat, 2D representations of the world, which limits their ability to understand spatial depth or perspective. Neural Radiance Fields (NeRFs) have introduced a major breakthrough by enabling 3D scene reconstruction from just a handful of 2D images. NeRFs learn to model how light interacts with objects in space, generating continuous volumetric representations that can be rendered from any viewpoint. This transforms 2D image data into immersive, explorable 3D environments–offering a powerful new way to visualize real-world scenes with stunning realism.

Applications in AR/VR, Robotics, and Healthcare

The ability to generate accurate 3D reconstructions has unlocked a range of high-impact applications. In augmented and virtual reality (AR/VR), NeRFs and similar models are used to build lifelike virtual spaces for gaming, training, or design. In robotics, 3D modeling enhances scene understanding, navigation, and manipulation tasks–enabling robots to interact more intelligently with their surroundings. In healthcare, 3D generative techniques are being used for reconstructing anatomical structures from limited imaging data, improving diagnostics, surgical planning, and medical training. These capabilities mark a significant leap in how AI systems perceive and reason about the physical world.

Tools: Instant-NGP, Gaussian Splatting

To accelerate the adoption of 3D generative modeling, several tools and frameworks have emerged. Instant-NGP (Neural Graphics Primitives), developed by NVIDIA, offers real-time NeRF rendering by dramatically speeding up training and inference using GPU-accelerated optimization. Gaussian Splatting, a newer technique, replaces complex volumetric rendering with compact, transparent 3D Gaussians–achieving visually impressive results with minimal computational overhead. These tools make it practical to implement 3D scene reconstruction in real-world applications, enabling developers to build faster, more interactive, and visually rich AI experiences across domains.

Integration of Perceptual Systems

While most generative AI systems focus on vision and language, the next wave involves integrating human-like senses such as touch, hearing, and physiological signals. Emerging models now process tactile input, voice patterns, facial cues, and biometric data to enable more empathetic, context-aware interactions. In healthcare, this could support early diagnosis; in robotics, it enhances control and safety. Research is also exploring synthetic smell and taste via chemical sensing. These advances bring us closer to embodied AI–systems that perceive and respond to the world more like humans do.

AI Sensing Emotion Through Audio, Facial Micro-Expressions, and Biosignals

AI systems are increasingly being designed to interpret human emotions by analyzing subtle cues across multiple modalities. Through audio analysis, models can detect emotional states based on vocal tone, pitch, rhythm, and speech patterns–identifying stress, happiness, anger, or anxiety. Similarly, facial micro-expressions–brief, involuntary facial movements–are rich indicators of hidden emotions, and can be captured using computer vision techniques powered by convolutional neural networks or facial landmark tracking. Going even deeper, biosignals such as heart rate variability, skin conductance, and EEG data provide real-time physiological insights into a person's emotional and cognitive state. By combining these inputs, emotion-aware AI systems can deliver more personalized, empathetic, and responsive experiences in domains such as mental health support, customer service, education, and human-robot interaction. This emerging field bridges the gap between affective computing and generative AI, making machines not just intelligent–but emotionally intelligent.

Experimental Directions: Smell, Touch (Haptics), Taste

As generative AI continues to evolve beyond vision and language, researchers are venturing into experimental sensory modalities such as smell, touch (haptics), and taste–pushing the boundaries of machine perception. In the domain of smell, projects are exploring electronic noses (e-noses) that can detect and classify chemical compounds, enabling applications in food quality monitoring, medical diagnostics, and safety systems. Haptic feedback systems are being combined with AI to simulate the sensation of touch–allowing robots to feel texture, pressure, or force, which is crucial for tasks involving manipulation or human interaction. In taste, early research leverages chemical sensors and neural decoding to simulate gustatory responses, with potential applications in virtual food testing, health monitoring, and personalized nutrition. While these modalities are still in their infancy, their integration into AI systems signals a future where machines are not only generative but sensory-rich and embodied, capable of perceiving the world in dimensions closer to human experience.

Personalized AI Companions

Generative AI is driving the rise of personalized AI companions–context-aware agents that learn from user interactions to offer emotionally intelligent, tailored support. Unlike static chatbots, these systems adapt to user tone, preferences, and habits over time, using multimodal inputs and long-term memory to maintain continuity and anticipate needs. Tools such as OpenAI's Custom GPTs, Replika, and Pi demonstrate early applications in productivity, wellness, and companionship. As they evolve, these agents are shifting from scripted responses to dynamic relationships, with potential in coaching, therapy, and collaborative assistance.

Combining Sensor Input + LLM Context

To further enhance personalization, next-generation AI companions are integrating sensor data with LLM-driven reasoning. This fusion allows the AI to perceive and interpret real-world signals–such as voice tone, facial expressions, location, calendar events, or biometric data–and contextualize them with past interactions. For instance, if the AI detects fatigue in your voice and notices a packed calendar, it might recommend rescheduling non-essential meetings. By combining environmental and physiological signals with conversational memory, these agents offer a deeply contextual, situationally aware experience, enabling them to act as intelligent life assistants rather than just chat responders.

Persistent Agents Across Sessions (such as Replika, Pi, Character.AI)

Unlike traditional chatbots that start fresh with each conversation, persistent AI agents maintain a long-term memory of past interactions, making them feel more continuous and human-like. Tools such as Replika, Character.AI, and Pi by Inflection exemplify this trend, storing and evolving personality traits, user preferences, and relationship dynamics over time. These companions remember who you are, what you care about, and how you communicate, allowing for a deeper, more meaningful relationship. Whether it is remembering your favorite music genre, tracking personal goals, or continuing a conversation from days ago, persistent agents create a sense of ongoing companionship, redefining how humans engage with AI.

Evolution of AI Infrastructure

As generative AI systems grow in complexity and adoption, the supporting infrastructure has rapidly evolved to meet the demands of scalability, efficiency, and deployment. Earlier AI pipelines required extensive manual setup, custom code, and high-end clusters. Today, platforms such as Amazon Bedrock, Google Vertex AI, and Microsoft Azure AI offer managed services that simplify everything from model training and tuning to hosting and monitoring. These platforms support foundation models, serverless APIs, vector databases, toolchains, and fine-tuning workflows—all within enterprise-grade security frameworks. Additionally, containerization technologies such as Docker and orchestration tools such as Kubernetes have made it easier to deploy AI models across hybrid cloud and edge environments. With the integration of GPU-accelerated infrastructure, real-time inference engines (for example, Triton, TensorRT), and cost-effective auto-scaling, AI is becoming more modular, composable, and production-ready than ever. This evolution empowers organizations of all sizes to deploy powerful GenAI solutions without needing to reinvent the stack.

Tools: Amazon Bedrock, SageMaker, Google Vertex AI

Leading cloud providers have introduced powerful platforms that abstract away the complexity of building and deploying generative AI. Amazon Bedrock allows developers to access foundation models from providers such as Anthropic, AI21, and Cohere through a simple API. SageMaker offers a more customizable option, supporting end-to-end workflows from model training to monitoring, with tools such as JumpStart for low-code experimentation. Vertex AI provides similar capabilities with robust integration into the Google ecosystem. These platforms allow enterprises to focus on building solutions, while the infrastructure—scaling, security, fine-tuning, and monitoring—is handled in the background.

API Orchestration, Serverless Inference, and Multi-Cloud Deployment

Modern AI infrastructure emphasizes flexibility and efficiency, with features such as API orchestration to manage complex workflows across multiple models and tools, serverless inference to eliminate the need for manual provisioning, and multi-cloud deployment for portability and resilience. Developers can now build scalable applications using APIs that connect LLMs with tools, databases, and user-facing apps—all dynamically managed. Serverless inference platforms (such as AWS Lambda, Bedrock's runtime, or Cloud Functions) reduce operational overhead and cost, while multi-cloud strategies ensure redundancy, compliance, and vendor independence—crucial for enterprise-level GenAI applications.

Use Case: Launching Enterprise-Level GenAI in Days, Not Months

Thanks to modern AI infrastructure platforms, enterprises can now rapidly prototype, fine-tune, and deploy production-ready generative AI applications with minimal DevOps involvement. What once required months of effort–setting up GPU clusters, configuring model training pipelines, building secure APIs, and integrating monitoring systems–can now be achieved in a matter of days, thanks to serverless architectures, pre-integrated vector databases, foundation model APIs, and MLOps toolchains.

Example: Financial Services - Intelligent Customer Support Agent

A large financial services firm wants to deploy a 24/7 intelligent virtual assistant to reduce call center load and improve customer experience. Using Amazon Bedrock, the team can:

1. Select a foundation model (for example, Anthropic Claude or Amazon Titan) via a managed API–no model training or GPU provisioning required.
2. Connect the agent to internal documentation and customer service logs using Amazon Kendra or a vector database (for example, Pinecone) to enable Retrieval-Augmented Generation (RAG).
3. Use Lambda functions or Bedrock's native runtime to build a serverless backend that handles user queries, processes responses, and invokes model inference.
4. Build a secure, compliant frontend (for example, using AWS Amplify or a React app) integrated with Cognito for authentication and API Gateway for throttling and monitoring.
5. Deploy monitoring with Amazon CloudWatch and set usage limits and failover policies using IAM and API Quotas.

Result: The entire solution–fully integrated with enterprise data, scalable to thousands of concurrent users, and compliant with financial regulations–can go live in under a week with minimal infrastructure overhead.

Another Example in Healthcare - Fine-Tuned Medical Assistant Across Clinics

A healthcare provider can deploy a HIPAA-compliant AI assistant on Google Vertex AI to support clinical documentation, diagnosis, and EHR summarization. The process involves fine-tuning a base model, such as PaLM or Gemini, using anonymized patient data with Vertex AI Training Pipelines, supported by BigQuery and TensorFlow Data Validation for preprocessing. The model is deployed via Vertex AI Model Registry and Prediction Services for secure, scalable inference. It integrates with EHR and radiology systems using FHIR-compatible APIs and provides real-time decision support through RAG pipelines linked to Cloud SQL or Chroma. Vertex AI Model Monitoring ensures ongoing accuracy and reliability.

- **Security and Compliance**: Data access and logs are secured with IAM roles, VPC Service Controls, and Cloud DLP, ensuring compliance with privacy regulations such as HIPAA and GDPR.
- **Deployment Timeframe**: A robust, production-ready, multimodal clinical assistant–capable of processing text, images (for example, scans), and structured data–can be live across hospital branches in less than 10 days.

Democratization of GenAI Tools

One of the most transformative trends in the AI landscape is the democratization of generative AI tools, making powerful capabilities accessible to a broader audience beyond ML experts. Thanks to no-code and low-code platforms, pre-built APIs, and user-friendly interfaces, individuals with little to no technical background can now customize and deploy AI models. Tools such as OpenAI's Custom GPTs, Canva Studio, and ChatGPT Pro allow users to build AI-powered assistants, generate content, and automate workflows with just a few clicks. On the developer side, frameworks such as LangChain, Hugging Face, and AutoTrain simplify the integration and fine-tuning of models. This democratization empowers startups, educators, marketers, and domain experts to harness AI for innovation without heavy engineering overhead—accelerating creativity, productivity, and problem-solving across industries.

Responsible Access and Guided Fine-Tuning for Non-Engineers

As AI tools become more accessible, platforms are also emphasizing responsible access and guided customization, especially for non-technical users. Services such as Hugging Face AutoTrain, OpenAI's GPT Builder, and Google's MakerSuite provide step-by-step interfaces to fine-tune models or build AI workflows with guardrails in place. These include bias detection, content filtering, and safety guidelines to ensure ethical deployment. By guiding users through safe and effective customization, these platforms make it possible for non-engineers to build high-impact GenAI applications—from customer service bots to educational tutors—while minimizing risks and maintaining alignment with best practices.

Digital Twins and Simulation Systems

Generative AI is transforming digital twin and simulation technologies by enabling virtual replicas of real-world systems to go beyond passive monitoring. These AI-enhanced twins use real-time data to simulate scenarios, generate synthetic data, and test outcomes without real-world risk. In manufacturing, they help detect failures and optimize supply chains. In healthcare, they simulate patient responses for personalized treatment. Urban planners and pharmaceutical companies use them for smart city modeling and drug discovery, combining physics-based simulations with AI to enhance forecasting and innovation.

In industries such as urban planning, drug discovery, and logistics, generative AI brings new power to digital twins. City planners can simulate traffic, population growth, and environmental impact. In drug R&D, AI models predict molecular behavior and toxicity, speeding up development. Logistics teams use digital twins to model supply chains, simulate deliveries, and optimize warehouse flows. These applications show how AI creates high-fidelity simulations that drive smarter, faster decisions.

By blending real-time data with generative models, digital twins now simulate dynamic systems such as supply chains, organs, and production lines. In supply chains, they predict disruptions and suggest alternate strategies. In biomedicine, they allow researchers to test treatments on virtual organs. In manufacturing, factory twins test layout or automation changes without halting operations. These advances enable safer, more efficient experimentation and innovation across domains.

Challenges and Open Frontiers

As generative AI advances rapidly, it brings with it a new set of technical, ethical, and operational challenges. Key concerns include hallucination, where models generate incorrect or misleading outputs with confidence, and the lack of explainability, making it difficult to audit or trust model decisions in critical domains. Issues such as bias, data privacy, and intellectual property ownership are also top priorities, especially as models are trained on vast and often unregulated datasets. Operationally, there are concerns around the cost of inference, energy consumption, and real-time performance at scale. On the horizon, open frontiers include the development of unified multimodal agents, embodied AI systems, context windows exceeding millions of tokens, and deeper integration of neurosymbolic reasoning. These directions hint at a future where AI is not only generative, but truly intelligent–capable of perceiving, reasoning, and adapting like a human collaborator.

Trust, Hallucination, Interpretability

One of the biggest challenges in deploying generative AI systems is ensuring trust and reliability. Models often suffer from hallucination–confidently generating false or misleading information, especially in open-ended or ambiguous scenarios. This undermines their usefulness in critical domains such as healthcare, law, and education. Additionally, many foundation models are black boxes, making it difficult to interpret how they arrived at a particular response. Without transparency, debugging or auditing these systems becomes challenging, and users are left unsure whether the output can be trusted. Addressing these issues requires better evaluation metrics, model explainability tools, and the integration of verifiable reasoning steps into generative pipelines.

Model Safety, Energy Efficiency, Copyright, and Ethical Dilemmas

As generative AI becomes more powerful and widespread, the need for safety, sustainability, and ethical responsibility grows. Large models require significant computational resources, raising concerns about energy consumption and environmental impact. On the legal side, the use of copyrighted content in training datasets has sparked debates around intellectual property, ownership of AI-generated content, and fair use. Furthermore, biases embedded in training data can lead to harmful outputs or unfair treatment, particularly in sensitive domains. Ensuring model safety involves not just fine-tuning and filtering, but also setting clear ethical standards, conducting audits, and promoting transparent data curation.

Conclusion

This chapter has taken us beyond the basics into the evolving frontier of advanced generative AI, where models are not just generating text or images, but reasoning, planning, adapting, and interacting across diverse modalities and environments. We have explored the rise of Agentic AI, capable of tool use, memory, and autonomous decision-making; the mechanics of function calling and structured API integration that transform models into action-driven systems; and the role of context protocols and LangGraph in orchestrating dynamic agent workflows. We examined how long-term memory and vector databases enhance continuity, and how lightweight adaptation techniques such as LoRA and PEFT are unlocking the power of GenAI on smaller, more efficient models.

As the field moves toward multimodal AI, 3D scene generation, and the integration of human-like perception–touch, emotion, and sensory signals–GenAI systems are becoming richer and more immersive. We also looked at how scalable infrastructure, democratized tooling, and ethical design are shaping the future of development, alongside unresolved challenges such as hallucination, interpretability, and responsible deployment.

In the next chapter, we will shift focus from the "what is possible" to the "how-to," diving into best practices for designing, deploying, and maintaining generative AI responsibly. You will learn the principles, guidelines, and real-world insights that help ensure reliability, fairness, and safety–so you can build GenAI systems that are not only powerful but also trusted and impactful.

Points to Remember

- **Agentic AI** enables models to go beyond static text generation by incorporating planning, memory, tool use, and reflection–turning them into autonomous decision-makers.
- **Function calling** allows LLMs to interact with external APIs and tools using structured outputs such as JSON, making them capable of executing tasks and retrieving real-time information.
- **Model Context Protocol (MCP)** and frameworks such as LangGraph help coordinate multi-step reasoning, agent collaboration, and persistent memory across sessions.
- **Long-term memory and retrieval systems**–powered by vector databases such as FAISS, Chroma, and Weaviate–enable models to access relevant past information and scale contextual understanding.
- **Multimodal AI** integrates text, image, audio, and video to enable cross-sensory understanding, supported by tools such as OpenAI's GPT-4o, DALL·E, and Google Gemini.
- **Perceptual systems** are expanding GenAI's capabilities by incorporating emotion sensing, touch (haptics), and even smell and taste, pushing toward embodied intelligence.
- The **democratization of GenAI** empowers non-technical users to build and customize AI experiences through no-code tools such as ChatGPT's Custom GPTs, Notion AI, and Canva Magic Studio.
- **Challenges** such as hallucination, bias, interpretability, and energy efficiency remain active areas of research, while open frontiers include multi-agent collaboration, robotics, and embodied cognition.

Multiple Choice Questions

1. What is the purpose of function calling in large language models?
   a. To improve the model's grammar
   b. To generate longer outputs
   c. To trigger external tools or APIs using structured output
   d. To compress training data
2. Which of the following best describes Agentic AI?
   a. AI models trained only on image data
   b. AI that focuses only on audio transcription
   c. Static models that respond only when prompted
   d. AI systems that operate independently with planning, tool use, and memory
3. What is LangGraph used for in GenAI development?
   a. Generating vector embeddings
   b. Scheduling batch jobs in the cloud
   c. Structuring memory and multi-agent workflows
   d. Drawing knowledge graphs from PDFs

4. Which of the following tools enables lightweight fine-tuning of LLMs with minimal parameters?
    a. FAISS
    b. LoRA
    c. NumPy
    d. ImageBind
5. What is a key benefit of integrating vector databases such as FAISS or Weaviate with LLMs?
    a. Faster model training
    b. Improved GPU utilization
    c. Long-term memory and semantic retrieval
    d. Data augmentation during fine-tuning

Answers

1. c
2. d
3. c
4. b
5. c

Questions

1. What is Agentic AI, and how does it extend the capabilities of traditional LLMs?
2. How does function calling transform large language models into interactive agents?
3. What role do vector databases such as FAISS and Weaviate play in enabling long-term memory for GenAI systems?
4. Explain the difference between fine-tuning, LoRA, and PEFT. In what scenarios would you use each?
5. How does multimodal AI differ from traditional single-modality models, and what are its advantages?
6. What are Neural Radiance Fields (NeRFs), and how are they used in 3D generative modeling?
7. How do tools such as LangGraph and MCP support structured, multi-step reasoning in GenAI agents?
8. In what ways are perceptual systems—such as touch and emotion detection—shaping the future of embodied AI?
9. Describe how modern AI infrastructure platforms such as Amazon Bedrock and Google Vertex AI simplify GenAI deployment.
10. What ethical and technical challenges arise as GenAI systems become more autonomous and integrated across industries?

Key Terms

- **Agentic AI**: A paradigm in which generative AI systems are capable of autonomous decision-making through planning, memory, tool use, and reflection—going beyond passive response generation.
- **Function Calling**: A mechanism that allows LLMs to output structured data (for example, JSON) to invoke external APIs, tools, or functions, enabling real-world actions and integrations.
- **Model Context Protocol (MCP)**: A protocol for maintaining and exchanging structured memory and contextual information across interactions with AI models to support longer conversations and agent workflows.
- **LangGraph**: A framework for building multi-step, memory-aware workflows using language models as agents; it enables complex reasoning, coordination, and event-driven state transitions.
- **Vector Database**: A specialized database (for example, FAISS, Weaviate, Chroma) designed to store and retrieve high-dimensional vector embeddings, used for semantic search and long-term memory in GenAI.
- **Low-Rank Adaptation (LoRA)**: A lightweight fine-tuning method that updates only a small portion of model parameters, making adaptation efficient and suitable for edge deployment.
- **Parameter-Efficient Fine-Tuning (PEFT)**: A set of strategies that allow large models to be adapted with fewer trainable parameters, reducing resource requirements during model updates.
- **Multimodal AI**: Generative AI that processes and combines different types of data—such as text, image, audio, and video—to enable richer, context-aware interactions.
- **Neural Radiance Fields (NeRFs)**: A technique used in 3D generative modeling to reconstruct volumetric scenes from 2D images, enabling applications in AR/VR, robotics, and medical imaging.
- **Perceptual Systems**: AI systems that simulate or process sensory inputs such as vision, touch, audio, and biosignals to enhance human-AI interaction and enable embodied intelligence.
- **LangChain Expression Language (LCEL)**: A high-level abstraction used to build and chain complex workflows and agents with LLMs using LangChain, simplifying orchestration.
- **Custom GPTs**: Personalized versions of GPT models configured with specific instructions, knowledge, or tools, allowing users to build domain-specific AI assistants without coding.
- **Digital Twin**: A virtual model of a real-world system or object that simulates its behavior in real time, often enhanced by GenAI for prediction, optimization, and testing.

CHAPTER 21
Best Practices for Generative Models

Introduction

Throughout this book, we have explored the foundations of generative modeling – from the mathematical underpinnings of latent variable models and adversarial training, to the practicalities of implementing diffusion models and large language models. Now, in this final chapter, we shift our focus to what often determines real-world success: how generative models are developed, debugged, deployed, and continuously improved in practice.

Developing generative models is not just about selecting an architecture or tuning a loss function—it is about making disciplined, context-aware decisions across the entire lifecycle. This chapter extracts lessons from production systems, research prototypes, and industry-standard toolchains into a coherent set of best practices for practitioners.

The implementation section outlines practical tips on selecting the right model for the job, reusing pretrained components efficiently, and applying modular design principles that accelerate experimentation and simplify debugging. We then highlight common technical, operational, and ethical pitfalls and provide clear strategies for navigating them. Finally, we explore security and compliance concerns and take a look at emerging frontiers such as hardware-model co-design, enterprise adoption trends, and next-gen architectures.

This chapter serves as your operational playbook. It is intended to help you build generative systems that are not just state-of-the-art in performance, but also reliable, interpretable, and production-ready. Treat it as both a checklist and a strategic guide—one that bridges the gap between proof-of-concept and long-term impact.

Structure

In this chapter, we will cover the following topics:

- **Practical Tips for Developing Generative Models**
  - Best Practices in Generative Modeling
  - Strategic Foundations for Effective Gen AI Development
  - Resource Allocation Guide
- **Data-Centric Best Practices**
  - Importance of High-Quality Training Data
  - Handling Missing Data, Noise, and Biases
  - Data Normalization and Standardization
  - Data Augmentation

- **Tips for Efficient Implementation**
  - Model Selection Framework
  - Pretrained Model Adaptation
  - Architecture and Design Checklist
- **Debugging and Evaluation**
- **Common Pitfalls and How to Avoid Them**
- **Strategies for Continued Learning and Innovation**
- **Security and Ethical Best Practices**
- **Emerging Frontiers in Generative AI**

Practical Tips for Developing Generative Models

Generative modeling is as much an art as it is a science. Success hinges on combining robust data pipelines with thoughtful model design, rigorous evaluation, and a culture of continuous learning. Best practices in this space emphasize quality over complexity: well-curated data, modular and scalable codebases, meaningful evaluation beyond raw metrics, and deliberate reflection after each deployment. As the field rapidly evolves, practitioners must stay grounded in fundamentals while remaining agile enough to absorb breakthroughs. The best models are not just technically advanced—they are thoughtfully built, critically tested, and transparently improved.

Best Practices in Generative Modeling

- **Data-Centric Best Practices:** The foundation of any successful generative model lies in its data. Adopt the CLEAN framework: Complete (no missing features), Labeled (or reliably self-supervised), Evenly distributed (minimize bias), Annotated (rich metadata), and Normalized (consistent scales). For image generation, this means curating datasets with balanced demographic representation—tools such as Google's REVISE can audit for hidden biases. In text generation, ensure token diversity by measuring type-token ratios; anything below 0.2 suggests oversimplification. Always version datasets using tools such as DVC, tracking transformations and provenance to enable reproducibility. Remember: Garbage in equals garbage out, but with generative AI, the garbage often looks deceptively plausible.
- **Implementation Best Practices:** Model architecture choices should follow a problem-first approach. Before defaulting to diffusion models, ask: Does the task require iterative refinement? For real-time applications such as game asset generation, GANs or VAEs often outperform slower alternatives. When fine-tuning, employ parameter-efficient methods such as LoRA—a single A100 GPU can adapt a 7B-parameter LLM in hours versus days for full retraining. Structure your codebase with modular components (separate data loaders, loss functions, and evaluation modules) to enable rapid experimentation. NVIDIA's StyleGAN3 codebase exemplifies this, allowing researchers to swap attention mechanisms or noise injection strategies with minimal refactoring. Always benchmark against a baseline; if your novel architecture cannot outperform a fine-tuned ResNet-50, it is not ready for production.
- **Evaluation Practices:** Move beyond single-metric myopia. For image models, combine Fréchet Inception Distance (FID) with human evaluations—assessors should spot-check 5% of outputs for artifacts or incoherence. In text generation, supplement BLEU scores with BERTScore to capture semantic fidelity. Implement failure catalogs: Document common error modes (for example, GANs generating broken limbs or diffusion models ignoring spatial relationships) and create targeted test suites. Adobe's Firefly team, for example, maintains a "hallucination registry" of bizarre outputs to guide model updates. Quantitative metrics alone will not reveal

if your dog generator accidentally creates five-legged specimens–always pair numbers with qualitative scrutiny.

- **Learning Practices:** Generative AI evolves weekly. Dedicate 20% of project time to deliberate upskilling: Reverse-engineer one arXiv paper (or similar) each month (reimplement key equations), and maintain an innovation journal that tracks three unsolved challenges in your domain. Participate in red team exercises–attack your own models to uncover weaknesses before adversaries do. For teams, institute model autopsy meetings after each project: What worked? What failed catastrophically? Anthropic's practice of publishing model cards with failure modes provides a template for transparent learning. Remember, mastering generative AI is not about memorizing architectures; it is about cultivating a mindset of disciplined experimentation and ruthless self-assessment.

Strategic Foundations for Effective Generative Model Development

One of the most important principles in generative AI development is the 80/20 Rule–allocate 80% of your effort toward data preparation and experiment design, and only 20% toward actual coding. The success of models such as StyleGAN2-ADA is a testament to this approach; it was not just architectural innovations that led to breakthroughs, but meticulous dataset pruning and augmentation strategies that made the difference. In generative modeling, thoughtful data curation often has a greater impact than model tweaks or code optimizations.

Another critical concept is Progressive Complexity. Rather than jumping directly into state-of-the-art architectures such as StyleGAN3, it is more effective to begin with simpler models such as DCGAN. This staged approach allows developers to understand the behavior of generative models incrementally and make informed adjustments. Each new iteration should be validated rigorously–aim for at least a 15% improvement in Fréchet Inception Distance (FID) to justify architectural changes. This disciplined scaling strategy helps avoid overfitting, wasted compute, and unnecessary complexity.

Resource Allocation Guide

In the fast-evolving landscape of generative AI, success is less about how much you build and more about where and when you focus your efforts. One of the most consistent patterns observed across high-performing teams is a strategic allocation of resources–spending more time refining data pipelines, evaluation methods, and experimental design, and less time over-engineering architectures from day one. This asymmetry might seem counterintuitive, but time and again, projects that invest early in data cleanliness, distribution balance, and labeling fidelity outperform those that obsess over model complexity too soon.

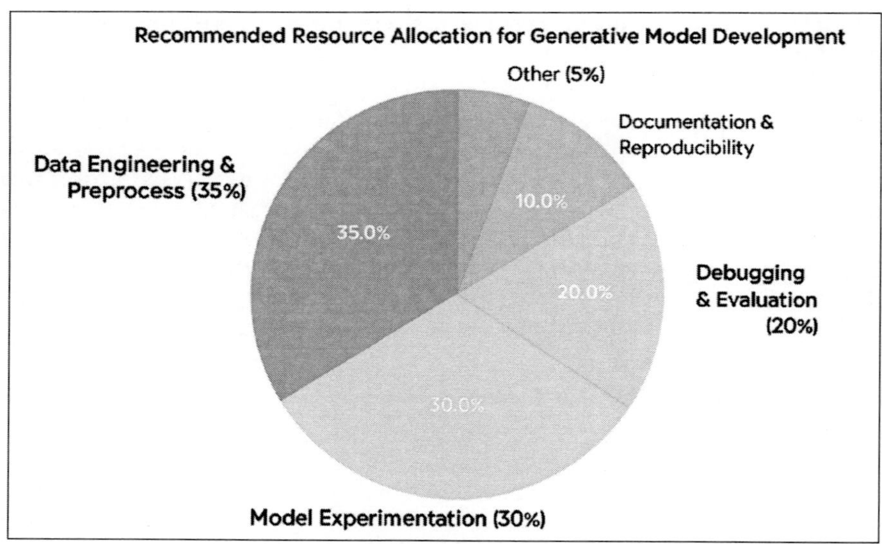

Figure 21.1: *Resource Allocation Guide for Generative AI Development*

The path from prototype to production is rarely linear. Effective resource allocation requires a staged approach. Start with lightweight architectures such as DCGANs or VAEs to test data readiness and baseline feasibility. Use evaluation metrics such as Fréchet Inception Distance (FID) or classifier-based proxy tasks to gauge whether the project is ready for more compute-heavy methods such as diffusion models or transformer-based generation. Compute-intensive models should only be introduced when simpler ones plateau, ideally showing at least a 15% improvement in validation metrics with each major upgrade. Leveraging pretrained models with parameter-efficient fine-tuning techniques (for example, LoRA, adapters, or prompt tuning) can also dramatically reduce the cost of iteration without sacrificing quality.

Beyond compute, team time is another critical resource. A well-balanced development workflow typically allocates 30–40% of effort to data engineering and preprocessing, 30% to model experimentation, 20% to debugging and evaluation, and 10% to documentation, compliance, and reproducibility practices. Automating experiment tracking with tools such as DVC, Weights & Biases, or MLflow helps conserve both time and mental overhead. Ultimately, your team's effectiveness is shaped not by the raw horsepower of your models, but by how thoughtfully you deploy your time, compute, and attention. Generative modeling is as much a strategic game of prioritization as it is a technical challenge.

Data-Centric Best Practices

In the realm of generative models, the adage "garbage in, garbage out" holds especially true. The effectiveness of any model largely hinges on the quality and preparation of the data it is trained on. Data-centric best practices focus on optimizing and maintaining the quality of data throughout the lifecycle of model development and deployment. These practices emphasize the importance of careful data collection, cleaning, preprocessing, augmentation, and management, ensuring that the generative models learn from diverse, accurate, and relevant datasets. Adopting data-centric best practices ensures not only better model performance but also more ethical, scalable, and adaptable AI systems.

Importance of High-Quality Training Data

High-quality training data is crucial for the success of generative models. It ensures the model learns accurate, diverse, and meaningful patterns, leading to better performance in real-world applications. Key reasons include:

- **Improved Model Accuracy**: High-quality data helps the model understand the target distribution, leading to more accurate outputs, whether for images, text, or other content.
- **Reduction in Overfitting**: Rich and varied data allows the model to generalize better, avoiding overfitting to specific examples.
- **Capturing Nuanced Patterns**: Diverse datasets help the model capture intricate features, such as textures or sentence structures, for more realistic outputs.
- **Enhanced Creativity and Diversity**: For creative tasks, high-quality data ensures the model generates varied and innovative results.
- **Ethical Implications**: Sourcing high-quality data carefully helps reduce biases, ensuring more ethical and inclusive outputs.
- **Real-World Applicability**: Data that reflects real-world scenarios ensures the model performs effectively in practical applications.

Key Characteristics of High-Quality Data:

- **Representativeness**: Covers a wide range of real-world scenarios.
- **Diversity**: Includes varied examples to enhance generalization.
- **Accuracy**: Free from errors and inconsistencies.
- **Consistency**: Clear, structured, and uniform labeling.
- **Ethical Considerations**: Avoids bias and ensures inclusivity.

Practical Steps:

1. **Data Collection**: Source data that is diverse, accurate, and representative.
2. **Data Labeling**: Ensure accurate, consistent, and expert-driven labels.
3. **Regular Data Audits**: Periodically update data to avoid outdated examples.
4. **Data Enrichment**: Supplement datasets to enhance diversity and coverage.

In summary, high-quality training data is essential for generative models to produce meaningful, reliable, and ethical outputs.

Handling Missing Data, Noise, and Biases

In any dataset, missing data, noise, and biases can severely impact the performance of generative models. Addressing these issues is crucial for ensuring that the model learns from reliable, representative, and clean data. Here is a look at how to handle each of these challenges effectively:

Missing Data

Missing data is a common issue in real-world datasets and can arise for various reasons, such as errors in data collection, inconsistent formats, or incomplete records. In generative models, missing data can distort the training process, leading to biased or unreliable outputs. Several approaches can address missing data:

- **Imputation**: One of the most common methods is imputing the missing values using statistical techniques such as mean, median, or mode imputation, or more advanced approaches such as regression or k-nearest neighbors (KNN). However, imputation should be done carefully to avoid introducing artificial patterns.

- **Data Augmentation**: For image or audio data, techniques such as image inpainting or audio interpolation can be used to fill in gaps in the data.
- **Modeling the Missingness**: In some cases, missing data can be treated as a feature, modeling the "*missingness*" itself as an indicator, which can sometimes improve the model's robustness.

Noise

Noise in the data refers to irrelevant or random information that can interfere with the learning process. Noise can come from various sources, such as sensor errors, human error in data labeling, or irrelevant features. If left unaddressed, noise can lead to overfitting, where the model learns spurious patterns that do not generalize well.

- **Data Smoothing**: In time-series or signal data, smoothing techniques such as moving averages or Gaussian filters can help reduce noise while preserving the underlying trends.
- **Feature Selection**: By eliminating irrelevant features through feature selection or dimensionality reduction techniques (for example, PCA or L1 regularization), you can reduce the impact of noisy data on the model's performance.
- **Regularization**: Regularization techniques such as L2 (Ridge) or L1 (Lasso) regularization can help the model focus on the most important features, preventing overfitting to noisy data.

Biases

Biases in the dataset can arise from various sources, such as sampling bias, labeling bias, or societal biases, and can lead to discriminatory or unfair model behavior. It is essential to identify and mitigate these biases to ensure that the generative model produces equitable and ethical outputs.

- **Fairness Audits**: Regularly auditing the dataset for potential biases, such as gender, race, or age bias, can help identify problematic areas. Tools and frameworks such as Fairness Indicators can assist in evaluating and correcting biases.
- **Balanced Datasets**: Ensuring that the dataset represents all relevant groups equally can help reduce bias. For example, in facial recognition models, a dataset should include images of people from diverse ethnicities to prevent racial bias.
- **Bias Mitigation Algorithms**: In some cases, specialized algorithms can be applied to reweight training examples or adjust the model's decision boundaries to reduce biased outcomes.

In conclusion, addressing missing data, noise, and biases in generative modeling requires a combination of data preprocessing, advanced algorithms, and continuous monitoring. By implementing robust techniques for handling these issues, you can ensure that your generative models are not only accurate but also fair and reliable.

Data Normalization and Standardization

Data normalization and standardization are essential preprocessing techniques in the development of generative models. Both methods help scale the data into a consistent range or distribution, ensuring that the model can learn efficiently and produce reliable results. While they are often used interchangeably, they serve slightly different purposes and are applicable in different contexts. Below are the best practices to ensure these techniques contribute effectively to model performance:

- **Always Fit on Training Data Only:** To prevent data leakage, compute scaling parameters (mean, standard deviation, min, max, and so on) only on the training set. These parameters should then be consistently applied to the validation and test sets to ensure the model is evaluated under realistic conditions.

- **Align Preprocessing with Model Architecture:** Choose normalization or standardization based on the model's architecture and activation functions:
  - Use normalization (for example, Min-Max Scaling) when using activation functions such as sigmoid or tanh, which expect bounded input values.
  - Use standardization when the model benefits from zero-centered input, such as in deep networks using ReLU or models relying on gradient-based optimization.
- **Be Consistent Across the Pipeline:** Maintain a consistent scaling approach across the entire ML pipeline, including during feature extraction, training, and inference. Inconsistencies here can lead to unpredictable model behavior or degraded performance.
- **Choose Scaling Techniques Based on Data Characteristics**
  1. Use Robust Scalers for datasets with outliers.
  2. Apply log transforms or power transforms for highly skewed distributions before normalization or standardization.
  3. Validate assumptions (for example, near-Gaussian distribution for standardization) before applying.
- **Avoid Blind Application:** Do not apply normalization or standardization uniformly to all features. Categorical or one-hot encoded variables usually do not require scaling, and doing so might reduce model performance or interpretability.
- **Document and Version Preprocessing Steps:** Track the exact method and parameters used for scaling (for example, min, max, mean, std). This ensures reproducibility and consistency across experiments, retraining, or deployment.
- **Integrate Scaling into Deployment Pipelines:** For real-time inference, incorporate the scaling process as part of the deployed model pipeline. Ensure the same preprocessing steps used during training are replicated exactly during prediction.
- **Monitor Impact on Model Outputs:** Validate how changes in scaling affect the outputs of generative models. In tasks such as image generation, scaling artifacts can lead to visible distortions. In text or time-series generation, inconsistent scaling can disrupt learned sequences or patterns.

In summary, both normalization and standardization are crucial preprocessing steps for generative models, ensuring that the data is in an appropriate scale for efficient and effective learning. The choice between the two depends on the model's requirements and the data's characteristics, and applying them correctly can significantly enhance the model's performance.

Data Augmentation

Data augmentation is a crucial tool for enhancing training datasets, especially when working with limited, imbalanced, or noisy data. However, its effectiveness depends heavily on how thoughtfully it is applied. Below are best practices to ensure augmentation strategies truly benefit your generative models:

1. **Align Augmentations with Task Objectives:** Augmentations must preserve the semantic meaning of the data in the context of your task. For generative models, this is even more critical, as learning incorrect patterns can lead to incoherent or unrealistic outputs. For example, rotating an image might be valid for object detection but not for digit generation (for example, 6 versus 9).
2. **Prioritize Realism in Transformations:** Ensure that augmented data mimics real-world variability. Avoid artificial or excessive transformations that deviate too far from real

scenarios. Generative models trained on unrealistic data will produce outputs that fail to generalize or appear unnatural.

3. **Use Controlled Randomness:** Introduce variability through random transformations, but keep it controlled. Apply probabilistic augmentations with set boundaries (for example, rotate images within ±15°). This maintains diversity while preserving label integrity and data fidelity.

4. **Apply Augmentation Consistently Across Pipelines:** For multi-modal data (for example, image + caption pairs), ensure that augmentations are applied in a synchronized manner across modalities. Inconsistencies can break alignment between inputs and targets, especially during conditional generation tasks.

5. **Monitor Model Performance with and without Augmentation:** Always benchmark model performance using both augmented and original datasets. If augmentation degrades performance, revisit your strategy–it could be introducing noise rather than meaningful variation.

6. **Avoid Augmenting Validation and Test Sets:** To maintain the integrity of model evaluation, do not apply augmentations to validation or test sets. These sets should represent the real-world distribution and provide an accurate assessment of how well the model generalizes.

7. **Use Augmentation as a Tool for Bias Mitigation:** If your dataset lacks diversity (for example, demographic imbalance), targeted augmentation can help. However, ensure the augmented samples genuinely expand representation and do not reinforce existing biases or introduce artificial patterns.

8. **Automate and Version Your Augmentation Pipelines:** Treat augmentation pipelines as critical components of your data pipeline. Use automated, reproducible workflows and maintain version control to ensure consistency across experiments.

9. **Evaluate Augmentation Impact During Early Experiments:** Rather than applying augmentation indiscriminately, test its impact during early-stage training. This helps determine which techniques actually improve generative quality or diversity.

In summary, data augmentation is a powerful best practice for enhancing the diversity, robustness, and generalization ability of generative models without the need for additional data collection. By carefully selecting augmentation techniques that preserve the underlying semantics of the data and applying them consistently and appropriately, you can significantly improve model performance, reduce overfitting, and enable more creative and resilient generative outputs.

Tips for Efficient Implementation

Prompt engineering has emerged as a critical skill for effectively interacting with generative AI models. By crafting precise, thoughtful prompts, users can greatly influence the quality and relevance of the model's output. This section delves into essential techniques for prompt engineering, providing actionable insights to maximize the potential of generative models.

Model Selection Framework

Selecting the right generative model is not a one-size-fits-all task; it depends heavily on your specific use case, data characteristics, deployment constraints, and desired output quality. A structured model selection framework helps reduce trial-and-error, accelerates development, and improves downstream performance. Below are the best practices to guide efficient and effective model selection:

1. **Define the Objective Clearly:** Start by articulating what the generative model is supposed to do—text generation, image synthesis, audio generation, data imputation, and so on. Knowing whether you need realism, diversity, controllability, or speed will influence whether you choose GANs, VAEs, diffusion models, transformers, or hybrids.

   Best Practice: Use a requirements checklist that scores objectives such as fidelity, diversity, latency, interpretability, and memory footprint. This guides objective-aligned model choices.

2. **Match Model Type to Data Modality:** Different model families are better suited for different data types:

   - **Text**: Transformer-based models (for example, GPT)
   - **Images**: GANs, Diffusion Models, or VAEs
   - **Audio**: Autoregressive models or diffusion-based audio models
   - **Multimodal**: Combine architectures such as CLIP or VQ-VAE with cross-modal transformers

   Best Practice: Maintain a decision matrix that maps data types to proven model architectures, validated through experiments or literature benchmarks.

3. **Prioritize Resource Feasibility:** Consider available compute, memory, and time. Training large generative models is resource-intensive. Smaller or more efficient models (such as distilled transformers or lightweight GAN variants) may be more appropriate for constrained environments.

   Best Practice: Benchmark models against your hardware budget early. Favor architectures with modular scaling (for example, transformer layers or convolution depth) to adjust based on available resources.

4. **Favor Simplicity in Early Stages:** Resist the urge to start with cutting-edge or overly complex models. Simpler architectures often yield quick insights, faster iteration, and easier debugging.

   Best Practice: Prototype using lightweight or open-source pretrained versions before committing to large-scale models. Validate feasibility and value before scaling up.

5. **Leverage Model Benchmarking Tools:** Use public model evaluation platforms (such as Papers With Code, HuggingFace Leaderboards, or OpenML) to compare how models perform on similar tasks.

   Best Practice: Maintain a living repository of comparative performance metrics (FID, BLEU, Perplexity, and so on) and update your framework periodically as new models emerge.

6. **Align with Long-Term Maintenance Needs:** Select models that have active community support, stable APIs, and documentation. This reduces technical debt and facilitates ongoing improvement.

   Best Practice: Prefer models backed by strong ecosystems (for example, PyTorch + HuggingFace for transformers, or TensorFlow + KerasCV for diffusion models).

In summary, a structured model selection framework ensures that the generative model you choose aligns with your problem scope, resource constraints, and output goals. By combining clear requirements, modality-specific knowledge, benchmarking tools, and practical constraints, you can drastically reduce implementation cycles and build more reliable and scalable generative systems.

Pretrained Model Adaptation

Using pretrained models is a powerful way to reduce development time, lower compute costs, and achieve strong performance with limited data. However, effective adaptation is key to unlocking their full potential.

Start by selecting a model suited to your domain and data type–text, vision, or multimodal. Prioritize models trained on similar datasets and architectures that offer fine-tuning flexibility. Before committing, assess zero-shot performance to estimate how well the model generalizes to your task. Freeze early layers to retain useful features and reduce compute, gradually unfreezing based on validation performance.

When fine-tuning, even small amounts of task-specific data can help. Use discriminative learning rates and monitor for overfitting. Prefer parameter-efficient methods such as LoRA, Adapters, or Prompt Tuning to adapt large models on limited hardware. Stick to the original preprocessing pipeline to avoid input mismatches. Finally, document everything–layer settings, learning rates, and tuning strategies–to ensure reproducibility and easier iteration. Thoughtful adaptation turns pretrained models into domain-specific powerhouses with minimal resource overhead.

Architecture and Design Checklist

Designing a scalable, maintainable, and performant architecture is essential for the success of any generative AI application. An ad hoc design often leads to technical debt, inefficiencies, or poor model performance in production. A structured checklist ensures your solution is built on solid architectural principles from day one.

1. **Align Architecture with Problem Scope:** Choose an architecture that matches the complexity and type of the generative task (text generation, image synthesis, audio generation, and so on).

   Best Practice: Avoid over-engineering. Use lightweight models for simple use cases and modular, scalable architectures for complex or enterprise-grade applications.

2. **Ensure Modularity and Separation of Concerns:** Decompose your system into well-defined modules–data ingestion, preprocessing, model serving, logging, and so on. This simplifies updates, debugging, and scaling.

   Best Practice: Use a clean interface between components (for example, APIs or message queues) so individual modules can evolve independently.

3. **Support Offline and Online Inference:** Generative models can be resource-intensive. Depending on latency requirements, support both batch (offline) and real-time (online) inference.

   Best Practice: Use a model-as-a-service design with asynchronous queues for heavy generation tasks, while supporting low-latency endpoints for quick responses.

4. **Optimize for Resource Efficiency:** Generative models are often compute-heavy. Choose efficient deployment strategies such as quantization, pruning, or knowledge distillation to reduce cost without sacrificing quality.

   Best Practice: Always profile your model before and after deployment using tools such as TensorRT (for vision) or ONNX Runtime (for transformers).

5. **Design for Extensibility:** Anticipate future changes–new data modalities, larger models, more user types.

   Best Practice: Create plug-and-play hooks for experimentation–such as interchangeable model components or a unified configuration system for easy hyperparameter changes.

6. **Implement Observability and Monitoring:** Track performance metrics (latency, throughput), usage patterns, and quality indicators (for example, coherence for text, fidelity for images).

   Best Practice: Set up automated alerts and dashboards for model degradation, drift, or failures using tools such as Prometheus, Grafana, or Datadog.

7. **Incorporate Human-in-the-Loop (HITL) When Needed:** Generative models often need human review or correction, especially in creative or regulated applications.

   Best Practice: Integrate feedback loops for human validation, annotation, or correction to continually refine model behavior and improve outputs.

8. **Support Versioning and Rollback:** AI systems evolve rapidly–always plan for rollback when updates go wrong.

   Best Practice: Use model versioning systems (for example, MLflow, DVC) to track artifacts, and CI/CD pipelines to promote reproducibility and safe deployment.

9. **Include Safety, Privacy, and Bias Controls:** Generative models can produce unsafe or biased outputs.

   Best Practice: Use content filters, differential privacy, and fairness audits during both training and inference stages. Embed ethical safeguards from the design phase onward.

In summary, a robust architecture for generative AI is modular, scalable, and resilient. By following a clear checklist–from model efficiency to human oversight–you can build systems that are easier to manage, faster to deploy, and more adaptable to real-world complexity.

Debugging and Evaluation

Evaluating and debugging generative models requires a balance of both quantitative rigor and qualitative judgment. Unlike traditional models, generative models may produce outputs that are plausible but incorrect, or statistically valid yet meaningless. Best practices in this area help teams catch subtle failures, improve model behavior, and ensure alignment with real-world expectations.

Quantitative Metrics

Quantitative evaluation metrics are indispensable for objectively measuring model performance. However, in generative modeling, these metrics should be selected and interpreted carefully.

Best Practices:

- **Choose Task-Specific Metrics**: Use metrics suited to the generative task–BLEU or ROUGE for text, FID or IS for images, and perplexity for language models. Avoid over-relying on generic scores.
- **Complement with Multiple Metrics**: No single metric tells the whole story. Combine diversity, quality, and coherence metrics to get a balanced view.
- **Track Progression**: Use metrics to monitor performance trends during training rather than relying only on final values. This helps detect overfitting or instability early.
- **Normalize Scores Across Datasets**: If comparing models across datasets or versions, normalize or standardize the metrics to maintain a fair comparison.
- **Automate Evaluation Pipelines**: Incorporate automated metric computation into CI/CD workflows for consistency and speed in experimentation.

Qualitative Evaluation

While quantitative metrics offer objectivity, qualitative evaluation remains essential in generative modeling–especially when dealing with outputs such as images, text, or audio, where human perception plays a critical role. However, subjective assessments can vary widely, so it is important to standardize the process.

Best Practices:

- **Curate a Fixed Evaluation Set**: Use a consistent, representative subset of prompts or inputs to compare model outputs across versions.
- **Use Human-in-the-Loop Reviews**: Involve domain experts or user panels to assess outputs for realism, relevance, creativity, or appropriateness.
- **Define Clear Evaluation Criteria**: Specify what constitutes a "*good*" output– for example, relevance, fluency, coherence, visual fidelity–to ensure consistent human reviews.
- **Employ Structured Rating Systems**: Use Likert scales or binary accept/reject ratings to minimize subjectivity and make comparisons easier.
- **Conduct Blind Comparisons**: Hide model identities during manual review to avoid bias toward a particular model version or training iteration.
- **Visualize Failure Cases**: Systematically log and visualize edge cases or poor outputs to guide debugging and iterative improvements.
- **Capture User Feedback**: If deployed, collect real-user feedback in production to validate how the model performs in the wild.

Debugging Workflows

Debugging generative models can be particularly challenging due to their complexity and the subjectivity of outputs. To maintain efficiency and systematically resolve issues, structured debugging workflows are essential.

Best Practices:

- **Start with Data Inspection**: Always verify the quality and format of your training data. Many issues originate from mislabeled, imbalanced, or inconsistent data.
- **Check Intermediate Outputs**: Visualize or log intermediate layers (for example, attention maps, latent vectors) to verify if the model is learning meaningful representations.
- **Track and Version Experiments**: Use experiment tracking tools (such as MLflow, Weights & Biases) to compare model versions, training parameters, and performance over time.
- **Enable Detailed Logging**: Implement extensive logs during both training and inference to capture anomalies, divergences, and resource bottlenecks.
- **Isolate Variables**: Change one component at a time (for example, architecture, data, loss function) when debugging, to pinpoint the root cause of errors or degradation.
- **Use Synthetic Inputs for Probing**: Craft test inputs with known expected outputs to detect regressions or instability in generative behavior.
- **Validate Loss Curves and Gradients**: Sudden spikes or vanishing gradients can signal architectural or optimization issues–monitor them closely throughout training.
- **Create a Failure Taxonomy**: Categorize failure cases (for example, incoherent outputs, repetition, bias) to prioritize and debug in a focused manner.

Common Pitfalls and How to Avoid Them

Despite the growing maturity of generative AI tools and practices, many projects still stumble–not because the models are fundamentally flawed, but due to avoidable mistakes in how they are implemented, managed, or understood. In this section, we explore three broad categories of common pitfalls–technical, operational, and ethical–and share practical best practices to help you steer clear of them.

Technical Pitfalls

Technical pitfalls often arise from gaps in model training, poor data handling, or unsuitable architectural choices. For instance, teams might use a complex architecture when a simpler model would suffice, leading to excessive training time and difficulty in interpretability. Another common error is insufficient pre-processing–neglecting normalization, not addressing missing or biased data, or failing to validate data consistency–all of which compromise the model's ability to learn effectively.

Best practices to avoid these issues include starting with a clear hypothesis for model design, benchmarking with simpler baselines before committing to deep architectures, and using automated data validation tools. Additionally, maintaining thorough documentation and using modular code design ensures that your technical foundations are sound and debuggable.

Operational Pitfalls

Even the best model can fall short if operational execution is flawed. Operational pitfalls include poor collaboration across teams, unclear ownership of data pipelines or model assets, lack of reproducibility in experiments, and skipping key stages such as model monitoring or rollback plans after deployment.

To avoid these issues, teams should adopt collaborative development practices, such as version-controlled code, shared experiment logs, and CI/CD pipelines. Implementing strong observability into production models–through logging, alerting, and performance tracking–helps detect anomalies early. Finally, ensuring that operational decisions such as model updates or retraining cycles are governed by clear processes can prevent unintentional regressions or downtime.

Ethical Pitfalls

Ethical pitfalls are highly relevant in generative modeling, as these models can perpetuate or even amplify biases found in their training data. Models trained without diversity checks can produce harmful, offensive, or unfair outputs. Similarly, ignoring licensing issues or privacy regulations when using datasets can lead to legal and reputational risks.

To mitigate ethical risks, teams should proactively audit their datasets for bias and representativeness. Establishing ethical review practices, including fairness testing and red-teaming of generative outputs, can help identify edge cases where harm might occur. Transparency with users–through disclosures about model limitations and responsible usage–also fosters trust and accountability.

Strategies for Continued Learning and Innovation

The field of generative AI is evolving rapidly, with new models, techniques, and tools emerging almost every month. In this dynamic landscape, staying relevant requires more than just building one successful system–it demands a mindset of continuous learning and a structured approach to innovation. This section outlines practical strategies for cultivating a culture of lifelong learning and maintaining an innovative edge in your generative AI journey.

Skill Development Paths

To remain effective in generative AI development, practitioners must continually expand their skill set. Skill development does not have to mean going back to school–it can take many forms, including online courses, reading research papers, participating in hackathons, or joining focused communities.

A thoughtful skill development path often starts with identifying gaps in one's current knowledge–such as understanding transformer architectures, mastering diffusion models, or deepening knowledge in data handling and ethics. Teams can also benefit from cross-training across roles–for example, a data scientist learning the basics of MLOps or a product manager getting familiar with model evaluation metrics. Regular skill audits and learning plans can ensure that both individuals and teams stay current and adaptable.

Micro Experiments for Practical Learning

While learning theory is important, much of the true understanding in generative AI comes through experimentation. Micro experiments–small, low-risk, quick-to-implement projects–are a powerful way to test ideas, explore new model types, or experiment with novel datasets. These experiments can be designed to run in short cycles, with limited scope and resources, making them ideal for continuous innovation without disrupting core development efforts. For instance, a team might run a two-week sprint to fine-tune a pretrained model on a niche dataset or evaluate a new image augmentation technique. The key is to make experimentation a regular habit–encouraging curiosity, documenting learnings, and applying successful insights into larger production pipelines.

Innovation Strategies

Innovation in generative AI does not just happen–it needs to be fostered deliberately. One effective strategy is to allocate dedicated time and space for research and exploration, such as "*innovation Fridays*" or monthly hackathons. Teams can also set up a formal innovation pipeline, where promising ideas from micro experiments are evaluated, prioritized, and scaled. Collaborating with academic institutions, participating in open-source communities, or contributing to benchmark challenges can also spark fresh ideas and open up new directions. Importantly, innovation should be aligned with user needs and ethical considerations–solving real problems while staying aware of societal impact. Building a feedback loop between users, researchers, and developers ensures that innovation remains relevant and responsible.

Security and Ethical Best Practices

As generative AI systems become more powerful and widely adopted, ensuring safe, fair, and lawful use is no longer optional–it is foundational. Building responsible AI systems means not only designing for accuracy and performance but also anticipating how the technology could be misused or cause harm. This section outlines essential best practices to help developers and organizations integrate security, fairness, and legal compliance from the outset.

Defending Against Adversarial Attacks

Generative models, especially those deployed in real-world applications, are vulnerable to adversarial attacks–manipulations that cause the model to produce incorrect or harmful outputs. These can range from slight perturbations in image pixels that fool classifiers to prompt injections that mislead large language models. Best practices to defend against such threats include adversarial training (exposing models to crafted attacks during training), robust input sanitization, and regular vulnerability testing. Additionally, deploying runtime safeguards such as anomaly detectors or model output filters can further minimize the risk of exploitation. Security should not be an afterthought; it must be integrated into every phase of model development and deployment.

Bias Mitigation Framework

Bias in generative models can stem from many sources–imbalanced datasets, subjective labeling, or reinforcement of societal stereotypes. To avoid harm, it is crucial to establish a bias mitigation framework early in the development process. This involves auditing training data for representational gaps, diversifying input sources, and employing techniques such as reweighting, resampling, or adversarial debiasing. Ongoing evaluation with fairness metrics (for example, demographic parity, equalized odds) and stress-testing across diverse user scenarios can uncover hidden biases. Importantly, this work must be iterative—bias mitigation is not a one-time task, but a continuous process as models are updated and user contexts evolve.

Legal Compliance Checklist

Beyond ethics, compliance with legal and regulatory standards is a practical necessity. Depending on the jurisdiction and application, generative AI systems may fall under privacy laws (for example, GDPR, CCPA), copyright and IP regulations, or sector-specific rules (such as HIPAA for healthcare). Best practices include maintaining transparent data usage documentation, securing informed user consent, and implementing robust data anonymization techniques. Tracking model provenance—knowing what data went into training and how outputs are generated—is also key to ensuring traceability and accountability. Keeping a legal compliance checklist and involving legal advisors in the development cycle can help teams avoid costly oversights and ensure the product is deployable in all intended markets.

Emerging Frontiers in Generative AI

As the field of generative AI continues to evolve at a rapid pace, it is vital for practitioners, researchers, and organizations to stay aware of the cutting-edge developments shaping its future. The next wave of innovation is being driven not just by smarter algorithms, but by the convergence of architectural advancements, hardware evolution, and growing enterprise use cases. This section outlines some of the most significant trends and opportunities emerging in the generative AI landscape.

Next-Generation Architectures

The architecture of generative models is undergoing a transformation. While transformer-based models have dominated the last few years, new architectures are now being explored to address their limitations—particularly in terms of efficiency, scalability, and interpretability. Mixture of Experts (MoE) architectures, sparsely activated networks, and retrieval-augmented generation (RAG) models are just a few examples leading to this innovation. These architectures aim to reduce computational costs without compromising performance and open new possibilities for domain-specific customization, real-time response generation, and multi-modal capabilities.

Hardware-AI Coevolution

The future of generative AI is not shaped by software alone. The underlying hardware plays a crucial role in determining how fast, efficient, and accessible these models can be. We are witnessing a coevolution where custom AI chips—such as GPUs optimized for transformer workloads, TPUs, and neuromorphic processors—are being designed in tandem with model requirements. Edge computing is also becoming increasingly relevant, as smaller and more efficient models enable generative capabilities on mobile devices, AR/VR platforms, and embedded systems. Staying informed on this synergy between hardware and AI will be essential for teams aiming to optimize performance and reduce operational costs.

Enterprise Adoption Trends

Enterprises across industries are rapidly experimenting with generative AI to automate content creation, enhance customer support, design new products, and streamline knowledge management. However, success in enterprise adoption depends heavily on well-defined use cases, responsible deployment practices, and tight integration with existing IT and data infrastructure. Trends such as model-as-a-service (MaaS), prompt engineering platforms, and industry-specific fine-tuning are accelerating adoption. Organizations looking to leverage generative AI at scale must prioritize governance, security, and explainability to build trust and drive ROI.

Competitive Landscape Analysis

The generative AI race is not just technical–it is strategic. A diverse mix of players, from big tech companies to agile startups and academic labs, is pushing boundaries in different directions. Open-source ecosystems are gaining momentum with models such as LLaMA, Mistral, and Stable Diffusion, which provide flexible alternatives to proprietary offerings. At the same time, proprietary models from companies such as OpenAI, Google DeepMind, and Anthropic continue to set benchmarks in capability and scale. For practitioners and decision-makers, understanding this competitive landscape is key to selecting the right tools, partners, or positioning strategies. Strategic decisions on model selection, IP control, and platform dependency should be made with a clear view of how the generative AI field is evolving.

Conclusion

In this chapter, we focused on best practices for building, deploying, and maintaining high-quality generative models. Rather than diving into theoretical foundations, our goal was to equip you with practical strategies that ensure efficiency, robustness, and ethical integrity throughout the generative AI lifecycle.

We began by examining data-centric practices such as handling missing data, mitigating noise and biases, and ensuring consistent normalization and standardization. We then explored data augmentation techniques that help improve model generalization, especially in low-resource or imbalanced scenarios. These foundational practices are critical for creating reliable training pipelines.

Moving into implementation, we discussed frameworks for informed model selection, effective reuse of pretrained models, and design checklists to align architectural choices with project goals. We also addressed debugging and evaluation, highlighting both quantitative metrics and qualitative methods, along with systematic workflows to trace and resolve performance issues.

In the operational context, we explored common technical, operational, and ethical pitfalls and how to proactively avoid them. The chapter also emphasized continuous learning through structured skill development, micro-experiments, and innovation strategies that foster creativity and adaptation.

Finally, we concluded with an exploration of emerging frontiers–from next-generation model architectures and hardware evolution to enterprise adoption trends and competitive landscape dynamics–highlighting how the field is rapidly evolving across both technological and strategic dimensions.

Armed with these best practices, you are now better prepared to build scalable, efficient, and ethically responsible generative AI systems. Whether you are fine-tuning an existing model or designing a new solution from scratch, these principles serve as a reliable foundation for sustained success and innovation in this dynamic domain.

Points to Remember

- Data preprocessing is foundational–handling missing data, noise, and bias effectively leads to more robust and fair generative models.
- Normalization and standardization help models train faster and generalize better by aligning feature scales and distributions.

- Data augmentation techniques such as cropping, noise injection, and text paraphrasing improve model diversity and resilience, especially in low-data settings.
- A structured model selection framework ensures alignment with task requirements, data constraints, and deployment needs.
- Leveraging pretrained models accelerates development and reduces resource costs, but requires careful adaptation and fine-tuning.
- Architecture and design checklists help avoid common implementation errors and promote scalable, modular development practices.
- Debugging generative models demands both quantitative metrics (for example, BLEU, FID, accuracy) and qualitative analysis (for example, visual inspection, user feedback).
- Common pitfalls span technical (for example, overfitting), operational (for example, versioning issues), and ethical (for example, biased outputs) dimensions–proactive planning helps mitigate them.
- Continuous learning through micro-experiments, self-assessment, and upskilling fosters innovation and long-term capability in generative AI development.
- Ethical and security best practices–including adversarial defense, bias mitigation, and compliance with legal standards–are essential for responsible AI deployment.
- Staying informed about emerging trends in architectures, hardware integration, enterprise applications, and market dynamics positions you for future readiness in the generative AI landscape.

Multiple Choice Questions

1. Why is data normalization important in training generative models?
   a. It increases the number of data samples
   b. It eliminates the need for data augmentation
   c. It reduces model complexity
   d. It ensures all features contribute equally by scaling them to a common range
2. Which data preprocessing technique transforms features to have zero mean and unit variance?
   a. Standardization
   b. Binarization
   c. Augmentation
   d. Normalization
3. What is a key consideration when adapting a pretrained generative model?
   a. Always freezing all layers
   b. Ignoring the original training domain
   c. Increasing model depth
   d. Fine-tuning on task-specific data to avoid overfitting

4. Which of the following is NOT a recommended debugging technique for generative models?
    a. Checking reconstruction loss or output fidelity
    b. Training without a validation set
    c. Visualizing intermediate model outputs
    d. Comparing generated outputs with ground truth examples
5. Which of the following is considered a technical pitfall in generative model development?
    a. Ensuring legal compliance
    b. Model overfitting due to inadequate regularization
    c. Ethical misuse of generated content
    d. Workforce resistance to AI integration
6. What is the goal of a bias mitigation framework in generative AI?
    a. To identify and reduce unintended model biases in output
    b. To improve computational speed
    c. To defend against adversarial attacks
    d. To ensure faster convergence during training
7. Which of the following is a strategy for practical skill development in generative AI?
    a. Relying solely on theory
    b. Avoiding experimental changes
    c. Running micro-experiments with real-world datasets
    d. Using only synthetic benchmarks

Answers

1. d
2. a
3. c
4. d
5. b
6. b
7. a

Questions

1. Why is data normalization or standardization important when training generative models?
2. How does data augmentation help improve the performance and generalization of generative models?
3. What factors should be considered when selecting a model architecture for a generative task?

4. Explain the benefits and limitations of using pretrained models for generative applications.
5. What are common quantitative and qualitative methods used to evaluate generative models?
6. Describe a basic debugging workflow when a generative model is producing poor outputs.
7. List two technical and two operational pitfalls that teams often face when building generative models.
8. What are some ethical issues associated with generative AI, and how can they be addressed early in development?
9. How can micro-experiments support practical learning and innovation in generative modeling?
10. What are some current trends in enterprise adoption of generative AI models?

Key Terms

- **Data Normalization**: A preprocessing technique that rescales input features to a common scale, often between 0 and 1, to ensure consistent training behavior.
- **Standardization**: A method of preprocessing that transforms input data to have zero mean and unit variance, improving convergence in many models.
- **Data Augmentation**: The process of expanding training datasets by applying transformations such as cropping, rotating, or flipping, especially useful in generative tasks to improve generalization.
- **Quantitative Metrics**: Objective measures such as BLEU, FID, and Perplexity used to assess the quality and performance of generative outputs.
- **Qualitative Evaluation**: Subjective assessment of generative outputs focusing on fluency, relevance, creativity, or human-likeness.
- **Technical Pitfalls**: Common implementation or configuration errors, such as poor data preprocessing or unstable training settings, that negatively affect model performance.
- **Operational Pitfalls**: Challenges related to deployment, maintenance, or scalability of generative models in production environments.
- **Ethical Pitfalls**: Risks such as content hallucination, deepfake misuse, or societal bias in outputs that require proactive design and governance.
- **Innovation Strategies**: Systematic methods to drive creative exploration and breakthrough ideas in generative AI, including cross-disciplinary collaboration and problem reframing.
- **Adversarial Attack**: A technique used to manipulate the output of generative models by inputting specially crafted data, often exposing vulnerabilities.
- **Bias Mitigation Framework**: A set of strategies and tools to detect and reduce harmful biases in generative model outputs.
- **Legal Compliance Checklist**: A guideline to ensure adherence to privacy, copyright, and AI governance regulations when building or deploying generative systems.
- **Hardware-AI Coevolution**: The interplay between advances in model complexity and specialized hardware (for example, TPUs, GPUs, edge devices), enabling scalable deployment.
- **Enterprise Adoption Trends**: Patterns in how businesses are integrating generative AI for efficiency, creativity, and decision support across industries.
- **Competitive Landscape Analysis**: Evaluation of the key players, technologies, and market trends shaping the rapidly evolving field of generative AI.

Index

A

C

D

E

F

G